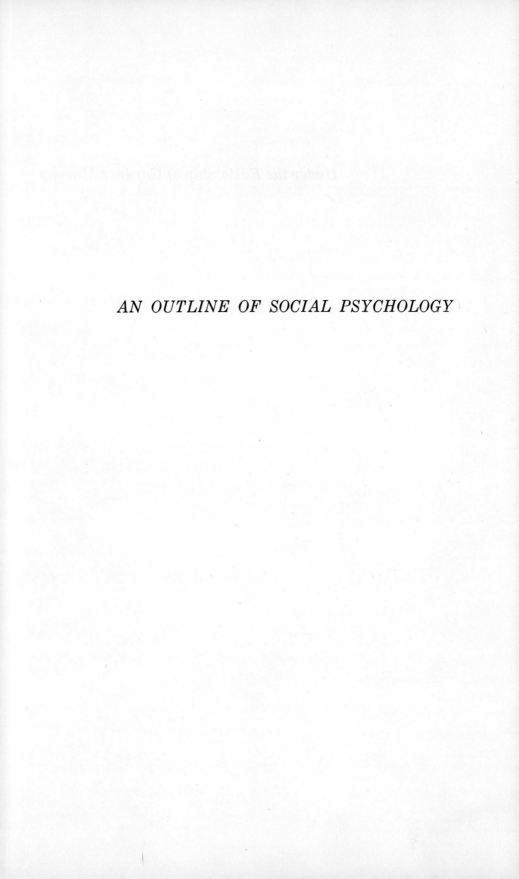

AN OUTLINE OF SOCIAL PSYCHOLOGY

Under the Editorship of Gardner Murphy

MUZAFER SHERIF
Research Professor of Psychology
and Director, Institute of Group Relations
The University of Oklahoma

and

CAROLYN W. SHERIF
Research Associate,
Institute of Group Relations

AN OUTLINE OF SOCIAL PSYCHOLOGY

REVISED EDITION

With a new introduction by
GARDNER MURPHY

HARPER & ROW, PUBLISHERS
NEW YORK AND EVANSTON

Library of Congress catalog card number: 56-6102

For Sue, Joan, and Ann

For Sue, Jane and Ann

CONTENTS

EDITOR'S INTRODUCTION TO THE REVISED EDITION   *xi*

PREFACE TO THE REVISED EDITION   *xv*

I. INTRODUCTION

1. *Introduction to Social Psychology*   3

   Social Psychology Defined—The Typical Level of Human Interaction—Social Stimulus Situations—Sociocultural Topics Studied at Different Levels—Social Psychology Today—Concluding Remarks

II. BASIC FACTS AND PRINCIPLES

2. *Some Basic Facts for Social Psychology*   37

   Behavior Studied Within Its Appropriate Frame of Reference—Relations Among Factors in Various Psychological Events—Anchorages in the Structuring of Experience—Cultural Variations in Anchorages—Concluding Remarks

3. *Some Principles to Be Applied*   77

   What We Attend to at a Given Time: Psychological Selectivity—Differential Effects of Structured and Unstructured Stimulus Situations—Concluding Remarks

III. HUMAN INTERACTION AND ITS PRODUCTS: GROUP STRUCTURE AND NORMS (VALUES)

4. *Experience and Behavior in Social Situations: Laboratory Studies*   119

   Differential Experience and Behavior in Social Situations—Differentiating Social Situations: Togetherness Situations—Group Situations—Experiments on Togetherness Situations—Concluding Remarks

5. *Properties of Groups*   143

   Informally Organized Groups as Prototypes—Essential Properties of Small Informal Groups—Reference Groups

6. *Formation and Functioning of Group Structures*   181

   Gradations from Togetherness Situations to Groups—Whyte's

Study of the Street Corner Boys—Experimental Production of Group Structures and Attitudes—Experimental Study of Expectations Based on Status Differentiation—Concluding Remarks

7. *Formation and Functioning of Group Structures* (Continued) *Leadership, Power, Communication*   209
   Leaders and Other Members of the Group—Power Relations in Group Structures—Communication and Status Relations

8. *The Formation of Social Norms*   237
   Group Norms Are Social Products—Group Norms and Individual Behavior—The Problem of Norm Formation—Norm Formation in the Laboratory—Further Experiments on Norm Formation—Formation of Social Norms in Actual Groups

9. *Intergroup Relations*   280
   Problem of Intergroup Relations Specified—Experimental Approach to Intergroup Relations—Experimental Production of Intergroup Friction—Bull Dogs and Red Devils (1949 Study)—Assessing Intergroup Stereotypes Through Judgments—Production of Intergroup Conflict and Its Reduction—Robbers Cave Experiment —Concluding Remarks

10. *Collective Behavior*   333
    Accentuated Differential Behavior in Collective Interaction—Focal Factors in Various Types of Collective Interaction—Conditions Conducive to Collective Interaction

IV. MOTIVES OF MAN

11. *Motives in Relation to Social Psychology*   365
    The Importance of Motives in Controversies Over "Human Nature"—Biogenic Motives—Relative Weights of Various Motives— Emotional Motivation—Concluding Remarks

12. *Motives and the Socialization Process*   388
    Trends of Motivational Influences: Developmental Picture—Orientation to Sociogenic Motives

13. *Motives and Deprivations in Human Behavior*   412
    Trends in the Study of Motives—Experiments on Motivational Factors in Experience and Behavior—Effects of Prolonged Deprivation—Effects of Deprivation in Social Life

V. MAN AND PRODUCTS OF HIS INTERACTION

14. *Man and His Words*   449
    Human Groups and Their Words—Language Concepts and In-

dividual Behavior—Language Is Distinctly Human—Learning to Communicate—Concepts in Formation—Concluding Remarks

15. *Social Attitudes*   488
Studies of Social Attitudes—Direct Techniques for Measuring Attitudes—Experimental Check with Implications for Attitude Measurement

16. *Attitude Formation and Change*   538
Factors in Formation and Change of Attitudes—Attitude Change With Shifts of Reference Groups—Norms Emerging in Decisions by a Group Are Binding—Conditions in Which "Contact" Is Conducive to Attitude Change—Studying Attitudes in the Process of Formation and Change—Changing Attitudes Through Communication—Mass Media of Communication in Perpetuating and Changing Attitudes—Relating Internal Factors and External Factors in Attitude Change

17. *Ego-Involvements*   579
Personal Consistency Largely a Matter of Ego-Involvements—Unique Individual Nuances in Ego-Involvements—Cultural Variations in Ego-Relevant Behavior—Ego Is a Developmental Product—Motivational Character of Ego-Attitudes—Ego-Involvements in Social Relationships

18. *Ego-Involvements and Reference Groups*   619
Ego-Involvements in Group Relations—The Ego of the Individual and Reference Groups—Reference-Group Concept Applied to Specific Problems

19. *Group Prejudice*   648
Norms of Social Distance—Formation of Attitudes of Prejudice—Individuals and the Social-Distance Scale—Attitudes of Prejudice and Behavior Toward Out-Groups—Problems of Changing Prejudiced Attitudes

VI.   INDIVIDUALS AND SOCIAL CHANGE
20. *Effects of Technology*   685
Some Elementary Effects of Technology—Differential Contact with Modern Technology—Technological Changes Conducive to Changing Organizations and Behavior—Interacting Effects of Technological and Organizational Changes

21. *Men in Critical Situations*   715
Social Movements—Crystallization of New Values in Great Social Movements

x CONTENTS

VII. PRESENT-DAY SOCIAL PSYCHOLOGY

22. A Glance at Social Psychology, Its Backgrounds and Present
Trends   747
The Background in a Glance—Current Social Issues and Social
Psychology—Three Overall Trends in Present-Day Social Psy-
chology—Concluding Remarks

Index of Names   773

Index of Subjects   783

EDITOR'S INTRODUCTION TO THE REVISED EDITION

The impact of the basic ideas of Muzafer Sherif upon social psychology has been so great that it would be ludicrous to attempt to "introduce" him to a world of social psychology which he has done so much to create. The purpose of my introduction is quite different.

Having developed an experimental social psychology in terms of the way in which human beings observe their social surroundings—integrating field studies with laboratory studies and providing ingenious experiments to show the relationship between laboratory behavior and everyday life behavior—Sherif's task in the first edition of this volume became the comprehensive integration of all the main factual materials of social psychology, whether they dealt with motivation, with language, with attitude, with propaganda, with ego-involvement, or with social roles and participation in social groups. What more was there to do? Why should a new edition be more than a pruning and perfecting of the first edition?

The answer to this question lies in noting the direction in which research in social psychology has been moving since 1948, and, in particular, in noting what Muzafer and Carolyn Sherif have been contributing to this development. Less and less has it been possible for social psychology to extend the methods of the psychological laboratory out into the marketplace. More and more it has been necessary to plan *within the marketplace* a systematic observational and experimental program. This has meant that experimental psychology has accepted the challenge of a conception of human nature which is one, whether represented in laboratory behavior or in life behavior; and has attempted not the transposition of the classical laboratory methods into areas for which their fitness is unknown, but in its place, the cultivation of a laboratory spirit, an experimental atmosphere, in the life settings upon which direct information is needed.

This movement, already vaguely suggested in much of the experimental work of the 1920's and 1930's, was magnificently advanced by several ingenious leaders, including especially Lewin, Moreno, and Sherif, each in his own way heralding a new era in which experimental social psychology becomes less and less the study of the socialization of the individual person, and more and more the experimental study of social groups. No psychologist today needs to be told that "small group research" is one of the largest and most significant divisions of social psychology and of sociology; the defense contracts alone and the industrial installations into which these ideas have penetrated would make it impossible to escape from them. What is more likely to be overlooked is the fact that ways have been found to use small group research—and large group research, too, for that matter —as ways of deriving basic information about human nature, the social potentialities, the social fulfillments of mankind. It is the contribution of Sherif and his collaborators in recent years to the experimental study of natural social groups, in their natural habitat, that constitutes the most exciting of the many exciting things offered in the new edition of this work. To maintain a broad perspective, in which every aspect of modern social psychology can find a place, and at the same time to present so vividly these newest aspects of the subject, is in itself a remarkable achievement.

Without taking the edge off of the full and challenging reports offered here by the authors, depicting the systematic observational and experimental studies of natural groups, it will nevertheless be appropriate to note that the great central concepts of the social sciences relating to culture, to social institutions, to the definition and enactment of social roles, are thrown in a new light by the ingenious discovery of ways of experimenting upon naturally constituted groups. The Sherifs' work reminds me vividly of the great phrase of Wesley C. Mitchell: "All of the social sciences have a common aim—the understanding of human behavior; a common method —the quantitative analysis of behavior records; and a common aspiration —to devise ways of experimenting upon behavior."[1]

The culmination of a series of brilliant ideas about experimental group psychology appears in a series of studies of boys' summer camp groups, first undertaken in Connecticut in 1949—with gradual perfection of method, learning by mistakes, broadening the theoretical structure, discovering variables that could be observed and quantified—and finally coming to a magnificent culmination in the Oklahoma summer camp studies of 1954. The result of all this is a social psychology that accepts the challenge of the complexities of life and meets the challenge with infinite sources of

[1] W. C. Mitchell, "Quantitative Analysis in Economic Theory," *American Economic Review*, 1925, p. 6.

ingenuity, patience, and adaptation of the experimenter to a fluid and dynamically changing situation.

The result is that we have a social psychology which is theoretically coherent and moves all the way from the tissues of the individual to the pattern of a changing society; and, in the matter of method, moves all the way from the sharply defined laboratory study of the influence of one or another social variable upon a responding subject to the investigations of complex social groups in their natural habitat. Social psychology has come a long way in the last twenty years and, particularly, in the last ten; and the reader will see that the Sherifs, both in their experimental reports and in the present volume, have done much to give the science its present form. It is a pleasure to say that there is both wisdom and charm in the manner in which this task has been executed.

GARDNER MURPHY

The Menninger Foundation,
Topeka, Kansas
February, 1956

PREFACE
TO THE REVISED
EDITION

Social psychology as a scientific discipline is still in a formative stage, even though many of its problems must be almost as old as human history. The background of this formative stage and trends that seem to be making effective headway are sketched in the last chapter of this book. In recent years, research and applied activities have accelerated.

The impetus for current thriving activity in social psychology does not come entirely from within the discipline. Probably a greater impetus to accelerated growth stems from the increased urgency of human relations problems faced by men of practical affairs, who have turned to social science with questions and with means to support their investigation. Many of these questions have concerned human groups, their organization, leadership and followership, morale, power relations, and communication channels. Research on relations between groups has interested men in community, industrial, and governmental affairs, as well as practitioners in the traditional area of tensions between ethnic groups. In a changing world marked by conflict between the old and the new, problems of attitude change came to the foreground. Problems of personal conflict, inconsistency, and marginality stemming from membership in multiple groups with conflicting values led to preoccupation with the topic of reference groups. Serious studies of collective behavior, crises and disasters were undertaken. An adequate picture of contemporary social psychology must reflect these interests and developments. Accordingly, proportional space is devoted to their treatment in this revised edition, in which approximately seventy percent of the writing is new.

The impetus from a world with serious practical problems has brought social psychology into more intimate contact with the actualities which it aims to understand. Another consequence has been crossing and recrossing traditional boundaries between the social sciences. However, along with these developments, the accelerated pace in social psychology encouraged and sponsored by action organizations has created numerous theoretical and methodological difficulties. If social psychology has claims to come of age as a scientific discipline, its varied activities must be related to established concepts and principles. Its findings must contribute to the development of a coherent body of knowledge. Only then can predictions of wide validity and applicability in various interpersonal, social, and cultural contexts be made. With this aim in mind, principles and generalizations which have proved their usefulness in laboratory and other research are spelled out early in this book, more specifically in Chapters 2 and 3. They are applied to treatment of various topics throughout the book with the addition of supplementary concepts and generalizations as needed.

In line with the interdisciplinary approach stated in Chapter 1, relevant material from sociology, anthropology, and history is utilized to cross-check generalizations based on laboratory and other research. The concept of "levels," as discussed in Chapter 1 and throughout the book, provides a basis for an integrative interdisciplinary approach. When the units of analysis employed at different levels of study are delineated, interdisciplinary comparison becomes an aid in checking the validity of findings and conclusions.

An integrating development for viewing individual and group in a functionally related way has emerged through analysis of the individual's ego formation and of his ego-involvements in given social settings. Conceptualization in terms of ego-involvements and reference groups, within the framework of the properties of group relations, is providing effective tools toward resolution of the long-standing controversy between proponents of an "individual approach" and of a "group approach." Therefore, these concepts and relevant material are further elaborated in this revision in the treatment of motives (Chapter 12), attitude formation and change (Chapter 16), and in chapters dealing with ego-involvements and reference groups (Chapters 17 and 18).

In the thriving state of social psychology today, textbook writers are necessarily put under heavy obligations to many people who provide time and support, good judgment, helpful suggestions, source material, encouragement, and personal kindness. It is a pleasure to acknowledge at least the outstanding ones in presenting this revision.

The group relations experiments reported in Chapters 6 and 9 were carried out under my direction in a research program underway since 1948. The first experiment completed in 1949 was jointly sponsored by the Attitude Change Project at Yale University, which is under the general direction of Professor Carl I. Hovland, and a grant from the American Jewish Committee, Department of Scientific Research, which was then directed by Dr. Samuel H. Flowerman. Continuation of this research program at the University of Oklahoma from June, 1952, to October, 1954, was made possible by a grant from the Rockefeller Foundation, for which I am grateful. As originally proposed to the Foundation, a survey of relevant literature, a theoretical approach based on the survey, and a report of the 1949 group experiment were presented in our *Groups in Harmony and Tension* (Harper, 1953) which served as the basis for plans followed in the 1953 and 1954 intergroup experiments. My gratitude to those who collaborated in the preparation, execution and analysis of the 1949 experiment, the incomplete 1953 study and the 1954 Robbers Cave study cannot be fully expressed. It is a particular pleasure to mention the collaboration of Dr. Marvin B. Sussman, Dr. Robert Huntington, Dr. O. J. Harvey, B. Jack White, William R. Hood, and Carolyn W. Sherif.

Several experiments summarized in this book were conducted under my direction with support from the Office of Naval Research. These include experiments on insecurity with the collaboration of O. J. Harvey and by Virgil Hill in Chapter 17; on status expectations by O. J. Harvey in Chapter 6; on conflicting anchorages by Norman Walter in Chapter 3; and on gradations of stimulus structure by James D. Thrasher in Chapter 3.

Members of the various social psychology seminars at the University of Oklahoma since 1950 have contributed surveys and illustrations, some of which have been utilized. O. J. Harvey, James Thrasher, Daniel Taub, Edwin Cohen, Charles Shedd, Vera Gatch, Arlene Gibson, Victor Harnack, Norman Walter, B. Jack White, William R. Hood, William Combs, James O. Whittaker, William Prado, and Lawrence LaFave were particularly helpful.

During the actual writing of this book, I was fortunate to have graduate assistants who searched for illustrative material untiringly and discerningly. William R. Hood and B. Jack White served in this respect beyond the call of their official duties.

I want to express special gratitude for the never-failing contributions of Dr. O. J. Harvey, who started in the fall of 1950 as graduate research assistant in our various projects at the University of Oklahoma and later was research associate. Even after leaving Oklahoma in 1954, he continued to lend a hand, notably by securing the pictures revealing group identification in Chapter 5 and material on intellectual movements, some of which was used in the section on intellectual aspects of social change in Chapter 21.

We are indebted to Professor T. C. Schneirla of the American Museum of Natural History for many stimulating discussions. We hope that their benefit is reflected in the introduction of the levels of organization concept in the first chapter and in spelling out the import of man's conceptual capacities in his sociocultural relations. Our appreciation is extended to Professor Lewis M. Killian, now of Florida State University, who made some of his material on multiple group membership available when he was preparing it for publication. Professor Paul David of the University of Oklahoma read a portion of the manuscript and made valuable suggestions for clarification.

Mrs. Betty Jane Frensley typed the manuscript. We are indeed grateful for her efficiency and alertness.

We are especially indebted to Mr. William R. Hood and Mrs. June Hood for their personal kindness in many ways which were invaluable. The personal efforts of Mr. and Mrs. L. A. Wood, Sr., for us and their grandchildren made it possible to complete the manuscript on schedule.

Acknowledgement for the illustrations in this book is made in the appropriate context throughout. In locating pictures, we were aided by Professor A. S. Luchins of the University of Oregon, who provided prints of his material used in Chapter 3; by Mr. Fred Snyder, The Menninger Foundation, and Dr. N. H. Pronko, University of Wichita, who provided the print of their work used in Chapter 3; by Professor Robert Bales of Harvard University, who supplied views of his work used in Chapter 7; B. Jack White, who made a number of first drawings; Frank Garner of the Norman *Transcript*; and Mr. and Mrs. James H. Bragg, Mr. R. Boyd Gunning, Professor Leonard H. Haug, and Professor Edith Mahier of the University of Oklahoma.

Time and support required for writing this book were provided by the administration of the University of Oklahoma. I am grateful for this opportunity and the generous encouragement of Dr. George L. Cross, President; Dr. Lloyd E. Swearingen, Vice President; and Dr. Laurence H. Snyder, Dean of the Graduate College. The establishment of an Institute of Group Relations in 1955 through their insight and administrative judgment added further encouragement for concentrated efforts on the central topics of social psychology presented in this volume.

Since 1947 I have had the good fortune of collaborating with Professor Carl I. Hovland in several research units. His searching and exacting questions in our discussions of attitudes and attitude change sharpened my thinking on these topics, which I hope is reflected in appropriate places.

In this undertaking, as in *The Psychology of Social Norms* and the first edition of this book, I have received encouragement and insight from Gardner Murphy. He has followed the growth of the manuscript chapter by chapter. We have incorporated some of his suggestions concerning organization and many of his editorial suggestions in the various chapters.

My wife, Carolyn Wood Sherif, refused my suggestion to join me in signing the 1948 edition, although she had written major parts of several chapters. This time, I took it upon myself to recognize that she wrote various chapters of this book, and then presented the fact to her.

MUZAFER SHERIF

Norman, Oklahoma
February, 1956

I

INTRODUCTION

CHAPTER 1

Introduction to Social Psychology

Social psychology is a new scientific development. Yet the problems it studies are among the most vital, intricate, and fateful human problems. Both the nature of its problems and the fact that social psychology is still in its formative stage make it a challenging area of study.

Consider just a few of our representative topics: How does a helpless infant eventually become a responsible member in organized undertakings with other people which require prolonged efforts and perhaps sacrifice of sleep and food? How do leader-follower relations develop and operate in a clique, a club, a management organization, or a labor union? Why are some people influenced by propaganda at a meeting while others reject it as absurd? Consider the topics of prejudice, segregation, and group conflict which involve millions of people throughout the world today.

Of course, social psychologists are not the first or only people concerned with such human problems. Philosophers, politicians, and writers on social topics have offered ideas and solutions for hundreds of years. In fact, almost all of us have our own formulas and solutions, whether or not we are engaged in studying them. We are personally involved in these problems in our daily lives.

Therefore, it is especially important that we begin with a clear conception of our subject matter and make the effort at the start to avoid some common pitfalls of the past. Building a social psychology that is valid requires special care in the approach, tools, and methods used. Throughout this book the importance of scientific methods is emphasized through concrete examples of research which has pushed forward the frontiers of social psychology as a scientific discipline.

Results of scientific studies are not sufficient by themselves to build social psychology, even though a science must stand on solid facts. It is necessary to have an appropriate set of concepts and principles to use in formulating problems and hypotheses, in collecting data, and in drawing conclusions. Otherwise social psychology would be no more than a rag bag of unrelated findings.

In this chapter we will gain some familiarity with our subject matter. Then we will turn to the task of clarifying some basic facts, concepts, and principles that are utilized throughout this book.

SOCIAL PSYCHOLOGY DEFINED

Historically, both psychologists and sociologists have been concerned with social psychological topics, and of course they are still so concerned. Among the topics in which both have been interested are socialization of the child, social attitudes, communication, propaganda, relations within groups and between groups, leadership, and prejudice. In colleges and universities, courses in social psychology are offered in departments both of sociology and of psychology.

Because of this common interest, concepts and terms have arisen and multiplied in a way that leads to difficulty in communicating and to some confusion in the use of psychological and sociological concepts. Our characterization of social psychology should, therefore, make clear the kind of concepts used in the discipline, and the ways in which psychologists and sociologists can supplement each other. In this chapter our aim is to characterize social psychology in such a way that sociological and psychological concepts and modes of analysis can be utilized to give a rounded picture of our topics.

Social psychology is the scientific study of the experience and behavior of individuals in relation to social stimulus situations. Social stimulus situations are composed of people (individuals and groups) and items of the sociocultural setting.

Considering each of the main terms in this characterization of social psychology will clarify the relationship of psychological and sociological concepts in social psychology. In the rest of this chapter we will take up the terms "experience and behavior of individuals," "social stimulus situations," and discuss reasons for choosing the terms in this characterization.

In dealing with experience and behavior the unit of analysis in social psychology is necessarily the individual. "Experience and behavior" are always experience and behavior of individuals. The only way of studying experience and behavior of individuals is through psychological activities, such as perceiving, judging, learning, remembering, imagining, thinking,

willing, acting, and the like. Adequate explanations of these psychological activities can be attained only on the basis of psychological concepts and principles. Therefore, the designation "social" in its title does not signify that social psychology uses concepts and principles all its own. Valid concepts and generalizations in social psychology should be congruent with valid concepts in general psychology. Whenever necessary, additional concepts and principles are added on the basis of more general ones.

Let us dispel right away any notion that "psychological concepts and principles" imply studying individuals alone or in isolation. Valid general principles in psychology are derived from relationships between functioning of the individual and properties of stimulus situations. The designation "social" means that social psychology is primarily interested in experience and behavior as related to social stimulus situations. Just as the stimulating conditions are an essential consideration in reaching valid generalizations concerning any psychological process, the properties of social stimulus situations become a crucial aspect of our study.

Experience and Behavior

The terms "experience" and "behavior" were mentioned together in defining the subject matter of social psychology. Historically, there have been tendencies to study experience and behavior separately, or to exclude one or the other. Let us consider some important reasons for taking experience and behavior together, rather than "experience" alone or "behavior" alone.

Experiences of an individual cannot be observed directly by other people. They are inferred from some overt behavior by the individual, such as his words, a movement, or an act. But if we restrict our subject matter to behavior alone, we ignore those important cases of reactions to social situations which remain implicit, at least for a time. Human experience is not always followed immediately by overt behavior; but later behavior may be understandable only in terms of that earlier experience. In every case, observed behavior follows a central patterning or organization of influences. The correlate of such internal patterning is some kind of experience. Therefore, experience and behavior are considered together as essential aspects of our subject matter.

Social psychology was defined as the scientific study of experience and behavior in relation to social stimulus situations. Terms like "determination of experience and behavior by social stimulus situations" were avoided deliberately. At first glance, this may seem a minute, hair-splitting distinction; however, it leads to fundamental questions in social psychology. The "determination" of experience and behavior is seldom, if ever, a one-way street. Determining influences cannot be assigned wholly to external conditions impinging on the individual, because the individual is not a passive entity (8).

From birth onward, an unmistakable characteristic of psychological activity is that it is *goal-directed* toward satisfying certain needs and motives and later toward fulfilling aspirations. From birth, the individual has a physiologically unique pattern of needs, unique sensory equipment, capacities, temperament, and the like. Therefore, his modes of organizing influences impinging on him are unique. Because of this and because the particular pattern of social influences any individual faces in his life history differs from that of others, the pattern of motives and aspirations which he develops in response to social influences is also distinctive to the individual.

This point need not be carried to the extreme of declaring each individual so unique that he must be studied in his own right. There are uniformities and regularities in the functioning of needs, sensory equipment and the like; there are uniformities in particular social environments. But the fact that psychological activity is characteristically goal-directed does indicate that an individual does not become a social person simply through receiving imprints of social influences, as though he were a blank tablet. From the time he is born, the way he responds to and assimilates external influences (social and otherwise) is determined *jointly* by the properties of external stimulus situations and by his own *selectivity* as well.

Interaction of Influences from Individual and Culture

The conception of experience and behavior as an outcome of interacting influences stemming from the individual himself and impinging from outside makes it futile to speak of the "determination of experience and behavior by culture or society" or to say that "experience and behavior are determined by individual motives."

In the history of social psychology, there is a time-honored controversy between partisans of the "individual approach" and partisans of the "cultural approach." One view considers social phenomena, even culture and social systems, as the outcome of the individual's deep-seated instincts and their vicissitudes. The opposing view takes the individual as simply the recipient of social imprints. Both views are one-sided and hence erroneous. Controversy based on these two positions becomes meaningless.

This sharp categorizing of the individual and culture, placing emphasis

on one at the expense of the other, resulted in one-sided views both of the nature of social influences and of the individual's reaction to them. The tendency was either to see the individual as an empty receptacle for culture or to regard his reactions to social influences as a constant struggle between a coercive society and a resisting individual, who succumbs only in spite of himself.

Of course, socialization may at times involve conflict for the individual between the demands of a social situation and his own desires. It may be unpleasant, and even painful, for the growing individual to conform to standardized schedules for eating, sleeping, and other vital activities. It is difficult to postpone eating because of some social etiquette when he is hungry and the food is before his eyes. It is deadening for a person to keep awake and appear to be enjoying a conversation when he is bored stiff in the company of guests. It is painful to postpone satisfaction of pressing motives until he gets a diploma or until the requirement of some social custom is observed. There are times when the individual, filled with resentment, may be boiling to say what appears to be the truth, while outwardly he is doing his best not to appear too far out of line with an outrageous discussion, because of the demands and pressures of the situation. The individual often resists conformity during his socialization until correctives applied are stronger than his resistances, or until the social values or norms become his own personally cherished values.

Such examples indicate that it is one-sided to consider the individual a passive recipient of culture. But it is similarly one-sided to view social influences as always *coercive*—to conceive of socialization as a struggle in which the individual is always the loser. From earliest infancy, when the individual is completely helpless, satisfaction of his needs is through other individuals. As he grows, his strivings for acceptance as a welcome person, for security, his efforts to earn a livelihood, his aspirations to prove his own worth are always in relation to other people and groups. Conformity to the values of his groups is not always brought about in spite of him.

We must also take note of cases in which the individual actively seeks to belong, to be an integral part of groups or institutions. Such strivings imply active efforts to make the values and standards prevailing in his groups his own values and standards (9). When a child's kindergarten class goes to Sunday School, he does not have to be pushed into going. In fact, he may feel resentful if he is kept from attending. A typical American boy does not have to be told to learn the rules of baseball. He astounds grownups by his demands that the fine points of the game be observed meticulously. On the whole, membership in colleges or universities is so valued by the student that he need not be exhorted to have loyalty toward and pride in his Alma Mater. His sense of self-esteem and of amounting to something are not independent of such ties.

In short, we can achieve a balanced understanding of relationships among influences coming from individuals and from social environments if we avoid a stand that glorifies the individual and a stand that glorifies culture. By viewing experience and behavior as joint products of influences coming both from within him and from groups and the culture surrounding him, we can approach our study of social psychology prepared to note the interplay of both sets of influences in shaping any particular experience and behavior. Following such an approach, we find cases in which strong impulses coming from within the individual are dominant and also cases in which sociocultural influences are dominant. We find no basis for claiming in advance a sovereign, immutable determination of the outcome of every situation.

Social life, culture, and all that they imply are first external to every newborn human baby. But if he has no contact with social life, he cannot develop into an individual possessing the personal qualities valued by the proponents of the individualistic approach. Such a creature is vastly different from socialized man. Social life is the natural habitat of the human individual; it is not alien to his nature.

Therefore, how an individual learns the requirements and values of his social groups is not the sole problem of social psychology. Man is not only a culture-learning organism. He is constantly involved with others in the process of culture growth and change. Man is a creator of culture as well as a learner of culture. Even as children assimilate the standards of behavior, schedules, and etiquette of the grown-up society in which they live, they are actively engaged in culturally creative activities in groups of their age-mates.

THE TYPICAL LEVEL OF HUMAN INTERACTION

If social psychology seeks understanding of man as both a learner of culture and a builder of culture, the starting point must be through his capacity to function in these ways. Man is the only member of the animal kingdom who learns, creates, and passes on a cultural heritage to future generations. The key to this distinctive human behavior lies in the capacities governing his typical level of functioning.

The typical functioning of human individuals is on a conceptual level.

What does conceptual level mean? It refers to the fact that after early infancy human beings communicate through words, and that this development has enduring consequences which permeate every phase of his psychological functioning. Concepts are standardized generalizations—groupings of objects, events, relations, experiences on some general basis which can be used in different specific situations. In language systems, concepts are crystallized as words.

Let us consider just two of the consequences of conceptual functioning for any human being as he develops. First, when concepts are attained, particular objects, persons, groups, events, relationships are dealt with in terms of a generic class to which they belong. For example, when a child learns the word "book," he applies it not only to books he has seen or handled but to all such objects on later occasions.

Likewise when the name of an ethnic, religious, or national group is learned (be it Mexican, English, Chinese, Navaho), the individual tends to ascribe to any member of that group the characteristics embodied in the concept as he learned it. As this example indicates, it is not necessary that the individual have actual contact with the objects or persons in question in order to learn a concept. At times he does learn concepts with little or no first-hand experience with the specific objects, persons, or events to which they refer.

Second, because of the typical level of human functioning, experience and behavior are possible in relation to stimulus objects and situations which are not immediately present, and may be far distant in space and time (5). Ends which the child achieves at first by crying until parents "guess" correctly, or by tugging at mother's skirts until she follows to another room, are soon accomplished by using words. In a matter of a few years a child begins to speak, think, feel, and act in terms of events past. He comes to experience breathless anticipation of future events, like "next Christmas." The significance of this development is difficult to overestimate. After early childhood a considerable portion of the individual's experience and behavior takes place in terms of past, absent, or future events and situations. Adults make plans far into the future, perhaps with anticipated consequences which may outlast their own lives.

The significance of this typical mode of human functioning is grasped more easily if its uniqueness in the animal kingdom is considered. Many of us have grown up interested in animals and pets. We have seen them do things which seemed remarkably like things human beings do. But in scientific study of human experience and behavior we must heed one of the lessons from the comparative study of various species: The comparative capacities of various species cannot be understood if we look only at their similarities and skip over the enormous differences between them (11, 12).

Even if behaviors of two different species appear similar, the capacities and processes underlying them may be vastly different. Therefore, our understanding is not advanced by giving two apparently similar acts, one by a dog and one by a man, the same name.

The capacities underlying man's functioning on a conceptual level provide the means for an overall organizing system which differs from that of other animals. The human child normally acquires an organized system of concepts and relationships (language) which he can then elaborate, rearrange, and use in ways appropriate to his own needs in a variety of situations. This capacity, writes Schneirla, "apparently depends upon the relative development of the cerebral cortex as a basis for advances in perceptual and conceptual learning. The chimpanzee's inability to use vocal sounds as language cues in anticipatory ways thus seems attributable to his failure to reach the essential level of organizing meaningful perceptual and conceptual relationships, a level which the human infant normally attains before the end of the first year" (11, p. 101).

Because of this difference in capacity and hence in underlying organizing processes between man and other animals, human social psychology is studied in terms of human experience and behavior. The comparative study of behavior of different species will continue to clarify problems at various levels of organization and functioning. The behavior of subhuman organisms may be suggestive for certain lines of investigating human experience and behavior. But in studying the interaction and social life of humans, the easy pleasure of simple comparison and analogy between human behavior and the behavior of pet dogs, laboratory rats, or chimpanzees has to be forgone.

Conceptual functioning is not a "faculty" or a compartment or an "additional factor" to be called upon for convenient explanation. Rather the conceptual level influences other aspects of human functioning profoundly. Thus, "there exists no such entity as 'instinctive man' or 'emotional man' considered as an 'animal nature' with a 'cortical component' overlaid" (11, p. 87). The fact that man's typical level of functioning is conceptual means that seeing the world, feeling, discriminating, wanting, and desiring attain properties not found in subhuman animals.

Man's unique capacity for functioning on a conceptual level does not make him a supernatural creature. He is a part of the animal kingdom.

The conceptual level affects other functions but it does not eliminate them. Therefore, the fact that humans typically interact through exchanging symbols does not mean that "everything is verbal," or "all we have to do is understand the way words are used." Far from it.

As we have seen earlier in this chapter, human experience and behavior are characteristically goal-directed. A minimum of man's needs has to be satisfied in order that he may exist. The capacity for conceptual functioning enables men to produce cultures and to pass accumulated knowledge, behavior standards, superstitions, art forms, formulas, and the like on to future generations. But human interaction is not devoted entirely to learning, creating, or accumulating cultural products. Men cannot live on concepts.

New concepts arise when human beings interact with one another in new situations involving objects, inventions, or relationships which have significance in their day-to-day scheme of living. Concepts often reflect inner urgency stemming from the relevance of objects or events to vital aspects of life. For example, the Masai, a cattle-raising group in Africa, have standardized seventeen concepts to refer to different conditions and states of a cow—a cow carrying a calf, after the birth, and so on. Such fine differentiations are important to them because cattle are highly significant in their whole scheme of living (7).

Human individuals originate concepts in interaction with one another in significant activities. Typically, interaction between human beings takes place on a conceptual level, that is, through exchange of words, conversation, written language, etc. *Interaction between individuals relies chiefly on communication.* Therefore, when we speak of human interaction, *communication* is necessarily implied.

SOCIAL STIMULUS SITUATIONS

Earlier in the chapter, social psychology was characterized as the scientific study of experience and behavior of individuals in relation to social stimulus situations. As a general introduction to its subject matter, the terms of this characterization are being discussed. Thus far, certain of the typical properties of human experience and behavior have been mentioned. Special emphasis was placed on the goal-directed character of experience and behavior. The implication of this characteristic is that influences coming from within the individual (his needs, motives, desires) take part in shaping his social experience and behavior. Then we considered some implications of the distinctive human capacity for producing and standardιzing concepts and for functioning from day to day on a conceptual level. As we have seen, individuals and groups (society) cannot be considered as necessarily antagonistic parties, alien to each other by nature. The satisfaction of man's needs is dependent on others from birth. Because of this and his typical (conceptual) mode of functioning, man is "in his element" in social life, even though the requirements of culture and of his needs may conflict at times.

Now we turn to some essential facts concerning another term in the characterization—"social stimulus situations." An introduction to the kinds of stimulus situations involved and a general specification of their properties will aid in gaining insight into the problems, tasks, and scope of social psychology.

Experience and behavior of individuals are always in relation to a given set of stimulating conditions, whether they are social or not. Therefore, it is not sufficient to specify only influences coming from within the individual in understanding man's experience and behavior. It is also necessary to know the exact scope and properties of the stimulus situations the individual faces. In experimental psychology, the experimenter describes the mazes to be learned, or the length and number of nonsense syllables to be recalled. It is considered essential to specify exactly what influences are introduced by the experimenter as stimulus agents and to record the state of the person (emotion, fatigue, hunger, etc.) and his motivation in relation to stimuli at hand.

But in dealing with social influences we have not always been so careful in specifying stimulating conditions. Not infrequently social stimulus situations are referred to by such general terms as "society" or "culture." In order to specify the social stimulus conditions which individuals actually face during their day-to-day activities throughout their lives, our first task is to look into the broad area of "culture" and "society" to see what sorts of stimulating conditions are involved.

Some sociocultural influences become so much a part of us that we take them for granted, just as we take our hands and head or the air we breathe for granted. Of course, such influences are not a part of us in a genetic or biological sense. They are not carried through our genes and do not blossom out simply through our maturation. All of these sociocultural influences are at first *external* to every human individual. But he later comes to feel or experience them as part of himself.

In this connection, an observation by the anthropologist Malinowski is instructive. Malinowski wrote of his experiences while studying a complicated system of exchange among island groups in the western Pacific (6). He commented that the individual plays his part in the whole game without knowing his relationship in the entire complex affair. The individual islander is immersed in the exchange system in much the same way that he is immersed in a physical atmosphere; that is, he is not aware of it. Those who take part in the Kula exchange system, Malinowski concluded, "have no knowledge of the *total outline* of any of their social structure. They know their own motives, know the purpose of individual actions and rules which apply to them; but. . . . Not even the most intelligent native has any clear idea of the Kula as a big, organized social construction. . . . If you were to ask him what the Kula is, he would answer by giving a few details, most likely by giving his personal experience and subjective views on the Kula. . . . Not even a partial coherent account could be obtained. For the integral picture does not exist in his mind; he is in it, and cannot see the whole from the outside" (p. 83).

An idea of the variety and scope of social stimulus situations may help to make us aware of some of these influences. The following list is borrowed from the anthropologists Kluckhohn and Kelly, who presented it in their discussion of the concept of culture:

. . . age-grading, athletic sports, bodily adornment, calendar, cleanliness training, community organization, cooking, cooperative labor, cosmology, courtship, dancing, decorative art, divination, division of labor, dream interpretation, education, eschatology, ethics, ethnobotany, etiquette, faith healing, family, feasting, fire making, folklore, food taboos, funeral rites, games, gestures, gift giving, government, greetings, hair styles, hospitality, housing, hygiene, incest taboos, inheritance rules, joking, kin-groups, kinship nomenclature, language, law, luck superstitions, magic, marriage, mealtimes, medicine, modesty concerning natural functions, mourning, music, mythology, numerals, obstetrics, penal sanctions, personal names, population policy, postnatal care, pregnancy usages, property rights, propitiation of supernatural beings, puberty customs, religious ritual, residence rules, sexual restrictions, soul concepts, status differentiation, surgery, tool making, trade, visiting, weaning, and weather control [4, p. 124].

Classification of Social Stimulus Situations

The specific social stimulus situations that individuals encounter in their day-to-day living are so numerous that it is useful to group them under a few generic categories. In actual study, of course, we have to make an effort to treat each stimulus situation in terms of its concrete properties and characteristics.

Social stimulus situations can be classified under two broad headings: (I) other people and (II) cultural products. Each of these headings can be further differentiated into two subunits, giving us the following classificatory scheme:

I. Other people.
  1. Other individuals as stimuli.
  2. Groups as stimulus situations. Group relations, in turn, can be specified as:
    2a. Intragroup relations (relations within groups).
    2b. Intergroup relations (relations between groups).
  3. Collective interaction situations.
II. Cultural products.
  4. Material culture.
  5. Nonmaterial culture.

When social stimulus situations are enumerated under different headings, the various items are separated from their context. In grouping social stimuli for convenience, no mutually exclusive categories are intended.

In actual social situations the individual usually participates in some social activity with other individuals or fellow members of a group in an appropriate physical atmosphere, as regulated by the values or norms of his group; and he utilizes appropriate means (lighting, seating arrangements, sound effects, communication, and the like). For example, when members of a family go to church, they enter a building especially designed to yield an atmosphere suitable for the occasion; they sing hymns and read verses. Their interpersonal relations, the ways they speak, keep silent, or greet others are regulated by social norms appropriate to the occasion. Here interpersonal relations, group relations, shared attitudes toward the particular religion, the norm-regulated nature and sequence of activities, the physical setting (including the architecture, organ, pulpit, etc.) are interrelated parts of the entire religious event. However, for purposes of analysis, the place or influence of these various parts could be analyzed.

Various chapters of this book are devoted to the experience and behavior of individuals in relation to representative social stimulus situations classified here in broad categories. Here we shall present a brief characterization of the various kinds of social stimulus situations.

I. Other People as Stimuli

1. OTHER INDIVIDUALS AS STIMULI: This kind of social stimulus situation is the one of which we are most aware. We know that other people serve

as stimulus agents for us, and we for other persons. This may be the case even in transitory encounters on a street or in a bus or store. When an individual comes to stand in a certain capacity to another, an interpersonal relationship has begun to function. A rather definite affective and motivational relationship exists between them, as typified in a love relation, for example. Frequently interpersonal relationships take place within and as parts of larger social settings. For example, parent and child are parts of a family. Relationships between teacher and pupil, siblings, supervisor and worker, neighbors, schoolmates, buddies in the armed forces are other examples of interpersonal relationships. Often it is necessary to know something about the larger groups or organizations in which individuals interact in order to understand their personal relationship.

2. GROUPS AS STIMULUS SITUATIONS: Of course, groups consist of individuals, and there would be no groups if there were no individual members. However, the mere presence of a number of individuals does not make a group. In the luxurious dining room of a hotel one's behavior is certainly influenced by the demeanor and attire of the other diners. But the collection of individuals in a public dining room is not necessarily a "group." The reason we cannot deal with groups simply as "other people as stimulus agents" is that human groups have characteristics which have profound and lasting consequences on the experience and behavior of individual members.

The "groupness" of a group is due to (a) the interdependence of members, which becomes more or less stabilized into a pattern linking every member in the group, and (b) the fact that the members share values, standards of behavior, or norms of the group. The pattern of relationships, in which each individual stands in some capacity or function to others, is called the *group structure*. Group structure consists of a system of relative positions or functions, that is, status and role relationships.

When individual members cherish the values of the group, their behavior is regulated in terms of these values, standards, or "ideals" for behavior. Deviations from the behavior implied by these values are responded to in negative ways. The shared values, behavioral standards, or ideals of groups are referred to as group norms or *social norms*.

When we study individuals participating in groups, our topic is group relations. Interpersonal relations of individuals within the group, their reciprocal status and role relations (for example, leader-follower relations) are referred to as *intragroup relations*. Relations between members of one group and members of other groups are referred to as *intergroup relations*.

FIG. 1.1. Individuals in interpersonal relations.

The currently important topic of prejudice is a special aspect of intergroup relations.

3. COLLECTIVE INTERACTION SITUATIONS: Collective interaction (exemplified in audiences, crowds, rallies, revival meetings, riots, mobs) involves other people as stimuli. Strictly speaking, such situations cannot be classified under interpersonal or group relations as characterized above. *Initially,* individuals participating in collective interaction may or may not be related to one another with personal or group ties. Collective interaction situations are considered in Chapter 10.

II. Cultural Products as Stimulus Situations

Social stimulus situations that individuals encounter are not exhausted by all possible cases of interpersonal and group relations. In any sociocultural setting, in addition to people, the individual encounters stimulus situations which do not exist in nature but are products of the past or current interaction of people in groups. He has some dwelling (primitive or palatial); he wears something; he uses some tools, uses some means of communication and transportation; he is moved by some melodies or rhythms. He is exposed to some language; as a consequence, he comes to deal in terms of categories and structure of that language and to communicate with other individuals in terms of that language. He worships some god that has acquired value in the scheme of things in his group. He cherishes and observes at least some values of a group. In many instances the practices, values, or norms of his groups, their importance, the aura which surrounds them is not referable simply to face-to-face group situations. Some groups are parts of larger organizations and of institutions. A particular religious congregation is but one part of a larger institution. The legislative body of a nation is not merely a face-to-face group; it is part of a government.

The above activities all imply man-made products which are referred to as cultural stimuli. The anthropologist Herskovits has defined culture in concise terms: "Culture is the man-made part of the environment" (2, p. 17). As individuals interact with one another in groups and participate in varying ways in group activities, they produce new cultural stimuli as well as learning and utilizing whatever has survived from previous generations. Since, as we have noted, the human species is the only one which has the capacity to function on a conceptual level, man is the only member of the animal kingdom who can produce culture, accumulate cultural products, and pass them on to future generations.

mothers' club at work.

FIG. 1.2.   Individuals in group relations.

tergroup relations after a contest.

Frank Garner, Norman, Okla.

FIG. 1.3. Individuals in groups and crowds.

Post-Dispatch from Black Star.

The New York Times.

A new kind of audience.

Restricting the definition of social psychology to the study of experience and behavior in relation to other people, leaving out their cultural products as stimulus situations, would amount to writing social psychology as though people were living in a pre-Stone Age (whatever that might have been).

If sociocultural influences were always mediated through communication in face-to-face situations or by word-of-mouth means, they might be studied through such interpersonal contacts. Certainly a good many sociocultural influences are mediated through parents, teachers, age-mates, and other people.

But consider for a moment the furniture surrounding a child, the size and type of his house, the kind and variety of his toys. These play important parts in shaping his tastes. Yet his perception of their size, proportion, limitation, or luxuriousness is not necessarily dependent on someone's telling him about them.

We drive through towns and cities at times without stopping to converse with anyone there. Still we form definite impressions concerning these places, and say "shabby," "poor," "prosperous," and the like, sometimes with considerable finality.

In modern civilization many influences impinging on us come through newspapers, books, radios, etc. Such influences may be experienced as "personal" by the individual. But to say that they are mediated through other individuals is stretching the meaning of interpersonal relationships. An individual in Broken Bow, Oklahoma, may feel the influence of a Hemingway (through his novels) or an Arthur Godfrey (through his radio program) in a personal way. But it can hardly be said that an interpersonal relationship or personal influence exists in these cases.

It is convenient to consider cultural products under two headings: material culture and nonmaterial culture. Thus, in addition to (1) other individuals and (2) groups as social stimulus agents, we have (3) material culture and (4) nonmaterial culture.

4. MATERIAL CULTURE: Material culture consists of those products of human interaction and labor which can be observed, handled, or manipulated as physical objects or structures. Buildings, playgrounds, technological products like the tools used in production (machines), means of transportation (oxcart, train, bus, boat, airplane), means of communication (books, newspapers, radio, television), furniture, cooking facilities, plumbing facilities, sleeping facilities are among these products that constitute material culture.

Courtesy of Martin's of Brooklyn.

Courtesy of Sabena Belgian Air Lines.

FIG. 1.4. Which of these women looks queer to you?

As the individual repeatedly faces and uses the various items of material culture in his environment, he forms attitudes toward them or standards of judgment concerning the "proper" or "essential" items for living and doing things. It is not necessary for another person to point out these items or pass judgments on them in order for the individual to form attitudes related to them. He himself may not be fully aware of his attitudes in these matters until he finds himself in a situation "too primitive to bear" or "splendid" beyond his wildest dreams—until he sees man-made means for doing things which contrast sharply with those he is accustomed to. Since much of the material culture is so closely related to carrying on essentials of living, items of material culture and new developments may exert a telling effect in the formation or change of viewpoints, attitudes, conceptions of basic aspects of man's living or of its minimum essentials.

The cooking unit of a Navaho kitchen. (From Laura Thompson, *Culture in Crisis*. New York: Harper & Brothers, 1950. Photograph by Milton Snow.)

FIG. 1.5.   Contrasts in man-made environment.

A modern kitchen with built-in appliances for cooking, washing dishes, washing and drying clothing, and disposing of garbage. (Courtesy of General Electric.)

L'Habitat au Cameroun. Paris: Office de la Recherche Scientifique Outre-Mer

From Tetsuro Yoshida, *Das Japanische Wohnhaus.* Berlin: Ernst Wasmuth G.m.b.H., 1935

FIG. 1.6A. Which house do you prefer?

From Werner Weisbach, *Die Kunst des Barock in Italien, Frankreich, Deutschland, und Spanien.* Berlin: Propyläen-Verlag, 1924.

From Frank Lloyd Wright, *The Future of Architecture.* New York: Horizon, 1953.

Ezra Stoller.

FIG. 1.6B. Which room is furnished in the "best taste"?

From Max Osborn, *Die Kunst des Rokoko*, Berlin: Propyläen-Verlag, 1929.

From Tetsuro Yoshida, *Das Japanische Wohnhaus*, Berlin: Ernst Wasmuth, 1935.

FIG. 1.7.   In this church scene, the demeanor and actions of other people, organizational symbols, music, verse, ritual, and architecture form an integrated pattern of social stimulation for an individual. (Courtesy of St. John's Episcopal Church, Norman, Okla.)

5. NONMATERIAL CULTURE: Nonmaterial culture consists of products of human interaction like language systems, various social organizations (e.g., family, kinship, political organizations), religion and its organization, art forms, music forms, schedules regulating vital activities, conceptions of man and the universe. One central area of nonmaterial culture is a system of values or norms.

Social norms are standardized to regulate experience and behavior in almost every activity that counts in social life and in regard to interpersonal and group relations. A social value or norm is standardized in the course of human interaction in relation to those aspects of life that have some consequence in the scheme of things of the particular group. Social norms imply an affectively charged generalization, that is, a "value judgment" concerning expected or even ideal modes of behavior. They are the outcome of interaction of human beings. These value judgments or norms are usually expressed in short-cut dicta of the language: "Thou shalt not steal," or "Honor your flag." The formation of social norms is possible because of man's conceptual level of functioning. They are transmitted through the vehicle of language to succeeding generations. Thus man lives not only in the present but also in terms of the past. His activities are regulated not only by the exigencies of the living present but also by the standardized generalizations of past generations and by his long-range aspirations for the future.

SOCIOCULTURAL TOPICS STUDIED AT DIFFERENT LEVELS

In social psychology, groups and their products constitute social stimuli for the single individual. But groups and their products become the subject matter of social sciences in their own right and on their own level. Groups and items of material and nonmaterial culture do not drop out of the blue; they are man-made. They are the product of human interaction and labor.

Groups possess cultural products whether a particular individual acquires them as his own or whether he has become "deaf and dumb" to certain of them for some reason. Denying the reality of cultural products amounts to ignoring facts reported by men who spent their lives studying archaeology, architecture, musicology, folklore, and the like.

In this connection, a point made by Herskovits while discussing the reality of culture is instructive:

There is little doubt that culture *can* be studied without taking human beings into account. Most of the older ethnographies, descriptions of the ways of life of given peoples, are written solely in terms of institutions. Most diffusion studies—those which give the geographic spread of a given element in culture —are presented without any mention of the individuals who use the objects, or observe given customs. It would be difficult even for the most psychologically oriented student of human behavior to deny the value of such research. It is essential that the structure of a culture be understood, first of all, if the reasons why a people behave as they do are to be grasped; unless the structure of custom is taken fully into account, behavior will be meaningless [2, p. 21].

To be sure, if there were no human beings to interact, there would be no cultural or social products. But once such products come into existence and accumulate, they take their places as stimulus conditions setting certain limits, certain perspectives, for the very human beings who were originally responsible for them. It is man who made machines: we can also say machines, in turn, make man. Man creates social organization; we can also say that social organization recasts man. Man is in the beginning of these things, but his products are not man himself. His products (social organization, technology, language, etc.) become subject matters of new disciplines which can be, and are, studied on their own level in a meaningful way without reference to single individuals. Thus, economics is a discipline in its own right, and so is ethnology, philology, fine arts, or music. To think otherwise would lead us to the absurd position of saying that everything is psychology—including physics and chemistry.

Let us illustrate the point with the human group as a topic of study. The topic of groups is central both in sociology and in social psychology. In social psychology the individual is the unit of analysis. On the other hand, as Freedman, Hawley, Landecker, and Miner stated in their recent work, "Sociology is the social science which takes the human group as its central problem" (1, p. 52). Further, they define the group as the unit of analysis for sociology: "The human group is an organization of two or more individuals in a role structure adapted to the performance of a particular function. As thus defined, the group is the unit of sociological analysis" (1, p. 143). In social psychology, the group constitutes stimulus situations for the individual member.

Necessity of Interdisciplinary Approach

Since the individual is its unit of analysis, psychology tries to attain valid concepts and principles pertaining to experience and behavior in terms of established facts about motives, perception, judgment, learning, and remembering. In order to establish valid concepts and principles for the lawful functioning of human experience and behavior, psychology borrows from biological and physical sciences in addition to working on its own level of analysis.

A few examples will illustrate the point. The psychologist learns from the physicist the necessary information concerning the physical nature of stimuli (light, sound, etc.), from the biochemist the nature of glandular functions and the like, from the geneticist the necessary information concerning man's genetic endowment, from physiologists what he needs to know about sensory and motor activities and the functioning of the neuromuscular system.

Likewise, social psychologists need to learn about the properties of social stimulus situations from social scientists. There is good reason for social psychologists to understand cultural products as they are studied by social scientists (sociologists, ethnologists, linguists, and so on). If social products as stimuli are studied only in terms of their discrete aspects, the relationships and proportions which give them as well their psychological reality may be missed. Even such a simple thing as a melody is not just a succession of tones (e.g., 3). A melody which reflects the times, yearnings, and aspirations of a generation consists of a definite relationship in terms of the given component tones. Cultural stimuli cannot be analyzed merely in terms of discrete patches of light, bits of radiant energy stimulating our retina, or separate sound vibrations producing resonance in our basilar membrane, even though such analysis may be useful in the study of sensory processes. They have to be understood on their own meaningful level, as studied by various social scientists.

Of course, social scientists may be interested in the component parts of groups, namely, individuals. When thus preoccupied, the social scientist is working on a psychological level. In achieving a rounded picture of human behavior and relations, the social scientist (e.g., sociologist) interested in the individual needs to turn to psychology for established concepts and principles, rather than improvising psychology. Psychological improvisations advanced by social scientists pertaining to basic motives of man, perceiving, the nature of attitudes, and the like have not fared well. Individualistic improvisations by psychologists concerning such things as the properties of group structure, social organization, etc., have not fared better.

On the one hand, the social psychologist needs to borrow from social science a rounded picture of groups, social organization, and cultural products in order to achieve the perspective of the group setting in which the individual functions. On the other hand, the sociologist can profitably borrow from the psychologist in those aspects of his work where he deals in terms of experience and behavior of individuals—the component parts of groups. Hence, *interdisciplinary coöperation becomes a necessity to tie together solid information obtained through these different levels of analysis using the individual or the group and its products as their units.*

It seems to us that the notion of *levels* (10, 13) is a useful one in making interdisciplinary coöperation really effective. As we have seen, psychologists and sociologists work on different levels, using different units of analysis. An understanding of levels of analysis will give men working on human relations the realization that they are approaching similar or even the same problems using different units of analysis and necessitating approaches and concepts appropriate for events and processes on that level. In this way it is possible to avoid making a patchwork of unrelated ideas from various disciplines and to eliminate fruitless arguments concerning the units of analysis and concepts to be used in interdisciplinary attempts.

With the notion of levels in mind, we can proceed to check findings obtained on our level of approach with findings obtained at other levels of approach to the same or related topics. If it is valid, a generalization reached at one level on some topic is not contradicted, and in fact is supported, by valid generalizations reached at another level of analysis. For example, if a person is found to be color blind by a psychological approach (exposing him to a series of discriminable colors), there must be something wrong somewhere with the structure or functioning of his visual apparatus or related organs. If a physiologist then declares that there is nothing physiologically the matter with the man in this respect, and that he should be able to discriminate colors, there is something wrong with either the psychology or the physiology in question—or with both.

Valid findings on one level cannot be contradicted by valid findings contributed at another level on the same topic. Let us take an illustration closer to social psychology. The sociologist's finding that collective action of a group has properties peculiar to itself should be and is in fact verified by the findings of the psychologist in his analysis of the unique experience and behavior of the individual member participating in the group activities. Such checking and cross-checking of findings obtained at one level against findings obtained at some other level on the same topic will make interdisciplinary collaboration the integrating meeting ground that it should be.

SOCIAL PSYCHOLOGY TODAY

Social psychology is still in its formative period. During the last three decades rapid strides have been taken in building social psychology as a scientific discipline. Perhaps the flourishing activity in our field has been accelerated by the growing realization that man's most vital problems today concern himself and his relations to others. Coherent results in the field have resulted especially from three developing trends which are reflected in varying degrees in most contemporary research and theory. Here we will simply note these trends:

1. Studying experience and behavior as joint products of *interaction* between man and his environment (social and otherwise). As noted in this chapter, this approach contrasts with either an "individual" approach or a "cultural" approach. Through this approach it has been found that the

interplay of internal influences coming from the individual himself and external influences coming from his setting is not an accidental process. In Chapters 2 and 3 some basic facts and principles regulating such inter-action are summarized and illustrated. In later chapters man's interaction with other men, groups, and their products is discussed in detail.

2. The increasing *use of scientific methods and techniques*. Scientific methods are essential in building a solid basis for future development. Through scientific methods significant factors can be specified and their functioning investigated in ways that can be checked by future research. Scientific method is not just a bag of techniques. In fact, in tackling prob-lems with so many complicated factors, many techniques have been used, including observation, experiment, questionnaires, rating scales, tests, inter-views, sociometric assessment, content analysis, and others too numerous to list. Whenever possible, experimentation is preferable, if it can be used without mutilating the essential characteristics of the problem studied. Experimentation is controlled observation which allows systematic varia-tion of just that aspect (variable) or those aspects crucial to the problem, holding others constant. But the sound precaution in social psychology today is to use a combination of techniques whenever possible. When results obtained by one technique are checked against those secured by others, we are on much sounder grounds to draw conclusions.

3. The increasing attempts to achieve balanced *perspective* on prob-lems and findings through checks against the *ethnocentrism* of the investi-gator. The tendency to view problems and findings from the viewpoint and premises of one's own setting (ethnocentrism) is a problem in other fields too; but it is nowhere more blinding than in social psychology. By their nature our problems are pertinent to vital concerns of men and groups. Every group has premises concerning human problems. Therefore, one of the primary and continuing tasks of the social psychologist is to guard against the influences of his own premises as a member of various groups. There are procedures which can help in this task, if used in formu-lating problems and hypotheses and drawing conclusions. In brief, these procedures involve comparisons of findings in *different cultures*, in *different groups* within the same culture, and at *different historical periods* within the same society.

Throughout this book these three developing trends are reflected in approach, specific research, and conclusions. In the final chapter dealing with the background and developments in present-day social psychology they are discussed in more detail.

CONCLUDING REMARKS

Social psychology was defined as the scientific study of experience and behavior of individuals in relation to social stimulus situations. In discussing the various terms in this characterization, the goal-directed character of experience and behavior and the typically human capacity of conceptual functioning were noted.

Following brief discussions of various social stimulus situations, the complementary nature of psychological concepts (referring to experience and behavior of individuals) and of sociological concepts (referring to properties of social stimulus situations) was emphasized. While the properties of individual experience and behavior and of sociocultural influences are studied on their own levels, social psychology does not place the individual and culture (or groups) in a sharp dichotomy as though each were alien to the other.

Throughout, emphasis was placed on the joint determination of experience and behavior through interacting influences coming from within the individual and from the sociocultural settings in which he moves.

The present formative stage of social psychology is gaining a more solid basis through developments made possible by three trends in its study: (1) conceiving experience and behavior as products of interaction between the individual and his setting; (2) applying a variety of scientific methods; (3) growing perspective in evaluating results rather than ethnocentric acceptance of results as embodying universals.

REFERENCES

1. Freedman, R., Hawley, A. H., Landecker, W. S., and Miner, H. M. *Principles of Sociology*. New York: Holt, 1952.
2. Herskovits, M. J. *Man and His Works*. New York: Knopf, 1949.
3. Katz, D. *Gestalt Psychology*. New York: Ronald, 1950.
4. Kluckhohn, C., and Kelly, W. H. The Concept of Culture, in R. Linton (ed.), *The Science of Man in the World Crisis*. New York: Columbia University Press, 1945.
5. Lewis, M. M. *Infant Speech*. New York: Harcourt, Brace, 1936.
6. Malinowski, B. *Argonauts of the Western Pacific*. London: Routledge, 1922.
7. Merker, F. *Die Masai*. Berlin, 1904.
8. Murphy, Gardner. *Personality*. New York: Harper, 1947.
9. Piaget, J. *The Moral Judgment of the Child*. London: Kegan Paul, Trench Trubner, 1932.

10. Schneirla, T. C. Problems in the biopsychology of social organization, *J. abnorm. & soc. Psychol.* (1946), 41:385–402.
11. Schneirla, T. C. The "Levels" Concept in the Study of Social Organization in Animals, in J. H. Rohrer and M. Sherif (eds.), *Social Psychology at the Crossroads.* New York: Harper, 1951.
12. Schneirla, T. C. A consideration of some conceptual trends in comparative psychology, *Psychol. Bull.* (1952), 49:559–597.
13. Sherif, M. Introduction, in J. H. Rohrer and M. Sherif (eds.), *Social Psychology at the Crossroads.* New York: Harper, 1951.

II

BASIC FACTS AND PRINCIPLES

CHAPTER **2**

Some Basic Facts for Social Psychology

Experience and behavior take place within a frame of reference of interrelated influences coming from within the individual and from stimulating conditions outside the individual. Therefore, social psychology studies the functional interrelationships of these various factors. In actual practice this huge task requires singling out social and other influences coming from the surroundings as they are related to one another, and also influences coming from the individual himself as they are affected by one another. If the external and internal influences operating at a certain time are specified, then an analysis of the functional interplay of these two sets of factors in shaping experience and behavior can be made. Overpreoccupation with influences coming from the surroundings (social and otherwise) or overpreoccupation with influences coming from the individual has given us distorted accounts of the determination of experience and behavior.

The growing knowledge in various areas of psychology and social science constitutes the basis for general principles pertaining to the interplay of external and internal influences in shaping experience and behavior. To proceed on solid grounds, this chapter gives some representative facts underlying these principles. The next chapter outlines a conceptual scheme based on an array of facts like those presented in this chapter. This conceptual scheme will make it possible to discuss specific topics in the various chapters of this book in a coherent way.

In developing principles, it is necessary to use concepts which are abstract, and which may appear far removed from actualities. Practical-minded people who want to do something about human relations tend to feel impatient with what appears like just "academic talk" about human problems. At times such impatience is justified. To be sure, scientific con-

37

cepts are abstractions; but they should not be abstractions for the sole purpose of confounding people. They are or should be generalizations about actualities. Their main justification is that they enable us to handle a mass of facts in a short-cut and related way.

Therefore, we will begin in a simple way with statements about the unity of the human person and some illustrations of the ways his experience and behavior are shaped by interrelated influences.

Perceiving and Acting

At any given time there is a focal aspect in what we attend to. We cannot see or hear everything at the same time; we cannot think of everything or imagine everything at the same moment. Psychologists refer to this fact as the "span of attention" or span of perception (48). Likewise, we can carry on only one pattern of activity at a given time.

The pattern of activity at a given moment is not divorced from what we see and how we feel at the time. What we do follows what we perceive, the way we "size up" the situation, and what we want to attain in the situation. We are not always aware of all of the internal influences that take part in shaping our perception, our appraisal of situations. In some circumstances we may not express by word or deed what we see in a situation, how we feel about it, how we size it up. But when we do react overtly by word, deed, facial expression, or bodily posture, our reaction is always related to our motives and perceiving. This relatedness, or functional unity of motivation, perception, and action, makes it possible to study each in terms of the others.

Nobody observes the intentions, motives, attitudes, perceptions of other people *directly*. Motives and experiences are always inferred from behavior, like words, deeds, or some subtle expressions of the face or body. Therefore, when dealing with a person's perception or experience, a psychologist is dealing at the same time with his behavior and motivation. Insulating motivation, experience, and action from one another is a remnant of the tightly compartmentalized psychology of the past, as exemplified by various "faculty" psychologies.

These are the underlying reasons why perception and experience are given a prominent place in the treatment of so many aspects of social behavior. It will become evident that investigation of many major topics through indices of perceiving, judging, and the like has proved highly effective and parsimonious.

Typical Illustrations of Interrelated Influences Shaping Behavior

Sometimes we arrive at a theater after more than half of the featured movie has been shown. Before we get the drift of the plot, the audience laughs at an apparently ordinary word or gesture by one of the actors. This laughter is meaningless to us at the time. We wonder what is so funny, and wait eagerly to see the sequence of episodes that preceded this scene so as to "make sense" of the laughter and to participate genuinely in it.

At a social gathering, those present find remarks by one person inappropriate. A chill goes over those assembled. Yet the same remarks on some other occasion are taken for granted or even regarded as highly enjoyable.

The humor of the ordinary word or gesture in the movie is relative to the unfolding of the plot; and the inappropriateness of the remarks at the gathering is understandable in terms of the bounds of relevance or propriety in the situation. These are simple examples of the fact that stimulus items and behavior items do not have absolute significance in and of themselves. Their significance is explainable only against the background or within the system of relations of which they are a part. The principle implied here is encountered in many human events.

Before turning to laboratory findings, let us glance at other recurrent events in social life representing a few major problem areas in social psychology which illustrate this point. Consider the experience of success or of failure. One student may be satisfied with a C on an examination while another feels miserable when he gets anything below an A. One person aims at making $4000 a year to pay the bills necessary for the essential business of living and to keep his children in school. Another person is unhappy because he is not able to spend $20,000 on a private swimming pool. It is said that the composer Wagner, who considered himself a great writer, thought he was something of a failure because others did not stand in awe of his literary ability. Such feelings of failure or success are the products of many interrelated factors, including the sort of goals the person has set for himself in various capacities, the standards of other people and groups he feels related to, the opportunities available, and others.

Even a simple judgment of what is "long" or "short," "heavy" or "light" is made in relation to a number of standards, including those built up through experience. A college professor lifts an object and says it is "heavy," but to a professional weight lifter the same object is "light." In places with good roads a husband and wife with means jump in their car and go for a week-end excursion of two or three hundred miles without thinking it extraordinary. In other "less developed" areas of the world there are millions of people for whom a trip of this distance, as far as they are concerned, would be like going to the ends of the earth.

Human beings everywhere are equipped with eyes and ears which function in very much the same way. Yet accounts of an incident, like a fatal quarrel between two people, are sometimes given in contradictory ways by different observers in newspapers or even in the courtroom. Such distorted reports indicate that "we don't see with our eyes alone" or "hear with our ears alone." We see and hear with our whole person; and under certain conditions our eyes and ears become instruments which serve our desires, partisanships, and biases.

Distorted pictures take shape in the minds of men, but not because men are gullible by nature and not because they cannot see events with accuracy under proper conditions and orientations. Seeing things is not independent of the person's desires and biases or prejudices. In a complex social world where there are many alternatives to be noticed, he is likely to notice those things which are relevant to his intentions and attitudes.

A telling case in point was reported in the vital area of relations between groups (29, pp. 149–152). In India several months after certain Moslem-Hindu riots, Hindu members of the community reported that relations between the two groups had been peaceful since the riots. They denied that further "incidents" had taken place between the two groups. On the other hand, Moslems could cite instance after instance of mistreatment and discrimination by Hindus. There was little correspondence between the events Moslems saw or heard about and the way Hindus perceived the situation after the riots.

The common-sense way of explaining experiences and events like those mentioned above is to say "he's used to doing things that way" (habit), or "he has a need to see things and act that way," or "he is biased." But such common-sense tags have not advanced analysis and understanding of such events effectively. Experience and behavior do not take place in terms of discrete influences.

BEHAVIOR STUDIED WITHIN ITS APPROPRIATE FRAME OF REFERENCE

Experience and behavior cannot be explained only in terms of factors impinging on the individual from outside, or merely in terms of influences coming from within the person. Both external and internal influences act and react on one another to shape a particular psychological patterning (integration, organization), which is revealed in judging, perceiving, imagining, and so on. Behavior follows central psychological integration, which is jointly determined by both external and internal factors.

Discrete stimuli impinging on the organism and internal impulses (desires, attitudes, motives) do not have absolute values in a particular psychological product or in behavior that follows as a consequence. The properties of these factors in the organized psychological product are determined by their functional relation to other parts of the pattern or organization as well as their own characteristics. Therefore, experience and behavior are studied in relation to both external and internal influences taken in an interdependent way. It should be noted that the individual need not be aware all the time of all or even the major influences, especially those stemming from within himself.

We shall refer to the totality of external and internal factors operating in an interdependent way at a given time as the *frame of reference* of the experience and behavior in question. Buxton has given a similar characterization: "The frame of reference may be defined as the background of stimulation which influences our behavior in a particular situation. It may include external or internal stimuli other than the outstanding ones. It may include ideas or memories. But an important assumption is implicit in our simple definition, namely, that the effects of any given stimulus upon a person are *not independent* of the effects of other stimuli" (6, p. 17).

Frame of reference refers, then, to the system of functional relations consisting of influences operative at a given time. It is not a psychological event, like a judgment or perception. Since the factors (external and internal influences) contributing to a psychological event will vary from case to case, it is helpful to use the concept in specific treatment of various topics as "the frame of reference of given experience and behavior." The concept "frame of reference" cannot be used in an abstract way to "explain" behavior, simply by labeling it. It becomes useful in functional analysis of specific influences operating at a given time and their interrelationships.

The following sections focus on well-verified facts from various areas which demonstrate the necessity of studying any particular experience and behavior in the appropriate frame of reference. Such facts have accumulated for many years. It will be noted that the number and variety of *reference points* which are operative at a given time will vary from case to case.

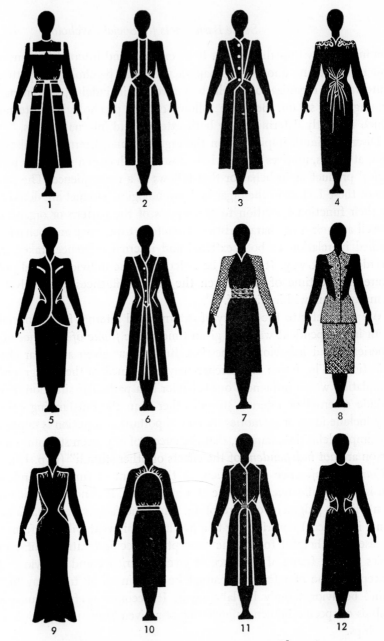

Designs which enhance or minimize a wide waist.

Fig. 2.1. How designers use lines and patterns to enhance the figure. (From *Clothes Make Magic*. Copyright, 1949, by Emmi Cotten. Published by E. P. Dutton & Co., Inc.)

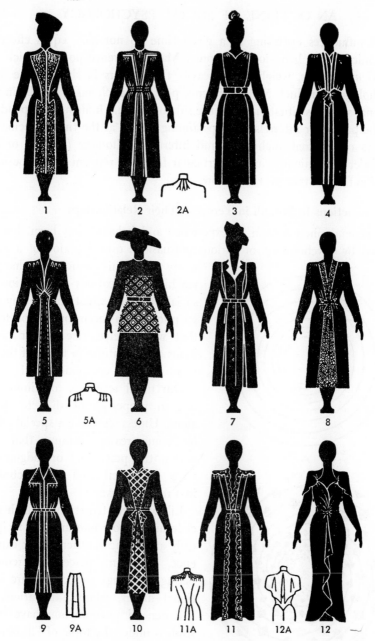

Contrasting treatments of a heavy figure.

Fig. 2.1. Continued.

All influences operating at a given time do not have equal effect in determining the behavioral outcome. Major reference points, which are called *anchorages*, weigh more heavily than others in shaping the final psychological product. Major reference points or anchorages may be in the external stimulus situation or on the side of internal influences, depending on the particular interrelationships among factors at the time. Specific instances of external anchorages and internal anchorages (that is, of the weightier determinants in the particular frame of reference) will be indicated in the illustrations that follow.

Reactions to Stimuli in Terms of Their Relationships

A general phenomenon of experience and behavior has been demonstrated by psychologists of various persuasions over a period of a good many years. This phenomenon has far-reaching implications for reaction to social stimulus situations of any description. It has been found repeatedly that we perceive, size up, or judge items and situations in terms of the relations of their component parts.

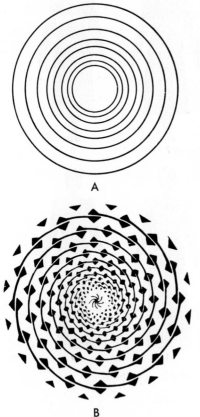

Our usual reactions to stimuli are not to properties of discrete items alone. Unless we make a special effort for some reason, stimuli that fall within the perceptual or judgmental range are experienced and reacted to in a relational way.

Likewise, related stimuli which precede and follow one another reciprocally affect one another in our experience. Judgment, perception, remembering of things and events are relational affairs. Many illustrations of this general phenomenon have been studied under the topic of "illusions."

Take two equal lines, say, four inches long. When arrows are added to the ends of one line pointing inward at a given angle and to the other

Fig. 2.2. (After Fraser.)

line pointing in the opposite (outward) direction at that angle, the same lines no longer look equal. The result is the well-known Müller-Lyer illusion. In our experience they are not the same lines; they are lines with those particular arrows. Each line and its arrows are part and parcel of a unit. To ascertain the objective reality, we can apply a ruler to the straight line in each unit and establish the fact that the lines are equal. This effect can be studied further in terms of judgmental variations brought about by changing the angles and lengths of the arrows.

FIG. 2.3. How big is the locomotive?

Dressmakers know well this general psychological phenomenon that things are experienced in a relational way. Utilizing this knowledge, they accentuate certain lines and curves (of course within limits) (Fig. 2.1). Architects have long known it and used it to create certain impressions of height, spaciousness, curves, and patterns in buildings.

In 1908 the British psychologist Fraser presented a series of illustrations showing the relational effects of stimuli within a perceptual unit (*11*). Look at the concentric circles of Figure 2.2. Look at the spiral in *B*. The spiral consists of the same concentric circles. In *B* they appear to be spiral because of other stimuli in the perceptual unit.

Show the locomotive in Figure 2.3 to a friend, without hinting why you are doing so. (Keep Figure 2.4 out of sight while doing this.) Ask him to estimate its length and other dimensions. Then show him Figure 2.4

with the engineer seated in the locomotive. Ask him to guess the length again. This engine of the children's train in the Oklahoma City park will appear to shrink to its physical size. Of course the presence of the engineer serves as the objective standard or anchorage.

The implication for social psychology is rather obvious. Even relatively simple objects are experienced in a relational way. There is no reason to believe that the more complex, more dynamic area of human relations in which individuals interact with one another is an exception. The implica-

Fig. 2.4.   Now how big is the locomotive?

tions will be elaborated when various properties of social situations are treated (Chapters 4–10).

RELATIONS AMONG FACTORS IN VARIOUS PSYCHOLOGICAL EVENTS

Principles underlying perception, judgment, remembering, and the like are not basically different. There is every reason to consider these activities as interrelated events. For the sake of convenience, and convenience only, the following factual findings are presented under the usual labels utilized in psychology.

Some Relations in Judgment

A large part of daily activity consists of discriminating between objects and persons, of passing judgments in financial affairs, of estimating expenditures within limits of our purse, of judging political issues or ethical matters, of sizing up performance in daily tasks. These activities all involve judgment. In carrying them out, we use standards, many of which are derived from our groups or built up during our life history.

All judgments, from the simplest discriminations of physical objects to the most complex social judgments, have a basic principle in common: They all involve comparison between two or more items. In order to judge something, there has to be something else to compare it with. In Chapman and Volkmann's words, the general fact is that "all judgmental activities take place within . . . referential frameworks" (7, p. 225).

Time and space localizations require certain comparison or reference points. For example, it is difficult if not impossible to localize a single point when no other points, objects, or contours are in view. If this isolated stimulus is a small fixed point of light located in completely dark surroundings, it seems quite unstable and appears to move. This phenomenon, called "autokinetic movement," is experienced by almost everyone, even though the person knows the light is stationary. Since this situation is so unstable, it has been utilized in social psychology as a laboratory situation to study the effects of standards provided by verbal suggestions, interpersonal and group influences, and the like.

If no objects, points, or contours are available as reference points, it may be well-nigh impossible to determine our location in space or to decide whether we are moving or standing still. Captain Charles E. Yeager's account of the first test flight to reach and maintain supersonic speed illustrates such a difficulty. His plane flew at an altitude so high that the earth was not visible through the atmospheric haze. Captain Yeager saw his instruments indicating speed faster than sound. Yet he did not experience great speed. On the contrary, he reported: "I had a hard time judging my speed. The little Mach needle and other instruments kept telling me that no one had ever gone faster, but I was so high and so remote, and the airplane was so very quiet that I might almost have been motionless. You sense speed in terms of something stationary, something outside yourself" (49, p. 16).

On some occasion almost everyone has said, "It is getting too late; I must rush." The particular time cannot be designated as "early" or "late" by itself. It is early or late in relation to other points in time which the person may or may not make explicit.

Studies on temporal judgment show that a standard is always involved in judging time. Whether a particular time seems long or short depends in part on the length of preceding temporal stimuli (47). Judgment of a time interval is also relative to what goes on during that interval. For example, Gulliksen found that individuals estimated a certain time as much longer when they did nothing than when they worked or even had an unpleasant experience (14). In short, time and its passage are experienced in relation to standards, many built up through past experiences and affected by the significance of events transpiring in time.

Localization of points touched on the skin is not free of the influence of other points on the body. The French psychologist Henri studied localization on the skin over a period of years. He first carried on his experiments at the Sorbonne in 1892–1894 (under Binet's direction) and continued them at Leipzig in 1894–1897. The results led him to conclude that certain parts of the body, such as the joints, serve as reference points for localization. Spots are localized in terms of distance from parts of the body. The errors of localization cannot be interpreted without recognizing the role of the reference points. In Henri's own words, "Almost always the error of localization is committed in the direction of the points of reference (*points de repère*) which the subject uses in the localization of the spot touched" (18). He further reported that when the subject used one reference point within a cutaneous area, there appeared a *constancy* in the direction of errors. With the shift of reference there was a corresponding shift in the direction of errors of localization (19).

Such findings establish the fact that judgment of an item is not determined solely by properties of that item but also in reference to other items with which it is functionally related. Judgment of an item is affected by its functional value in the scheme of relationships at the time. The study of judgment affords some of the most clear-cut examples of *membership character* of the constituent items in a functioning system.

REFERENCE SCALES: In recent years it has been customary to refer to this basic fact as the "relativity of judgment" (20, 26, 31). Relativity of judgment does not mean at all that judgment is an arbitrary affair, or that it merely follows the whims of the person passing the judgment. On the contrary, relativity of judgments means determination of the discriminations of particular items by their relationships to other stimuli or standards.

The relativity of judgment was illustrated by Postman and Egan in this way:

We see a movie and we call it interesting or dull without comparing it with some standard movie. We call a person's voice loud or soft without comparing it to a standard voice level, and so on. But even though we may be judging one object at a time, such judgments are, nevertheless, relative to a response scale which we have acquired in the course of daily living. We have seen a large number of movies and so have acquired a personal response scale for rating them, ranging from very interesting to very dull. We have heard a great many voices and, again, have acquired a personal response scale, ranging from very soft to very loud. When we judge any single object, we place it, often without making an explicit comparison, somewhere along the range of similar objects which we have experienced [*31*, p. 223].

This general tendency for judgment to be determined in terms of a whole background of relevant items gave rise to a new method in psychophysics. In classical psychophysics, the usual procedure was to present each stimulus (e.g., weight, tone) in a series together with a standard stimulus of a given value. It was thought that a standard stimulus was needed for making precise comparisons. The accumulating work on judgment of single stimuli shows that the use of a standard stimulus for each comparison is not needed to permit the observer to judge each stimulus in the series. After the series of stimuli (weights, tones, etc.) is presented for a few rounds, the observers establish a scale internally. Henceforth the position of a particular stimulus is judged against the background of that scale.

An example reported by Wever and Zener is pertinent. Using the method of single stimuli (which is sometimes called the "absolute method"), they gave an observer a "light" series of weights (84, 88, 92, 96, and 100 grams). When this series had become an "established" scale, they suddenly introduced a "heavy" series (92, 96, 100, 104, and 108 grams). "The effect of the first series on the judgments of the second was quite evident for 20 or 25 presentations, i.e., for four or five rounds judgments of the 'heavy' predominated for all the stimuli; from this point on, however, the judgments showed a redistribution conforming to the second stimulus series" (*46*). In other words, when the "light series" (84–100 grams) is the reference scale for the individual, a particular stimulus (e.g., 96 grams) is experienced as heavy; but when the same stimulus is related to the "heavy series" (92–108 grams), it is experienced as light.

A more recent study by Tresselt directly connects the work on reference scales in judgment with learning. Tresselt had her subjects practice first with a given scale of weights. After varying amounts of practice (learning) with this scale, she introduced a new scale. She found that at first the practiced scale had a significant effect on the judgments of the values in the new scale, until the subject adjusted himself to the new scale. Further, there was a definite effect of different amounts of practice upon judgment of the new series. "The greater the amount of practice, the more slowly does the scale of judgment shift to its new position" (39, p. 260). This finding has a bearing on the experience of individuals during a period of adjustment to new surroundings, and on the difficulty that people with rigidly established routines undergo in making such adjustments.

Since a single stimulus is judged against the background of functionally related stimuli, this background for judgment can be called the individual's *reference scale* for the special item in question. The placement of a particular stimulus is dependent to an important extent upon the range of stimuli presented in a series. If the stimuli presented for judgment vary within a narrow range, the categories which can be used are few. On the other hand, a wide range of stimuli leads to broader categories and the possibility of utilizing a larger number of them. As Volkmann has suggested, the fact that placement of a particular item is necessarily relative to the width of the stimulus range confronting the individual has important implications for social psychology and educational procedures (41). For example, this fact bears on the reactions of individuals when they face new devices, ideas, or events which have never been present in their environments. It can be utilized in understanding differences between the reactions of individuals who have been consistently exposed to a narrow range of devices, ideas, and possibilities and those of individuals who have been consistently exposed to a great variety of stimulation encompassing broad areas.

A reference scale generally has one or more salient or outstanding items which have more influence than others in the judgment of something else. These salient or outstanding reference points may be called *anchorages* or anchoring points.

When a standard stimulus is presented along with the items to be judged, the standard stimulus becomes the primary anchorage. When the method of single stimuli is used (each item being presented separately in a series), the end points in the stimulus series serve as anchorages, and other stimuli are judged according to their appropriate place somewhere between these anchoring points. Thus in a series of weights, the heaviest and lightest objects serve as anchorages for the reference scale.

During the last two decades, study of the effects of anchorages has been extended, especially by Volkmann and his associates (26, 34, 40, 41). In this work, anchoring points have been introduced at and beyond the end points of the stimulus scale. The shifts of the reference scale and placement of items produced by such anchorages are related to problems of attitude formation and change, to the differential effects of propaganda, and to the analysis of reference groups. Their implications become so important in these topics that an introductory treatment of the effects of various anchorages and reference scales is given in a separate section later in this chapter (pp. 64–66).

AFFECTIVELY CHARGED JUDGMENTS: The relative nature of judgment is not restricted to discriminating weights, lines, or other stimuli seemingly devoid of affective significance. Beebe-Center and his associates demonstrated that the pleasantness or unpleasantness of a particular stimulus, such as odor, depends in part on the pleasantness and unpleasantness of other stimuli preceding it. This is referred to as the "principle of hedonic contrast" (3).

Years ago, William James called attention to the fact that the experience of success or of failure is relative to the goals one sets for himself. A series of experiments, starting with the work of Hoppe, Frank, and others, showed that the level of performance in a task is not judged as "success" or "failure" in terms of the absolute degree of accomplishment but in terms of the "level of aspiration" or goal one sets in that particular line of achievement. If he reaches or surpasses that level, his experience is success; if he falls short of that level of attainment, the experience of failure follows. Setting aspiration levels or goals for oneself and for others with whom one stands in definite relationship (as friends, loved ones, competitors, enemies) implies judgment of future attainment. In shaping such judgments, it has been found that past levels of performance in the task in question, the general state of one's self-esteem, one's sensitivity in respect to his own successes and failures, the place of the task in one's scheme of personal values, the positive or negative interpersonal relationships with other people involved, the level of achievement and goals of one's group all may come into the picture.

In Chapman and Volkmann's words, "the conditions which govern the setting of a level of aspiration . . . in the sense of an estimate of one's future performance in a given task, may be regarded as a special case of the effect upon a judgment of the frame of reference within which it is executed" (7, p. 225). The operation of some specific factors involved in passing judgments about one's own performance and the performance of others with whom one is related in negative or positive ways is discussed in Chapter 17.

Relations in Perceptual Structures

One of the most prolific areas of research in psychology has been perception, which concerns experience of present objects and events. Contrary to the conception of some early philosophers and psychologists, the bulk of evidence led psychologists to conclude that perceiving objects and events does not consist of synthesizing a disconnected conglomeration of sense impressions. Patterning, integration, or organization seems to be an immediate psychological process (24, 25).

FIG. 2.5. When we see a vase, the shape stands out clearly, the rest forming the background. When we see two profiles, the contours of the faces are conspicuous in the foreground, and aspects that are not relevant to the profiles recede into the background. (From E. Rubin, *Visuellwahrgenommen Figuren: Studien in psychologischer Analyse.* Kobenhavn: Gyldendol, 1921.)

When we look around, we do not experience patches of disjointed impressions. We see distinct objects, persons, continuity of contours in definite directions and proportions. Even in the subway station at rush hour, certain units, like objects and people, "stand out" for us. As Köhler stated: "Visual fields tend to be clearly organized in the sense that they contain objects with well-defined boundaries" (25, p. 44).

Objects or persons which constitute clearly defined or organized perceptual units stand out as *figures* against the background of other stimuli.

This *figure-ground* delineation of the stimulus field was first studied systematically by the Danish psychologist Edgar Rubin (35). It has furnished some of the clear-cut evidence demonstrating the direct and immediate structural properties of perception.

The figure is distinct and stands out from the ground, which lacks distinctiveness. The figure has more clear-cut boundaries than the ground. Things and persons perceived as figures tend to be recognized and remembered later with distinct features, whereas stimuli that constitute the ground are sometimes hardly remembered (30).

For example, look at the picture in Figure 2.5. If a person has seen the two profiles facing each other, the white area in between them is just an empty space. If he has seen the goblet, this same white space has "body" to it. Similarly if the person saw the profiles first, the two white lines opposite each other at the lower part of the picture are meaningful as openings of the mouths. However, when the goblet is seen as "figure," these white lines are merely decorative details on the goblet.

FIG. 2.6. Napoleon and the trees. (By permission from *Psychology*, by Stagner and Karowski. Copyright, 1952. McGraw-Hill Book Company, Inc.)

If in Figure 2.6 one sees the figure of Napoleon in characteristic posture, the white area gains imposing prominence as the body of the French general. If the black tree is seen, "Napoleon" is an empty space between the branches.

Such examples show once more that stimuli do not have absolute stimulating values. Their significance is derived in an important way from being located in the figure or in the ground at the time, and from their particular membership character within a given figure or ground. The properties of an item in a perceptual structure are determined not only by the properties it has when studied by itself but also by its relation to other parts. This is analogous to the finding that items in a judgmental scale are experienced in relation to others in the scale.

EXPERIENCE IS SELECTIVE: Why do certain stimuli or events in actual life acquire more distinct figure character in experience at a given time while others remain in the background? Or, in plain language, why do we attend to certain items or events rather than others? This question leads to the important problem of *psychological selectivity*. Experience seems always to be selective. Psychological selectivity, as much as any phenomenon, drives home the inseparable relatedness of motivation and cognition, or in ordinary terms, of "affective" and "intellectual" processes. In the next chapter a special section is devoted to this problem, which has great importance for social psychology.

Whatever the stimuli or events which are focal or figure at a given time, the tendency to experience events in an organized way is found even if the stimuli and events in the external world are not clearly patterned or structured themselves. However, cases in which the stimulus field has objective structure will be considered first.

STIMULUS PROPERTIES AND PERCEPTUAL STRUCTURES: When the stimulus field has definite objective pattern or structure, the structure of perception corresponds to it rather closely. The objective factors or determinants conducive to the formation of corresponding perceptual structures have been studied since the 1920's (45). Newman (30) discussed such factors in the following terms: (1) similarity, (2) proximity, (3) symmetry, (4) good continuation or "common fate," (5) common movement, and (6) what can be expressed as consistency of moving patterns or formations. (7) In addition, following Wertheimer and David Katz (22), it may be convenient to refer to a number of perceptual patterns as determined by the factor of "closed forms." (See Figure 2.7.)

These factors explain in part the impressions we get watching formations made up of human individuals (like commencement and church processions, military parades, formations of college bands at rest or moving in football stadiums). Short characterizations of some of these external factors are in order.

Those items or objects *closer to one another* will be grouped together, if other factors do not work against it too heavily.

When some items or objects in the stimulus field are similar and some are dissimilar, those which are *similar* will be grouped together, if other factors do not operate against it.

Parts of an object or pattern which have clear *continuity* will be perceived as belonging together. This factor may work against proximity and similarity, and (as we shall see) against internal factors from past experience.

Objects and items bound together with sharply defined boundaries are likely to be perceived as perceptual units.

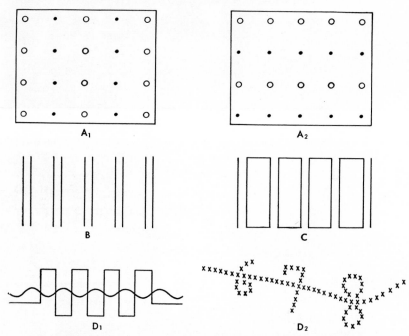

FIG. 2.7. Structural factors in external stimulus situations. A_1. Because of similarity, items are seen more easily in vertical order. (After Wertheimer.) A_2. Because of similarity, items are seen more easily in horizontal order. (After Wertheimer.) B. Lines are perceived in five pairs because of proximity. (After D. Katz.) C. Vertical lines are the same as in B. Factor of closed form dominates over factor of proximity. (After D. Katz.) D_1. Good continuity of contours dominates over proximity. (After Wertheimer.) D_2. Despite proximity, distinct numbers and a curved line are seen because of good contour. Familiarity (an internal factor) also favors distinctiveness of contours here. (After Prothro and Teska.)

These various objective factors conducive to perceptual structures corresponding closely to objective structure may be mutually supporting or destructive, either singly or in combination. For example, good continuity may work against proximity. The formation of persons standing or moving close to one another in an academic procession or a uniformed band affords

FIG. 2.8. (Above left) Note "700" in crowd at left, favored by similarity in continuous dark pattern against light ground. Note also the dollar sign formed by band members, favored by similarity and continuity. (Courtesy of Professor L. H. Haug, University of Oklahoma.) FIG. 2.9. (Middle left) Here continuity works against proximity. Members in the middle of the first line in the *U* are not seen as parts of the bottom line of the *O*, even though they are closer to them. (Courtesy of Professor L. H. Haug, University of Oklahoma.) FIG. 2.10. (Lower left) Continuity more clear-cut at a distance. (Courtesy of Professor L. H. Haug, University of Oklahoma.) FIG. 2.11. (Top above) Pattern of trophy illustrating closed form. Note that the three closed forms within the loving cup are seen as subordinate parts of the larger pattern. (Courtesy of Professor L. H. Haug, University of Oklahoma.) FIG. 2.12. (Above) Band stands out distinctly against the crowd. Note that the band formation stands out from the bulk of the crowd because of proximity of band members in lines and similarity of uniforms. (Courtesy of Professor L. H. Haug, University of Oklahoma.)

a good example of proximity, similarity, good continuity, and common movement all working together to produce a compelling perceptual structure (Figs. 2.8–2.12).

For economy of expression, let us refer to these objective factors (like proximity, similarity, closed form, and common movement) as *structural properties* of stimulus situations. At times they are so imposing, so compelling that objects or items which have long been familiar are not recog-

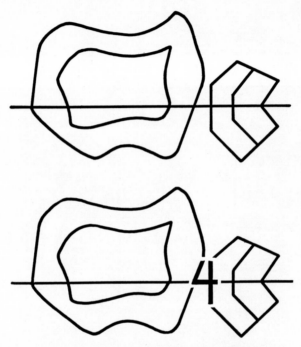

FIG. 2.13.   Hidden 4. (After W. Köhler.)

nized when they are part and parcel of a larger structure. When parts of larger structures, these items are no longer the ones with which we have been so familiar in other connections; they are now perceived in the capacity of their membership in the total structure. When social stimulus situations are considered, certain of their structural properties which have been defined by social scientists will be discussed.

In their zeal to prove the overwhelmingly greater effectiveness of the structural properties of figures than of past experience or learning, Gestalt psychologists presented numerous examples of hidden figures which do not appear with their familiar identity (13).

Indeed, it is difficult to find the 4 in Figure 2.13, although we have been familiar with this number ever since our first grade in school. Or take the word *nationality* hidden in Figure 2.14. In classroom demonstrations, it sometimes takes students several minutes to isolate it, with partial success, even after they are told that the word is in the figure.

In similar fashion, the skillful propagandist presents his main points in such an irrefutable pattern that at times we tend to swallow the hook with the bait.

When the overall scheme of relations in the interaction process is considered, this compelling determination of experience and behavior by the

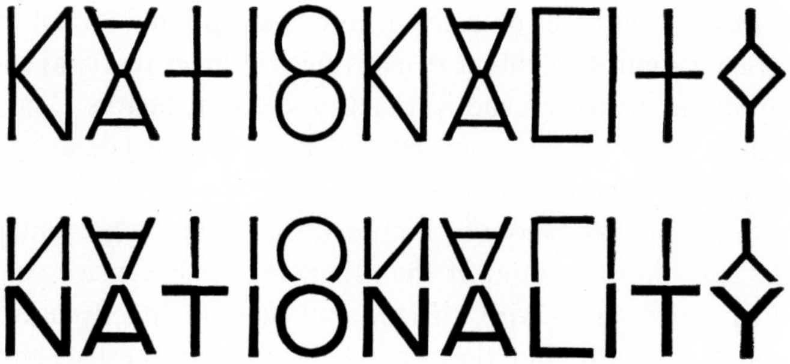

FIG. 2.14. Hidden word. (After Prothro and Teska.)

structural properties of stimulus situations becomes an important part of the picture but by no means the whole picture. To complete the picture, we have to bring to the foreground the facts that experience is selective and that all stimulus situations do not have compelling structural properties.

GRADATIONS OF STRUCTURE AND SHIFTS IN FIGURE-GROUND RELATIONSHIPS: An objective test of the relative structure of a stimulus can be obtained in terms of the number of *alternatives* in perceptual structuring that are possible in relation to it. Highly structured patterns, like a circle, probably produce the same perceptual structure for individuals anywhere. At the other extreme, ink blots or movement dimly seen in darkness offer alternatives, and structuring of experiences in relation to them may reflect our major expectations, desires, and worries. Between these extremes there are various gradations of stimulus structure.

In the reversible figures, like Figures 2.5 and 2.6, there are *two* alternatives for structuring, even though the contours are clear in themselves. Figure 2.5 can be seen either as two profiles or as a goblet.

Even when there are only two feasible alternatives in structuring, social factors, such as instructions from another person or socially derived attitudes, become important determinants of which alternative will be perceived. If, before showing Figure 2.5 to someone who is not familiar with it, you say, "Tell me how tall the goblet is," he will probably see the goblet as figure. On a later encounter, it will probably still be a goblet to him, at least at first. But if you had asked, "How do you like these profiles?" he would probably have seen the profiles first.

Thus, even with two possible alternatives, other factors besides the objective properties of the situation operate jointly with them to determine the character of the perceptual structure. When the alternatives increase owing to a lack of clear-cut objective factors, perception does not ordinarily end up in confusion. Perceptual structuring still takes place, as influenced to an important degree by motivational and social factors. The implications of these facts have opened fruitful lines of research in motivation and other crucial areas of research.

SIGNIFICANCE OF THE GROUND: Figure and ground are not independent; each influences the properties of the other. In a public place you may be absorbed in conversation with a friend and may be directly noticing only his face and his words. But the general structure of the background, the gaiety or solemnity of the group, the quietness or noise around you will have an effect on you and your friend, despite your absorption in each other. In Koffka's words, "The ground serves as a general level (niveau) upon which the figure appears" (23).

The ground becomes especially important in social psychology. Studies on social interaction gain in significance if the subtle relationship between figure and ground is taken into consideration. When two people are talking in a public place, their conversation and behavior may be tinged by the properties of the whole atmosphere. There are even instances in which the character of the general atmosphere is an important determinant of what will be perceived as figure. For example, during the daytime shopping hours a woman walking along the sidewalk in formal evening clothes is noticed by the shoppers, simply because all other persons are wearing street clothes.

Relations in Remembering

The relational character of experience is revealed clearly in remembering some past object, person, or event. Many years ago the French psychologist Ribot pointed out that remembering takes place in terms of certain reference points. "These reference points form for each of us different series corresponding to the events that make up our life; daily occupations, domestic incidents, professional work, scientific investigations, etc., the series becoming more numerous as the life of the individual is more varied" (33, p. 52).

Because remembering occurs in the absence of the original stimulating conditions, the main reference points, as Ribot indicated, frequently stem from the significance of events remembered in the individual's life.

In his pioneering studies of remembering, Bartlett pointed out that the form of the original stimulus (for example, story form or clear-cut figure) exerted influence on subsequent reproductions, along with a variety of internal factors. Of course, if remembering takes place in a social context and concerns events with significance for other people, the context and other people serve as further reality checks in the process.

Bartlett's work broke down the artificial boundaries between perceiving, remembering, and even imagining. "In passing from perceiving and imaging to remembering we do not enter a field of new psychological problems. . . . We have seen that in perceiving the data presented have to be actively connected with something else before they can be assimilated. In remembering the task is made more specific. That with which the immediate stimuli of the reactions have to be connected is more narrowly defined, and must now be some specific thing or event which was presented before at some specific time" (2, pp. 45–46).

Bartlett concluded from his series of experiments that remembering is hardly ever exact, and that it does not consist of simply arousing "fixed, lifeless and fragmentary traces" of past events. Rather, remembering "is an imaginative reconstruction, or construction, built out of the relation of our attitude towards a whole active mass of organized past reactions or experience, and to a little outstanding detail which commonly appears in image or in language form" (2, p. 213).

Thus remembering an object or event with certain structural properties occurs in relation to certain reference points, which may include the structure of the original stimulus and internal influences operating when the individual perceives the object or event and when he later recalls it.

Although experiments in remembering have not specifically investigated it, there is little reason to doubt that the situation in which past events are remembered also becomes an important determinant, especially if it is a social situation.

ANCHORAGES IN THE STRUCTURING OF EXPERIENCE

The findings on various psychological activities summarized in the preceding sections are illustrative of many others. It is established that a stimulus or event is not experienced merely in terms of its absolute properties but as it is related to other factors operating at the time. The influence of a particular factor, whether in the figure, in the ground, or originating within our body (internal), can be understood only in terms of the frame of reference of which it is a functioning part.

However, in numerous examples it was evident that all of the various factors operating in an interdependent way do not contribute equally to the final psychological product. Certain factors play a greater part in determining the character of a given experience than others. These dominant factors have been referred to as *anchorages*.

The dominant factors or anchorages may be external, particularly when the stimulus situation has compelling structural properties. In actual life the main anchorages vary in different instances. At times the anchorage is a physical stimulus and its properties (like a loud noise). It may be a social influence, like the words of another person. A social standard or norm serves as an anchorage when it becomes a factor in a frame of reference. Sometimes the principal anchorage is internal, stemming from the individual's attitudes or motives.

There may be more than one anchorage at a given time. When one looks at a reversible picture with a specific "set" or expectation of what he will see, both structural properties and the set or expectation are crucial determinants of experience and response. In such cases there are both external and internal anchorages.

Wells gave examples of judgment in which the anchorage was internal and in which the anchorage was in the stimulus situation. He reported that when individuals arranged ten pieces of music in order of preference, the ranking would be done according to each person's *own standard*, whereas if they ordered graduated weights, the standard used would be in the objective stimulus series (44).

When a person looks at some nonsense form or a familiar figure which is altered in some detail, he relates it to the familiar form of which he is reminded. Later when he is asked to recall and reproduce it, the drawing will resemble the familiar object more closely, or it may even be transformed into the familiar object, in terms of anchorages coming from within the person. This has been shown time and again by Bartlett (2) and others. The internal anchorages may be provided by some motive or attitude of the person. In many cases the internal anchorage is in the form of a name given by the individual or suggested by the experimenter. Gibson found that the nonsense form on the left in Figure 2.15 "might be interpreted by one observer as a woman's torso, by another as a dumbbell, and by a third as a violin" as shown in the drawing on the right (*12*, p. 20). As Gibson remarked, evidently these persons had differing interests in life.

Of course, it can be shown that nonsense forms and even an ink blot can be correctly perceived and drawn if left in plain view while the subject

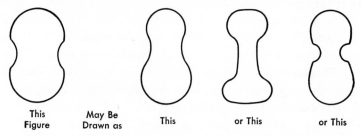

This   May Be
Figure   Drawn as   This   or This   or This

FIG. 2.15. The effects of personal concerns in determining form.
(After J. J. Gibson.)

is drawing, or if presented for a longer time. Such a demonstration may be a useful test of cognitive ability. But ordinarily this opportunity is not available when remembering takes place in actual life.

The reproduction of past events cannot be explained simply on the basis of a tendency to structure things in the direction of simpler and more pronounced forms. If the tendency for reproductions to be simpler and more clearly shaped is treated only in terms of an abstract trend toward more pronounced structure (*Prägnanz*), the various factors operating in memory are kept in insulated compartments. The direction and kind of transformations of forms, items, and events remembered vary from person to person, revealing the special training, desires, or attitudes of the individual in question. The available evidence indicates that such transformations do have a definite direction and relevance to the person's pressing motives and attitudes at the time. These variable factors function as anchorages in the system of related factors determining the experience.

When we think of a loved one, primarily good things and events arise as figure. At a later date, if our relationship with the same person has changed to enmity, incidents that were part of the background before come persistently to the foreground to acquire figure character.

Seeing things (perception) is subject to reality checks in the objective stimulus situation. But in remembering, the effect of reality checks is lessened. The character of experience may be determined primarily by the nature of internal anchorages operative at the time.

Interrelationship of Anchorages and Reference Scales

The functional significance of anchorages in the patterning of experience and behavior becomes clearer in terms of some specific ways they influence and are influenced by other factors. As noted earlier in this chapter, reciprocal effects of anchorages and other factors are critical in social psychology, particularly in the areas of attitude formation and change, reaction to propaganda, and other social situations and events. The most clear-cut examples of the interrelationships of anchorages and other factors come from the experimental study of judgment. These findings can be utilized for orientation to the general problem.

In discussing some relations in judgment, it was stressed that formal standards or anchorages are not needed to judge stimuli in relation to one another. When individuals are exposed to a series of discriminable stimuli, they establish a reference scale; they place each stimulus according to its membership character within the particular reference scale.

In this placement of stimuli within a reference scale, it is the end points of the scale which serve as main anchorages. When the end points are changed, and hence when the scale changes, the same stimuli are placed differently, according to their relative position in the new reference scale.

The placement of the same stimulus by two different individuals will correspond rather closely if they are using the same anchoring points; it will differ if they are judging the stimulus in terms of different anchorages. As Volkmann indicated, one of the most effective ways to bring about agreement between individuals judging an item is to insure common anchorages (41). The implication of this fact in social controversy is obvious: as long as people make their judgments in terms of divergent premises, agreement is impossible.

The most dramatic demonstrations of changes in psychological values of stimulus items with shifts in major anchorages come from the work of Volkmann and his associates (26, 34, 41). In this work the individual is exposed during various trials to a series of stimuli. Also stimuli are introduced whose values lie at the ends of the scale or at various distances from the ends of the stimulus scale. Volkmann refers to these specially introduced stimuli as "anchoring points."

The findings are understandable in terms of the functional value of the end points of the reference scale (*41*).

1. It is primarily the end stimuli which govern the placement of other stimuli in the series.

2. The items that have objective values closer to those of the end points are more finely discriminated. The farther away from the end points the objective values of items (that is, the nearer the middle segment of the stimulus series), the greater is the variability and hence error in the placement of items.

3. The introduction of procedures which accentuate the end points makes finer discrimination of stimulus items into more precise classes or categories possible. This may be done by presenting the end stimuli more frequently than others; and it may be done by deliberately instructing the subjects that a particular stimulus is the lowest value (weight, pitch, etc.) and that another is the highest.

The findings obtained when anchorages are introduced at various distances beyond the end of the scale are particularly important for social psychology. Anchorages outside of the stimulus scale consist of the same kind of stimuli, but their objective values exceed the objective value of the end point in varying amounts. They may be presented with each stimulus to be judged, that is, paired with each item in the series. They can also be presented only occasionally throughout the series.

As the objective value of the anchorage increases beyond the end point of the stimulus scale, the whole reference scale of judgment expands in the direction of the anchorage, up to a certain point. Correspondingly, up to that point the class or category widths increase, or become wider. Rogers found this expansion of the reference scale using weights and visual inclinations (*34*). McGarvey found the same tendency using verbal material, such as statements of offenses and crimes varying in seriousness (*26*).

If the anchorages are removed excessively beyond the end of the stimulus series, instead of expanding, the whole reference scale of judgment contracts or shrinks (*17, 37*).

The expansion of the reference scale when the anchorage is not too far from the end of the individual's reference scale is a case of psychological *assimilation*. A counterpart in social life is our tendency to assimilate new ideas if they are not too far from our own ideas.

The contraction of the reference scale when the new anchorage is too distant from our own reference scale is a case of psychological *contrast*. A counterpart in social life is our tendency to react negatively in the face of ideas or items of propaganda which differ greatly from our own.

These assimilation and contrast effects are operative in other areas besides judgment. They are produced by simultaneous stimulation as well as successive stimulation. In perception, there are differential contrast effects depending on the place of items in the figure or in the ground (4).

However, it will be one-sided to emphasize only the effects of anchorages on the reference scale. As noted earlier, the magnitude of the reference scale itself, the degree of practice with it, and the intensity of the person in relation to his reference scale or some segment of it are matters to be noted carefully. Anchorages, reference scales, and personal involvements affect one another reciprocally.

There is good reason to believe that these reciprocal effects occur in relation to social situations as well. In addition to studies like McGarvey's utilizing socially significant material, basis for this expectation can be found in experiments utilizing weights, tones, etc. The crucial finding in this respect is that anchoring effects can be produced by verbal means (41). In short, words, instructions, verbal categories function as anchorages in the perception and judgment of objects.

In actual social life individuals learn a system of verbal categories and relationships (language) which enters at every step into their perception and judgment of the social world.

CULTURAL VARIATION IN ANCHORAGES

This chapter is concerned with a factual basis for generalizations pertaining to the interplay of external and internal influences in determining experience and behavior. Findings have come chiefly from experiments using weights, tones, simple forms, single lights, pictures, lines, or relatively simple verbal material as stimuli.

Someone primarily interested in social phenomena might ask, "What does reaction to little pictures, weights, or tones have to do with social behavior?" If no effort is made to extend generalizations and concepts reached on this basis and to apply them to social stimulus situations, indeed they can have no bearing on social psychology. The illustrations in this section were chosen to demonstrate that such generalizations from experimental findings are useful in handling certain cultural variations in experience and behavior, without using different concepts for each variation.

We have seen that, within the particular frame of reference of interrelated factors determining behavior, certain factors have greater weight in affecting the properties of others and the total outcome. These salient reference points or anchorages may be internal or external; or there may be both internal and external anchorages within the relational system of factors operating at the time.

In venturing into the broad area of cultural variations, the starting point is relatively simple but basic phenomena in which various features of social life in different cultures provide compelling anchorages. Since these features will vary from culture to culture, experience and behavior are subject to variation as influenced by differing anchorages. Perception and judgment of time, space, and distance provide such a starting point.

Time Perception

Modern societies have calendars based on careful observation of astronomical events. Time localizations are made in terms of days, months, and years of calendars computed on this basis. When a calendar is not available, other reference points are used. In some cultures periodicity of events in the economic life may serve as anchorages in reckoning time. Throughout central Africa, neighboring communities meet periodically to exchange their produce. On these days ordinary work stops while the trading is done. The Wagiriama of British East Africa have a market day every four days. Therefore they mark off the weeks in terms of the market day and intervals between, the week consisting of four days, each with a name. Other groups have weeks of different lengths, depending on the intervals between market days.

"With the regular market is inseparably connected the market week, the length of which varies from three to ten days. The shorter intervals of three, four, and five days reflect the simple economy of primitive life, since the market must recur with sufficient frequency to permit neighboring communities, who keep on hand no large stocks of food and necessaries, to obtain them from one another. The longer cycles of six, eight, and ten days, much less common, apparently arise by doubling the earlier periods" (43, p. 117).

In other cultures, events in nature which recur with some regularity are taken as anchorages for time reckoning. The Andamanese, for example, had rather unusual reference points for time based on the blossoming of plants. The anthropologist Radcliffe-Brown observed: "In the jungles of Andamans it is possible to recognize a distinct succession of odors during a considerable part of the year as one after another the commoner trees and lianas come into flower. . . . The Andamanese have therefore adopted an original method of marking the different periods of the year by means of the odoriferous flowers that are in bloom at different times. *Their calendar is a calendar of scents"* (32, pp. 311 ff.). As he explains, scents play an important role, connected with magic, in the life of the Andamanese. Odors, therefore, are relatively more important as stimuli than in some other groups.

Before the development of reliable mechanical clocks, the history of time-keeping records the use of many devices for reckoning the duration of events. The accuracy of these devices improved especially with the need for uniformity and precision brought on by modern industrial development. Fire, water, and sand have all been used to aid in computing the passage of time. Such devices are still needed in less developed cultures when the periodicity of events is not sufficiently clear-cut or when sun, stars, or moon are obscured. Hough observed the use of fire among Pacific Islanders: "Most of the Pacific Islanders burn torches of the oily nuts of the 'candle-nut' tree, *Alensites triloba*, by skewering a number of the kernels on a long palm-leaf midrib and lighting the upper one. The kernels are of nearly uniform size, and burn with a clear bluish flame, consuming in about ten minutes to a fungus, which, when the nut below is ignited, must be removed by someone in attendance. The Marquesans tie bits of tapa at intervals along the torch, and thus have invented a clock" (21, p. 207).

The external events which become anchorages in experience of time may not be as reliable as mathematically computed calendars based on observations of various heavenly bodies through precise instruments. As a result, the experience of time and localization of events in time may be vague and confused. For example, discrepancy between the lunar month and reckoning of the solar year was not taken into account by the calendars of some American Indian groups. Therefore, after a time, a familiar event like a celebration or observance would fall in the "wrong" month. "In the calendars which have only twelve months, the Indians may unconsciously lengthen a month when it does not tally with the event for which it was named, or they may insert another period. That the discrepancy was felt is shown by frequent reference in the literature of the Indians to discussion and quarrels about which month it is or ought to be at a given time. The arguments apparently continue in such cases until, through a comparison with the natural phenomena, matters are set right" (8, p. 137).

Space Orientation

Just as differing events or regularities serve as anchorages in the experience of time, conceptions and experiences of space in various cultures are regulated by various objective relations and limitations in the life of the people. "The Dobuan concept of space is that of a large garden clearing. Just as the garden has its inland border *kaikai*, its seaward border *kunnkumwana*, and its sides *nana*, so also has space in its widest extension" (10, p. 131).

It will be recalled that the ancient and medieval conceptions of space centered around the known lands of Europe, Asia, and Africa, which were believed to be surrounded by waters that teemed with monsters and eventually dropped off into space. The concept of a spherical world had been developed by scholarly men; but it was by no means common to the masses of people even when Columbus journeyed westward. Fears of reaching the end of the earth were expressed.

Estimates of Distance

Until standard units of length and distance were adopted, measures of length were often based on parts of the body and consequently varied from person to person. Standardized units were at first adopted on a local basis and became uniform when trade between localities, resulting in confusion and disagreements, necessitated uniform and more precise measures (1).

When no standardized measuring units and devices are available, experience of distance is vague. In a relatively isolated Turkish village, distances up to three or four kilometers were expressed as "within a bullet's reach," or "as far as my voice can go," or "as far as (it takes) to smoke a cigarette." Long distances were referred to by such expressions as: "You start early in the morning and reach there by sunset," or "You reach there (by the time) you work on crops of one dönum (of land)." These estimates were based on how long it took to make the trip on foot. Those villagers who had been on trips by bus or train (usually for military service) referred to the distances in terms of the days and nights spent on the vehicle. They could not translate these experiences into walking times, which served as anchorages in their ordinary experiences of distance. As a result, there were great discrepancies between their experience of some distances and the actual distances as measured in kilometers. For example, a neighboring town, to which these villagers had to walk, was considered farther away than Istanbul, which by railroad was almost twice as far (see pp. 692–694).

Similarly Hallowell found great difficulty in conveying the distance he had traveled from Philadelphia to the region of the Saulteaux, an Indian group he studied. The Saulteaux reckoned long distances in terms of "sleeps." Hallowell traveled by train and boat to a point within 260 miles of these people, where he proceeded by slower means. Thus, the number of nights he had slept gave a very distorted picture of the total distance. It had taken him as long to travel the remaining 260 miles as it had to come that far by modern transportation. Yet the distance during the first part of the journey was more than six times the remaining 260 miles (15).

Color Classifications

It is well known that, largely owing to their relative significance or importance in vital group activities, various features of the environment are accentuated by people in different cultures. As noted above, odor is an important feature of Andamanese life. Other features, however, may be less important and are conceptualized more vaguely. Color is such a feature in some cultures. Boas observed that in some cultures color is classified into distinct groups, without differentiation of various shadings. "What we call green or blue are often combined under some such term as 'gall-like color,' or yellow and green are combined under one concept, which may be 'young-leaves color'" (5, p. 199).

It is not implied that under proper conditions the individuals who utilize these color classifications could not see different shadings or differentiate between them. The point is that their experience of color is referred to categories differing from those which serve as anchorages in our color classification. Probably it has not been important for them to make finer distinctions.

In our own culture, artists and others who utilize color in their work may make finer distinctions than our common color classification does. Most of us ignore or do not notice these finer distinctions. Similarly, Wallis noted: "Not infrequently the savage *ignores* distinctions observed by us or cross-sections our distinctions. This frequently happens in color designations. The Ashantis have distinct names for the colors black, red, and white. The term *black* is also used for *any dark color*, such as blue, purple, brown, etc., while the term *red* does duty for pink, orange and yellow" (42, p. 421).

At a more complicated level, experience of differing skin colors varies in different societies. Such variations are not always due entirely to positive or negative stereotypes of people with different skin colors. Some may be traced to a reference scale built up through exposure to a narrow range of skin colors. It seems likely that initial reactions to light-skinned people as "pale" or "sickly" by darker-skinned groups were to an important extent a function of contrast of the light complexion in relation to their own reference scale. Such a contrast effect was experienced by the white journalist H. M. Stanley upon his first sight of Europeans (Portuguese) after his famous stay among the dark-skinned people of Africa: "As I looked into their faces, I blushed to find that I was wondering at their paleness. . . . The pale color, after so long gazing on rich black and richer bronze, had something of an unaccountable ghastliness. I could not divest myself of the feeling that they must be sick; yet, when I compare their complexions to what I now view, I should say that they were olive, sunburnt, dark" (38, p. 462).

However, in a world of functionally related groups, perception of skin color and reactions toward individuals with various skin colors are affected in decisive ways by socially standardized concepts (stereotypes) concerning those groups and their "place." Such concepts function as anchorages for reaction to skin color by those who have internalized them. In some cases the effect of these anchorages may be conducive to glossing over objective color differences. White persons in the United States undoubtedly are able to differentiate between light brown and dark brown, yet, as Faris noted some years ago, mulattoes in the United States are classified as Negroes and reacted to as Negroes. In Brazil, on the other hand, mulattoes are not classified with black-skinned peoples and are not reacted to as Negroes (9).

In an experiment on judgments of skin color by Negro subjects, Marks traced the variations in judgment to two main reference points. One was the social value placed in American culture on a light skin. Subjects revealed attitudes reflecting this cultural value by displacing their judgments of themselves and preferred associates toward the lighter color. The other anchorage affecting judgment was the objective color of the rater's own skin. If he was very dark, for example, this fact served as a check on how light he rated himself. Thus the reference scale of judgment varied somewhat from person to person in terms of the shade each person assigned to his own skin. The *relative* ranking of individuals on the various reference scales tended to correspond, but their absolute ranking in terms of skin color varied. This study gives clear-cut evidence of the joint effects of several related anchorages within the frame of reference determining judgment (28).

Perception of Patterns

The names given to different objects and structures serve as anchorages to individuals who have internalized (learned) those names. Hallowell gives an interesting example in this culture in relation to patterns which are clear but do allow for alternatives in structuring. He was lecturing to a group of students and discussing the different names which had been given to the constellation Ursa Major (dipper, bear, otter, plough, etc.) and their influence on perception of this group of stars. When he finished, feeling he had made the point, one student spoke up and said: "But it *does* look like a dipper." As Hallowell's remarks indicate, it probably *does* look like a plough to those who use that label (*16*, pp. 171–172).

Examples of cultural variations in experience and behavior illustrating that socially standardized anchorages exert a telling influence on perception, judgment, and reaction to objects, persons, and events could be piled up almost indefinitely. Only two more examples will be noted, illustrative of many which might be chosen.

A striking case of variation in the perception of similarity and differences between people was observed by Malinowski. From his study of the Trobriands, Malinowski reported that perception and judgments of resemblance between parents and offspring, or between children of the same parents, are regulated by strict social norms, which sometimes controvert evidence and our expectations in two respects.

First, resemblance to the father is considered "natural, right and proper. . . . Such similarity is always assumed and affirmed to exist." But it is a great offense to hint that a child resembles its mother or any of its maternal kinsfolk. "It is a phrase of serious bad language to say, 'Thy face is thy sister's,' which is the worst combination of kinship similarity."

Second, brothers are not considered to resemble one another, although each is said to be exactly like the father. Malinowski relates a specific incident illustrating this. When he commented on the striking likeness of two brothers, "there came such a hush over all the assembly, while the brother present withdrew abruptly and the company was half-embarrassed, half-offended at this breach of custom." In another case, five sons of a chief were each said to be exactly like the father. When Malinowski pointed out "that this similarity to the father implied similarity among themselves, such a heresy was indignantly repudiated" (*27*, pp. 87–92).

Here we see the influence of a taboo which resulted in ignoring a similarity that might otherwise have been perceived, and a positive norm emphasizing a similarity which might not otherwise have been noticed.

Remembering

The internal influences which, as Bartlett's studies showed, invariably enter into remembering some past experience are not necessarily unique for the individual. Many are derived from standards or significant values of his group. Bartlett was told that the Swazi of South Africa had wonderful memories. He accordingly devised several little test situations which were meaningful to the Swazi, like carrying a message in their language from one end of the village to another. He found, however, that recall in these test situations was no better or worse than that he had found among English subjects.

It was suggested to him that this remarkable memory for which the Swazi were noted applied only to objects and events which had considerable significance in their life, in particular to their cattle, which were the center of their economic life. Therefore, a European settler offered a test case: Bartlett would ask his Swazi herdsman, who could not read, for a description of the cattle which the settler had purchased a year earlier. The owner had a written record of the transactions, which the herdsman had merely observed and overheard. Circumstances were arranged so that there was no way for the herdsman to be informed concerning the transaction. Upon Bartlett's request, the herdsman recited each of twelve transactions made a year earlier, including a description of the animal, the price paid, and from whom it was purchased. In checking the account book, only two errors were found—an error of a few shillings in one price and a mistake in color of one animal. Bartlett concluded that "the individual peculiarities of the cattle can be recalled freshly and vividly, because herds, and all dealings with them are of tremendous social importance" (2, pp. 250–251).

CONCLUDING REMARKS

This chapter has drawn on a large body of literature for illustrations of the factual basis for concepts and generalizations applicable in handling the joint determination of experience and behavior by functionally related internal and external influences. Examples were drawn both from experimental literature on reactions to relatively simple stimulus material and from ethnological literature revealing cultural variations in experience and behavior. The rationale for the selection was twofold: concepts and generalizations in social psychology must be congruent with findings of general psychology and must also be applicable to facts of cultural variation.

These illustrative findings, basic to the concepts and relationships utilized in treating various topics in social psychology, are to be considered in relation to a conceptual scheme encompassing diverse specific examples. Such a conceptual scheme is outlined in the next chapter.

REFERENCES

1. American Council on Education. *The Story of Weights and Measures.* Washington, 1932.
2. Bartlett, F. C. *Remembering: A Study in Experimental and Social Psychology.* Cambridge: University Press, 1932.
3. Beebe-Center, J. *Pleasantness and Unpleasantness.* New York: Van Nostrand, 1932.
4. Benary, W. The Influence of Form on Brightness Contrast, in W. D. Ellis (ed.), *A Sourcebook of Gestalt Psychology.* New York: Harcourt, Brace, 1939.
5. Boas, F. *The Mind of Primitive Man.* New York: Macmillan, 1924.
6. Buxton, C. E. The Frame of Reference, in R. H. Seashore (ed.), *Fields of Psychology.* New York: Holt, 1942.
7. Chapman, D. W., and Volkmann, J. A social determinant of the level of aspiration, *J. abnorm. & soc. Psychol.* (1939), 34:225–238.
8. Cope, L. Calendars of the Indians North of Mexico, *Univ. of Calif. Publ. in Amer. Archaeol. and Ethnol.* (1919), 16:137.
9. Faris, E. The concept of social attitudes, *J. appl. Sociol.* (1935), 9:404–409.
10. Fortune, R. F. *Sorcerers of Dobu.* London: Routledge, 1932.
11. Fraser, J. A. A new illusion of direction, *Brit. J. Psychol.* (1908), 2:307–320.
12. Gibson, J. J. *The Perception of the Visual World.* Boston: Houghton Mifflin, 1950.
13. Gottschaldt, K. Gestalt Factors and Repetition, in W. D. Ellis (ed.), *A Sourcebook of Gestalt Psychology.* New York: Harcourt, Brace, 1939.
14. Gulliksen, H. The influence of occupation upon the perception of time, *J. exper. Psychol.* (1927), 10:52–59.
15. Hallowell, A. I. Some psychological aspects of measurement among the Saulteaux, *Amer. Anthropol.* (1942), 44:67.
16. Hallowell, A. I. Cultural Factors in the Structuralization of Perception, in J. H. Rohrer and M. Sherif (eds.), *Social Psychology at the Crossroads.* New York: Harper, 1951.

17. Heintz, R. The effect of remote anchoring points upon judgments of lifted weights, *J. exper. Psychol.* (1950), 40:584–591.
18. Henri, V. Recherches sur la localisation des sensations tactiles, *Année Psychol.* (1895), 2:168–177.
19. Henri, V. *Über die Lokalisation des Tastempfindungen.* Berlin: Reuther, 1897.
20. Hilgard, E. R. *Introduction to Psychology.* New York: Harcourt, Brace, 1953.
21. Hough, W. Time keeping by light and fire, *Amer. Anthropol.* (1893), 6:207.
22. Katz, D. *Gestalt Psychology.* New York: Ronald, 1950.
23. Koffka, K. Perception: An introduction to Gestalt-theorie, *Psychol. Bull.* (1922), 19:531–585.
24. Köhler, W. *Gestalt Psychology.* New York: Liveright, 1929.
25. Köhler, W. *Dynamics in Psychology.* New York: Liveright, 1940.
26. McGarvey, H. Anchoring effects in the absolute judgment of verbal material, *Arch. Psychol.* (1943), No. 281.
27. Malinowski, B. *The Father in Primitive Psychology.* New York: Norton, 1927.
28. Marks, E. Skin color judgments of Negro college students, *J. abnorm. & soc. Psychol.* (1943), 22:3–14.
29. Murphy, Gardner. *In the Minds of Men.* New York: Basic Books, 1953.
30. Newman, E. B. Perception, in E. G. Boring, H. S. Langfeld, and H. P. Weld, *Foundations of Psychology.* New York: Wiley, 1948.
31. Postman, L., and Egan, J. P. *Experimental Psychology.* New York: Harper, 1949.
32. Radcliffe-Brown, A. *The Andaman Islander.* Cambridge, England: Cambridge University Press, 1922.
33. Ribot, T. *Diseases of Memory.* London: Appleton, 1893.
34. Rogers, S. The anchoring of absolute judgments, *Arch. Psychol.* (1941), No. 261.
35. Rubin, E. *Visuellwahrgenommen Figuren: Studien in psychologischer Analyse.* Kobenhavn: Gyldendol, 1921.
36. Sherif, M. *The Psychology of Social Norms.* New York: Harper, 1936.
37. Sherif, M., Taub, D., and Hovland, C. I. Assimilation and contrast effects of anchoring stimuli on judgment (in preparation).
38. Stanley, H. M. *Through the Dark Continent.* New York, 1878, Vol. II.
39. Tresselt, M. E. The influence of amount of practice upon the formation of a scale of judgment, *J. exper. Psychol.* (1947), 37:251–260.
40. Volkmann, J. The anchoring of absolute scales, *Psychol. Bull.* (1936), 33:742–743 (abstract).
41. Volkmann, J. Scales of Judgment and Their Implications for Social Psy-

chology, in J. H. Rohrer and M. Sherif (eds.), *Social Psychology at the Crossroads*. New York: Harper, 1951.

42. Wallis, W. D. *An Introduction to Anthropology*. New York: Harper, 1926.
43. Webster, H. *Rest Days*. New York: Macmillan, 1916.
44. Wells, F. L. On the Variability of Individual Judgment, in *Essays Philosophical and Psychological in Honor of William James, by his Colleagues at Columbia University*. New York: Longmans, Green, 1908.
45. Wertheimer, M. Laws of Perceptual Forms, in W. D. Ellis (ed.), *A Sourcebook of Gestalt Psychology*. New York: Harcourt, Brace, 1939.
46. Wever, E. G., and Zener, K. E. Method of absolute judgment in psychophysics, *Psychol. Rev.* (1928), 35:466–493.
47. Woodrow, H. Time Perception, in S. S. Stevens (ed.), *Handbook of Experimental Psychology*. New York: Wiley, 1951.
48. Woodworth, R. S., and Schlosberg, H. *Experimental Psychology*. New York: Holt, rev. ed., 1954.
49. Yeager, C. E. I Flew Faster Than Sound, New York *Herald Tribune*, Magazine Section, August 22, 1948.

CHAPTER **3**

Some Principles to Be Applied

The last chapter presented illustrative facts basic to the pyschological principles which will be utilized in handling the various topics of this book. The facts and principles selected for emphasis here are the basic minimum. They do not include all of the principles that are utilized in social psychology. Auxiliary concepts and generalizations are necessary in the application and extension of these essential principles to the social field. In addition to those made focal here, others will be used as required by particular topics and problems.

This chapter summarizes principles illustrated in the last chapter. Concise propositions are stated which together constitute the main outlines of a conceptual approach to social-psychological problems. Later in the chapter, two of these propositions are elaborated further because of their crucial implications for various specific topics. These two pertain to *psychological selectivity* and to the relative effects of *structured and unstructured stimulus situations*. These basic problems prepare the ground for discussion at the end of the chapter of some consequences of the *loss of stable anchorages* and *conflict of anchorages*, which are prevalent in the contemporary social scene.

1. *Experience and behavior constitute a unity*. The conceptual approach starts with the conception of the unity of experience and behavior (20, pp. 354–359). This assertion becomes necessary because of certain lines of argument advanced in recent years.

Some investigators have demonstrated that there are cases of discrepancy between what people *say* their attitude is on an issue and how they behave in matters related to that issue. For example, hotelkeepers who wrote in response to a written inquiry that they would not accommodate Chinese did accommodate Chinese individuals who appeared on the scene with the investigator. Bartenders who said they would not serve Negroes did actually serve Negro individuals who dropped in, usually in the company of white companions.

Such cases need not indicate that experience and behavior are independent of each other. Discrepancy between verbal statement (behavior) in one situation and behavior in another situation does not mean that attitude and action are unrelated. There are several possible explanations of these cases without such an assumption. It is possible that direct verbal inquiry in letter or oral form arouses other attitudes (for example, the businessman's conception of "good public relations"). In this case his persistent attitude on the issue at hand is not ascertained by the methods employed. Or if his reply does indicate a persistent attitude, it is possible that other factors came into the picture on the later occasion which weighed more heavily at that time in determining the line of action he took. Attitudes are not the only factors influencing experience and behavior. Other motivational and situational factors are also involved, often in decisive fashion. In any case, it is not necessary to assume a sharp separation between experience and behavior.

In the analysis of such apparent discrepancies, more effective methods of tapping attitudes are needed. Point-blank verbal questions requiring an all-or-none stand on an issue usually arouse motives other than the attitude in question. There is ample evidence that when individuals take a definite positive or negative stand they do react rather consistently on related issues. (See Chapter 15.)

Such apparent discrepancies have sometimes been taken as evidence for the advantage of a "phenomenological" (experience) approach, as opposed to an "objective" (or behavior) approach. Advocating divorce of experience and behavior is akin to saying that the muscles function independently of the central integrative processes. To be sure, every experience is not immediately translated into action. There are times when one finds it inappropriate or even risky to act in terms of his cherished position on a topic. But whenever action is taken, it is the outcome of central integrating processes, which are shaped by diverse, functionally related factors. The dissociation of experience and action which appears in some pathological cases is not typical of man's relations of consequence in human affairs.

2. *Behavior follows central psychological structuring.* Ordinarily, behavior is the consequence of central structuring or patterning; hence the unity of experience and action. In the accompanying diagram central psychological structuring is represented by PS (Fig. 3.1).

Action is not a direct function of external stimuli or of internal impulses (motives, desires, and the like). Behavior follows the central organization or patterning of all of these factors. In the patterned product, the individual need not be aware of separate contributing items coming from external stimulating conditions or from inside himself.

3. *Psychological structuring is jointly determined by external and internal factors.* Perceptual structuring may be taken as a prototype of all psy-

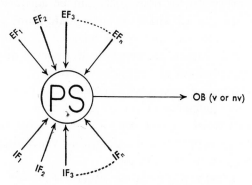

Fig. 3.1.   Diagrammatic representation of the frame of reference of an observed behavior.

OB (v or nv): Observed behavior (verbal or nonverbal).

EF: External factors (objects, cultural products, persons, groups, etc., in the external stimulus situation).

IF: Internal factors (motives, attitudes, emotions, various states of the organism, effects of past experience, etc.).

PS: Psychological (perceptual) structuring.

chological processes (judging, learning, remembering, imagining, decision making, and so on). Perceptual structuring is not only a "cognitive" affair. It is jointly determined by the totality of functionally related external factors and internal factors coming into the structuring process at a given time (25, p. 32).

In 1929 Köhler pointed out the "bipolar character" of psychological structuring (13). This view is exemplified in the following statements: "We may say that, apart from drowsiness and similar state of low vitality, the organization of the total field will almost always have just that bipolar character, the self being directed to something else or from it" (p. 323).

"Evidently it is not only the external situation which in a great many cases has to be considered, but the internal situation of the organism as well" (p. 325). In spite of this theoretical orientation, the major emphasis of Gestalt work on perception until recent years has been on the structural properties of the external field.

The functionally interrelated external and internal factors operating at a given time constitute the *frame of reference* of the ensuing reaction. Observed behavior (verbal or nonverbal) can be adequately understood and evaluated when studied within its appropriate frame of reference, or system of relations. The sequence of the relations is shown by the direction of the arrows in Figure 3.1. However, this simple diagram does not indicate the interrelatedness of the various factors.

The concept "frame of reference" does not refer to a specific psychological product, like judgment or perception. It does not refer merely to an attitude or to a social norm. Rather it denotes a system of functional relations among factors operative at a given time which determine psychological structuring and hence behavior.

The *external factors* are stimulating situations outside of the individual—objects, events, other persons, groups, cultural products, and the like.

The *internal factors* are motives, emotions, attitudes, general states of the organism, effects of past experience, etc. The limit between the two sets of factors is the skin of the individual—the skin being on the side of the organism.

4. *Internal factors (motives, attitudes, and so on) and experience are inferred from behavior.* The psychologist's data consist of items of observed behavior (verbal and nonverbal) and external stimulus situations. Motives, attitudes, etc., and experience are inferred from observed behavior in specific situations. Overt action, words spoken or written, subtle expressions of face and body are all behavior. The unity of experience and behavior is again implied.

No one has directly observed an attitude, a desire, a complex. These internal variables are not witnessed in the same way that one observes an overt expression of approval or disapproval, a word or deed, a person's verbal report of perception, an explicit statement of one's expected performance, a slip of the tongue, a narrative of someone's dream, an action or a series of actions.

5. *The psychological tendency is toward structuring of experience.* There is a tendency toward structuring in the experience of present objects and events (perception) and also in the experience of objects and events

not immediately present (remembering, imagining, and the like). Of course, perceiving and judging are not identical with remembering or imagining. Experience and behavior in relation to actual objects and events are subject to the correctives of reality checks. In remembering, on the other hand, the physical object or event is not present and the role of objective factors is necessarily reduced, though not absent altogether.

We tend to see definite forms, definite patterns, definite sequences and structure in events. In time, our memory of them may be modified and even transformed, yet still further structured.

Experimental evidence has shown that psychological structuring, whether in perceiving, judging, or remembering, is not an additive affair. The properties of various parts in a structure are different from their properties when they are parts of another structure, and different from their properties when they are studied alone by themselves. The point was illustrated in various ways in the last chapter. This characteristic is referred to as "membership character." The membership character of parts is as true of motivational impulses as of sense impressions of situations outside the body.

This principle and the concept of membership character are basic to understanding the differential effects of social interaction and the consequences of membership in a human group.

6. *Structured stimulus situations set limits to alternatives in psychological structuring.* The stimulus world around us consists of objects, streets, buildings, contours in space, and so on. When we are concerned with such structured stimulus situations, the structure of perception corresponds, on the whole, to physical structures. Some objective factors that determine corresponding psychological structure were illustrated in Chapter 2 (pp. 54–59). Objective properties of stimulus situations limit the possible *alternatives* in experiencing them. The shape of steps and their sequence on the staircase are compellingly perceived as such. Very few people will recklessly tumble down a staircase. Such situations are referred to as *structured stimulus situations*.

7. *In unstructured stimulus situations, alternatives in psychological structuring are increased.* There are stimulus situations which lack objective structure in various degrees. The contours, the beginning and end points in space or time, the sequence of characteristics, or the objects and events are not sharply defined. They lack stable objective anchorages. Therefore, various alternatives in psychological structuring become feasible.

The simplest illustrations of stimulus objects which are conducive to alternatives are the reversible pictures which are constructed so that two or more different objects can be perceived in them. The Rubin reversible picture, which can be seen either as a goblet or as two profiles facing one another, is an example (Fig. 2.5, p. 52). If the individual is told to expect two profiles, he will be more likely to see two profiles first. If set to expect the goblet through instructions or some other influence, he will see the picture first as a goblet. The objective properties of this picture allow only two alternatives.

As the objective structure, the pattern, of the stimulus situation decreases, as it becomes more ambiguous, more complicated, as the demarcation lines of the situation or event become more uncertain, the *alternatives* for perceptual structuring increase. Stimulus situations of this kind are referred to as *unstructured* stimulus situations.

8. *The more unstructured the stimulus situation, the greater the relative contribution of internal factors in the frame of reference.* As stimulus situations become more unstructured, the relative contribution of internal factors (motives, emotions, attitudes, identifications of the person, other products of past learning) to the ensuing psychological structure becomes greater. Accumulating laboratory evidence substantiates this assertion. Some of the evidence is summarized later in this chapter (pp. 100–106). To the frightened person in the dark, there are many hostile movements in the shrubbery.

9. *The more unstructured the stimulus situation, the greater the relative contribution of external social factors in the frame of reference.* The more unstructured, the more uncertain, the stimulus situation, the greater are the effects of social influences (personal suggestion, information, group demands, majority opinion, and the like) in psychological structuring.

In studying the effect of social factors, the motives or attitudes of the individual in relation to the stimulus situation, which includes the social influences at hand, have to be taken as related to one another. Otherwise, some important internal factors operative as parts of the frame of reference at the time will be neglected. The increasing relative weight of social influences as the structure of the external stimulus situation decreases can be understood in terms of the relationship between these external social anchorages and internal factors (motives, attitudes). In situations providing few physical reference points, social influences tend to become effective anchorages because of their relevance to the individual's motivations, attitudes toward persons, groups, or social products involved.

Whether the objective situation is well structured or not, the tendency is toward psychological structuring, as indicated under point 5 above. Uncertainty, chaos, and confusion are psychologically avoided if possible. As Murphy stated, "The ordering of events in time and space gives satisfaction" (*20*, p. 359).

10. *Various factors in the frame of reference have differing relative weights.* If the aim is to go beyond giving a general picture of the psychological tendencies revealed in perception and behavior, the mere citation of external and internal factors operative within the frame of reference at a given time which give rise to particular psychological structuring is not sufficient. If the aim is the prediction and eventual control of events, then the *relative weights* of various external and internal factors in a given frame of reference have to be discovered by systematically varying this factor now, that factor then.

This point seems similar to a hypothesis stated by Murphy and Hochberg and expressed in terms of raw impressions received from outside through the sense organs and impulses stemming from within the organism. "Exteroceptive, interoceptive, and proprioceptive components, enter fully and on an equal footing, but not always with equal weight, into the dynamics of perception" (*21*).

Even though all of the various factors that function as parts within a frame of reference influence other parts, certain factors, or a certain factor, are operative as *limiting* influences in determining the main character of the structure. If the limiting factors are changed or eliminated, the whole character of the structure and of other parts will change or be transformed. These limiting, weighty factors are referred to as the main *anchorages* in the frame of reference. The discussions under points 6, 7, 8, and 9 above are related to this problem of the relative weights of external and internal factors under various conditions.

As noted in the last chapter, recent work in judgment dealing with the effects of experimentally introduced anchoring stimuli demonstrates the importance of such weighty factors in determining the character of the structure and of other parts (pp. 48–51).

The concept of anchorages is crucial in understanding the consequences of becoming a member of or relating oneself to a social group. Change in the major group anchorage of an individual, that is, a change of reference groups, brings about alterations in many other attitudes which were not specifically challenged by the individual himself or by appropriate communication from others.

11. *Psychological activity is selective*. In laboratory situations the indi-vidual's stimulus field is circumscribed to the specified items meticulously prepared and delimited by the experimenter. The more exclusively the external field is limited to the experimental variable—the more others are excluded—the more successful the experiment. Consequently, the subject is forced to attend only to the stimuli prepared for him by the experi-menter. The structured or unstructured nature of the stimuli affects the organization of judgment or perception along the lines outlined above (under 6, 7, 8, 9).

However, on a street, in a department store, on a college campus, in a concert hall there are literally hundreds of objects which are well struc-tured. The structural properties of some are so compelling that they are likely to be noticed by most people. The others, if noticed, would arouse perceptions corresponding, on the whole, to the objective structure of those objects. However, only a small proportion of these structured objects are perceived during a particular period. Those objects or persons that are perceived are likely to be the ones related to our motives, attitudes, pre-occupations at the time, in addition to those whose structural properties are sufficiently compelling so that they "hit" almost everyone in the eye.

Take a young man whose flow of energy is flooding the banks of his ex-istence; a social climber restless in his upward moves; a pretender to the title of best-dressed lady in town; a person deeply concerned with human affairs. As they come from the lecture hall, from the address of an invited celebrity, ask them to jot down all the items they perceived in the hall. Classify the items in terms of their frequency and relevance to major per-sonal goals. There will be significant differences in the frequency of items under each classification for these persons, in line with their major goals. This rather trite example shows a psychological tendency well known for decades. It embodies the major principle of *psychological selectivity*, brought to the foreground by dramatic demonstrations that "we do not see with our eyes alone" or "hear with our ears alone," but see and hear as well with all the person we are at the time—with our desires, attitudes, and ambitions.

In short, of all the potentially "perceivable" objects, those are likely to stand out as *figures* with distinct contours which have relevance to the ob-server's preoccupations, desires, attitudes, or ambitions at the time. Other objects or persons, which are potentially just as "perceivable" as structured objects but which have little relevance to interests or motives at the time, will generally stay in the perceptually rather indistinct *background*. Like-wise, of all the potentially discriminable aspects of the world, the individual is likely to discriminate, and to learn to make finer discriminations of, those which have some relevance to his enduring or temporarily pressing desires, interests, or ambitions.

The above facts point to certain limitations in the work practice of psychologists, who deliberately reduce the stimulus world of the subject to experimentally introduced items. This is the only feasible way to study "cognitive" abilities (such as discriminatory and perceptual abilities) and their physical correlates. But the natural psychological tendency is to perceive *selectively*, not as determined by an exclusively restricted stimulus field but as determined by internal factors and external factors which are reciprocally relevant.

The starry sky with its constellations of rather definite grouping was always there, but man did not always attend to its distinctive features. Man's vision was not any different formerly; but he attended rather to the distinctiveness of other structures in his surroundings. Historically it is found that certain structures had little or no relevance in terms of the preoccupations of individuals living in human groups at a given place and time. But when the preoccupation of the group changed, at times some generations later, these stimulus structures came to the foreground. All parts were keenly perceived by individual members and relevant aspects were sharply differentiated.

Perception and judgment are not only cognitive affairs. They are jointly determined by external and internal factors operative at a given time. Ordinarily both cognitive and motivational factors contribute to the structuring of experience. In actual life conditions, motivational factors are implicitly operative even in cases of perceptions whose structures correspond closely to the structure of stimulus objects, or judgments which follow the objective stimulus series. This implicit participation of motivational factors becomes clear if we ask: Why is this object perceived at this time rather than other possible objects in the situation which are equally well structured? Why is this aspect discriminated rather than other aspects which are equally discriminable? The answer lies in psychological selectivity, which is tuned by desire, attitude, passion, interest, preoccupation, and the like, operative at the time.

WHAT WE ATTEND TO AT A GIVEN TIME: PSYCHOLOGICAL SELECTIVITY

The facts of psychological selectivity deserve further discussion, for they pervade man's experiences and reactions in every phase of social life. This discussion will start at a simple level as preparation for handling more complicated problems concerning the role of man's motives, attitudes, and interests in his selective reactions to social situations.

First the problem is summarized. In experiments the conditions are set for the individual before he enters the laboratory. The particular tasks he will perform and the stimuli he will respond to are prepared in advance. The aspects of the situation and the manner in which he should be concerned with them are carefully planned in the experimental procedures and instructions. He is exposed to carefully prepared hidden figures in structured visual forms or a precisely graded series of weights at one extreme, or at the other extreme he is presented with ink blots, a single point of light, or other unstructured stimuli. After agreeing to take part in an experiment, he ordinarily tries to do his best to follow instructions in relation to the task and stimuli prepared; and not infrequently he goes farther and tries to prove that he is not a back number. By and large, present psychological generalizations pertaining to perception and judgment of various types of stimulation are based on this type of situation.

However, in actual life circumstances, the individual's stimulus field is not thus circumscribed. He is exposed to literally thousands of stimulus objects. Some of them are well structured, some are not, and there are all kinds of shadings in between these extremes.

Yet at any given time what the individual attends to is circumscribed. And this circumscribed stimulus object or person need not be in itself the most conspicuous of those present. Anyone who watches people on Times Square in New York, the most crowded intersection of the world, sees individuals who succeed in carrying on a conversation and attending only to the words exchanged, individuals who look intently at tiny wrist watches in a drugstore window, someone reading a newspaper against the competition of noise, massive and incessantly moving traffic, huge billboards, colored lights, and a flowing stream of humanity.

The initial problem becomes, therefore, why we attend to certain stimuli rather than thousands of other possible ones. This is the problem of psychological selectivity. After studying it, the problems of how a particular stimulus is perceived, the effects of its structural properties, and other influences can be studied adequately. If the order of study follows the sequence of psychological events, the problem of psychological selectivity has to be taken up first. On the whole, research and theory have been overpreoccupied with how things are perceived and reacted to after they have become focal. Therefore, the matter of selectivity, which should be the first problem, has not received due consideration in proportion to its significance in the sequence of events.

In dealing with the important problem at hand, the term "psychological selectivity" is used rather than "perceptual selectivity." *Perceptual selectivity is a special case of general psychological selectivity. Perception is selective, and so are learning, thinking, remembering, and imagining.*

The Span of Focal Experience Has Definite Bounds

The selectivity which makes a certain unit focal in experience is necessary for integrative psychological functioning. When two or more units, each consisting of various parts, become focal at the same time, the functioning of integrative processes becomes cluttered or even disrupted. Instances are seen even in simple discrimination of two objects.

Faced with the task of discriminating when we cannot readily resolve one object as the bigger figure and the other as the smaller, we feel strain in the task. When we are caught between two important decisions and find that neither stands out as the preferred line of action, we are caught in the strain of a conflict. The smoothness of our functioning is disrupted; our confidence becomes shaky.

The bounded, limited nature of the unit of experience which is focal at a given time was referred to as *focus* as distinguished from the *margin* or *fringe* of experience as early as the days of William James.

Figure and ground are delineated in remembering, thinking, and imagining as well as in perceiving and discriminating (pp. 52–54). What is selected as focal in remembering and thinking stands out as figure against its appropriate ground or fringe. Particular items or events do not acquire figure character in a haphazard way. Selectivity may be largely due to the sheer compellingness of external events, or it may be chiefly due to the relevance of the figure for a task engaged in, a desire, attitude, or preoccupation which has greater relative weight at the time. There are times when some internal urge is so strong that certain items become focal in spite of one's intention to concentrate on a task at hand. The individual need not always be aware of all of the internal factors which brought a certain item to the foreground of experience.

Span of Attention or Apprehension

The clearest demonstrations of psychological selectivity have been in the area of perception and judgment. In one rapid glance, a person's perception encompasses only a unit of the external field consisting of a number of parts or items. Since the last century this fact has been referred to as the span of attention or apprehension. The items included within the span of attention become parts within the contours of the figure, as distinguished from the ground. Thus the span covered by attention may be the figure of the perceived external situation or the distinct reference scale of judgment consisting of so many items.

Facts demonstrating the limiting nature of the span of attention have been reported for almost a century. In 1859, Sir William Hamilton told his students that if they threw a handful of marbles on the floor they would "find it difficult to view at once more than six, or seven at the most, without confusion; but if you group them in twos, or threes, or fives, you can comprehend as many groups as you can units because the mind considers these groups only as units" (37, p. 90).

In 1871 Jevons tossed a handful of black beans, some of which fell on a tray. He immediately estimated the number of beans on the tray and recorded his estimate. He then checked his estimate against the actual number of items on the tray. The number of items correctly comprehended in one glance did not exceed 5 or 6 items. With the use of a tachistoscope, which enables the experimenter to project objects on a screen for brief exposures of fractions of a second, it is established that the average span of attention for scattered objects for keen adults is about 8 objects (37, p. 94).

However, the number of objects grasped in one glance can be increased by exposing them in objective patterns, say in 2's or 5's. If the items are objectively grouped in 5's, an observer can grasp and report correctly that there are 25 objects in a limited area. In this case, however, they are not perceived as 25 separate items but as 5 units each consisting of 5 items.

Beyond 6-8 items the individual does not discriminate them as one unit; he makes an estimate based on a general impression. If he tries to be exact, he counts one by one or by 2's; or if conditions allow, he counts by groups in 5's or 6's. Counting means attending to items in successive steps.

If letters are the stimulus material, the span of perception is increased when they are in meaningful words. It is increased many times more when the words are related to one another in a meaningful way (37, p. 101).

The most extensive recent studies concerning the span of judgment for a number of objects in one glance are those by Reese, Volkmann, and their associates (12, 24). The trend of previous findings was confirmed and extended in their work to the study of the effects of anchorages introduced by the experimenter. The findings concerning the role of anchorages in the span of judgment are full of implications for the problem of selectivity as it is related to social psychology.

These investigators found that up to 6 items the number is immediately and correctly perceived in one glance (when exposed for a fraction of a second). They gave a technical name, *subitizing,* to this immediate and correct perception of 5–6 distinct items to distinguish it from *estimating,* which occurs beyond this point. Larger numbers of objects were judged by global impression, and errors increased abruptly. Judging the number of objects at a glance in this general fashion was called *estimating,* as distinguished from the direct perception of a smaller number (subitizing).

The direct perception of number is influenced by such external factors as the *area* in which objects are scattered, the *density* of scatter, the *size* of objects (within limits), and the *order of presentation.* For example, starting with presentations of small numbers (1–5) is more favorable to direct perception than starting with larger numbers.

On the side of internal factors, past experience (practice, for example) decreases report time and variability and increases the confidence with which individuals judge the number of objects.

External social influence in the form of instructions that "most people tend to overestimate" causes the subjects to underestimate the number of objects presented. The suggestion that "most people tend to underestimate" produces the reverse effect, namely, overestimation. However, suggestion by the experimenter is effective *only when the number of objects is beyond the perceptual* (subitizing) *range* or span. When the number presented is within the span of perception (up to about 6 items), suggestion is not effective, and subjects report the actual number of objects, which, within this range, they are able to perceive immediately.

One research unit dealt with the effect of experimentally introduced anchorages in estimating large numbers of objects exposed briefly. There were 35 collections of dots presented, each collection differing in number. The collections ranged at appropriate intervals from 1 dot to 210. When a standard (anchorage) of 210 items was given with each presentation, its effect was to decrease errors in estimates and to decrease variability of the estimates in the middle and upper range of numbers. When the anchorage consisted of 49 dots, numbers just below 49 were overestimated, and those just above 49 were underestimated. In short, an assimilation effect was produced by the anchorage for numbers just below and above it. The anchorage had the further effect of reducing variability for estimates of most numbers, and of quicker responses given with greater confidence.

In social life, individuals frequently make immediate on-the-spot judgments of surrounding objects or persons, of performance and achievement of other people. They estimate future events. The anchorages involved in making such judgments come from past experience, from one's positive or negative stand on an issue (attitude), from positive or negative relationships with persons in question, or from a favorite radio or newspaper commentator.

In brief, the material summarized above indicates that perceiving, judging, and the like are circumscribed at a given time within certain bounds. What is distinct, focal, or figure in experience and even its span are influenced by available anchorages, which may be external, internal, or both.

Psychological Selectivity in Various Activities

Thus, one basis of psychological selectivity is the fact that only a more or less bounded structure (figure) consisting of a limited number of items can become focal or distinct in experience at a given time.

The generality of psychological selectivity was stressed by William James in his memorable treatment of the stream of consciousness. James chose selectivity as one of the four essential characteristics of experience. "It is interested in some parts of its object to the exclusion of others, and welcomes or rejects—*chooses* from among them, in a word—all the while" (*11*, p. 152).

"The phenomena of selective attention and of deliberative will are of course patent examples of the choosing activity. But few of us are aware how incessantly it is at work in operations not ordinarily called by these names. . . ."

"But we do far more than emphasize things, and unite some, and keep others apart. We actually ignore most of the things before us" (*11*, p. 170).

External and Internal Factors in Determining What Is Focal in Experience

What will stand out more distinctly as focal or figure in experience is not an arbitrary affair. The facts of selectivity have to be analyzed in terms of external and internal factors and the interplay of these two sets of factors.

Combining and extending the factors variously proposed in standard works (e.g., 22, 29), we may cite such factors under the following broad headings without attempting to be exhaustive:

I. External factors.
   1. Intensity, size, novelty, repetition, contrast, movement, and change of objects and events.
   2. Social influences, such as instructions, suggestions, group pressures, and group participation.
II. Internal factors.
   1. Momentary set, personal interest, motives (hunger, thirst, sexual desire, and the like), states of the organism (emotion, fatigue, and the like).
   2. Socially derived factors, such as positive or negative social attitudes, identification with or prejudice against persons or groups, linguistic repertory, internalized social norms, and the like.

When we walk down a street, skim through a newspaper or magazine, turn on the radio or television, we are faced with a flood of advertising which utilizes the effectiveness of the above external and internal factors in varying combinations to gain our attention.

In billboards, papers, radio, or television, the size, intensity, novelty, contrast, movement, and change of external stimuli (singly or in combination) are usually not presented in abstract form. The form and colors or the sounds are usually those of an attractive female or male, or of some distinguished folks with their brightly colored car. In other words, size, novelty, contrast, change, and other external factors which gain our attention are not used in abstract form but in forms related to internal factors (hunger, sexual desire, social distinction, bias, and identification).

In the great metropolis of London there are huge things, colored and moving things, novel things—millions of objects to attract the notice of visitors from Africa. A commission of Swazi, a tribe of Zulu origin in South Africa, visited London. The thing that remained most vividly fixed in the recollection of these Swazi chiefs was their picture of the English policeman regulating traffic with uplifted hand. Bartlett, who reported this incident, raised the question which helps to clarify the implications of this selective recall:

"Why should this simple action have made so profound an impression? Certainly not merely because it was taken as a symbol of power. Many other illustrations of power, far more striking to the European mind, had been seen and, for all practical purposes, forgotten. The Swazi greets his fellow, or his visitor, with uplifted hand. Here was the familiar gesture, warm with friendliness, in a foreign country, and at the same time arresting in its consequences. It was one of the few things they saw that fitted immediately into their own well-established social framework and so produced a quick and lasting effect" (5, p. 248).

Of course, these Swazi individuals certainly could not help perceiving other stimulus structures and events during their stay in London. Yet the special selection of the traffic officer with uplifted hand as something clearly recalled indicated that this particular event was among those which stood out vividly at the time in their perception, because it aroused warm internal resonance as well.

Earlier it was noted that the structural properties of bright stars in definite groupings are not sufficient to insure that an individual will experience the groupings as figure. There are many objective groupings and structures. Which one of these will be focal at a given time can be explained only with reference to internal factors and, in many instances, to social factors as well. The point is illustrated by an ethnological observation. Among some of the Northern Rhodesians ". . . remarkably little attention is paid to the stars (intongwezli). When one thinks of the magnificently brilliant nights and their habits of sitting around the evening camp fires, one wonders that they should not have figured out constellations and formed myths of the stars. We have many times drawn their attention to the stars and tried to get their names, but without success. It is not reckoned taboo to attempt to count the stars, but any one who should try it would be laughed at as a fool. The only planet they name is Venus; but knowing that she appears as the evening and as morning star, they give her two names" (27, p. 66).

Külpe's Demonstrations of Multidimensional Selectivity

In the experiments reported earlier on span of attention, only one dimension was to be reported, namely, the number of the objects. Usually in a perceptual figure the component parts or items have various discriminable aspects (e.g., color, shade, intensity, size, form) which are also subject to selective accentuation. Finer and more detailed differentiation of these various aspects or dimensions is significantly influenced by various internal and social factors operative at the time (e.g., past experience, someone's instructions telling what to look for, motives, internalized norms). A homely illustration of the point may be the aspects or dimensions of an attractive young woman that are perceived by young men, old ladies, or young ladies.

A well-known line of research furnished convincing experimental demonstrations of the principle involved. Experiments in Külpe's laboratory studied the influence of *Aufgabe* (task or instruction) on perception of the stimuli presented (*14*). In these experiments, begun in 1900, Külpe briefly presented his subjects with different stimuli, such as printed syllables, about which different aspects or "dimensions" could be reported. For example, the *number* of letters, the *location* of the colors, or the *total pattern* composed by them could be reported.

Külpe found that more items were noted and more correct judgments made by the subject about that aspect of the stimuli which had been emphasized by the *Aufgabe.* The subjects noticed more fully and in more detail the aspects of the stimulus field that they were "set" to see. Subsequently Yokoyama (*38*) and Chapman (*8*) verified Külpe's results. All of these experiments indicate that "the efficiency of report for all tasks is lower under an indefinite *Aufgabe* than under a definite instruction" (*8*).

In these studies the individual is "set" to respond to certain aspects because of the instructions given by the experimenter. To speak of a "set" means nothing more than that certain expectations make the individual's behavior at a given time selective. Such a "set" may be established by other prior stimulation or by a variety of internal factors (motive, attitude) as well as by instructions.

Selectivity of Remembering in the "Psychology of Testimony"

Selectivity in the observation and memory of events was the subject of systematic study early in this century by Binet, Stern, Münsterberg, Whipple, and others. The pioneering experiments in this research were done by the French psychologist Binet (*35*, p. 293). Using "description-tests," he investigated many aspects of observation and memory and directly related this work to the problem of testimony in his *La Suggestibilité* (1900). He noted that reports of subjects concerning the stimulus material were reached through a "process of selection" (*6*).

Binet was interested further in the effect of social influences in the selectivity of recall. Using different sorts of questions which ranged from "neutral" to "leading" types, he found that the amount of error in the report could be substantially affected by the type of question asked. Thus error for recall in response to the least suggestive questions was 26 percent but increased to 61 percent for the most "leading" questions (*6*). Stern's results showed that young children were most responsive to such suggestion from an interrogator and that adults were similarly influenced, but to a lesser degree.

Stern (*30*) and later Münsterberg extended this line of work to more complicated situations. In addition to laboratory tests using pictures, objects, and the like, real-life "incidents" like a quarrel or infraction of some regulation were carefully arranged and staged before naïve spectators, who were then asked to report what had happened. (Stern also suggested that it might be fruitful to use the "moving picture show" as the stimulus material to be reported.)

Münsterberg's work *On the Witness Stand* (1908) gives colorful descriptions of this kind of study. Here is an example:

There was, for instance, two years ago in Göttingen a meeting of a scientific association, made up of jurists, psychologists, and physicians, all, therefore, men well trained in careful observation. Somewhere in the same street there was that evening a public festivity of the carnival. Suddenly, in the midst of the scholarly meeting, the doors open, a clown in highly colored costume rushes in in mad excitement, and a negro with a revolver in hand follows him. In the middle of the hall first the one, then the other, shouts wild phrases; then the one falls to the ground, the other jumps on him; then a shot, and suddenly both are out of the room. The whole affair took less than twenty seconds. All were completely taken by surprise, and no one, with the exception of the President, had the slightest idea that every word and action had been rehearsed beforehand, or that photographs had been taken of the scene. It seemed most natural that the President should beg the members to write down individually an exact report, inasmuch as he felt sure that the matter would come before the courts. Of the forty reports handed in, there was only one whose omissions were calculated as amounting to less than twenty per cent of the characteristic acts. . . . But besides the omissions there were only six among the forty which did not contain positively wrong statements. . . . Only four persons, for instance, among forty noticed that the negro had nothing on his head; the others gave him a derby, or a high hat, and so on. In addition to this, a red suit, a brown one, a striped one, a coffee-coloured jacket, shirt sleeves, and similar costumes were invented for him. . . . The scientific commission which reported the details of the inquiry came to the general statement that the majority of the observers omitted or falsified about half of the processes which occurred completely in their field of vision. . . . The judgment as to the time duration of the act varied between a few seconds and several minutes [18, pp. 51–53].

On the theoretical side, Münsterberg stated: "The reports of the witness are always combinations of objective and subjective factors. Emotions, decisions, thoughts may influence his account of the past experience, and even where the interest is entirely devoted to the external stimuli, the subjective apprehension and attention must play a role" (19, p. 396).

An example of the influence of internal factors is the finding that training or practice in reporting, accompanied by "interest" or "desire to improve," was effective in extending the range of things reported as well as the accuracy of report (34, pp. 167–168). This is an instance of what is often called "perceptual learning" today, in the sense of improved discrimination of "figures" and items within the figure stemming from active practice, that is, practice in which subjects are motivated.

In recent years several experiments have demonstrated the influence of an individual's attitude toward objects or persons perceived and later recalled. Very much as the observers of the scene reported above by Münsterberg invented various bizarre costumes for the Negro involved, a number of observers who recalled pictures in a recent experiment transferred a razor from the hand of a white person in one picture to the hand of a Negro, in line with their stereotyped notion of who would be likely to hold a razor (2).

Selectivity in Recognizing Items with Motivational Relevance

We tend to single out objects and persons in our environment that we love or hate, depend upon or fear, esteem or despise, almost in no time. We are "tuned" to pick out items which involve us in positive or negative ways.

An author is quick to note favorable or unfavorable references to his work. A person who feels "let down" by his friends becomes sensitive even to slight insinuations which may have passed unnoticed during a period of greater confidence and stability of these ties. The frightened person is quick to see moving things or threatening signs in his surroundings. In short, objects, persons, and events which have positive or negative motivational relevance to us readily assume figure character.

One way of studying such selectivity is by observing an individual's reaction to stimulus items, some of which are relevant in positive or negative ways to his motives, attitudes, and interests and some of which are not. This has been done by briefly exposing words and seeing how easily an individual recognizes those with varying motivational relevance. By this technique it was found that the ease of recognition of words about equally familiar to the individual varies in terms of their motivational relevance.

There has been a tendency in recent social-psychological literature to subsume selectivity of this sort under various distinct "mechanisms," like "perceptual defense." For example, it was maintained that recognition thresholds were lower for welcome items but higher for unwelcome items.

That is, favorable items were supposedly recognized more easily than un-favorable items (23). Therefore it was suggested that "perceptual defense" caused the slower reaction to unfavorable items.

It is true that not infrequently unpleasant items are glossed over, or a dis-liked person is avoided. On the other hand, there are numerous circum-stances which lead an individual to go out actively to ascertain his ad-versaries, to seek out and exaggerate the odds against him.

In an experiment by Allport and Kramer, it was found that individuals who are prejudiced against an ethnic group may see more persons belong-ing to that group than less prejudiced persons do (1). Twenty slides show-ing photographs of male college students were shown to students at Har-vard and Radcliffe, who were asked after a 15-second exposure to say whether they thought each pictured a Jew, or a non-Jew, or if they did not know. Those students with high "prejudice scores" judged more faces to be Jewish than did students with low scores. Further, these more preju-diced students tended to be more correct in their judgments. This suggests that persons who do not have attitudes of prejudice toward an ethnic group are less selective of those aspects which the prejudiced person em-ploys in discrimination. Such results are extremely difficult to explain in terms of contrasting mechanisms which defend the person from unpleasant stimuli and sensitize him to pleasant items.

The variations in selectivity are too diverse to be handled in terms of distinct "mechanisms." A recent experiment by Gilchrist, Ludeman, and Lysak (9) shows that under certain circumstances items with motivational relevance, either positive or negative, may be perceived more readily than neutral items. This study is among those demonstrating the serious limita-tions of handling psychological selectivity in terms of "mechanisms." Stu-dents at the University of Wisconsin were shown a series of words, all about equally familiar. Some words pertained to "positively valued" char-acteristics, some to items of neutral value, and some to "negatively valued" characteristics. When these words were exposed briefly, it was found that "both positive and negative values lowered word-recognition thresholds in comparison with neutral value" (p. 426). In other words, the subjects recognized words with both positive and negative value more readily than "neutral" words.

Rather than compile an inventory of "mechanisms," the parsimonious and valid analysis of psychological selectivity has to proceed in terms of the relative weights of various internal factors (motive, attitude, past learning) and external factors operating at a given time within a particular frame of reference. In such analysis, the functional relations between motives, stimuli relevant to them, and other factors in influencing selectivity should be included.

Only through analysis of this type can the wide variations in selectivity be understood. Variations in selectivity for individuals under differing conditions are not surprising unless the investigator is set to find and defend certain fixed "mechanisms." They are to be understood and even predicted in terms of the interrelated factors operating at the time, including the degree of motivational relevance of stimuli, the relative weight of the motive in question, the compellingness of other internal influences, the structural properties of the stimulus, and other external factors, including social relationships, suggestions by other persons, etc.

In Chapter 13 the problem of psychological selectivity is considered specifically in relation to motivational factors (pp. 429–433).

DIFFERENTIAL EFFECTS OF STRUCTURED AND UNSTRUCTURED STIMULUS SITUATIONS

After certain objects or events become the focus of experience, after something is attended to, experience of that something and reaction to it is affected in important ways by its characteristics. The differing effects of stimulus situations with various degrees of structure were mentioned earlier in this chapter (pp. 82–83).

The differential effects of stimulus situations of varying objective structure are significant from several points of view. This topic yields rather definite evidence for a regularity or lawfulness of the conditions in which external factors or internal factors carry greater relative weights in a frame of reference. The principle which has emerged serves as the basis for much experimental work pertaining to the functioning of internal factors, as inferred from behavior in specified conditions.

Well-structured stimulus situations have been referred to as "compelling," "strong," "clear," etc. in the literature. Unstructured stimulus situations have been referred to as "equivocal," "weak," "ambiguous," "indeterminate," "vague," or "impoverished." The characteristics are subsumed under the terms "structured" or "well structured" and "unstructured" or "lacking in structure." As noted in point 5 above (p. 81), the psychological tendency is toward structuring of experience, whether or not the stimulus situation is well structured. Perception and the like tend to be organized affairs. The concepts of structure and lack of structure in stimulus situations refer to the extent to which the stimulus condition allows for *alternatives* in the structuring of experience (perception, judgment, remembering, etc.).

In some cases the external field of stimulation is well structured. We see definite shapes in buildings, tables, and books. We hear definite melody and rhythm in the music coming from radio, choir, and orchestra. The field of stimulation is organized into definite structures, the rest forming the background on which these structures stand out with figure character. In the organization of response to stimulation, an essential principle is the grouping of different parts of the stimulus field.

Some sort of psychological grouping or structuring takes place whether or not the stimulus field itself imposes the essential or limiting conditions for grouping. When the field of stimulation is well structured, the special characteristics of a psychological grouping are determined by the structural properties of the stimulus situation. The shape of a square with clear-cut lines will be perceived by everybody. In this case the sharp contours of four lines unmistakably connected at their extremities are determining factors. In the preceding chapter such structural properties of the stimulus field were discussed and relevant findings mentioned, many from the work of Gestalt psychologists (pp. 54–58). Stimuli which are well structured allow for few alternatives in the structuring of experience (point 6).

There are well structured social situations, like a line of people or massed formations in motion or standing still. Man is surrounded by tools, furniture, buildings, means of transportation, timetables, and other definite social schedules regulating vital activities. These are well-structured stimulus situations with compelling structural properties. The individual responds to them in terms of their definite magnitudes, proportions, limiting time spans, definite scopes, and so on. Such compelling aspects of the "man-made" world produce in the individual definite reference scales and standards, which, once formed, constitute a major source of the formation of his tastes and expectations in relation to things, his conception of the scope of his world, his degree of mobility, his major sense of the proportions of things, his conception of speed, riches, and the like. In Chapter 1 this area of social stimulation was referred to as material culture, or technology. Together with its psychological effects, namely, the technology and mentality relationship, it is a sorely neglected topic in social psychology. This important topic is the concern of Chapter 20.

Unstructured Stimulus Situations

When objective factors are lacking, that is, when the stimulus field is *unstructured* in various degrees, the individual does not usually perceive chaos. Organization of some sort still takes place. Even in a moment of great confusion an individual tends to experience events in a structured way, probably after an initial experience of instability which may not disappear for some time. (This point is elaborated in a following section on "Loss of Stable Anchorages.")

When an individual is put in a situation of complete darkness except for one tiny pinpoint of light, he does experience considerable uncertainty. As noted in Chapter 2 (pp. 46–47), the light appears to move (autokinetic movement). It may seem to move very erratically, or slowly or quickly for different people. Nevertheless, when repeatedly faced with such apparent movement, any one individual establishes in time some range within which movement is perceived; and the extent of movement varies around a modal point (25). In such cases the internal or internalized factors play the dominant role in psychological structuring or organization. The individual's emotional state, pressing motives, and motives aroused by the situation are examples of such internal factors.

As noted earlier, ambiguous puzzle pictures provide two (or more) alternatives for psychological structuring. Which alternative is perceived can usually be determined by prior instruction. The Rorschach pictures are good examples of an unstructured field of stimulation. These pictures consist of ink blots. The subjects are asked to report and trace whatever they see in them. Since the ink blots are irregular and complex, they allow for a large variety of alternatives which may reveal certain internal factors in the subject himself. One of the early studies by Bleuler and Bleuler shows concretely how habitual ways of looking at things may cause people to interpret the Rorschach blots in a way that reveals characteristics of their well-established culture products. These investigators gave Rorschach tests to a group of Moroccan subjects. The important result for this discussion is that the Moroccans gave "such a wealth of small-detail responses" as is not usually found in European subjects. This very probably reflects the "love for beautiful detail" in Moroccan art (7).

Some good examples of the tendency toward grouping and the dominance of internal factors are found in the experimental work on "subjective" rhythm. The essential condition in perceiving rhythm is grouping of stimuli. Usually accent is decisive in determining rhythmic patterns. But even when sounds follow one another fairly rapidly at a uniform rate without intensity or time-interval differences, the individual experiences rhythm although rhythm is objectively lacking. The rhythmic grouping of the puffs of the locomotive or the grinding of the train wheels is an example of "subjective rhythm."

This was experimentally demonstrated by Sherif in 1933 (25). The stimulus was a succession of ticks coming from behind a screen at a uniform rate. The groups of subjects were instructed to move their hands in time with the ticks, and to count aloud in a particular grouping given to them by the experimenter: 1–2 or 1–2–3 or 1–2–3–4, as the case might be. While this was in progress, another subject was brought into the experimental room. This new subject was ignorant of the fact that the rhythm was prescribed by the experimenter; he was told merely to listen to the rhythm. For a few minutes the other subjects continued in his presence, after which all but the naïve subject were sent out of the room. He was then instructed to beat time to the rhythm of the ticks. Most of these subjects conformed to the grouping that had been suggested by the hand movements and oral counting-off of the other subjects. The usual introspective reports from the naïve subjects revealed a tendency to experience intensity (accent) and time-interval differences. (It would be interesting to compare the reactions of musically naïve subjects with the reactions of musically sophisticated subjects. Perhaps musically sophisticated subjects would be more concerned with the objective properties of the sound pattern, hence less affected by the suggested rhythm than were naïve subjects.)

Gradations of Stimulus Structure

There are an almost infinite number of *gradations* in the relative structure of the stimulus field—from, say, the imposing mass and contour of Rockefeller Center in New York to the confusing chaos or complexity of a devastated town in which buildings are reduced to rubble and public services disrupted. (Figs. 3.2 and 3.3.)

The work of Luchins gave a clear demonstration of the graded effects of the degrees of structure. Luchins studied the effects of social factors (e.g., suggestion) in relation to stimulus objects with various degrees of structure. The studies show that the greater the degree of vagueness or indefiniteness of the stimulus object, the greater the effect of the social factors (15, 16, 17).

Such experimental evidence underlies two of the propositions stated earlier in this chapter, namely, points 8 and 9. These propositions are that the more unstructured the stimulus situation, the greater the relative contribution of internal factors in the frame of reference and the greater the relative contribution of external social factors operative at the time. Social influences, like suggestion or group pressure, have relatively greater

FIG. 3.2. New York

A contrast in stimulus structure.

Standard Oil Co. (N.J.)

G. 3.3. Hiroshima

Wide World

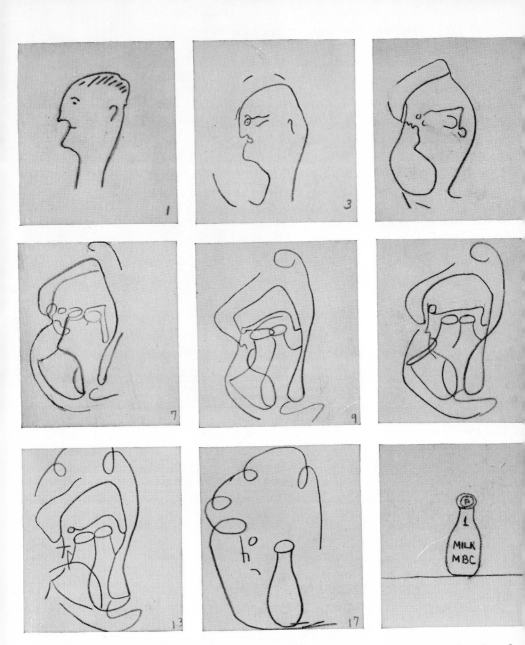

FIG. 3.4. Gradations of stimulus structure (selected drawings). Drawings 1 (man) and 21 (bottle) are the most structured in this series. Perception of them is least affected by social influences, e.g., suggestion. Perception of the ambiguous drawings in the middle of the series is most affected by social influences. (Courtesy of A. S. Luchins.)

weight in psychological structuring in unstructured stimulus situations partly because of their relevance to internal motives or attitudes and partly because they provide compelling and clear anchorages.

In a recent study James Thrasher investigated the interplay of internal factors and degree of stimulus structure in judgments of the position of lights (32). Variation of internal factors was studied by comparing the reactions of individuals who judged the location of lights with friends toward whom they held positive attitudes and those of individuals who made judgments with strangers. Variations in degree of stimulus structure were studied by securing judgments in three situations: In situation A, the lights to be localized appeared within a luminous circle. In situation B, two short portions of the circumference of the circle were luminous. In situation C, only one luminous portion of the circumference was visible. (Fig. 3.5.)

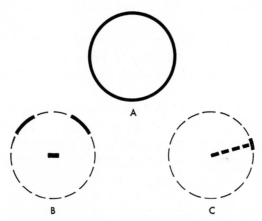

Fig. 3.5. Three degrees of stimulus structure. Phosphorescent lucite visible to subjects during conditions A, B, and C is indicated by heavier lines. (After J. D. Thrasher.)

Seventy-two students at the University of Oklahoma served as subjects. Half of the subjects were pairs of good friends; half of the subjects were pairs who were not acquainted.

The overall findings of Thrasher's experiment were as follows:

1. As the degree of stimulus structure decreased, the correspondence between objective location of the lights and judgments of their location decreased. In short, the number of alternatives in judgment increased progressively from the relatively most structured situation (A) to the most unstructured situation (C).

2. As the degree of stimulus structure decreased, the range and variability of judgments increased. In other words, in situation C individual differences in judgment were generally more pronounced.

3. On the other hand, when pairs of individuals who made their judgments together were compared, it was found that as the structure of the stimulus situation decreased, the influence of internal factors (attitudes of friendship) was significantly greater. In situation A (more structured) there was no significant difference between the influence of individuals who were friends on each other's judgments and that of individuals who were strangers. But in the less structured situations (B and C) judgments by individuals who were personally involved as friends were influenced significantly more by each others' judgments than were those of individuals who were not acquainted.

Thus, as the objective stimulus field became more unstructured, the influence of internal factors (personal involvement as friends) became greater.

A series of experiments on perception and judgment of the upright position demonstrates the interplay of internal and external factors in determining experience and the relative weights of each in situations of varying stimulus structure (36). These experiments were begun by Wertheimer (1912), who had subjects look through a tube at a mirror tilted to reflect a scene 45° from the vertical (upright). Since his subjects came to accept the upright of the tilted scene as the true upright, he concluded that the upright position is perceived chiefly in terms of the framework of the stimulus situation. Apparently contradictory findings were reported by Gibson and Mowrer (1938), who found that their subjects continued to perceive some tilt to the mirror image and concluded that the perceived upright is largely based on impressions coming from the body.

This discrepancy in experimental findings has been resolved through a series of studies by Asch and Witkin. The later units were carried out by Witkin. In successive experiments, the conditions were varied in such a way that the relative contributions of the stimulus field and of bodily impressions and pressures could be studied. The stimulus situations presented to the subjects varied in structure. In addition, the internal bodily impressions were varied by tilting the subject's head or body and in Witkin's later studies (1950) by moving the experimental room (which could be tilted) around a circular track at different speeds, thus varying bodily impressions due to gravitational forces.

The general finding of these experiments pertinent to this discussion was that both the structure of the external stimulus field and bodily impressions and other internal factors were involved in perception of the upright. However, the relative contribution of these varied in situations of differing stimulus structure (36, p. 6). In a well-structured situation (like a room in which subjects sat), what was perceived as upright depended both on the structure of the visual field and on internal factors (e.g., bodily impressions); but the structure of the visual field tended to play the dominant role.

At the other extreme, in a perfectly dark room, subjects relied on bodily impressions, making more errors as their heads or bodies were tilted. When a luminous framework was presented in a dark room, other internal influences became prominent. For example, some subjects became so confused about the position of their bodies and the stimulus that they adhered to the only available external anchorage (the luminous frame) even when it was tilted to one side. In an extreme instance one subject judged the position as horizontal when it was actually vertical.

Not all individuals perceived these situations in the same way. Individuals reacted selectively, some relying more on the stimulus situation and others more on their bodily impressions and other internal factors. Witkin and his collaborators extended the study of upright to learn more about such variations.

The individual does not necessarily start living in a dream world just because the stimulus situation he faces is unstructured. He may try actively to follow the few anchorages in the external situation. He will respond to social suggestions having relevance to his motives and attitudes or from sources he considers "reliable." Whether or not the resulting reaction is realistic will depend both on the nature of the internal factors and on the properties of the external anchorages.

In between the extremes of well-structured and unstructured situations there is a tremendous range of possibilities which are being studied experimentally. In general, experience and behavior at a given time are determined jointly by interrelated influences; the relative weight of internal and external influences in the frame of reference will vary with the degree of structure of the stimulus situation. As the degree of stimulus structure decreases, the relative weight of internal factors increases. The differential effects of social influences in structured and unstructured stimulus situations may be understood in terms of the effect of external anchorages with *relevance* to important internal factors (like attitudes toward other people, groups, values).

This leads directly to a brief consideration of social stimulus situations. Whether well structured or lacking in structure, social stimulus situations are usually not experienced neutrally by socialized individuals. Rather, social stimulus situations—even such well-structured stimuli as technological devices, regularities of work and living, schedules, and the like—ordinarily have motivational relevance. Thus social stimulus situations are particularly likely to be experienced *selectively*.

A good many facts pertaining to social behavior become meaningful in terms of the differential effects of given gradations of stimulus structure. Therefore, the main theme of this discussion recurs frequently throughout this book.

Loss of Stable Anchorages

As stated in the fifth proposition (p. 80), the overall tendency is toward structuring of experience at any given time. This tendency is related to the goal-directed character of experience and behavior, to the conceptual level of functioning, and to the fact that experience develops in the course of dealing with an environment which is usually ordered, clear, structured.

At times, however, a person finds himself in circumstances in which not only is external structure lacking but customary anchorages for experience are missing altogether. Some of man's most painful and distressing feelings are caused by loss of stable anchorages in his physical and social bearings. When he is unable to find or establish landmarks in his orientation in space, he flounders about to find some secure anchorages. When social ties with friends, loved ones, associates in some capacity are disrupted, he tosses in uncertainty. His very feeling of self-identity is shaken. Such facts are significant in understanding the development of a conception of self. In later chapters their implications will be discussed more fully. Here a few cases illustrating the consequences of loss of stable or customary anchorages are reported for a general orientation.

In 1949 the newspapers reported that engineers working on a "silent chamber" designed to measure sound found "dead silence" difficult to bear. This room was completely silent. "About 30 minutes of absolute silence was just about all anyone could stand. After 30 minutes the engineers became uneasy. After a few hours, the Army said, the dead silence produced 'pronounced adverse psychological effects'" (3). This is an example of the painful effects of situations in which no customary anchorages are available.

In an experiment planned to study the progressive elimination of stable anchorages, one phase took place in an average-sized experimental room which the subjects glimpsed briefly before the lights were turned off. Other phases took place in a large hall in utter darkness. The physical anchorages available varied. In the situation with fewest anchorages, the individual had to find his way to his place in darkness with no guides other than preliminary verbal directions. The subjects became very confused and disoriented. Some thought they were walking north when they were actually moving south. One subject said afterward that he "felt helpless, ill at ease —very puzzled." Another said he had been "completely confused. Lost as heck." This experience of great uncertainty produced by eliminating anchorages resulted in pronounced variations in judgment. In comparison to the situations which provided a few anchorages for orientation, like a glimpse of the room or guidelines to one's place, judgments of autokinetic movement indicated that the light appeared to move over much greater distances and that judgment was highly variable. Thus loss of anchorages and the uncertainty it produced were reflected in judgments as floundering around in an extreme way, in comparison to judgment in other situations (26).

Not long ago a botany professor lost his bearings in the woods in Oregon while searching for specimens. Finding no familiar guides and being unable to reach any by following the sun, he felt increasingly uncertain and insecure. In desperation he built a fire with the hope that it would be noticed by someone who would rescue him. But in his frightened state of mind he let the fire get out of hand. Running away from the fire, he stumbled onto a path only a few hundred yards away. But his panic resulting from the lack of any familiar anchorages or guides caused a forest fire which destroyed acres of forest (4).

During World War II a series of airplane accidents occurred at a training base in which a common feature appeared to be that "the pilot may have been confused or disorientated at the time of the crash." Since it was thought that the autokinetic phenomenon (see pp. 46–47) might have contributed to some of these accidents, a series of investigations in the laboratory simulating flight conditions and in actual night flights was carried out. When flight in a Link Trainer was simulated in a large laboratory using the airplane and various lights (targets), it was found that apparent movement was indeed perceived, making it difficult for the pilot to maintain the proper instrument readings in the Trainer.

The experiments in formation flights at night indicated that the autokinetic phenomenon and the resulting disorientation "probably offers the explanation for some of the accidents which have occurred." Apparently a pilot flying at night with no available anchorages other than one (or even two) lights on a lead plane may sometimes become sufficiently disoriented so that his judgments of position and the like are unreliable. For this reason, methods of reducing the phenomenon were investigated. The recommendations are given here because they consist of efforts to establish effective anchorages: "(1) using some fixed object (for example the framework of any opening or part) as a reference point, (2) periodically interrupting any steady fixation of a target light, and (3) in case of doubt regarding the reality of an observed movement, reliance should be placed on instruments if these conflict with the pilot's perceptions" (*10*, p. 151).

The consequences of loss of stable anchorages were noted well by the authors of *The American Soldier: Combat and Its Aftermath*. They noted that in combat a soldier was subject to violent stimulation much of the time; but his environment provided few if any "firm constants." He seldom knew just what was going on or what was likely to happen next. Thus even with good communication, discipline, and administration he experienced "insidious anxieties." "All people need some stability in their environment; it has been repeatedly shown that personality integration and the development of regularized patterns of behavior are strongly conditioned upon the existence of stable referents for activity. One of the prime functions of any sort of social organizations is to provide the individual with a dependable set of expectations. Unless one knows, at least within broad limits, what behavior to expect from others, the very concept of adjustment becomes meaningless" (*31*, pp. 83–84).

In times of uncertainty and confusion people do search for "something to hold on to." They make desperate efforts to establish their orientation, to find something secure to which they can relate themselves and events both in a physical sense and in the realm of social and ideological ties. Until they are able to attain stability, they feel uneasy, tense, even jittery. They may respond to striking or decisive movement of other people, even though it means taking part in a panic; they may become easy prey of demagogues who hold out clear-cut standards and solutions. Until stability is established, they are highly sensitized to expect extraordinary happenings, like "moving statues" of significant religious figures or "flying saucers."

Times of uncertainty, like those created by war, the possibility of war, depression, or some other social crisis, are ripe for the spread of rumor, as keen observers have long noted and as has been demonstrated in carefully conducted studies.

Such times are periods of loss or weakening of stable and customary anchorages. The implications of their consequences and their relation to man's motives are significant for understanding the rise of new slogans, values, and social movements. Such problems are discussed in Chapter 21.

Conflicting Anchorages and Frameworks

In the frame of reference at a given time, some factor or factors carry greater weight than others in determining psychological structuring. Such anchorages may be either internal factors or external factors, or both.

In actual life, more than one influence usually serve as main reference points (anchorages) in the patterning of experience and behavior. The interplay among various anchorages operating at a given time may not be a harmonious affair. At times anchorages are conflicting or mutually contradictory.

The stimulus situation may be well structured; but two aspects of it whose influences are opposite in effect may become focal. Or aspects of the stimulus situation may conflict with internal factors, such as motives or standards built up through past experiences. Two conflicting internal influences may be aroused simultaneously. For example, a strong urge to satisfy hunger may conflict with strivings for social position. Conflicting anchorages (internal or external) are discussed in appropriate contexts in various chapters. As an introduction to this general problem, rather clear-cut examples are considered here briefly.

Suppose that you put on glasses which turned the world upside down, with the result that everything was in reverse relationship to your accustomed experience of position in space. What you had seen as the floor would now be "up," and what you had seen as ceiling would now be "down." An object which appeared at your right would actually be at your left; if you moved to the left to avoid it, you would bump into it instead. The anchorages and frameworks of your visual world would directly contradict inner influences built up through long experience and learning about the physical world from childhood on.

A few investigators have actually tried this experiment. In 1896 Stratton wore an inverting optical lens (on one eye). In his second attempt, he wore the device for 67 hours over an 8-day period. In 1928 Ewert and two other subjects wore inverting lenses on both eyes for longer periods (covering 14–16 days). More recently Snyder and Pronko (28) carried out an experiment in which Snyder wore inverting lenses for a 30-day period, not seeing at any time without them. The findings reported by these investigators are similar on the whole; but since the more recent observations by Snyder and Pronko are more controlled, some of their results are summarized here.

Before putting on the inverting lenses Snyder practiced a number of standard eye-hand coördination tests, so that his performance on them could be compared before, during, and after wearing the lenses.

The initial and early reactions to the inverted visual field were those of considerable confusion and disorientation. Ordinary tasks, like walking or going up and down stairs, became quite difficult. A guide was needed to steer him along a sidewalk. Performance on all of the standardized tasks was disrupted appreciably for a time. (Performance on these tasks was made all the more difficult because the inverting apparatus also reduced the usual range of vision considerably.) Figure 3.6 shows the subject trying to follow a painted maze outline on the floor. This task proved now to be hopelessly confusing: "I could not decide which foot I was to move next" (28, p. 128).

Now what happened during the 30-day period? Did confusion, disorientation, and difficulty in making appropriate movements persist? In the standardized test situations performance began to improve rather rapidly to the previous level and finally exceeded the previous level. Improvement in performance seemed to be related to how familiar the activity had been before the lenses were put on. Eating and walking under ordinary circumstances, for example, improved quickly. On the other hand, improvement in walking the maze pattern in Figure 3.6 was much slower and remained different in quality, although time required was shortened a great deal. During the period, in his usual surroundings Snyder became able to walk around, board a bus, walk in a crowded store, and even to drive a car.

How did the world look to him as he continued to wear the inverting lenses? Even by the fourth day some familiar scenes began to appear normal. By the twenty-fifth day, when watching divers at a swimming pool, he found that they seemed to be diving quite normally. In fact he thought of this only when someone asked if things looked "upside down." He then found that he had to make a conscious effort to realize that in his vision the divers appeared to move upward. Until asked, he had been seeing them plunging "downward" into the water.

Snyder and Pronko's conclusions were concerned with how the conflict was handled between anchorages and frameworks already established and those perceptually present through the inverting lenses. At first, it should be noted that behavior patterns had to be *translated* deliberately to fit the

FIG. 3.6. Conflicting anchorages and frameworks of inverted visual field and past experience make this task extremely difficult. (From F. W. Snyder and N. H. Pronko, *Vision with Spatial Inversion*. Wichita, Kan.: University of Wichita Press, 1952.)

present perceptions. In their words: "At first, reaching, walking, turning, and other responses had to be translated into a new framework. But soon these were fairly automatic and homogeneous with the perceivings that were developed under the circumstances. Toward the end of the 30-day experiment, it was not necessary to think, the obstacle ahead appears to my *right*; I must turn to my *right* to avoid it. A new and immediately perceived frame of reference was available for responding" (28, pp. 112–113).

CONFLICT IN SOCIAL ANCHORAGES: The acquisition of a new immediately perceived framework for responding to the physical world is no mean achievement in terms of the concentration required in "translating" responses into the framework or coördinating bodily movements. However, ordinarily the physical world, even when inverted, is clear cut, well structured, and seldom conflicting in itself.

The same cannot be said of social life, which presents a variety of alternatives, many of them contradictory or conflicting. Even though social life too has regularities, modern complex societies present aspects which are contradictory.

What happens when an individual is faced with equally effective but contradictory anchorages in his social surroundings? Suppose two eminent professors come to contradictory conclusions on the same topic, or two respected commentators present opposite interpretations of some political event. This was the general problem of a study by Norman Walter on judgment in an unstructured stimulus situation (33).

At least a week before the experiment college students were asked to rate the schools or universities which had high prestige in their eyes. These ratings were not connected to the experiment by the subjects. They enabled the experimenter to determine which two schools had the greatest prestige for each subject.

In the first experimental session, the subjects simply reported their judgments of the distance which a point of light appeared to move (autokinetic situation). Before the second session, the experimenter mentioned casually that the distance judgments of students at one of the schools which the subject had rated high in prestige were "such and such." The actual figure named for each subject was arrived at by taking a value in either the upper or lower 10 percent of that subject's judgments in the first session. Thus the judgments attributed to students at the prestige institution conflicted with most of the subject's own judgments previously, but were within the range of his own judgments. A group of control subjects received no suggestions from the experimenter.

What happened in this second experimental session? The subjects shifted their modal judgments in the direction of those they believed were being made at the "prestige" institution. At the same time, variability or spread of their judgments was sharply and significantly reduced. Control subjects tended to keep the same norm of judgment as in the first session, with a slight decrease in variability which was not statistically significant.

Now came the crucial procedure of this study. Before the third session, the experimenter casually dropped word that students at a second school of high prestige for the subject in question were making certain judgments, the figure given being directly opposite in direction to that given in the previous session for another prestige institution. Now the subject faced two standards from institutions of high prestige which were conflicting.

The result was that the subjects in this session distributed their judgments over a wide area; that is, variability increased sharply. Variability in the control group (no suggestion) stayed about the same. Did the subjects accept the new suggestion or stick with the first one? In this conflicting situation, a few stayed with the first suggested norm, but more often there was a shift to some place in between the two.

Before the final session, the experimenter remarked that apparently there had been errors in the results he had reported previously, due to equipment failure or errors in calculation, and that both studies he had mentioned were being repeated. This suggestion was aimed at *discrediting* both experimentally introduced anchorages. The result was another sharp increase in variability of judgment, which on the basis of other studies can be attributed to uncertainty experienced by the subjects. The judgments of control subjects were distributed around the same modal point throughout, and variability decreased gradually from session to session.

Such results indicate that one important consequence of contradictory or conflicting social anchorages is a state of uncertainty accompanied by increased variability in behavior. One of the tasks which social psychology undertakes is investigating various consequences of such uncertainty aroused by conflicting anchorages under varying conditions, and whether or how they are resolved. Conflicting social anchorages confronting individuals have important implications for feelings of personal stability and security of social ties. These problems are among those most vital in the contemporary scene of conflicting values.

CONCLUDING REMARKS

In this chapter a conceptual approach to social psychological problems was stated in the form of propositions (pp. 77–85). Then two of these propositions, pertaining to *psychological selectivity* and to the relative contributions of internal and external factors in *stimulus situations of varying structure,* were elaborated with specific illustrations. Finally, the crucial role of main reference points (anchorages) was emphasized with examples showing certain consequences of the *loss of stable anchorages* and of *conflicting anchorages.*

These concepts and propositions were stated at this point in order to provide some tools for analyzing various specific problems treated in the chapters of this book. It is sometimes difficult to plunge into a conceptual scheme before increasing one's familiarity with specific topics; but it is even more difficult to avoid treating each topic in a separate compartment if one has no conceptual tools available. Acquaintance with some coherent and related concepts enables one to apply them in a consistent way to various specific topics. Of course, additional concepts and principles are needed along the way. This chapter touched on the minimum necessary for venturing into the concrete subject matter of social psychology.

Concepts are necessarily abstract. They are generalizations encompassing a wide range and variety of specific facts. In the last two chapters the concepts presented were tied to the more basic and simple of the facts which they encompass. Often these facts concerned experience and behavior in relation to simple physical stimuli (forms, weights, tones, etc.). Illustrations of related findings in social stimulus situations were included to show the applicability of the concepts to topics in social psychology. This applicability is extended in future chapters. The approach to social psychological problems is through functional analysis of the interrelated external and internal factors (variables) operating at a given time—in short, through analysis of the frame of reference of experience and behavior.

REFERENCES

1. Allport, G. W., and Kramer, B. M. Some roots of prejudice, *J. Psychol.* (1946), 22:9–39.
2. Allport, G. W., and Postman, L. *The Psychology of Rumor.* New York: Holt, 1947.
3. Associated Press, April 14, 1949 (from the New Haven *Register,* April 14, 1949).
4. Associated Press, August 8, 1952 (from the New York *Times,* August 9, 1952).
5. Bartlett, F. C. *Remembering: A Study in Experimental and Social Psychology.* Cambridge: University Press, 1932.
6. Binet, A. *La Suggestibilité.* Paris, 1900.

7. Bleuler, M., and Bleuler, R. Rorschach's ink-blot test and racial psychology: mental peculiarities of Moroccans, *Character and Personal.* (1935), 4:97–114.

8. Chapman, D. W. Relative effects of determinate and indeterminate Aufgaben, *Amer. J. Psychol.* (1932), 44:163–174.

9. Gilchrist, J. C., Ludeman, J. F., and Lysak, W. Values as determinants of word-recognition thresholds, *J. abnorm. & soc. Psychol.* (1954), 49:423–426.

10. Graybiel, Comdr. A. (MC), USNR, and Clark, Lt. B. H. (S), USNR. The autokinetic illusion and its significance in night flying, *J. Aviation Medicine* (1945), 16:111–151.

11. James, William. The Stream of Consciousness, in *Psychology*. New York: Holt, 1892.

12. Kaufman, E. L., Lord, M. W., Reese, T. W., and Volkmann, J. The discrimination of visual number, *Amer. J. Psychol.* (1949), 62:498–525.

13. Köhler, W. *Gestalt Psychology*. New York: Liveright, 1929, esp. chaps. 5 and 9.

14. Külpe, O. Versuche über Abstraktion, *Bericht über den I. Kongress für experimentelle Psychologie* (1904), pp. 56–68.

15. Luchins, A. S. On agreement with another's judgment, *J. abnorm. & soc. Psychol.* (1944), 39:97–111.

16. Luchins, A. S. Social influences on perception of complex drawings, *J. soc. Psychol.* (1945), 21:257–273.

17. Luchins, A. S. The stimulus field in social psychology, *Psychol. Rev.* (1950), 57:27–30.

18. Münsterberg, H. *On the Witness Stand*. New York: Doubleday, Page, 1914; McClure, 1908.

19. Münsterberg, H. *Psychology: General and Applied*. New York: Appleton, 1916.

20. Murphy, Gardner. *Personality*. New York: Harper, 1947.

21. Murphy, Gardner, and Hochberg, J. Perceptual development: Some tentative hypotheses, *Psychol. Rev.* (1951), 58:332–349.

22. Newman, E. B. Perception, in E. G. Boring, H. S. Langfeld, and H. P. Weld, *Foundations of Psychology*. New York: Wiley, 1948.

23. Postman, L., Bruner, J. S., and McGinnies, E. Personal Values as Selective Factors in Perception, in G. Swanson, T. M. Newcomb, and E. L. Hartley (eds.), *Readings in Social Psychology*. New York: Holt, 2nd ed., 1952.

24. Reese, E. P., Reese, T. W., Volkmann, J., and Corbin, H. H. *Psychophysical Research—Summary Report (1946–1952)*. Mount Holyoke College: Psychophysical Research Unit, January, 1953 (lithoprint).

25. Sherif, M. *The Psychology of Social Norms*. New York: Harper, 1936.

26. Sherif, M., and Harvey, O. J. A study in ego functioning: Elimination of stable anchorages in individual and group situations, *Sociometry* (1952), *15*:272–305.

27. Smith, E. W. *The Ila-Speaking Peoples of Northern Rhodesia.* New York: Macmillan, 1920, Vol. II.

28. Snyder, F. W., and Pronko, N. H. *Vision with Spatial Inversion.* Wichita, Kan.: University of Wichita Press, 1952.

29. Stagner, R., and Karowski, T. F. *Psychology.* New York: McGraw-Hill, 1952, pp. 194–202.

30. Stern, W. Abstracts of lectures on the psychology of testimony and on the study of individuality, *Amer. J. Psychol.* (1910), *21*:270–282.

31. Stouffer, S., et al. *Studies in Social Psychology in World War II.* Vol. II. *The American Soldier: Combat and Its Aftermath.* Princeton: Princeton University Press, 1949.

32. Thrasher, James D. Interpersonal relations and gradations of stimulus structure as factors in judgment variations: An experimental approach, *Sociometry* (1954), *17*:228–241.

33. Walter, Norman. A study of the effects of conflicting suggestions upon judgment in the autokinetic situation. Doctorate dissertation, University of Oklahoma, Norman, 1952; *Sociometry* (1955), *18*:138–146.

34. Whipple, G. M. The observer as reporter: A survey of the "psychology of testimony," *Psychol. Bull.* (1909), *6*:153–170.

35. Whipple, G. M. *Manual of Mental and Physical Tests.* Baltimore: Warwick and Work, 1910.

36. Witkin, H. A., Lewis, H. B., Hertzman, M., Machover, K., Meissner, P. B., and Wapner, S. *Personality Through Perception.* New York: Harper, 1954, chap. 1.

37. Woodworth, R. S., and Schlosberg, H. *Experimental Psychology.* New York: Holt, rev. ed., 1954.

38. Yokoyama. Reported by E. G. Boring, Attribute and sensation, *Amer. J. Psychol.* (1924), *35*:301–304.

III

HUMAN INTERACTION
AND ITS PRODUCTS:
Group Structure and Norms (*Values*)

Experience and Behavior in Social Situations

LABORATORY STUDIES

When a person is asked to walk across the room or to perform some familiar task before a class, he may find that his feet fail to "track" just right, or he is "all thumbs." Almost everyone knows that when other people are about, a person feels and acts differently from when he is alone. In some social situations he may experience a sense of unusual keenness. The words flow into just the right combinations; the argument is brilliant. In others he feels inept or inadequate; even familiar acts are awkward.

This chapter introduces the topic of social situations involving other people. A social situation may consist simply of other people going about their business, or all doing the same thing. It may consist of interpersonal relations of two or more individuals. It may involve collective interaction of a good many people or of an organized group.

Specifically the focus in this chapter is on laboratory studies of *transitory* social situations. Some of these experiments were aimed toward the study of human groups and their influence on experience and behavior. However, the study of groups in the laboratory is feasible only to the extent that the properties of human groups are brought to the situation or created during the experiment. Chief among these properties of human groups are stabilized relationships and expectations among the individuals participating, and common decisions, standards, or group norms. Regardless of their varied purposes, experiments on the effects of other people in transitory social situations have been fruitful in demonstrating the variety of social influences which can enter into psychological structuring.

DIFFERENTIAL EXPERIENCE AND BEHAVIOR IN SOCIAL SITUATIONS

In social psychology the effects of social situations on experience and behavior are studied in terms of the reactions of single individuals. For experience and behavior are always activities of experiencing and behaving individuals. Apart from the participating individuals, audiences, groups, crowds, mobs do not have experience or behavior.

Yet experience, and hence behavior, in social situations is not identical with experience in solitary situations plus so many items added from the social situation. Experience and behavior in judging, perceiving, remembering are always in terms of relations among factors, and not of discrete items in an additive way.

In Chapters 2 and 3 we emphasized that reacting to relations rather than to discrete items is a general psychological principle. The individual perceives, sizes up, judges stimulus items or situations in terms of relations among component parts. Unless he makes a special effort to dismember particular items in the situation, stimuli are experienced as functionally related to one another. When compelling new anchorages are introduced, they produce differential effects on experience and behavior. Such differential effects do not pop up only in social situations. It is helpful here to recall the illustrations presented earlier (Figs. 2.2, 2.3, 2.4, pp. 44, 45, 46). The concentric circles look like a spiral when presented in the presence of the other patterned stimuli. The size of the same locomotive appears considerably different with and without a stimulus of known size. This relational nature of experience and behavior holds true for all psychological phenomena (see pp. 40–64).

Therefore, the *psychological principles involved in experience and behavior in social situations do not constitute a sharp break from general psychological principles*. They are extensions of general principles. Starting with the least complicated cases, the experience of simple figures is altered and even transformed when they are perceived in relation to other stimuli. Hence, it would be foolhardy to assume that experience of things and tasks when others are present will be the same as when the individual is alone. Experience in social situations cannot be handled by adding up the new elements in the new (social) situations.

The relational nature of experience and behavior in social situations is further accentuated by the fact that the new factors in such situations are not restricted to external stimuli like forms or geometric patterns in which the individual is not personally involved. In social situations the individual acts and reacts to other individuals, who are not ordinarily perceived in neutral fashion, particularly when a person stands in competitive, coöperative, friendly, hostile, superior, or inferior relationship to them. No wonder, then, that both observational and experimental studies have almost always reported differential properties of experience and behavior in social situations.

Some authors have stressed differential improvement and some have stressed differential deterioration of performance in social situations. Some dwelled upon beneficial effects of social interaction for human relations; others drew dramatic pictures of its degrading effects. One can find piles of evidence to point to *positive effects* of social situations; he can do the same to point to *negative effects*. Different writers have come to different conclusions, depending on which pile they chose. Both represent selective choices of material reflecting the "individual-centered" or "group-centered" predilections of the author, his affiliations, and his times.

Various Factors in Social Situations Function Interdependently

The one outstanding fact in the evidence marshaled by "individual-centered" and "group-centered" authors is that social situations have consequential effects for experience and behavior, whether positive or negative. The assertion that such effects are preponderantly in a positive direction or in a negative direction for all cases does not square with the facts.

The differential effects of social situations and their direction are not determined by just the presence of others in the performance of a task or by the sheer fact of participation in a discussion or a meeting. Interrelated factors pertaining to the motivations which brought individuals into the particular situation, the task or problem involved, various aspects and characteristics of the participating individuals—all these have to be brought into the picture. When these various factors are brought into the analysis in an interrelated way, the properties of experience and behavior of single individuals in a given social situation and its positive or negative effects begin to be coherent.

Among the interrelated factors which can become important in social situations, the following are cited without attempting to be exhaustive:

Factors related to individuals involved: Their number (size of the aggregate); homogeneity or heterogeneity in terms of their backgrounds (e.g., sociocultural, economic, educational affiliations and ranks); age, sex, and the like.

Their relationships to other participating individuals: previous acquaintance and the existence or nonexistence of established relationships among all or some of the individuals.

Their particular motives related to participating in the situation, including the extent to which some motives are common to various individuals.

Factors related to the problem or task: Whether it is new or habitual; the degree of its structure (number of possible alternatives for attainment or solution); proportion of individuals present necessary for the activity; the capacities in which individuals function.

Special communication related to it, such as suggested lines of action or instructions; the content and source of communication.

Factors related to the site and facilities: The physical setting (laboratory, open space, auditorium, tavern, club, church, hotel lobby, etc.); tools and technological means available; the presence of nonparticipating individuals or groups in the surroundings and their relation to the individuals and events taking place; opportunities the site affords for movement and contact with others.

Factors pertaining to relations of an individual to others, the site, the problem or task: Relation of the problem or task to the individual, its significance to the individual and within any existing scheme of relationships among the individuals, the related abilities and talents of individuals; the individual's relation to the content and source of any special communication; the existence or nonexistence of standards of conduct or social norms relevant to the locale, situation, problem or task, and other individuals.

These factors in social situations are listed to give some idea of the scope of interrelated influences which may become important in the analysis of a social situation and its effects on experience and behavior. Ordinarily some are important only as related to other factors; some are so weighty that when they are operative the whole outcome is colored accordingly. The order in the listing above does not indicate their relative importance even for a single instance. Nevertheless, surveying the gamut of factors reminds us that social situations entail a variety of interrelated factors and not just one feature which invariably produces this or that effect, this or that harmful or beneficial result. For this reason, the sociological and psychological studies which have furthered our understanding of experience and behavior in social situations most effectively are those which have brought various factors to the focus of study as they are related to one another.

A concrete example of the interrelated functioning of factors in social situations will clarify the point. The particular factor chosen for this purpose is the number of individuals. The comparison is not between a few and a great many, but within the range that can be termed a small aggre- gate of individuals. The sociologist Simmel pointed out early in this cen- tury that the "numerical factor" can determine both form and quality of activities in certain circumstances (27, p. 2). However, the number of individuals does not function as a factor independently. As Becker and Von Wiese noted, this factor operates with others to establish certain optimal limits for social functioning. The most prominent other factors pertain to the purposes of activity and the relationships among individuals in the situation (3, p. 500). Thus, in investigations varying the number of individuals (or any other single factor) in social situations, the nature of other influences and their relative weights must be specified if the effects of size are to be evaluated.

In a study of the influence of number of individuals upon agreement (consensus) reached in discussion, Hare reported that within a given time the degree of agreement reached was less for groups of 12 members than for groups of 5 members (10). The given time in this case was 20 minutes. The particular social situation studied took place in a summer Boy Scout camp. The task and discussion concerned a *hypothetical* camping trip which required each boy to select 10 pieces of camping equipment. Leaders were appointed on the basis of observed experience and ability. Their past relationships to the particular individuals in the discussion and the relationships among other individuals taking part were not specified. Un- der these conditions the larger groups, of 12 individuals, were less satisfied with results of discussion, and the degree of agreement reached was less than in the smaller groups.

In one of our studies comparable individuals interacted with each other in a camp setting toward goals with common appeal value to all over a period of time sufficient for relationships among them to become stabilized. It was observed in one instance that groups of 11 individuals reached com- mon agreement on a real problem they faced in less than two minutes. The issue at hand was related to strong and persistent motives common to the individuals. This group of 11 boys had received a sum of money as a reward for performance in a task. They agreed enthusiastically and unani- mously within a brief time to spend the money in repairing their boat, which they had all used before it was damaged and had all missed during the previous days. (This study is summarized in Chapter 9, pp. 301–328.)

Such apparently divergent results indicate that generalizations concern- ing the effects of particular factors in social situations must specify precisely other factors operating, their nature, degree, and interrelationships. In this instance the number of individuals as a factor in reaching agreement seems dependent on the significance of the problem at hand to those individuals and the kind of relationships among them.

DIFFERENTIATING SOCIAL SITUATIONS: TOGETHERNESS SITUATIONS— GROUP SITUATIONS

Since the end of the last century and especially since the appearance of the works of Moede in Germany and F. H. Allport in America, there have been hundreds of experiments on the effects of social situations on individuals taking part in various tasks. Factors like those mentioned in the previous section have been studied.

These studies have been surveyed under different classificatory schemes. A survey can be made in terms of the number of individuals participating, the capacities in which individuals take part (differing from passive spectators to active initiators of activity), the psychological functions studied (judgment, association, attention, and the like), or independent variables involved (such as nature of the task or problems introduced). Such surveys are useful reference works.

In this book no attempt will be made to review this body of research in an exhaustive fashion. A thorough review would occupy the space of several chapters, and convenient summaries are available—in surveys by Murphy and Murphy (18), Murphy, Murphy, and Newcomb (19), Dashiell (8), Roseborough (21), Kelley and Thibaut (13), and Riecken and Homans (20).

In discussing social situations, representative research is arranged around the existing relationships of participating individuals. On the whole, the experiments included in this chapter represent those in which the experimental situation either prevented interaction among subjects or allowed only transitory interaction among them.

Without reference to the relationships among participating individuals, the effects of other factors, such as the task or problem, number of individuals, communication among them, and so on, cannot be analyzed adequately. Ordinarily, satisfaction of the individual's motives is either in relation to other individuals or through the mediation of other individuals. No one is self-sufficient or wholly independent of others in satisfying daily needs or in strivings he may have for acceptance, status, recognition, prestige, accomplishment, and so forth. Performance of a task is usually dependent to some extent on one's relation to other persons in the situation, or his conception of what other related individuals are doing or would do in the task.

Especially in the modern world, differentiations in terms of division of labor, of status and role relations, or of intergroup demarcations are the general rule. One's acceptance and rejection in a given social situation, his role in a task and its performance, his standards and claims are always colored by the nature of his relationships to other people involved.

On the whole, the nature of relationships in a situation is a limiting factor. Ordering relevant material around this variable brings a great deal of coherence to a welter of data which appear inconclusive and even contradictory if presented as separate, discrete factors.

Seemingly contradictory results reporting increases and decreases of performance in social situations become much more meaningful when viewed in terms of the individual's conception of his relation to other people. Thus, it makes a great deal of difference to a person with specific ability in a task whether he is performing it in the presence of strangers or of fellow group members, who have definite expectations of his performance.

One major fact that has made the topic of groups so vital in the study of human relations today is the membership of individuals in established group structures, which consist of stabilized, reciprocal relationships among individuals. Membership in established group structures colors one's experience and behavior in interpersonal relations, in carrying out activities in group situations, and in intergroup relations.

It was noted in Chapters 2 and 3 that experience and behavior are regulated by anchorages within a frame of reference, which consists of those functionally related internal and external factors operative at a given time. Major anchorages of the individual's reactions in social situations are provided by his membership in particular groups or by his psychological relatedness to these and other groups. Needless to say, these major anchorages derived from membership in groups do not operate unaffected by other factors in the situation.

Thus, one has to be extremely cautious in extending implications of findings concerning behavior in *transitory* social situations directly to functioning of individuals as members of established groups. The nature of the task, the effect of number, and patterns of interaction or communication in speech and writing do have different relative weights in transitory or temporary social situations and in established groups.

Therefore, there is a decided advantage in referring to social situations under the two general headings of *togetherness situations* and *group situations*.

1. *Togetherness situations* are transitory social situations in which participating individuals do not have stabilized status and role relationships and established standards or norms peculiar to the people involved and to the situation at hand. In such cases, situational factors and the immediate task or problem take on greater relative weights than when individuals are related to one another and to the task and situation in terms of certain established expectations and norms.

2. *Group situations* are those social situations in which individuals participate as members of a delineated group structure with specified status and role relationships to one another and with certain shared norms or ways of carrying out the task at hand.

In time, togetherness situations may develop into group situations. The crucial condition for this change involves interaction of individuals over a time span in relation to problems which have motivational significance to them. As this statement implies, there are *gradations* in the structure of relationships among individuals, ranging from the chance encounter of strangers to interaction in highly stabilized and closely knit groups. This chapter focuses on experiments on togetherness situations. In the next chapter properties of group situations are discussed. Various gradations of structure of relationships are focal in treating the formation and functioning of group structure in Chapter 6.

EXPERIMENTS ON TOGETHERNESS SITUATIONS

For decades psychologists and sociologists have noted that there are differences in the performance of tasks and reactions to stimuli in social situations in comparison to behavior in solitary or alone situations. In the early works of sociologists like Le Bon (*14*), Ross (*23*), and Durkheim (*9*) one finds dramatic demonstration of the fact. These early descriptions dealt largely with extreme interaction situations, the kind that will be discussed in Chapter 10 of this book.

On the other hand, early laboratory work concentrated on the study of rather discrete effects of social situations on various activities, such as motor output, association, attention, judgment, and the like. For example, August Mayer (1903) compared reasoning, memory, and imagination in alone and togetherness situations. Meumann (1904) made similar comparisons for rote memory of words.

Among these studies, F. H. Allport's series of experiments carried out from 1916 to 1919 are particularly noteworthy. They gave impetus to considerable work along the same lines. Allport compared performance in vowel cancellation, attention to reversible perspective, multiplication, association, thought, and judgment of odors and weights in alone and togetherness situations. The subjects were male and female graduate students. The general procedures used in these experiments were similar.

In alone situations each subject carried out assigned tasks in a separate room. In togetherness situations the same task was performed at the same time by four or five individuals, each working independently, seated around a table. Performance time was the same for all subjects and was controlled through buzzers by the experimenter. An appropriate and constant time was allowed for the performance of each task, and individual scores were computed in terms of amount and quality of work completed during that time. An attempt was made to reduce rivalry, so that "pure effects" of the togetherness situation could be measured, by having all subjects finish at the same time, by prohibiting comparison and discussion of results, and by specifying that the test was not a competition and that no comparison of individual results would be made (*1*, pp. 265–266).

In view of this deliberate attempt by the experimenter to eliminate rivalry between individuals and comparison of performances, the results obtained are significant in showing that performance of a task in the presence of others is not identical with its performance in isolation. The presence of other individuals becomes a factor in the structuring of experience and behavior.

The overall finding of this series of experiments was that there were increases or "social increments" for the majority of subjects in speed and quantity of work produced in the togetherness situation, the increase being greater for simpler tasks than for "purely intellectual" tasks. In reasoning, Allport reported that there was a lowering of quality (social "sub-valuents") in the togetherness situation for two-thirds of the subjects, while quantity increased, on the whole.

In the judgment experiment, subjects in alone and togetherness situations gave their estimates of the degree of pleasantness or unpleasantness of five series of ten different odors, ranging from perfumes to putrid odors. In the togetherness situations extreme judgments of pleasantness and unpleasantness were generally avoided. "The unpleasant odors, therefore, were estimated as *less unpleasant* in the group than when judging alone; and the pleasant were estimated as *less pleasant* in the group than in the solitary judgments" (*1*, pp. 275–276). Thus, in the togetherness situation there was a "leveling effect" revealed in avoidance of extreme judgments. Similar results were obtained in judgments of weights (see Fig. 4.1).

In view of the tendency to draw overall conclusions concerning the beneficial or harmful effects of social situations from studies carried out

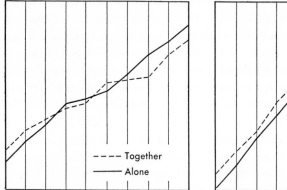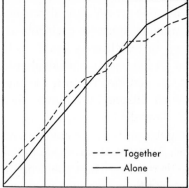

FIG. 4.1.   *Left:* Influence of the group upon judgments of pleasantness and unpleasantness; *right:* Influence of the group upon judgments of weight. (After F. H. Allport.)

under specific conditions, a few words of caution are necessary. The direction of differential effects, such as increase or decrease of quantity or rise or fall of quality, has not been conclusive or in the same direction in the results of various investigators since Allport's studies. Even in Allport's experiments the direction of differential effects was not the same for all subjects. For example, in his experiments on thought, in which nine subjects took part, six individuals gave arguments showing best reasoning in alone situations. On the other hand, three individuals gave arguments showing best reasoning in the togetherness situations. Therefore, the safe conclusion to draw from Allport's experiments and similar studies carried out since is that social situations do produce differential effects on behavior. In order to specify the positive or negative direction of such differential effects, other factors, like the motivation of individuals in the task, significance of the situation to them, and appraisal of others, have to be brought into the picture in a systematic fashion.

Social Influences and Conceptual Factors

In most studies of performance in togetherness situations the task, number of subjects, time allowed, instructions by the experimenter, and other factors in the immediate experimental setup are carefully specified. However, the subject's appraisal of the experimental situation and task and his relations to the experimenter and other subjects have been neglected. Current research on social situations is not free of such neglect, even though psychologists have become more aware of the many factors which can influence the direction and extent of their findings. Yet knowledge concerning such factors may be essential in interpreting results. Uncontrolled influences probably account for some of the rather substantial variations in results of different experiments on togetherness situations which have been found even when the tasks and the instructions were similar.

One possible effect of uncontrolled factors was demonstrated by Dashiell (7). His experiment extended procedures like those used by F. H. Allport and others to ascertain the effects of togetherness situations, rivalry, and being under close observation on performance by the same subjects. In alone situations, subjects performed the tasks in separate rooms simultaneously, the time being regulated by a central buzzer controlled by the experimenter. The togetherness situation was essentially like Allport's. In rivalry, subjects were told to compete with each other. In the observation situation, two other people watched the subject closely while he performed. The tasks were multiplication, mixed relations or analogies, and word association.

In this experiment consistent increases in speed in the simplest togetherness situation over the alone situation were not found as they had been in previous studies. However, instructions to compete (rivalry) and especially the fact of being observed by others produced rather pronounced increases in speed.

Dashiell's significant finding came from a second series in which the crucial comparison was between two "alone" situations. He reasoned that perhaps being alone in a room when others were also performing the same tasks in other rooms did not eliminate social influences. Therefore, he compared this "alone" situation with one in which each subject came to the laboratory at a different time and worked in a private room, his performance being regulated by an automatic timing device. Comparison of these two "alone" situations indicated that performance in the situation where subjects worked in different rooms at the same time was more nearly comparable to performance in the togetherness situation. Performance when subjects worked alone and at different times was slower than either the togetherness or the alone but simultaneous performance.

The important implication of Dashiell's experiment is that knowing that other individuals are performing the same task can influence experience and behavior even when the other individuals are not physically present in the room. When a professor works alone in his study on a learned argument, he is not unmindful of the related activities and opinions of his colleagues. The mother making her child's dress rushes with her greatest care and skill to complete it by Easter, when it will be on display with similar products by Mrs. Jones and other neighbors. Because of the human capacity for conceptual functioning and for forming social attitudes at that level, the individual's experience and behavior in social situations cannot be treated adequately without specific and direct consideration of such factors.

When individuals grow up as participants in social situations where competition and rivalry are emphasized rather strongly and consistently, they form attitudes at a conceptual level which do become factors in a social situation even though no one specifically instructs them to compete. In Leuba's study of competition between pairs of children from ages 2 to 6 years, the children were invited to put pegs in a pegboard (15). Performance was compared in terms of output when children were alone with the experimenter and when they came to the situation in pairs. The nursery school they attended had a general policy of not encouraging rivalry. For the 2-year-old children, who were just beginning to master language, the task assumed minor importance in the social situation. Participating to show they could do something, much less competing with another child, was somewhat beyond their level. They were interested in the other child, however. Most children from 3 to 4 years (9 out of 13 subjects) exhibited social responses to the other child, which interfered with performance. The few who did compete in this age group increased their output. By the age of 5 (kindergarten age), the predominant reaction in the togetherness situation was to compete with the other child. Most 5-year-olds showed an increased performance with another child.

Thus, by the age of 5, these children had formed certain attitudes relating to performance with others that led them to perceive the situation as competitive. Studies of competitive situations in America from Triplett's (1898) on have revealed differential effects, their degree and direction varying from individual to individual.

Such findings by Dashiell, Leuba, and others demonstrate that the investigation of behavior in togetherness situations necessarily involves factors besides the mere presence of other persons and the task to be performed. Human conceptual functions enable an individual to relate himself in certain ways and capacities to the situation, other individuals, the task, and the experimenter, whether or not the experimenter considers such factors in designing the procedures and reporting the results.

There are important implications for the methods used in obtaining data in social situations. Direct, close observation, like that in the Dashiell experiment summarized above, produces differential effects on behavior even when the observer is not an "experimenter" or a "psychologist" or a "sociologist" in the subject's eyes. Therefore, a common practice is to watch individuals perform a task or discuss some topic through a one-way mirror or screen which hides the observer. This seems to be fairly satisfactory when subjects are children or adults who do not know or suspect such devices. However, an experiment by Wapner and Alper indicates that under some circumstances observation through a one-way mirror produces a greater effect on behavior than when the individual sees that he is being observed (29).

The task in their study involved choosing a word appropriate for a given phrase. The measure was the time taken for decision. The 120 subjects took part in three different situations. In one, only the experimenter was present in the room. In another, the individual knew he was being observed through a one-way mirror but could not see the observers. In the third, the illumination behind the mirror was increased so that the subject could see several observers.

During the first half of the 20-minute session, the longest time for decision was in the situation with unseen observers behind the one-way mirror, the next with observers who could be seen, and the shortest time with only the experimenter present. Thus, the individual's awareness that "someone" was watching, when he was uncertain who that someone might be, was of relatively greater significance than the presence of definite persons whom he could see observing him. These differential results tended to disappear during the second part of the sessions, in line with previous indications from experiments by Allport and others that the effects of such transitory and relatively mild social influences tended to diminish with time.

From the viewpoint of methods in experimenting, it is important that the effects of being observed be studied when the situation, the task, and the relationships among individuals involved are of greater and more lasting significance to the subject. Would he become accustomed to or "forget" the fact that he was being observed when the situation, task, or other people were more closely related to his conceptions of his personal worth, self-esteem, and social position? There is evidence that when these are sufficiently involved the individual may actively resent being observed (16). The subject's word on this matter cannot be taken as conclusive evidence, since the situation may produce differential effects without his being aware of its influence and since he might understandably be reticent to confess that he was "self-conscious" or disturbed by being observed. There is a need for studies systematically varying the methods of observation, relationships among individuals, and the problem or task and its significance along the lines of the Wapner and Alper study. A further comparison needed is between different methods of observation and "no observation" so far as subjects are concerned.

Reactions of Other Individuals and of a "Majority"

A considerable body of research concerns variations in behavior when the subject knows the performance of other people in the situation or when others react in certain ways to his performance. Since this research concerns a host of varying social influences and different tasks and psychological functions, much of it will be considered in appropriate contexts in later chapters. This section summarizes representative experiments which studied behavior in togetherness situations when the behavior of others in the situation was the main variable.

The influence of expectations relating to the task and other individuals was revealed in H. Clark's experiment with 168 students in a large classroom nearly 40 years ago (6). Clark opened a bottle containing water and asked for student response when they "smelled" the odor of the liquid. (It should be noted in evaluating the results that, relatively speaking, smell is not a very discriminatory sensory modality.) In a previous session alone with the experimenter, only one out of nine individuals had said he smelled something. But in the classroom, the experimenter's behavior was not the only factor. Within 10 seconds, some response came on the front row of seats; in 15 seconds some on the second row responded; by half a minute, response was made on the third row; and so on, until, by the end of three minutes, 33 students had responded. Those who responded were scattered around the first five rows of seats and were predominantly on one side of the room (23 subjects). Thus, it seems fairly certain that response was not merely in terms of an expectation aroused by the experimenter but also in terms of expectations relating to the entire classroom situation, in which the response of other individuals was a weighty influence.

In F. H. Allport's experiments on judging odors and weights in togetherness situations, a tendency was noted for extreme judgments to be avoided. This tendency and the resulting "leveling" of individual judgments is revealed in the graphic representation of these data (Fig. 4.1). The presence of other persons affected the individual's appraisal of the task and situation.

From 1928 to 1930, A. Jenness carried out several experiments under Allport's direction in which individuals made judgments alone, then *discussed* their judgments with the assigned task of reaching agreement, and finally gave individual judgments a second time (*11, 12*). Judgments were made of the number of beans in a sealed bottle, the actual number being 811 in every case. The actual number was a "matter of fact"; however, making a judgment was open to various *alternatives*, as indicated by the fact that over 90 percent of all subjects, both experimental and control, changed their initial estimates. Control subjects did not discuss their judgments.

Besides discussion to reach agreement, the other main experimental variable was the diversity or homogeneity of judgments given initially by individuals who were placed in the togetherness situations. In one condition, subjects from the same psychology class were placed in "committees" of three, the criterion for placement being that their initial alone judgments were divergent. In a second condition, four subjects in each committee were chosen so that initial judgments were close together. In a third condition, the experimenter read initial judgments of every individual in the whole class aloud, then passed out eight bottles; subjects gathered around informally in eight "committees" of differing sizes. The fourth condition was the "control."

Fifteen minutes of discussion were allowed. Each "committee" was instructed (1) to elect a chairman, (2) to "decide on a number to represent the consensus of the committee," and (3) to return to the classroom and write individual reports on the meeting and a final individual judgment (*12*, p. 281). Two aspects of the procedures are particularly important in evaluating the results. The first is that the subjects were instructed to reach agreement on one figure in the togetherness situation. The second is that the grade of "A" was to be given to the individual whose judgment was most accurate and to the chairman whose committee gave the most accurate figure; in addition, they were to be excused from writing up the experiment as a class report.

Like many experiments of this period, a primary interest was on increases and decreases in accuracy as a result of the social situation. Here it need only be noted that in this task and situation over half of the individuals in the control group, about half in the second experimental condition, and about three-fourths of those in the other two experimental conditions improved their accuracy in the second "alone" judgments.

Jenness was also interested in determining what effect the togetherness situation in which the subjects were required to reach a common agreement would have in increasing or decreasing "typicality" of individual judgments, and whether individuals would avoid extreme judgments afterward, as they had in Allport's experiments. The overall findings may be summarized as follows: When the subjects were aware of divergent estimates by others and discussed them with the explicit purpose of reaching agreement, the subsequent individual judgments showed increased similarity or "typicality," and the direction of change was toward more "conservative" estimates. The latter finding is similar to the leveling of judgments found by Allport. When individuals were not aware of widely divergent opinions and discussed their rather similar estimates with the explicit purpose of reaching agreement, differential results were obtained following the togetherness situations. The range of individual judgments within committees decreased in only two committees out of six, increased in three, and remained the same in one. While overall variability for all subjects combined was reduced, it would not seem safe to conclude that the effect of the togetherness situation and discussion was the same or consistent in the different "committees." Apparently unspecified relationships among various factors operating produced these variations.

When the stimulus situation lacks objective structure, the effect of others' judgments is more pronounced, even though individuals are not instructed to reach a common agreement. In one part of Sherif's study of social factors in perception utilizing the autokinetic phenomenon (p. 251), an individual judged distances of apparent movement first alone and then with two or three other subjects (25). This unstructured situation arouses considerable uncertainty. Even though they were not told to agree and were *cautioned against being influenced*, the individuals in togetherness situations shifted their judgments toward a common standard or norm of judgment. Unlike the increased leveling or conservative trend in the studies summarized above, the convergence here did not result in a trend toward the average. Rather the influence of various individuals differed, and the emerging common norm for judgment was in various instances above or below the average of individual judgments in the initial alone session. Such variations in the level of convergence are evident in the graphs of results, as presented on pp. 256–260 in the fuller report of this study.

Recently such convergence of judgments in the autokinetic situation has been demonstrated without the actual presence of other persons making judgments. Blake and Brehm presented through earphones recorded judgments which the subjects were told came from another subject in a different room (5). The important implication is that a common standard for judgment can be reached through conceptual means even though other individuals are not present.

It was further shown by Sherif that the direction of shifts in judgment of autokinetic movement in a togetherness situation could be prescribed by varying the range and norm of judgments given by one subject coöperating with the experimenter. Such shifts were particularly pronounced in the prescribed direction if the coöperating subject had some definite relationship (prestige) to the individual (26). Variations due to relationships among subjects are considered in detail in future chapters.

Whether or not there are existing relationships or definite interactions among individuals, the behavior of another person seen as part of the same situation can serve as an anchorage or standard for judgment. This was demonstrated also by Rosenbaum and Blake, who investigated the effect of another person's response on an individual's decision whether or not to serve as a voluntary subject in an experiment (22). An assistant to the experimenter chose a seat in the university library among a number of persons studying. As far as these persons were concerned, he was just another student at work. Five minutes later, the experimenter approached the table and asked the assistant to take part in an experiment, speaking just loud enough so that others could hear the request. In one condition, the assistant accepted, followed the experimenter from the room, and returned in four minutes to his seat. In another condition, the assistant replied, "No, I'd rather not" to the request. The critical subject was the person sitting next to the assistant. After the assistant accepted and returned or after he refused, this naïve person was then requested to participate in the same manner. As a control, the assistant was eliminated and the experimenter approached a naïve person directly.

There were 15 subjects in each condition. When the assistant accepted, 13 individuals subsequently agreed to be subjects. When the assistant refused, only 3 persons accepted the invitation. In the control condition, 8 persons agreed to the experimenter's request. Since these differences are statistically significant, it was concluded that the reactions of another person did serve as one anchorage for the individual in making a decision.

The effect of the preponderant reactions by individuals in a togetherness situation or by the "majority" has been the topic of much research, especially since Münsterberg's classroom demonstrations, showing shifts after majority judgments were given. Ordinarily the stimulus material was not well structured, in the sense that discrimination was not easy or various alternatives were feasible. In such a situation, as in the autokinetic situation, an individual may respond to the reactions of other people in choosing an alternative without being aware that his appraisal of the task has been influenced by others and without experiencing personal conflict.

Experiments like that by Moore demonstrated that merely presenting "majority" opinion to an individual could be effective, even though other individuals were not present (17). Moore also compared the relative effects of "majority" opinion (others apparently similar to oneself) and the opinion of "experts" in the field in question (individuals superior to oneself in this respect). The relative effect of the "majority" opinion was greater in matters of language usage and moral or ethical judgments than for musical preferences. Judgments were shifted in the direction of the "expert" opinion just about as frequently as toward the "majority," except for judgments of language usage, where apparently the opinions of someone more or less like oneself were more valued than those of an "expert."

Such differential results produced by the opinions of others who stand in different relationships to oneself and to the task indicate that the individual's appraisal of the task and behavior in it would vary in terms of relationships among subjects. This is indicated also in a study by Saadi and Farnsworth, in which subjects tended to accept "dogmatic" statements most readily when they were attributed to someone they liked and least readily when they were attributed to a disliked person (24). However, most studies of majority influences in togetherness situations have not specified any existing relationships among subjects or differentiations which developed in the experimental situation, beyond the general indication that subjects were all graduate students, in the same class, etc.

When there was an opportunity for some discussion and hence interaction among individuals, Thorndike found a tendency for an individual who differed from others on judgments of verbal material to change in the "majority" direction, the likelihood of his changing becoming greater as majority size increased (28).

In a series of experiments by Asch, the size of the "majority," the number of individuals disagreeing with the "majority," and the structure of the task were systematically varied (2). The task was judging the length of lines by matching a given standard line to one of three lines presented on a card. The experiments focused on the effects of an erroneous judgment made unanimously by about eight other persons on the judgments of a naïve individual. The persons who gave the wrong judgments were instructed prior to the experiments concerning the choices they were to make.

Consider first the influence of the degree of stimulus structure of the task. Just as previous studies have shown, Asch found that when differences between the stimuli did not provide an objective basis for discrimination, various alternative judgments were feasible; the subjects were influenced significantly by the erroneous judgments of the planted majority without feeling upset or disturbed.

At another extreme, when the discrepancies between the correct lines and those chosen by the majority were large (say, 2–4 inches), the influence of the majority judgments became a subordinate factor influencing the judgment of the naïve individual. The clear-cut differences between lines were the dominant stimulus factor in the situation. The discrepancy between this clear-cut stimulus factor and the judgments of others produced considerable conflict for some subjects. Only a few subjects shifted their judgments in the majority direction on some occasions, however.

When judgments by the majority differed from the correct length by ½ to 1¾ inch, their judgments carried relatively greater weight among the

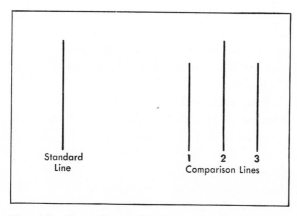

Fig. 4.2. Examples of the order of differences between lines used in study of majority influence. Subjects were instructed to choose the comparison line equal in length to the standard. (After Asch.)

factors determining the naïve individual's estimates. The differences between the lines chosen by the majority and the correct choices were, by and large, sufficient so that almost all individuals could discriminate on that basis, as control subjects demonstrated. Figure 4.2 shows an example of order of these differences. Yet eight other individuals were unanimously announcing a different choice from that which looked correct. The situation was almost a bizarre one for the individual—something he confronted, as Asch said, for possibly the first time in his life. Even those subjects who did not respond to the others by altering their judgments did react to them by feeling disturbed to some degree. They felt relieved when the situation was explained to them at the conclusion of the experiment.

Apparently this disturbance or uneasiness was a significant factor in the situation. Since there seemed to be no good reason why others were acting as they were, some subjects concluded that perhaps the others were subject to some illusion to which they were not. In this situation, a little less than one-third of the estimates made by 50 naïve subjects were errors in the direction of majority errors, and 68 percent of their estimates were correct. There were broad differences between individuals, both in their overall reaction to the situation and in the relative influence of the erroneous majority estimates.

When two naïve subjects took part with a planted majority giving erroneous judgments, the proportion of errors in the majority direction decreased to 10.4 percent. Withdrawing the additional naïve subject in the middle of the series of judgments resulted again in an increased proportion of error in subsequent judgments (28.5 percent), while introducing him midway in the series reduced errors to 8.7 percent. One planted subject instructed to respond correctly while the other planted subjects continued to make erroneous choices reduced the proportion of errors by the naïve subjects to 5.5 percent.

In order to check whether the errors of the naïve subject were attributable to the influence of the other subjects, several series were carried out using only 1 planted subject, 2 planted subjects, 3, 4, 8, or from 10 to 15. The influence of 1 other subject making erroneous judgments was rather slight, though not absent altogether. Errors in the direction of the judgments of 2 planted subjects were 12.8 percent of the total estimates. When 3 planted subjects made erroneous judgments, the proportion of errors in the majority direction made by the naïve subjects increased to the level reported above (about one-third) and stayed about the same regardless of the number added to the majority (up to 10–15).

As a further check, the relationship of majority subjects and the single individual to the task was reversed. A naïve majority of 16 found 1 (instructed) subject in their midst giving erroneous judgments. In this situation the naïve subjects did not feel personally disturbed. The incongruity of this situation became so obvious that contagious laughter swept through the room. The planted subject was looked upon as odd, an object of ridicule or of pity by various subjects.

A repetition of the experiment by R. Berenda indicated that the influence of the unanimous estimates by others which were at variance with the correct estimate had substantially greater effect on children's judgments than they had for the adults that Asch studied (4). Younger children (7–10 years) in particular tended to err in the majority direction more frequently. Furthermore, the young children were not so upset at being confronted by a situation which had seemed bizarre and highly out-of-the-ordinary to the adult subjects. This would indicate that the child's relation to the task and to other people was perceived by him somewhat differently. There is a possibility also that the existing relationships among subjects in Berenda's experiment were relatively more significant factors than in the experiments using adults. The children were from the same classes, and the report refers to relationships among classmates in evaluating results.

Earlier in this chapter various factors which can enter in structuring experience and behavior in social situations were enumerated. On the basis of the differential effects observed in various studies of togetherness situations, it is clear that these factors do not function as discrete influences but operate interdependently in structuring the individual's perception and judgment of a task in a given situation. In certain circumstances when the external stimulus situation does not provide clear-cut anchorages the behavior of other persons taking part may serve as the main anchorage, which affects in decisive fashion the way other factors are related to each other. Even when the objective situation is clearly structured, arousal of internal factors, like uncertainty, bewilderment, anxiety, may result in a tendency to take the behavior of others as a standard. In actual life such a situation is probably exceptional.

"Majority opinion," "rivalry," and "social pressure" are not blanket terms. Their effects differ with varying relationships among all of the factors operating at the time. By varying the relationships among individuals involved and particularly their stability, further differential effects are produced, as we shall see when group situations are discussed. To illustrate this point, consider that in some situations the acknowledged leader of a small informally organized group can swing the other members (majority) toward his proposal for a line of action. Typically, two or more alternatives are feasible before a choice becomes a real problem in such a setting. The leader's influence does not mean that he is "authoritarian" or employs threats. Rather, group members have observed his skill in making decisions and pursuing activities significant in their scheme of things on various occasions. In fact, this was an important basis for the particular individual's achievement and maintenance of the leader position. Henceforth, his opinions, suggestions, and behavior serve as weighty factors, always as related to the task and situation and the entire scheme of relationships among members of the group.

If group members see that a leader's decisions are contrary to facts or reality or are detrimental to their aims, he will begin to lose his power to influence them. In actual group situations the choice is seldom between a clearly perceived reality and the contradictory behavior of so many individuals. Instead, choice involves selecting among real alternatives whose appropriateness to lasting concerns of the members can become apparent only through a period of time and whose selection is made by individuals functioning in a differentiated scheme of relationships.

CONCLUDING REMARKS

The study of experience and behavior in social situations was introduced in this chapter through reviewing representative laboratory experiments on various influences in *togetherness situations*. The presence of other individuals observing or performing the same task has differential effects on experience and behavior, depending upon the interrelationships among factors operating at the time. Since social situations typical of actual life involve individuals who stand in more or less definite relationships to one another, caution is indicated in extending specific findings on togetherness situations to other social situations. Investigation of social situations in which individuals function as members of a scheme of established relationships implies the study of human groups, which is the topic of the next chapter.

REFERENCES

1. Allport, F. H. *Social Psychology*. Boston: Houghton Mifflin, 1924.
2. Asch, S. E. Effects of Group Pressures upon the Modification and Distortion of Judgments, in G. E. Swanson, T. M. Newcomb, and E. L. Hartley (eds.), *Readings in Social Psychology*. New York: Holt, 2nd ed., 1952.
3. Becker, H. *Systematic Sociology on the Basis of Beziehungslehre and Gebildelehre of Leopold von Wiese*. New York: Wiley, 1932.

4. Berenda, R. H. *The Influence of the Group on the Judgments of Children.* New York: King's Crown, 1950.
5. Blake, R. R., and Brehm, J. W. The use of tape recording to stimulate a group atmosphere, *J. abnorm. & soc. Psychol.* (1954), 49:311–313.
6. Clark, H. The crowd, *Psychol. Monogr.* (1916), 21:26–36.
7. Dashiell, J. F. An experimental analysis of some group effects, *J. abnorm. & soc. Psychol.* (1930), 25:190–199.
8. Dashiell, J. F. Experimental Studies of the Influence of Social Situations on the Behavior of Individual Human Adults, in C. Murchison (ed.), *Handbook of Social Psychology.* Worcester: Clark University Press, 1935.
9. Durkheim, E. *Elementary Forms of Religious Life.* London: Allen and Unwin, 1915.
10. Hare, A. P. A study of interaction and consensus in different sized groups, *Amer. sociol. Rev.* (1952), 17:261–267.
11. Jenness, A. Social influences in the change of opinion, *J. abnorm. & soc. Psychol.* (1932), 27:29–34.
12. Jenness, A. The role of discussion in changing opinion regarding a matter of fact, *J. abnorm. & soc. Psychol.* (1932), 27:279–296.
13. Kelley, H. H., and Thibaut, J. W. Experimental Studies of Group Problem Solving and Process, in G. Lindzey (ed.), *Handbook of Social Psychology.* Cambridge: Addison-Wesley, 1954, Vol. II.
14. Le Bon, G. *The Crowd.* London: T. Fisher Unwin, 1917.
15. Leuba, C. An experimental study of rivalry in young children, *J. compar. Psychol.* (1933), 16:367–378.
16. Miller, F. B. "Resistentialism" in applied social research, *Human Organiz.* (1954), 12:5–8.
17. Moore, H. T. The comparative influence of majority and expert opinion, *Amer. J. Psychol.* (1921), 32:16–20.
18. Murphy, G., and Murphy, L. B. *Experimental Social Psychology.* New York: Harper, 1931.
19. Murphy, G., Murphy, L. B., and Newcomb, T. M. *Experimental Social Psychology.* New York: Harper, rev. ed., 1937.
20. Riecken, H. W., and Homans, G. C. Psychological Aspects of Social Structure, in G. Lindzey (ed.) *Handbook of Social Psychology.* Cambridge: Addison-Wesley, 1954, Vol. II.
21. Roseborough, M. E. Experimental studies of small groups, *Psychol. Bull.* (1953), 50:275–303.
22. Rosenbaum, M., and Blake, R. R. Volunteering as a function of field structure, *J. abnorm. & soc. Psychol.* (1955), 50:193–196.
23. Ross, E. A. *Social Psychology.* New York: Macmillan, 1908.
24. Saadi, M., and Farnsworth, P. R. The degree of acceptance of dogmatic

statements and preferences for their supposed makers, *J. abnorm. & soc. Psychol.* (1934), 29:143–150.

25. Sherif, M. A study of some social factors in perception, *Arch. Psychol.* (1935), No. 187.

26. Sherif, M. An experimental approach to the study of attitudes, *Sociometry* (1937), *1*:90–98.

27. Simmel, G. The number of members as determining the sociological form of the group. I (trans. by A. W. Small), *Amer. J. Sociol.* (1902), 8:1–46.

28. Thorndike, R. L. The effect of discussion upon the correctness of group decisions, when the factor of majority influence is allowed for, *J. soc. Psychol.* (1938), 9:343–362.

29. Wapner, S., and Alper, T. G. The effect of an audience on behavior in a choice situation, *J. abnorm. & soc. Psychol.* (1952), 47:222–229.

CHAPTER 5

Properties of Groups

The individual's behavior in whatever he is doing is appreciably affected even by the mere presence of other persons. In the last chapter this fact was referred to as the differential effects of social situations.

Differential effects are not uniform in direction, and they are not fixed quantities for all occasions. In a given situation, they may be positive or negative in different degrees. They vary according to the nature of the task or problem, whether it is objectively clear-cut or subject to interpretation, and according to its significance for the individual.

Differential effects on experience and behavior vary also according to the nature of the social situation. And the nature of the social situation in producing differential effects is our concern. The nature of the social situation is not defined only by whether other people are present or absent. It makes a difference whether the individual knows that the others are engaged in the same task as he. The mere awareness that others are engaged in the same task may put him in a rivalry situation, even though he has not been instructed to compete.

The number of those present, whether they are spectators or active participants, and whether they are in the majority or in the minority facing a problem are among other factors which determine the direction and amount of differential effects.

Among the social determinants of differential behavior, the ways the individual is related to others in the situation are of particular importance for social psychology. As noted in the last chapter, his relationships to others who are parts of the situation in various capacities (e.g., as strangers or as fellow group members) influence all other factors in an interrelated way.

It makes considerable difference in the performance of a task or in tackling a problem if persons present are hostile, if they are indifferent, or if they are fellow group members.

With such considerations in mind, we differentiated social situations as (1) togetherness situations and (2) group situations. In a togetherness situation, participating individuals do not have stabilized status and role relationships—and hence established expectations toward each other. In a group situation, interaction among individuals takes place against the background of established relationships among them and hence reflects stabilized expectations among them.

The "groupness" of the group consists primarily of established reciprocities (statuses and roles) among individual members and a set of norms (standards or values) that they share in common. One can speak of a group to the extent that there are definite status and role relations among a number of individuals and that these individuals have a set of values or norms in carrying out relevant activities.

An extensive survey of available findings on human groups reveals the above properties among the essential characteristics of groups. These properties weigh heavily in determining the experience and behavior of individual members. Therefore, we shall use the concept *group* in a technical sense and define it accordingly.

A group is a social unit which consists of a number of individuals who stand in (more or less) definite status and role relationships to one another and which possesses a set of values or norms of its own regulating the behavior of individual members, at least in matters of consequence to the group.

This is a long definition, as definitions go. But if the minimum properties of the referent of the concept *group* are to be included, we have no choice. Otherwise, *group* is a blanket term to refer to any aggregate of individuals.

A few points in this definition need to be made explicit now. Others are clarified later in the chapter. "A social unit" delineates a given group from others and draws boundaries for it as a structure. Yet the phrase "consists of a number of individuals" makes this unit concrete and specifiable in space and time. It implies that there can be groups only with individuals, thus ruling out the possibility of misinterpretations like "group mind" doctrines.

In referring to relationships within the group, the qualification "more or less" is included because status and role relationships are not fixed and immutable. Literally, they may be stabilized to greater or lesser degrees.

A group does not have "values or norms" in relation to every conceivable task or situation that individual members might face. But in matters like activities frequently engaged in, the relationships among members, and perpetuation of the group as a unit, every group has standards or norms for experience and behavior. Therefore, the definition specifies that "in matters of consequence to the group" experience and behavior are regulated in terms of group norms.

The key concepts in the definition, namely, status, role, and norms, are characterized and illustrated later in this chapter.

Groups Are Products of Interaction Among Individuals

Groups do not drop out of the blue with stabilized relationships among members and a set of norms. Much work on socialization has concentrated on groups as they exist and on how new members learn the prevailing status and role relations and norms through a series of rewards and punishments. In this kind of study, the socialization process is chiefly confined to the problem of learning existing social norms through a series of positive reinforcements and of dropping out socially disapproved types of behavior through negative reinforcements or lack of reinforcement. Such work starts by taking for granted the existence of a given set of status and role relations and the norms that prevail in a given group.

This is only a part of the story. The other part is the problem of the *formation* of status and role relationships and the rise of norms. The study of the formation of groups with distinct properties gives crucial leads for a more adequate understanding of learning processes applicable to socialization. The socialization process does not consist only of learning this or that social norm concerning existing social arrangements and the "right" way and "wrong" way of doing things through linkages with reward or punishment.

When a number of individuals interact facing problems for which they do not have ready-made solutions or established ways of behaving, a set of reciprocities among them and a set of standards develop that regulate their relationships and modes of behavior. The status and role reciprocities and set of norms are these individuals' own doing from their very beginnings; they are experienced as their own.

It was stressed in the first chapter that social organization and cultural values are not things that come into existence in spite of man. He cannot help producing such social products when he interacts with others. His personal stability and his feeling of being a person in his own right are not independent of these products. If the implications of these points are kept in the foreground, tackling the *problem of the individual-group relationship* takes a more realistic bent. Otherwise, conclusions are likely to be just so many individual-bound or group-bound verdicts. The propositions stated above in summary form will be supported in the following pages and substantiated throughout the book.

INFORMALLY ORGANIZED GROUPS AS PROTOTYPES

The study of experience and behavior of individuals in group situations is not a simple task. On one hand, it is necessary that the social situation actually embody properties of groups. On the other hand, the investigator has to be able to specify these properties and other variables operating.

In modern societies almost everyone belongs to a number of groups. He is a member of a family, of one or more clubs, of a professional or work group, a fraternity or sorority, a church group, a study group. Some of the groups are small; some are quite large. Various of these groups are related to others in specified ways. Their memberships may overlap in varying degrees. Many of the small units are functioning parts of larger organizations, whose established purposes, relationships, and rules include specifications and limits for the functioning of their subunits.

Such complications indicate one reason why it is advantageous to single out small informal groups as representative of group situations. In small groups, like cliques, gangs, friendship clusters, clubs of various sorts, the individuals who participate, their interaction and reciprocal relationships, their problems, activities, and related factors operating at a given time can be observed and specified more directly and easily.

This is not the only advantage in studying small informal groups. Another is that such social units can be observed while in the process of formation. The stabilization of reciprocities and of traditions (norms) can be traced over a period of time. Their change and even their disintegration can be studied. Both the properties of the group situations and their effects on individuals can be specified. Thus, the "past history" of the group and of individuals as members of the group is brought within the scope of actual observation.

Sociologists interested in group properties and functioning, as well as socialization of individuals, have studied small informally organized groups over a period of many years. Especially since the 1920's under the impetus given by Park of the University of Chicago and his associates, empirical results on actual informal groups have accumulated. Observations of such groups and case histories of individual members provide a gold mine for social psychology. The growing research interest in small groups in social psychology followed studies of groups in industry initiated by Elton Mayo and his associates at the Harvard Business School in the late twenties, J. L. Moreno's studies of role relations (1934), and later the experiments of Kurt Lewin and his associates.

Small Informal Groups and Large Organizations

Taking small informally organized groups as prototypes in the study of group situations does not imply that such social units are identical with large, formal organizations. In the first place, many large organizations have long histories which have been enacted by generations of individuals. As Whyte pointed out in discussing industrial organizations, "bigness" in itself brings distinctive problems (57). The face-to-face interaction and communication among individuals characteristic of small groups tends to be replaced by indirect, even mass, communication. Flexibility in meeting problems, in changing to meet the demands of new situations may be drastically curtailed. The compelling structural properties of large-scale, formal organizations cannot be minimized. Their inescapable impact, especially that of mass communication, is emphasized in later chapters.

Many small groups in actual life are functioning parts of large organizations. Therefore, the relationships and major norms in these smaller parts stem from the larger organization or institution to an important extent. A Ladies Aid society of an established church, a union local, a local Chamber of Commerce are examples of such groups. In informally organized groups the specific interactions of members and their reciprocal relationships assume relatively greater importance as the *source* of influences affecting members. However, the necessity of referring to larger social units in explaining the nature and functioning of small groups is not specific to small units in larger formal organizations. As we shall see later, small groups, whether formally or informally organized, are *always* related to larger social units. Juvenile gangs spring up informally within larger community and institutional structures (47). In any final analysis, these larger social units and their relationship to other larger structures have to be specified, in order that we may comprehend fully the formation and functioning of small informal units within them (49).

Therefore, if the central problem is understanding man's behavior in group situations, it is not always feasible to make a sharp dichotomy between *formally* organized groups and *informally* organized groups. In terms of this problem, the chief basis for differentiating sharply between formally and informally organized groups is their origin, and the origin of the norms governing their functioning. Even on this basis the differentiation is not clear-cut.

As Barnard stated: "Informal association is rather obviously a condition which necessarily precedes formal organization" (4, p. 116). Many formal organizations of today started as informally organized groups. Many if not most Protestant sects began as relatively small groups on an informal basis. The Mennonites, Quakers, and Mormons are specific examples. One of the early labor organizations in the United States, the Knights of Labor, grew on an informal basis and functioned for 12 years in secrecy (29). The beginnings of the modern coöperative retail movement grew from the informal meetings of 12 unemployed weavers who, after a time, were instrumental in establishing the first coöperative store in England (21).

Generality of Informal Group Formations

The choice of small informally organized groups as prototypes is amply justified by their importance in the socialization process and in individual behavior from childhood on. Especially since the writings of Cooley, sociologists have been aware of their significance in this respect. Their empirical studies, as well as observations by keen reporters of human life, provide impressive documentation of the prevalence of informally organized groups in all walks and conditions of life. Robert Faris has pointed to the almost universal tendency for individuals sharing common circumstances in life to interact in informally organized groups as one of the impressively verified generalizations about social life (10).

Even at preschool ages, children begin to form small friendship and play groups with reciprocal relationships and traditional ways of doing things which have some stability (32, 33). Thirty years ago Parten carried out her studies on the participation of preschool children in group play. Her findings showed that organized group activities become possible only with the development of conceptual capacities and some facility in language. Characteristic play by 2-year-olds is side by side; that is, it involves simply "togetherness." With age there is an increasing frequency of group activity, its organized forms appearing definitely at around three years of age and increasing thereafter (38).

The capacity to form and function within organized groups increases markedly with age from kindergarten through the eighth grade (34). Piaget has traced this tendency to the attainment of a conceptual level of functioning which enables the child to relate himself to others in a reciprocal way (39). That is, taking part in the formation and functioning of organized groups presupposes the formation of an ego structure (as characterized on pp. 581–583).

Informally organized groups, cliques, or gangs become especially widespread and important during adolescence in modern societies. When one is not yet an adult and conceptions of self in relation to others are being reformulated, informal groups of age-mates may become the center of the experience of personal identity and stability. Investigations of adolescence in all walks of life have revealed this fact (50). Adolescents themselves are frequently well aware of the great importance of their age-mate groups in their lives (20).

Among the most fruitful sources of empirical observations on informally organized groups are the sociological studies of gangs formed in the deteriorating slum sections of large cities by youngsters who are frequently deprived of some essentials of life and of close social ties with either a family, an organized community, or the respectable sections of society. As the studies of Thrasher, Zorbaugh, Clifford Shaw, and others demonstrated, in such circumstances the youthful gang of individuals with a common destiny becomes the central anchorage for individual satisfactions, aspirations, preoccupations, and actions (44, 45, 46, 54, 58).

The prevalence of small informal cliques within college dormitories and fraternity or sorority houses has been documented in many studies utilizing sociometric techniques. They also arise in community housing projects of young married students (11). Zorbaugh's study of the near North Side in Chicago revealed informal groups in every area. Thus, the Gold Coast had its exclusive clubs; artists had their little Bohemian groups. Areas with heavy foreign populations had numerous "mutual protection" societies; the slum had its gangs. Even that loneliest of areas, the rooming-house district populated by single, unattached individuals, had its cults and sects; and every pool hall or cigar store was the center for some sort of grouping (58, p. 192).

Informally organized groupings are also found in rural settings. Now that rural life is more mechanized and communication and transportation are more modernized, these informal groupings are based to a lesser extent simply on family units and proximity in the rural community. There is a trend to include the townspeople, who used to seem more remote and different (27).

Those most formal of formal organizations—the military—provide the settings for informal groups throughout their various branches and units. No doubt the nature of these groupings varies considerably, from clusters of "buddies" to larger units. The observations of reporters like Ernie Pyle and Bill Mauldin during World War II indicate that in wartime such informal groups frequently included the whole unit or crew sharing common experiences, hardships, and risks. These observations were verified by the investigations of social scientists, which showed that high morale, esprit de corps, and unit pride were based on the formation of informal group structures within the unit, and that individuals' feelings of security were intimately tied to these informal structures (52).

These findings can be exemplified in the words of Ernie Pyle: "The hundred men in that camp were just like a clan. They had all been together a long time and they had almost a family pride in what they were doing and the machinery they were doing it with" (40, p. 122).

"Private Wolfson, Sergeant Harrington, and Major Robb had one thing in common with every soldier in the army—they thought their division was the best extant. Since I was a man without a division, I just agreed with them all" (40, p. 233).

There are, therefore, two main reasons why small informally organized groups are utilized as prototypes in the study of experience and behavior in group situations. First, small informal groups are advantageous for methodological reasons. For example, the individuals, their interaction and relationships, their problems and activities, and related factors operating at a given time can be observed and specified directly. Further, such informally organized units can be studied while in the process of formation. Second, informally organized groups are so prevalent and important in social life that their study constitutes a necessary aspect of social psychological research in itself.

Utilizing small informally organized groups as prototypes to derive properties of group situations and to study individuals in group settings does not mean that such units are identical with formal social structures. In terms of origins of group products, of the compellingness of various structural properties, and other respects there are decided differences. At times, structures that come into existence as a consequence of contemporary interaction among individuals may not be in line with existing formal organizations and regulations "on the books." However, the central problem at present is the effects of group situations on individual experience and behavior, and the purpose is to discover relevant principles which can be elaborated for application.

ESSENTIAL PROPERTIES OF SMALL INFORMAL GROUPS

In order to specify the effects of group situations on individuals as they become functioning parts or members, it is necessary to single out the minimum properties in the formation and functioning of the groups. Four properties essential in group formation and functioning are discussed in this chapter. They are based on an extensive study of sociological literature and actual small groups over a period of years. Other properties have been proposed in various treatments of the topic. Those presented here seem to be a minimum.

All of these properties presuppose that a number of individuals interact with one another. *Interaction* is basic to group formation. However, it is not distinctive to group situations. It is, in fact, a feature common to any form of social contact between people, whether it is interpersonal, like that between two friends or lovers, or casual, like the chance conversation of two strangers on a bus.

Interaction between human individuals (beyond the age of 3 or so) is characteristically carried out by persons functioning at a conceptual level and utilizing standardized symbolisms as exemplified by gestures, insignia, flags, musical patterns, and spoken or written words of a language system. Therefore, human interaction characteristically involves *communication* in one form or another. When human individuals interact, communication is an integral part of the process.

The minimum properties essential in the formation and functioning of small informal groups are:

1. Common motives conducive to interaction among individuals.
2. Differential effects of interaction on participants, determined increasingly by the structure and norms peculiar to the group as togetherness situations tend toward group formation.
3. Formation of a group structure (organization) consisting of roles and hierarchical statuses and, consequently, a clear-cut demarcation of the in-group from others.

4. Standardization of values or norms which regulate relationships and activities of consequence to the group.

Each of these essential properties is discussed briefly in the above order.

1. Common Motives Conducive to Interaction

Informal organization of groups takes shape through the interaction of individuals with common motives and goals. The potential variety of these covers the range of human needs, desires, interests, and aspirations which may be common to more than one individual. They may be deprivations of the bodily needs common to all, like hunger and need for shelter and adequate clothing. For example, youngsters in communities where the families are unable to provide means for relieving major deprivations may gravitate into gang formations, whose chief activity is securing these means, perhaps by stealing. Or adults in a prisoner-of-war camp where food is insufficient band together in their personal misery to devise means for distributing the little food available or for obtaining more. A common threat or danger to life itself or to the means of livelihood may bring people together for mutual protection and aid. Thus, the early formation of the Knights of Labor united in the statement: "When bad men combine, the good must associate, else they will fall, one by one, an unpitied sacrifice in a contemptible struggle" (29, p. 4).

Individuals facing uncertainty or pervasive insecurity in their social ties may gravitate toward one another to establish some stable anchorage of their own, in terms of which they may achieve clarified and more stable personal identities. This is a common basis for interaction in a modern world of rapid change where old loyalties overlap and conflict with the new, where thousands of people feel "alone" in cities teeming with life, where youth struggle through a long transition to adulthood amid the clashing of old and new in themselves and in the social world of adults and age-mates. A desire for some place in life, any place at all, or a better place, for prestige, distinction, power—all of these and many others have brought people together to interact as a group.

All individuals who gravitate toward each other to interact need not come with the same predominant motives. But one or more motives are central in the process, and these usually weigh heavily in determining the type of activities engaged in, the sort of status structure which develops, and the traditions and new goals which are standardized in the interaction process. Thus, Thrasher observed that gangs tended to specialize in certain activities appropriate to their dominant interests. Some were organized around sex, some around stealing, picking pockets, junking, athletics, gambling, and so on. In each case specialized structures, "codes" of conduct, and special "techniques" developed, in line with the dominant interest. The Gold Coast of Chicago, which Zorbaugh studied, was the setting for numerous cliques with differing levels of distinction, each intent on attaining more social standing and recognition or maintaining that already achieved.

The individual who interacts with others but does not share the motives which were predominant in bringing them together soon finds himself out of place and a misfit. At the same time, however, certain motives distinctive to an individual member may be satisfied in a group which is specialized along other lines.

The phrase "common motives conducive to interaction" is a disarming one. It seems obvious enough. Yet all motives experienced by a number of individuals in the same place at the same time are not conducive to their interaction. In certain instances, a bodily need may become so pressing, a deprivation so keenly experienced by an individual that for the time being he can see no advantage in attempting to deal with his problem along with other people similarly affected. This seems to be the upshot of an examination of group formations in concentration camps during World War II. There were all sorts of complicating factors in these situations, many intense personal problems, and their effects varied for different individuals. However, it seems that group interaction was more likely to occur in those situations where bodily needs were deprived to lesser degrees. People slowly starving to death in these situations were not prone to interact as groups, and individualistic efforts to get food, even if this meant stealing from fellow sufferers, were not uncommon. Throughout history, there have been deprived people, people caught in common circumstances, who have not come together in groups on the basis of their common problems.

Other examples can be cited. Some motives by their very nature are incompatible to interaction among individuals having the same desire. Take five vice-presidents all set upon having the presidency. Since only one can have the position, the common desire to be president is actually antagonistic to interaction on any but the most polite and formal basis. In accounts of the California and Klondike "gold rushes," we find that those who went to build fortunes had the same or similar motives. In many instances the common motive was the cause of conflicts, to the point of harmful acts to one another. However, there were also times when the aspirants joined hands. These were times when they realized that only by doing so could they achieve their purpose.

Therefore, "common motives conducive to interaction" necessarily implies that the individuals perceive, even though dimly, that others also face the same problems and that coöperation with them has some relevance for the problem, even if only that of providing mutual solace. The phrase implies experience by individuals, functioning on a conceptual level, of a set of circumstances or a problem which can be faced, escaped, ignored, or dealt with in some fashion by coöperating individuals. Of course, in some cases coöperation may lead to nothing. If a group starts to form and then finds a blind alley or meets with completely crushing obstacles, there is a tendency toward disintegration for the time being, unless another basis for interaction has evolved in the meantime.

As we shall see when motives are discussed, human motivation (at least after early childhood) always involves conceptual and perceptual functions (Chapters 11–13). Thus "motives conducive to interaction" does not imply new factors not found in other cases of human motivation. Even though goals may be perceived or conceived only vaguely by individuals, human motives are not typically "blind, irrational forces" in the sense that they operate in separate compartments from cognitive functions. If they were, it would be difficult to explain differentiation of individuals sharing a common fate into group structures based on different attitudes and different ideologies.

For example, individuals with homogeneous backgrounds living in a housing project and attending college may cluster into little groups on the basis of sheer *proximity* in the project. But when individuals having different beliefs and heterogeneous backgrounds face a common problem, they will tend to form groups centered around different attitudes toward it and different modes of meeting it. In one German prison camp the initial groupings of individuals caught in these difficult circumstances were on the basis of living units. But these temporary groupings gave way to more enduring formations centered around different motives (attitudes toward the situation and the Germans). Thus different groups were formed based on the wish to defy the Germans (refusal to work), or on desires to escape, or on the wish to have it as easy as possible or to gain the favor of the guards (1).

EMERGENCE OF NEW MOTIVES IN GROUP INTERACTION: Before taking up the second property of group formations, another aspect of motivation in human groups must be noted—the problem of what keeps individuals together once they interact to form a group. It is true that initial motives and goals (e.g., economic gain, sexual satisfaction, political ambition, distinction, etc.) which brought individuals together in the first place frequently remain important factors in the continuance of group activity.

On the other hand, once group formation begins, once an "in-group" takes shape, new motives and goals arise which must be included in accounting for the persistence of the group. Emerging in the process of group formation and functioning, these new motives may even acquire greater importance to the members than those which were central in first bringing them together. They are central in the solidarity and maintenance of the group.

Motives related to integral membership in a group are not imposed from outside. In the first place, the very fact of *belongingness* in a group provides the individual with a sense of being somebody in the situation, of having some place in the scheme of things. The importance of satisfactions derived from group membership is seen dramatically in cases of individuals who lack such a sense of belongingness and turn heaven and earth to be accepted as part of some group in their surroundings.

One's sense of amounting to something and his experience of his worth in life are closely tied with the functions he serves in various capacities in groups of which he is a member. To maintain his belongingness implies loyalty to the group and the furthering of its interests.

Relationships with other individuals within a stable system of reciprocities are, in themselves, satisfying forms of human association. In addition, group interaction offers many other pleasures and opportunities for activities and achievements which are impossible in isolation.

But the explanation for the emergence of new motives in the process of becoming a member lies in the products of group interaction and the formation of attitudes related to these products by individual members. Once a system of reciprocities arises among members and values or norms are stabilized, the members of the group form appropriate attitudes, within a range set by these group products. Henceforth, these attitudes, relating to the individual's position and functional relations in the group, to ways of doing things, to desirable ends of activity, to belongingness, become functional parts of his conception of himself (his "ego"). Ego-attitudes define his relatedness in those aspects of his life in which the particular group functions.

From childhood on, the individual is involved in establishing and maintaining, in changing and forming new modes of relatedness with his surroundings. It is difficult, and it may be exceedingly painful, to have one's ego-attitudes upset. One's whole sense of personal identity and stability may be shaken. Therefore, once an individual becomes a member of a group and thus forms appropriate attitudes relating himself to other members and to the group products, it is not a pleasant experience for him to have these upset or to sever the relationships.

He feels uneasy, disturbed, confused when his group ties are rendered shaky by changing relationships or circumstances. The process of deliberately destroying his relatedness to the group, of severing ties with it, of looking for new forms of relatedness elsewhere is a formidable task, particularly if the group has been central in his scheme of values. Conversely, the stability and continuity of group ties is a proportionately pleasant and satisfying experience—a state to be desired, maintained, and improved.

These considerations concerning the rise of new motives in group interaction and the individual-group relatedness are to be elaborated further. (The problem is discussed in Chapters 17 and 18, which deal with ego-involvements.)

2. Differential Effects of Interaction on Members

When individuals interact with one another, the interaction process and its properties produce differential effects upon their experience and behavior. "Differential effects" means changes in perception, discrimination, emotions, thinking, "personality" features, and action which result from becoming a functioning part or member of social interaction. These differential effects may be qualitative changes, as well as increases or decreases in behavioral tendencies.

Such differential effects are found in most empirical investigations of behavior in groups which are concerned with more than simply the immediate situation. For example, Thrasher reports the case of Ellman, who belonged to a juvenile gang called the "Dirty Dozen." When he went out with his girl, Ellman was courteous and pleasant. But in the gang he liked to appear very tough, loud, and bragging. He was one of the "meanest fellows" in it (54, p. 50). Another boy in a different group could always be counted upon to respond to "an appeal for the best for himself and the gang," but outside of the group he showed little responsiveness to the requirements or appeals of others (54, p. 295). Thrasher and Clifford Shaw (44, 45, 46) report many instances verging on self-sacrifice by individuals in the interests of group solidarity and in line with the group's code (set of norms).

Group situations are not the only situations in which differential experience and behavior occur. As we saw in Chapters 2 and 3, shifts, reversals, and even transformations in experience and reaction occur whenever compelling new factors become anchorages in the frame of reference at a given time (especially pp. 62–66). In the last chapter we found that even the presence of another person engaged in a similar task or the judgments of a number of other individuals produce differential effects. The considerable sociological literature on crowd situations reveals differential effects, including qualitative changes in experience and behavior, even when the crowd is not involved in an organized activity, like attending a football game or witnessing a prize fight. (This and other aspects of collective behavior are discussed in Chapter 10.)

Since differential experience and behavior are found even in simple perceptual situations, their explanation in group interaction does not require involving mysterious forces or hypnotic influences from the group. Some early writers considered differential effects quite unique to group or crowd situations and accounted for them by considering the individual as the prey of omnipotent group influences or hypnotic effects. Others, like Freud, simply denied that there was anything new and significant about the characteristics of experience and behavior in groups and stated that the individual was expressing tendencies he had already stored in his "unconscious," tendencies built up on an individual basis and ready for release when his inhibition or social veneer was stripped away (*13*).

The distinguishing feature of differential effects in group situations is that they become referable to an increasing extent to the organizational properties and norms of the group. They become more consistent and predictable. However, in togetherness situations or transitory groupings where relationships among individuals and group norms are not stabilized, factors producing differential effects can also be specified. The process is not mysterious or magical.

In the so-called "leaderless group" studies, a number of individuals are placed in a situation and faced with a task or problem which requires some coöperation or coördination for completion. The task or problem may involve discussion of some topic, or solving a puzzle which requires manipulation, or getting across a stream with the aid of only crude material. Such situations have been studied by many investigators, including military personnel in various countries (*3*), an O.S.S. team of social scientists during World War II (*37*), Gibb (*17*), Carter (*9*), industrial personnel, and others (*5, 42*).

In these situations the *task* or *problem* at hand and the *special skills* it requires assume considerable importance. In the process of interaction to complete the task or solve the problem, reciprocities among the individuals develop, largely in terms of their functions in the situation if there were no established relationships among individuals at the outset. Even in its beginnings, this state of reciprocities produces expectations toward others in relation to oneself. The expectations tend to shift as new phases of the task are tackled, as new difficulties arise calling for different skills and abilities, or as various individuals offer proposals or take actions which prove effective or ineffective, as the case may be (9, 42).

Such togetherness situations thus tend toward some stabilization of reciprocities and expectations which are more or less specific to the situation, task, and its duration. Even though the reciprocities and expectations are temporary and conditional on task and situation, they are sufficiently stabilized in many cases so that they produce differential effects on individual participants. Thus, it happens that some individuals, whom investigators could not designate as likely "leaders" in the situation and task through prior interviews or tests, emerge in the temporary interaction process as the chief initiators of action. These studies started with the practical intent of selecting likely candidates for leadership posts in organized groups and have been continued by many with such practical interests (3, 5). It is clear that differential behavior in interaction of a transitory nature is sufficiently specifiable in terms of reciprocities and expectations arising among individuals in a given task or problem situation to have some predictive value for similar practical situations. Practical persons who utilize such findings are not at all interested in mysterious group forces or in the contents of an uninhibited "unconscious."

Of course, the reciprocities and expectations among individuals arising as a consequence of the immediate situation and the nature of the task are not the only factors which produce differential effects in transitory interaction. It has been demonstrated, for example, that previously established status relations among individuals and their particular attitudes and personal characteristics formed prior to interaction also lead to substantial differences in the resulting interaction and the behavior of participating members (6, 19, 24). Since structural properties of transitory situations are incipient rather than stabilized and clear-cut, one would expect that any of a host of variables might result in pronounced shifts in interaction and behavior.

In contrast to such transitory situations, if individuals interact over a period of time in joint efforts to deal with a common problem or attain a common goal which has genuine and lasting significance to them, the reciprocities and expectations among them become more stabilized. Partly because groups tend to "specialize" in activities and tasks in line with their central purposes or problems, and partly because of the stabilization of reciprocal expectations among members, the specific task faced at a given moment carries *relatively* less weight in determining interaction toward its completion.

Differential effects on experience and behavior are determined more and more by the role and status relationships (organization) and norms stabilized in the group. The effects of structural properties of group situations can be contrasted to bit-by-bit additions or changes in this factor or that factor. In group situations the individual becomes a *part* of a functioning system, the properties of which become major anchorages for his experience and behavior.

Since the relationships within a group are organized along hierarchical lines, the particular nature of these anchorages will also vary in terms of the individual's functional position in the group. Thus, a person who sees himself and is perceived by others as being at the top in his group is affected differently from a person who is "low man on the totem pole."

The differential effects of group properties on experience and behavior as the individual comes into contact with them and becomes a functioning member are illustrated by Bill Mauldin's description of men in combat units he observed during World War II. Note the changes which a man might have to make while he is being accepted, and the consequences group belongingness has even when the individual is not actually in the presence of the group:

Combat people are an exclusive set, and if they want to be that way, it is their privilege. They certainly earn it. New men in outfits have to work their way in slowly, but they are eventually accepted. Sometimes they have to change some of their ways of living. An introvert or a recluse is not going to last long in combat without friends, so he learns to come out of his shell. Once he has "arrived" he is pretty proud of his clique, and he in turn is chilly towards outsiders.

That's why, during some of the worst periods in Italy, many guys who had a chance to hang around a town for a few days after being discharged from a hospital where they had recovered from wounds, with nobody the wiser, didn't take advantage of it. They weren't eager to get back up and get in the war, by any means, and many of them did hang around a few days. But those who did hang around didn't feel exactly right about it, and those who went right back did it for a very simple reason—not because they felt that their presence was going to make a lot of difference in the big scheme of the war, and not to uphold the traditions of the umpteenth regiment. They went back because they

FIG. 5.1. "I guess it's okay. The replacement center says he comes from a long line of infantrymen." (From *Up Front* by William Mauldin. Copyright, 1945, by Henry Holt and Company, Inc. Reprinted by permission of the publishers.)

knew their companies were very shorthanded, and they were sure that if somebody else in their own squad or section were in their own shoes, and the situation were reversed, those friends would come back to make the load lighter on *them* [31, pp. 58–60].

To sum up, in group interaction, differential effects are produced by the stabilized relationships and norms of the group. Differential effects may appear in any situation in which compelling new factors become anchorages in the frame of reference determining an individual's behavior at the time. When the situation embodies no consistent or lasting rela-

FIG. 5.2. "By th' way, what wuz them changes you wuz gonna make when you took over last month, sir?" (From *Up Front* by William Mauldin. Copyright, 1945, by Henry Holt and Company, Inc. Reprinted by permission of the publishers.)

tionships among individuals in terms of their mutual expectations, goals, values, or norms, differential effects are produced by immediate factors in the specific situation. When a persisting group structure and norms are stabilized, these provide organized, enduring, and motivationally significant anchorages which produce consistent differential effects on behavior and affect, in varying degrees, the relative contribution of situational factors, like the task or minor changes in the situation.

3. Formation of Group Structure

When individuals with common motives and goals interact repeatedly over a period of time, a group structure consisting of roles and hierarchical statuses (relative positions) takes shape and becomes stabilized in some degree. Interaction among individuals for the solution of a common problem or attainment of a common goal necessitates coöperation among them, differentiation of functions, and coördination of efforts.

In its broadest sense, group structure refers to a more or less stabilized system of interdependent relationships (status and role) among individuals according to their respective contributions to interaction toward a common goal. These relationships are interdependent and reciprocal, linking a given individual to every other individual in the group in certain definite ways (roles). In terms of the individuals' respective contributions in various capacities relevant to the tasks, problems, or goals significant in the interaction process, reciprocal expectations are stabilized for each member in relation to other members. These stabilized expectations for behavior in the group define the *roles* of the group members.

We use the term "role" to refer to the expected behavior of a given individual in the scheme of established reciprocities of a group. Therefore, role is a relational concept which has meaning in terms of expected, reciprocal modes of behavior among members constituting a group. For example, the leadership role implies certain expected modes of behavior in relation to "lieutenants" and other group members.

Individuals differ in personal, social, or material capacities, skills, and resources. In any interaction process involving a common problem or goal, some capacities and resources are more pertinent to the central focus of interaction than others. By virtue of such capacities, skills, and resources, some people exert greater weight, or control, or authority than others. Therefore, when interaction continues over a period of time among individuals with persistent, common motives or problems, the reciprocal expectations among them fall into a hierarchical pattern or scale. A differentiated position in this hierarchy is called *status*.

People everywhere function as parts or members of such group structures, whether they are aware of it or not. Even in the most "disorganized" sections of society, organization among individuals is stabilized on an informal basis. Noting this fact, Whyte observed that in every informal organization "there was a hierarchical structure of social relations binding the individuals to one another and that the groups were also related hierarchically to one another" (55, p. viii). In the most informal groups where individuals were not always aware of their relationships, the group structure was revealed through the predictable patterns of interaction among them. As we shall see in Chapters 6 and 7, stabilization of group structure necessarily implies stabilized interaction patterns and *lines of communication* among members.

The statement that group structure tends always to be hierarchical along some dimension does not imply that brute dominance, suppression, and ruthless competition always rule supreme in determining group structure. Anthropologists have taught us that in order to achieve status in groups where coöperation is highly valued an individual must excel in that respect. Even when men in groups explicitly set out to abolish all distinctions whatsoever, a group hierarchy develops on some basis. Thus, the three men who originally banded together on the isolated Atlantic island of Tristan da Cunha signed an agreement that "No member shall assume any superiority whatsoever, but all to be considered equal in every respect . . ." (35, p. 19). But within the space of five years, as new members found themselves on the island, a new contract was drawn specifying by name the status hierarchy which had developed in the meantime. The basis of this hierarchy was chiefly proficiency and diligent pursuit of work. A hierarchy of statuses is necessitated by division of functions and *coördination* of functions.

The reciprocal expectations pertaining to function and behavior in the group become stabilized in time for each position in the group structure. Such stabilized expectations regulate both the behavior of other members toward the person occupying a particular role and status position and his own behavior toward others. One of the early experimental studies of informal groups, begun in 1926 and carried out by Newstetter, Feldstein, and Newcomb, found higher relationships between status and kind of treatment *received* by the person occupying that position than between status and various personality "traits" (36). The particular individual, in turn, comes to expect certain treatment and may be shocked if he is treated in a manner varying from it widely. His aspirations are likely to be colored by his role and status. If he does attempt to substitute his own definitions and aspirations for those stabilized in the group for him, he must be prepared to face obstacles and resistances in varying degrees, depending on the stability of the group structure at the time.

In the sense implied above, the reciprocal expectations for behavior among members in a group structure become standardized. They constitute norms for the group governing reciprocal relations among the various individual members. Thus, as Freedman, Hawley, Landecker, and Miner pointed out, the stability or unity of groups requires both "functional integration" and "normative integration" (12). Here functional integration refers to status and role relationships, while normative integration refers to values, standards, norms which serve as criteria of conduct for members. These aspects, namely, functional and normative integration, are not discrete or independent of each other.

The social norms defining reciprocal relationships, functions, and positions in the group hierarchy are not absolute, cut-and-dried affairs. They define *ranges of tolerable behavior* within which the behavior of a member in a given position is expected to fall. The range of tolerable behavior will vary both in terms of the particular member's position in the hierarchy (status) and in terms of the nature of the behavior involved. These variations will be touched upon in the next section when social norms are discussed, and in Chapter 8.

LEADERSHIP IN GROUPS: Since the next chapter elaborates the formation of group structure in some detail, such important aspects as leadership and power relationships will receive little more than recognition here. The leadership position is at the top of the status hierarchy. Since the status hierarchy is stabilized in terms of relative control or ability to affect the interaction and behavior of others, it necessarily implies *power relationships* as an integral aspect. The dimension of status pertains to effective initiative in coördinating reciprocal functions, in carrying out activities and starting new activities. In this sense, the status dimension represents the power invested in various members, from the leader on down through the group.

The focus of power resides in the leader position. For this reason, the leader is clearly the most important single *part* of the group structure from the point of view of influencing activity and maintaining stability of the structure. But a *part* of the structure he is. Leadership is a role within the scheme of relations and is defined by reciprocal expectations between the leader and other group members. The leadership role is defined, like other roles, by stabilized expectations (norms) which in most matters and situations of consequence to the group are more exacting and require greater obligations and responsibility than those for other positions. A section is devoted to leadership in Chapter 7.

IN-GROUP DELINEATION AND SOLIDARITY: Once a group structure takes definite form, it may be characterized as an *in-group* from the point of view of members. The in-group is delineated clearly from other groups or *out-groups*. Individuals not belonging to the group are viewed as outsiders. In-group demarcation becomes concrete in the following observation by Bill Mauldin:

> While men in combat outfits kid each other around, they have a sort of family complex about it. No outsiders may join. Anybody who does a dangerous job in this war has his own particular kind of kidding among his own friends, and sometimes it doesn't even sound like kidding. Bomber crews and paratroopers and infantry squads are about the same in that respect. If a stranger comes up to a group of them when they are bulling, they ignore him. If he takes it upon himself to laugh at something funny they have said, they freeze their expressions, turn slowly around, stare at him until his stature has shrunk to about four inches and he slinks away, and then they go back to their kidding again.
>
> It's like a group of prosperous businessmen telling a risque joke and then glaring at the waiter who joins in the guffaws [31, p. 58].

When an in-group delineation has taken shape, a regalia of objects, things, places, and practices is appropriated by members. Thus, a meeting place, a certain table, a soda fountain becomes "ours" to the group. Even an area of activity with certain boundaries may be defined, as reported in many studies on cliques and gangs.

It should be emphasized, however, that in-group delineation in itself does not necessarily imply any particular kind of relationships with out-groups. It does imply formation of attitudes toward out-groups and their members with whom the group has functional contacts. But hostility or antagonism toward outsiders need not be a universal accompaniment of in-group formation. The kind of positive or negative attitudes formed in relation to a given out-group and its members is determined by the nature of functional relationships with that out-group. This point is made here because of its importance in understanding intergroup relationships (Chapter 9).

That state of affairs referred to as *solidarity* or "high morale" is largely a consequence of a stabilized group structure in which the various members meet the expectations defining their particular functions and positions. In emphasizing stabilization of structure, there is the danger that it be conceived in static terms as frozen. It is far from that. In varying degrees, the reciprocal relationships within a group change and shift as the group faces different problems or tasks and as different members participate in different ways. Through internal frictions or the pressures of conditions outside, the group structure may be weakened and may even disintegrate (55).

The importance of stable structure in which reciprocal expectations are met consistently is illustrated by the famous Carlson Raiders of World War II—a deliberately fostered informal organization within the Marine Corps (7). In this unit, reciprocal expectations were stabilized among men in terms of the functions necessary for an explicitly formulated goal. This stabilization process involved minimizing or eliminating those traditional distinctions between officers and enlisted men which did not seem essential for coördinated action and clear outlining of the plans followed and their purpose. Officers were expected to demonstrate their worth as leaders of activity. Carlson, in particular, made himself the model in consistently meeting high expectations for his behavior.

The result of these efforts to foster an in-group structure in which high expectations for behavior were standardized and consistently met was astounding group solidarity, even under terrible combat conditions of Guadalcanal and other battles which broke down many other units and individuals in them. It became virtually unnecessary for Carlson to exert formal disciplinary measures. Modes of behavior were standardized and internalized by members of the units. Thus, activities toward group goals were carried out with zeal and enthusiasm stemming from the men themselves, and not from direct external compulsion.

The dependence of group solidarity and high morale upon the fulfillment of stabilized reciprocal expectations among members is revealed in a dramatic fashion by what happened to the group after a year of difficult combat. As noted above in the general discussion, the leadership role ordinarily carries relatively greater obligations and responsibilities than roles lower in the hierarchy. This is particularly the case in a military group because of the great importance of coördination and control in the serious situations the group faces. Carlson had set extremely high standards for himself and made an explicit point of meeting them.

There came a time, when the men were weary of combat and expecting a rest period, when Carlson could not fulfill the high expectations that his role demanded. Apparently this was beyond his control; his outfit was ordered back into combat and his requests for material comforts for the men were denied. Being a loyal Marine officer, he answered the men's questions and complaints evasively, refusing to put the blame on the higher echelons. As far as the men were concerned, he was "letting them down." His previous behavior seemed like trickery; he was just another "brass hat."

As a result of this breakdown in stabilized expectations, morale was low. In contrast to the earlier period of solidarity, there was "hell in the ranks." Carlson and the values emphasized in the Raiders became objects of ridicule and resentment. It was not until Carlson was removed to another duty and a more orthodox Marine officer sent to replace him that the men realized what had happened. When he left, a correspondent reported seeing men "cry like babies." They were aware that the in-group and its norms were "dead." In the ranks they put it in a song: "Give up your Raider schemes, Give up your Raider dreams, In the memory of men, there were those who were brave. . . ."

This account illustrates the rise of an in-group structure with stabilized and consistently met expectations. The solidarity of the group depended on this state of affairs. When behavior began to deviate markedly from the expected standards and dissatisfaction spread through the group, the in-group began to disintegrate. Therefore, this example has implications for individual experience and behavior. It is through achieving a stable position in a system of reciprocities that the individual experiences a feeling of "belongingness" in the group. Becoming a member and occupying a definite role and status imply that he forms attitudes appropriate to the reciprocal expectations relating to various functions and positions in the group. Thus, the expectations standardized in the group as social norms become his own expectations, personally experienced whether he is physically in the group or not.

Herein lies the most elementary condition in groups through which the *social* (stabilized reciprocities and values) becomes *personal*. Any dichotomy between the strictly "social" and the strictly "individual" becomes untenable. The process of becoming able to participate as a part of a functioning system of relationships and of becoming a member with a differentiated position is basic to socialization.

We shall have a great deal more to learn about the process by which the individual comes to experience the relationships and values of a group in intensely personal ways. Here it can only be noted that in the formation of group structure and achievement of stable reciprocal relationships within it, this is precisely what happens. The group values become one's own cherished values. Achievement of group goals is experienced as personal victory. Failure or defeat of group efforts becomes one's private misfortune.

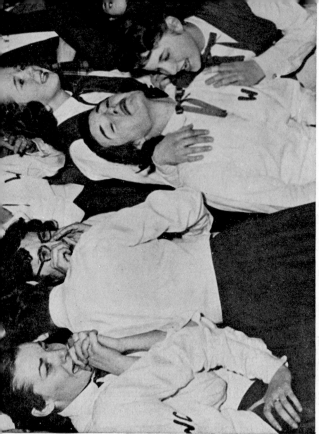

FIG. 5.4. Defeats of our group become our frustrations.

"Tears, cheers and anxiety were crowded into the frantic last minute of last night's W—— - H—— basketball thriller before 2,800 fans in the P—— W—— Gymnasium. Heartbroken W—— cheerleaders shed tears at the right as the gun ends the game with H—— a 40–38 winner. As cheerleaders on the left screech with glee at their team's eighth triumph in a row, while a policeman tries to keep the bubbling crowd from spilling upon the court." (By permission from the New Haven *Evening Register*, Jan. 14, 1955.)

FIG. 5.3. Victories of our group become our victories.

Fig. 5.5. Injury to one of us is our personal concern.

"In the center, a W—— manager (left) has his head bowed and hands folded as if in prayer as Coach —— and Dr. —— (with glasses) examine knee of W—— star M——. Mrs. ——, mother of the player, is at right. ——'s injury was not serious and he was able to finish the game." (By permission from the New Haven *Evening Register*, Jan. 14, 1955.)

This fact is illustrated in the accompanying pictures by the expressions of joy and grief that go with victory and defeat of one's own team (Figs. 5.3–5.5).

4. Formation of Group Norms

When individuals with common motives or problems interact over a sufficient time span, a group structure evolves. Concomitant with differentiation of group structure, *by-products* of the interaction process are stabilized in the form of catchwords, nicknames, jargon, slogans, customs, traditions, values, and the like. Most of the significant by-products thus stabilized may be referred to under the generic term *social norms*.

Social norms refer to any criteria of experience and behavior formed in group interaction which regulate the behavior of individual members in relevant stimulus situations. Thus, norms represent *standardized generalizations* concerning expected modes of behavior in any matter of consequence to the group. As standardized generalizations, norms are *concepts*. They are concepts which are evaluative by nature. They not only encompass given ranges of behavior in relation to persons, objects, and situations but incorporate value judgments concerning them. Therefore, norms denote *expected* behavior, or even ideal behavior. Social norms do not refer to an average or central tendency, like a test norm, for example. Average behavior of members in a group may or may not coincide with its social norms at a given period in its history (*12*).

In a given group structure, norms may not be standardized for every single item of behavior or for every task or situation. However, if the group functions regularly or continuously for a period of time, norms or group standards are formed in relation to any matters of consequence to the group. The central focus of the group, its persistent problems and goals are crucial in determining what situations, tasks, and activities are consequential to the group.

One consequential area of behavior, as we have seen, pertains to the reciprocal relations of members in carrying out differentiated functions in the group. Stabilization of norms for the various statuses and roles in the group structure is a necessary by-product of group formation. These norms crystallize in short-cut forms how individuals should behave in relation to others in the group and in other matters of importance.

As the in-group comes into functional contact with other groups and persons, norms are formed pertaining to ways of behaving and treating the out-group. These norms toward various out-groups constitute the social distance scale of the group. The nature of norms toward out-groups varies in terms of the positive or negative, friendly or antagonistic relations with the particular out-groups in question.

Social values or norms seldom specify just one point or one single way of behaving. Like all concepts, norms encompass a *range* of behavior which is tolerable (permissible) to the group. The *range of tolerable behavior* varies in extent, specificity, or permissiveness both in terms of the importance of the matter a norm pertains to and in terms of the position of a particular member in the group hierarchy. Norms which are minor, in the sense of being incidental to central issues, may allow extensive variation. But in vital matters concerning the identity, major goals, continued existence of the group, the range of tolerable behavior is proportionally narrow. It would be feasible to construct a scale for the range of tolerable behavior for various norms of a group. The more consequential the norms, the narrower the range of tolerable behavior.

Norms arise in group interaction even in groups organized around rebellion or deviation from the "rules" of organized society. The Labadist Colony in Maryland, an offshoot of the Reformed Church of the Netherlands, centered around a belief in freedom from all law other than Divine Law. In the course of time, a hierarchical structure developed and "freedom from law," though applied to laws external to the group, was not applicable for norms standardized within the in-group (26). Thus, a group of people who started with rebellion against established social order ended up in rather strict institutionalization of their own affairs.

In summarizing some characteristics of sects which isolate themselves socially or geographically through nonconformity to the norms of larger society, Gillin noted: "In the beginning, their tenets are negative in their origin. They do *not* swear, do *not* take arms, do *not* wear gaudy clothing or ornaments, do *not* baptize infants, and do *not* have church sacraments. Then gradually they build up a body of positive doctrines and practices which easily can be seen to have been brought into the circle of social consciousness by their opposition to the social class holding the other doctrine" (*18*, p. 429).

Even such fluctuating groups as migrant workers ("hobos") have definite norms which developed as they came together in work situations and in their camps ("jungles"). For example, there are standard norms concerning the proper ways to act when using a camp (which may be nothing more than a place where cooking and sleeping can go on without detection by authorities). Anderson listed seven norms for behavior in hobo jungles whose violations constitute "jungle crimes" (2).

If the norms of a group are not codified in the form of written rules, constitutions, and bylaws, how can we know that they exist? In raising this question, Freedman, Hawley, Landecker, and Miner suggest three lines of evidence for the existence of social norms (12). The first is simply the observation of striking similarities in the behavior of different individuals in a group. Thus, social norms are revealed in sociological studies, like the gang studies by Thrasher, through the repeated observation that the various members behave in certain ways in relation to particular persons, objects, symbols, groups, or situations. Whether or not the individuals can express it in so many words, a group standard or norm is regulating their behavior. Good members of juvenile gangs, for example, do not "squeal" on others to outsiders, particularly the police. They may keep quiet even though they are personally resentful of a particular member. Thrasher reported the case of a gang member whose head was gashed open by a lead pipe wielded by a fellow member. But when the police arrived to investigate, the boy said he had fallen and hit his head on a rock (54).

The second line of evidence cited for the existence of norms comes from experiments like that by Sherif demonstrating that individuals facing an unfamiliar or unstructured situation tend to form a common basis for reaction to it, rather than each individual developing a unique mode of reaction, as he does when he is alone (48). This line of evidence is reviewed in Chapter 8, which deals with the formation of social norms.

The third line of evidence is that every stable group establishes special categories of rewards for behaving in certain ways and penalties or punishments for behaving in other ways. Such rewards and penalties are called *sanctions*. Praise, prestige, special favors, and recognitions may be accorded to members living up to behavior prescribed by group norms. Penalties are invoked by group members for deviation from the norms.

It should be noted that *deviation* does not refer simply to variations in behavior, but specifically to variations which are outside the range of tolerable behavior for a particular norm. Members' behavior may vary considerably in the group. However, variant behavior does not ordinarily provoke group sanctions unless it lies at the limits or beyond the range of tolerable behavior for the norm in question.

In the Roethlisberger and Dickson study of informal work groups in industry, group norms for production or amount of work done were observed. Such norms are typical in industrial plants. Even though more could be produced, individual members were expected to produce within a limited range, and those who exceeded this range were "rate busters." The rate buster or deviate was viewed with disfavor. Various forms of correctives were applied to try to pull him into the fold—disapproval, ridicule, scorn, warnings, and even physical punishment. The physical punishment was given a standardized name—"binging." Binging consisted of striking another person and was "used to regulate the output of some of the faster workers" (*41*).

In a community which has been more or less isolated over a long period, group sanctions are clear-cut, well-known, and relatively rigid as long as life goes on in the familiar pattern. Brummitt surveyed such a community in Casey County, Kentucky. People who came into the community with new ideas from outside saw them "laughed out of use." "People who do not live as it is generally felt would be best for themselves and everyone else concerned are almost forced to move away. There is certainly order in what will follow as a result of all action. . . . Every social sin has a punishment well-known to any member" (8, p. 126).

Depending on the importance of the norm to the group and the degree of deviation, nonconformity is reacted to with various measures: ridicule, scorn, "silent treatment," ostracism, physical punishment, or even death. In adult criminal gangs, requirements for conformity to norms are more exacting than in most groups. Deviates are punished more ruthlessly, in proportion to the seriousness of consequences which their deviation might have for other gang members. In his study of organized criminal gangs in Chicago, Landesco cites concrete examples of death penalties meted out by the gang to deviating members (28).

Group Norms and Social Attitudes: The preceding examples of pressures applied by group members to secure conformity to norms indicate the existence of norms. However, in groups with stabilized reciprocal relationships, in groups where mutual expectations of members are consistently fulfilled and solidarity is high, external means for maintaining conformity are seldom necessary. Gardner reported that in one industrial plant pay rates were established in terms of work finished by the group, but the foreman checked on individual output. In this situation the faster workers in the informal work groups would let others have part of their output. If the individual's production was too high, he would either "give it away" or just not report part of the work actually done (*15*, p. 157). Thus, even when external correctives are not applied, group members may regulate

their own behavior in terms of group norms, although other personal benefits are reduced.

An individual member may internalize group norms which run counter
to individual capacities and trends. Then he is in for a difficult time, even
if other group members understand his conflict. In a German prisoner-of-
war camp a tall Basque prisoner who was unusually powerful and skillful
in work assigned tried to slow his work performance in accordance with
the group norm of equalizing work production for each member so that
none would be punished by the guards. No one had to tell him to conform
to this norm; he was a good member of the prisoner group and wanted to
do so. "Try as he might to control his movements, little by little his energy
would get the better of him and he would resume his normal rhythm. 'I
don't know how to slow down' he would say with sincere embarrassment.
So when the foreman's back was turned he would throw shovelfuls into
his neighbor's wagon in order to satisfy both his need to expend himself
and his spirit of solidarity" (1, p. 37).

In the preceding section we noted that becoming a member of a group
implies forming attitudes appropriate in terms of reciprocal relationships
(status and role) in the group. The individual becomes a good member to
the extent that he abides by its norms, upholds them, and serves their aims.
When he forms attitudes whose content derives from the group norms, his
behavior is regulated by them and, therefore, falls within the range of
tolerable behavior in the group. He does not need to be coerced. If he is a
good member, he actively strives to approach the ideal of expected behavior. By forming attitudes in relation to group norms, he assimilates
group influences. What was an external influence on his behavior becomes
an internal factor, regulating behavior in consistent fashion in relevant
situations.

The meaning and significance of the above remarks will become clearer
when we discuss social attitudes in Chapters 15–17. Here a word of caution
is necessary. *Social norm* is a sociological designation referring to a product
of group interaction. When an individual forms attitudes relating to them,
he does not swallow group products like a pill. In the process of attitude
formation his past history, particular temperament, intellectual capacities
and other characteristics, and position in the group structure come in to
make his attitude distinctive and in some sense unique to him. But the
content of the attitude is derived from social products; it falls within a
range denoted by the norm. It is in this sense that we speak of "internali-

zation" of social norms or active "assimilation" of social influences. Such phrases are sometimes convenient when it is necessary to specify the *source* of the content of a social attitude.

Social norms and other social influences are important sources of the individual's attitudes, hence of his motives. Attitudes, psychological relatedness in various respects, aspirations, and strivings can be understood as parts of larger processes when they are related to the groups and group products from which they are derived.

REFERENCE GROUPS

The general discussion of group formation and functioning and particularly of their effects on the experience and behavior of individual members will acquire clarity and balance if the concept of reference groups is introduced at this point. *Reference groups are those groups to which the individual relates himself as a part or to which he aspires to relate himself psychologically.* In everyday language, reference groups are those groups with which he identifies or aspires to identify himself.

When an individual has motives in common with others and interacts with them toward the formation of a group structure of which he is an integral part, when he internalizes the values or norms which he had a hand in forming, it is obvious that the group in question is his group and the norms are his own norms. His sense of identity, his desire to amount to something, his pride are intimately related with his membership in the group in question. Its norms are his cherished personal values. As a consequence he willingly and with zeal regulates his experience and behavior accordingly. Such cases are typical of the kind of groups discussed in this chapter; the groups of which the individual is a member are his reference groups.

But such is not always the case. In complicated modern societies, in which the individual is a registered "member" of multiple groups, the anchorages regulating his behavior are not always derived from these "membership" groups. The concept *reference group* arose from the necessity of ascertaining precisely the groups which provide the main anchorages for experience and behavior. In fact, the first use of the concept was directly linked to experimental work concerning frames of reference and anchorages (25). The concept of reference group is a useful one. It directs investigation toward the actual group anchorages of an individual. Without such investigation the individual's psychological relatedness might be sought only in groups of which he is a registered member. Such membership is frequently determined largely by external circumstances; it may or may not coincide with the individual's psychological relatedness.

Reference Groups and Membership Groups

During the last three decades the fact that group effects arise which are understandable only in terms of the interdependence of individuals and norms peculiar to the group has become established in psychology. This basic orientation, perhaps more than any other single development, helped to save social psychology from being a compendium of discrete facts and brought it in line with the reality of the phenomena of concrete social relationships at the level of the social sciences.

But from here we have to go farther. Especially today, groups are not closed systems. The integrated or contradictory nature of different groups which are functionally related in positive or antagonistic ways has to be faced as one of our major problems at the psychological level. The currently vital issues of socioeconomic class groupings and antagonisms, issues of prejudice based on these groupings and on other less significant ingroup and out-group formations, the agonizing issues of "marginality" (51), of "dilemmas and contradictions of status" (23), of self-hatred so prevalent today in "casually patterned" Western societies (30) impose this task on us in a forcible fashion. We can no longer be complacent and satisfied by announcing as a major finding that the individual experiences and behaves differently in group situations as determined by the structural properties of the group. Many a person today necessarily moves in multiple groups which may and *do* place different and contradictory demands on him. They tend to pull him in different directions, to arouse different and even contradictory values, loyalties, conformities, and aspirations. They certainly contribute their share to conflict situations with unfortunate consequences for the individual.[1]

This state of affairs is mainly responsible for the appearance of a *discrepancy* for the individual in regulating his attitudes, loyalties, conformities, and aspirations. This discrepancy has far-reaching consequences. It may be summarized as follows: Ordinarily the attitudes and loyalties of an individual are derived from the values, norms, and status regulations of the group or groups of which he is an actual member. These groups to which a person actually belongs—as a son of a family, member of a clique or gang,

---

[1] Psychoanalytic literature is replete with material showing the consequences of this state of affairs. See, for example, K. Horney (22), E. Fromm (14), H. S. Sullivan (53).

student of a college, member of a club, or unit in a socioeconomic class in the choice of which he had no part—may be designated as *membership groups*. Ordinarily his attitudes and relatedness, and subsequently his diverse specific reactions, are regulated and determined by them. But not always. He may actually be a member of a particular group but psychologically *refer* himself to a different group and regulate his attitudes and aspirations accordingly, that is, in reference to that other group. The case of a member of the working class or the middle class who, consciously or unconsciously, relates himself to a higher class and tries to adjust his living and his experiences accordingly is a concrete illustration of the point. Particularly since Veblen's *The Theory of the Leisure Class* the problems that arise from this discrepancy have been dealt with in various sociological and psychological works.

In short, evidence indicates that the individual's standards and aspirations are regulated in relation to the reference group to which he relates himself. Usually, the reference group is his actual membership group. But, especially in competitive societies (such as the highly differentiated and stratified societies of America and Europe), where the hierarchical arrangement is based on sharp and yet not impregnable vertical class lines, this is frequently not the case; there may be a discrepancy between the individual's actual *membership group* and the *reference group* which he uses to regulate his standards and aspirations.

Membership in multiple groups and active choice of a reference group which may not be within the individual's perceptual range are distinctly human phenomena. Societies in the modern scene are differentiated into many groups. Man is endowed with conceptual capacities which enable him to relate himself to anchorages beyond his perceptual range—anchorages not immediately observable at a given time. If man were not susceptible to the influence of words coming from books, newspapers, radio, and other media of communication, if he did not live in a highly differentiated social world, there would be no need to raise the problem of reference groups. J. P. Scott, a contemporary authority on animal behavior, pointed out that subhuman organisms do not face problems related to reference group behavior (43).

Most of the groups dealt with in these chapters may be considered membership groups which are also reference groups for individual members. Before we can give a satisfactory presentation of topics related to reference groups, including those which are not membership groups, treatment of the effects of concepts and an account of ego development are necessary.

Therefore, their fuller discussion is postponed until these topics are discussed. The fuller account of reference groups is given in Chapter 18.

REFERENCES

1. Ambriere, Francis. *The Long Holiday*. Chicago: Ziff-Davis, 1948.
2. Anderson, Nels. *The Hobo: The Sociology of the Homeless Man*. Chicago: University of Chicago Press, 1923.
3. Ansbacher, H. The history of the leaderless group discussion, *Psychol. Bull*. (1951), 48:383–391.
4. Barnard, C. I. *The Functions of the Executive*. Cambridge: Harvard University Press, 1948.
5. Bass, B. M. The leaderless group discussion, *Psychol. Bull*. (1954), 51:465–492.
6. Bass, B. M., and Wurster, C. R. Effects of company rank on LGD performance of oil refinery supervisors, *J. appl. Psychol*. (1953), 37:100–104.
7. Blankfort, M. *The Big Yankee*. Boston: Little, Brown, 1947.
8. Brummitt, Jessie A. A survey of an isolated community, Casey County, Kentucky. M.A. thesis, Sociology Department, University of Chicago, 1942.
9. Carter, L. F. Leadership and Small Group Behavior, in M. Sherif and M. O. Wilson (eds.), *Group Relations at the Crossroads*. New York: Harper, 1953.
10. Faris, R. E. L. Development of the Small Group Research Movement, in M. Sherif and M. O. Wilson (eds.), *Group Relations at the Crossroads*. New York: Harper, 1953.
11. Festinger, L., Schachter, S., and Back, K. *Social Pressures in Informal Groups*. New York: Harper, 1950.
12. Freedman, R., Hawley, A. H., Landecker, W. S., and Miner, H. M. *Principles of Sociology*. New York: Holt, 1952.
13. Freud, S. *Group Psychology and Analysis of the Ego*. London: Hogarth, 1922.
14. Fromm, E. *Escape from Freedom*. New York: Rinehart, 1941.
15. Gardner, B. B. The Factory as a Social System, in W. F. Whyte (ed.), *Industry and Society*. New York: McGraw-Hill, 1946.
16. Gardner, B. B. *Human Relations in Industry*. Chicago: Irwin, 1947.
17. Gibb, C. A. The principles and traits of leadership, *J. abnorm. & soc. Psychol*. (1947), 42:267–284.
18. Gillin, J. S. A contribution to the sociology of sects, *Amer. J. Sociol.* (1910), 16:236–252.
19. Haythorn, W. The influence of individual members on the characteristics of small groups, *J. abnorm. & soc. Psychol*. (1953), 48:267–284.
20. Hollingshead, A. B. *Elmtown's Youth*. New York: Wiley, 1949.

21. Holyoke, G. J. *The History of the Rochdale Pioneers.* New York: Scribner, 1893.
22. Horney, K. *New Ways in Psychoanalysis.* New York: Norton, 1939.
23. Hughes, E. C. Dilemmas and contradictions of status, *Amer. J. Sociol.* (1945), 50:353–359.
24. Hurwitz, J. R., Zander, A. F., and Hymovitch, B. Some Effects of Power on the Relations Among Group Members, in D. Cartwright and A. Zander (eds.), *Group Dynamics.* Evanston, Ill.: Row, Peterson, 1953.
25. Hyman, H. The psychology of status, *Arch. Psychol.* (1942), No. 269.
26. James, B. B. The Labadist Colony in Maryland, *Johns Hopkins Studies in Historical and Political Science* (1899), 17:7–45.
27. Kolb, J. H., and Marshall, D. G. *Neighborhood-Community Relationships in Rural Society.* University of Wisconsin, Agricultural Experiment Stations, Research Bull. 154, November, 1944.
28. Landesco, J. Organized Crime in Chicago, in *The Illinois Crime Survey.* Illinois Assoc. for Criminal Justice. Chicago: Blakely, 1929.
29. Lindsey, Almont. *The Pullman Strike.* Chicago: University of Chicago Press, 1942.
30. Lynd, R. S. *Knowledge for What?* Princeton: Princeton University Press, 1939.
31. Mauldin, B. *Up Front.* New York: Holt, 1945.
32. Merei, F. Group leadership and institutionalization, *Human Relat.* (1949), 2:23–39.
33. Moreno, F. B. Sociometric status of children in a nursery school group, *Sociometry* (1942), 5:395–411.
34. Moreno, J. L. *Who Shall Survive?* Nervous and Mental Disease Monogr. Series, No. 58. Washington, 1934; Beacon, N.Y.: Beacon, rev. ed., 1953.
35. Munch, P. A. *Sociology of Tristan da Cunha.* Oslo, Norway, 1945.
36. Newstetter, W. I., Feldstein, M. J., and Newcomb, T. M. *Group Adjustment: A Study in Experimental Sociology.* Cleveland: School of Applied Social Sciences, Western Reserve University, 1938.
37. O.S.S. Assessment Staff, *Assessment of Men.* New York: Rinehart, 1948.
38. Parten, M. B. Social participation among preschool children, *J. abnorm, & soc. Psychol.* (1932), 27:243–269.
39. Piaget, J. *The Moral Judgment of the Child.* London: Kegan Paul, Trench, Trubner, 1932.
40. Pyle, E. *Here Is Your War.* New York: Holt, 1943; World, 1945.
41. Roethlisberger, F. J., and Dickson, W. J. *Management and the Worker.* Cambridge: Harvard University Business Research Studies (1939), 21, No. 9.
42. Roseborough, M. E. Experimental studies of small groups, *Psychol. Bull.* (1953), 50:275–303.
43. Scott, J. P. Implications of Infra-human Social Behavior for Problems

of Human Relations, in M. Sherif and M. O. Wilson (eds.), *Group Relations at the Crossroads*. New York: Harper, 1953.

44. Shaw, Clifford R. *The Jack-Roller*. Chicago: University of Chicago Press, 1930.
45. Shaw, Clifford R. *The Natural History of a Delinquent Career*. Chicago: University of Chicago Press, 1931.
46. Shaw, Clifford R. (ed.) *Brothers in Crime*. Chicago: University of Chicago Press, 1938.
47. Shaw, Clifford R., and McKay, H. D. *Juvenile Delinquency and Urban Areas*. Chicago: University of Chicago Press, 1942.
48. Sherif, M. A study of some social factors in perception, *Arch. Psychol.* (1935), No. 187.
49. Sherif, M. Sociocultural influences in small group research, *Sociol. and soc. Res.* (1954), 39:1–10.
50. Sherif, M., and Cantril, H. *The Psychology of Ego-Involvements*. New York: Wiley, 1947, chap. 9.
51. Stonequist, E. V. *The Marginal Man*. New York: Scribner, 1937.
52. Stouffer, S. A., et al. *The American Soldier: Combat and Its Aftermath*. Princeton: Princeton University Press, 1949.
53. Sullivan, H. S. *Conceptions of Modern Psychiatry*. Washington: William Alanson White Psychiatric Foundation, 1947.
54. Thrasher, F. M. *The Gang*. Chicago: University of Chicago Press, 1927.
55. Whyte, W. F. *Street Corner Society*. Chicago: University of Chicago Press, 1943.
56. Whyte, W. F. *Human Relations in the Restaurant Industry*. New York: McGraw-Hill, 1948.
57. Whyte, W. F. *Patterns for Industrial Peace*. New York: Harper, 1951.
58. Zorbaugh, H. W. *The Gold Coast and the Slum*. Chicago: University of Chicago Press, 1929.

Formation and Functioning of Group Structures

In the course of repeated interaction over a time span among individuals with common motives or problems, togetherness situations become group situations. The appearance of a group is marked by the formation of structure (organization) and a set of norms. As individuals become group members in this process, differential effects of the interaction process become more pronounced and more predictable in direction and degree.

These generalizations are based on field studies dealing with the formation and functioning of groups. In this chapter, one intensive field study of group structure in real life is summarized. More recently, generalizations derived from field studies have been subjected to experimental verification under conditions which were controlled and which approximated real-life circumstances. A summary of one experiment on the formation of in-groups with distinct structures and norms follows the representative field study.

Further experiments have demonstrated that differential effects of group interaction can be measured in terms of individual behavior through laboratory techniques. These are summarized in the final sections of this chapter.

GRADATIONS FROM TOGETHERNESS SITUATIONS TO GROUPS

The distinctive group properties generated in the course of interaction are a group structure (organization) and norms regulating reciprocal relations and relevant activities. For such properties to arise, for a mere togetherness situation to become a group, interaction has to continue beyond

181

the transitory social situations represented in traditional laboratory experiments. Interaction must continue over a time span.

The other aspect essential for the rise and *stabilization* of group properties is a common motive or a common problem for the individuals. This common problem arises through the nature of actual circumstances in which individuals interact. It is not assigned from outside the group, as it would be in the typical procedure used in laboratory experiments.

When a number of individuals have a common deprivation or motive with goals which cannot be attained through individual effort, they tend to interact with each other. Interaction centers around the common problem(s). If extraneous conditions do not disrupt the interaction process, the common problem is conducive to prolonged interaction. In actual life, the goals conducive to interaction cannot be attained in an hour's or a day's interaction.

Interaction among individuals with a genuine common motive typical of real life produces differential effects from the very start. In the initial stage of interaction, individual characteristics in expressiveness, "showing off," reticence, initiative, or enthusiasm are revealed in less restrained ways. Participants make suggestions and ineffective and effective moves toward solution. In short, in this initial stage there is a heightened social activity, reminiscent of F. H. Allport's "social increments." At this time interaction has no definite pattern as yet. The lines of communication are not established; they shift, perhaps from moment to moment.

Then interaction goes through a selective process—bringing to the foreground the participants who contribute effectively toward the goals with their words and deeds and shifting to the background those who just make some noise or who prove to be a nuisance from the point of view of goal attainment.

In actual life, group interaction is not a one-episode affair. Therefore, the choice of unit activities and the sequence of steps in problem solution are greatly affected by what has gone on before, by the trends that have already taken some shape.

With the succession of episode after episode, with the demonstrated resourcefulness of certain participants in pursuing common goals and with the repeated ineffectiveness of others, stabilization of statuses begins. The end points that stabilize first in this status polarization are, usually, the leader position and the bottom position. There is quite a bit of active bickering and jockeying for "lieutenant" positions near the leader. The middle and lower-middle statuses are subject to fluctuations for a more prolonged period.

In this interaction process, group structure takes shape with differentiation of statuses for various participants. At the same time certain catchwords, expressions, and relevant standards or group norms arise. A plausible sequence of status *stabilization* for various members is represented in Figure 6.1.

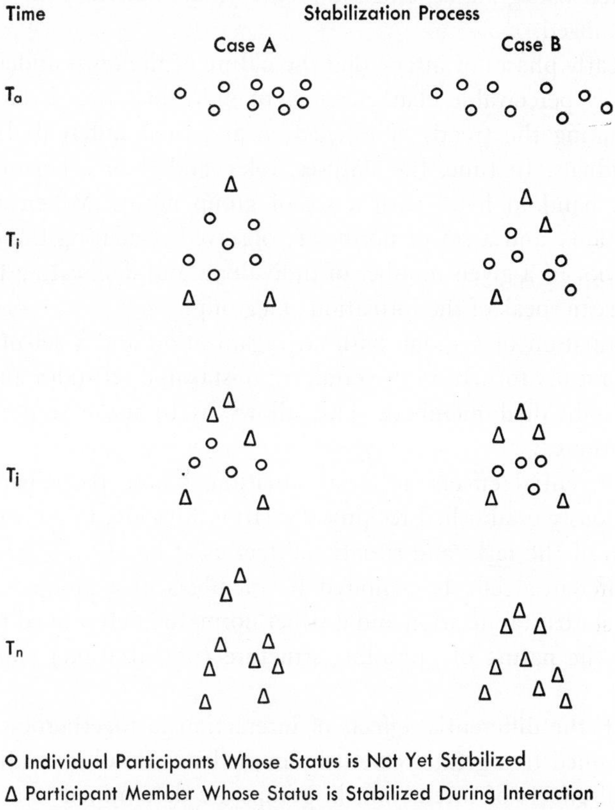

O Individual Participants Whose Status is Not Yet Stabilized

Δ Participant Member Whose Status is Stabilized During Interaction

FIG. 6.1. Diagram of two representative sequences of status stabilization with interaction in time. Note that hierarchical arrangements in A are steeper than in B. In A, the leader and bottom statuses are stabilized first. In B, leadership and "lieutenant" positions are crystallized simultaneously with bottom position. The diagram is based on data of experiments reported in this chapter and Chapter 9.

These diagrams were suggested by experiments carried out in 1949 and 1953, which are summarized later in this chapter (pp. 191–202), and in 1954 (pp. 312–316). The sequence of stabilization may be accelerated or retarded by various circumstances, such as the compellingness of the common goals, internal harmony or friction, an emergency situation, outside influences against group formation (resistances and pressures of other groups), and so on. The particular pattern varies with the individuals involved, their backgrounds, and the problems and activities in which structure is stabilized.

In the early phases of interaction the nature of the *tasks* undertaken and immediately perceivable characteristics of individuals weigh more heavily in determining the trends of interaction and their differential effects on the individuals. In time, the statuses, roles, and their occupants become stabilized, hand in hand with a set of group norms. When a structure (organization) and a set of norms are observed regulating the experience and behavior of a given number of individuals and delineating them from others, we can speak of the formation of a group.

The formation of a group with an organization and a set of standards or norms means formation of certain unmistakable attitudes and expectations by individual members. This allows us to make some important generalizations:

The differential effects in social situations whose participants do not have previously established reciprocal relationships are, to a greater extent, a function of the tasks and situational factors at hand.

The differential effects exhibited by members of a group with a high degree of status stabilization and distinct norms are determined to a greater extent by the nature of prevailing structure (organization) and norms of the group.

In short, the differential effects of interaction in togetherness situations are determined to a greater extent by immediate stimulus conditions. The differential effects of interaction in groups are determined to a greater extent by the status and role arrangements and group norms.

WHYTE'S STUDY OF THE STREET CORNER BOYS

In the field work of Whyte carried out in the thirties, we find a first-hand account of the formation and functioning of informal group structures against the background of a slum area (11). The Street Corner groups that he studied show in high relief the properties of group situations:

1. Motivational factors conducive to interaction among individuals in the same boat.
2. The formation and workings of a group structure (organization) with statuses and roles (leader-follower relations) for the individual members.
3. The formation of group standards or norms that come to regulate the behavior of the members in various matters of concern to them all.
4. The differential effects of interaction among group members, acquiring more pronounced proportions and predictable directions in terms of the group structure (2) and norms (3).

Motivational Factors Related to Sociocultural Background

The group (clique) of Street Corner Boys which this account concerns arose from conditions existing in a slum area of a large Eastern city in America. As F. Thrasher and Clifford Shaw pointed out, such areas are particularly conducive to the spontaneous formation of informal group structures. The slum areas are looked down upon and segregated in various ways by respectability. Cornerville (this particular slum area) has a high percentage of foreign and American-born Italian inhabitants. The district "has become popularly known as a disordered and lawless community. He is an Italian, and the Italians are looked upon by upper-class people as among the least desirable of the immigrant peoples" (*11*, p. 273). So the inhabitants of the slum area have had to build up their own business and social hierarchy.

For the people who live in Cornerville, social life does not present a picture of confusion and lawlessness. To them it is fairly well organized.

The Street Corner Boys, also known as the Nortons, came from the representative mass of people in Cornerville—the little guys. Several of these boys frequently did not have any money to spend. At the time the study was carried out, some of the Nortons including the leader, Doc, did not have steady jobs even though they were well over 20 years old. All the Norton boys grew to adolescence and adulthood with the uncomfortable feeling of being little guys even in their own community. From occasional encounters with the more respectable and highbrow groups in their own community they knew that they were treated as rough little guys, and the tendency was to put them in their "place." These circumstances certainly helped to make them gravitate toward each other, to seek a standing in the world and to secure mutual help from their fellow men. The group was not a creation peculiar to Norton Street. In almost any city with a similar street, on which boys grow up with various kinds of deprivations and lack social belongingness in relation to society in general, there is a similar sort of group.

Still on the fringe of the main vertical current of social organization of the huge socioeconomic scheme, still left to themselves, these boys gravitate toward each other in their search to relieve their deprivations and to achieve some sense of the belongingness that is one of the essential conditions of psychological security.

Formation of Group Structure

In the course of interaction among such individuals in the same boat, a group structure is stabilized with its peculiar hierarchical arrangement of statuses. As Thrasher pointed out, the emergence of the leader in the group is a function of group structure. Usually the group makes the leader, of course, on the basis of some special capacity which he has for coping with its particular problems. In one case it may be physical strength; in another it may be shrewdness; in a third it may be something utterly different.

In the case of the Corner Boys the capacity that was primary in determining the choice of the leader was toughness. On the basis of this characteristic the leader emerged. Doc was first a lieutenant of the leader. But when Doc repeatedly licked the leader, Nutsy, the group centered around Doc.

Once a group is stabilized in the course of interaction in events of significance to the members, some sort of in-group formation emerges. The higher the status of the member in the group, the more stringent are the expectations placed upon him. The hierarchical positions of the membership of the Nortons are represented by Whyte in a simple diagram shown in Figure 6.2.

Once group structure is stabilized, group action is determined along certain lines. Whyte noted that group activities were usually originated by the men with the highest standing in the group. These individuals encouraged suggestions for activities in which they excelled and discouraged those in which they did not excel.

A more or less lasting set of expectations from each member and to each member in the group is stabilized in terms of the relative statuses in the group. This can be illustrated concretely by incidents in one of the major activities of the Nortons. At one time the Nortons were seriously interested in bowling. The performance in bowling became, more or less,

THE NORTONS
Spring and Summer 1937

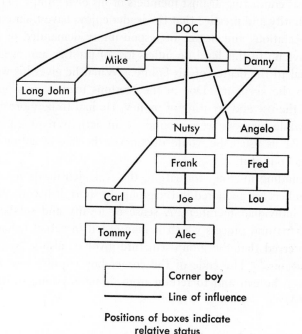

FIG. 6.2. Hierarchical arrangement of members'
positions and lines of influence in the Nortons. (Reprinted from *Street Corner Society* by W. F. Whyte
by permission of The University of Chicago Press.
Published, 1943.)

the sign of distinction in the group. As a consequence, the high performance of the top-ranking members was accepted as natural and was encouraged. But not so with the high performance of members with low
status. That their performance might surpass the achievement of high-
ranking members was something that simply did not fit into the picture of
established expectations. Hence, they were put "in their place."

Take the case of Frank, a member with relatively low standing. Frank
was a good player in his own right, yet "he made a miserable showing"
when playing in his own group. In his own words: "I can't seem to play
ball when I am playing with fellows I know, like that bunch. I do much
better when I am playing for the Stanley A. C. against some team in Dex-
ter, Westland, or out of town." Whyte concluded: "Accustomed to filling

an inferior position, Frank was unable to star even in his favorite sport when he was competing against members of his own group" (*11,* p. 19).

The authority and prestige that the leader enjoys have their counterparts in the expectations and degree of responsibility demanded of him. If he does not live up to this level he suffers loss of prestige and even of status, proportional to the degree of his failure. "When he gives his word to one of his boys, he keeps it." Doc in the Nortons made very strict rules for himself in the use and securing of money. He had to be more generous in spending while his boys were around. If an activity required money and he was broke as usual, he would discourage the line of action or find an excuse to get out of it.

In the binding in-group formation, the real identifications of the individual members are anchored in the group. In short, it becomes a reference group for individual members. A sense of loyalty and solidarity is generated as a natural process which is manifested in actual behavior. Thus, Whyte observed that the group structure involved also a "system of mutual obligations." "The code of the corner boy requires him to help his friends when he can and to refrain from doing anything to harm them" (*11,* p. 256).

Formation of Group Standards or Norms

In the interaction of members in forming an in-group, a set of standards or norms invariably arises to regulate the activities of the group as a whole and of the individual members. In the preceding pages we have seen various concrete instances of regulation of in-group relationships in terms of group norms. One of the interesting norms that arose among the Nortons was their "sex code" defining their attitudes toward various types of women and putting limits on whom they could date and could not date (*10*). For example, a Corner Boy would not have extramarital relationships with a relative of a fellow group member. Chapter 8 is devoted to this central topic, namely, the formation and functioning of group norms.

Disintegration of the Group

Groups, especially informally organized ones, are not fixed, immutable entities. Almost constantly factors are operating which tend to break down the grouping. From within the group, these may be friction between members over status, failure of those in high positions to fulfill expectations, dominance of individual motives over the group goals. From without, the impact of other groups and society at large may lead to disintegration of the group.

"Getting settled down" in other groupings and positions not compatible with the preoccupations of the group is one of the major factors in the disintegration of gangs. The "settling down" may result from getting married or obtaining a steady job or holding a position in the hierarchy of society at large. In a negative way this indicates the function that the informally organized gang serves in the life of individual members. The group provided its members with a feeling of belongingness and security, among other benefits. When these are achieved elsewhere, identification with the informal gang drops away. But as long as "settling down" is not achieved elsewhere, evidence indicates that no amount of preaching and punishment by those outside of the group can change group affiliation and activities.

In the Norton group, disintegration came when the leader suddenly let the boys down. Doc, the leader, was running for a political office with the knowledge and enthusiastic support of all the Nortons. Without his boys' knowledge, Doc announced abruptly one day that he was withdrawing from the contest. This was a clear case of letting down the boys who had looked up to him and were doing their level best for his election.

"The news of Doc's withdrawal hit the Nortons with devastating effect." Their faith in him was shaken. The immediate suspicion in such cases was that a candidate who withdrew had made a bargain with another politician and had used his support for some material advantage. The shocking effect of Doc's withdrawal was proportional to the level of expectations for his behavior. The higher the expectations, the greater the reaction when the expected course of action is not followed. Doc was no longer the leader of the Nortons: he was not even in a position to discuss politics. He lost his magic and became a nobody, though he continued to hang around as an unattached individual.

The Nortons then disintegrated as a group unit temporarily. Some of the boys formed a new gang around a new leader, Angelo. This is an instance of the recurrent fact that members of a disorganized group do not stay long in a state of disintegration or chaos. They usually form new groups or join other groups. One night Doc happened to be in the hangout of Angelo and his boys. Doc suggested to some of them, among them his former lieutenants, that they go some place together. His word carried no weight. The boys answered separately that they preferred to hang around with Angelo.

Doc's decision to withdraw from the political race was due to the demands of situations outside of his group to which he exposed himself by becoming a candidate in the main current of sociopolitical life. As Whyte pointed out, one cannot be a good member of the informal groups in Cornerville and of the respectable groups outside at the same time. The two come into conflict, with subsequent reverberations on the individual. The two worlds are not harmoniously integrated, even though they are functionally related in the whole socioeconomic setup. It is tough, especially on a sensitive man like Doc.

Impact of Functionally Related Out-Groups and Situations

One of the great merits of Whyte's study of the Corner Boys is that he did not confine himself to in-group influences in accounting for the formation and functioning of the group. Especially in differentiated modern societies, groups are not closed systems. Whyte deliberately made a point of studying the impact of outside groups and situations on the group and on individual members.

No matter how well structured a small group is, no matter how strongly it influences its members, the psychology of groups is doomed to remain academic if factors almost constantly impinging from the general social setting are not brought organically into the picture. Only by considering the impact of the general social setting in which group formations function can we hope to do justice to the total situation. Otherwise, insistence on including major features of the total situation in our analysis will not promote this excellent methodological stand, except by paying it lip service.

The rise of various types of gangs in large cities is due, in Clifford Shaw's words, to "processes more or less common to American cities" (2, 3). Further evidence, from Cornerville, shows that the main activities the Nortons engaged in are characteristically American activities—in spite of the fact that this particular group happened to belong to an Italian ethnic group in a predominantly Italian slum.

In Cornerville itself, social life was hierarchically organized with a minority of "big shots" and a great majority of little fellows. Our Street Corner Boys stemmed from the lowest stratum of working people. During the depression, when group activity was at its height, most of the members were totally or partially unemployed. There were innumerable other boys' gangs of their class and of higher classes, up to college boys and their clubs. The Settlement House on the Nortons' street was above their social level. As Long John, one of the Nortons from the lowest level of society, remarked during a short period when they frequented the Settlement

House: "I think that everybody that goes in there thinks they're a little better than the next fellow."

The relationship of the Nortons with a group of girls (the Aphrodite Club) which ranked a little higher in the social ladder illustrates how relations with other groups could be disruptive of group unity. For these girls, education, good manners, and appearance had great value. They were anxious to make friends with the regular boys at the Settlement House, whose position was still a little higher than their own.

The Nortons, after considerable discussion, created a situation which enabled them to meet these girls. For a time, association with the girls became the chief preoccupation of the boys. Then the top members in the Nortons, who were more concerned with keeping group solidarity intact, began to worry lest living up to the girls, preoccupation with them, and the jealousies they might arouse among the boys be disruptive of their unity. Therefore, the top members went to work to get their boys away from the girls' group. After much effort and friction they succeeded. The group regained its solidarity, but not without a loss. A few boys remained loyal to the girls, and their place in the Corner group became "rather tenuous."

As we have seen, it was the impact of the larger social setting which led to the ultimate disintegration of this group. When Doc let the boys down by withdrawing from the political race, it was because of the conflict he faced in the outside world. Doc was encouraged by his own boys to run for an office and he was loyally supported by them. But his campaign required money; and he was penniless. He could not bring himself to sell out to outside politicians. His way out of the conflict between the two worlds was to drop out of the contest, saying that there were too many candidates and he had no chance. But his real reason, the conflict between the Corner Boys' world and the world of the politician, came out in his own simple description:

"The more there were in the fight, the better it was for me. . . . It was the social demands that were too much for me. When I'm down at Jennings' with the boys, somebody comes up to me and wants me to buy a ticket for something. I'm batted out, so I have to refuse. . . . You can't be that way in politics. They hold it against you" (11).

EXPERIMENTAL PRODUCTION OF GROUP STRUCTURES AND ATTITUDES

Sociological field studies on spontaneously organized small groups furnish experimental social psychologists with fruitful hypotheses to be tested egarding formation of group structure and internalization of group norms which *become* personal attitudes of individual members, regulating their behavior in interpersonal and group relations.

If our aim is prediction and control, hypotheses derived from such empirical findings must be specified in terms of the conditions and relations upon which group formation, attitude formation, and change depend. Effective prediction and control is made possible through experimental study permitting precise specification and control of conditions and interaction processes among individuals whose backgrounds, existing attitudes, and motives in the particular setting are known.

Following suggestions derived from attitude formation among the members of informally structured groups, an experiment was undertaken in 1949 which aimed at producing conditions conducive to the formation of groups and later to relations between groups. A summary of the main procedures and results of this study is given in this section. A more complete account is reported in Sherif and Sherif (7). The results obtained in this experiment concerning in-group formation were substantiated in repetitions of the experiment in 1953 and again in 1954 (6, 8). These three experiments were carried out under the direction of M. Sherif.

On the basis of findings from field work on small groups, it was plausible to formulate the following hypotheses:

1. When individuals having no established relationships are brought together to interact in activities with common goals, they produce a group structure with hierarchical positions and roles within it.

   The interaction process tends to produce common norms for the group, which constitute the basis of attitudes of individual members, at least in matters of consequence to the group.

2. When two in-groups are brought into functional relationship under conditions of competition and frustration, negative out-group attitudes toward the out-group and stereotypes will arise and be standardized.

In this section, we shall be concerned primarily with the first hypothesis. The properties mentioned in it are the criteria of groups specified in our definition of group (p. 144).

Subjects

In order to test these hypotheses in terms of experimental conditions, it was necessary to eliminate as much as possible other bases for group formation. Specifically, the possibility had to be avoided that in-groups would form on the basis of (1) background factors (differences in age, sex, ethnic affiliations, class, religion, education); (2) previous bonds of friendship or hostility among individuals; or (3) personal characteristics of the individuals. In short, subjects had to be as *homogeneous* as possible in background and individual characteristics and unrelated prior to the experiment. Through selection of subjects from different communities in the New Haven area, interviews with parents and other adults in the environment, and clinical tests prior to the experiment, these criteria were met with considerable success.

Twenty-four boys of about 12 years of age were selected. All came from settled Protestant American families of the lower-middle-class income group. Educational opportunities and backgrounds of the boys were similar. There were no established friendship bonds among them. The group had a mean IQ of 104.8. All might be called more or less "normal" boys; none were "behavior problems."

Design and Procedures

The possibility remained that group formation and relations between groups might be primarily determined by personal preferences, attractions or dislikes among the boys, or common personal interests. Therefore, the experiment was planned so that spontaneous groupings would begin to form on the basis of such personal factors and could be deliberately separated when the experimental groups were formed.

The experiment was carried out in an isolated camp site in northern Connecticut during the summer of 1949 (see Figs. 6.3, 6.4). The nearest town was eight miles away. No visitors were allowed. Thus there were no immediate outside influences to alter experimental conditions. The subjects did not know that any manipulation of conditions for experimental purposes would be done or observations of behavior made.

The sequence of experimental conditions was planned as follows:

Stage I: Friendship clusters. This period was planned to permit the beginning of spontaneous or informal groupings on the basis of personal inclinations and interests of subjects. All activities were camp-wide, with maximum freedom allowed in choosing bunks, seats, buddies, athletic teams, etc. Thus, it became possible to ascertain budding friendship groups and to minimize the weights of personal preferences as factors in the experimental formation of groups in Stage II.

Stage II: Experimental in-group formation. This period was designed to produce the formation of two groups as similar in composition as possible, in terms of number of budding friendships, in size and athletic skill, intelligence, and personal characteristics of individual members. Each experimental group was to participate separately in specified activities which involved all members of the group. Activities for this period were selected on the basis of their motivational appeal to the subjects, as revealed in the boys' preferences, and the extent to which they involved all individuals. Activities were varied enough so that each boy had a chance to show his worth in some line of activity.

Stage III: Intergroup relations (friction). The third period was planned to study intergroup relations between the two experimental groups produced in Stage II. Specifically, intergroup relations were studied when the groups were brought into contact (1) in a series of competitive activities (athletic and camp competition) and (2) in mildly frustrating situations. The procedures and findings during this stage are summarized in more detail in Chapter 9.

PROBLEM SITUATIONS AND THEIR SOLUTION: The experimental conditions and their alteration during the experiment were manipulated through the introduction of specified activities within this isolated camp setting. The goals introduced were intrinsic to the activity. For example, cooking a meal outdoors when subjects were hungry, hiking, and camping overnight were typical activities.

Each activity constituted a problem situation for all individuals with a definite goal which they could not ignore easily. For example, ingredients of food were made available in bulk form at a time when they were hungry. Eating depended on various individuals' getting to work in a coördinated way (building a fire, cutting and proportioning food in bulk, cooking, and serving). Another example is the problem one group faced when they wanted a large table in the camp grounds for their own hide-out in the woods, about half a mile away. Figure 6.5 shows the coördinated action which they undertook in executing their plan. Figure 6.6 shows the other group at their swimming place, which they found too shallow and therefore took coördinated action to improve.

Thus the attainment of goals necessitated *discussion, planning,* and *execution* in an effective and coördinated way. A common goal which is not artificial but arises as an intrinsic aspect of the situation provides a real problem situation. Its solution necessitates effective and to-the-point discussion, planning, and execution. These considerations have been a cardinal point in the present experimental approach to group processes.

TECHNIQUES FOR OBTAINING DATA: The bulk of observational data was

Fig. 6.3. Overall view of camp site. (From M. Sherif and C. W. Sherif, *Groups in Harmony and Tension*. New York: Harper & Brothers, 1953.)

Fig. 6.4. Camp grounds. (From M. Sherif and C. W. Sherif, *Groups in Harmony and Tension*. New York: Harper & Brothers, 1953.)

Fig. 6.5. Red Devils carrying table to their hide-out.

Fig. 6.6. Bull Dogs at the swimming pool which they improved and appropriated. (From M. Sherif and C. W. Sherif, *Groups in Harmony and Tension*. New York: Harper & Brothers, 1953.)

obtained by two participant observers who acted as counselors to the two experimental groups. Each participant observer had the assistance of a junior counselor experienced in camping who was under his supervision. The participant observers were, therefore, comparatively free to observe their groups throughout the camp period. They were instructed not to make notes in the boys' presence unless the situation clearly called for writing—say, "minutes" of a cabin meeting. Otherwise, they withdrew to jot down short notes which were expanded each evening.

This observation technique was followed for good reasons. The objective was to obtain reactions as natural as possible under specified yet life-like conditions. Awareness of being observed by a personage with authority in the situation cannot help but be a factor influencing behavior (Chapter 4). It would be a little too much to expect spontaneous reactions when a person feels that his moves toward establishing friendships or his unflattering words and deeds are under scrutiny.

The staff was instructed not to plan *how* activities should be carried out, and not to delegate authority to any boy. Rather, the aim was to leave such questions up to the boys for discussion, planning, organization, and solution. The leaders and "lieutenants" emerged from the ranks of the two experimental groups in the course of group interaction.

Summary of Main Results

Stage I: Friendship clusters. During Stage I (three days) there were evidences of budding friendships among the boys, and of leaders emerging in these clusters in specific situations. At the end of this period, popularity ratings (sociometric choices) were obtained during informal interviews held on the pretext of getting suggestions for favored activities and improving the camp. As would be expected from sociometric studies, the result was that boys were clustering into groups of two, three, or four boys, as the case might be.

The division of subjects into two experimental groups preparatory for Stage II was made deliberately to split these friendship groups so that the results of the periods of group formation and intergroup relations could not be explained on this basis. For example, if two boys showed preference for each other, one was put in one group and the second in the other group. Or, if more than one friendship choice was made, the boy was put in that group holding the *fewest* of his friendship choices. Therefore, at the start of Stage II, the number of friendship choices given to members of the experimental "in-group" was substantially fewer than the number of friendship choices given to members of the experimental out-group (see Table 6.1).

In addition, the two experimental groups were equated as much as possible, without violating requirements of the sociometric results, in respect to members' size, strength, ability in games, intelligence, and ratings on personality tests obtained prior to camp (by two psychologists).

TABLE 6.1.   Total Choices of Friends at the End of Stage I and End of Stage II. (Note the reversals of proportions)

| | | Choices Received By: | |
| | | Eventual | Eventual |
	Choices Made By:	In-Group	Out-Group
End of	Eventual Red Devils	35.1%	64.9%
Stage I	Eventual Bull Dogs	35.0%	65.0%
		In-Group	Out-Group
End of	Red Devils	95.0%	5.0%
Stage II	Bull Dogs	87.7%	12.3%

Stage II: Experimental in-group formation. This stage lasted five days. After division of subjects into two groups on the basis of the considerations outlined above, each group chose a bunkhouse. Then both groups left immediately for hikes and cook-outs in opposite directions. These activities had been chosen as most attractive by the boys and were introduced at that time so that the division into two groups would not be strongly resisted by the boys. There was some resentment shown by several boys at being separated from their newly found friends.

One of the major findings of the study was the formation of well-defined in-group organizations or structures. The accompanying sociograms reveal the hierarchical positions of the boys within each experimental group in terms of popularity (Figs. 6.7 and 6.8) as determined by friendship choices at the end of Stage II.

The particular index of structure used in constructing these sociograms does not adequately reflect the *power relations* within the groups. For example, in the Red Devil group, L was more popular than S, who was second in popularity; however, S was the acknowledged leader of the group and became the focus of power because of his undisputed authority over L and other high-status members. In the Bull Dog group, H exerted more power than his popularity rating indicates because of his ability and acknowledged leadership in athletic events. He was "team captain" for that

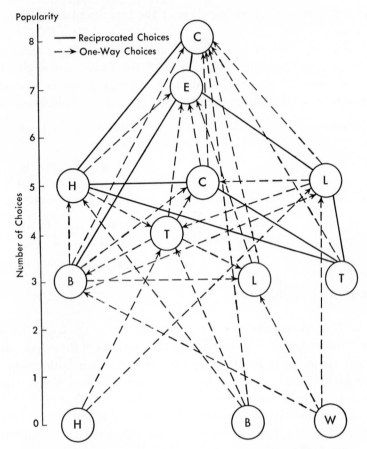

Fig. 6.7. Bull Dogs—end of Stage II, in-group formation. (From M. Sherif and C. W. Sherif, *Groups in Harmony and Tension*. New York: Harper & Brothers, 1953.)

group, although he always yielded to the overall leadership of C, the Bull Dog leader. Even in athletics, H deferred to C's expressed wishes or decisions if C stepped in.

As these sociograms indicate and observations substantiate in detail, the status structures of the two groups were different. Chiefly because of the particular leadership role achieved by C, the Bull Dog group tended to be more stabilized and better coördinated in specific activities than the Red Devils. In the Red Devil group, the leader, S, was more of a daredevil. Though admired by all, his control was exerted chiefly by manipulating his lieutenants, who swung the rest of the group into line.

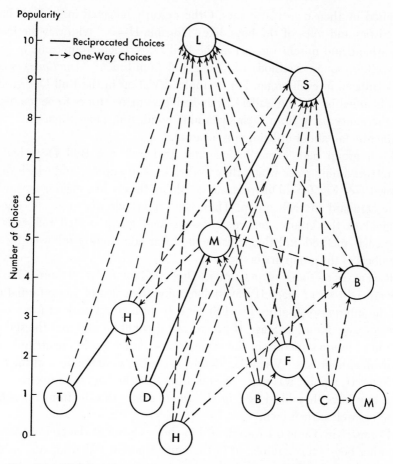

FIG. 6.8.   Red Devils—end of Stage II, in-group formation. (From M. Sherif and C. W. Sherif, *Groups in Harmony and Tension*. New York: Harper & Brothers, 1953.)

As the group structure formed, members achieved positive attitudes toward the in-groups. *Norms* peculiar to each group were stabilized. Examples of such norms were the names of the groups. The choice of these particular names was undoubtedly influenced by the immediate and the larger settings. Blue and red colors were assigned the groups for identification purposes in the camp. The Bull Dog name was standardized for the group of boys assigned the blue color, which was the color of a nearby institution with a bulldog as its symbol.

Most boys were quickly given *nicknames* in their group. Some were

inspired by their own real names. Others clearly reflected individual characteristics and roles of the boys, like "Horrible H——" who was the leading athlete and mischief-maker in the Bull Dogs. Each group came to prefer certain songs. Methods of praise and punishment (*sanctions*) were
standardized in each group. For example, deviation in the Bull Dog group
was handled by C (the leader) by assigning so many stones to be removed
by the guilty party from their swimming pond. Bull Dogs thought C was
eminently fair about utilizing this measure.

Each group had "secret" hide-outs. As noted, the Bull Dogs had a
secret swimming place which they worked hard to improve and which they
named (see Fig. 6.6). Different ways of doing things, like making lanyards,
were standard in each group. These work methods were not, of course,
original to the groups; but members in each group started following a
particular method and then this method was consistently followed by all
members of the group in question.

REVERSALS OF FRIENDSHIP CHOICES DUE TO GROUP MEMBERSHIP: One of
the crucial tests of Stage II was to determine the effect of group formation
on the interpersonal attitudes of Stage I. If shifts or reversals of friendship
choices were found as Stage II progressed, it could be said that the stabilization of group structure in this stage produced changes in the attitudes of
individual members. When the friendship choices were obtained at the end
of Stage II, a point was made of indicating that the boys were free to mention any boys they liked best *in the whole camp*, that is, from the other
group as well as their own.

Compare in Table 6.1 the friendship choices given at the end of Stage I
to other boys who were placed in the same experimental group and in the
other experimental group with the choices at the end of Stage II given to
boys in the in-group and in the out-group. This comparison reveals that
friendship preferences of these boys were at first predominantly for boys
who were placed in the other experimental group (nearly two-thirds of the
choices in each group). After the stage of in-group formation, members of
each group predominantly preferred to associate with members of their
own in-group. The result is a reversal in direction of preferences. After Stage
II, 95 percent of the Red Devils and 87.7 percent of the Bull Dogs chose
friends who were members of their own respective groups.

Stage III: Intergroup relations (friction). Stage III was devoted to relations between the two experimental groups under specified conditions. It
lasted about five days. The two groups were brought into functional relationship (1) in a tournament consisting of a number of competitive events

and (2) in situations which were reciprocally somewhat frustrating to the two groups. Each member of the winning group in the tournament was given a highly valued reward which had been announced at the start of the tournament.

In the course of interaction in these competitive and reciprocally frustrating events, negative intergroup attitudes, name-calling, and unflattering types of reactions developed toward the out-group. The name-calling tended to be standardized in the form of derogatory stereotypes. Since intergroup relations, the production of negative intergroup attitudes, and their reduction will be the main topic in Chapter 9, we will postpone discussion of these results until then.

Summary and Conclusion

The main results can be summarized as follows: When individuals of similar backgrounds and no previously established friendship bonds were brought together, they tended to cluster into small friendship groups, in line with sociometric findings on clique formations (Stage I).

The individuals in these budding friendship groupings of twos, threes, and fours were deliberately split and put into two separate experimental groups, so that a great majority of preferred friends (about two-thirds) were assigned to the other experimental group (Stage II). Only one-third of the friendship choices remained in the experimental group of the person making the choices.

In the course of interaction within the assigned experimental groups in activities which had common goals whose attainment depended on cooperation and pulling together, definite in-group structures arose with hierarchical statuses and roles within them. Along with the appearance of in-group structures, individual members developed common attitudes. One of the most important consequences of these new attitudes was revealed in the reversals of friendship choices, in the direction of the members of the newly formed in-group and away from the choices made when subjects interacted without common group goals. Group norms were stabilized which regulated behavior of members within the group in matters of consequence.

Finally, when the two in-groups were brought into contact in competitive and frustrating situations, attitudes of hostility and rudiments of negative stereotypes toward the out-group and its members were formed (Stage III).

These results confirm the hypotheses which were derived from field studies on small groups concerning stabilization of statuses, roles, and norms within group structures as a consequence of interaction toward common goals over a period of time.

EXPERIMENTAL STUDY OF EXPECTATIONS BASED ON STATUS DIFFERENTIATION

Sociological field studies and the experiment on the formation of group structure just summarized indicate that individual members develop expectations or attitudes as they become functioning parts of a group structure. These attitudes effectively regulate and motivate the individual member's experience and behavior in group interaction.

In Chapter 3 one of the main propositions stated that psychological structuring is jointly determined by interrelated external and internal factors operating at a given time within their appropriate frame of reference (p. 79). The relative contribution of internal factors in psychological structuring is greater when the objective stimulus situation is unstructured, that is, when it permits alternative modes of psychological organization (proposition 8, pp. 97–106).

Therefore, it was feasible to predict that the differentiation of group structure and the differential expectations of individual members in relation to various positions in that structure would be reflected even in relatively simple perceptions, discriminations, and other reactions of individual members (4). A concrete instance was Whyte's observations of Frank, the lower-status member of the Nortons whose high performance in bowling violated expectations stabilized in the group (p. 187). This prediction was tested in two experiments which are summarized in this section.

Prior to these experiments, a number of studies had shown that interpersonal relationships, like friendship and love or hostility, were reflected in a person's expectations for the achievement of a friend, loved one, or rival. This experimental work developed from studies on the setting of goals for performance by an individual, or his "level of aspiration." It had been found that setting such goals for one's own future performance, like other judgments, was relative to the standards or anchorages operating at the time. Thus, the level of aspiration set by an individual for his performance shifted upward or downward when the performance achieved by members of "superior" or "inferior" groups was introduced as an anchorage. (These studies are summarized later in this book, pp. 624–626.)

In order to tap differential expectations within group structures, several definite steps were followed. First, clearly differentiated group structures had to be ascertained. Following the underlying theoretical background, individuals who were part of such structures had to be brought together in a situation where perceptions or judgments of a simple and measurable kind could be made. Certain characteristics of the task were indicated. If internal factors were to be tapped, the task had to be sufficiently unstructured so that it would allow alternative reactions. Furthermore, the task had to seem relevant or of some importance to the individuals in the group.

In preliminary work by W. Simpson, at the University of Oklahoma, a few high-school cliques were ascertained through actual observations of the members, teacher ratings, and sociometric choices. Three members of each clique were chosen to throw darts in turn while the others watched and estimated future performance on each trial. The trials showed the tendency for the estimates of future performance to be regulated by the relative status of the person performing and the person estimating his performance.

Following the indication of this work, a more extensive and systematic study was carried out by O. J. Harvey (1). Through teachers' ratings, observations by the experimenter, and sociometric techniques, 16 adolescent cliques were selected. Since clearly differentiated groups were necessary, individual subjects were taken from only 10 of these, in which all 3 ratings agreed. Three members were selected from each clique—the leader, the member with the lowest standing, and a member with a middle status in the group.

The task was throwing darts at a target and making estimates of *future* performance. Each of the 3 clique members, in turn, threw the darts and estimated his own performance on the next trial, then watched while the others threw and made estimates of their future performance. The target board for the darts did not have the concentric circles usually painted on such targets. However, subjects were shown a board with scored circles prior to the session. In this situation, most persons can estimate the score they have actually made on a trial with fair accuracy. The aspect of the situation which allowed for variations in judgment was that estimates were made of *future* performance, in which some alternatives are always feasible.

In this experimental situation, a high and positive relationship was found between the individual's status in the group and expectations for his performance ($r = .828$). Expectations for an individual member's performance were highest for the leader, next for the person of middle status, and lowest for the member with bottom status. Expectations for the low-status members were so low that on the whole their future performance was actually *underestimated* by the leader and middle-status members. In brief, the higher the individual's status in the group, the higher were the expectations for his performance, as revealed in *over-estimation*. The lower the individual's status, the lower were expectations for his performance, to the point that at the bottom-status level future performance was *under*estimated.

The differential expectations stemming from stabilized reciprocities within the group were revealed also in the individual's estimates of his own performance. In these clearly differentiated group structures, the leader had higher expectations for himself than he did for the other members. Likewise, the middle- or lower-status member held expectations for his own performance which were in line with those stabilized by others in the group in regard to him. Thus, the higher the individual's status in the group, the higher were his expectations for his own performance. The lower the individual's status in the group, the lower were his expectations for his own performance.

Sociological literature indicated a tendency for differential effects of group structure to be revealed more clearly in groups with highly stable structures and great solidarity, like the gangs in large city slums whose members centered their personal identity in the group (as surveyed in 5). Therefore, some of the cliques in this experiment were chosen from a poor neighborhood in a city of about 200,000 and some from a school attended by children of professional parents. The findings for the cliques from these two different backgrounds were suggestive in indicating that the relationship between status and differential expectations for individual members was somewhat higher in cliques from the poor area than in cliques composed of adolescents from professional families.

Status in Experimentally Produced Groups Studied Through Direct Judgments

The next step in tapping the differential expectations and attitudes of individuals who function as members of a group structure was to create conditions for group formation, to observe the formation of a group structure among individuals who were not previously related to one another in any established way, and then to tap the reciprocal attitudes among them through precise laboratory-like techniques. In this way the past history of relationships among individuals and their behavior in a specific situation could be specified.

This experimental unit was carried out under M. Sherif's direction as part of the large-scale experiment on group formation in 1953 (8). In the large-scale experiment two in-group structures composed of boys about 12 years old were produced through experimental manipulation of conditions in which they interacted. These conditions for interaction were similar to those of the 1949 experiment reported in some detail in the last section. The individuals interacted over a period of time in relation to tasks and goals which had common appeal value and which required coöperative and coördinated efforts.

Status structures in both groups evolved sufficiently so that the independent ratings of status made by several observers were in significant agreement. However, it was also clear that the structure in one group was relatively more stable and solidarity was higher than in the other, as shown by the fact that this group spontaneously adopted a group name which members used in a self-glorifying fashion: the "Panthers." The other group later came to call themselves "Pythons." We will refer to it in this summary as the Py group, to indicate both that this name was not yet standardized in the group and that solidarity was less than in the Panther group. Therefore, one of the variables in this unit was a difference in relative stabilization and solidarity of group structure.

As the next step in testing the proposition that differential attitudes stabilized in a group would be reflected in perceptions, judgments, and behavior of members, the task in this unit involved *direct judgments of performance*, not of future performance. That is, the individuals judged their own achievement and that of others just after the task was performed. In order to tap expectations stabilized in activities which had common motivational appeal to the members, the task chosen was one of significance to the group. It was presented to the subjects as an integral part of the camp situation in which they were functioning.

The task was throwing a handball at a target. It was introduced just before a softball game planned between the two groups. To the subjects, it was natural and important as a practice session before the game. The objective structure of the task was reduced by covering the target with blue denim, and by the fact that the ball rebounded from the target, leaving no trace of where it had hit. This was done so that internal factors (attitudes) operating in the situation would contribute relatively greater weight in psychological structuring (arriving at a judgment of performance in this case).

Each group took part separately at different times. Every member of a group threw the ball at the target 25 times. To make it "more fun," both he and other members estimated his performance each time.

The overall finding for both groups was that judgment of an individual's performance was significantly related to that individual's place in the status structure of his group. At the top level, the performance of members of high status was overestimated by other group members; the performance of individuals with low status tended to be underestimated by other members. The extent of over- or under-estimation was related to relative position in the group. Thus, the attitudes of group members toward any given individual in their group were stabilized in line with that individual's role and status in the group. (Rank correlation between variations in judgment and status rank in the Panthers was .737 and in the Py group was .676.)

In this situation, where objective structure was reduced and the task had considerable relevance and significance to group functioning, the judgments of performance by group members were not significantly related to actual skill, as indicated by scores recorded by the experimenter but not announced to the subjects. Of course, this does not mean that skill displayed does not become a factor in group activities or in judgments by individuals. Skill in activities of importance to the group is significant in the very stabilization of group structure. An individual's judgments are not made without reference to objective facts when these facts are clearly apparent. But in this experiment the primary concern was tapping attitudes stabilized by members on the basis of repeated experiences with various individuals in different tasks and functions. Therefore, the objective basis for judgment was deliberately reduced in the experimental situation. However, even when the situation was as clear-cut as a baseball game, attitudes like those tapped in this experimental situation were revealed in tendencies to over-evaluate the high-status members' performance, to expect greater contributions from them than from lower-status members, and to gloss over or even ignore the contributions of low-status members.

In terms of the difference in relative stability and solidarity of the two groups, the finding of note was that the relationship between status and judgment in the Panther group was higher than in the less coördinated Py group. Further, skill or actual performance score was related to judgment in the Py group more closely than in the Panther group. Thus, among interrelated influences operating for a member of the Panther group in this situation, his attitude formed on the basis of stabilized relationships in the group functioned as an anchorage for judgment. Individuals in the Py group were just beginning to form attitudes in relation to all members of their group on the basis of reciprocities in the group. For a particular individual, the apparent skill of another member carried somewhat more weight in making a judgment than it did for a member of the Panther group.

In the less stable Py group, there was little relationship between an individual's own judgment of his performance and the judgments made by other group members of his performance. But in the Panther group, an individual's attitude toward his own performance in the group was more likely to be moving toward similarity with the attitudes of other members relative to him. This was revealed in a higher relationship between an individual's judgments of his own performance and the judgments made by other group members of his performance.

In both groups, the data indicate that in the process of group formation the various individuals form stabilized expectations for a given member before he forms a definite attitude toward himself as a group member. Thus, the expectations the individual member has for his own behavior are influenced by and toward the relationships and expectations stabilized in the group pertaining to him. Possibly this tendency varies for different individuals in various positions in the group. Observations of groups in real-life situations indicate that if individuals do not accept the group's expectations and attitudes toward them, they suffer considerably over the discrepancy between them.

Implications

These experiments tapping differential expectations and attitudes of individuals stemming from stabilized and reciprocal relationships in group structures verify behavioral observations. Beyond this, they offer the opportunity for more refined and precise specification of variables involved in becoming a member of a group structure. Rather simple perceptions and judgments may become useful as indices of group products and their psychological consequences for individual members. This line of development is based both on general theory of psychological structuring and on the properties of group formation and functioning. In pursuing it further, it is essential that tasks and techniques be utilized without destroying motivational factors and the structural properties of groups which make these topics and their refined study so crucial to social psychology.

CONCLUDING REMARKS

In this chapter the formation and functioning of group structures over a time span was discussed in terms of empirical findings. First, a field study of group structure in real life, its functioning and eventual disintegration, was summarized. Generalizations derived from such field studies were tested through an experiment in which conditions of interaction were controlled and altered over a time span. In both field observations and experimental findings, psychological effects of becoming a functional part of a group structure were noted. Such psychological effects were tapped through laboratory-like techniques in experiments concerning the differential attitudes of members based on stabilized reciprocities within the group structure. These attitudes and their consistency are intimately related to the degree of stability and solidarity of the group structure. These findings constitute further evidence for differentiating social situations in terms of gradations ranging from mere togetherness situations to stabilized groups.

REFERENCES

1. Harvey, O. J. An experimental approach to the study of status relations in informal groups, Amer. sociol. Rev. (1953), 18:357–367.
2. Shaw, C. R. Delinquency Areas. Chicago: University of Chicago Press, 1929.
3. Shaw, C. R., and McKay, H. D. Delinquency and Urban Areas. Chicago: University of Chicago Press, 1942.
4. Sherif, M. A Preliminary Experimental Study of Inter-Group Relations, in J. H. Rohrer and M. Sherif, Social Psychology at the Crossroads. New York: Harper, 1951, esp. pp. 421–423.
5. Sherif, M., and Cantril, H. The Psychology of Ego-Involvements. New York: Wiley, 1947, chap. 10.
6. Sherif, M., Harvey, O. J., White, B. J., Hood, W. R., and Sherif, C. W. Experimental Study of Positive and Negative Intergroup Attitudes Between Experimentally Produced Groups. Robbers Cave Study. Norman: University of Oklahoma, 1954 (multilithed).
7. Sherif, M., and Sherif, C. W. Groups in Harmony and Tension. New York: Harper, 1953, chaps. 9, 10, 11.
8. Sherif, M., White, B. J., and Harvey, O. J. Status in experimentally produced groups, Amer. J. Sociol. (1955), 60:370–379.
9. Thrasher, F. The Gang. Chicago: University of Chicago Press, 1927.
10. Whyte, W. F. A slum sex code, Amer. J. Sociol. (1943), 49:24–31.
11. Whyte, W. F. Street Corner Society. Chicago: University of Chicago Press, 1943.

Formation and Functioning of Group Structures (Continued)

LEADERSHIP, POWER, COMMUNICATION

The process through which group structure is stabilized and its significance for behavior are grasped by the study of individuals interacting over a time span in conditions conducive to group formation. Through such studies, various aspects of group functioning were touched upon in the preceding chapter.

Certain aspects of structure are so crucial in group functioning that they have been topics of lively discussion and research activity. Accordingly, these aspects are singled out for separate treatment in this chapter.

First, the bulk of research on *leadership* is approached in terms of leader-follower relations within group structures. The topic of *power* is a logical extension from the problem of leadership and followership. In this extension, social psychology is dependent on increasing conceptual and empirical analysis at the level of the social sciences. A highly condensed picture of power relations within group units follows the section on leadership. Finally, patterning of *communication* within group structures is considered briefly.

LEADERS AND OTHER MEMBERS OF THE GROUP

Leaders have been subjects of history, social philosophy, and politics for several thousand years. To one person a "leader" may mean a person of accomplishment in the arts, science, business, or athletics. To another a "leader" is simply a phenomenon to be understood in his own right in terms of his unique capacities and talents. To a third a "leader" is anyone holding a public office. To still another a "leader" is anyone who behaves in certain ways. Or a person who influences other people may be taken as a "leader."

If the aim of leadership study is to understand actual leaders in social life, the term "leadership" must refer to those realities which make its investigation important. It is rather obvious that leadership can occur only in relation to other people. No one can be a leader all by himself. Beyond that, leadership implies rather definite kinds of relationship to other people.

An individual who becomes a leader is one part of a social group. The particular relationships he bears to other individuals are status and role relationships (see definition of *group*, p. 144). In togetherness situations, certain individuals may be more prominent, more influential than others. Possibly one of them will become a leader if interaction pertaining to significant problems continues. He becomes a leader to the extent that his high status and reciprocal relationship to other individuals are stabilized. Typically, the leader position is among the first to be stabilized in the process of group formation. However, this need not be the case. When it is not, a longer period of flux, struggle, and perhaps even conflict is implied for the formative stages of the group.

A leader is the individual highest in the status relationships of the group. He is *part* of a group structure which may be more or less stable, more or less enduring. As such he carries on reciprocal relationships with other members of the group. These reciprocal relationships and expectations define his leadership role in the particular group.

When leadership is viewed as a status in a group structure and a role defined by reciprocal relations with others in the particular structure, it is not difficult to understand why the numerous studies of leaders' personal characteristics or "traits" have failed to find a consistent pattern which distinguishes leaders (23, p. 889). In 1940 Bird summarized a list of 79 traits found characteristic of various leaders (8). This list revealed little overlapping among traits. After surveying the accumulated studies, Jenkins concluded that there were wide variations in the characteristics of individuals who are leaders in similar situations, and even greater variations in different situations (30).

However, both Jenkins' and Stogdill's reviews of this research reveal that leaders excel other group members in at least one of various abilities, skills, or personal characteristics relevant in the activities and values of the particular group (30, 54). The abilities and skills which are prominent in the group seem to depend upon the values, goals, and traditions of the

group quite as much as on the personality of the leader. A concrete example will make this clear. In a study of school children, the first-grade leader
was the boy who could spit the farthest. The fourth-grade leader was the
child who dared to "sass" the teacher. And so on, up to high school, when
the inconspicuous little girl of grade school became a leader because of
superior "dating power" (16).

Specificity or Generality of Leadership

Measurement of personal characteristics of leaders had been stimulated
particularly by the practical problem of selecting leaders for various organizations (military, industrial, and the like). As it proved unrewarding,
many investigators employed "situational" methods for studying leadership
and selecting potential leaders.

With situational techniques, a number of individuals are placed together
in a situation and instructed to perform some task, solve a problem, or discuss an issue. No person among the subjects is appointed to take responsibility. Observing which individuals take effective initiative and influence
the activity of others in such situations seemed more feasible than tests
and rating of personal traits in isolation as a means of selecting potential
leaders.

Such situational methods of selection were studied in the German army,
the British armed forces, in industry, in the Australian armed services by
Gibb in particular, and in the O.S.S. Division of the United States Army.
As Gibb observed, the general finding is that leader or follower "traits"
are not exhibited in isolation. They are relative to a specific social situation.
The person who becomes a "leader" surpasses others in some qualities
required by the problem or the goal in the particular situation. "Leadership
is both a function of the social situation and a function of personality, but
it is a function of these two in interaction; no additive concept is adequate
to explain the phenomenon. There is no justification for saying that personality qualities which make for leadership exist in latent form when not
being exercised in a social situation" (21, p. 268).

Similarly, the O.S.S. research found that leadership varied from situation
to situation and from group to group. It was not always the most "assertive" individual who gained a leadership role, although many designated as
"leaders" were assertive. The leadership position sometimes shifted from
one individual to another as the demands of the situation changed. For
example, a man who took the lead in discussing the problem might be in
the background when attention was turned to actually carrying out the

manipulations involved in solving it (43). (Examples of situations employed are portrayed in Figures 7.1 and 7.2.)

This line of research served as a significant corrective to traditional and stereotyped notions of leaders as uniquely superior individuals who would lead in whatever situation or time they might find themselves. The corrective is clear in Gibb's words quoted above. Thrasher's study of juvenile gangs was among the sociological research bearing the same implications for traditional views (58). Sociometric studies led to a similar conclusion concerning the relationships between personal characteristics and leadership. Thus, Helen Jennings concluded that the " 'why' of leadership appears . . . not to reside in any personality trait considered singly, nor even in a constellation of related traits, but in the interpersonal contribution of which the individual becomes capable in a specific setting eliciting such contributions from him" (31, p. 205).

However, one by-product of the situational studies of leadership or "leaderless" groups was the view that leadership is specific to a specific situation. In extreme form, such a conception is at an opposite pole to a traditional view of unchanging leadership traits. On the basis of findings revealing that in togetherness situations different individuals took initiative in different tasks or in different phases of the same task, it seemed to some investigators that leadership was a way of behaving exhibited by individuals in differing degrees in different situations. That is, leadership as a sociological concept was equated to types of behavior observed in the so-called "leaderless" group situations, in which conditions are insufficient, on the whole, for interaction over a time span around problems with motivational relevance to the participants.

A caution against the view that leadership is behavior entirely specific to a given situation was made by Carter (12). On the basis of his studies and others, he noted that even in situational studies of leadership there was some generality as to who would be rated high on actions defined as leadership behavior for different situations, depending in part on the skills and abilities required by the task. Further, Carter noted correctly that if leadership is absolutely unique to a given situation, then it cannot be subjected to scientific analysis and generalization.

The crux of the issue for a comprehensive approach to leaders and leadership lies in the referents of these concepts. So long as leadership is equated with certain types of behavior exhibited by individuals interacting in a togetherness situation, of course leadership will seem to depend largely on factors in the *immediate* situation, like the specific nature of the task

FIG. 7.1. Getting a "delicate" instrument across a brook.

Situational tests in O.S.S. study. (From *Assessment of Men*. New York: Rinehart, 1948.)

FIG. 7.2. Surmounting an obstacle.

or problem, and the distribution of the abilities these require among the individuals present.

If such behavior as effective initiative, individual prominence, sociability, consideration, and the like exhibited in the performance of specific tasks in togetherness situations is equated with a leadership role in group structures, one will conclude that more than one individual acts like a leader in various situations or at different times. There is no reason to doubt Gibb's conclusion that in "traditionless" laboratory groups unequivocal leadership by one person rarely, if ever, occurs, and that the question of who are "leaders" in such "groups" can be answered only by drawing some arbitrary dividing line on a frequency continuum of behaviors (24). Certainly, it would not seem possible to identify one person as the leader of a group if no status relationships or group norms have developed.

However, if the terms "leader" and "leadership" refer to functions in actual groups in social life, there can be little doubt that one person typically does occupy the leader position and perform leadership functions. It is also true that different individuals may and do occupy this position and carry out these functions at different times in the group's history, whether it is relatively brief or long. As group members face new situations, as new goals or values emerge in interaction, leadership may change hands if the present leader does not exhibit the abilities or skills or suggest solutions required by these new conditions. But leadership changes hands in a group structure with stabilized norms (traditions) only when the changed conditions facing it are urgent and pressing, when they are related to significant motives of individual members, or when the leader fails to live up to existing norms or meet new conditions.

If a leader of an informally organized group cannot cope with some aspect of a task the group faces, he ordinarily *delegates* authority to a competent member at that time. But he does not thereby vacate the leader position. In our experimental studies of group formation like the Bull Dog and Red Devil study (summarized on pp. 191–202), the leaders who emerged in the groups during the experimental period of formation were not in all cases the best in their groups in athletics. Therefore, when the groups were brought together in a tournament of competitive games, the leader of each group delegated authority to another high-status member to act as the athletic "captain." But, while the tournament progressed, the leader did not drop out of the picture. The athletic captain directed team activities with the leader's approval. When this delegation of authority occurred, the group members recognized it as such. In general, in the instances in which the group leader and the athletic captain disagreed, the leader's word was followed by the captain and other members. These examples illustrate group structure in the process of functioning. Delegation of authority is a typical aspect of group functioning; it does not necessarily imply a change in the status hierarchy.

In one experimental group, leadership did actually change hands during the intergroup competition (1954 study, pp. 309–312). The athletic captain in this group became the new leader. In this case the change did not come about simply because the nature of activities changed. Actually, the initial leader was one of the better athletes in this group. He dropped down from the leader position during the course of intergroup competition largely because he did not live up to expectations of his fellow group members. In the intergroup competition he turned out to be a "poor loser"; he deserted the group when it needed his support and encouragement most. As this became apparent on several occasions, the athletic captain rose in position and began to take over the leadership functions. This did not occur on the basis of one incident alone.

The conception of leadership and of the leader depends, therefore, on the conception of *group*. As we have seen, a group characteristically has a structure of more or less stabilized status and role relationships and a set of norms. The leader is necessarily a part of a group. There is considerable truth in Stogdill's contention that leadership is an aspect of organization (55), if "organization" refers to both informal and formal organization. Informally organized groups have organization. Leadership is a status and role in an organized group, whether organization has developed informally or has become formalized. As a by-product of organization, values or norms are stabilized, and these are also essential to an understanding of leadership.

Reciprocal Relations Between the Leader and Other Members

When groups interact over a period of time in relation to problems of common motivational value, the leader position, other statuses, and reciprocal relations among them become more or less stabilized. One factor conducive to stabilization is that groups tend to specialize, engaging in tasks and activities chosen in line with group values or goals. This is one of the reasons why the leadership in social groups does not change frequently from specific situation to situation. As the person at the top of the status hierarchy, the leader is the most important *single* member of the group. As Whyte noted, significant changes in the reciprocities between leader and other members imply changes in the entire group structure (60). This was demonstrated in an experiment carried out in Japan by Toki, who studied groups of children in school and in camps (59).

The general question in Toki's study was "What happens when the individual who has achieved the leader position in a group is removed?" If the leader was removed while the group structure was still in the process of formation, the developing group structure tended to disintegrate, with resulting helplessness on the part of the rest of the group. But the helplessness was temporary if the group continued to interact. A new structure began to take shape.

If the former leader was returned to the group soon after his removal and assumed membership in the group again, then the new structure tended to be replaced through the restoration of initial relationships in the group. However, if the former leader was not returned until the new structure was stabilized, the group members tended to continue functioning within the new, stabilized structure.

Communication among group members tends to flow in relation to the focal position of the leader. Disputes and frictions within the group, as well as positive actions, ultimately are settled or find expression through him. If some members are dissatisfied with the direction of activities or with the behavior of other members, they sooner or later complain to the leader, or the leader himself intervenes. As Whyte noted among the Street Corner Boys, the other members try to get the leader to act in the desired direction and bring pressure on others, for his approval is the best insurance of action (60).

Concomitant with the greater authority and power of the leader is his greater prestige. He need not be best at everything the group does, but he must have some skill in those pursuits which particularly interest the group and in some respects he must excel (58, 60). Once he becomes leader on the basis of excellence in some respect significant to group activities or in coördination toward attainment of common goals, his prestige, based both on these personal qualities and on his status, is an important factor in his relations with other group members.

When Doc moved to the leadership of the Nortons, a serious challenge came from Tony Fontana, who had become a professional boxer. One night Tony began "acting big" to Doc, who thought of Tony's prowess in the ring and decided to go to bed. But Doc could not sleep. He dressed and went down to Tony. In Doc's words: "I said 'Say that to me again!' He did and I let him have it—pow! . . . But he wouldn't fight me. Why?

Prestige, I suppose. Later we had it out with gloves on the playground. He was too good for me, Bill. I stayed with him, but he was too tough. . . . Could he hit!' " (60, pp. 4–5).

However, the relationship between leader and other members is not just a one-way affair, only from members to leader. The authority and prestige the leader enjoys have their counterparts in the responsibilities required and the expectations for his fulfilling them. The leader is expected to keep his word, to stick by the members, to uphold the group values or norms. The experiments tapping expectations for members of various statuses through laboratory-like techniques reported in the last chapter revealed the high level of achievement expected of the leader (pp. 202–207).

If the leader does not live up to the level expected, he suffers a loss of prestige and even of position in the status structure. This, as we have seen, is what happened to Doc when he "let the boys down." A loss in prestige was reported in the story of the Raiders in Chapter 5. When Carlson could not live up to his men's expectations, there were few good words for him (pp. 166–168). Whether or not the leader lives up to his obligations and responsibilities is a key factor in the solidarity and morale of the group.

RANGE OF TOLERABLE BEHAVIOR FOR THE LEADER: In general, the stabilized expectations (norms) defining the role of leadership in a group are more exacting, require greater obligations and responsibilities, than those of other positions in the group. The group members have higher aspirations for the leader, and he sets higher standards for himself. In addition, he is subject to a narrower range of tolerable behavior than are other group members, in those matters of consequence to the group in terms of its goals.

In general, closer adherence to the major values or norms of the group is found at the upper status levels. This was revealed in a study of a women's political group (39). The most active core of the membership adhered more closely to the major group values than did those who were less active or just hanging on.

In rather minor matters, the leader's prestige may permit considerable variation from relevant norms. However, in matters of importance to the identity, solidarity, or maintenance of the group, if the leader steps beyond the limits of tolerable behavior for his leadership role, he can look forward to a struggle to maintain his position. He may even wake up to find himself lower in the status hierarchy.

An extreme possibility can be illustrated by the fate of one O'Brien, who was leader of the elite ore-trimmers' union on a Lake Michigan port. As president of the union, he was sent to Cleveland to negotiate a pay scale for the coming season. Instead, O'Brien became involved in a deal to transfer his men to a new union—one which would trim ore for less than he was delegated to demand. When he began to carry out the scheme, a furor arose. When the men caught up with him, "O'Brien was ready for ten months in a hospital and nobody on the street seemed to know who had prepared him" (27).

Leaders initiate, direct, and manipulate activities of other members. But leadership in a particular group is effective only within the range of tolerable behavior determined by the leader's reciprocities with other members and by group norms established as the group interacts in relation to specified goals. It is important to specify just what sets the limits within which leadership is effective. Sometimes these limits are conceived as imposed by blind, unreasoning emotions of group members. Thus, we are told that leaders cannot influence their groups in matters of social prejudice, because the bulk of the membership is fundamentally prejudiced, emotional, and blind. But there are intelligent, rational persons who also have prejudices.

The sources of limits of a leader's power to direct or manipulate the group are illustrated by Merei's study of children's groups (40). Children were allowed to interact over a period of time until a *tradition* of ways of doing things, relations to one another, ritual, sequence of activities, and jargon had formed which were not found in their school as a whole. Then individuals who were somewhat older and larger and who had been definite leaders in other groups of children were brought into the situation. What happened?

In all groups, the person who had been a leader in other groups was "absorbed" into the new group, and he took up its traditions. A number of alternative possibilities were then observed. Some of the children who had been leaders in other groups were completely "absorbed" by the established group. Others were assimilated and followed the established traditions but became the ones who gave the orders of how to proceed or made the distribution of materials in accordance with custom. That is, these children became group members and then assumed a leadership role within the existing framework. Those few individuals who became leaders in their new group and succeeded in modifying the existing group tradition did so by first becoming a group member, accepting the established norms, and then introducing insignificant modifications in them. Once the norms were weakened by slight variations, it became possible to introduce new customs, although few leaders were able to do this.

Clearly the limits of the leadership role are set by the established norms of the group, both those concerning reciprocal relationships within the particular group and behavior in other matters of consequence to the group. Because of their greater responsibility to adhere to group norms, leaders are by necessity prone to be more aware of the social norms of the group than are other members (15). When an issue confronts the group, the leader may be more influential than other group members in shaping the group norm, thus being more cognizant of its nature and concerned with its maintenance (57). But the fact that he was initially more responsible than others in the process of norm formation does not mean that he can change the norm at will once it is formed.

Nevertheless, there are certainly cases, and very important cases, in which the leader does succeed in extending the limits of existing norms or is the key figure in the establishment of new norms. Merci's study gives a hint. If the leader is able to introduce slight modifications, it may be easier to shift the range of a norm or to alter it. But, as his results indicate, this probably is exceedingly difficult as long as the conditions in which the group functions remain the same.

When the conditions which the group faces change, as in critical times, social norms may become weakened because of their manifest inappropriateness to new conditions, the compelling push-and-pull of deprivations, and anxieties shared by the group. The result is widespread deviation from the norms. Study of periods of crisis and uncertainty indicates that such conditions are particularly conducive to the introduction of new values or norms, as we shall see in Chapter 21. That is, the limits placed on established leadership by social norms are extended by the weakening or even breakdown of the norms. If the established leader does not introduce new standards and solutions, he is likely to be deposed in favor of a new leader who does, depending in part on the seriousness of the situation to the group as a whole. Kelley has suggested that in times when established norms are out of touch with realities a group which is already weakened may have greater survival ability than a highly stable group (33). This may well be true, providing a leader arises in the weakened group who suggests solutions appropriate to the realities and succeeds in solidifying group structure in terms of these solutions.

Leadership in Formally and Informally Organized Groups

In the preceding paragraphs we have touched on problems which may become important in the functioning of both informally organized groups and formal organizations. There are, of course, differences in leadership in small informal groups and large formal organizations. In many formal organizations the membership make very little, if any, contribution to the selection of a leader or to the formal status structure in the group. But this alone does not mean that leaders who are appointed by authority outside of the group are in all cases altogether different from leaders who emerge in the course of interaction in informally organized structures.

The biggest difference between leadership in formal organizations and informally organized groups is in the leader's sources of power. In informally organized groups the leader's power is ordinarily derived from personal resources, his specific relations with the membership and to the resources of the group. However, as we shall see in the next section, power in actual groups is seldom unrelated to larger power structures. Even if a leader emerges informally in group interaction, some or much of his power in the group may stem from his relationships with persons and resources outside of the group.

In some formal organizations a leader comes to power solely by appointment of a board or by outside persons or groups. However, his position and role in the group structure require that he live up to certain obligations and carry out certain reciprocal relations with others with whom he interacts in the organization. If he does not a discrepancy will arise and may result in the growth of an informal organization with another leader position. Then the formally appointed leader is in danger of being leader "in name only," unless he changes his ways and/or utilizes his power derived from outside sources. Or the discrepancy may lead to prolonged friction within the organization, with all of the instability and confusion such friction implies.

Studies of Leadership Techniques

In 1939 and 1940, Lewin, Lippitt, and White conducted experiments on the effects of different leadership techniques on behavior in groups of 11-year-old boys (36). These groups were led by adults using three different methods or styles of leadership.

In one method, the adult determined the policy, procedures, and activities in the group; this technique was called "authoritarian." In another, the adult encouraged participation by members in deciding these matters and behaved in a friendly, helpful manner to the members, giving technical assistance and suggesting alternative procedures as they were needed; this technique was called "democratic." In the third, the adult leader allowed complete freedom for decisions and activity, keeping his own initiative and suggestions to a minimum; this technique was called "laissez-faire."

By rotating adult leaders using these different techniques systematically among the groups, it was possible to compare behavior in the different groups under the same techniques and to detect some effects of preceding techniques for the same group.

These studies demonstrated in a clear-cut way that the treatment by the adult leader had a significant effect on the behavior of members, in spite of individual differences among the members of various groups and possible differences in the personalities of the adult leaders.

It was found that some individuals reacted somewhat differently to the various leadership techniques used in terms of previously acquired attitudes. For example, the son of a military officer preferred the "authoritarian" leader. In comparing the same group under different adult leaders, it was noted that reaction to a particular leadership style was also affected by the group's previous experience with other techniques. Thus, one club was fairly passive under an "authoritarian" leader. But after it had a leader using a "democratic" technique, a second leader using "authoritarian" methods was reacted to with discontent.

From this and subsequent studies of different groups in different situations it is evident that the leadership technique exercised by an adult in a superior position (as "adult leader" or teacher) is a significant factor in behavior of individuals in groups. However, reactions to a particular treatment may vary with the established attitudes which individuals bring to the situation and with the situation in which the technique is exercised (9, 23, 49).

A given technique may not have the same significance when exercised by an adult and by an informal leader who is also a group member. Thus, informal leaders who emerge in "democratic" interaction may use more "authoritarian" methods than leaders appointed by persons outside the group (13).

As these findings indicate, there is considerable confusion concerning the use of the terms "democratic," "authoritarian," and the like in research practice. The same undefined terms are at times used to apply to certain leader techniques and behavior, to institutional forms, to ideologies of individuals, and to methods of reaching decisions in a group (28). In systematic consideration of the effects of leadership techniques on the behavior of members, it is clear that the techniques in question have to be related to the established attitudes of the membership, to the particular form of stabilized relations among the individuals including the leader, to the shared values or norms of the group, and to the situation in which the leader functions as a part of the group structure.

POWER RELATIONS IN GROUP STRUCTURES

Status has been characterized as a differentiated position in a hierarchy stabilized on the basis of control, authority, or relative weights of individual members in determining activities and decisions in the group (p. 162). This characterization delineated the status hierarchy from hierarchical arrangements in other dimensions. In most groups it is feasible to order members in terms of popularity or the extent to which they are liked, in terms of physical characteristics like size or beauty, or in terms of personal abilities or skills. These scales may or may not coincide with status arrangements, depending on the character of the group, its major interests, purposes, and activities.

In the account of the Bull Dogs and Red Devils in the last chapter, a concrete instance of a discrepancy between status and popularity dimensions was noted. Studies by Norfleet (42), Gibb (22), Carter (11), and Bales (2) indicate that sheer liking or pleasure of associating with others need not be closely related to contribution to a group's activities, to objective ratings by trained observers of effective initiative, or to rank based on volume of action initiated. Of course, it is possible that in some informally organized groups like friendship cliques or gangs with common goals of some importance to the membership a higher relationship would be found between the dimensions of popularity and status than that indicated by these studies.

Power relations in the group are an integral aspect of the status structure. The higher status levels are the focal levels for power. Individuals with high status in the group exert relatively more *control* over the activities and over the patterns of interaction in the group. Their words and deeds carry more weight or authority than those of members lower in the status hierarchy of the group. As noted in the discussion of leadership, this differential weight of the upper status levels is reflected in the treatment they enjoy. For example, in the Bull Dog group, the leader was the only boy in the group who was not given a nickname; he was respectfully called by his given name.

In time the upper status levels, particularly the leader, come to control the use and treatment of the physical resources of the group. Decisions requiring action by the group become final and binding only with the approval of the upper status levels. Action is initiated in group interaction by individuals at various levels; but if a course is suggested for the group, it is not followed until the members with high status and the leader in particular give their assent.

Thus, power denotes the relative weights of behavior by members in a group structure. In the technical sense, it is meaningless to speak of power or power relationships apart from the context of organization. For this reason, power is not equivalent with "influence" or with initiating change in another person's behavior without regard to the situation in which it occurs. A newborn infant can influence and change the behavior of his parents and family. A stranger on the street can influence the actions of others by calling out "Look out for that car!" But this influence is not equivalent with power in group functioning. Neither is power equivalent in all cases with "prestige." The local minister who joins a club may have considerable prestige in the eyes of the members but little power in the reciprocal relationships in the group.

Direct and Indirect Exertion of Power

Power influences may be exerted either in direct and imperative fashion or indirectly. The former occurs typically in a formalized relationship from a superior to a subordinate. When power is exerted indirectly, the individuals may not be aware that they are being influenced. Such indirect attempts to exert power are found both in face-to-face situations and within larger social structures, notably through the use of mass media of communication (52).

In informal groups in camp settings, Lippitt, Polansky and others found status hierarchies in cabin groups and showed that children at the upper status levels made more attempts at *direct* influence and were more successful in directing the behavior of others than children with low status. Children lower in the status structures were less likely to attempt to influence behavior of high-status members directly; their attempts were more indirect. Those low in status were more deferential in behavior toward those with high status. These relationships were found in camps both for "disturbed" youngsters and for normal children, although the personal characteristics associated with achieving status in the two types of groups differed (37, 45).

On the basis of sociological studies of established status relationships and observations, it is likely that the direct exertion of power occurs most frequently and is most often successful from a superior to a subordinate within the bounds prescribed by the established relationship. The superior may also attempt to exert power indirectly in matters not closely related to the established relationship with the subordinate. Thus, the leader of a political group exerts power directly to lower status levels through imperatives, orders, and the like; he may also use indirect means to influence his subordinates' social life, friendships outside the group, and so on.

Both the individual's response to direct and imperative exertion of power and his response to indirect attempts will become more clear when ego-involvements are discussed in Chapters 17 and 18. The explanation of willing and enthusiastic response to imperatives and orders by those with higher status in the group lies in the fact that, in becoming a member, the individual has related himself to the group, its established reciprocities, norms, and goals in definite ways and capacities. If he relates himself to the system of reciprocities in the group through forming appropriate attitudes, specific demands and instructions from others higher up in the scheme of things are willingly, even zealously, accepted and pursued. Indirect exertion of power which is successful likewise hinges on involvement of relationships or values which an individual considers as an integral part of himself. Through such means, persons high in the status structure of an organization can exert power indirectly in matters which do not fall within the bounds of their established relationships with subordinates.

Power Relations and the Larger Setting

The power dimension becomes especially useful in specifying the sources of status in the group. In groups of young children, these sources may be entirely within the group. Status stems directly from differential personal characteristics, skills, and resources of individuals in the particular interaction situation. But the sources of differential status and hence of power in groups of older children and adults are seldom solely within the sealed confines of the group.

This dependence of power relations in small groups on other power structures is found even in such "spontaneous" formations as juvenile gangs. In surveying the gangs of El Paso, Texas, Dorothy Dean found two gangs which were really "super-gangs." One was called the 2-X. This was the "best" gang in El Paso, the roughest, most daring, and most versatile. Its membership was carefully chosen from all over the city. Being chosen was an honor to the individual and to his gang. Therefore, the status relationships within smaller gangs containing one or more members of the

2-X would be decidedly influenced by the superior gang (17). Another example was reported by Rodhafer in Detroit. The Maling Street gang consisted of a number of smaller gangs with a total membership of from 200 to 300 members. This gang existed primarily as a mutual protection organization. The leader was a large man 26 years old; he directed and co-ordinated the efforts of smaller gangs which became involved in fights. When he put out a call for recruits, the various smaller gangs would respond in large numbers (47).

In actual life status and power relations within small group structures ordinarily are determined to some extent by power structures outside the group. In his study of informally organized groups and clubs, Whyte gave a detailed account of the consequences of power relationships in politics, business, and the rackets on status structure within the small informal groups. These power relationships in the larger community were altered in turn by shifts in the power structures of larger superordinates. For example, after the WPA had functioned for a time, the influence of the local politician upon the informal organizations declined, since his efforts to secure favors were relatively ineffective unless tied to power sources in the national capital (62).

The topic of power, therefore, presents immediately problems of inter-group relationships, particularly between larger superordinate units and their subordinate parts. This was shown in a study of supervisory leadership by Pelz (44). The relative power of supervisors in different units of a business organization could be understood only in terms of the supervisor's role in the larger structure. Thus, a supervisor whose word carried some weight in the larger organization was more effective in the group he supervised directly. He was able to help individual members achieve their goals; he met their expectations.

Because power relations, even in small group units, involve larger social organizations and ultimately the superordinate structures of socioeconomic, political, and cultural life, social psychology is necessarily dependent on the various social sciences dealing with structures and relationships at this level for a rounded account of the topic.

COMMUNICATION AND STATUS RELATIONS

Interaction among individuals typically involves communication. The usual mode of interaction among human beings after early childhood is through language and symbolic gesture, whether interaction is between strangers, between friends, or between fellow group members. Our present concern is communication among group members within a structure of status and role relationships.

In group situations, communicative behavior and the lines of communication among individuals become increasingly predictable in terms of reciprocal relationships stabilized in the group. In contrast, communication in togetherness situations tends to reflect influences immediate to the situation, the task, and the personal characteristics of individuals as they interact. This contrast between communication in transitory togetherness situations and that in stabilized group structures is consistent with the general observation that the properties of groups serve as stable anchorages affecting group functioning and individual behavior in more predictable fashion.

Direct comparisons of togetherness situations and organized groups have found greater consistency and coördination of reactions of members in organized groups to a problem or stimulus than of individuals who were not fellow group members. French compared individuals in organized groups and togetherness situations in reactions to insoluble problems and an apparent danger (smoke filling a locked room) (20). Individuals in organized groups tended to face these problem situations as a group, "pitching in" with greater equality and involvement of all, and feeling more frustrated at failure. Bovard reported that members of organized groups were influenced significantly more by the announced judgments of fellow members than were aggregates of unrelated individuals who simply came together to serve as subjects (10).

Experimental findings reported in the last chapter indicate that anchoring effects of group structure vary with different *gradations* of stability in status reciprocities and solidarity of members (pp. 162–170). Even in large organizations where various statuses and functions are formalized in regulations, charts, and the like, the relative stability of status reciprocities and expectations produces predictable differential effects on individual behavior.

Thus, investigation of organization in restaurants by Whyte (61) and in naval units by Scott (51) reveals differential effects stemming from relative lack of clarity within the status hierarchy. The naval units studied by Scott were all stabilized, efficient units. Yet in relative terms the organization marked by more confusion and lack of reciprocity within its structure was also lowest in morale and efficiency of members. The significant finding was not whether existing status reciprocities approximated formalized structure as indicated in regulations. Rather, the consequential feature of status hierarchy was the extent to which the existing pattern provided stable anchorages for individuals in it, whether it coincided exactly with the formal structure or not.

Differentiating between togetherness and group situations and conceiving of group structure in gradations of stabilization are particularly useful in approaching the mass of contemporary research dealing with communication or using indices based largely on communicative behavior to study other topics. In a typical experimental situation, individuals are brought together to discuss or solve some problem. The topic of discussion, task, or problem may or may not have intrinsic interest for the subjects. The degree of its significance and the extent to which it has common appeal value to all individuals are usually not specified, although some studies have manipulated these variables through instructions or rewards from the experimenter. Data relevant to the topic of investigation are secured through detailed ratings of behavior as it occurs, recording the directions of communications, questionnaires, or rating devices administered to subjects.

Such research typically does not embody the conditions essential to group formation in actual life, namely, interaction over a time span in relation to goals which are significant to all individuals. Therefore, direct extrapolation of findings from such transitory situations to behavior in organized groups is usually not warranted. However, in some studies interaction and communication are seen in the process of stabilization.

One noteworthy attempt in research is the development of generalized categories for behavior in problem situations that can be applied to any social situation. In his book *Interaction Process Analysis* (1950), Bales presented categories which have been found adequate to handle various specific behaviors of individuals involved in interaction. In abbreviated form, these categories were: (1) Shows solidarity, (2) Shows tension release (e.g. laughs), (3) Agrees, (4) Gives suggestion, (5) Gives opinion, (6) Gives orientation, (7) Asks for orientation, (8) Asks for opinion, (9) Asks for suggestion, (10) Disagrees, (11) Shows tension, (12) Shows antagonism. More recently the term "information" has been substituted for "orientation" in categories 6 and 7.* In practice, the categories are used by observers behind a one-way mirror (See Fig. 7.3). An interaction recorder is used to obtain a record of classified observations occurring in time sequence.

Conceivably, any of the factors which enter into social situations, like

---

* Personal communication from Dr. R. F. Bales.

FIG. 7.3A. Discussion situation as observed through a one-way mirror. (Courtesy of Robert F. Bales.)

FIG. 7.3B. The interaction recorder used by observers. Observations are recorded using generalized categories on the moving paper. Time intervals are marked automatically. (Courtesy of Robert F. Bales.)

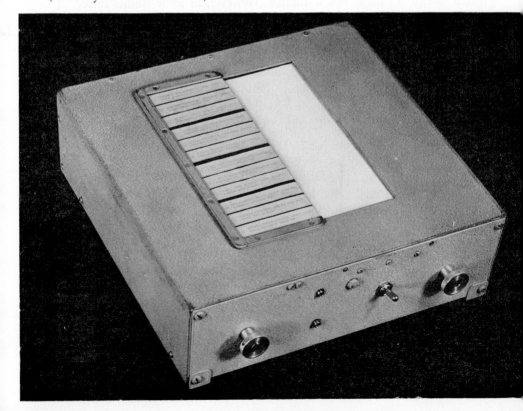

Fig. 7.4. Participants discussing a problem on the other side of a one-way mirror. (Courtesy of Robert F. Bales.)

those listed in Chapter 4 (pp. 121–124), could become important variables in shaping interaction initially. Since several surveys, bibliographies, and selected readings are available, no attempt is made to be exhaustive here (see 14, 34, 46, 48, 56).

Significance of Tasks to Interacting Individuals

On the basis of a number of studies dealing with communication in togetherness situations, the special importance of the task to the various individuals is evident. The typical procedure has been to vary the significance of the task in different situations or for various individuals in the same situation through instructions or rewards and punishments from the experimenter. In view of the primary importance of the motives of individuals in interaction processes and their stabilization, it might be expected that variations in task significance would lead to differential trends in communication. This is clearly the case.

By varying instructions and rewards to subjects which increased the significance of the task, Back demonstrated that patterns of communication between partners (two individuals) and their relative influence on each other were affected (1). Schachter varied motivations of individuals in interaction situations by having some discuss topics in which they had expressed interest and others discuss topics of little interest to them. Planted subjects in the discussions took positions on the topic which deviated markedly from those of the naïve subjects. The relative increase and decline in the amount of communication directed toward this deviating individual over a period of time (to 45 minutes) was found to vary with the significance of the discussion topic and its relevance to the main interests of the participants (50).

Kelley reported differences in the content and direction of written communications among individuals working on a task, depending on instructions given as to how important their functions in the task were and whether there was a chance of changing to a more important function (32).

In Deutsch's investigation of study units meeting for three hours over a six-week period, the main variable was the extent to which the significance of the problem faced was *common* to the individuals of the group (18). Some units were told that their efforts would be evaluated as a unit; others were instructed that individuals would receive grades in terms of their individual contributions. The repeated interaction of subjects over a period of time resulted in greater reciprocity, greater coördination of efforts and differentiation of functions, stronger feelings of mutual obligations, and more effective communication in the units which perceived the task as having common significance for all (coöperative units). In short, when individuals perceived the situation as embodying a common goal, reciprocities developing among them over a period of time tended to take more coördinated and stable form.

In line with field studies and experiments on group formation reported in the preceding chapter, these findings indicate that the significance of tasks and the extent to which this significance is common are crucial factors in patterning communication in groups. As Deutsch's study indicates, common significance of the task is central in the transition from togetherness to stabilization of structure.

Such considerations become crucial in practical work with groups, particularly when the aim is producing alterations in individual behavior in a predictable fashion. Progress in group psychotherapy is conditional to an important extent on the degree to which individual members come to experience belongingness and solidarity with the group (41, 53). Such experiences go hand in hand with interaction in relation to a common problem over a time span. In one study throughout a 12-month period, changes (improvements) in individuals were most marked in groups with common interests and objectives and with high solidarity (38).

Other Factors Affecting Patterns of Interaction

Findings in numerous studies reflect the importance of skills or abilities required by the task for interaction, the particular individuals who gain prominence, and the lines of communication among them (23, 34). For example, Bales and Strodtbeck suggested that interaction goes through different phases in different tasks and problem situations. Thus, the pattern of interaction and communication in one phase shifts as another phase is entered (3). Carter reported differences in interaction among individuals on tasks requiring intellectual efforts and tasks requiring manipulative skills (12).

Previously existing status and role relationships among individuals significantly influence the particular patterns of interaction and communication which begin to take shape in a transitory experimental situation. Bass and Wurster found that differentiation of behavior in discussion groups was highly related to established status ranks of the individuals in a large organization, particularly when the topic of discussion concerned matters relevant to that organization (6, 7). In discussions at a one-day conference attended by persons with varying prestige in the field of mental health (like social workers, teachers, psychologists, nurses, psychiatrists), Hurwitz, Zander, and Hymovitch reported that communication tended more frequently to be directed toward persons of high professional prestige, both by others with high standing and by persons with lower standing in the field (29).

The particular personal characteristics of various individuals elicited in the situation affect the patterns and kind of interaction among them, as shown in Haythorn's study, which systematically varied the individuals taking part in reasoning, mechanical assembly, and discussion tasks (26). Trends in communication among individuals in togetherness situations are also significantly influenced by their personal preferences for each other and the extent to which their interpersonal choices are perceived as reciprocal and relatively stable (19).

Even in a brief period of interaction among persons discussing a specific topic, the relative contributions different individuals make to the discussion and their recognition by others may lead to some consistency in the pattern of communication. A study by Bales et al. of discussions among individuals who met only once indicates such a tendency. Their results are the pooled findings for a number of discussion units. The same trends were not found in each of the transitory discussion units. The basis of ranking was in terms of frequency with which individuals initiated action (discussion). In terms of sheer volume of communication initiated, the individuals with higher rank tended also to receive more communication. These overall findings indicate that communication tends to be directed upward toward those who initiate action more frequently (4).

If the lines of communication, hence of interaction, are arbitrarily restricted by the experimenter to written form and to certain directions among individuals, differentiation of functions in a given task tends to reflect the positions in the prescribed communications network (35). Such imposed communication patterns may tend to speed up a coördinated attack on a problem over that when lines of communication are not restricted. However, the personal contributions of different individuals in insightful coördination toward solution may lead to tendencies differing from the arbitrary lines of communication (25). Thus, arbitrary lines of communication do not guarantee corresponding differentiation of functions, at least in temporary groupings working on a specific task.

Communication Within Group Structures

Investigations of transitory togetherness situations have indicated the importance of a number of factors in the patterning of communication. Among these are the tasks undertaken, their significance to individual participants, previously established status relationships, personal characteristics of the individuals, their impressions and preferences for each other, and the relative contribution various individuals make in the task at hand. When the tasks faced have common significance to individuals and interaction continues over a time span in relation to these tasks, communication becomes more predictable and more coördinated. In short, fluid togetherness situations shade into group reciprocities.

In actual groups, communication among members becomes stabilized in directions and ways reflecting the hierarchical arrangements and reciprocities in the structure. Henceforth, the various situational factors which significantly disrupt, divert, or improve communication in initial phases of interaction operate as affected by the properties of this stabilized structure.

Formation of a status hierarchy tends to polarize communication in the direction of the upper status levels. This is a reflection of the fact that upper status levels carry greater relative weights (power) in initiating action and in decisions concerning the course of action to be taken which stem from other levels of the hierarchy.

Perhaps the earliest manifestation of this polarization of the communication pattern is seen in the overall statistical tendency for communication to be directed toward those individuals in a togetherness situation who initiate most activity in the specific task at hand (4). If individuals in a togetherness situation are differentiated in terms of a hierarchy of prestige in the area under discussion, communication flows toward the higher levels (29).

In the experimental studies of group formation in lifelike conditions reported in the preceding chapter and in Chapter 9 (pp. 287–328), the tendency for communication patterns to stabilize in line with the status hierarchy was observed. As Whyte noted in studying the Street Corner Boys, communication concerning problems of significance to the group was eventually channeled toward the leader. A line of action or a decision made is dependent in the final analysis on at least a "nod" from the leader and is shaped by other members in proportion to their status in the group. Suggestions by low-status members are taken up, possibly in a form modified by those in higher positions, only when the assent of upper-status members is secured (60).

Thus, the patterning of communication in groups is necessarily dependent upon the status relations in the group and its stability is intimately related to the stability of the group structure.

REFERENCES

1. Back, K. W. Influence through social communication, *J. abnorm. & soc. Psychol.* (1951), 46:9–23.
2. Bales, R. F. The Equilibrium Problem in Small Groups, in T. Parsons, R. F. Bales, and E. A. Shils, *Working Papers in the Theory of Action.* Glencoe, Ill.: Free Press, 1953.
3. Bales, R. F., and Strodtbeck, F. L. Phases in group problem solving, *J. abnorm. & soc. Psychol.* (1951), 46:485–495.
4. Bales, R. F., Strodtbeck, F. L., Mills, T. M., and Roseborough, M. E. Channels of communication in small groups, *Amer. sociol. Rev.* (1951), 16:461–468.
5. Bass, B. M. The leaderless group discussion, *Psychol. Bull.* (1954), 51:465–492.
6. Bass, B. M., and Wurster, C. R. Effects of the nature of the problem on LGD performance, *J. appl. Psychol.* (1953), 37:96–99.

7. Bass, B. M., and Wurster, C. R. Effects of company rank on LGD performance, *J. appl. Psychol.* (1953), 37:100–104.
8. Bird, C. *Social Psychology.* New York: Appleton-Century, 1940.
9. Birney, R., and McKeachie, W. The teaching of psychology: A survey of research since 1942, *Psychol. Bull.* (1955), 52:51–68.
10. Bovard, E. W., Jr. Conformity to social norms in stable and temporary groups, *Science* (1953), 117:361–363.
11. Carter, J. H. Military leadership, *Military Rev.* (1952), 32:14–18.
12. Carter, L. F. Leadership and Small Group Behavior, in M. Sherif and M. O. Wilson (eds.), *Group Relations at the Crossroads.* New York: Harper, 1953.
13. Carter, L. F., Haythorn, W., Meirowitz, B., and Lanzetta, J. The relation of categorizations and ratings in the observation of group discussion behavior, *Human Relat.* (1951), 4:239–253.
14. Cartwright, D., and Zander, A. *Group Dynamics.* Evanston, Ill.: Row, Peterson, 1953.
15. Chowdry, K., and Newcomb, T. M. The relative abilities of leaders and non-leaders to estimate opinions of their own groups, *J. abnorm. & soc. Psychol.* (1952), 47:51–57.
16. Cunningham, R., and associates, Leadership and the Group. Reprinted from *Group Dynamics and Education.* Washington: National Education Association, Division of Adult Education, 1948.
17. Dean, Dorothy J. Juvenile delinquency in El Paso, Texas. M.A. thesis, University of Oklahoma, Norman, 1952.
18. Deutsch, M. An experimental study of the effects of cooperation and competition upon group process, *Human Relat.* (1949), 2:199–232.
19. Festinger, L., and Hutte, H. A. An experimental investigation of the effect of unstable interpersonal relations in a group, *J. abnorm. & soc. Psychol.* (1954), 49:513–522.
20. French, J. R. P., Jr. Organized and Unorganized Groups under Fear and Frustration. *University of Iowa Studies in Child Welfare* (1944), 20:229–308.
21. Gibb, C. A. The principles and traits of leadership, *J. abnorm. & soc. Psychol.* (1947), 42:267–284.
22. Gibb, C. A. The sociometry of leadership in temporary groups, *Sociometry* (1950), 13:226–243.
23. Gibb, C. A. Leadership, in G. Lindzey (ed.), *Handbook of Social Psychology.* Cambridge: Addison-Wesley, 1954, Vol. II.
24. Gibb, C. A. An Interactional View of the Emergence of Leadership. Paper read at the Annual Meetings, American Psychological Association, New York City, September, 1954 (mimeographed).
25. Guetzkow, H. Organizational Development and Restrictions in Com-

munication. Pittsburgh: Carnegie Institute of Technology, January, 1954, (mimeographed).

26. Haythorn, W. The influence of individual members on the characteristics of small groups, *J. abnorm. & soc. Psychol.* (1953), 48:276–284.

27. Holbrook, S. H. *Iron Brew, A Century of American Ore and Steel.* New York: Macmillan, 1946.

28. Hollander, E. P. Authoritarianism and leadership choice in a military setting, *J. abnorm. & soc. Psychol.* (1954), 49:365–370.

29. Hurwitz, J. R., Zander, A. F., and Hymovitch, B. Some Effects of Power on the Relations Among Group Members, in D. Cartwright and A. Zander (eds.), *Group Dynamics.* Evanston, Ill.: Row, Peterson, 1953.

30. Jenkins, W. O. A review of leadership studies with particular reference to military problems, *Psychol. Bull.* (1947), 44:54–87.

31. Jennings, H. H. *Leadership and Isolation.* New York: Longmans, Green, 2nd ed., 1950.

32. Kelley, H. H. Communication in experimentally created hierarchies, *Human Relat.* (1951), 4:39–56.

33. Kelley, H. H., and Shapiro, M. M. Conformity to group norms, *Amer. sociol. Rev.* (1954), 19:667–677.

34. Kelley, H. H., and Thibaut, J. W. Experimental Studies of Group Problem Solving and Process, in G. Lindzey (ed.), *Handbook of Social Psychology.* Cambridge: Addison-Wesley, 1954, Vol. II.

35. Leavitt, H. J. Some effects of certain communication patterns on group performance, *J. abnorm. & soc. Psychol.* (1951), 46:38–50.

36. Lewin, K., Lippitt, R., and White, R. K. An Experimental Study of Leadership and Group Life, in G. E. Swanson, T. M. Newcomb, and E. L. Hartley (eds.), *Readings in Social Psychology.* New York: Holt, rev. ed., 1952.

37. Lippitt, R., Polansky, N., and Rosen, S. The dynamics of power, *Human Relat.* (1952), 5:37–64.

38. Malone, T. P. Analysis of the dynamics of group psychotherapy based on observation in a twelve-month experimental program, *J. Personal.* (1948), 16:245–272.

39. March, J. G. Group norms and the active minority, *Amer. sociol. Rev.* (1954), 19:733–740.

40. Merei, F. Group leadership and institutionalization, *Human Relat.* (1949), 2:23–39.

41. Moreno, J. L. *Who Shall Survive?* Beacon, N.Y.: Beacon, rev. ed., 1953.

42. Norfleet, B. Interpersonal relations and group productivity, *J. soc. Issues* (1948), 4:66–69.

43. O.S.S. Assessment Staff, *Assessment of Men.* New York: Rinehart, 1948.

44. Pelz, D. C. Leadership within a hierarchical organization, *J. soc. Issues* (1951), 7:49–55.

45. Polansky, N., Lippitt, R., and Redl, F. An investigation of behavioral contagion in groups, *Human Relat.* (1950), 3:319–348.
46. Riecken, H. W., and Homans, G. C. Psychological Aspects of Social Structure, in G. Lindzey (ed.), *Handbook of Social Psychology*. Cambridge: Addison-Wesley, 1954, Vol. II.
47. Rodhafer, I. A. Gangdom—fists to reasoning, *J. educat. Sociol.* (1949), 22:406–415.
48. Roseborough, M. E. Experimental studies of small groups, *Psychol. Bull.* (1953), 50:275–303.
49. Sanford, F. H. *Authoritarianism and Leadership*. Philadelphia: Institute of Research in Human Relations, 1950.
50. Schachter, S. Deviation, rejection and communication, *J. abnorm. & soc. Psychol.* (1951), 46:190–207.
51. Scott, E. L. *Status Expectations and Organizational Behavior*. Columbus: The Ohio State University Research Foundation, 1953.
52. Sherif, M., and Sherif, C. W. Effects of power relations in molding opinion and behavior, *Southwest. soc. sci. Quart.* (1953), 33:287–296.
53. Slavson, S. R. *Introduction to Group Therapy*. New York: Commonwealth Fund, 1943.
54. Stogdill, R. M. Personal factors associated with leadership, *J. Psychol.* (1948), 25:35–71.
55. Stogdill, R. M. Leadership, membership and organization, *Psychol. Bull.* (1950), 47:1–14.
56. Strodtbeck, F. L., and Hare, A. P. Bibliography of small group research, *Sociometry* (1954), 17:107–178.
57. Talland, G. A. The assessment of group opinion by leaders and their influence on its formation, *J. abnorm. & soc. Psychol.* (1954), 49:431–434.
58. Thrasher, F. *The Gang*. Chicago: University of Chicago Press, 1927.
59. Toki, K. The leader-follower structure in the school class, *Jap. J. Psychol.* (1935), 10:27–56; English summary in E. L. Hartley and R. E. Hartley, *Fundamentals of Social Psychology*. New York: Knopf, 1952.
60. Whyte, W. F. *Street Corner Society*. Chicago: University of Chicago Press, 1943.
61. Whyte, W. F. *Human Relations in the Restaurant Industry*. New York: McGraw-Hill, 1948.
62. Whyte, W. F. The Changing Nature of Political Leadership, in A. W. Gouldner (ed.), *Studies in Leadership*. New York: Harper, 1950.

CHAPTER **8**

The Formation of Social Norms

During interaction among individuals in pursuit of life and its better-
ment, a group structure takes shape. The individuals take on different functions. Each acquires a relative status. A routine and rules for the conduct of
affairs are stabilized. Routines, rules, standards of conduct, values to uphold are thus by-products of group interaction. Such a superstructure of
rules, standards, and values is referred to generically as the social norms
of the group.

It is hardly possible to discuss group formation and functioning without
discussing their products. Therefore, group norms figured prominently in
our dealing with status relationships, leadership, and group functioning. In
this chapter the characterization of social norms given in Chapter 5 is further elaborated. After that we will be concerned chiefly with the formation
of social norms. A number of experiments and observations of norm formation in actual life illustrate this problem.

This chapter concentrates on the formation of norms for two principal
reasons. First, the nature of social norms can be grasped best by examining
their origins. Second, through the study of norm formation we can glimpse
the process through which the individual acquires standards, values, and
aspirations whose origins are social. One part-process of norm formation is
necessarily the formation of attitudes by the individuals participating.

Through participation in the formation of group norms, individual members take part in the production of new values, new goals, new ideals. The
individual acquires personally experienced motives which are truly social in
origin. To the new group member, social norms are initially external. They
are revealed in so many concrete stimulus situations during group interaction.

No matter what urgent pursuits brought individuals into interaction or
led them into an existing group, they form new motives as they become

functioning members of a group structure with particular norms. Men come into industrial plants primarily to earn a living for themselves and their families. If they are paid rates for each piece of work with a bonus for production above a certain level, it would seem that they would work and strive to produce as much as possible, within limits of their physical capacity and health. However, the worker in this situation finds himself in an informal work group. He soon learns from the others that one does not produce above a certain amount, even if he can. There is a social norm governing production output; the good member of the group keeps his production within a certain range, as governed by the norm (12, 29). If he does not, he will receive notice from others, in the form of comments, warnings, standardized physical annoyance (see "binging," p. 173), or ostracism by the group members. Those who persist in ignoring the group norm for production are the ones who do not relate themselves to the informal work groups. In other words, the "rate busters" do not take the work group as their reference group. Typically, they are either "lone wolves" in the factory and community or are hard set on moving upward in the social scheme (12).

The fact that the production norm in informal working groups may be below a feasible ceiling for production does not indicate that group norms usually bring a "leveling effect." In the case of this norm, there are reasons why adherence may result in lower production than is feasible for some individuals. This stems from the conviction, formed in many cases through experiences, that if the particular range set by the norm is exceeded the pay rates will be cut (31).

The social norms of the group make explicit a bottom and a ceiling for aspirations of individual members. They constitute a reference scale for the aspirations and experiences of failure or success of individual members. In any particular case, the limits of this reference scale may be above or below the realistic attainment possible by individual members. For example, a certain person may join a social club whose members are somewhat above him in social position and wealth and are doing their best to move up the ladder still further. For this individual, "keeping up with the Joneses" may be an almost impossible task. He will experience continuing feelings of frustration and failure, even though his goal was once simply to be a member of this elite crowd.

In contrast, young married couples in a housing development for young business executives who are moving upward, but are still at a critical stage in achieving financial and social success, may stabilize a norm of "keeping *down* with the Joneses." Then if the man with the financial means wants a fancy new car or a special kind of fence around his lawn, he has to face the disapproval of the other people living in his court of the housing development. Considerable sympathy is extended to people who do not yet have the means to acquire all of the usual home furnishings and automatic appliances. But the person who buys a Lincoln car, paints his garage fire-engine red where others are white, or puts up an elaborate fence is running the risk of being considered a person with "poor judgment" and no sense of "timing" by others in his court (48). In the particular housing development studied, the norms for appropriate household furnishings, decorations, automobiles, clothing, maintenance of privacy, and the like varied from court to court. The court unit tended to set the boundaries for interaction in the rather homogeneous population of young executives and their families.

The reference scale of aspirations and goals established by the social norms of a group regulates behavior in relation to satisfying biogenic motives as well. Just any edible substances will not do to satisfy hunger under normal circumstances. The individual satisfies his special personal tastes and regulates his longings within the bounds of those foodstuffs deemed edible, nourishing, or desirable in his particular group settings.

Consider the established norms for sexual strivings of the Corner Boys in the Italian slum area which Whyte studied (49). Women were classified by these boys in terms of their desirability along several dimensions. For each category, there were striking differences in behavior. The categories were continually being made explicit in both action and discussion. Various girls were discussed periodically in terms of their current place on these reference scales. Here is Whyte's scheme showing the categories and the scale for each, with the most desirable position at the top of each category:

Sex Experience	Physical Attractiveness	Social- and Ethnic-Group Position
1. "Good girls"	Beautiful	1. Superior groups
2. "Lays"		
(a) One-man girls	to	2. Italian nonslum
(b) Promiscuous		
(c) Prostitutes	ugly	3. Italian slum

The girls at the top of these scales were also the most inaccessible to the boys. Every Corner Boy knew that if he even called on a "good girl," her family would assume he intended to marry her. He could only dream about a blonde representative of respectability and wealth, because he had few means to meet or court her. A "good girl" was the type he wanted to marry eventually, and he could be respectful to her to the point of severe personal frustration. Whyte relates an incident in which a "good girl" became intoxicated and encouraged some boys. Even though she was inviting in that condition, they took her home and thus preserved her "good girl" standing. One of the same boys, however, felt no compunction at all about cheating a prostitute out of her fee. The prohibition of intimacy with a relative of a fellow clique member was also noted in summarizing the Corner Boy study (p. 188).

GROUP NORMS ARE SOCIAL PRODUCTS

A necessary condition for the formation of group norms is interaction of individuals with common motives or problems over a time span. One person cannot form a social norm all by himself. Since group norms are products of interaction, the concept is a sociological designation.

Social norms refer to any criteria of experience and behavior formed in group interaction which regulate the behavior of individual members in relevant stimulus situations. Since social norms are formed by individuals interacting in groups, the terms "social norm" and "group norm" may be used interchangeably. (Some authors use the term "group standard.") At some time in past or recent history social norms evolved in some specific group interaction. When that group and its membership can be specified, group norm is the more accurate term since it makes explicit the relationship between behavioral criteria and group membership.

As characterized here, social norm is a generic term, covering a host of products of past and contemporary group interaction. Among these are social values, standards, customs, traditions, mores, folkways, rules, fads, and fashions. However, referring to these various social products generically does not imply that they are identical. Entire books have been written about various kinds of social norms. When a social psychologist deals specifically with, say, fads or fashions as contrasted with more lasting mores or folkways, the first task is gaining intimate acquaintance with empirical findings on this topic on a sociological level of analysis. Detailed accounts of such social products are far beyond the scope of this book.

Social norms of any description represent standardized generalizations concerning expected behavior in matters of consequence to the group or groups in question. In other words, social norms represent one particular kind of *concepts*. Like all concepts, norms refer to groupings or classes of items. They do not usually refer to just one behavior for one specific situation. A concept denotes a generalization encompassing a range of items with more or less clear limits.

The feature distinguishing norms from concepts in general is their *evaluative* nature, as evident in the examples mentioned earlier. Social norms incorporate value judgments pertaining to a range of items. They imply evaluations of modes of behavior relative to persons, objects, or situations. Specifically, norms refer to expected or even ideal behavior in matters of some importance to the group.

Norms are not formed by all groups in relation to every kind of behavior and every possible situation. They are formed in matters of consequence to the group in question. Just what matters are consequential to a given group varies, in terms of the main purposes and goals of group functioning, the relationship of the group to other groups in society, and other conditions in which it operates. Ordinarily the relationships among members and the unity and continued existence of the group as a social unit are consequential to any group.

The scope of behavior regulated by norms varies considerably in different groups. For example, the norms of most Protestant churches in America today pertain chiefly to ethical matters. However, some sects, like certain Mennonite groups, have norms covering a much broader area of life, including apparel, modes of transportation, forms of entertainment, schools, and so on.

The average behavior of members in a group may or may not coincide with that denoted by its norms at any given period in its history. In fact, certain norms may set such a high level for desirable conduct that average behavior of members could approach it only at exceptional times. Nevertheless, the degree of adherence to major group norms by members is *one* index of solidarity in the group. When the behavior of members begins to diverge consistently from the bounds implied by group norms, it is safe to predict significant changes in group functioning. The nature of such changes depends, of course, on other factors. It may be that as a result of external conditions or internal frictions the group is in the process of disintegration. Or changed conditions facing a group may lead to weakening its norms and to the formation of new norms more congruent with the new conditions. In modern differentiated societies, the degree of adherence to norms in a particular group is affected by the fact that members frequently belong to a number of groups. These various groups may have conflicting or even contradictory norms. Therefore, the degree of adherence to norms in one group may be in part a function of the extent to which norms of other reference groups of the membership are congruent with them.

When informally organized groups function over a period of time, norms become formalized and may even be written down as rules, regulations, and laws. Analysis of formalized norms and legal regulations in large social organizations has to begin by specifying the different groups functioning within the larger structure, their norms, and the power relations among those groups most influential in establishing the laws and in enforcing them. Large organizations today are seldom composed of just one group encompassing all individuals, although this might still be the case in relatively small, isolated societies. As a recent analysis of French governmental structure indicates, persons within such a structure may be members of groups with widely differing norms and interests (15).

"Conformity" and "Deviation" Imply the Existence of Norms

Not all behavior of human individuals is regulated by social norms. As noted in Chapter 5, the existence of norms is inferred from two general sorts of behavior: conforming behavior, on one hand, and deviation or nonconformity, on the other (pp. 170–175).

The terms "conformity" and "deviation" (nonconformity) imply two definite conditions. First, they both imply the existence of some standard or norm in terms of which particular behavior is evaluated. Second, they both imply membership in a social group which possesses the norm in question.

It is obvious that an individual's behavior can be characterized as "conforming" or "nonconforming" only in relation to a relevant standard or norm for the behavior in question. Furthermore, "conformity" and "deviation" are meaningful characterizations of behavior only when the individual whose behavior is in question is a member of a group possessing the norm. It would be absurd to speak of a Methodist who refrains from dipping his fingers in holy water at a Catholic church as a "nonconformist" or "deviate."

Therefore, it is seldom feasible to refer in an overall way to the conformity or deviation of a large population for a particular social norm. Most large populations, like modern nations, are composed of diverse groups with different or even contradictory norms in some respects. Of course, some norms will be common to all groups in the general culture.

But the meaningful analysis of conformity to social norms in such large populations starts by referring specific norms to membership in specific groups. What appears at first sight to be deviation by large sections of a population or "patterned evasion" may in fact be conformity to other norms by members of groups who are at an advantage in the power structure at the time (50).

For example, a legal regulation exists in the state of Oklahoma today prohibiting the sale of intoxicating beverages. "Patterned evasion" or deviation from this legal norm exists. However, a recent referendum and continuing agitation for enforcement indicate that the law in question represents a functioning norm for a considerable portion of the population. This part of the population has identifiable group memberships. Certain other organized groups support the law for reasons related to their own interests. Widespread and continuing deviation from legal norms becomes possible when groups within the population do not possess the norm and when the membership of these groups is in a position to influence enforcement processes.

Typical examples of conforming behavior which reveal a group norm may be observed in functioning group units. Members of youthful gangs in New York City in the nineteenth century were identifiable through their conformity in matters of dress. The "Shirt Tails" all wore their shirts outside of their trousers. The "Plug Uglies" adopted large plug hats which they stuffed with wool and leather and drew down over their ears during fights. Some gangs wore stripes of a certain color on their trousers (3). The recent "zoot-suit" styles and their modifications are well known. However, the clothes of one youthful gang called the "Cougars" were chosen to resemble those of a Harvard undergraduate as closely as possible. "Sharp" styles were "out" in this group (21).

When workers taking part in a strike refuse to participate in the services of their church because a nonstriker is present, or when "strikebreakers" are ignored by people they have known for years, it can be inferred that a group norm formed in previous or current strikes is regulating behavior toward those who do not take part (18).

Other examples of conformity to group norms can be observed in fraternity or sorority houses on a college campus. These norms include a "dating hierarchy" which establishes in that particular group the most and least desirable kind of dates in terms of an individual's affiliations and extrinsic characteristics.

Clemmer made an extensive study of life in a large penitentiary and showed how the prison "code" governed communication among prisoners, treatment of fellow prisoners and officials, methods of satisfying sexual deprivations, and the like (9). Within the prison community hundreds of informal group structures were found, each with more distinctive norms. A significant finding of this study was that the individual's adjustment to prison life was highly related to the extent to which he took the norms of the prison community and informal groups within it as personal guides for behavior. A few individuals maintained strong ties and psychological reference to groups and persons outside of prison walls. When this was not possible, the men who could not accept the prison code as their "own" were the ones who suffered most personal difficulties and disorganization.

Both conformity and deviation are relative to a range of tolerable behavior implied in a group norm. While conformity refers to behavior within this range, deviation implies that the behavior is at or beyond the limits of a range of tolerable behavior in the group. In short, deviation is not simply variation in behavior. It is variation of a type characterized by other group members as "unwise," "threatening," "dangerous," or even "disloyal" or "traitorous."

A particular behavior is deviant in relation to the range of behavior implicit in relevant group norms. In functioning groups, the presence of nonconformity or deviation from norms of any consequence to the group is recognized and controlled as much as possible through *sanctions* (pp. 170–173). Standardized sanctions are also used to reward achievement and lines of action in approved directions. Examples of deviation and sanctions imposed by group members were noted in the discussion of Whyte's Street Corner Boys and the Bull Dogs and Red Devils in Chapter 6.

Gist's survey of secret societies in the United States indicates that when rules and regulations are formalized and written down, deviation and its penalties are also formalized for the membership (17). He lists 24 rather specific types of behavior which are defined as beyond the range of tolerable behavior taken from the regulations of 10 representative "secret" societies. Such behavior results in reprimand, fines, suspension, or even threat of expulsion for the member involved. Many societies grant the right of trial by fellow members.

If the aims of a secret society run counter to those of organized society, total secrecy becomes essential to preservation of the group. Therefore, deeds revealing group members and activities to outsiders may be punished with violent or even fatal means by the membership (36). The same is true in criminal gangs. Both the adherence to norms required of the membership and the severity of penalties for deviation are related to the serious-ness of such deviation for other members and the group as a whole.

GROUP NORMS AND INDIVIDUAL BEHAVIOR

As noted above, variations in behavior are not identical with deviation. Since they represent standardized generalizations, group norms typically pertain to a range of behavior varying in scope according to the importance of a particular norm in the group's scheme of things. Ranges or scales of tolerable behavior also differ from group to group. Behavior is reacted to as deviant when it approaches or exceeds the limits of the range of toler-able behavior.

A number of factors contribute to variability of behavior from individ-ual to individual in groups. Group norms are not the only factors influenc-ing a person's behavior at a given time. Typically, norms function as anchorages among the interrelated influences shaping experience and be-havior of group members. But this does not mean that the other influences can be ignored. In given situations, other factors may acquire greater weight. For example, a strong personal motive or compelling external con-ditions may be dominant at a given time.

Individual differences in abilities, in temperament, in past experience, in motivations operate in any situation to produce variability in behavior. Such individual differences also lead to differing perceptions and reactions to social norms. In addition, within a group structure different expecta-tions for behavior are stabilized for the various statuses and roles. As noted in discussing leadership, the range of tolerable behavior and thus the varia-tion permissible in matters pertaining to group norms differs at various status levels (pp. 217–219).

In modern differentiated societies, considerable variation in behavior of group members stems from their membership in and psychological ref-erence to other groups. That is, a particular individual has multiple group memberships. His various reference groups may have differing and even conflicting norms governing the same areas of behavior. As Stouffer has suggested, in differentiated societies where the individual functions as a member of various groups, knowledge of the range of behavior permissible in different groups and the extent of overlapping among these ranges is essential for understanding individual behavior in one particular group (40).

The solidarity, continued existence, and preservation of a group require that variation in matters of consequence fall within the range prescribed by its norms. Sanctions are the principal means for controlling behavior of members who get too far out of line. But in spite of factors leading to variability of behavior, members of groups with some stability and solidarity do not have to be brought into line through the constant exercise of overt rewards and punishments. The bulk of membership of an organized group which tends toward stability rather than disintegration regulates experience and behavior in terms of group norms and willingly upholds them. Overt pressures or coercion toward conformity are exceptional rather than usual in group life, unless solidarity is at low ebb.

The problems touched upon above are dealt with in some detail under the headings of attitude formation, ego-involvements, and reference groups in later chapters. They are mentioned here to emphasize their relevance to the formation of group norms. In the formation of norms the process of attitude formation by individuals, the attainment of psychological relatedness to social products, and the achievement of autonomous conformity are seen in clearest form.

Social Norms Are Initially External to the Individual

To a growing child or a new member of an organized group, norms are at first external and are revealed through the actions and words of other people. Awareness or knowledge of norms does not lead automatically to regulation of behavior by them.

Studies of children by Piaget and others (28, 32) have shown that young children first respond to the dicta of adults and rules of play set by older children in much the same way that they respond to physical restraints. Moral dicta and rules are external stimuli which the child responds to and regards in a rather absolute fashion. Although he lapses from them under the grip of momentary desire or in the flux of fantasy, they tend to be regarded as final and inflexible, resting on the authority of Mommy or Daddy. However, as the child matures and as he interacts with other children, he grasps the notion of reciprocity with others. Interaction in reciprocal relationships makes possible coöperative activities and coördination of individual efforts.

In the process of reciprocal interaction, the child comes to see rules or norms as based on mutual agreements. He finds that they can be changed and that new rules can be made. When he begins to take part in the process of changing and making rules himself, they truly become his "own" rules by which he abides through *inner autonomy*. Thus, the crucial condition for willing, autonomous, and even enthusiastic internalization of social norms is participation in reciprocal interactions with other people.

THE PROBLEM OF NORM FORMATION

In the process of group formation, norms are standardized as common property of the developing group. Sociological findings on groups of many descriptions reveal this fact. Thrasher's studies of youthful gangs are an example (41). It was observed in the experiment on group formation reported in Chapter 6.

Once a set of norms arises for matters of consequence to a group, it provides reference scales for action, strivings, and aspirations of group members. These norms are products of interaction. They cannot be predicted from the behavior of one individual, although various individuals contribute differentially to their formation. They cannot be predicted by getting an average of individual standards prior to the interaction in which they are produced.

Many sociologists recognized the fact that social norms are emergent products of group interaction. For example, in his *Elementary Forms of Religious Life*, Durkheim made a strong theoretical point of the rise of "collective representations" in interaction situations and their effects on the experience and outlook of individuals (13). But Durkheim and other sociologists went on to draw a dividing line between individual psychology and social psychology, and restricted the appearance of emergent properties to behavior in group situations. From that point of view, it would follow that to explain the behavior of individuals in group interaction altogether different and new principles would be necessary.

Now it is true that the properties of an interaction situation cannot be extrapolated from the properties of an individual's behavior. But it is quite another thing to say that individual behavior in an interaction situation requires altogether new psychological principles from behavior in other situations.

As we saw in Chapters 2 and 3, the emergence of new properties in experience and behavior is found even in the simple perception of form, melody, rhythm, and in judgments of distance, length, or weight. Such differential effects occur whenever a salient new reference point or anchorage enters into the frame of reference, which consists of functionally interrelated factors at a given time (pp. 62–64).

New psychological principles are not required to explain the emergent properties of behavior in group interaction. It is necessary, however, to bring the unique properties of the interaction process into the explanation.

For this reason, the systematic study of norm formation from a social psychological viewpoint starts with the problem of the ways individuals react alone in relation to a given stimulus situation, then goes on to study the effects of the interaction process with its unique properties.

The next step is to determine the characteristic of situations in which norms are formed. Social norms are formed in matters and situations in which there are alternatives for experience and behavior. This sounds like a truism, and it should. However, it brings into the problem the question of the degree of structure of the external stimulus situations, which was discussed at some length in Chapter 3 (pp. 97–106).

When the objective characteristics of external situations are clear-cut, individual reactions to them vary comparatively little. A circle or a normal human hand is perceived in similar ways by different individuals. There are compelling objective conditions and situations which limit alternatives in experience and behavior of various individuals.

In such compelling situations, anchorages in the external stimulus field will play an important role in structuring experience and behavior of individuals and in the normative concepts of interacting individuals (43). In a later chapter, we shall see numerous examples of the decisive effects of anchorages stemming from technological conditions on the psychological processes of individuals who face and use them (Chapter 20). For example, the social norms and the experience of individuals pertaining to wealth and poverty are affected by the actual range of wealth in their environment. Social norms pertaining to behavior in automobiles are not formed by individuals who know no means of transportation but the oxcart.

Group norms are typically formed in conditions which are unstructured in some or many aspects. If the particular situation or that aspect which is not clear-cut relates to a major concern of the group, particular alternatives for behavior selected through interaction among individuals are stabilized for the group. The complexity of social life provides many situations in which various alternative ways of behaving are possible. To the extent that these alternatives are limited by objective factors, to that extent objective factors enter into norm formation. Within the available alternatives, the stabilization of preferred or desirable ones is determined more heavily by the interaction process among individuals, their stabilized relations and goals, their motives, their past experiences, including knowledge about various alternatives and their consequences.

It follows that norm formation, and particularly the effects of the properties of interaction in this process, can be observed most clearly when the objective stimulus situation lacks in objective structure. The less the contribution of external factors, the greater the effects of the unique interaction process, of internal factors aroused by the interaction and by the stimulus situation. As noted above, it does not follow that all social norms are formed in situations which lack objective structure.

NORM FORMATION IN THE LABORATORY

The experiment to be reported in this section was carried out by M. Sherif to test empirical observations concerning norm formation and its effects on perception and judgment of individuals in a laboratory setting (33, 34). On the basis of the considerations outlined in the last section, a stimulus situation lacking in objective structure was chosen. The experiment was planned so that reactions by individuals before, during, and following interaction with others could be obtained and compared.

The first problem raised was: What will an individual do when he is asked to make judgments of an aspect of a stimulus situation which lacks objective structure, so that a basis of comparison in the external stimulus field is absent? Will he give a hodgepodge of erratic judgments? Or will he establish some standard of his own? By answering these questions first, the tendency of the individual could be determined and then compared with his behavior during and following interaction.

The next problem was, therefore: What will a number of individuals do in this same situation? Will the different individuals give a hodgepodge of judgments? Or will every person establish his own standard? Or will a common norm be established for the various individuals peculiar to the particular interaction and dependent upon the particular individuals and their influence upon one another? If during the course of interaction the judgments of individuals converge within a certain range and toward a modal point, we could say they have formed a common norm (standard) in their judgments of that particular situation.

It is possible, however, that such convergence may be due simply to immediate social pressure to adjust to the judgments spoken aloud by other individuals in the situation. Therefore, if it is shown that the common range and modal point established in interaction are maintained by the individual on a different day, when he is alone, then we can say that the norm formed in interaction with others has become his own norm.

The Autokinetic Effect; Its Possibilities for Our Problem

With these considerations in mind, the first task was to find a situation that was unstructured in some respect. From among other possible experimental situations that could be used, the autokinetic situation was chosen for this particular series of experiments.

The conditions that produce the autokinetic effect afford an excellent experimental situation. We can easily get the autokinetic effect. In complete darkness, as in a closed unlighted room, or on a cloudy night in the open when there are no lights visible, a single small light seems to move, and it may appear to move erratically in all directions. If you present the point of light repeatedly to a person, he may see the light appearing in different places in the room each time, especially if he does not know the distance between himself and the light.

The experimental production of the autokinetic effect is very easy and works without exceptions, *provided, of course, that the person or the experimenter does not use special devices to destroy the effect.* For in a completely dark room a single point of light cannot be localized definitely. There is nothing in reference to which one can locate it. The effect takes place even when the person looking at the light knows perfectly well that the light is not moving. These are facts which are not subject to controversy; anyone can easily test them for himself.

In this situation not only does the stimulating light appear erratic and irregular to the subject, but *at times the person himself feels insecure about his spatial bearing.* This comes out in an especially striking way if he is seated in a chair without a back and is unfamiliar with the position of the experimental room in the building. Under these conditions some subjects report that not only are they confused about the location of the point of light; *they are even confused about the stability of their own position.*

The autokinetic effect is not a new artificial phenomenon invented by psychologists. It is older than experimental psychology. Since it sometimes appears in the observation of the heavenly bodies, the astronomers had already noticed it and offered theories to explain it. A concise history of the autokinetic effect as a scientific problem was given by Adams (1). Several theories have been advanced by psychologists to explain the nature of the autokinetic effect. Recent studies have indicated rather clearly that it is not due merely to eye movements or other peripheral factors but is centrally determined (e.g., 10).

The study of the extent of movement experienced permits a quantitative index for the approach to the formation of norms. Therefore, this study reports on the extent of movement.

Procedures

The extent of movement experienced was studied in two situations: when the individual was alone, except for the experimenter, in order to get the reaction of the individual unaffected by other experimentally introduced social factors and thus to gain a basic notion about the perceptual process under the circumstances; and when the individual was together with others, in order to discover modifications brought about by interaction among individuals.

The subject was introduced into the group situation in one of two ways: He was brought into an interaction situation *after* being experimented upon when *alone*; this was done to find out the influence of interaction after he had had an opportunity to react to the situation first in accordance with his own tendencies. Or he was first introduced to the situation along with other individuals, having no previous familiarity with the situation, and was afterwards experimented upon individually; this was done to find out whether any norm or standard which might be established in interaction with others would continue to determine his reaction to the same situation when he faced it alone. This last point is crucial for our problem. The others lead up to it and clarify its implications.

The experiments were carried on in dark rooms in the Columbia psychological laboratory (see Fig. 8.1). The subjects were graduate and undergraduate male students at Columbia University and New York University. They were not majoring in psychology and did not know anything about the physical stimulus setup or the purpose of the experiment. There were 19 subjects in the individual experiments; 40 took part in the group experiments.

Individual Experiments

The stimulus light was a tiny point of light seen through a small hole in a metal box. The light was exposed to the subject by the opening of a suitable shutter controlled by the experimenter. The distance between the subject and the light was five meters. The observer was seated at a table on which was a telegraph key. The following instructions were given in written form:

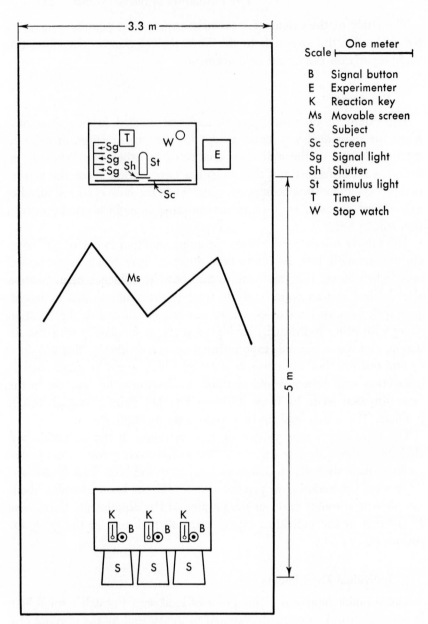

FIG. 8.1. Plan of the experimental room used in group experiments.

When the room is completely dark, I shall give you the signal READY, and then show you a point of light. After a short time the light will start to move. As soon as you see it move, press the key. A few seconds later the light will disappear. Then tell me the distance it moved. Try to make your estimates as accurate as possible.

These instructions summarize the general procedure for the experiment. (See Figures 8.1 and 8.2 for the experimental setup.) The exposure time

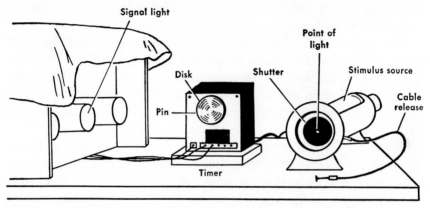

Fɪɢ. 8.2. Drawing of apparatus used in autokinetic experiments in 1934–1935 (point of light, timer, signal system.)

after the subject pressed the key to indicate that he had begun to experience the movement was two seconds in all cases. The light was physically stationary during the entire time; it was not moved at all during any of the experiments.

After the light had disappeared, the subject reported orally the distance through which he thought it had moved. One hundred judgments were obtained from each subject. The subjects reported their estimates in inches (or fractions of inches).

The results unequivocally indicate that when individuals perceive movements which lack any other standard of comparison *they subjectively establish a range of extent (a scale) and a point (a standard or norm) within that range which is peculiar to the individual.* The ranges and standards or norms established by the various individuals differ.

In other words, when individuals repeatedly perceive movement with no objective basis for gauging its extent, there develops within them during the course of successive presentations a standard (a norm or reference point). This subjectively established standard or norm serves as a reference point with which each successive experienced movement is compared and judged—short, long, or medium—within the range peculiar to the subject.

To express the same point more generally, we conclude that, in the absence of an objective range or scale of stimuli and an externally given reference point or standard, each individual builds up a range of his own and an internal reference point within that range. Each successive judgment is given within that range and in relation to that reference point. The range (scale) and reference point established by each individual are peculiar to him when he is experimented upon alone.

In a second series of individual experiments it was found that, once a range and point of reference within that range are established by an individual, there is a tendency to preserve them on subsequent days. A second and third series of 100 judgments each show a median for a given subject very similar to that found in the first series, but with a reduced variability.

The written reports obtained from every subject at the end of the experiment corroborate these conclusions. Reports of the following sort, which are typical, show that the subjects at first found it hard to estimate distance because of the lack of externally given reference points or standards:

"Darkness left no guide for distance."

"It was difficult to estimate the distance the light moved, because of the lack of visible neighboring objects."

"There was no fixed point from which to judge distance."

Other observations indicate that the subjects developed standards of their own in the absence of the objective ones:

"Compared with previous distance."

"Used first estimate as standard."

These findings reveal once more the general psychological tendency to experience things in relation to some reference point or standard, as we noted in reviewing evidence of this tendency in various functions in Chapter 2 (pp. 40–51).

Following the individual experiments, these findings of experimental psychology were carried into social psychology by noting the individual's reactions when in an interaction situation with others.

Group Experiments

On the basis of the results, the problem studied in the group experiments becomes self-evident. To recapitulate, the individual experiences the external field of stimulation in relation to anchorages within the frame of reference of factors operating at the time. When such an anchorage or reference point is given in the objective situation, it will usually determine in an important way the structural relationships of the experience. All other parts are organized as modified by it. But when objective anchorages are lacking—when the field of stimulation is unstable, vague, and not well structured—the individual perceives the situation as shaped by his own internally evolved standards or anchorages.

The process is reduced here to a very simple form; but the first fundamental problem is the way an individual perceives a stimulus situation. His behavior follows upon this perception rather than upon the simple fact of stimulation. There is no direct and simple correlation between the stimulus and subsequent behavior, especially on the level of behavior with which we are dealing. A simple perceptual situation is the first requirement for experimental analysis of the problem.

A stimulus situation was chosen purposely in which the external factors were unstable enough to allow the internal and social factors to dominate, within limits, in establishing the main characteristics of organization. In this way we can say that any consistent result in the experience of individuals in an interaction situation which differs from their experience as isolated individuals is a function of their interaction with others.

As we have seen, individuals do not face stimulus situations involving other people in an indifferent way. They are charged with certain modes of readiness, certain motives or attitudes which enter to modify their reactions. This important consideration shaped the plan of the group experiments. Reactions were compared (1) when the individuals first faced the stimulus situation with others, and (2) when they first established their individual ranges and norms alone and then joined others. Accordingly, 20 of the subjects began alone and were put into groups in subsequent experimental sessions; the other 20 started with group sessions and ended with individual sessions.

This rotation technique enabled us to draw conclusions regarding the following important questions:

How much of his independently established way of reacting to this situation does the individual carry over when facing the same stimulus along with others?

How will he experience the situation when he is alone after a common range and norm have been established peculiar to the interaction situation in which he participated? Will the common product developed in interaction serve as a determining factor when he subsequently faces the same situation *alone?*

The experimental setting was in general the same as in the individual experiments. Of course, additional devices were necessary to handle two or more individuals at the same time. One major addition was the use of signal lights. The experimenter could not tell from the voice who was giving a judgment; so as each subject gave his judgment aloud, he pressed a button connected with a dim signal light of a particular color by which the experimenter might identify who the speaker was (see Figs. 8.1 and 8.2).

There were eight groups of two subjects each and eight groups of three subjects each. Four groups in each of the categories started with the individual situation and then functioned in interaction. Four groups in each category started in group situations for the first three sessions on three different days (all members being present) and were then broken up and studied in individual situations.

In order to make the relation of individuals to one another as natural as possible, within the limits of the experimental setting, the subjects were left free as to the order in which they would give their judgments. In fact, they were told at the start to give their judgments in random order as they pleased. Whether the person who speaks first has more influence than the others becomes a study in leadership, which is a further interesting problem.

From the examination of the results, we can say that the reporting of the judgments has a gradual cumulative effect. Aside from whatever influence the first judgment may have on the second or third, the judgments of the third individual at a given presentation affect the subsequent judgments of the first subject in the round of presentations following. Thus the production of an established group influence is largely a temporal affair and not the outcome of this or that single presentation. We shall refer to this point again later.

Besides the quantitative judgments obtained, the subjects were asked at the end of each session to write down their observations. Questions were asked which aimed at finding out whether they became conscious of the range and norm they were establishing. These questions were: "Between what maximum and minimum did the distances vary?" "What was the most frequent distance that the light moved?"

Summary of Results

Certain facts stand out clearly from the results, and may be summarized in a few paragraphs.

1. When an individual faces a stimulus situation which is unstable and not structured in itself, he establishes a range and a norm (a reference point) within that range. The range and norm that are developed in each individual are peculiar to that individual and may vary from the ranges and norms developed by other individuals in different degrees, revealing consistent and stable individual differences.

2. When the person who develops a range and a norm within that range independently is put into a situation together with others who also enter the situation with their own ranges and norms established in their own individual sessions, the ranges and norms of the various individuals tend to converge. But this convergence is not so close as that which occurs when the subjects first work together and have less opportunity to set up stable individual norms. (See left-hand graphs, Figs. 8.3 and 8.4.)

3. When individuals face the same unstable, unstructured situation together for the first time, a range and a norm (standard) within that range are established which are peculiar to the group. If, for the group, there is a rise or fall in the norms established in successive sessions, it is a group effect. The norms of the various individuals rise and fall toward a common norm in each session. (See the second and fourth graphs of the three subject groups in Fig. 8.4.)

To this conclusion the objection may be raised that one subject may lead and be uninfluenced by other members of the interaction situation. The social norm may be simply the leader's norm. To this the only possible empirical reply is that in the experiments the leaders were constantly observed to be influenced by their followers—if not at the moment, then later in the series and in subsequent series. Although the objection has occasional force, the statement regarding social norms is in general true. Even if the social norm gravitates toward a dominating person, the leader represents a polarization in the situation, having a definite relationship toward others which he cannot change at will. If the leader changes his norm after the group norm is settled, he may thereupon cease to be followed. This occurred several times in our experiments. In general, cases of complete polarization are exceptional. (See the right-hand graphs, Figs. 8.3 and 8.4.)

The fact that the norm thus established is peculiar to the interaction situation suggests that there is a factual psychological basis in the contentions of those who maintain that new and supra-individual qualities arise in group interaction. This is in harmony with the facts developed in the psychology of perception, as we noted in Chapter 2 (pp. 51–60).

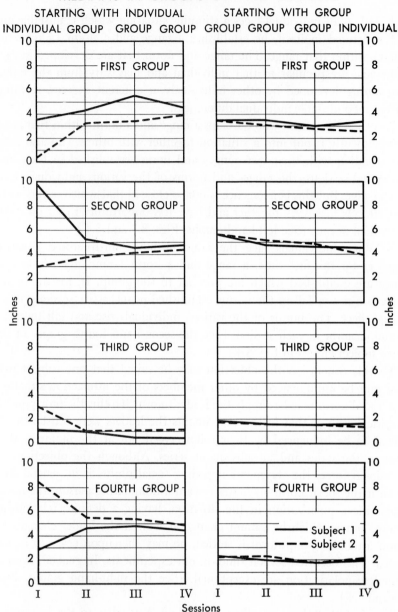

MEDIANS IN GROUPS OF TWO SUBJECTS

Figs. 8.3 and 8.4. Where individual sessions came first (I), divergent norms were established, giving rise to "funnel-shaped" figures as a result of the convergence of the subjects' norms in the subsequent sessions (II, III, IV). (See left-hand graphs in both figures.) Where the group sessions

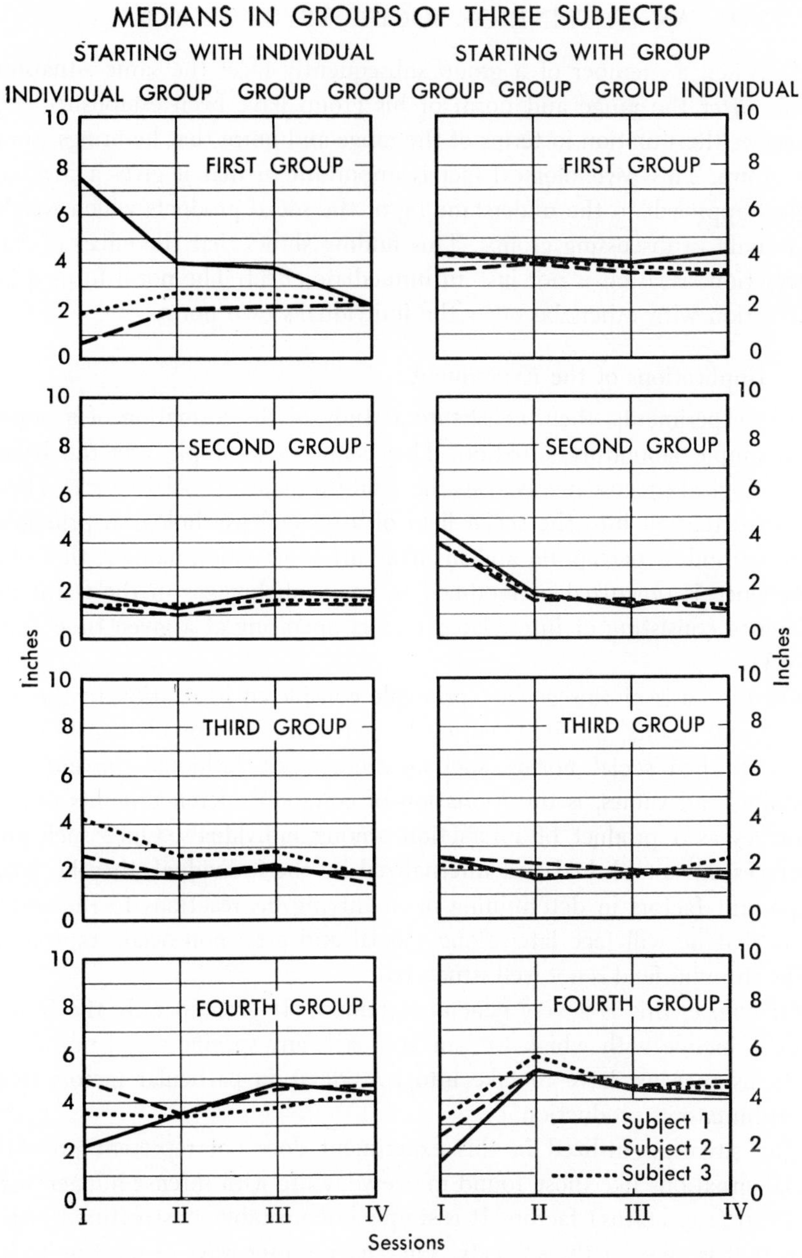
MEDIANS IN GROUPS OF THREE SUBJECTS
STARTING WITH INDIVIDUAL
STARTING WITH GROUP
INDIVIDUAL GROUP GROUP GROUP
GROUP GROUP GROUP INDIVIDUAL
FIRST GROUP
SECOND GROUP
THIRD GROUP
FOURTH GROUP
Inches
Subject 1
Subject 2
Subject 3
I II III IV
Sessions

FIGS. 8.3 and 8.4. Continued.

preceded the individual ones, the convergence of norms was apparent from the first session, and remained throughout, including the (final) individual sessions. (See right-hand graphs in both figures.)

4. When a member of a group subsequently faces the same situation *alone, after* the range and norm of his group have been established, he perceives the situation in terms of the range and norm that he brings from the group. This psychological fact is important in that it gives a psychological approach to the understanding of the social products which weigh so heavily in discussing groups. This finding shows that the effect of the interaction situation is not just an immediate effect. The norm formed in interaction with others becomes the individual's own norm.

Implications of the Experiment

The experiments, then, constitute a study of the formation of a norm in a simple laboratory situation. They show in a simple way the basic psychological process involved in the establishment of social norms. They are an extension into the social field of a general psychological principle that we find in perception and in many other activities, namely, that our experience is organized or modified by main anchorages in the frame of reference consisting of interrelated factors operating at a given time (pp. 79–83).

On the basis of this general principle considered in relation to the experimental results, we shall venture to generalize. The psychological basis of established social norms, such as stereotypes, fashions, conventions, customs, and values, is the formation of common reference points or anchorages as a product of interaction among individuals. Once such anchorages are established and internalized by the individual, they become important factors in determining or modifying his reactions to the situations that he will face later alone—social and even nonsocial—especially if the stimulus field is not well structured.

Of course, this is a very general statement. It gives us only the broad basic principle with which we can approach any specific social norm. In each instance we have to take into consideration particular factors that contribute to its production.

The situation utilized in this experiment does not represent pressing social situations like those found in everyday life with intense hunger, sex, and ego (e.g., status) factors. It is simply one unstable, unstructured situation that is new for the subjects. They have no set ways of reacting to it. Therefore it is plastic enough so that psychological structuring is affected by experimentally introduced social factors, such as suggestion, prestige, and other group influences.

In this situation, within certain limits, there is no "right" or "wrong" judgment. One subject demonstrated this spontaneously during the experiment by suggesting: "If you tell me once how much I am mistaken, all my judgments will be better." Not being sure about the correctness of his judgments, the subject feels uneasy, as we know from the introspective reports.

If, in the beginning of the experimental session, individuals start with widely different judgments, they come together in the course of the experiment, the divergent one feeling uncertain and insecure in the solitude given by his judgments. This convergence is not brought about instantly by direct influence of one or two judgments of other members of the interaction situation. It exhibits a temporal pattern. The following analysis by a member written in answer to the question "Were you influenced by the judgments of the other persons during the experiments?" illustrates the point. This subject wrote, "Yes, but not on the same observation. My judgment in each case was already made, and I did not change to whatever the other person said. But on subsequent observations my judgments were adjusted to their judgments. After a number of observations, the previous agreement or lack of it influenced me in adjusting my own perspective."

Despite the above case, every individual was not necessarily aware of the fact that he was being influenced by others, or that he and other individuals were converging toward a common norm. In fact, the majority of the subjects reported not only that their judgments were made before the others spoke, but *that they were not influenced by the others*. This fact is in harmony with many observations in the psychology of perception. As we have seen, the general setting of a stimulus influences its properties, and unless the individual takes a critical and analytic attitude toward the situation he need not be aware that its properties are influenced by its surroundings.

It must be said that in our experimental setting the subjects were not moved by a common interest or motive like a common danger, such as starvation, or the cruel authority of a tyrant, or some other pressing problem. In these vital situations there is a certain gap that has to be filled, some urgent deprivation to be satisfied. Until the motive is satisfied, to some degree at least, the instability of the situation continues. If the norms and slogans that arise under the stress of a tense and uncertain situation do not meet the situation adequately, the instability is not removed, and new norms and new slogans are likely to arise until the tension is relieved. For example, in a mass of hungry people searching for food, a leader or a small party may standardize certain norms or slogans as guides to outlook or action. But if these norms do not lead to the satisfaction of hunger, other leaders or interested parties spring up with other norms and slogans. This dynamic process moves on and on until norms or slogans are reached appropriate to the situation.

Before closing this discussion a word is in order about the positive and negative, or lowering and uplifting, effects of group products. Depending on the motivational factors, the background, and the general social setting in which the group interacts, emerging group products and group directions will vary. For example, delinquent gangs have harmful social consequences, yet they are perhaps among the most democratically formed groups. No norm is imposed on them from without. The leader and the group norms emerge in the process of group interaction. The mass meetings of the Hitler *Jugend* in which the conquest of the world became a fixed, standardized delusion illustrate the degrading effects of group products. A lynching mob is another good example. On the other hand, some of the loftiest deeds of human selflessness may emerge in group interaction. Therefore, we cannot take sides on the general question posed by some writers of whether group interaction and its products result in ennobling or degrading effects. A blanket answer either way is factually erroneous.

FURTHER EXPERIMENTS ON NORM FORMATION

During the years since the foregoing experiment on norm formation was carried out, a number of experiments pertaining to specific problems it raised and to related problems have been carried out. Since the plan of most of these studies was similar, representative results are summarized in this section in brief form.

Individual Standards

When an individual repeatedly gives judgments alone of a stimulus situation which lacks in objective structure in the aspect being judged, his judgments are distributed within a range and around a modal point peculiar to himself. This finding has been confirmed in various experiments. For example, Walter found that during four sessions on different days the individual's range and standard become increasingly stable, i.e., variability of individual judgments was consistently reduced from session to session (45).

This general finding has important implications for social psychological theory. The underlying psychological principle in the individual situation is not altogether different from that in interaction situations. There is a tendency to reach a standard for judgment of an unstructured stimulus situation in either case. Here we must correct the view that emergent properties appear only in interaction situations. In individual situations, emergent properties appear within the more limited frame of reference consisting of the stimulus situation and the special characteristics of the judging individual. In the interaction situation, the norm is a product of these as they relate to the particular interaction situation and its unique properties. The norm emerging in interaction is dependent on the special properties of the interaction.

What causes the differences in standards formed by various individuals? The work of Voth would indicate that individual differences in personal characteristics and probably motivations are certainly important factors (44). An experiment by Sherif and Harvey showed that increased insecurity aroused by reducing anchorages for bodily orientation in space produces wide and significant differences in judgments as compared to those made in a situation where the individual has some notion of his location in space. Reducing anchorages for bodily orientation in space yielded greater variability on the whole and individual judgments of perceived distance which were significantly greater in magnitude (35).

Hoffman, Swander, Baron, and Rohrer made a definite contribution to this general problem by demonstrating that prior training with a light that actually moved within a luminous framework produced individual standards for judgments of autokinetic movement very much like the actual movement perceived during training. In other words, the standard produced through training with *objective* movement was generalized to the autokinetic situation (19).

In terms of the effects of stimulus structure in limiting alternatives for individual standards, James Thrasher's experiment showed that with increasing availability of objective anchorages the individual's judgments approach the objective characteristics of the stimulus more closely (42). As noted in Chapter 2, studies of judgment and perception demonstrate that when objective stimuli are well structured, the individual establishes a reference scale which coincides closely with the stimulus scale presented to him.

Norms Formed in Interaction

The findings concerning norm formation for autokinetic movement in interaction situations have been confirmed in detail in various experiments

(e.g., 39). In addition, numerous points raised in the experiment as reported in this chapter have been clarified.

Perhaps the most significant of these is the substantiation of the finding
that after participating in the formation of a common norm the individual
takes this norm as his own standard, even when he is not in the interaction
situation. Bovard demonstrated that the effect of a common norm persisted when the individuals made judgments alone 28 days after the interaction situation in which it was formed. The extent of carry-over of the
common norm was related to initial individual differences among subjects.
The tendency was for *subjects whose initial individual judgments were
more variable to stick more closely to the common norm formed in interaction* (5).

Rohrer, Baron, Hoffman, and Swander found persistence of norms
formed in interaction for a much longer period. Following training with
a moving stimulus light, subjects participated together in interaction situations. Convergence of judgments toward a common norm was found, even
though this necessitated shifts from individual norms established through
training. A whole year later, these individuals made judgments alone. It
was found that the norms formed in interaction were carried over by the
individual, while effects of the training prior to interaction were negligible
after this long interval (30).

Through the use of different stimulus materials it has been demonstrated
that the findings concerning norm formation are not peculiar to the auto
kinetic situation. Similar findings have been reported for different stimulus
modalities, such as cutaneous perception of warmth (23), duration of
perceptual phenomena (37), estimates of size (6, 25) and of number
(7, 38), and aesthetic judgments (24). However, the stimulus situations
used have been relatively unstructured in at least one aspect.

One part of a study by Asch reported earlier shows that when naïve
individuals make judgments in each others' presence of stimuli which
present clear-cut objective differences their judgments coincide with objective factors (see pp. 136–139). A few studies substantiate the basic
assumption of Sherif's first autokinetic experiments, namely, that the
norms formed in social situations will be influenced by objective factors
to the extent that such objective standards are available. Sinha used a perceptual phenomenon that lasted from 5 to 45 seconds with a median duration of 25 seconds for individuals alone. When individuals who had established standards at one extreme in this range (say, above 40 seconds) were
confronted with judgments at the other extreme (in this case, below 10

seconds), the tendency to converge toward the other's judgments was greatly reduced (37).

Sperling obtained similar results for judgments of autokinetic movement when differences between judgments by a naïve subject and a "planted" subject differed by as much as 14–22 inches (39). Under the specified experimental conditions (exposure time, size of light, distance between subjects and light), most individuals do not experience movement as great as the 20–25-inch range used by the "planted subjects" in this experiment. Therefore, the naïve subjects were simply shocked at judgments which so violated what they took to be reality and what they actually experienced.

Using estimates of number, Sodhi observed that the tendency for convergence in interaction was a function of the level of difficulty in making judgments. That is, as the number of dots increased and hence the limiting effect of objective number in the time allowed decreased, convergence toward a common norm in togetherness situations was more marked (38).

As noted on page 250, subjects in the autokinetic situation feel somewhat insecure and unsure of themselves, and this motivational factor is related to the tendency to converge in interaction. In the Sherif and Harvey experiment varying available physical anchorages for space orientation, a tendency was found for convergence to increase when these feelings of insecurity were heightened owing to uncertainty in orienting oneself in space (35).

Since, within limits, there is no objective "right" or "wrong" in this situation, the experimenter can produce different degrees of confidence or insecurity by telling the individual that his judgments are correct or incorrect. Experiments by Kelman (22) and Mausner (25) found that variations in the subject's motivations produced by such different instructions lead to differing tendencies in interaction. Those subjects who have more confidence in the correctness of their judgments show less tendency to converge toward the judgments of others. If various individuals in the same interaction situation have been told that their individual judgments are correct, they may even react against each other's judgments, leading to divergence rather than convergence (25). Thus, in a situation lacking in structure, a standard which the individual has every reason to believe is objective (i.e., the experimenter's confirmation of his judgments) removes the realistic possibility that other alternatives are feasible.

Such experiences prior to the experiment and their counterparts in the individual's past history undoubtedly influence his motivations and reactions in interaction situations and probably account for many of the observed differences in individual reactions to the interaction situations reported in the original study and in later experiments (e.g., 5, 22).

It is evident that convergence toward a common norm by individuals in interaction is not due to any one sovereign factor, like a supposedly basic need to conform or innate suggestibility, but to a number of interrelated factors coming from the individuals, the objective stimulus situation, and the interaction process. In an experiment by Blake and Brehm, common norms were formed even when no other persons were actually present but the individual heard the recorded judgments of others, who he was told were in other rooms (4). This finding indicates that, although the individual is not usually aware that his judgments are shifting toward a common norm, the process occurs on a conceptual level of functioning.

RELATIONSHIPS AMONG INTERACTING INDIVIDUALS: As suggested in the autokinetic experiments (p. 257) and emphasized in the preceding chapters, the formation of social products and reactions of individuals in interaction are affected in decisive fashion by the unique properties of the interaction process. The extent to which relationships among individuals and hence interaction patterns are stabilized is a crucial determinant of these properties. In a further experiment by Sherif using the autokinetic situation, it was demonstrated that affective or prestige relationships among individuals produced predictable effects on norms formed during interaction (p. 609).

Recently, Mausner varied the relationships of partners and studied their effects on judgments of pictures (24). Whether an interacting partner was a "fellow student" or an "art director" made a decided difference on the tendency to converge toward his judgments. The supposition here is that an "art director" would be more likely to be "right" in aesthetic judgments than a fellow student. This supposition was substantiated in a further study by having individuals judge lines with others who had previously exhibited either "success" or "failure" in another task. The tendency for convergence toward a common norm was greater when the partner with whom one interacted was seen as "successful" than when he was seen as having failed (26).

But what of norm formation when interaction patterns among individuals are stabilized in a group structure? This is the point of departure for future significant experiments on norm formation. A lead is provided in two experiments by Bovard, which substantiate empirical observations concerning the effects of social products in group situations. In the first experiment, the interaction situation was in the classroom (6). The classes were taught by different techniques, one "group-centered" and one the more traditional "teacher-centered" instruction. The chief difference these methods made for relationships among individuals was in amount of verbal interaction among them. One type of group allowed interaction between individuals so that its incipient patterning was possible. The other restricted interaction between individuals. A total of 504 subjects in 30 different class units made individual estimates of the length of a green rectangle. They were informed of the judgments of others in their class and then were asked to make individual judgments again. The results showed differences in the extent of convergence toward a common norm in the two types of interaction situations. Convergence was greater in the situation which had permitted most interaction among individuals.

In another study, Bovard obtained estimates of number of dots on a card containing 500 dots by members of organized group units of considerable stability and members of temporary togetherness situations (7). Once again, convergence was greater in groups with stabilized relationships than in the transitory togetherness situations.

Experiments on the formation of groups in controlled yet lifelike conditions, like the Bull Dog and Red Devil study reported in Chapter 6, reveal the formation of group norms in actual social situations which present problems of motivational significance to group members. In Chapter 9, a further experiment is reported in which social norms formed by group members toward another group are analyzed in relation to the common motives of group members and the specific conditions of their interaction with the other group. Such experiments approximate conditions for norm formation in actual life and, as we shall see, make it possible to relate the process to factors which operate in actual group situations.

FORMATION OF SOCIAL NORMS IN ACTUAL GROUPS

The final test of the validity of generalizations in social psychology is their applicability to concrete situations and events. If the generalizations reached have no bearing on social life as it flows and rushes onward, then all of the thought, effort, experimentation that went into them are no more than academic ritual. For this reason, our work starts with immersion in the realities of social life and must be checked and rechecked against them at every turn.

It has been stated that group norms are formed in relation to situations which are vague, ill defined, or confusing in some aspect which has consequence to interacting individuals. Eventually these norms come to regulate the experience and behavior of individual members. In previous chapters the formation of social norms was noted in adolescent cliques, in youthful gangs so prevalent in large cities, in military groups isolated for the time being from the usual conditions of life, in a small community on an isolated island, in informal work groups. In Chapter 21 emphasis will be laid on the rise of new norms and slogans in times of crisis and rapid social change when old norms linger on through the inertia of a "social lag" or are perpetuated by small portions of a population until they lose their points of contact with urgent realities.

For many years we have surveyed material on the formation of new norms in history, sociological studies, journalistic accounts, and eyewitness reports. It is not easy to choose from these. There are the fascinating stories of new groups breaking off from the main stream of society to work out their own destinies and ways of life, sometimes isolating themselves by thousands of heartbreaking miles, as the Mormons did. There are the coöperative experiments, the New Harmonys, the Perfectionists of Vermont, and later of the Oneida Community, the Amana Society, the Ephrata community of Pennsylvania, the Labadists of Maryland, the 15 Shaker societies, the Harmonists of George Rapp, Brook Farm. All of these were in protest against some or many norms of a larger society. All formed new norms governing the major problem areas of life.

There are the little "bohemias" of large cities whose members shock respectable folks with flagrant violations of one or several social norms, but who respond in turn to violations of their own norms (27, 46). Thus a woman who decided to marry the man whom she had lived with for some time received the reproaches of her bohemian friends for abandoning their "ideals" (14). Thus too, visitors to Montparnasse in Paris of the twenties who wore evening dress found themselves as conspicuous as a dinner guest in shorts, and a celebrity was accorded indifference as assiduously as he was lionized in the fashionable salons elsewhere in the city (20).

Choosing examples of norm formation from life is not limited by their dearth, but by space between covers of a book. In making a choice, we have succumbed to the lure of the West—to the American frontier which was still developing and being transformed into organized social forms at the turn of the century. Men, women, children, families, groups moved westward for vital reasons. Whatever the reason they found a country and problems different from those left behind in the East or in other lands. They faced problems in earning a living and in social life in which the familiar rules and customs could not be followed. They found other problems that were new and altogether unlike any they had faced before. In response to such problems, new organizations and new social norms were formed.

An Example of New Norms Formed in Frontier Life

The eminent historian of the western frontier Walter Prescott Webb gives a number of examples of how "in meeting practical situations, solving immediate problems, men develop a workable practice, and later get the practice recognized and incorporated into law" (47, p. 256). One of these concerns the practices, rules, and rights of individuals to use water in the streams and lakes. These rules and rights developed in certain conditions in the old West.

Under the custom and law of eastern states, which were brought from the moist English climate, only the owner of the bank of a stream had rights to the water; and he was prevented from diverting the water from its natural channel in a way that interfered with the rights of other owners. This was called the "law of riparian rights."

The story of the modification of these customs, rights, and laws governing the use of water starts with the Gold Rush of California in 1848–1850. According to Gard, in the early days of the gold explorations crime was not a pressing problem in the gold camps (16). But as the rush swelled and brought with it fortune hunters with few scruples, the situation became desperate. In Webb's words, "neither life nor property was safe, and it demanded a remedy. Thoughtful men decided that some rules must be formulated to give protection to the survivors and to bring some order out of chaos" (47, p. 257).

So it was done. In smaller camps, all of the miners assembled to agree on rules, to judge the guilt of persons accused of violating them, and to mete out punishment (16). Since there were no jails, the usual penalties were banishment, whipping, or hanging. In larger camps, "miners' courts" were organized to perform similar functions. These were informal bodies which met irregularly and often kept no records. In other places, "committees of vigilance" developed on a voluntary and informal basis. Through all of these bodies, rules were agreed upon concerning property and human life, and violators were punished. However, none as yet had legally constituted authority. Their authority sprang from the camps in which they were located. They represent an "informally organized society" in the process of standardizing norms and taking necessary means to punish deviation from them (16).

One issue that was very common in these miners' assemblies, courts, and vigilance committees was the problem of protecting a gold claim (47). The decision in this regard was that the first man to discover a claim, stake it properly, and have witnesses should hold it. Others had to respect his claim, so that their claims as second or third comers were also protected.

Water was necessary for sluicing dirt and gravel from the gold. It was also scarce, and the streams were weak. It is not known how much these miners knew about the "law of riparian rights." In any case, as Webb pointed out, they ignored it. Indeed it would have been a little absurd at a time when landownership was tenuous and confused and in a place where water needed by all was so scarce. So the customs and rules which arose in informal gatherings regulating use of the land were transferred to water. The first man to claim the water should have the amount required, *but only as long as he used it*. When he ceased using it, the later comers had the right to its use.

In 1850 the state of California adopted English common law, including the law of riparian rights. A year later it gave legal status to rules and decisions of "miners' courts," thus adopting an entirely contrary principle concerning water usage. The rest of the story in California is a question of legal and political debate and litigation. The significant fact is that ways of behaving, conceptions of personal rights concerning the use of water, were standardized among people, at first on an informal basis. Norms were formed appropriate to the situation and were enforced by bodies ("miners' courts" and vigilance committees) which were organized informally as a means of dealing with common problems. These problems arose because there were alternative ways of dealing with the conditions which were urgent to the individuals involved. The fact that a particular alternative was chosen does not mean that the norms which formed were the only possible ones. However, in this instance the limiting effects of objective factors on the process of norm formation can clearly be seen.

The Oklahoma Run

Less than three weeks after he became President of the United States Benjamin Harrison proclaimed that the "unassigned" lands consisting of about two million acres in the heart of the Indian Territory would be opened for settlement at noon 30 days hence. Thus an issue of much controversy was decided in favor of those who had "boomed" this area for white settlement.

There had never been anything quite like this opening in the history of the country. Many people in both the bordering and distant states had hoped and waited for the news, and they began to congregate along the borders of the region. There were some families, but the pioneers were mostly men who planned to bring their families in after securing land (8).

The provisions for entry and securing possession were clear enough, having been established by federal laws concerning homesteading and by executive proclamation. The border of the region was guarded by federal troops, who would give the signal for settlers to cross. The land had been surveyed in 160-acre tracts and marked off. Possession was to be taken on a "first come, first serve" basis with the provision that anyone who crossed the boundary before the official entry time was to be barred from securing legal claim. There were two federal Land Offices in the area for filing individual claims.

However, the homestead regulations were not applicable to conditions for setting up organized communities. There were no organized towns, no courts, no rules for incorporation (2). This period was, therefore, a unique situation. Within half a day on April 22, 1889, from 40,000 to 60,000 people poured into these lands. In a score or more places, townsites were staked out with hundreds or thousands of people claiming building sites from 25 to 50 feet wide. The townsites which suddenly mushroomed on the rolling prairie were the fertile grounds for the formation of new organizations and new norms.

For over a year the people in this area literally governed themselves, setting up their own forms, establishing their own authority and rules for community life. Perhaps one of the most significant facts is that this could and did happen in a situation which was initially the very picture of chaos. Although there were controversies over claims, intergroup rivalry and struggle, and even some deaths before the period was over, the scene became organized. Chaos and excitement did not reign long (2, 8).

People came on horseback, in carriages, in wagons, on foot, and by train. In the north the border was well guarded; but along other borders it was possible to slip through and hide until the appointed hour for entry (11). Thus some found the claim they reached in such haste already taken. Those who crossed the border illegally were called "Sooners." In the years following the run, all one had to do to win a contested claim was to establish evidence that the other party was a "Sooner" (2). This unique designation become the nickname for all Oklahomans, although it originally had "evil connotation." This is an instance of a derogatory stereotype whose connotation was altered with changing conditions and whose scope was broadened to include all inhabitants of the area.

So it happened that at the townsite called Guthrie after a railroad stop there were about 200 people before noon of the deadline. Some of these were Sooners already staking out claims. A contemporary report says that in spite of this activity, with the exception of the railroad station, incompleted Land Office, and a few tents, the scene was one of "vast unbroken prairie" (11). Before three in the afternoon of that day the prairie on every side of this cluster of life was filled with people, horses, and tents. Figure 8.5 is a photograph of a part of the scene and shows a portion of the unorganized crowd of humanity. Figure 8.6 shows a part of the town five days later. In this short time several buildings were erected, others were started, and, despite pending disagreements over claims, the area was pretty well staked out.

One provision made by the Homestead Act did apply to these townsites. A townsite was to be an area about a mile long and a mile and a half wide. The 15,000 settlers at Guthrie proceeded, therefore, to stake out four adjacent townsites which were given different names. Accordingly, organization proceeded in these areas separately and along different lines.

In Guthrie itself, groups of men assembled on the first evening after the run to discuss the question of town organization, "which was a perplexing problem since no basis of law existed upon which action could be authorized" (2, p. 17). The next morning, riders circulated through the area announcing a meeting. Four thousand people assembled in the open. The first procedure was a roll call of states. It was found that 32 states and territories were represented. Each area was asked to designate a spokesman. Thus a "Committee of Thirty-two" was set up to make nominations for mayor.

After considerable discussion, three candidates were chosen and the chairman of the "Committee of Thirty-two" opened the contest. Facing this unique situation, the committee and candidates found that usual methods simply did not work. There were, of course, no provisions for balloting and no safeguards to insure fair voting. Attempts at voice votes were discarded when the threat of physical combat developed among these men, who were carrying guns. Therefore, *a new method of balloting was devised and agreed upon.*

Figure 8.7 shows this method in action. Three farm wagons were drawn up and the candidates each mounted a wagon. As each line marched past the wagon, it was counted. This would seem like a clear-cut method for evaluating a perceptual situation. However, a new form of "ballot stuffing" soon became apparent. After passing the wagon, many voters returned to the end of the line and marched up to the wagon again. In desperation the meeting adjourned.

The next day the procedure was similar and had similar results. Therefore, an entirely new method was devised. Each candidate chose three representatives. Then the representatives of all candidates agreed upon an additional person. This group was a selection committee, and its choice was unanimously adopted at a final mass meeting on April 25, two days after the start of the contest. Although city councils of this period and region were ordinarily limited to 4–8 members, the election of council members continued with enthusiasm until 17 had been selected (2).

One of the first actions of the council was to prohibit gambling on the public streets and provide fines for violators. Although the council itself was worried about its authority, as evidenced by its decision to confer with the United States marshal concerning this problem, it was successful in establishing rules and enforcing sanctions for about a month. In the middle of May, objections began to pour in demanding an election. The issue was the council's decision creating arbitration boards to decide contests for building lots and charging fees for title certificates.

Therefore a new election was set for June, at which time a "charter commission" was also chosen. This group agreed upon rules under which the inhabitants lived for over a year, until Congress made provisions for the territory and a "legal" government was organized.

Problems were faced and coped with in distinctive ways in the other townsites in this area. Lacking precedent, the modes of organization and norms adopted were the result of interaction between particular groups which came and which formed in the new towns, their conflicting and harmonious interests, and specific problems which developed as a result of their separate actions.

In Oklahoma City, a stable organization and rules by which the inhabitants agreed to regulate their activities were much slower in developing than in Guthrie. This process reflected the presence of two rival "town companies" and of groups which formed among individuals not affiliated with either one. One group from Seminole, Kansas, were Sooners who staked out lots before the legal opening time. A group which arrived at the legal time called the "Colony Company" proceeded to stake out an

FIG. 8.5. The first day of the run, Guthrie, Oklahoma, April 22, 1889. (Courtesy of University of Oklahoma Library, Phillips Collection.)

FIG. 8.6. Guthrie, Oklahoma, five days later, April 27, 1889. (Courtesy of University of Oklahoma Library, Phillips Collection.)

FIG. 8.7. One of the new methods of voting in the election of the first mayor of Guthrie, April 24, 1889. (Courtesy of the Oklahoma Historical Society.)

adjacent claim. As other legal settlers arrived, these two rivals began to come into conflict. The next day a group of men not allied with any town-site company met informally and called a mass meeting which lasted for three hours and was the scene of speeches and discussion. As a result of this meeting a "Committee of Fourteen" was selected to start a third survey of lots and streets.

When the Seminole group threatened armed resistance, this informal committee reconsidered and decided to call another mass meeting, at which the necessity of compromise was decided upon. A "Committee of Ten" composed of members from each of the rival companies was named to effect a compromise. As a result of the efforts of this committee, the results of all of the surveys were accepted. The disputed areas were drawn irregularly to accommodate the conflicting lines of the various surveys. The streets of present-day Oklahoma City conform to this decision, with those in the old area of conflict jogging in unexpected directions.

When an election for municipal organization was held four days later, it was evident that the Seminole Company had gained the upper hand. The first rules passed dealt with "lot jumping" and provided fines for those who attempted to claim a lot when there was evidence that anyone else claimed it.

As the new residents of this new town resisted the regulations and opposed the methods of the Sooner organization, sharp lines were drawn between anyone associated with the "Seminoles" and those opposing them. The "Seminoles" called their opposition "kickers." A member of the opposition substituted the Indian name "Kickapoo," in contrast to the Indian name "Seminole." Thus this intergroup conflict was given a standardized name by inhabitants: the "Seminole-Kickapoo War" (2). Some six months later the "Kickapoos" succeeded in electing their choice for mayor.

Thus in the face of unaccustomed problems, with no provision for organization, authority, establishing rules for behavior, or enforcing them, the thousands of new inhabitants of the various towns which appeared literally overnight did proceed to organize, to establish authority, to make rules for conduct, and to establish and enforce sanctions for their violation.

On June 14, 1890, the federal government made provision for municipal organizations in this area, and the existing organizations and their rules were made to conform to them. However, as Alley concluded, these legal communities and their laws were in no sense more real than those which had existed for the preceding 18 months (2). Once stabilized, the norms which were formed and standardized informally in the various new communities were as effective as the legally constituted authority and laws, because the people of the various communities took part in their formation, recognized their existence, supported their authority, and obeyed them.

Thus the formation of communities in the territory witnessed the formation of new norms as the people faced immediate, urgent problems with alternative solutions. After varying periods of discussion, planning, organization, friction, resistance, trying out methods in practice, these norms were standardized in the communities, the particular forms being more or less distinctive for different communities. As a result, individuals took these norms as their own and, for the time, regulated their behavior accordingly.

REFERENCES

1. Adams, H. F. Autokinetic sensations, *Psychol. Monogr.* (1912), No. 59, pp. 32–44.
2. Alley, J. *City Beginnings in Oklahoma Territory.* Norman: University of Oklahoma Press, 1939.
3. Asbury, H. *The Gangs of New York.* New York: Knopf, 1927.
4. Blake, R. R., and Brehm, J. W. The use of tape recording to simulate a group atmosphere, *J. abnorm. & soc. Psychol.* (1954), 49:311–313.
5. Bovard, E. W., Jr. Social norms and the individual, *J. abnorm. & soc. Psychol.* (1948), 43:62–69.
6. Bovard, E. W., Jr. Group structure and perception, *J. abnorm. & soc. Psychol.* (1951), 46:398–405.
7. Bovard, E. W., Jr. Conformity to social norms in stable and temporary groups, *Science* (1953), 117:361–363.
8. Buchanan, J. S., and Dale, E. C. A *History of Oklahoma.* Evanston, Ill.: Row, Peterson, 1924.
9. Clemmer, D. *The Prison Community.* Boston: Christopher, 1940.
10. Crutchfield, R. S., and Edwards, W. The effect of a fixated figure on autokinetic movement, *J. exper. Psychol.* (1949), 39:561–567.
11. Dale, E. C., and Rader, J. L. *Readings in Oklahoma History.* Evanston, Ill.: Row, Peterson, 1930, "The Run of 1889" (written in 1890), pp. 469–476.
12. Dalton, M. Summarized in W. F. Whyte, Economics and Human Relations in Industry, 1947 (mimeographed).
13. Durkheim, E. *Elementary Forms of Religious Life.* New York: Macmillan, 1915.
14. Faris, R. E. L. *Social Disorganization.* New York: Ronald, 1948.

15. Furniss, E. S., Jr. *The Office of the Premier in French Foreign Policy-Making: An Application of Decision-Making Analysis,* Princeton University, Organizational Behavior Section, Foreign Policy Analysis Series, No. 5, October, 1954.

16. Gard, Wayne. *Frontier Justice.* Norman: University of Oklahoma Press, 1949.

17. Gist, N. P. *Secret Societies: A Cultural Study of Fraternalism in the United States.* Columbia: The University of Missouri Studies (1940), *15,* No. 4.

18. Hiller, E. T. *The Strike.* Chicago: University of Chicago Press, 1928.

19. Hoffman, E. L., Swander, D., Baron, S. H., and Rohrer, J. H. Generalization and exposure time as related to autokinetic movement, *J. exper. Psychol.* (1953), 46:171–177.

20. Huddleston, S. *Back to Montparnasse.* Philadelphia: Lippincott, 1931.

21. Jones, S. V. The Cougars: Life with a Brooklyn gang, *Harper's Magazine* (1954), 209:35–43.

22. Kelman, H. Effects of success and failure on "suggestibility" in the autokinetic situation, *J. abnorm. & soc. Psychol.* (1950), 45:267–285.

23. McCord, F. The formation of group norms, *J. soc. Psychol.* (1948), 27:3–15.

24. Mausner, B. Studies in social interaction: III. Effect of variation in one partner's prestige on the interaction of observer pairs, *J. appl. Psychol.* (1953), 37:391–394.

25. Mausner, B. The effect of prior reinforcement on the interaction of observer pairs, *J. abnorm. & soc. Psychol.* (1954), 49:65–68.

26. Mausner, B. The effect of one partner's success in a relevant task on the interaction of observer pairs, *J. abnorm. & soc. Psychol.* (1954), 49:557–560.

27. Murger, H. *Latin Quarter.* New York: Dodd, Mead, 1930.

28. Piaget, J. *The Moral Judgment of the Child.* London: Kegan Paul, Trench, Trubner, 1932.

29. Roethlisberger, F. J., and Dickson, W. J. *Management and the Worker.* Cambridge: Harvard University Business Research Studies (1939), *21,* No. 9.

30. Rohrer, J. H., Baron, S. H., Hoffman, E. L., and Swander, D. V. The stability of autokinetic judgments, *J. abnorm. & soc. Psychol.* (1954), 49:595–597.

31. Roy, Donald. Quota restriction and goldbricking in a machine shop, *Amer. J. Sociol.* (1952), 57:427–442.

32. Şemin, Refia Ugurel. Moral behavior and moral judgment of children, *J. abnorm. & soc. Psychol.* (1952), 47:463–474.

33. Sherif, M. A study of some social factors in perception, *Arch. Psychol.* (1935), No. 187.

34. Sherif, M. *The Psychology of Social Norms.* New York: Harper, 1936.
35. Sherif, M., and Harvey, O. J. A study in ego functioning: Elimination of stable anchorages in individual and group situations, *Sociometry* (1952), 15:272–305.
36. Simmel, G. The sociology of secret societies (trans. A. W. Small), *Amer. J. Sociol.* (1906), 11:441–498.
37. Sinha, Durganand. An experimental study of a social factor in perception: The influence of an arbitrary group standard, *Patna University Journal*, Jan.–April, 1952 (reprint).
38. Sodhi, Kripal Singh. *Urteilsbildung in Sozialen Kraftfeld.* Göttingen: Verlag für Psychologie, 1953.
39. Sperling, H. G. An experimental study of some psychological factors in judgment. Master's thesis, New School for Social Research, 1946. Summarized in S. E. Asch, *Social Psychology.* New York: Prentice-Hall, 1952, pp. 487–490.
40. Stouffer, S. A. An analysis of conflicting social norms, *Amer. sociol. Rev.* (1949), 14:707–717.
41. Thrasher, F. *The Gang.* Chicago: University of Chicago Press, 1927.
42. Thrasher, J. D. Interpersonal relations and gradations of stimulus structure in judgmental variation, *Sociometry* (1954), 17:228–241. Complete report in Doctorate dissertation with same title, University of Oklahoma, 1954.
43. Tresselt, M. E., and Volkmann, J. The production of uniform opinion by non-social stimulation, *J. abnorm. & soc. Psychol.* (1942), 37:234–243.
44. Voth, A. C. An experimental study of mental patients through the autokinetic phenomenon, *Amer. J. Psychiat.* (1947), 103:793–805.
45. Walter, Norman. A study of effects of conflicting suggestions upon judgment of the autokinetic situation. Doctorate dissertation, University of Oklahoma, 1952; *Sociometry* (1955), 18:138–146.
46. Ware, Caroline F. *Greenwich Village.* Boston: Houghton Mifflin, 1935.
47. Webb, W. P. *The Great Frontier.* Boston: Houghton Mifflin, 1952.
48. White, W. H., Jr. The Transients, in L. Miller (ed.), *Prize Articles 1954.* New York: Ballantine; reprinted from *Fortune*, 1954.
49. Whyte, W. F. A slum sex code, *Amer. J. Sociol.* (1943), 49:24–31.
50. Williams, R. M., Jr. *American Society. A Sociological Interpretation.* New York: Knopf, 1951, esp. pp. 352–371.
51. Zorbaugh, H. *The Gold Coast and the Slum.* Chicago: University of Chicago Press, 1929.

CHAPTER **9**

Intergroup Relations

Relations between social groups, expressed in states of conflict and harmony, of domination and slavery, of war and peace, have always been consequential matters in human affairs. Among these, the problem of unfavorable attitudes (prejudice) or friendly attitudes toward out-groups has been a lively issue for social scientists and policy makers.

But at no time has the problem of intergroup relations been more vital than it is today. Relations between labor and management, between ethnic groups, between religious groups, between groups committed to given ideologies or ways of life are at the basis of grave uncertainties, conflicts, as well as misfortunes of millions of people.

The reason is that in the present world setting no human grouping functions as a closed system. No human grouping, no matter how weak or powerful, has an independent existence today. This state of affairs is ever bringing all social units into closer and closer functional relationship. Increasing interdependence among groups is the general rule both within nations and between nations.

In this chapter we shall deal with the process of the formation of intergroup attitudes and behavior. Our primary concern will be the step-by-step tracing of interaction between groups that gives rise to positive or negative intergroup attitudes. This step-by-step tracing will be presented in accounts of experiments deliberately designed to study intergroup relations.

Lasting end products of intergroup interaction, in the form of definite social distances from various out-groups, are grasped better after more adequate treatment of the topics of ego functioning and reference groups. The topic of group prejudice or social distance, therefore, will be discussed more concretely in Chapter 19.

PROBLEM OF INTERGROUP RELATIONS SPECIFIED

Every friendly or unfriendly item of behavior among individuals is not necessarily a case of intergroup relations. Accordingly, we have to differentiate those behaviors which can properly be called intergroup behavior.

Let us start this task of identifying intergroup behavior by specifying the main concepts involved. As we have seen, a group is defined as a social unit (1) which consists of a number of individuals who, at a given time, stand in more or less definite interdependent status and role relationships with one another and (2) which explicitly or implicitly possesses a set of values or norms of its own regulating the behavior of individual members at least in matters of consequence to the group. In order that this definition not be excessively bulky, common attitudes, common aspirations and goals were omitted. All of these shared attitudes, aspirations, and goals are related to and implicit in the common values or norms of the group.

An adolescent clique or gang, a college fraternity, a club, a church, a union local, a chamber of commerce, a political party are examples of social groups. From the point of view of members within the group, these social units may be referred to as *in-groups*. Again from the point of view of the individual member, those social units of which he is not psychologically a part or with which he does not identify himself may be referred to as *out-groups*.

The term *intergroup relations* refers to the relations between two or more groups and their respective members. Whenever individuals belonging to one in-group, collectively or individually, interact with another group or its members in terms of their group identification, we have an instance of intergroup behavior. Group relatedness and attitudes stemming from it become so much a part of the individual's psychological make-up in a personally experienced way that the fact of interaction in terms of group membership need not always be consciously recognized as such by the individual himself. Discriminatory practices, for example, are frequently put in terms of personal preferences.

Intergroup Relations of Small Groups in Their Setting

At this early stage of our knowledge, we are on safer grounds methodologically if we concentrate on relations between small groups, whose members can be singled out and studied concretely. But, especially in industrial societies today, relatively small groups are not closed entities, as isolated and stable tribes might have been.

A club, a neighborhood church, a union local, a manufacturers' organization in the community is usually a subunit of a larger organization. The large organization may have a good number of subunits, all tied to one another and to the central authority with definite rules, values or norms, loyalties, responsibilities, and a particular pattern of power relationships.

This fact forces us to take small groups, not as closed entities, but as parts or *subordinates* of larger social units, or *superordinates*. The properties of subordinates are determined at times decisively, in other cases to a lesser extent, by the nature of the larger social units of which they are a part. The determination of the properties of smaller units by those of larger units of which they are a part will vary, depending on the degree of integration of the various parts within the larger organization and the nature of power relations within it. Therefore, small groups and relations between them must be studied as they are affected by their relationship to larger units. In preceding chapters specific instances of such relationship and its effects have been noted. These considerations were raised cogently by Arensberg (*1*), Whyte (*18*), and others.

Framework of Intergroup Relations

In accounting for intergroup behavior, some authors have singled out as the determining factors deep-seated "instincts" supposedly inherent in human nature. Other authors pointed at frustrations of the individual with ensuing displaced aggressions. Some have placed major emphasis on "national character" and culture. Still others sought the explanation of intergroup issues primarily through the character of leadership.

Certainly individual motives, frustrations, the undeniable role of leadership, and characteristic modes of behavior due to culture do enter as factors in determining intergroup behavior in various ways. But the essential feature of intergroup relations noted above requires that these and other factors be considered as they operate within the setting of the particular case of intergroup relations. These various influences are factors interdependently related to one another and to other factors operative at a given time. Intergroup behavior is the outcome of internal factors (motives, attitudes, complexes, and the like) and external factors (situational, organizational, socioeconomic, and material), which jointly determine the unique properties of psychological structuring at the time. In short, intergroup behavior, like any behavior, can be understood only within its appropriate frame of reference.

The appropriate frame of reference for intergroup behavior necessitates the examination of functional relations between two or more groups. The functional relationship between groups whose members perceive them as in-groups has properties of its own. These properties are generated in the course of interaction between particular groups. Even though they are not independent of the relationships within the groups in question, the characteristics of functional relations *between* groups cannot be deduced from the properties of in-group relations alone. Prevalent modes of behavior within groups in the way of coöperativeness and solidarity or competitiveness and rivalry among members need not be the prevalent modes of behavior in intergroup relations. Hostility toward out-groups may, at times, be proportional to the degree of solidarity within the group. Also, there are cases of consequential intergroup relations which effect modifications in the structure of relations *within* the groups involved.

Main Problem of Intergroup Relations Is Not Deviate Behavior

In explaining intergroup relations there has been a tendency in recent years to bring to the foreground cases of individuals who have suffered unusual degrees of frustration, or who have been subjected to extensive authoritarian treatment in their life histories. There is good reason to believe that some persons who are brought up under unfortunate life circumstances may become more intense in their prejudices and hostilities. But this is not the crux of the problem of intergroup relations. At best these cases can explain the intensity of behavior in a given dimension. Established stereotypes toward out-groups are not the doings of a few frantic or neurotic individuals. When there is a conflict situation between two groups, such as a strike or a war between small or large groups, it is *usually* the most responsible, the most talented, the most exemplary members of the group who are in control. The conduct of activities in conflict is carried out by individuals who can withstand the strains and the wear-and-tear imposed by the conflict situation. When members of a group rightly or wrongly perceive threat, unjust treatment, or invasion of their rights coming from another group, opinion is crystallized, slogans are formulated, effective measures are organized, not usually by a few neurotic or deviate individuals, but by those recognized as the most responsible in their midst. The prejudice scale that is produced and the slogans that stick are not imposed by some deviate members. Such individuals ordinarily exhibit their intense reactions within the reference scales of prejudice, hostility, or sacrifice of their respective settings.

Intergroup behavior of members of any group is not *primarily* a problem of deviate behavior. If it were first and foremost a matter of deviate behavior, intergroup behavior would not be the issue of vital consequence that it is today. Intergroup behavior is primarily the matter of participation by individual members within the social-distance scale of their in-group in more stable times, and in the developing trends in relations between the respective groups in periods of flux and change characteristic of our own times.

The participation of individual members implies regulation of experience and behavior toward out-groups in terms of existing or developing anchorages provided by their reference groups. Attitudes and hence behavior of the individual toward out-groups and their members are regulated, on the whole, in terms of the proximity or distance prescribed by the social-distance scale or the developing friendship or hostility between the individual's reference groups and various out-groups. The motives, attitudes, complexes, frustrations, and aggressive tendencies of individual members do have a place in intergroup relations, as they are modified, deflected, and even transformed within the social-distance scale and developing trends of intergroup relations among their respective reference groups.

The organization of the experience and behavior of the individual when he is interacting as a member of an in-group has unique structural properties which cannot be extrapolated from his experience and behavior in individual situations.

Likewise, explanations of intergroup behavior have to bring into the picture the unique properties of the intergroup interaction in question. Only within their appropriate setting can the *relative weights* of various factors (motivational, socioeconomic, situational, etc.) be properly singled out. In more stable and established situations and times, the social-distance scale of the reference group in question is, on the whole, the weighty determinant. Thus, in the Indian village of Rampur, a research team determined the small groups (*dhars*) or factions among the villagers and ascertained the established social distances among them. On this basis, definite predictions were made about the reactions of individuals from the various factions in a meeting. Within half an hour after the meeting began, these predictions were fulfilled. Members of the factional groups made open attacks on each other in terms of their respective group alignments (9).

However, in more extraordinary times of changing group relations and group realignments, the dominant factor may be situational, socioeconomic, or even military. An illustration of intergroup behavior which contrasts with that stemming primarily from established relationships and social distances among groups will clarify the point. On October 29, 1953, a full-page advertisement by a leading television station appeared in the newspaper. It was headed "Color TV Is Coming" and forecast its arrival the following spring. Six days later (November 4, 1953), another full-page ad appeared in the same paper headed "All the Facts about Color Television." The items listed below this heading cautioned readers in detail that color television would not be available to them on a mass basis, in inexpensive and easy-to-see form for some time. The final appeal urged readers to purchase black-and-white television sets immediately. This advertisement was sponsored by distributors of the 12 brands of television which were ordinarily the keenest rivals in capturing the market (3). The impending arrival of color television and its public announcement created a *situation* with potential threat to each one of these traditional rivals. Therefore, they banded together temporarily to reduce the threat. Such cases are by no means unusual.

Positive and Negative Intergroup Attitudes in Formation

Positive and negative intergroup attitudes are derived from products of interaction between two or more groups. Norms of social distance are the end products of interaction between groups over a time span. They are not merely reflections of transitory relations (friendly or hostile) among individuals. Relations among individuals belonging to various groups have to be standardized as norms toward out-groups before they are reflected as intergroup attitudes by the membership of the given groups. History is full of illustrations of the formation of such norms (e.g., 15).

To stay within manageable limits, our discussion is restricted here to intergroup relations of small groups. In developing the theoretical approach which led to the experiments to be reported in this chapter, we relied rather heavily on leads derived from an extensive survey of actual small groups. Relations of small groups yield to intensive step-by-step analysis in the very process of formation. Their structural properties can be studied in terms of reciprocal status and role relations of all constituent members, including the leader. Therefore, informally organized small groups afford a basis for sound generalizations concerning the intra- and inter-group relations of in-groups in general.

As we have seen, when individuals with common motives interact with one another and the fulfillment of the common motives requires their continued interaction, in time there develops a group structure in which members occupy definite statuses. The very fact of stabilization of a system of reciprocities implies the demarcation of in-group structure from other groups.

The in-group thus delineated becomes endowed with positive qualities which tend to be praiseworthy, self-justifying, and even self-glorifying. Individual members tend to develop these qualities through internalizing group norms and through example, verbal dictum, and a set of correctives standardized to deal with cases of deviation. Hence possession of these qualities, which reflect their particular brand of ethnocentrism, is not essentially a problem of deviate behavior but a question of participation in in-group values and trends on the part of good members, who constitute the majority of membership as long as group solidarity and morale are maintained.

Functionally related out-groups and their respective members are attributed positive or negative qualities, depending on the positive or negative nature of functional relations between groups in question. The positive or negative nature of these functional relationships may result from actual harmony and interdependence or from actual incompatibility and conflict between the aspirations and directions of the groups in question. However, especially in the relations of larger group units, where face-to-face contacts are supplanted to a considerable extent by communication from the powerful mass media, the nature of intergroup relations may reflect a picture promulgated by powerful and interested parties within the groups involved or by other functionally related groups.

In time, the adjectives attributed to out-groups take their places in the repertory of group norms as a scale of social distance for the group in question toward so many out-groups. The lasting, derogatory stereotypes attributed to out-groups low on the social-distance scale are particular cases of norms toward out-groups.

Because they become integral parts of the group's norm or value system and are transmitted to new group members through short-cut dicta and verbal counsel, norms or stereotypes toward out-groups tend to outlast the conditions which gave rise to them. In this light it is easier to understand why, in times of changed relationships between former antagonistic groups, it is difficult for leadership to plunge immediately into the line of action direly necessitated by developing conditions. "Tradition" lies between them.

EXPERIMENTAL APPROACH TO INTERGROUP RELATIONS

The generalizations stated in the preceding paragraphs are derived from a historical survey of social-distance scales in formation, studies of prejudice, and intensive study of various forms of small groups in their in-group and intergroup relations (15). They were basic in the formulation of hypotheses and execution of the experiments to be reported in this chapter.

Briefly, whenever individuals interact in the face of a common goal or common misfortune or fate, they tend to stabilize their relations in a group structure delineated as an in-group or "we-group." This sets them off distinctly from others. In-groups inevitably form, in time, norms toward groups with which they are functionally related. These norms toward out-groups may be positive or negative. The positive or negative intergroup attitudes of members are derived from these norms.

For example, when the clash of vital interests between the American colonies and England in the pre-Revolutionary period finally led Britain to attempt to maintain her dominant position by force of arms, "the mother country began to appear in American eyes as a foreign, despotic, and 'Papist' power" (10, p. 374).

When a gang appropriates certain blocks in a city for its activities, it is considered "indecent" and a violation of their "rights" for another group to carry on its feats in that area. Intrusion of another group in the area is conducive to conflict, at times with grim consequences (17).

When a workers' group declares a strike, existing group lines are drawn more sharply. Other individuals and groups are evaluated and reacted to in terms of their stand on the strike. Those who are not actually for the strike are regarded as against it. And there is no creature more lowly than the man who works while the strike is on (7).

Literature on the formation of prejudice by growing children shows that it is not necessary for the individual to have actual unfavorable experiences with out-groups to form attitudes of prejudice toward them. In the very process of becoming an in-group member, the intergroup delineations and corresponding norms prevailing in the group are internalized by the individual (8).

In experimental literature one finds support for the general fact of in-group demarcation and attitude formation toward out-groups even in studies which were not primarily designed to investigate these topics. For example, in Sears, Hovland, and Miller's study of the effects of frustration caused primarily by sleep deprivation, with various other frustrations provided for the subjects as well, an in-group formation was observed in the making. Jokes and unflattering adjectives were bestowed not only on the experimenters involved but on psychologists in general (11). Likewise, in the Minnesota study of semistarvation during World War II, the men sharing semistarvation "built up a tremendous in-group feeling that tended to exclude both their non-starving friends and administrative and technical staff" (5, p. 31).

On the basis of leads from such empirical and experimental literature, a number of hypotheses concerning intergroup relations were formulated and an experimental program on intergroup relations was carried out. The rest of this chapter will concentrate on this research.

Methodological Guides Followed in the Experiments

The great advantage of experimentation lies in its rigorous control of conditions and precise specification of variables. If properly conceived and executed, experimentation provides a definitive basis for verifying or rejecting specific hypotheses and concepts advanced to account for intergroup behavior. Intergroup relations are new problems for experimentation. At this early stage we have to proceed cautiously. Therefore, it is extremely important that the main methodological guides followed in the experiments be specified. Only in this cautious way can prediction and control of social events be within our reach.

These considerations governed the formulation of hypotheses, selection of subjects, techniques of data collection, and design of longitudinal experiments on intergroup relations directed by M. Sherif in 1949 (12, 15), 1953 (16), and 1954 (14). Since these aspects were similar, this section serves as a general introduction to all of the experiments. Variations in detail are noted in presenting the results later in the chapter.

Problems of study which are organically related to actual intergroup relations can be formulated only through a great deal of familiarity with actual events in this area. Likewise, fruitful *hypotheses* which can be tested experimentally are derived through careful study of recurrent findings and trends in actual historical and current events. Hypotheses which are simply a priori hunches based on pet notions are likely to lack validity. The particular hypotheses formulated in these experiments are stated in their appropriate contexts.

Devising Experiments That Embody Essentials of the Problem: Even if the original problem is related to recurrent realities, there is a danger of destroying that problem and its significance in actual experimental work. In order to obtain valid results, the interaction situations must embody the main essentials of their counterparts in actual life. Experimental conditions are controlled. Yet they must also appear natural to the individuals functioning within them. Our concern for precision and rigor in procedures is balanced with equal insistence on keeping the main essentials of interaction processes intact, so that these features are not mutilated through formalism in procedures.

For this reason, subjects in these experiments were not made aware that they were subjects in experiments designed to study intergroup relations or that various problem situations were manipulated by experimenters. The experiments were announced as studies of camping procedures, group life, leadership, of how individuals get along in various activities with others, how they react when they are competing, when the going gets rough, and so on. As far as the subjects themselves were concerned, they were attending camps set up to study camping methods and group living in general.

As noted in earlier chapters, there are sound psychological reasons for this procedure (see pp. 131–132; pp. 191–196). If individuals are aware that the process of group formation, their strivings toward friendship, their hostility expressed toward others are being observed at every step, their self-awareness becomes an important factor in determining their behavior.

Experimental Control over Conditions of Interaction: Studying group relations as they develop in natural settings does not mean sacrificing experimental control over conditions. Control over conditions started in the selection of a site for each experiment. The site of experimentation was chosen (1) to be isolated from outside influences, (2) to afford opportunity for a variety of activities, (3) to allow manipulation of the conditions and circumstances of interaction. The latter included separate and comparable facilities for experimental groups. The isolation of the site and prior arrangements with relatives and friends of subjects and staff made it possible to eliminate outside visitors to the camps. The manner in which experimental situations were controlled and altered is outlined briefly below.

Problem Situations and Goals: The problem situations and related goals introduced at various stages of these experiments were not artificial to the subjects. The main interests and concerns of the subjects were studied both prior to the experiment and as it progressed. Thus, whenever feasible, activities and problems were introduced at specified times in such a way that they met the expressed desires of the subjects.

In keeping with the attempt to approximate life conditions, *goals* were introduced as integral aspects of the ongoing activities. For example, individuals were given undivided, unprepared ingredients of a sumptuous meal or refreshment when they were hungry, so that a situation of interdependence and coöperation for attainment of a goal desired by all of them was created.

Once activities or problem situations were introduced, the experimental staff was instructed to refrain from making suggestions concerning how to proceed or from singling out individuals to take responsibility. For the solution of problem situations no formal method, such as discussion or lecture, was utilized. The basic assumption was that the introduction of a problem situation that was urgent and could not be ignored would be conducive to interaction. *When individuals interact toward common goals, discussion necessarily has its place, lecture and exhortation from fellow members have their place, and action has its place.* In all cases, they do not follow an identical sequence. They may merge and overlap. Once a plan of action was undertaken, staff members provided technical assistance in carrying it out, if it was needed.

EXPERIMENTAL DESIGN IN SUCCESSIVE STAGES: Experiments concerning formation of group structure, in-group relations, and relations between groups are necessarily longitudinal. They involve interaction of individuals and groups over a time span. In order that the results of interaction processes could be related to systematic changes in the conditions of interaction, these experiments were designed in successive stages.

It will be recalled that those parts of the 1949 and 1953 experiments summarized in Chapter 6 (pp. 191–207) started with observation of the beginnings of informal friendship clusters on the basis of personal affinities. This initial period was introduced solely with the aim of assigning individuals to experimental groupings which split up the budding friendship clusters as much as possible. In this way the possibility that in-groups produced were formed largely on the basis of personal attraction, rather than the experimental conditions, was reduced. Since both the 1949 and 1953 experiments demonstrated that the experimental conditions prescribed by the hypotheses were sufficient to produce in-group formations among homogeneous individuals, this initial period was eliminated from the 1954 experiment.

In all of the experiments, in-groups were formed as a consequence of interaction among individuals before studying intergroup relations. *In order to study intergroup relations and their products, there have to be at least two delineated groups with hierarchical status and role relations and group norms.* In the stage of in-group formation, all activities introduced met the criterion for the experimental conditions in that stage. Thus, the activities during that period required interdependent, coördinated activity toward goals which had appeal value to all interacting individuals.

The next stage studied was *intergroup relations* in specified conditions conducive to *friction between groups*. This negative aspect was deliberately undertaken as the next step in studying intergroup relations. The major problem in intergroup relations today is the reduction of existing inter-group frictions. The problem of producing harmony or integration be-tween groups which are not in conflict is slight in comparison. By singling out factors in intergroup relations which are conducive to friction, realistic leads for reducing friction between groups can be formulated.

All activities during the phase of intergroup friction were selected (1) to embody goals whose attainment by one group meant failure or frustra-tion to the other group or (2) to involve frustration or blocking of goals shared by members of one group which appeared to result from the actions of the other group.

The final stage of experimentation was introduced in the 1954 experi-ment to be summarized in this chapter. This stage was the study of the *reduction of intergroup friction.* The activities in this phase required co-ordinated efforts toward commonly desired goals which could not be ig-nored by group members, but whose attainment was beyond the resources and efforts of one group alone. Such goals will be referred to as *superordi-nate goals.* Thus the experimental conditions in this stage embodied super-ordinate goals conducive to interdependent activity involving both groups.

SUBJECTS: In these experiments studying the formation of group struc-tures and relations between them, subjects were chosen in terms of the following criteria and for the reasons noted:

1. Normal individuals, so that results could not be explained in terms of individual abnormalities, excessive frustrations, and the like.
2. Individuals with no previous relationships as friends or co-members of an already existing in-group, so that relationships formed during the experiment could be traced to interaction during the experiment itself.

3. Individuals who were homogeneous in terms of age, sex, and backgrounds (educational, religious, socioeconomic, stability of family, etc.), so that trends in interaction among them could not be attributed to existing friendly or antagonistic attitudes stemming from these differences.

To insure isolation and to eliminate immediate external influences on the conditions of interaction, camp situations have decided advantages. These led to choosing as subjects preadolescent boys, for whom the activities in these situations are real and exciting.

DATA COLLECTION: The techniques of obtaining data were guided by the concern that experimental conditions capture the main essentials of their counterparts in actual life. Accordingly, data collected concerning individual and group functioning were secured without the subjects' knowledge that they were being observed at every step. As far as subjects were concerned, the observers were all personnel in functions customary for the situation. Participant observers were instructed to record observations in such ways that they could not be detected in the act of observing. Observations were jotted down in rough notes, which were expanded during the same day. In addition, data were secured whenever possible through "hidden microphones" and candid cameras. All other methods were those which could be used without cluttering the flow of interaction, once a problem situation was introduced. This methodological point was so central in the conception of the experiments that all techniques of data collection were subordinated to it.

USING A COMBINATION OF METHODS: There is always a danger that even trained observers may observe selectively, discounting items which reveal tendencies opposing the main hypotheses. Therefore, to check and cross-check the validity of results and to increase precision of data obtained, a combination of methods was utilized. If trends revealed through various techniques check with each other, then one is justified in concluding they are valid findings.

Both observational and sociometric techniques were used in all of the experiments. Trends observed were checked by introducing various situational and laboratory-like techniques as part of ongoing activities at crucial "choice points." One such check in the 1953 study concerned the emerging status reciprocities and attitudes within the experimental groups; it was summarized in Chapter 6 (pp. 204–207). In 1954, cross-checking of results by a combination of methods was carried still farther, in line with theoretical and methodological considerations stated at the initial period of this research (*12, 15*). Accordingly, observational data, status ratings, sociometric choices, situational tests, laboratory-like techniques at choice points were utilized for this purpose.

Personal data on subjects, their backgrounds and adjustments in school and neighborhood were secured prior to the experiments in such a way that they were not linked to the interaction situations during the study in the subjects' eyes.

EXPERIMENTAL PRODUCTION OF INTERGROUP FRICTION—BULL DOGS AND RED DEVILS (*1949 STUDY*)

In Chapter 6 the group relations experiment carried out in 1949 was reported with emphasis on formation of the group structures (pp. 191–202). These groups took the names "Bull Dogs" and "Red Devils." A more adequate summary of the period of intergroup relations in that study was reserved for this chapter.

It will be recalled that, when individuals were brought together and engaged in activities requiring coöperation for attaining common goals, unmistakable in-group structures developed, each with hierarchical positions and roles within it. As the groups formed, the members of each achieved positive in-group identifications as they acquired certain statuses and roles. This group relatedness resulted in shifts or reversals in the friendship preferences of group members *away* from previously budding friendships with individuals who were assigned to another group and *toward* friendship preferences within their own group. Thus the developing groups became the *reference groups* of the individual members. In the process of group formation, by-products of group interaction were standardized as social norms, which pertained to in-group relations and in-group activities. These main results on experimental in-group formation were confirmed in 1953 (*16*) and also in 1954 (see pp. 303–306 below).

Rise of Intergroup Friction

A period designed to study intergroup relations followed the stage of in-group formation. The Bull Dogs and Red Devils were brought into functional contact in competitive activities and in mutually frustrating situations. The main hypothesis tested in this phase was as follows:

When two in-groups are brought into functional relationship under conditions of competition and frustration, negative out-group attitudes and stereotypes will arise and become standardized.

This stage lasted nearly five days. At the beginning, a series of competitive games and camp contests was announced, as though granting the boys' expressed desires to engage in these activities with another group. Points were given for victory in games and excellence in performing camp duties. The winning group was to receive a much-admired prize: 12 four-bladed knives. Winning these prizes was contingent on being a member of the victorious team. They could be attained only by contributing to the achievement of the group as a whole. Figure 9.1 shows the two groups in a tug-of-war during the contest.

The effects of competitive games were not immediate. Rivalry between the groups was apparent; derogation of the other group was common. Yet observers noted considerable "good sportsmanship" on the part of both groups at first. For example, after the first and second contests, the winning group spontaneously gave a cheer for the losers, and the losers responded as a group with a cheer for the winners. However, as the series of contests progressed, this cheer changed from "2-4-6-8, who do we appreciate," followed by the name of the other group, to "2-4-6-8, who do we appreci-*hate*."

Effects of Intergroup Friction on the In-Groups

The series of contests tended, especially at first, to solidify further the groups which had taken shape in the previous stage. As intergroup rivalry became more intense, expressions of hostility toward the out-group became more and more frequent. Probably because of their more effective organization, the Bull Dog group pulled out into the lead and stayed there.

The Red Devils responded to their increasingly apparent losing position by labeling the Bull Dogs "dirty players" and "cheats." A common expression among the Red Devils was "At least we play fair." By the contest's end, the terms "dirty players" and "cheats" were almost synonymous with *Bull Dogs* as far as the Red Devils were concerned.

The results of the intergroup competition for the Bull Dogs were elation and heightened in-group pride and identification. The losing group of Red Devils suffered considerable frustration. Chiefly because the Red Devil leader became vindictive and began blaming defeat on low-status members of his own group, group failure was, in this group, conducive to signs of disorganization. Lower-status Red Devils were hostile to the Bull Dogs; at the same time, they resented the accusations of their own leader. Until the Red Devil group experienced broadside attacks from the Bull Dogs and fought with them later, there were frequent indications of in-group conflict.

Fig. 9.1. Tug-of-war. (From M. Sherif and C. W. Sherif, *Groups in Harmony and Tension*. New York: Harper & Brothers, 1953.)

Fig. 9.2. The Red Devils' table smeared with food by Bull Dogs. (From M. Sherif and C. W. Sherif, *Groups in Harmony and Tension*. New York: Harper & Brothers, 1953.)

Increasing Intergroup Hostility and Name-Calling

This contest was followed by a party proposed by the staff to let "by-gones be bygones" between the groups. Although each group claimed that the bad feelings between them were strictly the fault of the other group, both agreed to come. This party involved a frustrating situation planned by the staff so that it appeared to be caused by one group. It led to further frustrations experienced in common by group members.

The refreshments were placed on a table. Half were crushed and unap-petizing; half were whole and delectable. By careful timing (which was not suspected by the subjects), the Red Devils arrived first. When told to take their share of the refreshments, they took the good half and sat down to enjoy it. When the Bull Dogs arrived a short time later and saw the sorry-looking refreshments left them, they immediately protested. The Red Devils justified their actions with "first come, first served," which became the standardized justification for all Red Devils. The Bull Dogs proceeded to eat their refreshments, hurling taunts, insults, and names at the Red Devils. Particularly common was the term "pigs." Among the names used by most Bull Dogs for Red Devils on this and later occasions were "pigs," "dirty bums" or "Red bums," "jerks," and several more objectionable terms.

The next morning the Red Devils retaliated by deliberately dirtying their breakfast table to make K.P. duty harder for the Bull Dogs. Upon seeing the dirty table, the Bull Dogs decided to mess it up further and leave it. All Bull Dogs joined in by smearing the table with cocoa, sugar, syrup, and the like, and leaving it alive with bees and wasps (see Fig. 9.2). The Bull Dogs hung the walls with threatening and derogatory posters against the Red Devils. (See Figs. 9.3 and 9.4 for examples of posters made by members of the two groups during intergroup friction.)

At lunch that day the hostility between the groups increased to such a point throughout the meal that they soon were lined up on opposite sides of the mess hall calling names and then throwing food, cups, tableware, etc. The fight was broken up. Neither group was sure who started the fight, but each was sure it was someone in the *other* group.

At this point, the experiment proper was over. The conflict was not over, however. It took another two days of genuine and active efforts by the staff, involving "preaching" and coercion, just to stop the group fighting. The groups planned raids on each other's cabins (see Fig. 9.5). Green ap-ples were collected and hoarded by both groups for "ammunition," with

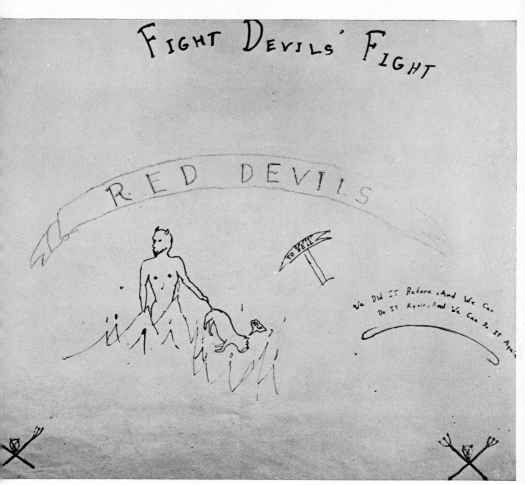

FIG. 9.3. One of the posters made by Red Devils. (From M. Sherif and C. W. Sherif, *Groups in Harmony and Tension*. New York: Harper & Brothers, 1953.)

FIG. 9.4. One of the posters made by Bull Dogs. (From M. Sherif and C. W. Sherif, *Groups in Harmony and Tension*. New York: Harper & Brothers, 1953.)

Fig. 9.5. Bull Dogs raiding Red Devil bunkhouse. (From M. Sherif and C. W. Sherif, *Groups in Harmony and Tension*. New York: Harper & Brothers, 1953.)

the explanation that this was done merely "in case" it might be needed. The Red Devils attempted "sneak" attacks when the other group and counselors were asleep. (The Red Devils had tended to show signs of disorganization after their defeat in the competitions. In this period the group was again united.) This fighting and raiding between groups took on a planned character. They were not merely outbursts upon momentary encounters of individuals.

Summary of Intergroup Friction and Its Aftereffects

Finally, the results of intergroup relations in competitive and frustrating situations were to solidify in-group belongingness and solidarity, to strengthen in-group attitudes, and to generate and increase attitudes of hostility toward the out-group. These attitudes of hostility included specific name-calling which came close to standardization of negative stereotypes. Thus the hypothesis concerning intergroup friction was supported.

In the course of interaction between the two groups in mutually frustrating and competitive activities, members developed negative attitudes and hostility toward members of the out-group. This happened in spite of the fact that, before these in-groups formed, friendship preferences of individuals were predominantly for other individuals who were assigned to the out-group.

A fact which may have practical implications in this connection deserves note. As we have seen, democracy and coöperation within the groups does not necessarily lead to democracy and coöperation with the out-group and its members, if the directions and interests of the groups are in conflict. In fact, the group in this experiment which had the more democratic in-group organization (Bull Dogs) was more consistent and concerted in expressions of out-group antagonism. There may be a substantial grain of truth in the contention by some sociologists that at times intergroup hostility may be proportional to in-group solidarity.

These results also have implications for an important line of theorizing in psychology as it applies to intergroup relations. It is sometimes suggested that hostility toward other people can be reduced through "catharsis" by giving vent to pent-up feelings of aggression in overt activities. Robert Faris called attention to the pitfalls of this view in interpreting group friction (4). Such a view misses the unmistakable effects of group membership on experience and behavior, both within the group and in relations with out-groups. The experiment summarized indicates that, once groups see each other as a source of frustration, a threat to themselves, and an obstacle to their goals, acts of hostility become conducive to the production of renewed hostility. Rather than reducing aggression toward out-groups, giving vent in overt activity actually increased hostility and its end products.

As noted, staff members were instructed after the period of intergroup friction to do away with the hostility as much as possible. Perhaps the most remarkable observation of this period was that in spite of their efforts to break up the in-groups by bringing the boys all together in camp duties and activities, campfires, birthday parties, and athletic events emphasizing individual rather than group competition, the preferences of the boys tended, on the whole, to follow the in-group lines. The old songs, names, and stereotypes derogatory to the out-group continued to crop up. Such observations indicate a strong tendency for attitudes toward in-group and out-group to persist even though the conditions which gave rise to them no longer exist. Such findings provided important leads for the methods used in 1954 for the systematic reduction of intergroup friction.

Probably the most effective event utilized for reducing friction between the Red Devils and the Bull Dogs was a camp-wide softball game, in which the best players were chosen by all boys from both groups to compete with an outside group of boys from a neighboring town. In this event, the boys participated as *campers*, not as in-group members. However, this lead was not followed in later experiments. Essentially, such a "common enemy" approach to reducing friction between groups by uniting them against another group amounts to producing friction between larger group units.

ASSESSING INTERGROUP STEREOTYPES THROUGH JUDGMENTS

Unfavorable stereotypes formed during intergroup conflict and favorable images of out-groups produced in intergroup coöperation were assessed in an experiment by R. Avigdor (2). This experiment was carried out in a settlement house in New York City in 1951 with friendship clubs of young girls.

A situation of coöperative interaction between groups was created by encouraging members to put on a show to raise money for club jackets. This much-desired objective could be reached only by having two groups join forces for a show. Two groups coöperating for this purpose came into conflict with another club, and this intergroup conflict was utilized by the experimenter.

During intergroup coöperation and at the height of intergroup conflict, Avigdor had each group rate the others on various characteristics. Some were favorable (e.g., *careful, considerate, fair*) and some were unfavorable (e.g., *bossy, cheaters, selfish*). The five categories used in rating ranged from "all of them are (e.g., *careful*)" through "some of them are . . ." to "none of them are. . . ." Thus, "all of them are (e.g., *fair*)" constituted an extremely favorable judgment when used with a favorable characteristic. "None of them are . . ." for the same characteristic was an extremely unfavorable judgment. The reverse appraisal held true for unfavorable characteristics (e.g., *cheaters*).

In brief characteristics attributed to the out-group in conflict were more unfavorable, more extreme ("all" or "none"), and selectively chosen in terms of their relevance to the in-group's particular stand in the intergroup friction. During intergroup coöperation, on the other hand, a generally positive image of the out-group was found with less tendency toward extreme, stereotyped conceptions.

The attribution of largely favorable characteristics to friendly out-groups and of unfavorable characteristics to negatively related out-groups was substantiated by O. J. Harvey in an experiment utilizing small cliques with existing intergroup relationships in a student dormitory (6). He further undertook to assess prevailing attitudes toward fellow clique members and toward friendly or unfriendly out-groups through judgments of performance.

On the basis of ratings by counselors and sociometric choices, 16 clearly differentiated cliques were selected. Half were on friendly terms; half were unfriendly or hostile. The performance was writing a list of items while listening to irrelevant recorded material which served as "dummy" to disguise the problem. By disguising the purpose as a "test" of attention span and projecting the achievement of each clique member briefly on a screen, the stimulus to be judged was relevant to group attitudes and allowed alternative modes of response.

The overall findings indicate that judgments pertaining to fellow group members made within the confines of the in-group differed from judgments made when members of an unfriendly out-group were present. When members of an unfriendly out-group were present, there was a greater tendency toward *overestimating* performance of fellow group members. In contrast, the presence of a friendly out-group led to no appreciable difference in judging performance by fellow group members. Thus these judgmental indices in numerical form confirmed the observed tendency for in-group members to "close ranks" and experience heightened positive evaluation of the group when interacting with an unfriendly out-group.

Unfriendly attitudes toward members of the out-group were revealed in judging their performance by the tendency to estimate their performance significantly lower than performance by fellow group members. Performance by members of an unfriendly out-group was underestimated. In contrast, the performance of members of a friendly out-group was not judged in a way appreciably different from that of fellow group members.

PRODUCTION OF INTERGROUP CONFLICT AND ITS REDUCTION—ROBBERS CAVE EXPERIMENT

In the summer of 1954, the third experiment on group relations was carried out under the direction of M. Sherif.[1] The general plan of the study followed the 1949 and 1953 experiments (pp. 193–196).

The crucial problem of the 1954 experiment was the *reduction* of intergroup friction and conflict. It was carried out in three successive stages:

[1] The account which follows is devoted only to a summary of main hypotheses and results. The experiment is reported more fully in 14.

I. *The stage of in-group formation.* In order to study intergroup relations, there have to be groups with definite structures and norms of
their own.

II. *The stage of intergroup friction and conflict.* Before tackling the main
problem, namely, that of changing unfavorable intergroup attitudes
toward friendship and coöperation, it was necessary first to produce
unmistakable manifestations of intergroup conflict.

III. *The stage of reduction of intergroup friction.* This stage is the crucial
one and constitutes the really new step beyond the previous experiments in this series.

The study was carried out in Robbers Cave State Park, about 150 miles
southeast of Oklahoma City. The 200-acre camp site is wooded, hilly, and
completely surrounded by the state park. Figure 9.6 gives an idea of the
site. The camp site and surrounding areas afforded ample facilities for
separate housing for the groups, varied activities, and lifelike problem
situations.

Subjects were 22 boys of about 11 years of age. They all came from
established, middle socioeconomic class, stable, Protestant families. None
came from broken homes. None was a problem case in school, home, or
neighborhood. They were all in the upper half of their class in scholastic
standing and had above average IQ's. They were all healthy, socially well-
adjusted boys.

Since the subjects came from a homogeneous socioeconomic, religious,
and ethnic background, the results cannot be explained on the basis of
social background differences. Neither can they be explained on the basis
of failure, excessive frustration, maladjustment suffered in their life histories, or scholastic retardation or intellectual ineptitude. Since the subjects
were not acquainted with one another prior to the experiment, groups
were not formed around previously existing personal relationships.

The subjects were divided into two bunches prior to the experiment.
These two bunches were matched in as many respects as possible (physical
size, athletic ability, swimming, cooking, musical proficiency, and so on).
The two bunches of boys were taken to the experimental site in separate
buses and at different times. Until the last days of Stage I (group formation), the two groups carried on in-group activities unaware of each other's
presence and activities in the camp.

The nature of goals introduced in each experimental stage was specified.
In the first stage, goals required coördinated activity conducive to division

of labor and hence to status and role differentiation. In the second stage, goals were conducive to friction between groups. In the third stage, goals were conducive to interdependent and coöperative activity between groups.

No special techniques by adults to manipulate interaction were used. There were no lectures, exhortations, emotional appeals, or discussions led by adults. Rather, carefully designed problem situations were introduced. When the group members reached a decision and took a course of action, they were given an effective hand by staff members in carrying it out.

Stage I: Formation of In-Groups

The predictions concerning group formation and the conditions of interaction conducive to it were formulated in the following hypotheses:

1. A definite group structure consisting of differentiated status positions and reciprocal roles will be produced when a number of individuals (without previously established interpersonal relations) interact with one another under conditions (a) which situationally embody goals that have common appeal value to the individuals and (b) which require interdependent activities for their attainment.
2. When individuals interact under conditions stated in hypothesis 1, concomitant with the formation of group structure, norms regulating their behavior in relations with one another and activities commonly engaged in will be standardized.

In line with the findings of the 1949 and 1953 experiments summarized in Chapter 6, these two hypotheses were once more verified in the Robbers Cave experiment. The change from togetherness situations to more and more stabilized groups took place during interaction in a series of problem situations over a week's period. Each of the problem situations had common goals which could not be ignored by the individuals and which required coördinated efforts for their attainment.

The emergence of differentiated statuses was ascertained in daily observations and independent status ratings made twice a day by staff members. The criterion for formation of group structures was stabilization of statuses occupied by members for two consecutive days, as revealed in high agreement between independent ratings of different observers. At the end of a week this criterion was satisfied. Each group had adopted a name, "Rattlers" and "Eagles" respectively. Each had appropriated a bunkhouse, hide-out, and swimming place as its own. The boys put the names of their groups on flags and T-shirts. The Eagles had named their swimming place

FIG. 9.6. Ledge overlooking camp area at Robbers Cave.

FIG. 9.7. Rattlers carrying their canoe to hide-out.

Some Eagles cut and distribute meat.

FIG. 9.8.   Preparing a meal.

Some Eagles cut watermelon.

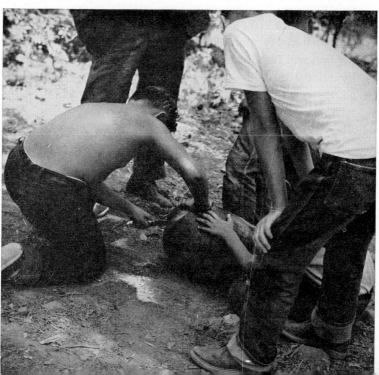

("Moccasin Creek"). The Rattlers appropriated the baseball field, which was closer to their area and which they had cleared for the coming competitive events when informed that another group was in the vicinity.

The sort of conditions which were introduced during this stage can be illustrated by representative problem situations. One was introduced by putting canoes near the bunkhouse of each group. When the group members discovered them, they wanted to take them to their special swimming place over rough terrain some distance away. The problem was discussed immediately and a plan carried out with the enthusiastic collaboration of group members. Figure 9.7 shows the Rattlers carrying out their plan.

Another typical problem situation was making available to the subjects the ingredients of a meal in unprepared form (e.g., meat, watermelon, Kool-Aid) at a time when they were hungry. Turning these ingredients into a meal required preparation, division into portions, and serving, in which participation of all was necessary. Figure 9.8, A and B, shows the Eagles in action on one such occasion.

Stage II: Production of Intergroup Friction

The formation of negative intergroup attitudes and stereotypes was planned in order to create the problem of reducing them. The main hypotheses for this stage were :

1. In the course of competition and frustrating relations between two groups, unfavorable stereotypes will come into use in relation to the out-group and its members and will be standardized in time, placing the out-group at a certain social distance.
2. The course of relations between two groups which are in a state of competition will tend to produce an increase in in-group solidarity.
3. Functional relations between groups which are of consequence to the groups in question will tend to bring about changes in the pattern of relations within in-groups involved.

To test these predictions, a series of competitive events and reciprocally frustrating situations was planned. As in the previous experiment, prizes were to be awarded to the group that accumulated the higher score in a tournament. There was great enthusiasm over this tournament in both groups. When the boys learned of the presence of another group during the last days of Stage I, each group to a man expressed intense desires to compete with that other group with a great confidence in themselves, and issued a challenge to the other group. Thus it appeared to the subjects that the tournament was the consequence of their own challenges. This strong tendency to want to compete with another group stemmed from their experiences and activities in the general culture.

In this experiment it proved unnecessary to introduce planned situations which were mutually frustrating. A series of mutually frustrating situations arose when the Eagles were defeated in a tug-of-war contest toward the end of the first day of the tournament. The Eagles burned the Rattlers' flag, which had been left on the backstop of the athletic field. The following morning the Rattlers arrived first at the athletic field and discovered their burned emblem. This seemed an outrage which must have been the vengeful deed of the Eagles. They drew up a strategy to destroy the Eagle flag if the Eagles admitted the misdeed.

So when the Eagles arrived at the field and admitted they had burned the flag, the Rattlers immediately went into action according to plan. The Eagles' flag was seized; the Eagles responded with some violence and in turn seized the remaining Rattler flag. Through all, the groups were scuffling and shouting derogatory names. Figure 9.9 was one of the pictures taken during this incident.

During the rest of this experimental stage, name-calling, physical encounters, and "raids" followed one another. After the skirmishes over the flags, the Rattlers staged a "raid" on the Eagle cabin, causing quite a bit of inconvenience and frustration to the Eagles. Figure 9.10 shows the Rattlers displaying blue jeans seized as booty on which they painted "The Last of the Eagles." This raid was later reciprocated by the Eagles, who left the Rattlers' cabin in confusion. However, this was a mild affair compared to the Rattlers' retaliation some days later, which took place after the Rattlers lost the tournament.

In the competitive events, the success of one group meant the failure of the other. In the reciprocally frustrating engagements that flared up, unfavorable invectives were hurled across group lines. Physical encounters intensified intergroup hostility. Within six days the intergroup conflict produced such an unfavorable image of the out-group, with accompanying derogatory stereotypes, that each group was dead set against having any more to do with the other. Thus there arose extreme social distance between the two groups.

ESTIMATION OF TIME BY GROUPS ON THE VERGE OF VICTORY AND DEFEAT: Each engagement in the competitive series implied considerable effort and zeal, which were reflected in characteristic psychological reactions and contributed to the building up of unfavorable attitudes toward

FIG. 9.9.   Incident after the flag-burning episode: Eagles seizing Rattlers' other flag.

FIG. 9.10.   Rattlers display blue jeans captured in raid on Eagles and inscribed "The Last of the Eagles."

the out-group. One of the noteworthy incidents is exemplified in the second tug-of-war. The Rattlers had won the first tug-of-war. The Eagles had retaliated by burning the Rattler flag, which initiated the series of conflict situations.

Before the Eagles came to the second tug-of-war on the next day, they devised a strategy to win. After the pulling started, on a prearranged signal the Eagles all sat down on the ground and dug in their feet. The confident Rattlers were on their feet pulling strenuously, but they were becoming exhausted and rapidly lost ground. After seven minutes, the Rattlers adopted the enemy strategy and dug in too (see Fig. 9.11, A and B).

Greatly exhausted during their initial pull in a standing position, the Rattlers were being pulled gradually across the line. At the fortieth minute of the contest, a time limit of an additional 15 minutes was announced. At the end of this time, the Rattlers had not yet been pulled completely over the line. The contest was declared a tie, to the indignation of the Eagles and the relief and satisfaction of the weary Rattlers.

The Rattlers, thus relieved of certain defeat had the contest lasted longer, were accusing the Eagles of employing "dirty" strategy and telling each other that the contest had appeared to them as if it would never end. The Eagles, on the other hand, were remarking to each other that the precious time flew too fast on the verge of their victory.

On the following day the participant observers of each group asked the members of their respective groups individually, "How long did the tug-of-war last after both groups sat down and dug in?" The actual duration was 48 minutes. The Eagle estimates ranged from 20 to 45 minutes. The Rattler estimates ranged from 1 hour to 3½ hours. Thus there was no overlapping at all between the estimates of time made by the two groups. Deliberately, the question was worded without specifying a time unit. The Eagles all gave their judgments in minute units. The Rattlers gave theirs in hour units.

IMPACT OF INTERGROUP EVENTS ON IN-GROUP RELATIONS: The nature of in-group relations is essential in understanding intergroup relations. The reverse is equally true; for an adequate understanding of in-group relations, the understanding of relations between groups is also essential. A striking illustration was the downfall of Craig from the leadership status in the Eagle group as intergroup competition and conflict developed during Stage II. Craig rose to leadership during Stage I, when more peaceful activities were engaged in. But with the advent of Stage II, which required leadership that could stand in the front line in contests and engagements against

FIG. 9.11A.   Eagles' strategy in tug-of-war: sitting down while Rattlers exhaust themselves standing.

FIG. 9.11B.   Rattlers adopt the Eagle strategy: both sides dig in sitting down.

an adversary, Craig did not live up to expectations. For example, he deserted the rope during the first tug-of-war when it became evident that the Eagles were losing. Several days later, he kept himself at a safe distance when the Eagles attempted a retaliatory raid on the Rattlers. Therefore, Mason, a high-status Eagle, rose steadily and took over leadership in the group with his exemplary daring and front-line action in various contests and conflicts with the Rattlers.

In various events, defeats caused temporary confusion, bickering, and blaming each other within both groups. On the whole, however, the cumulative effect of intergroup friction was to intensify in-group solidarity. Temporary dissension within the group was followed typically by renewed efforts at in-group coördination, planning new tactics or engaging in acts directed against the out-group, and the like.

The change of leadership in the Eagles, reciprocal bickering, and maneuvering for positions within groups were family affairs. The Eagles were like members of a family or good friends who join hands immediately against an outside intrusion.

One of the telling indications of increased in-group solidarity was exhibited in both groups at Carlton Lake, a public beach a few miles from the camp. At the end of Stage II, each group was taken there separately. This was a test situation. The public beach was crowded with people and full of other distractions. However, each group behaved there as if the boys were by themselves; they were altogether preoccupied with their own business and their own fun.

These are examples of the general finding that intergroup relations, both in conflict and in the period of friendship between groups which followed, had significant consequences for the properties of interaction and the relations of members within the group structures involved.

SUMMARY OF OBSERVATIONAL FINDINGS IN STAGE II: The recurrent observations during Stage II indicate that intergroup friction which is consequential in the scheme of group activities (1) brings about unfavorable attitudes and stereotypes in relation to the out-group, (2) increases in-group solidarity, and (3) changes the pattern of relations within groups when such changes become necessary for effective dealings in intergroup relations. These results substantiate further the findings concerning intergroup friction in the 1949 experiment.[2]

---

[2] In the 1953 study, this stage was not completed. In a frustration episode, the subjects attributed the plan to the camp administration. Since testing the hypothesis required that the source of frustration be attributed to the experimental out-group, the 1953 study was terminated at this point.

CHECKING OBSERVATIONAL FINDINGS WITH OTHER METHODS: At the end of Stage II, sociometric choices, ratings of stereotypes of the in-group and the out-group, and judgments of performance by in-group and out-group were obtained in order to check the validity of observational findings.

Sociometric choices. Sociometric questions were asked informally of every member of each group individually. Two of the criterion questions concerned friendship preferences. They were worded to specify choices from the *entire camp* and not just from one's in-group. The other two criterion questions concerned effective initiative in the group, i.e., choosing who gets things started and who gets things done.

The friendship choices were overwhelmingly toward in-group members. Sociograms constructed on the basis of weighted scores (4 for the first choices, 3 for second, 2 for third, and 1 for the rest) for the four criteria reveal clearly the unique hierarchical group structures formed among the Rattlers and Eagles (see Figs. 9.12, 9.13).

Stereotyped images of in-group and out-group. Ratings of fellow group members and members of the out-group were obtained on a number of adjectives, of which six were critical. These critical terms were chosen from those actually used by subjects in referring to their own group or to the out-group during the height of intergroup friction. Three were favorable terms (*brave, tough, friendly*) and three were unfavorable (*sneaky, smart alecks, stinkers*). The rating technique was essentially like Avigdor's, ranging from "all of them are . . ." to "none of them are . . ." (see pp. 300–301).

As predicted from observational data, ratings of fellow group members were almost exclusively favorable (100 percent by Rattlers and 94.3 percent by Eagles). In contrast, ratings of the out-group after the intense intergroup friction were predominantly unfavorable. The ratings made by Rattlers of Eagle members were 53 percent unfavorable and 34.9 percent favorable. The ratings made by the Eagles of the Rattlers were 76.9 percent unfavorable and only 15.4 percent favorable. (Other ratings fell in the category "some of them are. . . .") These significant differences between favorable and unfavorable designations of the in-group and out-group confirmed observational findings. They will be discussed further in giving results of Stage III, where shifts in these ratings brought about by changed intergroup relations constitute important substantiating evidence.

Judgments of performance by in-group and out-group. It was predicted that an individual group member would have formed attitudes toward his own group and the out-group which would influence significantly his ap-

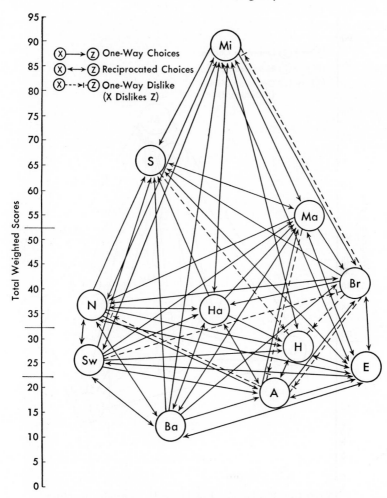

Fig. 9.12.   Rattlers—end of Stage II, in-group structure.

praisal of the activities of other individuals in the respective groups. This hypothesis was made on the basis of observations that the individual members tend to depreciate the achievements of the adversary and magnify the achievements of their fellows. This unit illustrates how precise methods derived from the laboratory can be utilized as an integral aspect of field study in lifelike conditions.

The task was introduced as a contest between the two groups, with a $5 reward to the winning group. Since social distance between the groups was so great that neither wanted to be in a situation with the other, this prize

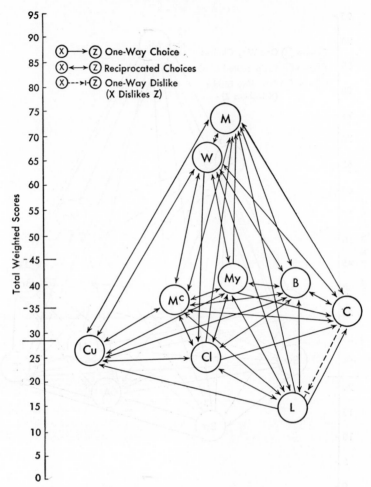

Fig. 9.13. Eagles—end of Stage II, in-group structure.

and the news that the staff had made wagers on the outcome of the event were inducements to take part. Once in the situation, members of each group participated with considerable zeal.

The contest was to be as follows: Each group was to collect beans which were scattered in two marked-off areas, one for each group, and then the number supposedly collected by each individual was to be judged. As far as subjects were concerned, both excellence in performance and accuracy in judgment were required to win the reward. The time for collecting beans was one minute. The beans were put in sacks with necks bound by a rubber hose so that they could not be counted (see Figs. 9.14 and 9.15).

Fig. 9.14. Bean toss contest.

Fig. 9.15. Experimental setup for estimation of performance.

After the collection the two groups went to a large hall where, according to announcement, the performance of each person (viz., beans collected) was projected by an opaque projector and judged by every other person. As each individual's supposed performance was projected, he stood up to insure proper identification.

Actually the same number of beans was projected each time for 5 seconds. Pretests with different subjects had shown that this number (35) could not be counted in 5 seconds but that subjects felt they could just about count if they tried a little harder. Thus, the number and timing reduced possible objections that exposure was too brief, but prevented accurate counting. Subjects did not suspect that the same number was projected each time. When the performance attributed to the Rattler leader was projected, admiring whistles were heard from his group.

The results of this unit were in numerical form, indicating the average amount of overestimation or underestimation of the number presented (35 in every case) as the performance by fellow group members or by members of the out-group. Thus the Rattlers tended to overestimate performance by fellow group members, the mean discrepancy between judgment and number projected being 3.40. In contrast, Rattlers tended to underestimate performance by Eagles with a mean discrepancy of − .29. Members of the Eagle group overestimated their own performance considerably more, the mean discrepancy being 11.80. In contrast, the Eagles' estimates of Rattler performance diverged from the actual number presented by only 4.56.

These differences between judgments of performance attributed to ingroup members and of performance attributed to members of the outgroup were highly significant and in the expected direction. It was concluded that the differing attitudes formed by individuals toward their own group and toward an antagonistic group affected their judgments. These results confirm the overall behavioral trends through reactions made in quantitative form by single individuals.

Stage III: Reduction of Intergroup Conflict and Stereotypes

By the end of Stage II, each group saw the out-group as the "villain" and placed itself on the side of the angels, justifying its deeds and unfavorable stereotypes toward the out-group. Solidarity and coöperativeness within the in-groups did not lead to coöperativeness and solidarity between groups.

CHOICE OF MEASURE FOR REDUCING INTERGROUP FRICTION: Various measures have been proposed for reducing the intergroup frictions that prevail today. A few of these are listed here with brief notes explaining why they were or were not included among the experimental conditions in Stage III:

1. Disseminating favorable *information* in regard to the out-group was not chosen as the experimental measure. As we shall see in discussing the general problem of attitude change in Chapter 16, information not related to the goals currently in focus in the activities of the groups in question is relatively ineffective.

2. In small groups like those in this study, it is possible to devise sufficiently attractive rewards to make individual achievement supreme. This may reduce tension between small groups by splitting the memberships on the basis of *"every man for himself."* Such a solution, however, has little relevance for actual intergroup tensions. In real life, social distance and intergroup conflict are in terms of membership in groups and of group alignments (pp. 283–285).

3. The resolution of conflict through leaders alone was not utilized. Group leaders, even when meeting apart from their groups around a conference table, cannot be taken independently of the dominant trends and prevailing intergroup attitudes of the membership in their respective groups. If the leader is too much out of step with these, he will cease to be followed. It is more realistic, therefore, to study the influence of leadership within the framework of prevailing trends and attitudes of the groups involved. This will give us leads concerning the conditions under which leadership can be effective in reducing intergroup tensions.

4. The "common enemy" approach is effective in pulling two or more groups together against another group. This was utilized in the 1949 experiment and yielded effective results. But bringing some groups together against others means larger conflicts, even though it may patch up frictions among a few groups temporarily.

5. Another measure advanced, both in theoretical and practical works, centers around social contacts among members of groups who stand at given social distances on occasions which are pleasant in themselves. This measure was tried out in the first phase of Stage III of this study.

6. In the second phase of Stage III, the measure that was effectively used was the introduction of superordinate goals which necessitated cooperative interaction between the groups.

Phase 1: Social contacts in reducing intergroup conflict. Before getting to the introduction of superordinate goals, contact in social situations was arranged. In this series of contact situations during the first two days of Stage III, both groups were left free in close physical proximity to interact with one another in situations which were pleasant in themselves. The staff members appeared to be out of supervision range on these occasions, as much as possible.

There were seven different contact situations, including eating together in the same dining hall, watching a movie together, and shooting fire crackers in the same area. These contact situations had no effect in reducing intergroup friction. If anything, they were utilized by members of both groups as opportunities for further name-calling and conflict. For example, they used mealtimes in the same place for "garbage fights," throwing mashed potatoes, leftovers, bottle caps, and the like accompanied by the exchange of derogatory names.

Thus, in line with our hypothesis to this effect, *contact between groups does not in itself produce a decrease in an existing state of intergroup tension.* Because of its implications for learning theories and for practitioners in the intergroup relations area, special note should be made of the fact that these activities, carried out by the two groups in close physical proximity, were satisfying in themselves.

Phase 2: Interaction between groups toward superordinate goals. Following the social contact situations, a series of superordinate goals was introduced which afforded challenging problem situations for both groups. These superordinate goals necessitated intergroup interaction toward common ends in problem situations which were real to the members of both groups. The goals were selected so that they would become focal to members in both groups; therefore, they could not be ignored or postponed easily. The attainment of superordinate goals could not be achieved through the energy and resources of one group alone but required the combined efforts and resources of both groups. This is why they are called *superordinate goals.*

The first of the two hypotheses tested during this period was:

1. When groups in a state of friction are brought into contact under conditions embodying superordinate goals, which are compelling but which cannot be achieved by the efforts of one group alone, they will tend to coöperate toward the common goal.

However, it is too much to expect that a state of friction, unfavorable stereotypes, and mutual social distance developed in a series of encounters over a period will be eliminated in a single episode of coöperation toward a common end. Therefore, the second hypothesis was:

2. Coöperation between groups necessitated by a series of situations embodying superordinate goals will have a cumulative effect in the direction of reduction of existing tension between groups.

Accordingly, during the following six days, a series of problem situations embodying such goals was introduced. The situations were varied in nature and required varied kinds of consideration, planning, and execution on the part of the subjects. But no matter how varied they were, all had an essential feature in common: they all involved goals that became focal for both groups under the given circumstances. These goals were urgent to the subjects; they had to be attended to. Psychological selectivity favored them. Yet their attainment clearly depended on communication, planning, and joint action by both groups. Thus the problem situations created a state of interdependence. The goal was highly desired by both groups, yet it could not be attained by the efforts and energies of one group alone.

All of the superordinate goals and problem situations introduced cannot be described here. Three of them are summarized below.

1. Both groups were warned several hours in advance that there was trouble in the water-supply system. Water came from a tank on top of a hill about a mile away. The tank was supplied with water pumped from a reservoir approximately two miles' walking distance from the camp. The terrain between camp and tank and reservoir was mountainous, rough, thickly wooded, and bushy. Both groups had had first-hand acquaintance with these places during Stage I, when each went on separate overnight camp-outs in the area. They had filled their canteens from a large faucet on the tank. So the water-supply system was real in the subjects' experience.

The problem situation was created by turning off a valve at the water tank and stuffing the open faucet on the tank with pieces of sacking. Several hours after a first warning, the water in the pipes leading to the camp was all drained through use. Therefore both groups were summoned to a central place at which the main pipe line in the camp divided into smaller lines supplying various points throughout the camp area. After demonstrating that the main pipe line and accessories were bone dry, the camp administration declared its inability to cope with the water situation within a reasonable time. It was explained that the defect might be leakage somewhere along the length of pipe line, at the pump by the reservoir, or in the supply tank. In order to make the outcome credible, it was stated that in the past vandals had been known to tamper with the supply system. Therefore, to solve the problem several parts of the system had to be attended to and about 20–25 men were required to discover the difficulty that day. By this time the Eagles were getting thirsty; the Rattlers still had a little water in their canteens.

Both groups promptly volunteered to tackle the situation. The details that volunteered for various segments of the water system were made up of either all Rattlers or all Eagles.

The announced plan was for all details to meet at the water tank after inspecting the pipe line and pump. In a little over an hour, all details congregated by the large tank. Since they were thirsty and hot, the first object of attention was the faucet on the tank. No water came out of the faucet. The members of the two groups took over the procedure. They tried to ascertain whether there was water in the tank.

When the faucet had been stopped up by the staff earlier in the day, the ladder, which leaned against the tank for climbing atop it, had been laid aside in the weeds about 30 feet away. Now the ladder was discovered by the boys. Almost to a man, Eagles and Rattlers were on top of the tank to look through the opening there and see if there was water in the tank (see Fig. 9.16). In short order, they came to the conclusion that the tank was practically full. Then the majority of both Eagles and Rattlers rushed again to the faucet. They discovered now that the faucet was stopped up with pieces of sack. Immediately they tackled the task of removing it. They pooled their available implements (mostly knives) and took turns at the work. Members of each group were mindful of and receptive to suggestions from members of the other group. There was common rejoicing at even the appearance of a few drops of water as efforts proceeded. This work lasted over half an hour. Then a Rattler suggested getting help from staff members. When the task was completed with staff help and the valve leading to the camp was turned on, there were expressions of satisfaction from all with the accomplishment, in which members of both groups had had an active and effective part.

This first coöperative action toward a common goal did not eliminate the stabilized intergroup friction. An hour later at supper, there was once again an exchange of invectives across group lines.

2. Another in the series of superordinate goals was the problem of acquiring the use of a much-desired feature-length movie. Both groups were called together and the possibility of procuring either *Treasure Island* or *Kidnapped* from the neighboring town was put to both groups. It was announced that the camp administration could put up half of the money to

Fig. 9.16. Members of Rattlers and Eagles climb to see if water tank is empty.

secure one film. (Since this was toward the end of the camp period, one group could not have provided the remaining sum alone without being destitute for the rest of the period.)

Following this announcement, suggestions poured in from both groups on a division of the needed sum. They made computations and agreed on a figure for each group to contribute. Then they computed the amount each member would have to pay to secure the desired film. Both groups decided together on the film to be selected.

After supper that evening the film chosen (*Treasure Island*) was shown. Both groups felt that they had chosen it and had a part in getting it. As a test situation, five rows of benches were placed in the hall with an aisle between them. Both groups were called to the hall at the same time. Despite the coöperative efforts they had carried out in getting the film, the seats chosen by individual members to watch it followed group lines on the whole.

3. The most striking episodes of intergroup activities toward superordinate goals took place during a camp-out at Cedar Lake, an out-of-the-way spot in the hills about 60 miles from the camp. Previously, both groups were asked separately to name the activities they would like to enjoy dur-

ing the last days of camp. Overnight camping was high on the list of both groups.

Cedar Lake had an attractive camping and picnic area overlooking a clear-water lake surrounded by hills. Since it was far off the main roads, there were no people, shops, or refreshment stands within miles. It afforded an ideal place for controlling experimental conditions for the introduction of superordinate goals.

Each group was taken in a separate truck to Cedar Lake early on the morning of the fifth day of this stage. Both groups were enthusiastic over the prospect of the overnight camp; but they stated a preference to enjoy the overnight camping by themselves, and not with the other group. Both groups, on their own initiative, loaded their respective trucks for an early start. When the trucks arrived in midmorning, each group went first to the swimming area, which is separated from the picnic area by a wooded valley. In the meantime, plans for the problem situations to be introduced were prepared in the picnic area.

Near lunch time, both groups returned to the picnic area. After the early breakfast, the trip, and the swim they were getting quite hungry by this time. At the picnic area there were separate tables and facilities and also a centrally located table on which eating and cooking utensils, mustard, and pickles had been placed. The groups rushed to this central table. The only means of transportation visible at the time was an old truck parked nearby.

A staff member announced in a voice audible to everyone that he was leaving to get food from a store some miles away. The groups were now standing about 15 yards apart. They watched the truck that was going to bring food. The truck made all kinds of noises, but simply would not start, as planned.

Several Rattlers suggested giving it a push so that it would start. This suggestion was not followed since the truck was parked facing uphill (as planned). The tug-of-war rope was lying piled up in plain sight. One Rattler suggested, "Let's get 'our' tug-of-war rope and have a tug-of-war against the truck." There was a little discussion of this idea and its practicality. Someone said: "Twenty of us can pull it for sure." Members in both groups voiced approval of this plan. Therefore they got into action. There was a little discussion concerning how to operate. This problem was settled by feeding the rope through the front bumper so that there were 2 lines for the pull. On the whole, the Rattlers pulled one line and the Eagles pulled the other (see Fig. 9.17).

It took considerable effort to pull the truck. Several tries were necessary.

FIG. 9.17. Rattlers and Eagles have tug-of-war against the truck.

During these efforts, a rhythmic chant of "Heave, heave" arose to accent the times of greatest effort. This rhythmic chant of "Heave, heave" had been used earlier by the Eagles during the tug-of-war contests in the period of intergroup competition and friction. Now it was being used in a cooperative activity involving both groups. When, after some strenuous efforts, the truck moved and started there was jubilation over the common success.

While the truck went for food, the question arose of taking turns in the preparation of meals or of joint preparation by both groups. The Eagles, with some dissensions, decided to prepare their own meals separately. Preparing food in their own areas implied two sets of activities: dividing food for each group; preparing it in their respective areas. A few days earlier, both groups would have insisted upon separate facilities and independent activities even though this implied more work for each.

Now, however, when the truck returned with the food, the groups did not bother to divide the food into two parts for meals in their respective areas. They simply started preparing it together. In this instance actual coöperation in preparing a meal proceeded without discussion and even in a direction contrary to the prior decision of one group. That evening at Cedar Lake the meal was also prepared jointly.

The truck pull was repeated in the afternoon when the truck "stalled" again before going to get supper provisions. This time both groups knew what to do, and carried out the plan with the same success. But on this second occasion the two lines of rope were not pulled separately by the two groups. Members from both groups intermingled on both lines of the rope. Henceforth group lines were blurred on such coöperative occasions.

THE SAME TOOL IN THE SERVICE OF FRICTION AND HARMONY: It will be remembered that the tug-of-war rope was used in the service of intense competition during Stage II. At the end of that stage the Rattlers used the same rope in activities within their own group. They had spent several days chopping at a dead tree at their hide-out. When the trunk was chopped through, the tree did not fall down. The fall was prevented by surrounding trees. As it stood, the tree was a hazard. It might have fallen down at an inopportune moment. Therefore the Rattlers used the tug-of-war rope to pull the trunk to a safe position. They rejoiced in loud tones over their victory in tug-of-war "against the tree."

As we have seen at the Cedar Lake campout, the Rattlers introduced "their" tug-of-war rope against the truck in a coöperative intergroup effort to get food for all. Here we see how the same weapon used in intergroup friction can be put into use for intergroup harmony.

SUMMARY OF OBSERVATIONS IN STAGE III: Only a few high points of the observations during this stage have been summarized. On the basis of the observational data, it was concluded: (a) When the groups in a state of friction interacted under conditions created by introducing superordinate goals, they did coöperate toward the common goal. (b) A series of such joint activities toward common, superordinate goals had the cumulative effect of reducing the prevailing friction between groups and unfavorable stereotypes toward the out-group.

In the closing hours of the experiment, the two groups decided together on their own initiative to put on a joint program at a campfire, entertaining each other with skits and songs. Also on their own initiative both groups requested that they leave the experimental site together in one bus. Thus, these two groups, which formed separately, met for the first time as rivals, engaged in sharp conflict which culminated in mutual antagonism and social distance, now appeared as friendly copartners.

CHECKING OBSERVED REDUCTION OF INTERGROUP FRICTION: The validity of observational findings was tested through other techniques at the close of this stage. These techniques were used specifically to check observations that repeated coöperation involving both groups toward superordinate goals resulted in (1) increased friendliness toward the out-group and its members and (2) reduction of the unfavorable stereotypes toward the out-group found at the close of intergroup friction.

Sociometric choices. The sociometric questions given informally at the end of Stage II were repeated (see pp. 312–314). The answers to the most general criterion which concerned friendship choices in the entire camp and an item tapping rejections (disliked individuals) provide clear verification of the changed attitudes toward members of the out-group. The change was from exclusive preference for the in-group and hostility toward the out-group toward increased preference for the out-group and reduced hostility toward its members.

Friendship choices were still largely for in-group members. However, when the choices for out-group members at the end of Stage III are compared with those after intergroup friction (Stage II), a substantial and significant change is seen. These comparisons are shown in graphic form in Figure 9.18. The Rattlers' choices of Eagles increased from 6.4 to 36.4 percent of their total friendship choices. In the Eagle group, the propor-

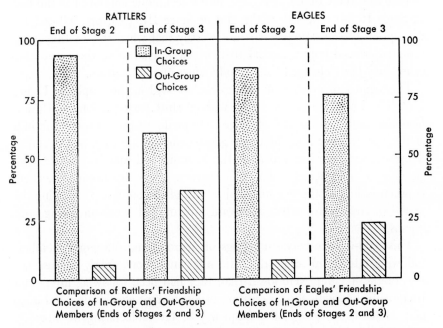

FIG. 9.18. Comparison of friendship choices by Rattlers and Eagles following intergroup friction and intergroup coöperation.

tion of choices for Rattlers shifted from 7.5 to 23.2 percent. These shifts are statistically significant.

Along with the increased tendency to choose out-group members as friends, there was a significant reduction in rejections of members of the out-group as persons disliked. At the close of intergroup friction (Stage II), 75 percent of the Rattlers' rejections were of Eagles. By the end of Stage III, only 15 percent were of Eagles. Similarly, 95 percent of Eagle rejections were of Rattlers at the end of Stage II, but this percentage fell to 47.1 percent at the end of Stage III.

These findings confirm the observations that the result of a series of situations embodying superordinate goals was increasingly friendly associations and attitudes pertaining to members of the out-group accompanied by reduced hostility.

Stereotyped images of in-group and out-group. Observations during the last several days of Stage III revealed a sharp decrease in the standardized name-calling and derogation of the out-group which was common during intergroup friction and the contact situations without superordinate goals early in Stage III. In addition there was less blatant glorification of the in-group and bragging about its accomplishments.

To check these observations, the rating technique employed at the end of Stage II was repeated at the end of Stage III. (See pp. 300–301 for description of the ratings.) It is noteworthy that when these ratings were repeated, several boys remarked that they were glad to do them again because they had "changed their minds" since the last ratings.

The significant changes in ratings are revealed in the graphs in Figure 9.19. The lower graphs show the marked shift from predominantly *unfavorable* ratings at the end of Stage II to predominantly *favorable* ratings at the end of Stage III. The upper graph demonstrates that, by the end of Stage III, ratings of members of the in-group and members of the out-group were both largely favorable. There were no significant differences between ratings of the in-group and ratings of the out-group following the period of coöperative activities toward superordinate goals involving both groups.

This resemblance between ratings of in-group and out-group members following intergroup coöperation did not come about simply because ratings of the in-group were lower than they had been following intergroup friction. In line with the observation of less blatant glorification and bragging about the in-group, the frequency of favorable ratings of in-group members was somewhat less than after Stage II. However, this change

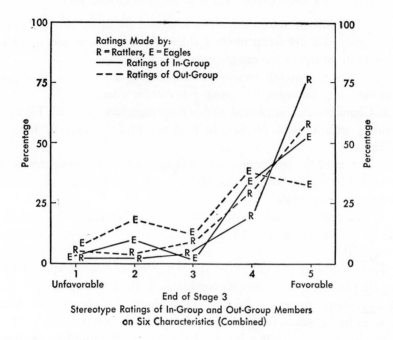

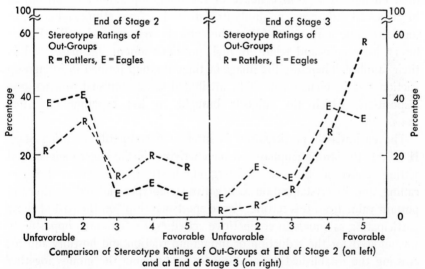

FIG. 9.19. (Top) Stereotype ratings of in-group and out-group members following intergroup coöperation (Stage III), six characteristics combined. (Bottom) Comparison of stereotype ratings of out-groups following intergroup friction (Stage II) and intergroup coöperation (Stage III).

was not significant statistically. The increased similarity between ratings of in-group and out-group resulted chiefly from the large and significant changes in ratings of the out-group in a favorable direction.

Therefore the overall conclusions concerning the images of in-group and out-group following intergroup coöperation were:

1. Characteristics attributed to in-group members were still highly favorable, with a slight decrease in tendency toward extremely favorable ratings.

2. Images of the out-group changed from highly unfavorable stereotypes following intergroup friction to a predominantly favorable image following intergroup coöperation.

3. As a result, the ratings of members of the in-group and members of the out-group did not differ significantly after intergroup coöperation (Stage III).

These shifts in the images of the out-group and stereotypes of them are attributable to the changed conditions as these altered the properties of intergroup interaction. Because the subjects were chosen from homogeneous backgrounds, the formation of negative stereotypes in Stage II and their change to a positive image of the out-group cannot be attributed to perceived differences or similarities stemming from ethnic, religious, or socioeconomic affiliations. All of the subjects were normal, well-adjusted boys with secure and relatively high positions among age-mates and in their families. Therefore the image of the out-group formed in intergroup friction and its change cannot be attributed to any unusual personal predispositions which the subjects brought to the experimental situations.

The enthusiastic participation in intergroup competition during Stage II reflects the strong emphasis on such activities in the larger sociocultural setting. However, the rise of intergroup hostility, the persistent name-calling, and its crystallization as negative stereotypes violated another important value from this setting: "good sportsmanship" on the part of those participating as equals in competitive activities. Even though opportunity was allowed for the reduction of intergroup friction and hostility and for crossing the established social distances by bringing the groups together in situations which were rewarding to each group, friction and the maintenance of a derogatory image of the out-group did not decrease until the groups interacted repeatedly in a series of situations embodying superordinate goals.

CONCLUDING REMARKS

The problem of intergroup relations is reflected in attitudes and behavior of the members of two or more groups toward each other, collectively or individually. Intergroup attitudes and behavior stem from the fact of an individual's membership in a group with particular relationships with other groups. This fact determines internalization by the individual member of the social-distance scale of the group and his participation in the trends of relations with given out-groups and their members. Internalizing the social-distance scale of his group, the individual member places the out-groups in question at certain social distances from his group and from himself. The placement is subject to individual variations within limits. If the individual is too much out of step with his group in his placement of a given out-group and its members, he is reacted to as a deviate.

Hence the problem of intergroup behavior is not primarily a matter of deviate behavior. The topic of deviate behavior in intergroup relations, as well as in relations within groups, is a significant psychological topic in itself. However, if the problem of intergroup behavior were mainly a matter of a few deviates, nonconformists, and neurotic persons in given groups, it would not be the vital topic that it is today.

The limiting factor in determining favorable or unfavorable intergroup attitudes is the nature of functional relations between groups. (In large group units, these relations may not be perceived directly by all individual members. Thus their conceptions may be dependent on communication from others, which may or may not reflect the actual state of affairs.) If the functional relations between groups are positive, favorable attitudes toward the out-group will be formed. If the functional relations between groups are negative, they will give rise to negative attitudes and stereotypes in relation to the out-group. In time, the attitudes and stereotypes are stabilized in the form of a social-distance scale for various groups and are perpetuated through the vehicle of language, even though the functional relations that gave rise to them are no longer operative.

Various theories are advanced to explain the intergroup behavior of individuals. Unusual frustrations or authoritarian treatment in the life history of individuals, deep-seated tendencies in human nature, the nature of leadership in groups are variously singled out as main determinants of intergroup behavior. Personal and sociocultural factors do count in shaping intergroup relations. But all of these influences should be taken within the framework of intergroup interaction and its products. The contribution of various influences is not an additive matter; they are affected and even modified in the process of interaction within groups and between groups.

Structure and norms within groups do influence and are influenced by the course of intergroup relations of consequence. However, we cannot jump to conclusions concerning intergroup trends and attitudes merely by concentrating on in-group customs and attitudes of individual members. Democracy and harmony within a group do not necessarily mean democracy and harmony with out-groups. There are demonstrated cases in which the nature of in-group relations and that of intergroup relations are at variance with each other.

These conclusions are based upon an extensive survey of evidence in social science. On that basis hypotheses were formulated and tested in a program of research. In the testing of hypotheses, lifelike yet controlled interaction situations were created. The results obtained in these situations through observation were cross-checked with sociometric data and laboratory-type techniques.

It was concluded that: (1) When individuals interact with one another toward common goals, *in time* a group structure emerges with definite hierarchical statuses and a set of norms to regulate activities within the group. These norms constitute the basis of individual members' social attitudes in regard to relevant objects and persons. (2) When two or more groups are in functional contact with one another in competitive and reciprocally frustrating situations, they develop negative attitudes and stereotypes toward one another. These negative intergroup attitudes cannot be explained simply on the basis of hardships and frustrations in the individuals' life histories. In the two experiments in which this generalization was verified the individuals were well-adjusted, healthy, successful persons whose upbringing had not involved unusual frustrations or uncertainties. (3) When groups in a state of tension interact with one another toward superordinate goals much desired by all which cannot be attained by the energies and resources of one group, they tend to coöperate. In a series of activities involving superordinate goals, intergroup conflict and unfavorable stereotypes do become markedly reduced.

Both in intergroup friction and in intergroup coöperation, the trends of relations between groups do have significant consequences for relations within the groups involved. Likewise, the trends in intergroup relations are not independent of relations within groups. For the reduction of intergroup friction, in-group and intergroup attitudes have to be in line with one another. If they pull asunder, the likelihood of reducing tension is diminished.

REFERENCES

1. Arensberg, C. H. Behavior in Organization: Industrial Studies, in J. H. Rohrer and M. Sherif (eds.), *Social Psychology at the Crossroads*. New York: Harper, 1951.
2. Avigdor, R. The development of stereotypes as a result of group interaction. Doctorate dissertation, New York University, 1952.
3. *Daily Oklahoman*, advertisement sponsored by distributors of Admiral, Arvin, Capehart, Crosley, Emerson, Hoffman, Motorola, Philco, RCA, Sparton, Sylvania, and Zenith, November 4, 1953.
4. Faris, R. E. L. *Social Psychology*. New York: Ronald, 1952, chap. 2.
5. Guetzkow, H. S., and Bowman, P. H. *Men and Hunger*. Elgin, Ill. Brethren Publishing House, 1946.
6. Harvey, O. J. An experimental investigation of negative and positive relationships between small informal groups through judgmental indices. Doctorate dissertation, University of Oklahoma, 1954.
7. Hiller, E. T. *The Strike*. Chicago: University of Chicago Press, 1928.
8. Horowitz, E. L. The development of attitudes toward Negroes, *Arch. Psychol.* (1936), No. 194.
9. Lewis, Oscar. *Group Dynamics in a North-Indian Village*. Delhi: Program Evaluation Organization, Planning Commission, Government of India Press, 1954.
10. Miller, J. C. *Origins of the American Revolution*. Boston: Little, Brown, 1943.
11. Sears, R. R., Hovland, C. I., and Miller, N. E. Minor studies in aggression. I. Measurement of aggressive behavior, *J. Psychol.* (1940), 9:277–281.
12. Sherif, M. A Preliminary Experimental Study of Intergroup Relations, in J. H. Rohrer and M. Sherif (eds.), *Social Psychology at the Crossroads*. New York: Harper, 1951.
13. Sherif, M. Integrating field work and laboratory in small group research, *Amer. sociol. Rev.* (1954), 19:759–771.
14. Sherif, M., Harvey, O. J., White, B. J., Hood, W. R., and Sherif, C. W. *Experimental Study of Positive and Negative Intergroup Attitudes Between Experimentally Produced Groups. Robbers Cave Study*. Norman: University of Oklahoma, 1954 (multilithed).
15. Sherif, M., and Sherif, C. W. *Groups in Harmony and Tension*. New York: Harper, 1953.

16. Sherif, M., White, B. J., and Harvey, O. J. Status in experimentally produced groups, *Amer. J. Sociol.* (1955), 60:370–379.
17. Thrasher, F. *The Gang.* Chicago: University of Chicago Press, 1927.
18. Whyte, W. F. Small Groups and Large Organizations, in J. H. Rohrer and M. Sherif (eds.), *Social Psychology at the Crossroads.* New York: Harper, 1951.

CHAPTER 10

Collective Behavior

Events referred to under the heading of "collective behavior" are out-of-ordinary forms of interaction. They have always attracted attention from both social scientists and laymen. Before discussing this topic, we shall summarize two rather different examples of collective behavior.

A Crowd at Buckingham Palace

On April 5, 1955, 3000 persons stood near the gates of Buckingham Palace. No public event had been announced. In fact, for 12 days the newspapers in London had not appeared, owing to a strike. According to the report of a news service, most of the people gathered there were "in the dark" about what might be happening. But they had the feeling that things were in the making. They were living through out-of-the-ordinary times.

"Pardon me," said a Scot, Malcom MacFie, "I've been standing here for two hours and I haven't the foggiest notion what all this is about."

His case appeared typical.

A mounted policeman moved into the crowd on the sidewalk before the palace and looked down on the throng massed around his horse.

"What are you doing here?" he asked.

"What are you doing here?" asked a woman who had a baby in her arms.

"I'm here because you're here," said the policeman.

This was about 3:40 P.M.

An exasperated mother turned to her teen-age daughter.

"Have you detected anything, or are we simply standing in this crowd for no good reason?" she asked.

"Mother," answered the girl, "something must be happening."

"Then I hope it happens in a hurry."

Fifteen minutes later more police arrived.

333

At 4:22 the Queen's car swung up before the gates.

"Ah," sighed the crowd.

Into the palace grounds she went, serene and beautiful but unsmiling, a lady-in-waiting beside her.

Eight minutes later, Churchill's car drove into view.

"Who is it, who is it?" was the cry in the crowd.

But it took only a second to recognize the round, pinkish face of the man in the back seat, the big black cigar and those mischievous eyes.

"It's Winston!"

Ten minutes later only a handful of people remained before the palace gates. The others drifted away.

But the little group stayed on. And the police stayed and again the crowd swelled.

Then Churchill's car returned into view.

Col. Sir Rhoderick Brinckman, a retired Grenadier Guardsman who as a young officer once commanded the palace sentries, exclaimed:

"Do you realize what you are seeing? These people in the crowd don't"[2].

The crowd felt that there was something out-of-the-ordinary in the air. Actually they were witnessing the resignation of the Prime Minister and his official retirement from public life.

A Revival Meeting

The scene is a mass revival meeting (21). Its setting has required nego-tiations for months or even years with local church organizations and with business and civic leaders. Two months ahead of time, advance representa-tives began to mobilize local ministers and laymen. From one to three thousand were chosen for the choir and began to rehearse. Another thou-sand or more were selected as ushers. Others began training classes as "counselors." The best became "front-row" counselors and the others the "reserve." Further classes were organized for "follow-up" work to insure the endurance of results of the meeting. Then posters, banners, cards, car stickers appeared all over the city announcing the event.

The hall or stadium is massive, all seats arranged toward the focal ros-trum. As the crowd begins to arrive, the choir is warming up. The flow of music and people swells as songbooks are circulated. The old beloved hymns are sung in growing chorus. Local figures and ministers appear, one offering a prayer.

On the rostrum, Billy Graham sits quietly, his head in hand. Then he comes forward, leads a short prayer, and plunges into his message. It is a simple message in simple words, repeated time and again in different form.

FIG. 10.1. A revival meeting. (Carl Mydans—Courtesy LIFE Magazine © TIME, Inc.)

Are you frustrated, bewildered, dejected, breaking under the strains of life? Then listen for a moment to me—say "yes" to the saviour tonight, and in a moment you will know such comfort as you have never known [1].

You laugh and you joke and all the rest, but when you're alone, there it is—that void, that aching, that empty space [21].

I beg you to come now before it is too late. You know you need Christ in your life. Leave your seat now and come forward [21].

As the first people start to respond to the plea to come forward, the advisers down in the aisles signal to a counselor seated nearby—a person of about the same age and the same sex as the new convert. As the stream toward the rostrum increases and the counselors are all busy, the advisers signal by planned gestures of their hands to the choir leader, who passes the signal along to the "reserve" counselors. No one has to make the long trip to the rostrum alone.

And they come—a housewife, a young boy, an athletic-looking young man, a mother with her baby—until finally there is a crowd around the rostrum. Since 1949, about 200,000 have come at various such gatherings. In different meetings in England, 38,447 pledged themselves as new converts. These are people who feel that the plea to the bewildered, dejected, and lonely is to them and who respond to the clear call to comfort. The words are not new. They are more or less intense, more or less formal versions of words they have heard many times before. But at the revival these words come at the crest of a rising structure of organized efforts, symbols, music, and spontaneous participation of thousands, all directed toward the same focus.

The event and its effects do not end at the rostrum. The new convert is taken to an "Inquiry Tent." Here he receives a packet of literature, counsel and encouragement. He fills out cards: one card for a current working file, one card for a follow-up file, one card for the pastor of a local church. The next morning he receives a personal-looking letter from Billy Graham. He finds further invitations and literature in his mail. People from his local church call on him. Continuing efforts are made to perpetuate the effects of the revival.

Collective Interaction Characterized

As these two examples indicate, "collective interaction" is used to refer to a broad range of social situations. Events with quite different backgrounds, focal aspects, behavioral manifestations, durations, and significance are treated under this heading.

In a general sense, collective interaction means behavior in social situations in which a number of individuals or groups actively participate and react to one another. In the literature, the term "collective behavior" usually refers to extreme cases of interaction exemplified by mobs engaged in lynching, by a riot launched against another group, by crowds carrying out a hunger march or a revolutionary move, by rallies voicing some mass protest in support of their demands, by crowds vowing that the last drop of their blood is committed to the incorporation of some territory within the bounds of their motherland. Revival meetings in which individuals participate with abandonment for the salvation of their souls, rites and ceremonies marking some memorable event—these are other examples of collective interaction.

Various schemes have been offered for classifying crowds, mobs, audiences, and the like. Representative classifications are noted later in this chapter. It is not easy to differentiate collective interaction situations into sharply defined types. In the course of interaction, the different types may merge. Under certain circumstances an orderly audience may become a frightened crowd or an unruly mob.

In a generic way, all cases of interaction consisting of a small (say a dozen) or a large number of individuals constitute instances of collective interaction. Collective interaction may be staged by some organized parties with special interests, or it may develop more spontaneously as a consequence of a give-and-take process or "milling" among participating individuals.

Collective interaction may involve hundreds or thousands of individuals. A small or a large proportion of the participants may be banded together to give a definite direction and plan of action to the process. But one thing is characteristic of collective interaction situations treated under the titles of crowds, mobs, revival meetings, mass meetings, etc.: some event, some issue, some problem, some danger, some threat, or some crisis which arouses motivational resonance in at least a good many of the participating individuals is always present.

In other words, collective behavior situations, like crowds, mobs, or mass rallies, are not merely togetherness situations in which individuals engage separately in twos or threes in their respective conversations or tasks. A hotel lobby, a railroad station, or Times Square in New York on ordinary days is a typical setting for togetherness situations involving large numbers of people. Such situations are social situations too. As we have seen, they produce differential effects on the behavior of individuals. How-

ever, the distinguishing mark of collective interaction situations, typical
in the examples mentioned above, is that give-and-take among people—
interstimulation—has a *focus* or acquires focus, centered around some
common interest, expectation, issue, problem, gripe, or crisis. This focal
aspect has been noted by various social scientists.

The particular focus of collective interaction is the main rallying point
in relation to which other aspects of the immediate situation acquire their
significance. The properties of the give-and-take, the "milling" process,

FIG. 10.2.   Tearing down an opponent's goal post. (Courtesy, University of
Oklahoma Photo Service.)

the duration of the event, the common excitement, the accentuated differential effects revealed at times in extreme forms of behavior are all affected by the main focus of the interaction situation.

ACCENTUATED DIFFERENTIAL BEHAVIOR IN COLLECTIVE INTERACTION

There have been stingy men who have contributed liberally in a revival meeting or rally. There have been persons who joined a riot in a half-hearted way and ended by committing violent deeds they had never performed in their lives. There have been kindhearted neighborhood boys who became heroes on the battlefield by destroying so many of the enemy. In a disaster, cases of panic have been reported; there have likewise been cases of men going to the help of the victims without regard to personal gain or their usual functions in life. For example, a postmaster in an Oklahoma town struck by a tornado left the post office unguarded, even though mail and money were strewn over the floor, to assist the victims. Merchants and clerks left money and goods on the counter to do likewise (13).

In the history of social science, such cases of accentuated differential behavior in extreme interaction situations were established through empirical observations even before cases of differential behavior in simple togetherness situations were documented by psychologists. Beastly, heroic, selfless, and other extreme kinds of behavior in crowds, mobs, and the like were described by various early writers. Outstanding among these early accounts was *The Crowd* by Le Bon, which was published in 1895 (15). The vivid and dramatic descriptions of behavior recorded there are still of interest. In these descriptions we find illustrations of how participants in a crowd "feel, think, and act in a manner quite different from that in which each individual of them would feel, think, and act were he in a state of isolation."

The defective aspect of the early accounts, as represented by Le Bon, lies in the psychological interpretations of behavior, which were mixed with current social philosophy of his time. For example, Le Bon talked of a "collective mind" or "group mind" and drew a pathetic picture of the degradation of intellectual functioning in collective action. This emphasis on the "irrationality" and "impulsiveness" and "inferior" capacities of crowds was shared by other writers, notably Martin (18) and Freud (10). In the sociology of Emile Durkheim the reality of qualitative changes in experience and behavior during the process of collective interaction, especially in periodic rites and ceremonies, was a cardinal aspect. Durkheim stressed the rise of "collective representations" (social norms), which were in his view at the basis of morality and any sense of responsibility of the individual (8, 9).

Earlier scholars, like Le Bon and Durkheim, made a sharp dichotomy between individual psychology and collective psychology. They based this dichotomy on a notion of "mental chemistry" prevalent during their times. In this scheme the individual represented the element, with certain properties in isolation. Qualitative changes in the properties of the element came about only in a compounding process, represented by collective situations. In the trend of social psychology influenced by Durkheim we find, therefore, a rather sharp differentiation of individual psychology and social psychology. The writings of Blondel are examples (3).

Psychoanalytic accounts of behavior in crowds noted the occurrence of extreme forms of behavior, especially of aggressiveness and brutality. However, the effect of collective interaction was attributed simply to stripping culturally derived restraints from participating individuals. Thus, differential behavior was not seen as new, but merely as the release and free expression of instinctive impulses and repressed desires.

The crux of the position taken by Freud in regard to collective behavior can be summarized in a few sentences. According to him, the main and, in fact, the only important effect of interaction situations on the individual is to strip from him the restraints of his conscience and to give free rein to the satisfaction of the libido. The only important thing that finds expression is what is stored in the unconscious. This idea is expressed in unequivocal terms:

> From our point of view we need not attribute so much importance to the appearance of new characteristics. For us it would be enough to say that in a group the individual is brought under conditions which allow him to throw off the repressions of his unconscious instincts. The apparently new characteristics which he then displays are in fact the manifestations of his unconscious, in which all that is evil in the human mind is contained as a predisposition. We can find no difficulty in understanding the disappearance of conscience or of a sense of responsibility in these circumstances [10, pp. 9–10].

According to Freud, the basic undercurrent of all social action and organization is the sex impulse; he finds: "First, that a group is clearly held together by a power of some kind; and to what power could this fact be better ascribed than to Eros, who holds everything in the world?" (10, p.

40). This means that, according to Freud, the direction of action in a group situation, as well as the emotional quality attained, is stored in the unconscious and ready in advance.

In short, in the psychoanalytic scheme, the sharp dichotomy between individual psychology and collective psychology was eliminated by simply reducing the accounting of behavior in collective interaction to pure instinct psychology. Contrary to this view, social psychology began to make headway in dealing with behavior in collective situations when due recognition was given to the characteristics and products of the interaction process. The new values or norms that arise in interaction situations become regulators of subsequent human relations.

Same Psychological Principles Applicable to Behavior in Collective Interaction

It has been stressed throughout this book that there are not two kinds of psychology, one applicable to individuals alone and one applicable to individuals in social situations. It is not necessary to posit new psychological principles to account for the undeniable facts of differential behavior or the appearance of new properties in behavior during social interaction.

In Chapters 3 and 4 we saw that experience and reaction to objects and persons are relational affairs, not the summed experience of so many discrete items. Things and events in the external situation are experienced and reacted to as they are functionally related to one another. In the structuring of experience and behavior, both the properties of external stimulus conditions and internal factors (motives, attitudes) take part in a functionally interrelated way (pp. 77–84). Every experience, and hence behavior, constitutes a structure which cannot be accounted for simply by totaling the properties of component external stimuli or the internal impulses, taken as separate and unrelated. Properties of constituent parts of the psychological structure are determined by their place in the entire frame of reference.

With a change of major anchorages in the frame of reference, the character of experience and behavior is modified and may even be transformed. Hence, the differential nature of experience and behavior is a general psychological phenomenon. In studying the differential effects of social situations (whether togetherness or collective interaction), the important task is description and analysis of functional relations between factors pertaining to external social situations and factors pertaining to the participating individuals.

As we learned in discussing differential behavior in organized groups, this task necessarily implies that the special properties of the particular social situation be included as an integral part of description and analysis. Included in such special properties are developing reciprocities among individuals, organizational structure, and group products, like social norms. In this approach, differential effects of social situations on individuals cease to be mysterious or to require entirely new psychological principles.

Differential Behavior in Disaster Situations

As noted earlier, both heroic acts to help others, and panic and beastly acts have been reported in response to sudden disaster facing large numbers of people. In recent years there have been a number of empirical studies of disasters, like tornadoes, explosions, and fires. In terms of the present discussion, the findings of such studies are revealing in indicating something about the conditions in which *panic* does and does not occur. These findings emphasize the inadequacy of traditional explanations in disaster situations in terms of the regressive effects of fear and the contagion of a "stampede."

In the first place, the studies revealed that panic is not necessarily the typical behavior of people faced with sudden disaster and that it occurs only under certain conditions (14). The various specific factors which may be associated with panic are numerous. Some types of situations have not even been systematically investigated. Nevertheless, certain recurrent findings suggest some of the conditions characteristic of panic. Killian mentioned two such conditions, namely, existing conceptions of the situation as "panic-producing" and ambiguity concerning the possibility of escape. The investigators at the National Opinion Research Center confirm the latter in concluding that panic actually occurred when the situation appeared to hold immediate threat and when escape seemed possible only at the moment, and not at a later time (11). Such perception of the danger by persons involved was found in actual panics.

In the case of the well-known "Invasion from Mars" radio broadcast by Orson Welles, panic resulted among those listeners who accepted the broadcast report of destructive Martians in their midst as a factual report. As Cantril noted, once this belief was accepted, the situation appeared to be one either of trying to escape by any means or of losing everything (6).

Such perception of a danger situation is contingent both on the individuals involved (their backgrounds, available guides for action, personal characteristics) and on the external situation. The NORC studies of actual disaster indicated that one external factor was *the amount of warning* of impending disaster. Warning in advance which allowed some time for preparation tended to decrease the likelihood of panic behavior. But warning too brief to prepare for the disaster was no more and probably less helpful than having no warning at all (*11*).

Among the crucial factors which affected the frequency of panic in the threatening situations studied by the National Opinion Research Center were the nature of the threat itself and the extent of coördination among individuals facing it. Two cases, one in which emotional reactions were rigidly controlled and the other characterized by considerable agitation, illustrate the importance of these factors. In the former, a coal mine explosion in West Frankfort, Illinois, killed 119 miners; but when the explosion was over, activities were highly organized and emotional distress was controlled. The people involved were organized to cope with disasters.

In the second case, individuals were unprepared for coördinated activity and the threat itself was not clear-cut in terms of its origin and duration. In this case, a series of explosions and fires caused by illuminating gas occurred intermittently over a two-hour period in Brighton, New York, killing only 2 persons and injuring 24. There was great uncertainty over what was causing the danger and what would happen next. The individuals were unprepared, uncertain, and not coördinated. Considerable agitation resulted.

The significance of such findings is that differential behavior in collective situations does not require new psychological principles or the invoking of mysterious collective forces. Rather, the course of behavior in the face of collective disaster can be specified in terms of factors operating at the time, such as the nature of the danger and the relationships (coördination) among participating individuals.

The importance of coördination of various individuals was found in a laboratory study by Mintz (*19*). A task which required coördination among individuals for solution was given to 15–21 persons in a togetherness situation. Each individual was to pull from a bottle a string attached to one of a number of solid cones through an opening large enough to permit only one cone to be withdrawn at a time. When no opportunity was given for the individuals to form a plan of action, jamming up of the cones resulted. On the other hand, when brief discussion was allowed and the task was presented as a coöperative activity, some plan was carried

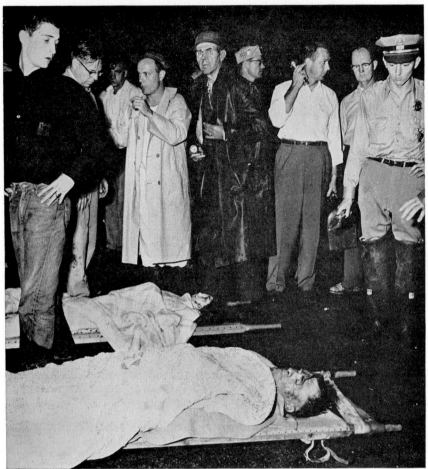

Staff photographer, Wichita *Eagle.*

FIG. 10.3. After a Kansas tornado disaster.

through quickly and successfully in every case. But when individual rewards and forfeits were introduced, so that individual efforts in the situation were antagonistic to coördination, jamming up was the characteristic result.

Such findings would indicate that relationships among individuals which encourage or maintain the pursuit of coördinated efforts in the face of common danger may be crucial in determining the type of behavior which will follow. This is confirmed by observations of panic among highly organized and differentiated groups, namely, army units.

Marshall studied the breakdown of organization and panic behavior occurring on the battlefield under enemy fire (17). His findings emphasize the great importance of maintaining effective communication among persons facing such intense and fear-provoking situations. Even the temporary inability of members of a unit to see each other clearly under fire disrupted organizational unity for a time.

Marshall observed 11 infantry companies and one reconnaissance troop to ascertain why enemy fire against an advancing infantry line frequently caused a delay of from 45 to 60 minutes. He concluded that the line did not proceed until effective communication was restored among the men. Because of the organized nature of relationships, this might be done simply by one person's standing up and shouting, "Follow me! We're going on." On the other hand, if the men saw one of their unit retreating without any explanation, panic was very likely to occur. Panic was largely avoided when withdrawal was accompanied by some explanation, however brief. This might be only "Get the hell out of here and follow me to that tree line on the far side of the creek" (17, pp. 129–130).

FOCAL FACTORS IN VARIOUS TYPES OF COLLECTIVE INTERACTION

In day-to-day social situations in a concert or lecture hall, in usual Sunday church services, in the classroom, the sequence of events and participation of individuals usually follows an orderly scheme as predetermined by the program, ritual, established routines, and prevailing status and role relations of individuals.

Out-of-the-ordinary types of collective interaction which assume properties and proportions beyond the bounds of prevailing grooves of daily living are always centered around some out-of-the-ordinary event or some incident which arouses commonly experienced motives or frustrations of individuals involved. Even in transitory instances in which people crowd together, impeding traffic or blocking the sidewalk, there is a focal aspect initially responsible for the congestion. It may be a slash in prices at a store below prevailing levels, or the sudden discovery of a celebrity in the midst of a crowd, or an automobile accident.

As we have seen, the focal problem conducive to interaction may be a disaster, like a flood, tornado, explosion, earthquake, fire, or circumstances through which a number of people are lost or stranded. Such situations arouse strong motivational and emotional problems which are faced suddenly by a number of individuals and problems which demand immediate attention. Such extraordinary events, being sudden, cannot be handled adequately by ordinary routines of life. While the machinery of organized social life is being geared to cope with the sudden disaster, informal banding together and leadership arise alongside the established machinery, as pointed out by Killian (13).

More precisely, collective interaction of any significance always has a focal aspect consisting of a common problem that urgently requires a solution, a commonly aspired-to goal, a commonly faced danger. This is an initial and central factor in ensuing collective processes. For the individuals, it constitutes the major anchorage. Activities and the sequence of events center around it.

In cases of prolonged and consequential collective interaction, the focal aspect acquires even greater significance. For example, the focal problem may stem initially from commonly experienced starvation, oppression, or uncertainty; or it may be the cherished aspirations of a group. Recognizing the crucial importance of the focal aspect helps us understand different specific cases and different types of collective interaction.

Types of Collective Interaction

In the literature on collective behavior, attempts have been made to differentiate between audiences, crowds, and mobs. Audiences are cited as more passive collectivities following certain routines. Crowds are taken to represent more spontaneous and emotional collectivities, which are said to become mobs when they move into action. Such classifications may be useful sociological designations. On the other hand, it should be noted that in the course of interaction these various types may be changed from one to another. At times the same collectivity may be transformed from an audience into a crowd and then into a mob. The reverse sequence is also possible. A mob may turn into a crowd and end up as an audience.

Proceeding along the lines of Blumer's classificatory scheme, Brown (5) recently typified acting crowds or mobs in terms of four categories: (1) "aggressive" mobs, as illustrated by those engaged in lynchings or riots; (2) "escape" mobs, as typified by both organized and unorganized collectivities faced with sudden danger which leads to panic; (3) "acquisitive" mobs, as represented by a collective rush to make withdrawals from a bank or to secure food for hoarding; (4) "expressive" mobs, characterized by emotional release and typified in revival meetings.

The first two of these types are characterized by rather specific behavioral manifestations during collective interaction. The third type is

FIG. 10.4. The focus in this street-corner interaction is an election.

characterized by a specific motivation. The last category—the expressive mob—seems to be more descriptive of behavior and implies a common emotional response.

From a social-psychological point of view, a more useful *analysis of crowds may be in terms of the focal issue of collective interaction* rather than in terms of a simple classification. A knowledge of the issue, problem, or motive which is the focus for participants in a particular collectivity will indicate, on the whole, the particular kind of collective behavior that will develop. For example, if this focus conducive to collective interaction is keeping certain people in "their place," or if it is establishment of the rights or position of one group in relation to others, the collective interaction will turn toward aggressive channels. If collective interaction is engaged in under circumstances of real or apparent common danger that is not too overwhelming to deal with, again an aggressive action will be taken, in relation to the danger or threat. On the other hand, if the common danger is experienced as too overwhelming, the end result will be a move to escape to safety. The escape may or may not take the form of a panic, depending on the anticipatory preparation and the degree of effective organization among participants. This mode of analysis emphasizes the fact that collective action (whether aggressive or escapist) is goal directed.

Collective interaction in religious revivals and various social formations which engage in diverse types of esoteric rites and ceremonies are also goal directed. This fact may be obscured by classifying them in terms of the "expressive" or emotional types of behavior that are manifested during interaction. Such formations and the esoteric and extreme practices they engage in constitute collective solutions of one kind or another for insecurities, uncertainties, and personal conflicts that participating individuals have in common. As prejudice and hatred held in common by a number of individuals and dangers faced jointly by a collectivity are conducive to interaction along given goal-directed lines, so too are the uncertainties, insecurities, and the experience of being "up in the air" without stable group anchorages conducive to the interaction of like souls and to the rise of religious and social formations with their particular modes of collective practices.

In this light, all kinds of esoteric-appearing practices, ceremonies, and festivities are seen as parts or components of goal-directed collective interaction. They are component parts of activities engaged in by participants in their strivings to establish some stable social (and personal) anchorages. This is evidenced by the satisfaction and sense of solidarity the participants

FIG. 10.5. Accentuated expression.

derive from these types of collective practices. In these expressive formations, the motives of the individuals which are necessary factors in understanding collective interaction are ego motives (pp. 600–602).

"Miracle at Sabana Grande"

Recently a case of collective behavior has been reported by social scientists which illustrates the advantages of analysis of collective interaction in
terms of its focal aspect. The collective behavior reported is clearly "expressive"; yet this example would be difficult to classify under any one
type because it served more far-reaching functions. Its other implications
for understanding collective behavior are considered in later sections.

This example was the topic of a research project which has not yet been
completely reported. However, definite statements have been made pertaining to the aspects of interest for the present discussion.

The actual event was summarized by Chapman and Eckstein (7). It
took place against the background of Puerto Rico, a largely Catholic
society in which poverty and persistent insecurity plague large numbers
of the people. Some poor country children reported that they had seen a
"beautiful lady" near a well. They said that she was the Virgin Mary and
that she promised to perform a great miracle on May 25, 1953, at 11 in
the morning. This is what happened on that day:

On May 25 approximately one hundred thousand persons assembled to witness the fulfillment of the Virgin Mary's promise. The crowd packed the valley
and spread up the sides of the surrounding hills. Though most of them were
too far away to see it, they faced a wooden platform which held the children,
the self-appointed priests, and many sick persons. The throng was tense, perspiring in the hot sun, and quiet. A few moments before eleven o'clock, they
pressed toward the platform, and those further away strained to see any sign of
activity on or near the platform where the "great miracle" might take place for
the children. Near the wooden platform was the well, and here too action of a
supernatural nature was expected. Seconds before the fateful hour, the silent
crowd stood, waiting, almost motionless. Suddenly a chilling wind swept over
the multitude, a cloud covered the blistering sun, and light cool rain fell. Cries
of, "the rain is holy" were heard. With outstretched arms, pointed fingers, and
rotating wrists, gestures initiated by one of the children on the platform, the
people beseeched the Virgin Mary to descend and bestow her blessings. The
place became a sea of raised, slowly turning arms. And some saw the Virgin
Mary. They saw her on the side and the top of a mountain north of the valley;
they saw her in the sky. Many who did not see the heavenly figure turned
anxiously, first one way, then another, trying to see. Here and there in the

midst of the crowd some of those who saw the Virgin Mary tried to help those who did not by pointing to her and describing her. Some prayed aloud, others prayed softly, and some sang to the Virgin. The silence was gone. Above the prayers, sighs, and occasional shouts of joy, one could hear applause—the clapping that meant someone had been cured. This applause came from various places in the throng; the loudest bursts came from those closest to the platform. Among the cures that took place on the platform that day, the most spectacular was that of "La Griega," an American citizen of Greek origin. Shortly after eleven o'clock she saw the Virgin Mary, felt a sharp pain, and removed the heavy neck brace that her doctor had ordered her to wear. Vivid descriptions of this cure and others spread rapidly through the crowd. Many who did not see any supernatural healing, heard the applause, and they clapped too. Other wonders were said to have taken place on this day of the "great miracle." Some believers saw crosses in the sky and heavenly lights, while others said that the rain that fell was colored and left the skin dry. A minority of those present said that they saw nothing that was supernatural. But, for the vast majority, it was a day of wonder and fulfillment. What they had seen and felt from eleven o'clock until about a quarter to twelve convinced them that the Virgin Mary had kept her promise. Before noon, the clapping, the gesturing, the seeing and trying to see the Virgin Mary, the praying, the singing had almost ceased; the pilgrims began to leave [7, pp. 204–205].

The focal aspects of this event have been studied by Tumin and Feldman (22). Their analysis starts with conditions which predisposed the individuals in this area to interact in terms of the focal aspect, the factors which enhanced the credibility of the event in advance, and the specific desires of those participating. They noted the following conditions which were effective in bringing individuals together with the belief that the children's prophecy would be fulfilled: "(1) widespread poverty; (2) persistent economic insecurity; (3) hard, tedious and long hours of work; (4) low educational levels and much ignorance; (5) widespread and disenabling illness. These factors combined to predispose the people to believe in Divinity; to accept the possibility of miracles; to hope that Divinity has a special eye for the poor; and to desire and seek miraculous cures" (22, p. 141).

The possibility of the fulfillment of desires was enhanced by widespread publicity given to the coming event through radio, newspapers, and the pronouncement of children, their teacher, parents, and the village officials. These investigators reported that the concrete desires of those who came were divided between those with religious impulses and those who specifically hoped for the cure of an illness.

Tumin and Feldman further report that the on-the-spot cures, the extraordinary events reported by various people in the crowd, the open repentance of disbelief by some, and the sheer fact of the crowd itself had the effect of strengthening the beliefs of those present, even those who doubted the "miracle." In spite of the presence of persons who did not experience the extraordinary events, they conclude that "genuine skepticism was rare."

If analysis in terms of the functions of collective interaction is made, it is important not to stop with the immediate event and the immediate reactions of participants. *Analysis has to be extended to the consequences of collective interaction.* In the case of the crowd at Sabana Grande, the following consequences were noted:

"Actual consequences included general enhancement of religiosity, implying positive functions for the Church in spite of its openly expressed official opposition; considerable enhancement of the prestige of the children, their parents, the teacher, the Mayor and the local community; a great though temporary uplift of the local economy; and a general reaffirmation of Community. There was also considerable expression of the belief that all of mankind, Catholics especially, would benefit" (22, p. 141).

The actions and events which take place at the actual time of collective interaction become more meaningful when related to the conditions for interaction, its focal aspect conducive to bringing individuals together, and its expected and actual consequences. Before continuing with such analysis, some of the processes which are typically reported in collective interaction will be summarized briefly.

Processes in Collective Interaction

Various accounts of the processes in collective interaction have been advanced by both psychologists and sociologists. Various explanations of the characteristics and processes of collective behavior have been offered. Among them are Tarde's notion of "imitation," Le Bon's idea of "suggestion" (which was closely related to notions of hypnosis of his time), McDougall's "primitive sympathy," Blumer's "circular reaction," and F. H. Allport's "social facilitation." The key term advanced by the sociologist Park was "rapport," in the sense of "mutual and exclusive responsiveness of each member of the crowd to the suggestions emanating from other members" (20).

There have been interesting descriptions of the processes during collective interaction. Blumer (4) described the interaction processes in crowds under the headings of "milling," "collective excitement," and "social contagion." Milling is considered as a "pure instance of circular reaction" which makes "the individuals more sensitive and responsive to one another, so that they become increasingly preoccupied with one another and decreasingly responsive to ordinary objects of stimulation." Collective excitement is "a more intense form of milling." Under the influence of this excitement people become emotionally aroused to a greater degree. The emotional arousal is said to make them more likely to be carried away by impulses and feelings. It is under these conditions that "social contagion" of feelings and behavior is enhanced.

Such descriptions of events in collective interaction can be evaluated when collective behavior is viewed as one event in a sequence of antecedent and subsequent events.

CONDITIONS CONDUCIVE TO COLLECTIVE INTERACTION

Analysis of collective behavior necessarily starts with the conditions conducive to collective interaction along certain lines. Ordinarily, human relations are carried on in stable groups regulated by established routines, expectations, and social norms. Especially in relatively stable times and societies, the give-and-take among individuals in their ordinary workdays follows established patterns of a division of labor, status and role relations according to the particular place of given individuals, and established ways of behaving and doing things.

Accentuated differential behavior like that manifested in collective interaction, as exemplified by riots, mass meetings, and successful revivals, does not happen every day. Extreme forms of collective interaction are out-of-the-ordinary events contingent on certain out-of-the-ordinary conditions.

There is some justification for the report that at times the immediate flare-up of extreme types of behavior in collective interaction may start with seemingly minor incidents, and that the interaction process grows in proportions in a spontaneous way. This mode of analysis, starting with the immediate, incidental events and the flare-up of interaction in them misses the antecedent factors which render incidental beginnings possible.

As we have seen, in order to understand collective behavior in the face of common disaster, an understanding of the background conditions, the extent of preparation, and the existing organizational structure is necessary.

While the immediate focal aspect is crucial for understanding the course of events, it is not sufficient to explain the occurrence of collective interaction.

Consequential recurrence of collective flare-ups, mass actions, riots take place on the whole at times and in places of pronounced social instability, times of pervasive insecurity, of widespread deprivations among large sections of the populace, times of heightened class or intergroup hostility, or times of havoc and confusion brought by prolonged war. Examples of such times are the pre-Revolutionary years in the American colonies; the Great Depression of the 1930's in industrialized America; the revolutionary period before the outbreak of 1789 in France and the two decades that followed; the 1840's all over Europe; the Civil War period in America; the years of inflation and economic and political instability in the twenties and early thirties in Germany.

The immediate incidents and processes in collective interaction situations acquire significance from the setting and times in which they take place. This point can be illustrated with a concrete study of collective riots which occurred during World War II. These riots took place in Detroit in 1943 and were investigated carefully by Lee and Humphrey (16). The

Detroit *Free Press.*

Fig. 10.6.　A glimpse from the Detroit riots.

rioting centered around intergroup conflict, starting with an incident, apparently a fairly minor incident, on the bridge of an amusement area called Belle Island on a humid Sunday evening in June. This incident swelled into larger proportions almost immediately, involving several hundred people, and the conflicts continued to expand in size and to spread across the city during the following days. In the end, 34 people were dead and more than 1000 injured.

What was the immediate incident which started the fighting on Belle Island? No one really knows, although it was apparently a violent encounter among a small number of individuals. The newspapers reported a fist fight; popular versions related that a Negro baby was thrown off the bridge by a white man, or from the other side that a white baby was thrown off the bridge by Negroes. There were further expanded rumors of its origin reflecting the viewpoint of those among whom the rumor was current.

As Lee and Humphrey pointed out, the beginning of these riots *is not understood by dwelling on the incident which set off the conflict.* Even before this particular incident, police had received a number of formal complaints of insults and injuries lodged by both Negroes and whites. For several years in wartime Detroit a growing Negro population and an even faster growing population of whites had found themselves crowded together in congested housing and recreational facilities, and in the war plants. On one hand, there were definite norms of social distance and segregation pertaining to Negroes and propaganda aimed against their aspirations. On the other hand, Negro boys were fighting in the war for their country, working in the war effort, and subjected to "second-class citizenship" in many aspects of living and working, a discrepancy which aroused dissatisfaction.

Hence, a relatively minor incident on the Belle Island bridge that Sunday evening was sufficient at the time to start an ever-growing chain of intergroup conflict. It becomes evident that, under the tense circumstances, another relatively minor incident at some other spot in the city might have set off such riots.

Accounting for Collective Interaction

The descriptive facts concerning the immediate, spontaneous interaction, milling, the rise of emotional tone, extreme forms of behavior, out-of-the-ordinary acts engaged in, and other differential products of interaction acquire greater significance when placed against the specific conditions in the setting as they relate to the focal aspects pertaining to the common motivations of individuals involved, and the existing organizational ties among them. Collective interaction does not take place every day. The mere "milling" of people in the same locality is not sufficient in itself to produce crowds, in the sense that makes their study important.

For a mere togetherness situation to turn into a crowd situation involving close interaction among participants there has to be a focal point centered around some common interest, issue, gripe, protest, indignation, or commonly cherished aspiration. Even transitory crowds interact as a consequence of some extraordinary happening that has common appeal value or threat to them, as noted earlier.

But a common motive, frustration, gripe, issue, demand, even though necessary, is not sufficient in itself for the formation of crowds. Existing social organization, tradition, social norms, and legal correctives stand against spontaneous translation of common motivational urges into action in collective behavior. Collective behavior is an out-of-the-ordinary type of activity which frequently constitutes deviation from the usual run of things. In its least deviate types, the populace is inconvenienced by the upset of routine or disorderliness. In order for participants with common problems to interact more spontaneously with one another, there are preparatory stages: weakening of existing norms, voicing of protests, exchanging of opinions in more limited interpersonal and group situations.

The importance of these preparatory conditions, stages, and events can be seen in the American Revolution. At the time when the American colonists were engaged in collective interaction for asserting their rights throughout the various colonies, there were other British colonies whose rights were invaded to no lesser degree. But in those colonies there was no collective action.

Thus the common issue or problem of interaction has to be considered in relation to other factors. Among them are the conditions of the general setting, their permissive or prohibitive character, the acuteness with which people with common problems have come to experience them, the degree of interaction among them, especially as expressed by some organizational pattern, and the intellectual or ideological level as this relates to the preceding factors. Even though the exact course of differential effects, such as extreme forms of behavior, and the direction of action are not always predictable in advance because of the possibilities of emerging proposals and leadership in the situation, activity in crowds is not an absolutely spontaneous affair. Almost always there is at least a *nucleus of leadership* which has a direct or indirect hand in shaping the crowd and its activities. The leaders may be prepared to function during the course of interaction. They may come to the foreground as a consequence of effective initiation of action in the situation.

In short, collective interaction does not take place in a void. The fluidity or stability of the times, the preoccupation with the issue by people in small clusters or groupings, their formal or informal organizational ties, and the nature of the focal problem or issue are all functionally related to one another.

Once interaction of individuals is initiated around a focal issue and their psychological selectivity is centered around it, *the togetherness of individuals begins to acquire a structure that is delineated from the surroundings.* Participating individuals henceforth become functional parts of the delineated crowd, in varying degrees. This is the fact noted by various social scientists and emphasized by various concepts, like "imitation," "suggestion," "rapport," "circular responses," and so on. As they become functional parts of a developing structure, participants are likely to perceive and to act in terms of their membership character in the developing trends.

Once the direction of experience and behavior starts taking shape in line with the developing structure of the interaction process, those who try to stand against the rising tide do become conspicuous as deviates. For the individual, being deviate in the midst of a rising tide of action is harder than being deviate when one is not related to a functioning system in the process of interaction. It is the fact of assuming membership in a delineated process of ongoing action which leads to the "social contagion" of ideas and behavior noted by so many writers.

When the delineated interaction process and developing trends of action acquire some definite structure, even the individuals who were initially responsible for crystallizing the issue and the line of action accepted by the membership have to act as parts of it. If a person who acquired leadership in the structure now attempts to act apart from these developing trends or to stop them, he faces the opposition of the irate members and, in some instances, runs the risk of being dropped from the structure.

Once it gets going in a structured fashion, collective interaction moves in the direction of short-cut solutions and direct, immediate action. Fine details of argument and qualifications of pros and cons are not looked upon with favor. Ideas and arguments elaborated in detail under routine conditions tend to be expressed in abbreviated, short-cut forms. The urgency toward clear-cut guides to action and solutions is seen in dramatic form in the circulation of *rumors*. This urgency is due in part to the interaction process but is understandable especially in terms of the prior conditions and central issues of interaction. Particularly in preliminary stages when structure and lines of action are still in fluid form, rumors, in the form of short-cut explanations, guides for action, and suggested solutions, originate and travel quickly from person to person. When external events lack clear-cut anchorages and when interaction is still fluid, rumors are accepted and passed on most quickly. At times they are started and circulated deliberately by parties interested in crystallizing events in a certain direction.

Various writers have stressed the "impulsive" and sheerly emotional nature of crowd behavior. The collectivity has definite directions, however, which cannot be explained in terms of mere "impulses" alone. The facts of heightened excitement and emotions in collective interaction are not discrete attributes independent of the cognitive or intellectual aspects of the participants. Collective interaction situations consisting of hundreds or even thousands of individuals develop a division of labor and a hierarchy of relations which can take place only through the utilization of the conceptual and intellectual resources of individuals. In short, the extreme types of behavior in human collective interaction cannot be likened to the milling and stampeding of cattle. In every case, the structuring of experience of individual members involves motivational and emotional components as they are related to cognitive or intellectual functions.

The intellectual level of participating individuals in collective interaction has been compared with their intellectual level in alone situations. Many writers have drawn conclusions concerning the effects of collective interaction. However, such a comparison is but one possible comparison at given points of time. If comparisons are to be meaningful, they should also be made longitudinally through the preparatory stages and after the given collective interaction. They should include individuals participating in various capacities—as leaders, organizers, carriers on of action, and onlookers. They should certainly include evaluation of the aftereffects of collective interaction for the intellectual level of participants as well as the effects in the immediate situation.

Rise of Organizational Structure and Norms in Collective Interaction

Many writers on collective behavior concentrated attention largely on one aspect of the topic: the psychological state of participants *at the time of* the actual interaction process. Detailed treatments of the topic have, therefore, concentrated to a disproportionate degree on the lowering of intellectual processes, the intense heightening of excitement and emotion, and the aggressiveness, impulsiveness, expressiveness, and other extreme forms of behavior. These, among others, may be the differential effects of actual interaction situations.

However, to restrict psychological analysis to differential behavior in the actual interaction situation amounts almost to describing the activities in construction work only in terms of the dust, disorder, and comings and goings during building operations. To complete the picture, the description has to include an account of the aftereffects or products of interaction. Of course, this is not to say that there will be a finished product in every case or that every product will be constructive. But this is certainly something that needs to be known. In some cases, the product of collective interaction may be in the direction of stabilizing existing institutions or values which have become shaky. In others, the direction may be destructive efforts to prevent changes.

In many cases, collective interaction situations, especially those which are not one-episode affairs, are the fertile grounds in which new social trends, organizations, values, or norms arise. At times, such new trends may not lead to realistic or effective solutions of the problems they center around. At other times, they may correspond more closely to the actualities of the period. The Boston Tea Party is an illustration of the point. If our analysis were restricted to the intellectual and emotional state of participants during the time of that engagement and were not followed by its subsequent effects on these and other individuals, we would be left with a very incomplete and erroneous account of the collective interaction (the Tea Party) in question. In itself, the excited activity of tossing tea into Boston Harbor would seem sheerly destructive, as no doubt it did to many people at the time.

This aspect of studying collective behavior was expressed concisely by Blumer: "Collective behavior is concerned in studying the ways by which the social order comes into existence, in the sense of emergence and solidification of new forms of collective behavior" (4, p. 169). This idea is also formulated clearly by the sociologist Hughes. In situations of collective interaction during periods of crisis, "institutions can be seen in the process of disintegration and formation" (12, p. 236).

In preceding chapters we have discussed the rise of organizational structure and social norms in small groups in the course of interaction among individuals working toward common goals. In the case of collective inter-action, which is most prevalent in periods of crisis in the face of common danger, common frustrations, or aspirations of groups of people, the rise of new types of social organization and norms comes through more dra-matic processes and at an accelerated pace. The short-cut *slogans* arising during collective interaction become new norms for participants and occa-sionally for others as well. Particular collective situations in critical times, like rallies, serve as landmarks for the snowballing of new social move-ments with their organizational ties and values. Since such more extreme and widespread forms of social interaction imply social change in one way or another, they are reserved for fuller treatment in Chapter 21.

REFERENCES

1. Associated Press dispatch, March 27, 1955 (*The Daily Oklahoman*, March 28, 1955).
2. Associated Press dispatch, London, April 5, 1955 (*The Daily Oklahoman*, April 6, 1955).
3. Blondel, C. *Introduction à la Psychologie Collective*. Paris: A. Colin, 1928.
4. Blumer, H. Collective Behavior, in A. M. Lee (ed.), *New Outline of the Principles of Sociology*. New York: Barnes and Noble, 1946.
5. Brown, R. W. Mass Phenomena, in G. Lindzey (ed.), *Handbook of Social Psychology*. Cambridge: Addison-Wesley, 1954, Vol. II.
6. Cantril, H. The Invasion from Mars, in G. E. Swanson, T. M. Newcomb, and E. L. Hartley (eds.), *Readings in Social Psychology*. New York: Holt, rev. ed., 1952.
7. Chapman, J., and Eckstein, M. A social-psychological study of the alleged visitation of the Virgin Mary in Puerto Rico, *Year Book of the American Philosophical Society*, 1954, pp. 203–206.
8. Durkheim, E. *Les Règles de la Méthode Sociologique*. Paris: F. Alcan, 1895. Trans. *The Rules of Sociological Method*. Chicago: University of Chicago Press, 1938.
9. Durkheim, E. *Les Formes Elementaires de la Vie Religieuse*. Paris, 1912. Trans. *Elementary Forms of Religious Life*. London: Allen and Unwin, 1915.
10. Freud, S. *Group Psychology and the Analysis of the Ego*. London: Hogarth, 1922.
11. Fritz, C. E., and Marks, E. S. The NORC studies of human behavior in disaster, *J. soc. Issues* (1954), 10:26–41.
12. Hughes, E. C. Institutions in Process, in A. M. Lee (ed.), *New Outline of the Principles of Sociology*. New York: Barnes and Noble, 1946.

13. Killian, L. M. The significance of multiple group membership in disaster, *Amer. J. Sociol.* (1952), 57:309–314.
14. Killian, L. M. Some accomplishments and some needs in disaster study, *J. soc. Issues* (1954), 10:66–72.
15. Le Bon, G. *The Crowd* (English trans.). London: T. Fisher Unwin, 1897.
16. Lee, A. M., and Humphrey, N. D. *Race Riot*. New York: Dryden, 1943.
17. Marshall, S. L. A. *Men Against Fire*. New York: Morrow, 1947.
18. Martin, E. D. *The Behavior of Crowds*. New York: Harper, 1920.
19. Mintz, A. Nonadaptive Group Behavior, in G. E. Swanson, T. M. Newcomb, and E. L. Hartley (eds.), *Readings in Social Psychology*. New York: Holt, rev. ed., 1952.
20. Park, R. E. In R. E. Park and E. W. Burgess, *Introduction to the Science of Sociology*. Chicago: University of Chicago Press, 1929.
21. *Time*, October 25, 1954, pp. 54–60.
22. Tumin, M., and Feldman, A. S. The Miracle at Sabana Grande (abstract). Papers of the 49th Annual Meeting, American Sociological Society, Urbana, Illinois, September 8–10, 1954, pp. 141–142 (mimeographed).

IV

MOTIVES OF MAN

CHAPTER **11**

Motives in Relation to Social Psychology

The modern trend in both biological and social sciences conceives of psychological development as a biosocial product. Behavior is a product of processes in which biological factors and social influences are inextricably interrelated—one of the main points in the frame of reference concept (pp. 77–84). This scheme for the study of human behavior specifically emphasizes that behavior is always a joint product of interrelated factors coming both from within the individual and from external influences.

The controversies over "human nature" and their far-reaching implications for the schemes of human relations advocated by various parties led us in this chapter to distinguish man's motives as to their origin. Especially in social psychology, the problem of origin becomes a meaningful one in the functional analysis of the *relative weights* of various internal factors. Also a consideration of the origin of motives will prove to be useful in comprehending the continuities and discontinuities in the characteristic consistency (type) of behavior of persons living under various cultural settings (pp. 588–591).

Motivated Behavior

The conceptual approach outlined in Chapter 3 specified that experience and behavior are the outcome of both external stimulus factors and internal factors operative at the time within their frame of reference, or system of relations. Motives are examples *par excellence* of internal factors.

Man's motives lend to his behavior its goal-directed character, which in turn is inferred from behavior. A great deal of the selective nature and other properties of experience and behavior are accountable only when motives are brought into the picture.

Many motives of man are products of social interaction and exposure to sociocultural products. These motives of social origin (sociogenic motives) are revealed in our preferences, in the favorable or unfavorable stand we take toward groups and social issues—in brief, in what constitutes our social attitudes. They are revealed in our identifications with various groups, in our susceptibility or resistance to influences in face-to-face human contacts or to influences from lectures, newspapers, books, radio, or television. Therefore, a general discussion of the problem of motives with special reference to social psychology is in order.

What motives operate as internal factors in the early years of human life? How do motives which have their origin in the physiology of the organism operate later in socialized man? How do new motives rise in social interaction? How do social motives come in as factors in the structuring of experience and behavior? These topics will be touched upon in this and the following chapters.

This chapter starts with the general problem of motives and the question of their origins. Why bother about the origin of motives? The human adult is, after all, a socialized, interrelated being. He is not part animal, part man, and part supernatural like the centaur of the Greek myths. Why not take him as he is, rather than inquire how he became that way? If the origins of man's motives differ, does this have any importance at all in the patterning of experience and behavior in adult life?

When we observe our fellow human beings in different cultures, we find individuals everywhere directed toward certain goals. These goals vary considerably and require shorter or longer times for their attainment. We see individuals invariably getting food or trying to get food at fairly regular intervals, although the length of the interval may vary. The meal time, its frequency within limits, the kind, place, atmosphere, and trimmings of the meal are determined usually by one's culture and by his social status and economic position within the social organization. What we observe about food getting and its social regulation is also seen in the matters of dwelling, clothing, and mating. We see individuals searching for sexual partners, using roundabout or direct approaches with all of the devices available for increasing their appeal value—masculine or feminine charm, position, power, riches, niceties, and the subterfuges of etiquette.

We see the individual striving to be a member in good standing of his group, whatever his particular group may be. The methods may vary from individual to individual, but each strives to excel in his group, whatever the requirements for excelling may be. Of course, different behavioral characteristics are at a premium in different social settings. In one, the degree of competitiveness or individualism or ability to outsmart others may be the established rule for excelling; in another, coöperativeness and solidarity, and so on.

One college student may aim at getting a C in his course; his classmate may feel frustrated unless he gets an A. The rich man may not feel satisfied unless his riches are second to none in his community, whereas a poor man who has difficulty making both ends meet may experience achievement if he is able to make a steady living for his family. The vice-president of a company may feel miserable until he becomes the president.

These everyday illustrations are cited to make our meaning clear. Whether directed toward food, clothing, shelter, the opposite sex, or toward status, acceptance, power, social distinction, recognition, trifles concerning dress, decoration, and etiquette, these are all cases of *motivated behavior*. In each case a motive is inferred. We shall use the term "motives" as a generic term to cover all of the internal factors which lead to different kinds of goal-directed (motivated) behavior, to designate such internal influences as the needs originating and embedded in the functioning of the organism, desires based upon them, as well as socially acquired desires, aspirations, and tastes.

THE IMPORTANCE OF MOTIVES IN CONTROVERSIES OVER "HUMAN NATURE"

Our present world is extraordinary for its epochal events and its developments in both sociocultural and technological fields. Problems of man's basic motives in relation to social institutions and social orders have come emphatically to the foreground. Friendly and antagonistic groups and individuals engage in heated argument and, at times, in open conflict over them. As typical illustrations of such flourishing controversies, we shall mention in passing two arguments between contending parties in many parts of the world today.

One argument centers around the relative effectiveness of incentives in competitive and in coöperative social groups. The implications of this argument have to be considered seriously in social psychology because they have a bearing on the individual-society relationship. The advocate of the individually competitive system argues that if you take away individual competition there will be no incentive to excel and, hence, progress will cease and Western civilization will stagnate. To prove his point, he cites the development of the highly competitive capitalist system during the past few centuries. His opponent argues with equal enthusiasm that this contention is not true and cites developments in the Soviet Union in confirmation. Is individual competition—the passion to outdo others in business, scholarship, or social life—the only possible incentive that can set a high pace for achievement?

The second argument is more comprehensive and goes to the core of the problem of the inherent compatibility or incompatibility of this or that social system with the basic tendencies of what contenders take to be "human nature." The person who is dissatisfied with the existing order of human relationships argues for a change in arrangements that are based on the private ownership of capital. He argues that the major ills plaguing people today, such as imperialism, war, economic crises, periodic scarcity, labor-owner strife, ruthless competition, are caused mainly by the private-ownership system. His opponent, in turn, points to the wonderful blessings of modern technology. He attributes these to the motives of profit and competition, arguing that without profit and competition progress would cease. Sooner or later in the course of the argument he reaches a conclusion that seems to him unanswerable: It is desirable to do away with economic crises, worker-owner conflicts, wars, etc., all of which cause hardships and misery to a great many people; but it is impossible to do away with the ownership system and individual competition because it is against "human nature" to do so. He may even attribute crises, conflict, and war to "human nature." His opponent may state with equal finality that, on the contrary, "human nature" is fundamentally opposed to competition, conflict, and war. The argument has reached a stalemate.

Controversies over "human nature" are old problems which have been heatedly debated for centuries without success. For example, Hobbes (8) gave a picture of the cruelty and selfishness of human beings on the one hand; Rousseau (22) depicted the innocence and spontaneous goodness of original "human nature" on the other. There have been innumerable variations on these main themes since then, usually couched in the currently fashionable intellectual expressions of their time. Thus, Kropotkin (11), in harmony with his social philosophy, looked at the living creatures around him and proclaimed a world of sympathy and coöperation. His contemporary, Herbert Spencer (23), who lived at the peak of the British Empire's power toward the end of the nineteenth century, painted a grim picture. Using the language of biological evolution, he sought to justify the might of the mighty, the fortune of the wealthy, the misfortune of the downtrodden, by the "laws" of the jungle.

Even now we are not far advanced from that stage of "scientific" justification for "human nature" in harmony with the picture of human relationships or society we fundamentally uphold. Of course, in pace with the more "scientifically minded" temper of modern times, more refined arguments are presented in the current controversies over original "human nature."

Not long ago it was fashionable to look for "original human nature" among more primitive peoples, the assumption being that the less developed a society is, the closer its members are to original "human nature." And what have been the results? Sure enough, observers were selective in their choice of facts; each found facts to support his own viewpoint. Methodologically, the vicious circle starts with the assumption that technically less-developed peoples are closer to original "human nature." On the basis of ethnological observations, it is safe to say that in general the members of less-developed groups tend to cling more closely and to conform more religiously to the values or norms of their society (no matter how strange or unnatural these may appear to outsiders) than do the members of societies at a higher level of technological development with their relatively more rapid changes and greater variations.

In spite of their refined methods and techniques, psychologists, even in recent times, have not been exceptions in this tendency to start with certain assumptions and then present elaborate facts in their favor. For example, it was not too long ago that some psychologists reported results which, if taken at face value, meant that the rich were rich because, without being appreciably affected by life circumstances of their upbringing, they were congenitally more intelligent.

The picture of "human nature" prevalent in any society at a given time corresponds rather closely to its established values or social norms regarding human nature and to the practice of human relationships sanctioned by these norms (13, 14). This can be seen from even a superficial comparison of the conceptions of "human nature" held by the French, Germans, or English in the ecclesiastically tinged feudal times with those held by these peoples today. It is particularly the superstructure of social norms and "social techniques which lend to a particular society a large part of its characteristic flavor, its 'myth,' as to the Nature of Man" (25, p. 23).

If this is true it becomes a superfluous preoccupation to indulge in futile controversies over whether or not "human nature" can be changed. The above considerations force us *first* to raise the question: What *is* this "human nature" about which argument rages?

When we start the argument with the question of whether or not human nature can be changed, we assume that we already know what it is. As yet, nowhere, including all of the books on psychology, do we find an adequate picture of "human nature." Therefore, the first essential task is the study of it. This necessarily becomes the study of the biological endowment, which includes congenitally given organic needs, the human capacity for conceptual functioning, and the limits of learning ability in the species.

Distinguishing Motives as to Their Origin

The endless controversies over "human nature" impose on us the task of distinguishing motives as to their origin. Real advance in this direction will help to clarify our study of the socialization process and our understanding of certain functional relationships among the psychological components of the socialized adult.

Distinguishing between universal motives and culturally derived motives of various sorts becomes imperative, especially in social psychology. The aim of the social psychologist is to achieve concepts and principles that are equally valid in different cultures, with their enormous diversity of social norms and values relating to various phases of life—from the most intimate kinship relationships to the trifles of social etiquette. Since this diversity gives rise, in turn, to a vast variety of goal objects and situations, the distinction between motives based on their origin has to be kept in mind throughout.

There are other good reasons for distinguishing motives as to their origin. In trying times of economic depression, poverty, and crises, people dispense with the pursuit of many goal objects and values which in better times they hold indispensable; they strive to keep barely alive. In periods of scarcity and privation, the motives of individuals become more and more directed toward those goal objects and situations that are closest to their organic needs. (See Chapter 13 for examples.)

Motives may be distinguished in terms of their origin as:

1. Biogenic motives. These originate in the physiological requirements and self-regulating processes of the organism that maintain equilibrium in the "internal environment," within certain limits. The self-regulating processes are referred to as homeostasis (3).

2. Sociogenic motives. These motives are acquired in the course of the individual's development in a social setting. They are formed in connection with interpersonal relationships, group relations, or established social values or norms and institutions.

It seems preferable to use the term "sociogenic" to indicate the origin of acquired motives, rather than "psychogenic," which some authors use. Motives that in a strict sense are personally acquired need not concern us much in social psychology. Specific kinds or types of sociogenic motives— such as tastes and desires for certain value objects, aspirations for a certain social position, ambitions, and the like—are so numerous that special terms are used for each. Behavior which reveals an established social attitude is taken as behavior aroused by a sociogenic motive inasmuch as such attitudes are directed toward certain values or objects.

After making the distinction between biogenic and sociogenic motives, one fact must be emphasized. Whether of biological origin (biogenic) or social origin (sociogenic), motives have consequences in the experience and behavior of the individual as long as they operate. Take the case of an ambitious politician who lives far above the subsistence level and who is set on obtaining some office. He certainly will turn heaven and earth to get it. His major elations or frustrations will be functions of his experienced proximity to the goal (the office). Or take a young person who is all set to attend a big football game or commencement week end. If for some reason he is prevented from going, he will feel miserable and betrayed. In short, whether of biological or social origin, once a motive is aroused, the individual experiences a sense of *urgency* to attain the goal (20). This urgency is, of course, proportional to the intensity of the motive.

Before closing these general remarks, a word about the place of motives in social relationships may be in order. It is a truism of everyday life that we enter into interpersonal relationships and participate in group interaction to achieve certain ends. The end may be to secure a livelihood, to find a mate, or to achieve social status or distinction. Certainly an account of interpersonal relationships or group interaction will miss major variables if motivational factors are left out.

On the other hand, we have seen that, once groups start to function, new values emerge (Chapter 5, pp. 154–156). These new values in turn become significant factors in shaping the experience and behavior of individual members, even in relation to the motives which were first responsible for bringing the individuals together. New values, hence new motives, do arise in the course of social interaction.

A concrete example will remind us of this point. A group of boys in a slum area, deprived of adequate food, clothing, and social ties, may meet as a gang to satisfy these deprivations, perhaps by stealing together. But once the group begins to function, once a "code" of conduct (social norms) appears in the group, the members willingly undergo hunger, deprivation, and temporary separation from the gang in accordance with its norms in order to preserve or enhance their status or to maintain the solidarity of their group (see also pp. 170–174).

BIOGENIC MOTIVES

No matter what the social setting or "culture pattern" may be—imperial or colonial, Western or Oriental, highly industrial or primitive, leisure-class or poverty-stricken, Christian or heathen—man eats, drinks, breathes, sleeps, and tries to keep warm simply in order to keep alive as a biological organism. No matter what other prosaic or refined, mean or noble, humble or distinguished activities and strivings he may be engaged in, he has first to achieve at least a subsistence level of living. And achieving a subsistence level means attending to such organic demands as hunger, thirst, and sleep.

The manner of satisfying these basic needs is subject to cultural variations. However, in spite of cultural variations and the emergence of altogether new practices and strivings in different societies, the fact remains that if there is a common substratum which may be labeled "human nature" it is these organic needs together with the ability to form concepts and the great plasticity in learning capacity of the human species. Therefore, one of our tasks of utmost significance is to try to specify these basic needs or motives.

Since the impact of the evolutionary teaching of Darwin began to be felt in academic psychology, many attempts have been made to achieve a classification or list of basic motives or "instincts" in psychology. For example, William James made such a list. Psychology owes a great deal to the influence of the work of McDougall and Freud for the beginning of the modern concern with problems of motivation. Both men drew up lists of "instincts" which they changed as they elaborated their systems.

McDougall's classification (15), which exerted a great influence at the time, now has only historical value. The instincts he listed were linked closely with his vitalistic speculation; and such instincts as ascendance and submission (16) have not survived the test of evidence. The dramatic instincts of life and of death (destruction) posited by Freud (e.g., 5) cannot be subjected to the check of controlled investigation. And, alluring though they are, the diverse central concepts (like the sexual libido of Freud, the "inferiority complex" of Adler, and the "collective unconscious" of Jung), which are used as magic keys to everything from personal troubles to the rise of social systems, blind us to the need of making room for other factors. The other factors stand as stubborn facts which cannot be assimilated by magic principles.

The confusion in regard to biogenic motives and the contradictory lists necessitate the application of some rigor in studying them. First, we must adhere to certain *minimal criteria* for including any motive in a list of biogenic motives.

1. The essential characteristics of a biogenic motive or need are as follows:

a. It constitutes a reaction to an organic demand, such as a chemical deficit (e.g., oxygen, food, water), or to some organic state (e.g., presence or excess of sex hormones in the blood stream). Biogenic motives signify states of the organism in which the constancy or equilibrium of the internal organic environment (homeostasis) is disturbed in various ways, as in hunger, thirst, or oxygen deficiency. Such states of disequilibrium stimulate neural impulses, emergency signals, or "warnings" proportional to the degree in which the internal environment is disturbed. In the case of bodily needs, the reaction "to deprivation of some stimulus presents the typical problem of motivation" (12, p. 448).
b. The reaction to impairment of internal balance constitutes an aroused state of the organism. The aroused state continues its prompting proportional to the degree of disturbance until equilibrium is restored by intake of oxygen, food, water, reëstablishment of normal temperatures, or discharge of excess sex hormones. All of these imply more or less specific patterns of neural and effector activity in relation to relevant stimuli.

2. Minimal criteria for including a motive in the list of biogenic motives are explicitly or implicitly accepted by almost everyone, but the requirements of such criteria are often neglected somewhere along the way. These criteria include at least its *universality* in the species, and its *unlearned* (innate) character in relation to a more or less definite range of stimulus objects or situations.

The second criterion needs some clarification. Probably human behavior aroused by any motive is to some extent modified through learning. Even such a simple basic pattern of activity as breathing has been regulated and modified through learning by singers, athletes, and enthusiasts of Yoga. The "unlearned character" of biogenic motives refers to the conditions of their appearance. To meet this criterion, a motive must come as a factor at birth or through maturation and not primarily as a *product* of learning. Hunger, thirst, and sexual urges are regulated and modified; the goals sought when they are aroused are subject to social influences, within limits. But learning is not the prerequisite for their initial occurrence.

Certainly eating, drinking, breathing, sleeping, and mating are universal in any social setting, no matter in what form these motives are satisfied in each case. Such universality cannot be claimed for motives like sharing, coöperation, competition, submission, domination, or wealth hoarding. The comparative studies of sociologists and ethnologists contain convincing evidence that the direction of these interpersonal and intergroup relationships is determined largely by the established practices and standards of the particular group at a particular period in its history.

On the other hand, no matter whether competition or coöperation, dominance or submission, individualism or solidarity is preponderantly required from the members of any society, we *universally* find human beings (after they reach a certain age) striving to belong to a group and to acquire a position or status, whatever the status may be. Then, because of the universality of activities connected with belongingness and status, shall we say that strivings for belongingness and status stem from biogenic motives? No. This brings us to the criterion of the *unlearned* character of the motive's origin.

The motives underlying strivings to belong and to achieve some status are formed in the course of the individual's development in a social setting. In the next chapter the problem of sociogenic motives is considered in some detail. If there is an innate basis for such strivings, it is to be found in the human species' capacity for conceptual functioning. For it is only in the human species that we find belongingness and status arrangements in the sense that they involve lasting reciprocal identifications, loyalties, and responsibilities.

The infant does not have these strivings in the early years of life. The essential condition for their appearance is development and learning within a social setting. The child acquires desires to *belong* and to be part of a group through social interaction. First he has to achieve the great feat of regulating his experience and behavior according to rules or norms other than his own whim. When he achieves this ability to grasp a set of norms, thus enabling him to see himself in a reciprocal relationship with those around him, *then* he begins to interiorize the status arrangements and norms of his family, his play group, his social setting. Hence, whatever pattern of interpersonal and intergroup relationships prevails in his specific social setting becomes his pattern too. The pattern varies from society to society. Of course, it also varies in terms of individual capacities, intensities, and limitations.

In short, motives related to the individual's status, belongingness, and ego problems are *sociogenic*. They cannot be called biogenic because they are products of learning in social interaction.

A List of Biogenic Motives

An adequate inventory of biogenic motives can be achieved only by keeping the basic problems and criteria of instinctive behavior clearly in mind. The essential earmarks of a biogenic motive are (1) that it constitutes a reaction to an organic demand such as a chemical deficit (e.g., oxygen, food, water, etc.) or other organic state (e.g., accumulation of sex hormones) and (2) that it leads to a more or less specific pattern of neural and effector activity in relation to relevant stimuli (*12*).

The minimal criteria of a biogenic motive in man are (1) its universality in the members of the species and (2) the unlearned character of its appearance. (Note that it cannot be stated that behavior aroused by a biogenic motive is not subject to modification. See page 373.) With this delineation of the essential problems of biogenic motives and their minimal criteria in mind, it may be safe to state that the following should be included among the biogenic motives, subject to corrections by investigators working in the biological sciences:

Hunger
Thirst
Activity-sleep (rest) cycle
Breathing[1]
Sex
Temperature regulation (avoidance of cold and heat differentials)
Suckling of young
Evacuation (urination and defecation)
Avoidance of organic injury (?)

These needs, and perhaps others that biological research will teach

---

[1] We have included breathing here in accordance with the following remarks by Morgan: "To be sure, respiratory behavior is not very relevant to most phases of psychology, for it probably plays an exceedingly minor role in learning and seldom enters into conscious experience. Respiration is, nevertheless, motivated behavior. Indeed, it is a model of such behavior in that it is relatively simple behavior whose mechanism is much better understood than other mechanisms of motivation; and its study offers some suggestions for the interpretation of other facts of motivation" (*18*, p. 438).

us about, are biogenic motives, which irrespective of the cultural setting and times have to be attended to at least to a minimum degree in carrying out and perpetuating the urgent occupation of living. They are all essential in varying degrees to the functioning of the organism. For example, disruption of the periodic function of breathing during a very short period, on the order of a few minutes, will be fatal, whereas the disruption of eating, drinking, and mating can be endured for much longer periods—differing of course from individual to individual.

When each need suffers deprivation or enjoys satisfaction, it comes to dominate the individual's experience and behavior to the exclusion or inhibition of other motives. After a long and hectic day, the need for sleep or rest usually dominates other needs and otherwise fascinating activities. If a normal person misses a meal or two for some reason, hunger may dominate his whole experience and behavior.

Behavior that is aroused by a biogenic motive may be characterized as behavior which is at first or *initially* unlearned and common to all members of the species. This behavior may appear at birth or later through maturation of the organism (like sex). It is aroused (in most cases) by some periodically recurring organic need (such as hunger for food, thirst for water) which activates and heightens the motor, sensory, and central

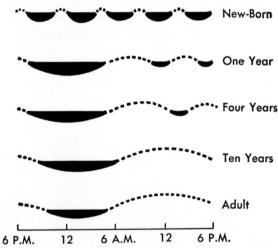

FIG. 11.1. Change from polyphasic to monophasic sleep as the individual grows up. (From N. Kleitman, *Sleep and Wakefulness*. Chicago: University of Chicago Press, 1939. Copyright, 1939, by the University of Chicago.)

(perceptual-symbolic) functions of the individual and renders him highly *selective* in the direction of an appropriate goal object or situation. If the need continues and grows more intense, such motivated behavior persists until the goal object or situation is reached; and it ends in a more or less specific pattern of behavior. This leads to restoration of equilibrium to the internal state involved (homeostasis).

Most of the biogenic motives (hunger, thirst, sleep, breathing, probably sex desire) recur periodically or cyclically within shorter or longer time intervals. Of course physiological rhythms are modified or regulated within limits by social and other factors. We see periodicity in the recurrent needs of the human infant, subject (within limits) to individual variations and to modifications as the child grows up under given social circumstances. One example of this periodicity and subsequent modification as the child grows older is the sleep cycle, as represented in Figure 11.1.

Biological Value of Stimuli and Their Social Significance

The social significance of stimuli, in the sense that they raise issues and complications in human relations, is not directly proportional to their biological value to the organism. As Cannon pointed out in his classic, *The Wisdom of the Body*: "Some of the needs are satisfied gratuitously. Oxygen and sometimes water also, we may have at will, without cost. It is noteworthy that in cities a supply of water is obtained only by community action and at public expense. There are other needs, however, which in the long run are quite as urgent as the needs for water and oxygen, and which at times cannot be satisfied because of the lack of social stability. These are the elementary requirements of food and shelter (clothing, housing and warmth) and the benefits of medical care" (3, p. 295).

Needs which depend on other individuals or on arrangements of the socioeconomic scheme for their satisfaction (like those for food, sex, warmth) are of particular concern as internal factors in the field of social psychology.

When an individual cannot meet the demands of biogenic motives because of his personal or socioeconomic circumstances, their deprivation has major psychological effects on his entire functioning. If deprivation is widespread among the population or among particular groups within it, the consequences are not only physiological and psychological but sociological as well. This is one of the most important fields in which the social psychologist may study genuine group formation and various aspects of collective phenomena and their emergence. At the present time, it is chiefly policy makers and politicians who are realistically treating these grim problems.

Therefore, in considering the significance of biogenic motives in social psychology, primary focus is on the extent to which satisfaction of motives is dependent on other human beings. The greater the dependence on other individuals in personal or group relationships for satisfying motives, the greater the social issues and complications they can arouse.

RELATIVE WEIGHTS OF VARIOUS MOTIVES

One problem in the area of motivation has been the relative importance of various motives in determining experience and behavior. Two of the issues involved here are (1) the "relative strength" of various biogenic motives (e.g., hunger, sex, thirst) or of various sociogenic motives (desires for recognition, wealth, power, aesthetic satisfactions, and so on) and (2) the relative weight of biogenic motives compared to sociogenic motives. The latter issue usually takes the form: "Which of these two sets of motives is more important in the lives of human beings?"

Some authors have suggested a hierarchy of motives, starting with needs of the organism and ranging upward through motives related to a sense of security and various social, aesthetic, and intellectual aspirations at differing levels of abstraction (e.g., 17).

Evidence supporting the relative dominance of one biogenic motive over others is sometimes taken from studies of animal motivation. An animal motivated by two different needs (e.g., hunger and thirst, or hunger and sex) is placed in a situation in which it can orient itself to only one of two incentives (26, 27). It is difficult to establish a fixed hierarchy for the strength of various biogenic motives. The point was made by P. T. Young after surveying the experimental literature:

"There is no doubt that hunger behavior dominates thirst if the animal has been long deprived of food and only recently of water, and that thirst dominates hunger under a reversal of conditions. Also, the preferential order for foods varies with the constituents of the animal's diet. Similarly, exploratory behavior inhibits sexual aggression, eating, and drinking, if rats are placed in a novel environment. Many such examples can be found to show that the relative dominance of behavior patterns is largely dependent upon circumstances. We are forced to conclude that *there is no immutable hierarchy of drives*" (28, p. 152).

The periodic or cyclical nature of biogenic motives is relevant to this point. Different needs appear in full strength at shorter or longer time intervals. For example, in the human adult, hunger and thirst are aroused in more or less regular cycles which are of shorter duration than the sleep cycle. They are also subject to some variation from individual to individual.

Ordinarily one motive becomes the weightier factor at a given time, and which motive it will be depends on both the state of the organism (degree of deprivation or frustration of various motives) and the circumstances at the time.

In regard to the relative weight of various sociogenic motives, a fixed hierarchy of importance under all conditions cannot be supported. Within broad bounds, the relative importance of different sociogenic motives varies from culture to culture. More specifically, it varies with the particular circumstances of development and living of individuals, into which both sociocultural and idiosyncratic factors enter in an interdependent way. Positing aspirations for power, wealth, recognition, or fame as the most potent motive, singly or in a given order, accounts for only a limited number of individuals in a particular place and at a particular time.

The discussion of the relative importance of biogenic versus sociogenic motives in shaping human experience and behavior has to be restricted in this context to one important aspect. Biogenic motives, like needs for oxygen, food, water, sleep, have to be satisfied to a minimum degree before other motives can be attended to. Prolonged hunger, thirst, or lack of sleep produces a state in which the functioning of the whole organism— his perceptual, intellectual, motor activities—becomes dominated by the deprivation in question. Some psychological consequences of such domination are given in Chapter 13 (pp. 433–443). Some consequences of prolonged deprivation of motives on a large scale or mass basis are dealt with in Chapter 21. People in favorable social circumstances may go through life without enduring prolonged or severe deprivation of biogenic motives. There are probably differences between the consequences of deprivation along one given dimension (for example, hunger or sex) and simultaneous deprivation of several, which is more characteristic of profound social crises or sufferings on the part of a sizable section of a population.

Barring prolonged deprivations of biogenic motives, their relative weights have to be studied in terms of the state of other motives at the time and of external influences operating simultaneously. Whether biogenic or sociogenic, a motive enters as an internal factor whose relative contribution in structuring of experience and behavior is determined by its functional relations to other factors, including other motives operating at the time. It cannot be said that biogenic motives are always weightier factors in a particular frame of reference. It can be said that under certain conditions and with intense degrees of deprivation biogenic motives will become the compelling determiners in the frame of reference.

An individual enters into interpersonal and group relations to attain certain goals, be they economic gain, a sexual partner, a sense of security or belongingness, or others. But interaction in interpersonal and group relations produces properties which modify and sometimes *transform* the particular functioning of the motive in question. Thus, at times individuals do undergo prolonged deprivation of certain motives in order to adhere to the values or goals which have emerged in social relationships of which these individuals are parts.

Motives Do Not Function as Isolated Units

In studying motives, one tendency in physiology and psychology has been to isolate various motives (like thirst, hunger, sex) for purposes of investigation, and to study them in their own right. To attain a base line for functional relationships involved, this mode of investigation is one of the steps that has to be taken. However, in actuality, a given motive ordinarily has a relation to other psychological functions and to social circumstances. Study of one motive as if it were independent gives at best a disjointed picture with little relevance to actualities. This touches on the major problem of "part-whole" relationship. It is necessary to study parts in their own right, and it is also necessary to study them as functioning parts of a system of relations, or a whole (2, 21).

In satisfying sexual needs, for example, we are dependent ordinarily on at least another person. An approach to another person is not simply a matter of the glandular and motor activities of the sexually aroused individual. Even to approach another person, matters of social etiquette, socially sanctioned and valued ways of making such an approach, the "appropriateness" or "inappropriateness" of words, gestures, and deeds directed toward the goal generally become parts of the whole functional scheme. This is true, by and large, even when male and female individuals are sexually attracted to one another. Sexual attraction in itself is to an important extent a question of socially defined standards of attractiveness, social compatibility, decency, and considerations pertaining to interpersonal and group affiliations of the parties (e.g., social, ethnic, religious, etc.). In any sociocultural setting these matters imply perception of the complicated interpersonal relations involved and evaluation of the circumstances. Perception of interpersonal relations and evaluation of circumstances are necessarily carried out on a conceptual level of functioning. This mode of functioning toward goal objects is distinctly human.

This is in line with conclusions reached by Ford and Beach on the basis of their survey of sexual activity of man:

> . . . In reviewing these topics it became apparent that human beings are less dependent upon sex hormones than are subhuman primates, and that the latter in turn are somewhat freer of hormonal control than are lower mammals. . . .
> . . . In particular, the cerebral cortex has assumed a greater and greater degree of direction over all behavior, including that of a sexual nature. It appears that the growing importance of cerebral influences accounts for the progressive relaxation of hormonal control over sexual responses. At the same time, increasing dominance of the cortex in affecting sexual manifestations has resulted in greater lability and modifiability of erotic practices. Human sexual behavior is more variable and more easily affected by learning and social conditioning than is that of any other species, and this is precisely because in our own species this type of behavior depends heavily upon the most recently evolved parts of the brain [4, p. 249].

As stressed before, behavior does not directly follow arousal of a motive state; neither does behavior follow directly an item of external stimulation. Experience and behavior follow central psychological structuring or patterning in which various external and internal factors participate in a functionally interrelated way. Motivated behavior is not independent of central integrative processes. Therefore, a motive operating at a given time is taken as an internal factor and studied in its appropriate frame of reference.

For such reasons, it is not sufficient to ascertain in isolation the properties of any motive (hunger, sex, and so on). Motives have to be taken in relation to other factors operative simultaneously stemming from external, social, and other circumstances, other dominant values of the individual's scheme of living, and effects of past experience in related matters.

When a person fasts because of his religious or political convictions, the homeostatic upset of the internal organism may not become the dominant factor. In some individual cases, completion of a book or a musical composition becomes such a dominant concern in regulating behavior that organically determined arousal of hunger or the need for sleep becomes subordinate for the time being to the overall goal at hand (cf. 6).

Therefore, the use of homeostasis as an *overall* explanatory concept in human motivation becomes questionable. Empirical evidence marshaled originally for demonstrating homeostasis was developed by Claude Bernard and Cannon for cases of constancy of internal bodily environment (3). Centrally aroused states of disequilibrium, like difficult discriminations, perception of complex and ambiguous stimulus materials or of those encountered when a person is caught between two vital decisions, should be specified as such. They may in turn lead to autonomic upset. But it will be stretching the application of the concept "homeostasis" too far if centrally aroused states of disequilibrium are subsumed under it. In such cases, the chain of events does not start with an imbalance in internal environment of the body. Rather, internal imbalance is a consequence of central motive states. Many sociogenic motives, such as those related to status and self-identity concerns, are aroused centrally through symbolisms made possible by human language.

The motivational activity of a human being in sexual strivings which involve other people or in food getting which involves also considerations related to his particular place, work, and talents in a socioeconomic setting necessarily implies factors on the conceptual level of functioning. Therefore, extrapolations from subhuman studies and from the pictures of a motive obtained by studying it in isolation have not been particularly rewarding in giving an adequate psychology of human motivation which can be applied to man's interpersonal and group relations.

EMOTIONAL MOTIVATION

Any strong motive state is experienced with pronounced affective tones, which may be either pleasant or unpleasant. As a state of deprivation progresses, the whole organism is mobilized, including autonomic, sensory, motor, and integrative functions, in relation to relevant goal objects. Strivings toward the goal by an individual thus mobilized are experienced in an emotional way. Approaches toward and attainment of a goal will be experienced affectively in varying degrees. Therefore, there seems to be a substantial truth in the position taken by McDougall and more recent writers that motivational strivings and acts are accompanied by appropriate emotional feelings.

Sociogenic motives and strivings related to them are also experienced emotionally to the extent of their central place in the individual's scheme of values.

A good many emotional experiences are aroused by external stimulus conditions. The feeling or emotion of frustration is aroused by obstruction of moves toward a goal object. Joy is aroused by rather sudden attainment of or finding the way clear toward a much-desired goal. Grief follows the loss of a valued object or person. These emotional experiences are all related to motives of the person. Understanding the arousal and consequences of such emotions requires specification of the stimulating conditions and their perception by the individual in question. Many fear-arousing and rage-arousing situations are socially defined. Perceiving a situation as dangerous or risky or infuriating implies conceptual as well as perceptual processes. The trend in physiological psychology has been toward emphasis of central functions, not only on a hypothalamic level, but also on a cortical level (*19*, pp. 350–356).

Once a situation is perceived as something to be feared or something to be experienced in pleasurable ways, the discharges produced bring about various autonomic and muscular reverberations which broaden the content of the emotional experience. To this extent, the well-known James-Lange theory of emotions still holds.

Because *frustration* has been brought so frequently into discussions of social psychology, particularly of prejudice and intergroup hostility, a note on its consequences is in order. Reaction to frustration will depend on the set of circumstances and on the individual's perception and evaluation of them. The following reactions have been observed in response to various frustrations in different studies: aggression, regression or lowering the level of performance, evading the situation by leaving it or "going out of the field," apathy, and resignation (especially for prolonged frustration). Reaction to frustration varies according to the circumstances and the individual's perception of them (*7*).

We are not in a position to list universal and unlearned emotions in man or original stimulus conditions ("unconditioned stimuli") that arouse them. Ever since Watson made his short classical list (fear, anger, and love), several authors have made attempts in this direction.

The functioning, form, expression, and very arousal of many human emotions are socially determined. The fact that many emotions are aroused by external stimulus conditions makes them particularly liable to social regulation and determination. No wonder, then, that "the explorer and anthropologist sometimes have difficulty in 'reading' native faces" (*20*, p. 152). Even the shedding of tears, which is usually elicited involuntarily under conditions of considerable grief and misfortune, may become voluntarily controlled and socially regulated: "Thus the Andaman Islander learns how and when to cry (without feeling sad). When an important man returns after a long absence, one weeps copious tears; the fountains are under control, can be released for exhibition to the ethnologist even when the normal occasion is lacking" (20, p. 154).

Even intense emotions involved in activities aroused by biogenic motives become socially regulated in the manner in which they are expressed. The different types of actions and expressions associated with sexual behavior in various cultures may be mentioned as one of the striking illustrations of the point.

The social regulation of emotional expressions is even more striking when we look at the manifestation of emotions in situations which take place in culturally prescribed channels. To cite one example: In America, it is customary to open a gift in the presence of the giver, to express appreciation of it in superlative terms, and to exhibit great joy over it whether you like it or not. In the Near East, until recently the established behavior under similar conditions was to thank the donor in rather humiliated terms and then to put the gift inconspicuously away until the giver had gone.

This illustration is representative of other culturally prescribed emotional expressions. At the celebration of a birthday or wedding, the expressions of pleasure or joy of the various guests are rather remarkably similar. Perhaps even more standardized are the expressions of pleasure and admiration of a newborn infant by friends and acquaintances of the parents, which seem to depend comparatively little on the actual characteristics of the baby. An appropriately solemn stance and expression are taken by those who attend the funeral of a public figure. In brief, *expression of feelings and emotions on social occasions is a means of communication* and of enhancing solidarity on important occasions or in the face of extraordinary events encountered by members of a group.

Not only are the forms of expressing emotions and the situations calling them forth socially regulated, but the degree of expression and even the amount of general expressiveness also run along prescribed social channels. An English gentleman in England and his highly expressive American grandson illustrate the point clearly. Examples of societies whose cultural norms prescribed limited expression of some emotions, at least in public situations, were the American Plains Indian and the traditional Chinese and Japanese cultures. In contrast, it has been found that Chinese and Japanese living in Hawaii and brought up as parts of a Western society tend to be more expressive than the traditional cultural prescriptions call for (10, pp. 174-179).

In spite of all these variations, the social psychology of emotional motivation should be the same for all cultures. There are established social norms in regard to emotions as well as other psychological functions, and certain situations are standardized to elicit characteristic emotional reactions and expressions.

An adequate account of the formation and functioning of attitudes should present essentially valid principles for the regulation of emotions and for the manifestation of emotional reactions. No amount of evidence concerning cultural variations in the expression of emotions (or in anything else for that matter) is sufficient to enable us to formulate a social psychology of emotion and feeling. We must first have a more rounded understanding of the baffling topics of feeling and emotion.

CONCLUDING REMARKS

Motives are examples *par excellence* of internal factors which enter jointly with other internal and external influences in the structuring of experience and behavior.

Man's motives have been a source of controversy in discussions of "human nature" for many years. If there is a common substratum which can be called "human nature," it is the biological endowment of the organism. Therefore, one task in studying human motives is delineation of those motives whose *origins* are biological (biogenic) and those whose *origins* are social (sociogenic).

Differentiation among motives on the basis of their origins must be made in terms of the essential characteristics of biogenic motives and definite criteria, including at least their universality in the species and the *unlearned* character of their initial appearance in the motivational repertoire. Whether biogenic or sociogenic, the arousal of a motive produces psychological consequences, involving sensory, motor, and central-integrative functions.

Behavior is not a direct consequence of motive arousal. Motives enter into a frame of reference of experience and behavior in interrelationship with other internal and external factors. Therefore, motivated behavior cannot be adequately understood through studies which isolate a single motive, even though such investigation is an essential step in the scientific study of motives. Likewise, this fact renders the attempt to establish any final or universal hierarchy of motives difficult if not impossible, since sociocultural and situational factors are inevitably involved in human motivation.

However, in cases of severe or prolonged deprivation of the bodily needs, the aroused motive state characteristically and significantly dominates psychological functioning, including central processes. This recurrent and established fact is a problem of special importance in social psychology. It indicates the importance of ascertaining the degree of deprivation, its relation to other motives, and particular circumstances in which biogenic motives become the compelling anchorages in the frame of reference.

The importance of social influences becomes apparent in considering emotions, since so many emotional reactions are evoked by external stimulus conditions and their expression is variously regulated in different sociocultural settings.

Some of the issues raised in this chapter are discussed in more detail in the next chapter, which concerns motives and the socialization process.

REFERENCES

1. Barker, R. G., Dembo, T., and Lewin, K. Frustration and regression, *University of Iowa Studies in Child Welfare* (1941), 18, No. 386.
2. Birch, H. G. Comparative Psychology, in F. L. Marcuse (ed.), *Areas of Psychology*. New York: Harper, 1954.
3. Cannon, W. B. *The Wisdom of the Body*. New York: Norton, 1932.
4. Ford, C. S., and Beach, F. A. *Patterns of Sexual Behavior*. New York: Harper, 1951.
5. Freud, S. *The Ego and the Id*. London: Hogarth, 1927.
6. Harlow, H. F. Motivation as a Factor in the Acquisition of New Responses, in *Current Theory and Research in Motivation*. Lincoln: University of Nebraska Press, 1953.
7. Himmelweit, H. Frustration and Aggression: A Review of Recent Experimental Work, in T. H. Pear (ed.), *Psychological Factors of Peace and War*. New York: Philosophical Library, 1950.
8. Hobbes, T. *Leviathan, or The Matter, Forme and Power of a Commonwealth, Ecclesiastical and Civil*. London: A. Cooke, 1651.
9. Kleitman, N. *Sleep and Wakefulness*. Chicago: University of Chicago Press, 1939.
10. Klineberg, O. *Social Psychology*. New York: Holt, rev. ed., 1954.
11. Kropotkin, P. *Mutual Aid: A Factor of Evolution*. London: Heneman, 1919.
12. Lashley, K. S. Experimental analysis of instinctive behavior, *Psychol. Rev.* (1938), 45:445–469.
13. Lynd, R. S. *Knowledge for What? The Place of Social Science in American Culture*. Princeton: Princeton University Press, 1939, esp. chaps. 3 and 4.

14. Lynd, R. S., and Lynd, H. M. *Middletown in Transition*. New York: Harcourt, Brace, 1937, pp. 176 ff.
15. McDougall, W. *Social Psychology*. London: Methuen, 1908.
16. McDougall, W. *Outline of Psychology*. New York: Scribner, 1923.
17. Maslow, A. H. *Motivation and Personality*. New York: Harper, 1954.
18. Morgan, C. T. *Physiological Psychology*. New York: McGraw-Hill, 1943.
19. Morgan, C. T., and Stellar, E. *Physiological Psychology*. New York: McGraw-Hill, 1950.
20. Murphy, G., Murphy, L. B., and Newcomb, T. M. *Experimental Social Psychology*. New York: Harper, rev. ed., 1937.
21. Riess, B. F. Physiological Psychology, in F. L. Marcuse (ed.), *Areas of Psychology*. New York: Harper, 1954.
22. Rousseau, J. J. *The Social Contract and Discourse*. New York: Dutton, 1916.
23. Spencer, H. *Illustrations of Universal Progress*. New York: Appleton, 1869.
24. Stone, C. P. Motivation, in F. A. Moss (ed.), *Comparative Psychology*. New York: Prentice-Hall, rev. ed., 1942.
25. Tolman, E. C. *Drives Toward War*. New York: Appleton-Century, 1942.
26. Tsai, C. The relative strength of sex and hunger motives in the albino rat, *J. compar. Psychol.* (1925), 5:407–415.
27. Warden, C. J. *Animal Motivation: Experimental Studies on the Albino Rat*. New York: Columbia University Press, 1931.
28. Young, P. T. *Motivation of Behavior*. New York: Wiley, 1936.

CHAPTER 12

Motives and the Socialization Process

Sociogenic motives are among the most important internal factors which enter into the structuring of experience and behavior of the human adult. They originate in interaction situations as the individual assimilates social influences, which are at first external to him. Therefore, to understand sociogenic motives we must examine the processes of development and learning in social interaction which result in the individual's internalization of social influences, so that they become "his own" preferences, tastes, and desires. To an important extent, this is what is meant by "socialization." A full account of sociogenic motives cannot be attempted in a single chapter. In this book, Chapters 15–18 deal with problems of sociogenic motives and their formation.

In this chapter we will seek orientation to the problem of sociogenic motives by starting with a picture of trends in motivational influences. At birth the child is endowed with certain bodily needs (biogenic motives). What changes occur in the patterning of experience and behavior as he comes into increasing contact with the physical and social world surrounding him? How are these changes related to his motives? This is our major concern in the first section of the chapter. To sketch these changes it is necessary to touch on behavior in the first weeks of life, on the social setting in which the child is born, on the early reactions to social influences, on the role of motivational factors in the child's perceiving and discriminating, and finally on the interdependence of motivational trends and developing conceptual capacities.

This quick survey of trends in development and increasing interaction with the social environment serves as preparation for a general orientation to sociogenic motives. A general summary of the problem of sociogenic motives constitutes the final section of this chapter.

TRENDS OF MOTIVATIONAL INFLUENCES: DEVELOPMENTAL PICTURE

A helpless infant finds contentment in suckling; in later life his enjoyment of food will depend on specific tastes for a variety of food, on the cleanliness and type of dishes, on his surroundings and companions at the meal. A baby lying in his bed becomes the boy whose thoughts and dreams are centered on the playing field, where he dashes about in skilled and highly coördinated actions with teammates.

The elegant lady who glories in the arts of conversation and the young woman whose life is devoted to singing the great music of the ages in different languages were once infants who cried when they were uncomfortable and babbled when contented. The tot crawling or toddling to explore everything within reach (whether toys, furniture, glass ash trays or poisonous fluids) will one day be a person who is cautious in approaching the edge of a precipice, fearful of certain small animals, and responsible in his dealings with other people.

The overall trend of experience and behavior through maturation and learning is toward increasing differentiation. We shall examine this trend briefly as it relates to motivational influences. The individual responds selectively to an increasing variety of stimulus objects and situations. Many of these are social products which have no immediate biological significance. Likewise, many of the individual's emotional experiences come to be aroused by external stimulus conditions which are socially defined as emotionally provoking.

The individual is born into a social setting which places different values on various objects, persons, and actions. As he becomes a participating member in social groups, he takes an active part in the process of defining what is socially significant. Selectivity is extended to a wider variety of stimuli and also becomes increasingly discriminatory within the range of significant stimuli. In these trends, a glimpse of the origins of sociogenic motives can be caught.

The Child's Behavior First Dominated by Biogenic Motives

During the first weeks of life, the baby's activity is determined chiefly by biogenic motives. Most of the infant's activity stems from the physiological states of his organism (23). For example, as hunger is aroused, his general activity increases and soon involves intense and continuous crying. At this point, external stimuli, like sounds or rocking, are only temporarily effective in reducing his general activity. While hunger is being satisfied at breast or bottle, potent stimulation is required to stop his sucking movements. During the quiet intervals between the rhythmic arousal of bodily needs, the infant is relatively more sensitive to external stimuli, like noises, colored objects, or a pinprick.

From a grownup point of view, an infant's behavior may seem chaotic, disorganized, mercurial. But, in Gesell's colorful words: "From the standpoint of 4-week-oldness his behavior is patterned, meaningful, significant" (8, p. 93). This standpoint centers around the physiological states of his organism.

As noted above, the infant responds to stimulation. But he does not respond in a *discriminatory* way to persons around him except as they come to satisfy or prevent satisfaction of the dominant need of the moment. Studies of infant response to various stimulus modalities (sound, light, color, touches) indicate that the normal infant is not blind or deaf in a literal sense. Yet, as Gesell observed, he is at first "socially deaf and blind to the approach of another person who bends over him and gives him every social provocation to respond" (9, p. 287).

Studies using various sorts of stimulation which are thought conducive to arousing emotional responses of infants under 4 or 5 weeks of age reveal lack of differentiation in emotional reactions (11). Many infants do not respond at all to treatment which would seem to be highly disturbing from an adult point of view. Bridges' observations led her to conclude that during the first month of life the infant is either quiescent or, in response to intense stimulation, generally agitated or excited (5).

In studying adult reactions to infant behavior, Sherman showed motion pictures of babies without revealing the conditions which had aroused the particular behavior (conditions like delayed feeding, sudden loss of support, pricking with a needle). He also had adults try to identify the cries of babies provoked by various stimuli when they were hidden behind a screen. Little agreement was found in adult judgments under these circumstances, indicating that emotional patterns are not differentiated at this age. Of course, when adults saw the stimulating conditions, they named the infant's reactions in conventional terms as hunger, pain, fear, and the like (30).

The Child Develops Within a Social Setting

From the moment a human child is born, he is dependent on other human beings, at first totally. This period of dependency is longer for man than for any other species. The fact of prolonged dependency of the human child has sweeping implications for problems of social development, and in particular for the formation of sociogenic motives.

The human adults who care for the child are socialized beings. They are parts of a social organization with established ways of behaving, with certain values and ideas which include the area of child care and upbringing. There are wide variations in all of these aspects of adult life from culture to culture, and from time to time within any one society. It takes a long time for a child even to perceive all of the aspects, much less to respond to them or incorporate them. However, some of them have implications for him even from the moment he is born.

Take a rather simple example. In some cultures a baby is fed whenever his mother thinks he acts hungry. Fifteen years ago an American mother who followed then current child-care practices based on statistical averages fed her baby every four hours. If he wailed during this period, she might hold him or rock him (though this too was frowned upon), but she would not feed him until the four hours was up. Later, a three-hour period was regarded as a more desirable interval for most infants. Then mothers were advised to rely entirely on a "self-demand" schedule: "Feed the child when he is hungry." The current view seems to be along these lines with somewhat lessened enthusiasm for the parent's ability to determine when the child is hungry and for complete disregard of adult schedules of living. Most hospitals continue to practice three- or four-hour feeding schedules during the first week or 10 days of life.

Such varying schedules practiced by adults do influence the child's behavior in time; he does adapt to them, of course in varying degrees. The degree of his adaptation depends in part on how realistic the schedule or practice is in terms of his physiological needs, his capacities, and his level of development. Even during the first 10 days of life some adaptation (learning) to feeding schedules has been detected. Marquis studied the bodily activity of infants during eight days of their stay in a hospital after birth. Eighteen babies were put on a four-hour feeding schedule, 16 on a three-hour schedule, and 4 on a "self schedule." The crucial comparison in this study was between the "three-hour" group and the "four-hour" group. Those on a three-hour schedule "learned" to be hungry at the end of three hours. Did those on the four-hour schedule also adapt to the feeding times? The test made was to switch the three-hour group to a four-hour schedule and to compare their activity with that of the babies who had been on a four-hour schedule throughout. As a result, the three-hour group showed a pattern of activity decidedly different from that shown by the regular four-hour group. This would seem to indicate that some adaptation to the four-hour feeding schedule had taken place in those babies whose feeding times were regularly four hours apart (18).

As indicated above, an adult society cannot impose just any arbitrary social schedule or practice on its young. If such practices diverge too far from the physiological rhythms and needs, there are behavioral consequences. A series of studies related infant crying to the gross measure of amount of time spent by adults in caring for them. When the amount of time spent on each baby by adults in a hospital nursery was increased from an average of 0.7 hours to 1.9 hours per day, the amount of crying decreased by 51.4 percent (1). These findings are not to be interpreted as meaning that the infants were crying to "attract attention," as may be the case for older children on occasion. On the contrary, they imply that a minimum amount of time must be spent by adults caring for an infant simply to keep him in a comfortable state. If adult schedules were to ignore entirely the child's needs, the organism would "kick back" with all its available capacities and intensity at the time.

Thus the human infant is affected by regulations of the society into which he comes even before he discriminates between people and other objects in his environment. His fleeting smiles after feeding at a month or 6 weeks of age are not directed *at* any particular person. Positive signs of recognizing a particular human face do not appear for most infants until between three and four months of age (9).

Human babies begin to show interest in people beyond merely looking at a face during this period. A human face and figure become more than a moving pattern of light and sound. Later dogs, cats, toys are objects of great interest. But at around 4 months, it is the persons who feed and care for the baby who are reacted to positively. This interest may be accorded also to children in the family who attempt to entertain or "play" with him.

It is significant, however, that some months must pass before a baby responds frequently or for any length of time to another baby (17). When the child begins to respond in a discriminatory and positive fashion to other human beings, he is not revealing an innate gregarious tendency to associate with his "kind." The most plausible sources of his early interest in other persons (of sociality) lie in the integral role played by other humans in satisfying his bodily needs and caring for him—an absolutely essential role because of his complete dependency. Thus the ones who feed and care for him (mother, nurse, father) receive the earliest positive signs of recognition, followed by other adults and children in his surroundings. As noted above, interest in those most like himself—other babies—ordinarily appears later. Aside from the breast or bottle, human beings are the first objects in his environment to acquire *value* for the child.

Studies of children in institutions who receive a bare minimum or even below minimum of adult care because of inadequate staff or other circumstances seem to indicate that if other human beings do not acquire value for the child during this early period his entire course of social development may be retarded. In extreme circumstances for some children, normal social development may be interrupted altogether (26). This might be expected if the sources of interest in other people or primitive sociality are traceable to the role played by people in caring for the child during his early development.

However, there is not clear-cut evidence pointing to the conclusion that the values acquired at this stage—the child's "character"—are formed once and for all during the first year of life, if he is spared gross deprivation, neglect, and disregard by adults. On the contrary, even as the relationship between mother (or adult) and child becomes a two-way affair in a limited sense, the bond between them, as Lewin observed, is one "in which, functionally, the needs of the baby have primacy" (12, p. 595).

Partly because the physiological states and needs of the organism continue throughout early childhood to weigh heavily among the various factors which influence behavior, the child's early relationships with other persons and the values he acquires are not stable in an adult sense. Let a mother delay a meal too long and her loving youngster will turn on her with all the explosive intensity of which he is capable. Even in preschool ages when the child begins to form social relationships with other children in play groups, these relationships and positive social attractions are particularly likely to be disrupted by quarrels if the children are getting hungry or tired.

From his birth, the child's biogenic motives are satisfied and regulated to an increasing extent by socialized human beings, who thus in time acquire value for the child. This process seems to be the first preliminary step to his socialization. Eventually his biogenic motives become socially regulated and even transformed within a matrix of sociogenic motives formed as he interacts increasingly with persons, groups, and other social stimuli in his environment.

Motivational Factors in Children's Perceptions and Discriminations

In discussing the frame-of-reference concept in Chapter 3, we emphasized that motives and other internal factors are inferred from observed behavior. Inferences about children's motives are derived by observing their discriminatory reactions (nonverbal and later verbal, also) to various objects and persons in specified situations. Children's perceptions and

FIG. 12.1. A suggestive photographic representation of the selectivity of the child's perceptions. (By LIFE photographer Herbert Gehr. © TIME, Inc.)

discriminations, like all experiences, are shaped jointly by internal and external influences.

The infant's physiological states and functioning are predominant during the first months of life. He responds on occasion to various external stimulation from birth; but the objects of his earliest discriminations and the objects which first acquire value are those intimately involved in daily satisfaction of his biogenic motives—faces of the people who care for him, the breast, bottle, blanket, or bed.

Perception in the first year of life has been characterized as undifferentiated and global (20, 33). The notion of the infant's world as a complete blur, however, finds little support. Infants respond early to bright or moving objects. As Gesell suggests, the infant "takes hold of the world" with his eyes before he is even able to do so with his hands (7, p. 253). After surveying available evidence, Vernon concluded that at least a primitive delineation of figure and ground is primary in experience (34). It is reported that individuals blind from birth with congenital cataracts experience "figures" immediately after operations removing the cataracts, even though great difficulty is experienced in *identifying* the objects, which had been familiar to them by touch (27).

Differentiation of perception and response proceeds as the child gains increased contact with his surroundings and mastery of his own body. Visual and auditory experiences become integrated before he moves out into these surroundings at all (7). At around the fifth or sixth month his hands become sufficiently adept at grasping that they take part in making contact with the world around him. Then come the fingers, touching, poking, patting. During the latter part of the first year or the early months of the second, the child is developed sufficiently to move out into his world —squirming or crawling and then walking. Thus differentiation of experience and behavior becomes possible as the child develops and interacts with his surroundings through integrated experience of perceptual, motor, and affective aspects.

Anyone who watches a baby during his first year or so of life sees him eagerly going out into the world as best he can at the time—poking with his fingers, reaching, banging objects. Almost anything he can lay hands on is an object of manipulation and temporary exploration. However, his selectivity is heavily dependent on his physiological states. Nothing but the bottle or food is of interest when he is really ready to eat. His more precise discriminations continue to relate to those objects and persons and events which have value for him. A study by Beaumont and Hetzer is illustrative. They observed children's reactions to cards, some plain, some with colored geometric figures, and some with pictures of a woman or a cup. Until the children were around 18 months of age, all of the cards were simply handled, with little evidence of any discrimination among them. However, children of that age or older began to respond differently to the pictures, which represented objects that had acquired value (3).

Like their early perceptions, the child's earliest generalizations tend to be relatively undifferentiated. His first words usually refer to objects and persons closely associated with motive satisfactions and may be so general that an adult has to know and observe the child's behavior rather regularly to understand their meaning. For example, one of our children learned "juice" in connection with her daily orange juice and then applied it to all liquids. A 2-year-old with whom we leafed through a magazine called all of the women in the pictures "mama." A year-old child, Cindy, used "mama" to designate anyone who cared for or waited on her, including her 3-year-old brother and 5-year-old sister.

The long-anticipated utterance which adults perceive as the child's *first word* may not be "mama" or "juice" or "bobbie" (bottle). It may be "bye-bye" or "kitty" or some other designation of an object which draws the child's interest. The early words pertain by and large to objects and persons which have acquired value, through involvement in the sequence of activities leading to satisfaction of biogenic motives. Gesell noted that the most frequent early words for children he observed at 52 weeks were for "things to eat" (9, p. 255). Shirley's records of concepts used by 336 children from 2 to 5 years old during a play period (30–45 minutes long) indicate that this close association between motive satisfaction and generalizations continues during early childhood. The four most common concepts pertained to mother, home, father, and brother or sister (31).

The relatively great weight of biogenic motives in the organization of children's experience can be demonstrated conversely by observing how children react to patterns which have *not* acquired value for them. A 2-year-old confronted with a Rorschach ink blot and asked to react to it tends to respond to the whole blot, giving a single word which may indicate a general impression (2, p. 289). Even children of 3 to 5 years do not tend ordinarily to perceive fine and minute details in abstract patterns or to notice irregularities in geometrical forms (14). When an experimenter requires a child to deal with stimuli or their qualities which have little value for the child (like length, color, shape), the child may make irrelevant or repetitive responses. Perseverative tendencies were reported, for example, by Brian and Goodenough when 2-year-olds faced the task of matching colored geometrical solids and forms (4).

What becomes figure for a young child tends to be an object which has relevance to his motives and the sequence of goal-directed activity. Within that figure he does not usually make fine discriminations of various dimensions (like line, weight, color, and so on) until some months or years later. Differentiation of response to various discriminable aspects or fine details within the figure seems to proceed throughout childhood. However, the fact that young children do not ordinarily discriminate fine differences within the figure does not mean that they *cannot* do so. On the contrary, when properly motivated, children can learn to discern quite fine differences. In a study by Munn and Steining a 15-month-old child learned to discriminate between two boxes on the basis of small black-and-white geometrical designs on the cover. He found a piece of chocolate in the "correct" box at each trial. When he had learned the discrimination, he continued to choose correctly when the figure on the "correct" box was rotated 45 degrees, when the background of the "correct" design was changed, and when a different form was used on the cover of the empty box (19).

Even finer discriminations were made by two fairly hungry 2-year-olds that Gellerman used in a similar study (6). He also found that when the children learned to respond positively to a vertical figure they tended to respond also when the figure was tilted. Children of this age are becoming intensely interested in objects; they can recognize familiar objects in various positions. A number of studies show that the conventional orientation of objects is even less important to a child than to an adult (34, pp. 77–78). To a child, the familiar object is the important, the significant aspect for discrimination. On the other hand, the position of the object seems to be very significant for a rat. To a rat, orientation and adjustment in space are of considerable importance. Vernon compares such findings in terms of the functional significance of these dimensions to the respective organisms. Thus the properties of objects which come to be significant vary: "Shape characteristics for children, spatial relations for rats" (34, p. 78). Of course, it is possible that structural and other functional differences between the species may also be involved in this finding.

As the above evidence indicates, insight into children's discriminatory reactions must be gained through analysis of their developing capacities and experiences (learning) with objects and their characteristics as these relate to their motives. Herein lies the key to understanding how social influences come to regulate the child's biogenic motives and to affect discrimination of objects perceived as goals.

The newborn infant possesses states of readiness to respond, determined by his biogenic motives. But how and where does he acquire other states of readiness, many in relation to stimuli with no immediate biological significance? This is the general problem of *attitude formation*, which is basic to any consideration of sociogenic motives.

Attitudes refer to functional states of readiness formed (acquired, learned) in relation to objects (persons, events, social products) of value to the individual. Attitudes are more or less lasting and imply a characteristic and selective response to relevant objects. The value attached to the object or person may stem from its relatedness to events of biological significance. However, value may be derived also from the object's social significance. Value may be invested in objects through social definition. Attitudes formed by individuals in relation to objects, persons, events, groups, concepts invested with social value are, therefore, social attitudes. Social attitudes, their formation and change are discussed in detail in Chapters 15 and 16.

In the next section the formation of social attitudes and their patterning as parts in the psychological make-up of the individual are considered briefly as they are related to conceptual development.

Motivational and Conceptual Development Are Interdependent

The trends in motivational influences, their patterning and functioning as internal factors can be traced only so far without reference to conceptual development and learning of language. The infant is a human from birth, endowed with the capacities of the species. But his native equipment is not mature. As he matures and develops, he learns about his surroundings, coming to grips with its physical and social aspects within the limits of his abilities and skills at the time.

Some characteristics of the child's "first words" were noted in the previous section. These early words are used in social interaction related to the child's inner urgencies and desires, but they are by no means conceptual or socialized in an adult sense. As M. M. Lewis pointed out, they are intimately bound to the child's affectivity, to his motor activities, and to immediate situations (13). A child may wave and say "by-by" when his daddy leaves, but not necessarily when others go out. These words can be "defined" only in terms of the functional significance incorporated in the child's generalizations. It will be some time before his usage approximates social definitions prevalent in his setting.

Words are added slowly during the second year of life, but toward the end of that year a sudden spurt in verbal activity takes place. In the space of two or three months the number of words the child uses increases about fivefold (see Fig. 12.2). This is the period some investigators of language

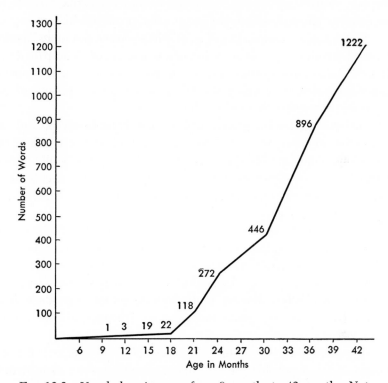

FIG. 12.2. Vocabulary increase from 8 months to 42 months. Note the sharp increase in size of vocabulary beginning at about 18 months of age. (Adapted from M. E. Smith, An investigation of the development of the sentence and the extent of vocabulary in young children, *University of Iowa Studies in Child Welfare* [1926], 3, No. 5, Table 8, p. 54.)

development have called the "naming stage" (16). Rather suddenly, the child begins to want names for everything. It is as though his level of development and experience had culminated in a new and sweeping generalization: that things have names. As he learns their names, he may ask the use of things, and even ask for definitions from adults. This attainment sets the stage for the increasingly instrumental use of concepts and for the approximation of the definitions prevailing in his social milieu.

The trend of conceptual development and functioning cannot be traced here. Our present interest is in some consequences of conceptual developments and trends. A more detailed discussion is given in Chapter 14.

In the first place, the process of attitude formation (acquisition of sociogenic motives) is thereby transformed. When symbolic gestures and spoken words are understood, the social value of objects and actions can be conveyed almost immediately. The relatively slower and more laborious process of building up values in infancy is telescoped. The parent who tells a child that "black children are dirty" is conveying a social evaluation which even a child of 3 can grasp. His attitudes toward persons of dark complexion will reflect this social value.

Second, striving toward goals which are not immediately present and, in time, toward future goals becomes possible. This characteristic of conceptual functioning implies also a greater stability and continuity of motivational influences. Concepts, and particularly children's concepts, are by no means immutable. However, they function as relatively stable and enduring internalized factors.

The conceptual level of functioning comes in time to affect, regulate, and even transform other processes. The motivation, perception, discrimination, learning, remembering of children who have attained some instrumental use of language are studied adequately when this fact and its implications are fully evaluated. One of its important by-products is the facilitation of increasingly fine and more precise discriminations (judgments).

Finally, conceptual functioning in terms of (standardized) language concepts makes it possible for the child to form a system of relatedness to the myriad objects, persons, groups, social norms, technological products, and social institutions in his surroundings. Through the first years of life, relatedness to many objects and persons is formed, though on the relatively unstable and mercurial basis of the child's own needs and desires and their attainment or blocking. But consistent and lasting relatedness to the many aspects of his environment becomes possible through conceptual functioning.

The individual's formation of a system of relatedness to various persons, objects, and groups in his environment is crucial in understanding sociogenic motives.

Formation of a System of Personal Relatedness (Ego)

To discuss the system of relatedness which the individual forms toward other persons, objects, and groups in his environment, some steps must be retraced. Let us go back to those months when a child makes his early positive discriminations of other persons and objects, revealing his earliest acquired values. At this time he starts touching his own hands, his body, feeling his ears and pulling at his hair, exploring them as he does other objects. He looks at his body and its parts and at other persons and objects and sees different things happening to them and done by them. He probably learns that sucking or biting a toy feels different from sucking or biting his own finger. As he begins to move actively out into the world on hands and knees and later upright, he encounters resistances from objects and other people. He also sees that he can "make things happen." Through such perceptual, discriminatory, affective, and motor aspects he begins to differentiate between his own body and other objects and persons.

The boundary between the body and the external world is, as Piaget wrote, the "result of a gradual and progressive dissociation, and not of a primitive intuition" (21, p. 128). During this period there is bound to be inconsistency, for the differentiation of self from other things is largely a perceptual distinction. Thus a year-and-a-half-old child, who was asked to give his foot while dressing, actually stooped and tugged at it, trying to hand his foot over as he had his shoe (24).

However, the perceived self is not a neutral object. If mother, father, and 5-year-old sister become valued through involvement in activities of significance to the child, it is equally likely that he should acquire value for himself (20). Indeed, at this period his body is the center and focus of his positive experiences.

In the process of attitude formation toward himself and others, concepts and social definitions enter early. Using Murphy's simple but illuminating account of the sequence of the developing self, we may say that the perceptual stage of self-awareness is followed by the acquisition of traits (20). And the acquisition of traits implies the formation of attitudes toward self in which concepts play a vital role. "Johnny is a good boy"; "Mary is a pretty little lady"; and so on. Thus the self notion expands through language and is elaborated with attitudes toward various ways of appearing and acting. As mastery of the instrumental and conceptual uses of language is attained, the attitudes defining the self and its relatedness to other things and people come to include social classifications. This implies drawing family lines, lines of membership in various groups and institutions (school, neighborhood, church, ethnic groups, etc.), and the formation of appropriate social attitudes.

These attitudes which relate the individual to different aspects of his surroundings in varying capacities are not discrete items in his psychological make-up. Their formation relates the individual as he comes to perceive himself to other persons and objects. They constitute, therefore, definitions and elaborations of a concept of himself, which is perceived and reacted to as valued. In short, such attitudes function as constituent parts of a system of relatedness with the individual's surroundings. The concept designating this constellation of functional relatedness is termed *ego*. Attitudes which function as constituents of this system are therefore termed ego-attitudes (29). Since they are formed by individuals in interaction with other persons, groups, and social stimulus situations of varying sorts (including material culture and social norms, institutions, and the like), many directive ego-attitudes are necessarily social in origin—that is, they are social attitudes.

When ego-attitudes are situationally aroused by some relevant object, person, event, task, situation, or group, the individual's experience and behavior are characterized as *ego-involved*. Ego-involvement means that one or more ego-attitudes have become functionally operative in a given frame of reference along with other internal and external factors. Ego-involvement is not an absolute process because the various attitudes functioning in the ego system are not all of equal weight or significance to the individual, and because particular situations and stimulus objects vary in their degree of relevance to the various ego-attitudes. Some ego-attitudes pertain to matters of relatively slight importance to an individual, while the significance of others may be so central that a relevant situational threat may lead to intense and violent reaction or attainment of a relevant goal may lead to boundless joy.

Thus one far-reaching consequence of conceptual development for the trend of motivational influences lies in the formation of an ego system. These interdependent trends make possible the individual's incorporation of social schedules, social norms for experience and behavior in so many aspects of living as *his own* preferences and desires. One of Piaget's contributions to social psychology was tracing moral development from the early period when rules are imposed on a child from without by grownups and older children (heteronomy) to the stage when he follows rules as his own rules (autonomy). This achievement is possible when the distinction between self and other is sufficiently clear so that the child can conceive of other points of view than his own. The achievement of such notions of *reciprocity* comes not just through adult intervention and guidance but through participation in group interaction with other children (22).

From the time that reciprocal relationships are grasped and engaged in, the trend of motivational influences is toward incorporation of social standards, values, or norms and other social influences into the ego system. The ego and its involvements are treated in Chapters 17 and 18.

ORIENTATION TO SOCIOGENIC MOTIVES

Sociogenic motives are those derived by the individual from his sociocultural setting. As grownups, we do not eat, mate, and sleep in just any old way. We eat, sleep, and mate in certain definite ways, with certain objects and persons and in certain places. These ways, objects, and places are prescribed mainly by our social setting, whatever it may be. If we are Chinese in China (under ordinary conditions), we may not be quite satisfied with our meal unless rice is included. If we visit a certain locality in the Near East, we may find that as honored guests at a banquet we receive as the choice portion the eye of a sheep. Under usual conditions, any old bed will not do. We want to live and sleep in a certain locality where the people are "nice," or in a hotel that meets our standards. We do not choose just anyone as a steady boy or girl friend. Our lasting mate has to be a person whose characteristics are socially prized and who does not constitute a threat to our standing in the group.

Established social norms may standardize definite relationships between men and the animals and plants about them, thus stamping a positive or negative social value on them. Rivers reported from Melanesia that "In Mota there are many persons, perhaps as many as half the population, who are not permitted by custom to eat the flesh of certain animals nor to eat certain fruits, nor to touch certain trees. The ground for prohibition in most cases is that the person is believed to be the animal or fruit in question, his mother having received an influence from an animal or plant of that kind before his birth" (25, p. 151).

Thus, in addition to certain delicacies and prized goal objects, the sociocultural setting includes definite prohibitions. Objects invested with such negative values tend to lose their appeal as goal objects. Under ordinary conditions the good Hindu would not eat the holy cattle wandering about the village, nor would the good Mohammedan eat pork. (Of course there are circumstances in which some individuals or even most individuals would taste "forbidden fruit.")

The range of goal objects with immediate biological significance is rather well defined—digestible foodstuffs, liquids, and so on. Objects and situations which become prized or prohibited in various cultures are not defined solely in terms of their biological significance. French champagne is not required to satisfy thirst, nor truffles for hunger, nor an elegant slender woman for sexual urges in any biological sense. Tastes for such goals are acquired as the individual develops and interacts with other people in a particular setting.

Acquired tastes and motives increase in number as the social organization becomes more highly developed and more highly differentiated. They are much more numerous for a person belonging to the upper stratum of a highly developed and wealthy society. He has to keep up with his exclusive set in a hundred ways. His tastes in beverages may discriminate wines and liqueurs of various colors, origins, and ages. His set may include diverse individuals of differing nationalities. If he is unable to entertain them on an exclusive yacht or at his private swimming pool, this may become his major concern.

These are only a few examples of the way that the tastes or motives acquired as the individual grows up in a social setting affect his experience and behavior. Many of these stem from the social norms of his particular sociocultural setting. Once he has formed attitudes incorporating these social norms, his behavior toward relevant objects, persons, and events becomes highly selective in characteristic ways.

The formation and functioning of attitudes is, therefore, basic to the problem of sociogenic motives. The objects which first have value for the child are those intimately involved in the sequence of activities impelled by biogenic motives and include other persons and his own body. Formation of these early preferences or attachments constitutes a preliminary step toward incorporation of many social values.

When the child begins to learn the language prevailing in his surroundings, the process of attitude formation is transformed. He acquires states of readiness in relation to definite stimulus objects and situations which are not dependent solely on the ups and downs of his affectivity. The affective properties and the content become crystallized in conceptual terms. Through language he forms attitudes in relation to objects, persons, and events with which he has had no first-hand contact. For example, very few children growing up in America have any first-hand contact with Turks. Yet attitude studies have shown that children form attitudes pertaining to Turks and attribute certain traits to them.

Obviously the problem of sociogenic motives involves learning. To say that sociogenic motives are acquired or to speak of attitude *formation* means that something is learned. At present, there is not a theory of learning which can adequately handle these acquisitions. However, it may be helpful to mention some of the facts which a theory of learning with utility in treating sociogenic motives (attitude formation) must consider.

Such a learning theory must account for modifications of experience and behavior in terms of interrelated factors (external and internal) which together determine psychological structuring. The properties of social stimulus situations assume an importance in human learning at least equaling that of the characteristics of the maze or puzzle box in animal experiments. On the side of internal factors, the nature of conceptual functioning and its interdependence with motivational development have to be considered fully. As a result, a learning theory useful in handling the problem of sociogenic motives cannot concentrate simply on modifications in motor aspects of performance. The modification of motor activities is only one aspect of human learning. For an organism capable of functioning on a conceptual level, modifications may occur internally before motor activity is involved. They can be inferred from subsequent behavior (verbal and nonverbal). There is nothing at all mysterious or subjective in the notion of restructuring of experience.

Learning does not necessarily occur only as an end result of a sequence of goal seeking and attainment. It also occurs at other points in the motive-goal sequence.

All motives have the property of directionality in space and time. Directionality can be comprehended in terms of the functional relevance of objects, persons, events, or groups to the motive in question. How can such functional relevance be ascertained? It is inferred from the more or less specific and coördinated reactions of the individual in relation to the goal object.

Searching for the goal object, approaching it, attaining it may imply such a diverse series of perceptual and overt activities in different places and over such a time span that the sequence has to be specified for each particular case of motive-goal relationship.

The nature of "goals" in human learning is severely limited when they are treated merely as rewards, like those one gives to a child for being good or receives for good performance in a game. Such rewards do serve as goals, of course; but all goals cannot be defined in terms of their characteristics.

A goal may be defined as any object, event, person, group, social value, product, situation which has positive functional relevance to a particular motive or pattern of motives.

Since man is capable of functioning on a conceptual level, a goal object may or may not be directly perceived. The arousal of a motive state and the individual's strivings need not depend on the immediate presence of a goal object. This is particularly evident in man's strivings for social position (status). It is also true of human hunger, human sexual desires, and the like, because attitudes are formed at a conceptual level in relation to socially selected goals.

Partly because of the variety of alternative goals, an individual may not have clear awareness of the goal objects and situations of his strivings. Between clear awareness of goal objects at one extreme and gropings for poorly differentiated goals at the other, there are all possible gradations of awareness.

Moves and circumstances which imply for the individual that he is getting closer to a goal or has attained a goal are experienced as satisfying in various degrees. Moves and circumstances which are felt as receding from the goal or preventing its attainment are experienced as unpleasant or frustrating.

In the sequence of activity encompassed by the motive state-goal relationship, those stimuli (objects, actions, events, persons, groups, etc.) that have functional relevance to the motive or the goal will be attended to as focal. They will stand out with figure character. This refers, of course, to psychological selectivity, which was discussed at length in Chapter 3 (pp. 85–97).

Any stimulus item which thus becomes focal (or figure) cannot help becoming part and parcel of a learning process in a way that will affect or modify experience and behavior in similar activities in the future. This seems to be true both for items that become focal in satisfying ways (felt as approaching) and for those that become focal in frustrating ways (implying to the individual reversals from the direction of the goal).

Emergence of New Motives in Social Interaction

All attitudes are not based on biogenic motives. Attitudes are also formed in relation to objects, persons, situations, events, values which are not and never could be directly relevant goals of motives originating in the physiological functioning of the organism.

A college student may feel utterly frustrated if he does not succeed in joining a certain fraternity. A girl may refuse the job of waitress as something beneath her dignity, even though she may urgently need money. Excellence in playing golf at the most exclusive club in town may become a man's major preoccupation. A person may sell his beautiful home at considerable financial loss if people whom he considers "undesirable" move next door.

When the child begins to function on a conceptual level, he acquires through the medium of language a host of attitudes which define his relatedness to diverse objects, persons, actions, situations. These attitudes are formed as he interacts to an increasing extent with the world around him and especially the world of people and their social relationships.

As we have seen, all of these attitudes become functional parts of a system of relatedness to the surroundings which defines the individual's conception of himself. This system of relatedness is called *ego*. Because the individual is born into a social group with an accumulation of tools, symbols, and social norms (values), the major part of the constellation of attitudes making up his personal identity is formed in relation to them. That is why the ego systems of individuals in different social groups and cultures are shaped in their major features much like those of others in their groups, of course subject to variations from person to person within given reference scales.

Social attitudes which come to function as parts of the ego are called *ego-attitudes*. These constitute the focal area of sociogenic motives.

Through various regularities and treatments and especially through short-cut verbal dicta, parents and other adults are indeed effective carriers of social values to the child, hence play a major role in the process of socialization. However, all attitudes are not formed through adult guidance and intervention.

There are attitudes which are formed in relation to social stimuli without direct adult influence. The nature of the setting in which a child develops, the man-made products which surround him, their nature and scope are reacted to even though no one tells him that they are desirable or undesirable. Through prolonged interaction with such settings and objects the child forms attitudes of what is "natural" for him, what is to be desired, what is undesirable—whether or not adults take an active role in instructing him. If his family owns a car, he does not need to be told that it is a desirable object. In a hundred experiences he sees its utility and desirability and comes to think of himself as a person who must have a car. Adults in an American family that does not own a television set do not need to point out its desirable features to their children. Usually communication takes the opposite direction, with children pressing strongly for acquiring one.

One's conception of the sort of living place he should be in or visit may be so well established that thrusting him into the midst of unaccustomed luxury or poverty may upset the stability of his whole experience of self-identity.

Studies of children's age-mate groups and of group interaction in general have important implications concerning the sources of social attitudes. Through interaction in group situations the developing individual grasps the notion of reciprocity—of "taking turns" and coördinating one's point of view and actions with those of other people. In this process he comes to accept group standards or norms as his own. Social norms are no longer perceived merely as arbitrary decisions and prescriptions of grownups or older children but as embodying his own tastes and preferences (pp. 594–598).

If he is to become a functional part (a participating member) of a human group, his ego must include attitudes relating himself and his activities to other parts (members) of the group. He forms attitudes relating to ways of doing things in the group and to its major goals.

Group interaction and its properties have another significant implication for the problem of sociogenic motives. It is sometimes said that all social motives are based on or are derivatives of basic needs (biogenic motives). Such a conception overlooks the stubborn fact of *emergences* in group interaction.

Individuals come together to interact as a group with certain motives. The particular motives of different individuals may vary, but one or more is usually common for all if group interaction is to last for any length of time. However, once group interaction is under way, values or norms are standardized in the group. The individual member forms attitudes incorporating these values, goals, or social norms of the group. In this way, new motives emerge in the process of group interaction. They are not necessarily identical with motives which brought the individuals into the group. They are not even derived from them.

Whether sociogenic motives are related to the satisfaction of bodily deprivations or not, they may all be studied under the general topic of attitude formation and functioning.

The learned or acquired character of sociogenic motives does not make them any less real or immediate or urgent when they are aroused. They mobilize other aspects of individual functioning toward the fulfillment of their goals. The person who is motivated by them does not ordinarily stop to think that he might easily survive without them. As long as he is in their grip, they are real and urgent. Thus a socialite will strive earnestly to keep slender and to be seen in fashionable spots wearing the latest styles, even if considerable food and sleep are sacrificed. A person whose mind is set on belonging to an exclusive group will move heaven and earth to become a member, even if membership offers little satisfaction other than social distinction.

There are men and women whose ego is so completely involved in a social ideal, a religious value, a movement, or a doctrine that they follow it in the face of any personal consequences, even death. Of course, such people are exceptional. Their lives are illuminating as examples of integration of all aspects of psychological functioning in terms of values central in their ego systems.

In modern complex societies, integration of sociogenic motives is the exception rather than the ordinary case. In the course of his development, the individual forms attitudes relating himself in many different capacities to many social groups (family, ethnic groups, church groups, clubs, professional groups, political groups, etc.). These attitudes become functionally related to each other. But their values and contents may be contradictory or even conflicting. In this case, functional relatedness of attitudes leads to experiences of conflict and sometimes personal instability. The adolescent in modern differentiated societies often experiences conflict between his attitudes as a child at home and in school, his strivings to establish himself as a person in his own right in his age-mate group, and his longing to appear and act as a grownup.

In some cases the individual may succeed in compartmentalizing conflicting attitudes, until he faces a situation which arouses two or more at the same time. A woman who functions as a wife and mother at home, a professional person or artist at work, and a member of ladies' clubs in her community may have appropriate attitudes for each of these roles and situations without experiencing much conflict. But sooner or later she will face a situation in which two or more do conflict. Her work is at an urgent phase when one of the children becomes sick. Or she finds that her role in a women's group demands that she submerge her professional or artistic pretensions.

The contradictory differentiations and group alignments of modern differentiated societies are reflected in contradictory but functionally related motives of an individual and are thus a source of many of his personal conflicts and dilemmas. Problems of multiple reference groups and statuses are discussed in Chapter 18.

REFERENCES

1. Aldrich, C. A., Norval, M., Knop, C., and Venegas, F. The crying of newly born babies: IV. Follow-up study after additional nursing care had been provided, *J. Pediat.* (1946), 28:665–670.

2. Ames, L. B., Learned, J., Metraux, R. W., and Walker, R. N. *Child Rorschach Responses: Developmental Trends from Two to Ten Years.* New York: Hoeber, 1952.

3. Beaumont, H., and Hetzer, H. Spontane Zuwendung zu Licht und Farben in ersten Lebensjahr, *Ztsch. f. Psych. u. Physiol. d. Sinnesorg* (1929), 113:239–267.

4. Brian, C. R., and Goodenough, F. L. The relative potency of color and form perception at various ages, *J. exper. Psychol.* (1929), 12:197–213.

5. Bridges, K. M. B. Emotional development in early infancy, *Child Developm.* (1932), 3:324–334.

6. Gellerman, L. W. Form discrimination in chimpanzees and two-year-old children. I. Discrimination of form *per se.* II. Form versus background, *J. genet. Psychol.* (1933), 42:1–50.

7. Gesell, A. Growth potentials of the human infant, *Scientific Monthly,* (1949), 67:252–256.

8. Gesell, A., and Ilg, F. L. *Infant and Child in the Culture of Today.* New York: Harper, 1943.

9. Gesell, A., and Thompson, H. *Infant Behavior, Its Genesis and Growth.* New York: McGraw-Hill, 1934.

10. Hicks, J. D., and Stewart, F. D. The learning of abstract concepts of size, *Child Developm.* (1930), 1:195–203.

11. Jersild, A. T. Emotional Development, in L. Carmichael (ed.), *Manual of Child Psychology.* New York: Wiley, rev. ed., 1954.

12. Lewin, K. Environmental Forces, in C. Murchison (ed.), *A Handbook of Child Psychology.* Worcester: Clark University Press, 2nd ed., 1933.

13. Lewis, M. M. *Infant Speech.* New York: Harcourt, Brace, 1936.

14. Line, W. The development of visual perception, *Brit. J. Psychol. Monogr.* (1931), No. 15.

15. Long, L. Conceptual relationships in children: The concept of roundness, *J. genet. Psychol.* (1940), 57:289–315.

16. McCarthy, D. Language Development in Children, in L. Carmichael (ed.), *Manual of Child Psychology*. New York: Wiley, rev. ed., 1954.
17. Mandry, M., and Nekula, M. Social relations between children of the same age during the first two years of life, *J. genet. Psychol.* (1939), 54:193–215.
18. Marquis, D. P. Learning in the neonate: The modification of behavior under three feeding schedules, *J. exper. Psychol.* (1941), 29:263–281.
19. Munn, N. L., and Steining, B. R. The relative efficacy of form and background in a child's discrimination of visual patterns, *J. genet. Psychol.* (1931), 39:73–90.
20. Murphy, G. *Personality*. New York: Harper, 1947.
21. Piaget, J. *The Child's Conception of Physical Causality*. New York: Harcourt, Brace, 1930.
22. Piaget, J. *The Moral Judgment of the Child*. London: Kegan Paul, 1932.
23. Pratt, K. C. The Neonate, in L. Carmichael (ed.), *Manual of Child Psychology*. New York: Wiley, rev. ed., 1954.
24. Preyer, W. *The Mind of the Child. Part II. The Development of the Intellect*. New York: Appleton, 1890.
25. Rivers, W. H. R. *The History of Melanesian Society*. Cambridge, England: Cambridge University Press, 1924, Vol. I.
26. Sarason, S. *Psychological Problems in Mental Deficiency*. New York: Harper, 1949.
27. Senden, M. V. Studies reported by D. O. Hebb, *The Organization of Behavior*. New York: Wiley, 1949.
28. Sherif, M. *The Psychology of Social Norms*. New York: Harper, 1936.
29. Sherif, M., and Cantril, H. *The Psychology of Ego-Involvements*. New York: Wiley, 1947.
30. Sherman, M. The differentiation of emotional responses in infants: II. The ability of observers to judge the emotional characteristics of the crying of infants, and of the voice of an adult, *J. compar. Psychol.* (1927), 7:335–351.
31. Shirley, M. M. Common content in the speech of preschool children, *Child Developm.* (1938), 9:333–346.
32. Smith, M. E. An investigation of the development of the sentence and the extent of vocabulary in young children, *University of Iowa Studies in Child Welfare* (1926), 3, No. 5.
33. Vernon, M. D. *Visual Perception*. Cambridge, England: Cambridge University Press, 1937.
34. Vernon, M. D. *A Further Study of Visual Perception*. Cambridge, England: Cambridge University Press, 1952.

CHAPTER 13

Motives and Deprivations in Human Behavior

This chapter deals with the demonstrated effects of motives and prolonged deprivations as factors in human experience and behavior. Human
behavior is typically goal directed. This goal-directed nature of psychological functioning is due to motives operative at the time. Whether biogenic
or sociogenic, motives participate as internal factors rendering man selective for certain objects, events, people to the exclusion of others (pp. 90–
97). *Within limits of alternatives set by the structure of external stimulus conditions,* motives bring about variations in perceiving, judging, and
reacting to objects, events, and people.

Prolonged deprivation and frustration of motives accentuate psychological selectivity and produce measurable changes or, at times, marked
transformations in man's relation to man, in his relations to groups, and
in other aspects of his life.

Until recently, systematic studies of motives concentrated on subhuman
animals. There are decided methodological and technical advantages in
the use of subhuman animals as subjects. One can do almost anything
with animals: bring them up under strictly controlled conditions, subject
them to specified frustrations and conflicts, or study them in any other
precisely controlled situation. Animal studies have a provocative effect in
refining approaches to problems of human motivation.

On the other hand, extrapolating generalizations obtained from animal
behavior to the motives of man has been singularly unrewarding. When
man eats, drinks, and mates, he cannot help involving his ego, with all its
symbolic ramifications. When you ask him a question concerning some

motive which concerns him in an intimate way, he first appraises your question and your intentions in asking it. His reaction to you is colored by his appraisal of your question and intentions. Not infrequently, the words he uses in response to the question are intended mainly to make a good showing or to live up to your expectations as he sizes them up. These indicate a few of the unique properties that are encountered in the study of human motives.

In recent years an increasing amount of work and ingenuity has been devoted to the study of human motives. It seems that a promising start in securing factual data has been made through the use of various direct and indirect methods devised by men in clinical, social, and experimental areas. The aim of this chapter is to provide an overall familiarity with the developing trends in the study of human motivation.

TRENDS IN THE STUDY OF MOTIVES

Citation of all recent developments in the empirical and experimental study of motives would require a full-length book in itself. Therefore, citations have to be restricted to a few which have a direct bearing on the representative material to be summarized in this chapter.

Social attitudes properly fall within the area of motivation studies. Attitudes derived from an individual's membership in groups and in a larger sociocultural setting make him highly partial in favor of or against individuals, groups, and various social, political, religious, and economic issues. The stands embodied in the individual's social attitudes are not merely cut-and-dried intellectual affairs. They are important determinants of the selective nature of his perceptions and judgments (discriminations) in relation to relevant stimulus materials. They are among the weighty determinants of his actual positive or negative behavior in relation to them.

For example, when an individual has an attitude of prejudice toward a group, he tends to see its members in an unfavorable light and to react in a discriminating way, putting them at a distance from himself and his kind. These discriminative reactions are revealed in employment preferences and in exclusion from his neighborhood, educational, and professional facilities. If a person has incorporated a prevailing reference scale in his particular setting concerning the amount of money necessary to prove himself a man to be counted, his attitude toward wealth becomes a main anchorage in evaluating his worth and the worth of others; it will be a factor in his choice of companions and in the kind of adjustments he follows in his human contacts. Some of the research units summarized here deal with sociogenic motives of this kind as factors in human behavior. Chapters 15 and 16 are devoted to more detailed treatment of social attitudes.

If one observes a man's behavior over a period of time and the conditions in which he functions, it is usually possible to see his motives and goals revealed in his words and deeds. Such observations can be made under experimentally controlled conditions. The Minnesota semistarvation study reported later in this chapter is a case in point. Such observational data may be obtained also from the reports of prolonged deprivation or frustration by persons who are caught in it through actual life circumstances. Prisoner-of-war diaries, first-hand accounts of experiences in concentration camps, or reports of other conditions brought on by war, famine, or other socioeconomic crises come under this heading.

One fruitful source of data pertaining to conditions of pronounced deprivation or frustration is ethnological literature. A survey of various cultures indicates that major deprivations and frustrations may vary according to prevailing economic resources, socioeconomic organization, and prevailing scales of socioeconomic, religious, political, or other social values.

One of the major tasks of a social psychologist studying motives is to discover precise, short-cut techniques to tap an individual's motives which will be valid in predicting future observed behavior. However, attempts to obtain indices of a person's motives or attitudes which are of intimate and serious concern through direct questions in face-to-face situations or by written forms have resulted in a mass of inconclusive data. When checked against behavior in relevant situations, there are frequently discrepancies between such data and the actual behavior in question. There is little wonder that some investigators have announced on the basis of these data a divorce between verbal response to questions and behavior in relevant situations.

Clinical studies utilizing methods like the Kent-Rosanoff word association, sentence completion, delayed reaction times in relation to stimuli with motivational relevance, various kinds of ambiguous materials as represented by Rorschach ink blots and other so-called projective techniques, psychoanalytic use of free association, slips of the tongue, interpretation of dreams constitute attempts to study motives or attitudes. Such devices and techniques are *indirect* methods which seek to obtain motivational data circumventing the disadvantages of direct questioning which were noted above.

Indirect Laboratory Methods in Assessing Motives

One of the remarkable developments from the psychological laboratory during recent decades has been the study of human motives and attitudes through selectivity and variations in relatively simple judgment, perception, learning, and recall of relevant stimulus material. The next sections are devoted to studies demonstrating this developing research trend.

The underlying assumption in all of these studies, whether explicitly stated or not, is that perception and other aspects of experience are determined jointly by external and internal factors (Chapter 3, pp. 77–84). In the study of motives or attitudes through judgment, perception, and the like, the usual device has been to use various sorts of unstructured stimulus situations, which are conducive to the greater contribution of internal factors in the structuring of experience. Because of the facts of perceptual selectivity, it is feasible to study motivation through perception of structured stimulus objects as well. However, in this case it would be necessary to present a larger, but specified, number of structured stimulus objects and either to expose them for a brief time or to include too large a number for all to be perceived in the time available (pp. 85–97).

In handling the demonstrated facts of perceptual and judgmental variations, this approach corresponds to the interdependent nature of psychological functioning more closely than does handling them in terms of separate "mechanisms." When perception and judgment, taken as prototypes of experience, are conceived as determined jointly by external and internal factors and the implications of selectivity are realized, the use of special mechanisms (like "defense," "projection," "introjection," and the like) becomes unnecessary.

Positing different mechanisms, even though they are recognized as mere labels, tends to freeze psychological processes into more or less separate compartments. The end result is likely to be discrete classification of hundreds of items as mechanisms, including "perceptual offense" as well as "perceptual defense" and many others. The rather negative labeling of consequential psychological processes as "defense mechanisms" reflects a gloomy conception of human nature built up chiefly on the basis of a selected sample of pathological cases. Recently Eysenck, a psychologist with close access to pathological cases, called attention to the fact that this pessimistic edifice of psychology built upon the study of pathological cases can scarcely be adequate for people as a whole (10). In actual practice there are quite a few individuals who do not just stay put and use their defenses in perceiving and acting as situations arise, but actively move out in their striving to make certain objects, persons, groups, and values focal in their experience.

It is not necessary or parsimonious to use terms such as "projection" which crop up frequently in discussion of variations or "distortions" of experience due to motivational factors. To be sure, perceptual variations under given conditions are facts too well established to be denied. Perceiving and judging are not cut-and-dried cognitive affairs. On occasion, the organization of experience and the sequence of organization are determined largely by the preoccupations, fixations, and attitudes of an individual. In some instances, in the face of harsh reality the individual may shut himself in to build castles within his own confined psychological horizon. In this case, his motives and passions reign supreme. That is why remembering, which in this case becomes imagining, is satisfying and frequently engaged in. The checks of external reality are reduced to a minimum. It is even true that as a consequence of frustrations experienced in the face of unjust treatment, of discriminations suffered, the whole world may be experienced as consisting of just a few friends and a great mass of all the rest, lumped together as unfriendly or hostile.

But there is no need for a clutter of separate mechanisms to handle the gamut of perceptual variations and distortions. They can be handled adequately in terms of a conception of experience as determined jointly by interrelated external and internal (motivational) factors, and in terms of the recurrence of particular events. In short, the psychology of motives and attitudes is included in this conceptual approach to experience and behavior.

EXPERIMENTS ON MOTIVATIONAL FACTORS IN EXPERIENCE AND BEHAVIOR

In Chapter 3 the fact of psychological selectivity as determined jointly by external and internal factors was introduced (pp. 85–97). Among the experiments demonstrating the part played by social attitudes acquired during the individual's development, those of Bartlett, started about 1912, were outstanding both in significance and in historical priority. Starting with the way individuals perceive their surroundings, Bartlett's experiments showed how social attitudes enter into perceiving, remembering, and imagining (2).

He found that variability of response increased as the stimulus material presented became more complex. "For the more complex the material, or its setting, the more varied is the play of interests and consequent attitudes which can be evoked" (p. 193). The complex material increased alternatives for perception. In remembering, the relative weight of attitudes increased because remembering takes place in the absence of the original stimulus. Sometimes the individual's attitude produced a "distortion" of the original percept. In other cases the end result was increasing accuracy of recall. Thus one subject, who was a student of mathematics, compared a rather unstructured pattern to a "mathematical function." He was subsequently able to reproduce it with a high degree of accuracy.

The role of attitudes derived from social norms or values in perceiving unstructured stimulus situations was demonstrated by M. Sherif (*44*). In this study of social factors in perception, numerous examples of selectivity influenced by such attitudes were presented, many from ethnological field studies. Selectivity, it was noted, is pronounced in states of deprivation: ". . . When the satisfaction of a basic need, such as food, is barred in a serious and lasting way, *the restless state of deprivation becomes the dominating factor*. The aspects we notice in the stimulus field are those which are connected in some way with the frustrated need, and which will ultimately lead to its satisfaction" (*44*, p. 192, italics in original).

Selectivity in imagining as a function of food deprivation was demonstrated by Sanford in a laboratory experiment which is summarized in the next section.

Experiments, stemming from the work of Egon Brunswik, by Zuk-Kardos, Fazil, and Ansbacher showed that perception and judgment of familiarly valued objects, like coins or stamps, were in some circumstances significantly influenced by the individual's attitude toward them, resulting in overestimation of the number of the more valued objects (e.g., *1*).

A series of coördinated experiments dealing with motivational and affective factors was initiated by Gardner Murphy and his students at the City College of New York. Since these various research units by Murphy with Schafer, Levine, Chein, Proshansky, and Postman were a direct stimulant for numerous later experiments by them and other investigators, they are summarized in some detail in appropriate contexts in this chapter. The problems of these studies concerned variability in perception and discrimination (*24, 35*), perceptual selectivity (*42*), and selective learning and recall as related to various internal factors (*25, 34*). The selective nature of remembering which had been demonstrated by Bartlett was also substantiated in relation to various specific attitudes by several investigators, including Seeleman (43), K. B. Clark (8), and Watson and Hartmann (46).

Laboratory Studies of Deprivation

Deprivation of food or liquids is an advantageous way to insure differential motivation. The experimenter can safely predict that a person deprived of food for a long period will be hungry. A like assumption in regard to most sociogenic motives, on the other hand, would be difficult to justify. Therefore, the effects of deprivation of biogenic motives are particularly appropriate for controlled investigation.

Because it is seldom possible to deprive subjects of food or water for a long period, the deprivation period in most studies varied within 24 hours. The controlled nature of laboratory work necessarily introduces factors not ordinarily found in real-life cases of deprivation. Therefore, the implications of laboratory experimentation for understanding prolonged deprivation of individuals caught in unfortunate life circumstances are limited to demonstrating suggestive trends and relationships.

FOOD DEPRIVATION: On the basis of the observation that abstinence from food leads to selective preoccupation and dreams of food, Sanford set out to test the hypothesis that the amount of imagining about food varies with the length of deprivation. As a first step, he tested a group of school children shortly before and after their regular meals. At both times, the children were presented with words, to which they were to respond with the first word that came to them, and with pictures of incomplete situations, like a pointing finger or a baby reaching out with its hands, which they were asked to complete. The children gave about twice as many food responses before meals as they did after meals (40).

Then, using college students as subjects, Sanford compared the variations in preoccupation with food (1) after a 24-hour fast and (2) during the normal eating cycle (41). All of the subjects were told that they were being tested for speed of response. After a few conventional speed tests, they were asked for word associations, interpretations of incomplete pictures, chain associations, completion of drawings, and completion of words of which two letters were given. Thus, all of the tasks permitted alternatives in response.

In the author's words, the findings were as follows:

"1. Food responses increase with time during the normal eating cycle and over a 24-hour period.

"2. Over a 24-hour period, the increase in food responses is not in direct ratio to the increase in time, the fasters' average being only slightly greater than that of subjects examined near the close of the normal eating cycle" (p. 155).

Whereas the physical need for food was surely greater, on the whole, for subjects deprived of food for 24 hours, the total food responses for this group were only slightly greater than for subjects before one of the regular meals. This established hunger cycle also accounts for the finding that subjects tested before breakfast, when they had not eaten for from 8 to 20 hours, made significantly fewer food responses than those tested during the latter half of their normal eating cycle prior to other meals. Breakfast is a meal which is often light or at times omitted, especially by college students.

Before leaving Sanford's study it is worth noting that the reactions he observed in subjects who fasted for 24 hours revealed certain aspects which some psychoanalysts tend to present dramatically as though they occurred only for sexual deprivation and to label as mechanisms. The following conversation between the experimenter and a subject shows one of the devices used to avoid preoccupation with food.

E. Well, how did it go?
S. It was kind of tough—thanks to my roommate.
E. What do you mean?
S. Well, it seemed that just about the time I got thoughts of food put out of my mind my roommate would say, "How would you like to have a nice, big, juicy steak?" [p. 158]

Another example of reaction to deprivation is seen in the subject who forgot that he was supposed to be abstaining from food: "I missed my supper, as I was supposed to do, and was driving home from a date when I thought, 'Gosh, I'm hungry.' I parked the car and went into a drugstore to get a sandwich, and then the thought struck me, 'Oh golly, I'm supposed to be fasting'" (p. 158).

In two more recent experiments, McClelland and Atkinson studied the influence of food deprivation for periods of 1, 4, and 16–18 hours in imagining. Their subjects were naval men awaiting admission to a training program they had requested. It was intimated that the tasks had importance in the type of work they had requested.

In the first unit (27), the subjects were told that "pictures" would be projected on a screen at very low intensities, and that it had been found that people could respond to such slight stimulation more correctly than chance alone permitted. Actually no pictures were projected, although the projector was running. Subjects were told that they must write down something for every projection. The results showed that the frequency of food-related responses increased with the hours of food deprivation, and that this increase was a function of increased naming of instrumental objects (like table service) rather than goal objects (food). In addition, the frequency of food-related responses varied significantly in response to suggestions or hints by the experimenter concerning the contents of the "pictures" which were supposedly projected.

In a second unit (28), the subjects were given actual pictures showing people in situations which could be variously interpreted. Some of these pictures were from Murray's Thematic Apperception Test and others were designed for the experiment. The task was to tell a story about each picture. Again it was shown that in imagining food-deprivation themes increased with the period of deprivation. The pictures which differentiated between hungry and non-hungry subjects most clearly were those which contained objects or situations *relevant* to hunger, while allowing various alternative interpretations.

Hunger and Perceptual-Judgmental Variations: The first of the experiments by Gardner Murphy and his students to be summarized here dealt with the effect of differential food deprivation in perception of relatively unstructured stimuli. This study, by Levine, Chein, and Murphy, sought to measure "the relation between the intensity of the food interest and the amount of perceptual distortion" (24).

College students were asked to verbalize their associations with pictures, some black and white and some colored. They included meaningless drawings, ambiguous food drawings, and drawings of various household articles. Both groups of pictures were shown behind a ground-glass screen, so that they could be "only vaguely perceived." Thus, the stimulus situation was highly unstructured and conducive to the relatively greater contribution of internal factors. However, of the two sets of unstructured pictures, the black-and-white ones were somewhat easier to see and tended to evoke relatively more food responses, regardless of the subjects' motivation. Many of these appeared "more or less round and so were called fruits." If arousal of a motive state leads to psychological selectivity toward *relevant* goal objects, then stimuli which are found by empirical means to be conducive to interpretation as food objects should be selectively perceived by hungry subjects.

Each subject was tested once a week at various periods after eating (1, 3, 6, 9 hours). These subjects were told that they would be fed after the session. Results for control subjects, who had eaten shortly before each session, were similar for each presentation. Results for experimental subjects are summarized in Figure 13.1.

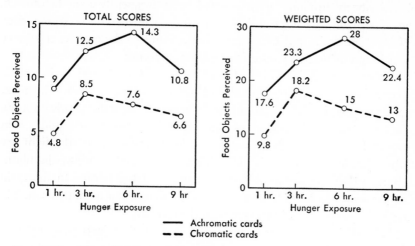

Fɪɢ. 13.1.   The effect of food deprivation on perception. These are the average scores of all experimental subjects. The total scores give the average of all food responses made. Weighted scores were computed by assigning different values to items referring to meat, fruits or vegetables, and eating utensils. (From R. Levine, I. Chein, and G. Murphy, The relation of the intensity of a need to the amount of perceptual distortion, *J. Psychol.* [1942], *13*:291.)

As this figure shows, the number of food responses to the unstructured pictures tended to increase with deprivation up to a certain point, after which there was a slight decrease in number. This drop occurred earlier (at 6 hours) for the colored pictures than for the black-and-white pictures.

In addition, the number of rejections, i.e., no meaningful associations with the pictures, increased progressively with the length of deprivation. Such rejections were consistently more frequent for the colored pictures than for the black-and-white pictures.

As the authors interpreted their findings, the differences in perception of black-and-white and of colored pictures as well as the decreasing number of food responses and increased rejections with time indicate that growing deprivation does not result simply in increased "wish fulfillment" or perceptual distortion, regardless of the stimulus situation. The wish fulfilling or "autistic" tendency was predominant for a time (up to 3 hours for the colored pictures and 6 hours for the black-and-white). But then the subjects became increasingly concerned with satisfaction of hunger. This "reality process" resulted in an overall drop in food responses (decreased distortion). The colored pictures, which were difficult to see realistically as anything, were rejected more frequently than before. On the other hand, the black-and-white pictures, which could be seen as food objects more easily and thus were more relevant to the motive, continued for a longer period to arouse food-related responses.

An experiment by Gilchrist and Nesberg investigated variations in judgment as a function of food and water deprivation (12). The maximum period of food deprivation was 20 hours and of water deprivation was 8 hours. Colored pictures of goal-related objects (foods or liquids) were presented for 15 seconds at a standard illumination. Then the light was turned off. After 10 seconds, the subjects were asked to adjust the illumination so that the picture looked the same as it had before. In short, the first presentation was a "standard" and the second was a comparison. The measure used was error in voltage from the standard.

The task involved judgment (matching) of illumination of pictures. Though the pictures were structured, the judgments were made from memory of one aspect (illumination), thus permitting variations in judgment as a function of deprivation.

The overall result was that errors in illumination matches increased with increasing periods of deprivation. The hungrier or thirstier the subjects, the greater were the errors in judgment of illumination of stimulus material relevant to the motive deprived. These errors were increasingly in the direction of underestimating the standard illumination. Less illumination was required to make the comparison resemble the standard for deprived subjects.

By varying the nature of the pictures presented, it was possible to specify that these judgmental variations as a function of deprivation occurred only in relation to relevant goal objects. Judgments, by deprived and non-deprived subjects, of illumination of homogeneous colored slides and landscapes did not differ significantly.

DEPRIVATION AND SELECTIVITY: The selective nature of response to stimuli relevant to a person's deprivations as contrasted with non-related stimuli was evident in the studies on imagining, in the Levine, Chein, and Murphy experiment, and especially in the experiment by Gilchrist and Nesberg summarized above.

The general finding that variations in experience as a function of deprivation occur in relation to relevant stimulus material was substantiated in Wispe's experiment on word associations by subjects deprived of both food and water for periods ranging from 0 to 24 hours (48). Subjects were told that deprivation and verbal fluency were being studied. A series of words was presented, half of which were "need-relevant" and half of which were "neutral" or not relevant to food or water deprivation. The relevant and neutral words were equated as much as possible for commonness of usage. As each word was presented, the subject was asked to give the first words which came to mind and to continue until told to stop.

The overall trend in terms of length of deprivation was that the number of food and water word associations increased significantly from 0 to 10 hours, with a slight drop for those subjects deprived for 24 hours, a rather general tendency found by other investigators.

A significant relation was found between the relevance of the stimulus word to hunger or thirst and the kind of associations given to it. Thus, "food-related stimuli beget more food-related responses, the water-related stimuli elicit more water association, and the neutral stimuli get more neutral word responses" (p. 231). Given a stimulus situation and task allowing some alternatives in response, the selective trend in response is, therefore, a function both of the internal deprivation and of environmental possibilities in the way of stimuli relevant to the deprivation.

Postman and Crutchfield (32) investigated selectivity in response to stimuli with varying structure, as influenced by the interaction of deprivation (hunger) and of "set" produced indirectly by varying the initial items on the task.

The task was carried out in a classroom situation and required completion of skeleton words, each with letters missing (e.g., gra − −, − − − − ing). Through a standardizing procedure, some skeleton words were chosen which showed a very high probability of food response by non-hungry subjects. Others yielded very low probabilities of food responses, and a third group was chosen with medium probability of food responses. In other words, the probability of certain alternative responses to the stimuli was determined before the experiment. The critical words were those of medium probability, with the supposition that response to these words would reveal selectivity as a function of deprivation and set most clearly.

Variations in "set" were produced by presenting from 0 to 5 skeleton words with very high probability for food responses as the first items on the task for different subjects. Such indirect hints or suggestions of the way to proceed in a task are ordinarily effective in the classroom, where subjects are concerned to perform "correctly." The periods of deprivation varied only from 0 to 6 hours, a fact which limited the effectiveness of deprivation as a factor in selectivity.

The significant finding was the overall tendency for both variables which increased selectivity toward food responses ("set" and deprivation) to have their greatest effect in relation to the critical words, where the initial probability of food responses was neither very high nor very low. On the other hand, responses to words which had previously been found to have high probabilities for food responses and those with very low probabilities for food responses did not differentiate clearly among subjects with varying periods of abstinence or experimentally induced "set." In the authors' words, "The extremes of the continuum of response probability define a floor and a ceiling for the operation of selective factors" (p. 216). For these words, the alternatives in response were limited by stimulus characteristics.

Judgments of Objects with Motivational Relevance

Several experiments summarized dealt explicitly with variations in perception and judgment of an unstructured aspect of the stimulus situation as a function of progressive deprivation of food or water. In studying variations in experience influenced by motives of social origin, it is more difficult to specify that a particular motive is involved as a factor in the behavior of all subjects. Most experiments have used a stimulus which has acquired value for most people in a society (like money) or have built up value of an initially neutral stimulus during the experiment by rewarding response to it with some generally valued object.

Proshansky and Murphy used a system of rewards and punishments (giving or forfeiting money) to produce value in the course of their experiment (35). This experiment has a direct bearing on the role of motivation in learning and discrimination.

In a pretraining period subjects were placed in a semidark room and asked to estimate the length of lines and to judge the heaviness of various weights. Some of the lines were "long" (5–7 inches), some were "short" (2–4 inches), and some were "intermediate," but some of the latter actually overlapped the lengths of the "short" lines. The weights were varied similarly.

During the training period the stimulus material was presented again.

However, this time the subjects were not asked to make judgments or other overt responses. They were simply rewarded with 15 cents each time a long line or a heavy weight was presented. When "short" lines and light weights were presented, the subjects had to forfeit 15 cents. These rewards and punishments were given to the "intermediate" lines and weights on a "planned haphazard" schedule.

In the final testing period, the subjects again judged the "intermediate" lines and weights (without reward or punishment). These judgments were compared to the initial judgments of the intermediate stimuli in the pre-training period. Whereas the judgments of control subjects, who were not rewarded and punished, showed no change, the judgments of the subjects who were rewarded during training increased significantly in the direction of greater length and weight. Thus, reward and punishment resulted in variations in judgment in the direction of the reward and away from the direction of the punishment.

Such variations can be called "distortions" in the sense that they do not correspond to the original stimulus items. However, the variations occurred in relation to a stimulus series which was not easy to differentiate. Alternatives in discrimination were possible. By building up differential values for the larger and smaller stimuli during the experiment, these valued stimuli at the ends of the series became anchorages for discrimination. After the establishment of affective anchorages, the intermediate stimuli tended to be assimilated toward the positively valued anchorage, even though they were objectively closer to the smaller (punished) stimuli. These results have suggestive implications for the study of affective anchorages and assimilation and contrast effects on judgment produced by them.

These findings were substantiated in an experiment by Haggard and Rose (15) using the autokinetic phenomenon of apparent movement (see p. 250). Judgments of direction and distance of movement were made. In half of the trials in which a subject responded that the light moved to the left, he was rewarded with five cents. Even with the relatively few and small rewards, a majority of the subjects reported movement more often to the left than to the right. The average distance which the light appeared to move to the left was longer than the average distance to the right. And all subjects were more confident of their judgments of movement to the left than to the right.

The stimulus material in these experiments lacked in objective structure in some aspect and in varying degrees. In 1947, Bruner and Goodman sought to test "the tendency for sought-after perceptual objects to become more vivid" by studying variations in judgment of the size of coins from a penny up to a half-dollar (4). The subjects were all 10-year-old school children, but one group consisted of children of prosperous parents and the other group came from the Boston slum areas. The children made estimates of the various coins and of cardboard disks the same sizes by adjusting a knob that regulated the size of a patch of light on a screen. The results showed wide differences in the tendency to overestimate the size of coins by the poor group and the rich group. For every value from a penny to 50 cents, the poor children's estimates deviated more from actual size than did the rich children's estimates. This tendency to overestimate increased with the value of the coin. When size estimates were made from memory, the well-to-do children overestimated quarters and half-dollars more than when the coins were actually present. On the other hand, poor children in this study overestimated coin size more when the coins were present than when estimating from memory (coins absent).

The large differences between size estimations of coins by the well-to-do and poor children and the somewhat surprising result that poor children overestimated coin size more when the coin was present than when it was absent led Carter and Schooler to undertake a similar experiment (7). Estimations of size were obtained for rich and poor children (1) with the coin present and (2) with the coin absent as in the previous study.

In this experiment, a general tendency was found to exaggerate the size of larger disks and to underestimate smaller disks whether they were cardboard, metal, or actual coins. The important finding with the coin present was that "when judgments are being made with the physical objects present as a standard of reference there are no significant differences in judgment between the rich and poor subjects" (p. 203). This conclusion may be viewed in terms of the discussion of relative weights of internal factors in structured and unstructured stimulus situations in Chapter 3 (pp. 97–99). In spite of the difficulties in adjusting the size of a patch of light to the size of a present coin, one would expect that objective size would be more compelling on the whole than internal factors which might operate in the direction of overestimation (or underestimation).

When the coin sizes were estimated from memory, however, the poor children did tend to overestimate size. On the other hand, the rich children made judgments from memory which were similar to their judgments when the coins were present. Carter and Schooler concluded: "The present results suggest that the value of a disk or the need associated with it is important as a determiner of judged size only when the stimulus object is equivocal or absent, as when judgments are made from memory" (p. 207).

Subsequently, Bruner and Rodrigues studied size estimates of present coins and disks of different materials by 10-year-old children from a middle-income group (6). They confirmed the finding that when objects were present judgments of valued objects did not differ consistently from judgments of similar objects with no value. However, their results suggested that in proceeding from smaller to larger objects, the relative extent of overestimation of coin size increased significantly more than overestimation of metal or paper disks.

The realistic implication of these studies does not seem to be that attitudes toward valued objects are not involved in reaction to them. Rather, the contribution of such attitudes to psychological structuring is checked by reality factors when the stimulus situation is well structured and is greater when stimulus structure is lacking or absent. Thus, attitudinal factors contribute relatively more in the interplay of influences determining judgment when the individual judges from memory. This finding was also confirmed by Rosenthal's study on the same topic (38).

One important shortcoming of these studies was that differential attitudes relating to the stimulus objects were assumed on the basis of the individual's background (well-to-do or poor). To make reliable predictions concerning the relative weight of an individual's attitude in perceiving and judging, it is necessary to know both the situation (relative degree of structure, social and other influences operating) and what the individual's attitudes toward the situation actually are. Conceivably some individuals from a wealthy background might regard money as more important, more central in life than some persons from a poorer background, as an experiment by Rosenthal and Levi indicates (39). Such methodological inadequacies were emphasized by Klein, Schlesinger, and Meister in a critical examination of previous findings on size estimation (21).

There is a decided methodological advantage, therefore, in building up a positive attitude toward the stimulus during an experiment. This method was used in the Proshansky and Murphy study summarized earlier and in experiments by Lambert, Solomon, and Watson (23). Young children acquired a positive attitude toward certain disks used as tokens during a training period. By turning a crank on a vending machine, the child received a disk. When this disk was inserted in the machine and the crank turned again a number of times, candy was ejected. After ten days of experience with this machine and the tokens, the children made estimates of the size of poker chips similar to the tokens, by turning a knob which controlled the size of a circle of light on a screen.

Size estimates by these children rose significantly from those made before the training period with the machine. However, when the candy was no longer received for the tokens, the size estimates fell significantly. When two disks of different color were required to secure candy, one serving simply to secure the token disk from the machine, only the token disk which brought the candy was significantly overestimated (22).

Studies of children at these early ages (3–5 years) indicate that their desires and interests are particularly likely to influence their evaluations. Therefore, it is likely that judgments of size by older children or adults in relation to such structured stimuli would, like those of Carter and Schooler's subjects, be influenced to a greater extent by objective factors than were these children's.

For this reason, the most clear-cut studies of motivation through perception and judgment by older children and adults utilize stimuli which are relatively unstructured, as in the Proshansky and Murphy study. The stimuli may be unstructured only in certain respects. Thus, in a study by Dukes and Bevan, older children (6–15 years) judged weights of stimuli which were well structured in every respect save their differences in weight (9). The weights in the series differed by six grams, a difference not easily discerned by these children. (The estimated j.n.d. or "just noticeable difference" for varying combinations of standard and comparison weights ranged from 11.5 up to 19.5 grams.)

The objects to be judged were open glass jars filled to the same height. Nine of the jars contained colored candies, a substance calculated to be desirable to children. The nine jars in the other series of weights contained a mixture of sand and sawdust and were considered to be neutral in appeal value. In each of the two series, the weights of the jars ranged from 176 to 224 grams. A standard weight of 200 grams was used against which other stimuli were estimated.

In discriminating these two series of weights, one candy and one a neutral substance, the children's attitudes toward the contents did play a significant role. "Valued stimulus objects appear heavier than neutral stimulus objects of the same actual weight." Attitudes toward the candy had still another important effect in their judgments. In some situations the standard weight of 200 grams was a candy-filled jar, and in others it was a jar filled with sand and sawdust. When both the standard and the particular stimulus to be judged were candy-filled jars, the variability of response was less than when the standard was neutral or than when both the standard and comparison stimuli were neutral (sand and sawdust).

Motives and Variations in Stimulus Structure: The experiments on perceptual and judgmental variations in relation to objects of motivational relevance summarized here indicate that internal factors (motives, attitudes) contribute relatively more in psychological structuring when the stimulus situation is relatively less structured (see Chapter 3, pp. 98–99). There is little evidence that just any stimulus is potentially equivocal or open to varying interpretations, as some investigators have claimed. Nor is there an indication that perceiving and judging in all situations are at the mercy of a person's values, wishes, and desires. Rather, these experiments point to the kind of circumstances in real life where individuals' motives do carry greater relative weight in perceptual and judgmental reactions, namely, situations which allow alternatives for response in some dimension.

When the stimulus situation is well structured, alternative modes of experience and behavior are limited or checked by reality factors. The individual's motives are revealed in such situations through his *selective* preoccupation with objects relevant to his motives rather than with other stimuli available in the environment.

Experiments on Selectivity

From various alternatives, what is attended to, noticed, and responded to? A number of the experiments on deprivation summarized earlier in this chapter concerned the problem of psychological selectivity. This section summarizes some experiments pertaining to selectivity as influenced by other motivational factors.

One unit in the series of experiments by Murphy and his students dealt specifically with selectivity in relation to two alternatives. In this experiment, Schafer and Murphy investigated the role of motives in the determination of the figure-ground relationship (42). For this purpose, reversible contour lines were designed which could be seen as one or the other of two profiles (Fig. 13.2). For the training series of the experiment, these profiles were separated so that there were four profiles in all, each bounded by a semicircle (Fig. 13.3). The profiles were presented in random order. The subjects were given a nonsense syllable for each profile which they were required to learn to associate with the appropriate face. When two of the faces were presented, subjects were rewarded, but when the other two were presented subjects made a forfeit. The two faces which were rewarded were determined by the experimenters and always included one profile from each of the drawings in Figure 13.2. Small sums of money were used as rewards.

After this training period, the subjects were shown the contour lines when placed together as in Figure 13.3 No rewards were given. The subjects were asked simply to write down the names of the profile they saw. The result was that subjects tended to perceive in the contour lines those profiles which had been rewarded previously. The profiles for which they had been punished tended to become the background for the rewarded profile. Since a significantly high number of perceptions after training occurred in connection with the profiles which had been rewarded, it was concluded that motives can function in the determination of a figure-ground delineation.

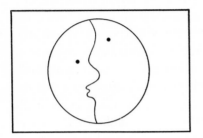

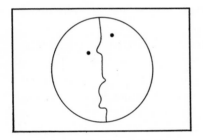

Fig. 13.2.   The two stimuli presented in the post-trainings series. (From R. Schafer and G. Murphy, The role of autism in a visual figure-ground relationship, *J. Exper. Psychol.* [1943], 32:337. Courtesy of the American Psychological Association.)

Rock and Fleck repeated the experiment with a modified procedure. Their results did not seem to confirm these findings (37). However, when the conditions of the Schafer and Murphy experiment were duplicated, their findings were substantiated (19).

Another in the series of experiments dealt with attitude as a factor in selective recall. The study by Postman and Murphy (34) is particularly instructive because it investigated the role of attitudes in recall of items which varied both in their affective relation to the subjects' attitudes and in the degree of this relatedness. The items which were recalled varied from those which were highly "compatible" or harmonious with the subjects' attitudes to those which were highly incompatible or conflicting, with various degrees of compatibility and conflict in between these extremes.

Subjects were bright eighth-grade students during World War II with varying attitudes toward the Axis powers and the United Nations. On the

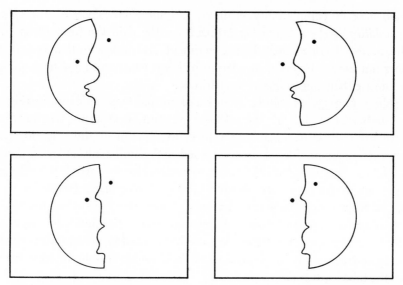

F*IG.* 13.3.   The four stimuli presented in the training series. (F*ROM* R. Schafer and G. Murphy, The role of autism in a visual figure-ground relationship, *J. Exper. Psychol.* [1943], 32:336. Courtesy of the American Psychological Association.)

basis of their ratings of statements about these nations on a five-point scale of intensity, pairs of words were selected. For example, if an individual agreed strongly with the statement that the German people are a kindly people, the pair of words "German—kindly" was given a compatibility value of +2. If he disagreed strongly, a value of −2 was given, and so on along the five-point scale from +2 to −2.

The pairs of test words and control words were presented to the subject one at a time, and he read them aloud to the beat of a metronome. To test for recall of these pairs, one word of each pair was exposed on a card for three seconds.

It was found that recall of these pairs was selective in the direction of items related to an emphatic or extreme attitude, whether this attitude was favorable or unfavorable to the relationship implied in the word-pair. "Pairs at either extreme of the scale—relationships completely endorsed and connections completely rejected—were retained in preference to other categories."

There was a tendency for pairs highly acceptable in terms of the subjects' attitudes to be recalled better than word-pairs which conflicted sharply with their attitudes. However: "Of the two factors operating, *ex-*

tremeness of compatibility or incompatibility, and *sheer degree of acceptability of the relationship* expressed in the pair, the former was . . . the more effective one." This experiment also indicates that selectivity does not always function in relation to items which are most harmonious or most enhancing to one's own attitude.

These findings on selectivity in recall are pertinent to consideration of a number of studies on the selective recognition of words presumed to have varying motivational significance. In experiments investigating perceptual selectivity for negatively valued and emotionally charged words, a tendency was found for the recognition times for such words to be longer than for positively valued words (5, 31). (*Recognition thresholds* were higher for the negatively valued words.) These results were interpreted as revealing "perceptual defense." Later, recognition thresholds for emotionally toned taboo words (terms not ordinarily used in polite society) were compared with those of neutral words, and higher thresholds were found for the taboo words (29).

Since words exposed for a brief time or with dim illumination are open to alternative interpretations, it was reasonable to suppose that motivational factors might be important factors in differential recognition thresholds. On the basis of common observations that people may "gloss over" or ignore unpleasant stimuli, it was feasible to suppose that in some circumstances internal factors might lead to slower recognition times. However, postulating a principle or mechanism of defense is justifiable only if the relationship between the internal factors and response to the stimulus is invariant and cannot be explained more parsimoniously.

Subsequent research indicated that one factor to consider in evaluating the explanations of experimental results in terms of "mechanisms" was the relative familiarity of the words presented, in terms of frequency of usage (17). This factor alone affects recognition thresholds. It is necessary to compare recognition of valued words and neutral words which are comparable in familiarity before a statement concerning the relative contribution of motivational factors can be made.

It was also possible that some of the words used in these experiments were sufficiently surprising to subjects in the experiment so that they hesitated to say them until they were quite sure of their perceptions. Studies by Whittaker, Gilchrist, and Fischer (47) and by Bitterman and Kniffin (3) indicate that such hesitation occurs in relation to taboo words presented in a laboratory by an experimenter. Of course, such hesitation is prompted by internal factors, but not those which are referred to by "perceptual defense."

Do motivational factors lead to perceptual selectivity of relevant words to a greater extent than to equally familiar words having little or no motivational relevance? A number of experiments indicate that they may, but that such selectivity is both for positively and for negatively related items and in varying degrees. Specifically, in relation to word recognition thresholds, motivational factors may lead to lowered thresholds for recognition of both positively and negatively related items (*11, 30*). In certain circumstances motivational factors may result in raised thresholds for recognition of positively or negatively related items (*33*). Among the other factors which enter into these relationships are familiarity of the words to the subjects, the kind of words that the subjects are set to see or not to see in an experimental situation, and other motives aroused by the experimenter, such as a desire to appear "normal" or socially well adjusted to a psychologist (*3, 11, 30*).

In short, experimental evidence does not warrant postulation of a mechanism of "defense" or of other special mechanisms. Like the previous work by Bartlett, Sanford, and Murphy and his students, these experiments have indicated that it is feasible to investigate the role of motivational factors in selective perception, imagining, learning, or recall of relevant stimuli. Such investigation necessarily involves more exacting specification of the internal factors in question and of the interrelationships among these internal factors, the characteristics of the stimulus, the task to be performed, and the experimental situation, including the subject-experimenter relationship. Understanding selectivity of experience and behavior is necessarily in terms of functional relations between motivational influences, other internal factors, and the external factors operative at the time.

EFFECTS OF PROLONGED DEPRIVATION

The consequences of prolonged deprivation due to famine, economic depression, foreign occupation, or chaotic socioeconomic situations are well known. Such prolonged deprivations of large groups of people will be discussed in Chapter 21.

No systematic treatment of prolonged deprivation is available as yet. For this reason, the one experimental study of prolonged semistarvation carried out at the University of Minnesota by Keys, Brozek, Henschel, Mickelsen, and Taylor on conscientious objectors during World War II constitutes a milestone in the scientifically controlled observation of prolonged deprivation (20).

The subjects were all volunteers from Civilian Public Service, coming from different states. Originally there were 36 subjects, but for various reasons four were eliminated. They were all informed about the aim, procedures, rigors, and dangers involved in the experiment. Their ages ranged from 20 to 33 years. They were all normal men in good physical health. In intelligence they were considerably above average.

After a three-month period of standardization, they were systematically subjected to semistarvation for six months. Unfortunately no space can be devoted here to the period of rehabilitation which followed. At the end of the period of semistarvation they had lost about 25 percent of their normal weights (see Fig. 13.4).

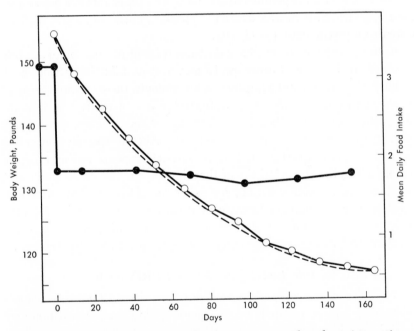

Fig. 13.4. Average loss of weight during six months of semistarvation. Average weights, 34 men. Predicted (broken line) and actual (solid line) body weights are shown as biweekly means for the entire group of 34 men. The actual food intakes, as calories, are also shown. Food intake in thousands of calories. (From A. Keys, J. Brozek, A. Henschel, O. Mickelsen, and H. L. Taylor, *Experimental Starvation in Man.* Used by courtesy of Dr. A. Keys, Director of the Laboratory of Physiological Hygiene, University of Minnesota.)

The major findings relevant to the psychological effects of prolonged deprivation should be interpreted with caution because of the relative security and purpose of the experiment. The conclusions drawn from this experiment are not directly applicable to cases of deprivation under conditions of actual chaos, insecurity, danger, oppression, and starvation. Guetzkow and Bowman, who collaborated in the experiment, pointed out that the subjects "had complete security, in that they were under constant medical supervision and knew that they would be taken out of the experiment if anything serious went wrong" (14). They were not exposed to any danger from enemy attack beyond that of the average American in the United States at the time. They were motivated rather highly by the belief that their participation in the experiment was a service to humanity, at a time when the war against fascism was being waged by their country. They felt considerable responsibility to "come through with flying colors." Furthermore, the experiment received world-wide publicity in the papers and on the radio, and the subjects took this as an opportunity to prove that "conscientious objectors were not slackers" (13).

The general effects of the period of semistarvation are indicated in the following broad description given by the main investigators:

> As starvation progressed they became more and more silent, apathetic and immobile. Movements were slow and restricted; stairs were mounted one at a time and the men sat or stood leaning against a wall while they waited. In discussion there was no evidence of confusion of thought or difficulty of expression but the attitude was frequently irritable and morose. Trivial incidents were productive of exaggerated annoyance and complaint. Favorite topics of conversation were food, farming and rural life, a fact which was bitterly resented by some of the men.
>
> All of the men continually complained of feeling cold, and even in the warm weather of July most of them wore heavy clothes. The conclusion was clear that any lack of heat in the building would have produced bitter suffering. Another frequent complaint was the sensation of being "old."
>
> A number of men were bothered by vivid dreams, particularly dreams of breaking the diet, with attendant great remorse [20, pp. 25, 26].

The deprivation did not affect all individuals identically. In general, Guetzkow and Bowman noted that the normal range of differences between individuals widened during semistarvation. However, in broad trend the effects took the same direction; each man experienced some of the tendencies which the investigators reported (14, p. 22).

One of the most revealing facts concerning individual differences was that the thresholds of the acquired value systems under these conditions of stress differed. Thus, a few of the men could not remain on the restricted diet voluntarily throughout the entire period. Some of the violations were so minor that they did not jeopardize the experimental controls. When major lapses occurred, the data for that individual had to be discarded.

This deterioration of their ethical control was all the more remarkable because these men had shown themselves to be sincere and upright throughout the two or more years of work they had performed in the civilian public service units before coming to the laboratory. . . . One of the individuals not only bought food, but also stole some from "locked" storerooms. Another individual sublimated his food cravings by stealing china cups from coffee shops. Although fasting is said at times to quicken one spiritually, none of the men reported significant progress in their religious lives. Most of them felt that the semi-starvation had coarsened rather than refined them, and they marveled at how thin their moral and social veneers seemed to be [pp. 31–32].

As noted in Chapter 11, under ordinary conditions of civilized life, various biogenic motives become dominant periodically as regulated by social schedules. Now the individual attends to hunger, now to thirst, and now to sleep or to sex. When these needs are satisfied, at least to a minimum degree, he strives for other higher and more refined ends. During the period of semistarvation it was noted that this process was upset, and that hunger came to dominate more and more of the individual's thoughts and activities. Along with this, there was less concern with other motives, like sexual urges. Guetzkow and Bowman noted that "it was the rare individual who continued courtship at the end of the starvation. Budding romances collapsed, and some men wondered how they could have been so interested in *that* girl. One fellow's girl friend visited him from a distant city during the low days of starvation, and she found his ostensible affection disappointingly shallow. His reservoir of affectional responses was drying up" (p. 24).

Even though intellectual capacities were not noticeably impaired, the psychological world of these subjects was more and more focused on food. "The intensive preoccupation with food made it difficult for the men to concentrate upon the tasks they had intellectually decided they would work on. If a man tried to study, he soon found himself daydreaming about food. He would think about foods he had eaten in the past; he would muse about opportunities he had missed to eat a certain food when he was at this or that place. Often he would daydream by the hour about the next meal. . . ." (p. 32).

Food and topics connected with food acquired almost a sacred halo for the men. Some of these grown-up men did not mind licking their plates

Fig. 13.5. A starving man's thoughts and fantasies center on food. (From H. S. Guetzkow and P. H. Bowman, *Men and Hunger*. Elgin, Ill.: Brethren Publishing House, 1946.)

in the presence of others to avoid waste. Some tried to avoid the everlasting topic of food and were disgusted by such behavior. These findings are revealed in the items which the men jotted down in their diaries at different stages of semistarvation. Here are a few of them:

The time between meals has now become a burden. This time is no longer thought of as an opportunity to get those things done which I have to do or want to do. Instead, it's time to be borne, killed until the next meal, which never comes fast enough [p. 19].

It wasn't what the boys did with their food that I didn't like but it was their method. They would coddle it like a baby or handle it and look over it as they would some gold. They played with it like kids making mud pies [p. 20].

This week of starvation found me completely tired practically every day. If they want to get any more work out of me, they're going to have to feed me [p. 20].

Stayed up until 5:00 A.M. last night studying cookbooks. So absorbing I can't stay away from them [p. 21].

During semistarvation the social relationships of these deprived individuals were altered. The facts of deprivation and their common fate produced a new social demarcation which is described in the following summary:

One of the more profound changes which took place was the decreased sociability of the men. There were important exceptions to this, but even the men who managed to continue their social contacts often felt animosity toward strangers, merely because they were strangers. The men built up a tremendous in-group feeling that tended to exclude both their non-starving friends and the administrative and technical staff. They were apart from others—those who had been well fed. They were especially alienated by the individual who supposed he knew what it was like to be hungry because he had gone without food for a couple of days. It was hard to sit near one's comrade who had extra food. They became provoked at the laboratory staff for giving "too much" food to some, and thought it criminal to restrict the rations of others, even though they clearly understood the experimental plan demanded such adjustments in rations [p. 30].

Evidence from Siriono Culture

The foregoing experimental results concerning the psychological effects of prolonged semistarvation are suggestive of observations in actual life situations. Ethnological field work in societies where securing food is a constant concern for all members demonstrates in a striking way the crucial role of persistent deprivation in determining major social values and practices. Holmberg undertook a comprehensive field study with this consideration in mind (16). Many investigators have recognized the effects of biogenic motives in shaping the characteristics and values of social groupings and thus their direct and indirect influences on the personality of individual members. However, the Siriono society which Holmberg studied offered an unusual picture of "a society in which the drive of hunger is so constantly frustrated as to have become the dominant motivating force in shaping habit and custom."

Although the food supply of the Siriono is sufficient for survival, it is persistently inadequate. The tropical climate in which they live is highly unfavorable for preservation or storage of food. Arduous hunts for food must be made almost daily, and about a fourth of them are unsuccessful. The Siriono have only the most primitive weapons and few agricultural tools or skills. Domestication of animals is unknown. In short, the Siriono's waking hours are occupied with the exhausting and dangerous job of hunting and collecting enough food to survive.

Here only some of the outstanding examples of the effects of this persistent deprivation can be mentioned. Food and food getting are the topics of the Siriono's major anxieties. When food is obtained, it is eaten without ritual, often furtively or at night so that it need not be shared. Quarrels over food constitute the greatest single source of conflict in the group. Almost no food preferences are shown; a hawk is devoured as voraciously as a partridge. The only stealing observed was the taking of food on those infrequent occasions when some was left unguarded.

Food and successful hunting almost dominate the *dreams* and *fantasy* of the Siriono. Holmberg noted that "sex dreams and fantasies are rarely encountered." Food is used as a lure for obtaining a partner in sexual activities. When food is scarce, there is little sexual activity. Sexual orgies follow a successful hunt.

The adult Siriono individual is characterized generally as aggressive, individualistic, and uncoöperative. There is no evidence that such characteristics develop on the basis of experiences in infancy or early childhood. The Siriono child is indulged considerably and frustrated little. His food supply is ample until he is weaned at about 3 years. Only as he grows older and younger children come into the picture does he share adult hardships. Typically by the time he is about 12, his behavior toward food is similar to that of the adults. "In general, he is aggressive in all matters that pertain to food."

The scarcity of food and the recurring problem of hunger are reflected in the practices and social values of Siriono culture. Since a man can seldom collect more food than is necessary for his family, the family is the functioning economic and social unit. The usefulness of the Siriono band is limited chiefly to serving as a source of sex and marital partners. Since the Siriono are often on the move in search for hunting grounds, individual ownership of a garden plot, tree, and the like is recognized only when such articles are used.

Status and prestige are based largely on hunting prowess and food-getting ability. The chief is always a good hunter. The best hunter or food collector is the most desirable mate. The sick and the aged are not able to obtain food well; therefore, they are treated as liabilities. People who are extremely ill and decrepit are no longer useful and are abandoned to die.

Finally, the almost constant preoccupation with food and the rigors of obtaining it have resulted in a sparse development of *art forms, folk tales,* or *mythology*. *Magic* relates chiefly to food. The Siriono's concern merely to survive leaves little time for intellectual activity or for speculations on deities or an afterworld.

EFFECTS OF DEPRIVATION IN SOCIAL LIFE

Facts concerning prolonged deprivation of biogenic motives observed by reporters and persons experiencing them in everyday life indicate the importance of tendencies noted in experimental situations. The validity of generalizations in social psychology must be tested finally on the basis of their adequacy in handling events of everyday life, when human beings carry on the business of living. Here rather simple examples of deprivations are given for illustrative purposes.

Ernie Pyle shared the lot of American GI's in combat in the North African campaign during World War II. The battle rations were adequate but lacked in variety. He reported an incident during this time in which a hog took on the halo which these GI's might ordinarily associate with the sight of a beautiful girl:

One day I was at a command post in a farmyard in a prosperous irrigated valley. The grounds were full of officers and soldiers who had just arrived. All of a sudden across the barnlot there came plodding a huge white hog.

It was touching and funny to see the wave of desire that swept over the soldiers. Everybody looked longingly at that hog. Everybody had some crack to make. . . .

A year before none of us would have looked twice at a hog. But then the mere grunting passage of a swine across a barnlot brought a flood of covetous comment [36, pp. 113–114].

People who were fascist prisoners of war for any length of time knew the pangs of real hunger. One ex-soldier, reporting his experiences as a German prisoner, emphasized the intensity with which hunger dominated the preoccupations of the prisoners with the following episodes:

When we were prisoners in Stalag Luft III in East Prussia, the food situation got bad during the winter of 1944. Red Cross packages were keeping us alive, but they weren't getting through regularly, and the Nazis were content to let us starve on a daily bowl of watery soup and a bit of bread.

Food became our principal topic of conversation; we planned menus, compared favorite dishes and reminisced on the last square meal we'd had, months, even years, before. Finally our senior officers and chaplains decided that this constant thinking about food was undermining morale, and a directive went around the compound that edibles were not to be talked about any more.

One day when several of us were sitting around shooting the breeze, a sergeant muttered, "Boy, I wish I had a nice thick steak."

A major, who was passing, turned around and warned him, "Hold it, sergeant! No more talk about food, you know."

The sergeant looked glumly at the ground, and somebody quickly changed the subject, "Well . . . I wonder what the new-model cars are going to be like?"

So we talked about cars, about new designs, probable speed, mileage, cost, and how soon we could get delivery after the war.

After a long time the sergeant looked up at us. "I wish I had one of those new cars right now," he said, "smothered in mashed potatoes and gravy" [18].

Similar preoccupation with food and actual dreams about it were reported by the men in Peary's expedition to the North Pole who were forced to live on the simplest diet (49), and by a group of fliers wrecked in the Antarctic on a more recent expedition to the South Polar regions (26).

In the stringently rationed prisoner-of-war camps of the Japanese during World War II, the men experienced and observed many instances of selectivity in perception, judgment, and memory shaped by their hunger. In describing his years of captivity under the Japanese, General Jonathan Wainwright recorded facts revealing such selective preoccupation and the weakening of social attitudes (45).

In prison camps at Tarlac and Karenko a group of high Allied officers underwent prolonged starvation. They began to be "haunted by hunger"; food "became a mania" with them. They "woke up each morning with hunger paramount" in their minds and "went to sleep to dream of food."

Under such intense and prolonged deprivation the range of stimuli which served as goal objects widened far beyond that which was culturally established. After a long period in which they had no animal protein, the officers greedily ate animal stomachs, intestines, and lungs. They searched the ground for large tough snails which, although dreadful to their taste, were "wolfed" down by those lucky enough to find them. Looking for the "tiniest nutrition," they ate worms and black weevils along with their meager rice portions.

Wainwright reported that relations among the men were seriously disturbed through this excessive concern with food. "We took to counting the two or three beans which sometimes appeared in the bottom of our soup pail, and if a man received a bean in his soup, and another did not, it made for hard feeling. This must be hard to imagine, but it is true" (p. 187). The men agreed on one man to divide the food as impartially as

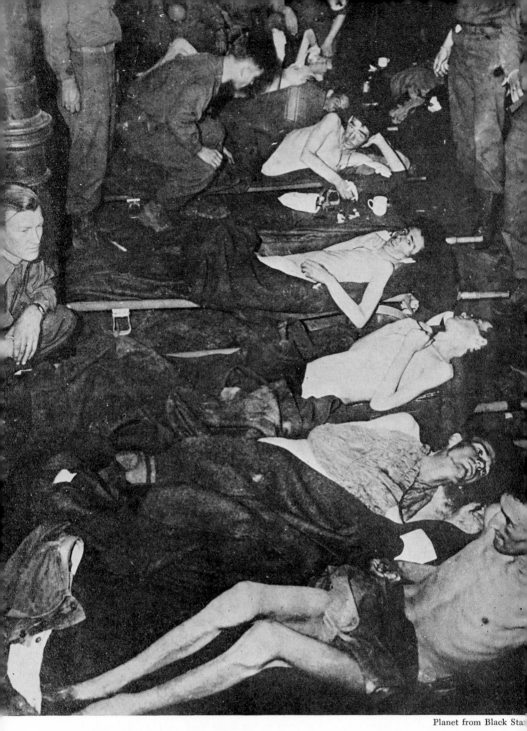

FIG. 13.6. These prisoners of war knew prolonged starvation well.

possible. However, he quit the job shortly because they all insisted on standing over him to watch. Finally another officer with the rank of major general accepted the job, but on the condition that he could divide the food behind a closed door.

When the Japanese kept Red Cross parcels from these men, "the frustration was more numbing than any beating we had ever taken." On one occasion the guards gave the prisoners a starved cow, which broke away as it was being unloaded. Frantically the prisoners chased after it as it ran out of the prison camp and brought it back. They were so absorbed in retrieving the cow that some of them did not even realize that they had been outside the bounds of the prison camp. Hunger obliterated even the much-desired freedom.

The fortitude with which these men stood on their dignity as Allied officers in captivity and, in accordance with the Geneva Convention, refused to work for the Japanese soon broke down when they were promised a small extra portion of "work rice."

Such "breakdowns" from standards or decisions agreed upon by a group when members are severely deprived of necessities of life becomes important in understanding group formation and collective action in such circumstances. Group formation and solidarity are extremely difficult or even impossible when the bodily needs of members are not met to some bare minimum and when external conditions offer no opportunity for fulfilling them through collective action.

Consideration of the effects of prolonged deprivation on a mass basis and its profound consequences are reserved for Chapter 21. These grim facts have not succeeded as yet in making their way to the ranks of major problems for social psychologists, even though men of action and policy makers seem to have considered their implications more realistically. Herein lies a fertile field for social psychologists, as their recent serious concern indicates. Aside from their realistic consequences, the facts concerning prolonged deprivations can lead us to a more adequate social psychology of motivation.

REFERENCES

1. Ansbacher, H. Perception of number as affected by the monetary value of the objects: A critical study of the method used in extended constancy phenomena, *Arch. Psychol.* (1937), No. 215.
2. Bartlett, F. C. *Remembering: A Study in Experimental and Social Psychology.* Cambridge: University Press, 1932.

3. Bitterman, M. E., and Kniffin, C. W. Manifest anxiety and "perceptual defense," *J. abnorm. & soc. Psychol.* (1953), 48:248–252.
4. Bruner, J. S., and Goodman, C. C. Value and need as organizing factors in perception, *J. abnorm. & soc. Psychol.* (1947), 42:33–44.
5. Bruner, J. S., and Postman, L. Emotional selectivity in perception and re-action, *J. Personal.* (1947), 16:69–77.
6. Bruner, J. S., and Rodrigues, J. S. Some determinants of apparent size, *J. abnorm. & soc. Psychol.* (1953), 48:17–24.
7. Carter, L. F., and Schooler, K. Value, need, and other factors in perception, *Psychol. Rev.* (1949), 56:200–207.
8. Clark, K. B. Some factors influencing the remembering of prose material, *Arch. Psychol.* (1940), No. 253.
9. Dukes, W. F., and Bevan, W., Jr. Accentuation and response variability in the perception of personally relevant objects, *J. Personal.* (1951), 20:457–465.
10. Eysenck, H. J. War and Aggressiveness: A Survey of Social Attitude Studies, in T. H. Pear (ed.), *Psychological Factors of Peace and War.* New York: Philosophical Library, 1950, pp. 64–65.
11. Gilchrist, J. C., Ludeman, J. F., and Lysak, W. Values as determinants of word-recognition thresholds, *J. abnorm. & soc. Psychol.* (1954), 49:423–426.
12. Gilchrist, J. C., and Nesberg, L. S. Need and perceptual change in need-related objects, *J. exper. Psychol.* (1952), 44:369–376.
13. Guetzkow, H. S. Personal communication.
14. Guetzkow, H. S., and Bowman, P. H. *Men and Hunger, A Psychological Manual for Relief Workers.* Elgin, Ill.: Brethren Publishing House, 1946.
15. Haggard, E. A., and Rose, G. J. Some effects of mental set and active participation in the conditioning of the autokinetic phenomenon, *J. exper. Psychol.* (1944), 34:45–59.
16. Holmberg, A. R. The Siriono. A study of the effect of hunger frustration on the culture of a semi-nomadic Bolivian Indian society. Doctorate dissertation, Yale University, July, 1946.
17. Howes, D. H., and Solomon, R. L. Visual duration thresholds as a function of word probability, *J. exper. Psychol.* (1951), 41:401–410.
18. Ivy, E. R. The Sergeant Changed the Subject, *Sat. Even. Post*, February 15, 1947, p. 62.
19. Jackson, D. N. A further examination of the role of autism in a visual figure-ground relationship, *J. Psychol.* (1954), 38:339–357.
20. Keys, A., Brozek, J., Henschel, A., Mickelsen, O., and Taylor, H. L. *Experimental Starvation in Man.* Laboratory of Physiological Hygiene, University of Minnesota, 1945.
21. Klein, G. S., Schlesinger, H. J., and Meister, D. E. The effect of personal

values on perception: An experimental critique, *Psychol. Rev.* (1951), 58:96–112.

22. Lambert, W. W., and Lambert, P. E. C. Some indirect effects of reward on children's size estimations, *J. abnorm. & soc. Psychol.* (1953), 48:507–510.
23. Lambert, W. W., Solomon, R. L., and Watson, P. D. Reinforcement and extinction as factors in size estimation, *J. exper. Psychol.* (1949), 39:637–641.
24. Levine, R., Chein, I., and Murphy, G. The relation of the intensity of a need to the amount of perceptual distortion, *J. Psychol.* (1942), 13:283–293.
25. Levine, J. M., and Murphy, G. The learning and forgetting of controversial material, *J. abnorm. & soc. Psychol.* (1943), 38:507–517.
26. McCarty, O. "Dead" Men's Diary. *Sat. Even. Post,* May 17, 1947, pp. 15 ff.
27. McClelland, D. C., and Atkinson, J. W. The projective expression of needs: I. The effect of different intensities of the hunger drive on perception, *J. Psychol.* (1948), 25:205–222.
28. McClelland, D. C., and Atkinson, J. W. The projective expression of needs: II. The effect of different intensities of hunger drive on thematic apperception, *J. exper. Psychol.* (1948), 38:643–658.
29. McGinnies, E. Emotionality and perceptual defense, *Psychol. Rev.* (1949), 56:244–251.
30. Postman, L., Bronson, W. C., and Gropper, G. L. Is there a mechanism of perceptual defense? *J. abnorm. & soc. Psychol.* (1953), 48:215–224.
31. Postman, L., Bruner, J. S., and McGinnies, E. M. Personal values as selective factors in perception, *J. abnorm. & soc. Psychol.* (1948), 43:142–154.
32. Postman, L., and Crutchfield, R. S. The interaction of need, set, and stimulus structure in a cognitive task, *Amer. J. Psychol.* (1952), 65:196–217.
33. Postman, L., and Leytham, G. Perceptual selectivity and ambivalence of stimuli, *J. Personal.* (1951), 19:390–405.
34. Postman, L., and Murphy, G. The factor of attitude in associative memory, *J. exper. Psychol.* (1943), 33:228–238.
35. Proshansky, H., and Murphy, G. The effects of reward and punishment on perception, *J. Psychol.* (1942), 13:295–305.
36. Pyle, E. *Here Is Your War.* New York: Holt, 1943; World, 1945.
37. Rock, I., and Fleck, F. S. A re-examination of the effect of monetary reward and punishment in figure-ground perception, *J. exper. Psychol.* (1950), 40:766–776.
38. Rosenthal, B. G. Attitude towards money, need, and methods of presentation as determinants of perception of coins from six to ten years of age, *Amer. Psychologist* (1951), 6:317 (abstract).

39. Rosenthal, B. G., and Levi, J. H. Value, need and attitude toward money as determinants of perception, *Amer. Psychologist* (1950), 5:313 (abstract).
40. Sanford, R. N. The effects of abstinence from food upon imaginal processes: a preliminary experiment, *J. Psychol.* (1936), 2:129–136.
41. Sanford, R. N. The effects of abstinence from food upon imaginal processes: a further experiment, *J. Psychol.* (1937), 2:145–159.
42. Schafer, R., and Murphy, G. The role of autism in a visual figure-ground relationship, *J. exper. Psychol.* (1943), 32:335–343.
43. Seeleman, V. The influence of attitude upon the remembering of pictorial material, *Arch. Psychol.* (1940), No. 258.
44. Sherif, M. *The Psychology of Social Norms.* New York: Harper, 1936.
45. Wainwright, General J. M. *General Wainwright's Story,* R. Considine (ed.). New York: Doubleday, 1945; Garden City, 1946.
46. Watson, W. S., and Hartmann, G. W. Rigidity of a basic attitudinal frame, *J. abnorm. & soc. Psychol.* (1939), 34:314–336.
47. Whittaker, E. M., Gilchrist, J. C., and Fischer, J. W. Perceptual defense or response suppression? *J. abnorm. & soc. Psychol.* (1952), 47:732–733.
48. Wispe, L. G. Physiological need, verbal frequency, and word association, *J. abnorm. & soc. Psychol.* (1954), 49:229–234.
49. Young, P. T. *Motivation of Behavior.* New York: Wiley, 1936.

V

MAN AND PRODUCTS OF HIS INTERACTION

CHAPTER **14**

Man and His Words

Human interaction and social life as we know it depend upon the use of words or gestures which are understood by the individuals taking part. Try inviting a friend to meet you on Saturday night for a party without using words. The most difficult part of issuing this invitation without words is specifying an action at a place you cannot point out and for a time in the future.

Through words, men communicate with each other in short-cut form, eliminating with a few syllables the need for a hundred separate actions. Through language, men make plans to be carried out in distant places at times far in the future. And using language, men bring to each other the accumulated achievement, knowledge, custom, and superstition of the past.

As noted in the first chapter, human interaction takes place typically on a conceptual level of functioning through words of a language. In this chapter we turn to the role of language in carrying social products to individuals in consistent and enduring forms. We will look briefly at the words used for communicating by men in different groups. Through experimental material we can learn something about the effects of words on the way the individual views his world, on his learning and other aspects of functioning.

Later in the chapter, trends in children's acquisition of conventional language will be summarized in terms of their consequences for social-psychological development. Finally, in order to appreciate man's relation to his language, we will discuss the formation of new words or concepts. Men not only learn and use words; they create them as well.

Symbols and Language Concepts

Words that men use are a particular kind of symbols. The word "cup" refers to all cups, not just to the one that holds our coffee. Most words are generalized labels which can be used to designate a group, a range or class of items or events. These labels embody generalizations or concepts.

Language concepts have another feature which distinguishes them from other symbols. They are *shared* by more than one individual. In human groups, concepts are standardized to denote a similar range or class of items, experiences, persons, or events to different individuals. In the words of Charles Morris, concepts of a language are not merely signs; they are comsigns—symbols common to members of a group (49).

Many gestures which men use in their daily dealings also have this shared or standardized character. Their use in communication hinges upon their common significance to various individuals in a group. For example, shaking one's head from side to side is a sign of "no" in this country. In parts of the Near East, "no" is signified by an upward toss of the head.

When gestures, words, and the generalizations they embody are not shared by individuals, they are not useful in communicating. In an experiment, children played together in small groups with a toy for which they had no name. Within a rather short time, the children in each group standardized a label for the toy. Different labels were standardized in the different groups. Therefore, when children in different groups tried to talk about the toy, they had great difficulty in communicating with each other. A common conclusion was that they had played with different toys. (This experiment is summarized later in this chapter, pp. 477–481.)

The meanings of words—that is, the generalizations they encompass— are not always identical for each individual. To the extent that they differ, communication between individuals is disrupted. By and large, common concepts are essential to the business of living in a group.

HUMAN GROUPS AND THEIR WORDS

Among the Northern Ojibwa Indians whom Hallowell observed, there is a word which means literally "snake berries" (23). This label is used by the Ojibwa for a number of plants which are not identical in appearance. When an Ojibwa child reaches for berries called by this name, a grownup takes them away or slaps his hand. Individuals learn these kinds of berries as a distinct category, and all are regarded as inedible. According to Hallowell, none of them are poisonous. But the individual Ojibwa does not learn about the berries and their properties through first-hand experience in eating them. He learns about them from grownups who use the name.

This illustration has two important implications. First, through the medium of language human beings can and do learn about the social and physical world they live in without always having direct, first-hand experience with all of its aspects. This possibility of a short cut in the laborious process of learning entirely through direct action and experience with every object and event has direct bearing on the socialization process, as we shall see later.

Second, this example of the Ojibwa concept of "snake berries" illustrates the finding that the generalizations, hence meanings, crystallized in a word are not necessarily based simply on compelling objective characteristics common to the various specific items included under it. Linguistic classifications are not given in nature. This fact and some of its implications are our main concern in this section.

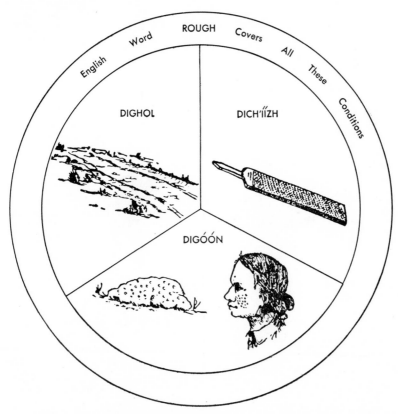

FIG. 14.1. Navaho language distinguishes between these three kinds of roughness, while English does not. (Reprinted by permission of the publishers from Clyde Kluckhohn and Dorothea Leighton, *The Navaho*. Cambridge, Mass.: Harvard University Press. Copyright, 1946, by The President and Fellows of Harvard College.)

Anthropologists and linguists have illustrated the differing classifications of objects, persons, and events in various societies through comparing the sort of items designated by words in one language with the referents of comparable words in English or other Indo-European languages. For example, the English word "rough" can be used to describe the surface of a road, a rock, or a file. In Navaho, three different words are needed to refer to these characteristics, and they are not interchangeable (35). This comparison is illustrated in Figure 14.1. On the other hand, one Navaho word can be used to describe both a pimply face and a rock with a bumpy surface, as shown in Figure 14.2.

Kluckhohn and Leighton give one example of a differing verbal category

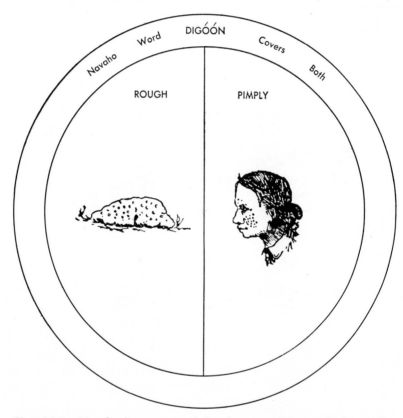

Fig. 14.2.   Navaho has one word for these conditions, which usually are referred to with two different terms in English. (Reprinted by permission of the publishers from Clyde Kluckhohn and Dorothea Leighton, *The Navaho*. Cambridge, Mass.: Harvard University Press. Copyright, 1946, by The President and Fellows of Harvard College.)

in Navaho and English which is traceable to a given set of historical circumstances. As shown in Figure 14.3, Navaho has one label which applies to flint, knife, and metal in general. This particular grouping of dissimilar objects stems from the fact that the Navaho implements of flint were replaced by metal objects after contact with Europeans. The old label was used to refer to the substance (metal) which replaced flint and knives made of it.

In Figure 14.4, contrasting categories in Hopi and English and in an Eskimo language and English are illustrated. As the linguist Whorf explained, Hopi has only one term that covers everything and everybody

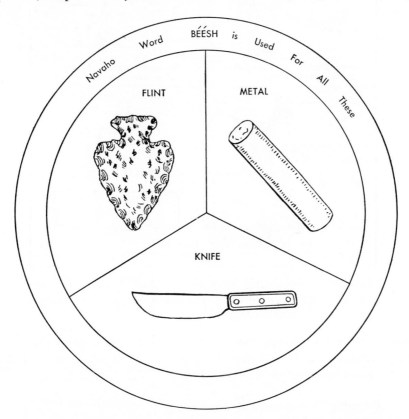

Fɪɢ. 14.3. Navaho refers to these with one word, while English requires three separate labels. Flint was replaced by metal in Navaho culture after European contact. (Reprinted by permission of the publishers from Clyde Kluckhohn and Dorothea Leighton, *The Navaho*. Cambridge, Mass.: Harvard University Press. Copyright, 1946, by The President and Fellows of Harvard College.)

that flies, except birds, which are designated separately. This Hopi word refers equally to an insect, an airplane, and the aviator who flies it. On the other hand, Hopi differentiates between still and running water with two different words, while English uses "water" for both. Eskimos use different

Hopi—One Word (Masa'ytaka)
English—Three Words

English—One Word (Snow)
Eskimo—Three Words

Hopi—Pāhe
English—One Word (Water)

Hopi—Keyi
Hopi—Two Words

FIG. 14.4.   Contrasting categories in Hopi, English, and an Eskimo language. (From S. I. Hayakawa, *Language in Action.* New York: Harcourt Brace, 1941.)

words to designate falling snow, snow on the ground, snow packed hard like ice, slushy snow, and wind-driven snow—all of which are included under the broad label of "snow" in English (74).

Differing Verbal Categories in History

The fact that men in groups categorize different features of their worlds in words can be seen also in historical surveys. The development and change in concepts of number, distance, and time afford clear examples.

There was a time in the early history of every society when no one could count. Some groups without accurate concepts of number exist today. A shepherd, for example, kept track of his sheep by calling each one by name. During the long history of numbers, different systems arose in different groups. Thus, the Old Babylonians developed a "sexagesimal system" in which 60 was a higher unit, as 100 is for us today.

One concept basic to the development of mathematics was evolved over a period of many years through the coöperation of many people. This is the concept of "zero." What is known of its fascinating history shows that it "came into use so gradually and its value was established by the cooperation of so many people that it can hardly be said to have had an inventor" (2, p. 16).

The history of concepts of measurement shows even more clearly that concepts are products of interaction of many people carrying on the important business of living in groups. In large part, the history of measures of length, area, and weight is a story of standardizing concepts for ever-enlarging groups of people.

In olden times, measures of length were frequently based on parts of the body and consequently varied from person to person. The ways which were worked out for reaching agreement on these concepts in a community seem very colorful today. In one German community, the following method was agreed upon: "Stand at the door of a church on a Sunday, and bid 16 men to stop, tall ones and small ones, as they happen to pass out when the service is finished; then make them put their left feet one behind the other and the length thus obtained shall be a right and lawful rood [rod] to measure and survey land with, and the sixteenth part of it shall be a right and lawful foot" (3, p. 11).

During the Middle Ages almost every town had its own measuring units. Of course, when people from different towns attempted to trade, considerable confusion could result. As trade between towns became more important, some agreement on these units became necessary.

In earlier periods of history, time concepts were exceedingly inaccurate and varied tremendously from group to group. Even as recently as 1850, people in America laughed at the idea of a factory producing seven watches a day. Who would want that many watches? In modern life, time and concepts which refer to precise units of time have become very important to people. Yet these concepts of time are not "natural" in the sense of corresponding with objective events in nature. Hours, minutes, and seconds are not given in any way by nature. The days of our calendar began as a natural unit (from sunset to sundown) but our present concept of a day is based on an *average* solar day (4).

Words and Realities in Group Life

The differing linguistic classifications of the environment in different historical periods and societies show us that concepts of a language are not based simply on objective similarities and differences among items they refer to. However, this does not mean that language concepts are just arbitrary classifications determined by sheer accident or the perverse whims of individuals.

Words do not drop from the blue. They are not typically formed by one person. On the contrary, the concepts of a language are social products. They arise and are standardized by people interacting in the vital matters of living, satisfying their needs, dealing with their environments, understanding the world they live in, and controlling or changing various of its aspects.

Studies of different societies have shown in detail that the vocabulary of a group, hence its classification of things, tends to reflect the practical activities of the group in its vital pursuits (26, 44). This is seen most clearly in rather small and relatively isolated human societies. In larger, more complex societies, words are spread from group to group within the society and borrowed from other languages. Another complicating circumstance is that, once standardized, words tend to persist even though they are no longer applicable to conditions and activities of group living. However, this persistence has limits. Outworn and inappropriate concepts do disappear in time. As we shall see later in this chapter, new concepts are formed when people face new and significant circumstances.

A group in Central Asia had names for each kind of horse they used, depending on its color and markings, but no word to refer to horses in general. At one time it was concluded that such fine classifications in "primitive" societies which cut across a broader concept used in more highly developed groups indicated that the "primitive mind" was more concrete and dealt more in terms of stimulus properties which are immediately perceivable. As Hocart pointed out in 1912, such differences are not indicative of the inferior generalizing capacities of people in less developed societies or of some other peculiarity of their mentality. Rather, such differential classifications reflect differences in the vital activities carried on by groups in certain definite environments (26). Concepts arise and are standardized to deal with such differences.

Here we can consider only a few examples of classifications that contrast with those familiar to us and that are clearly related to contrasts in the environments and activities of people who use them. For example, the Masai of East Africa were a group of people whose chief occupation was raising cattle. The Masai had at least seventeen terms for cattle. A cow with one calf, a cow with two calves, a sterile cow were all referred to with separate words. Each of the cattle was given a name of its own (45).

The Ifugao of the Philippines lived in valleys surrounded by mountains which for centuries isolated them effectively from the outside world. Their chief crop was rice, which was grown on irrigated terraces. In the Ifugao language, which is one of the Malay group, rice in various stages of planting, growth, and harvesting was given 20 different names (6).

Hocart related that in the Solomon Islands one of the staples was a nut. Two nuts, so alike in appearance that they seemed identical except for size, were given different names: *vino* and *ngari*. These names signified an important distinction. The two nuts, similar in appearance and both vital in the living of the islanders, had different seasons, were gathered differently, and were cracked and preserved differently. In fact, in terms of the activities which the islanders carried out in relation to them, the nuts were similar only after they were roasted and made into pudding. And at this stage, they were both called by the same name (26).

Differing classifications of the same objects are used by people with similar languages and cultures when the importance of these objects differs in the life of the particular groups. In many South Pacific islands, breadfruit is an important food, and it is usually referred to with several different names denoting important stages in its growth. Among the Mangarena, the supply of breadfruit is never quite enough. Therefore, the fruit is used in all stages of growth, ripeness, imperfection, and even decay. In this group breadfruit is designated by an even larger number of names, which refer to varied and finely differentiated stages in its development and deterioration (9).

In striking contrast to classifications which may seem minute, some groups have few or very vague names for objects and events that are not very important in their lives. Malinowski observed that groups whose activities center around gardening and raising animals had many names for single species of plants and animals designating various stages in their development and utilization. On the other hand, a tree, plant, or bird with no value to the group for food, clothing, or decoration was dismissed with some phrase like, "Oh, that is just 'bush,'" or "merely a flying animal" (44).

Groups whose chief means of livelihood is hunting or gathering, especially against great odds, like the Arunta of Australia or the Siriono of Bolivia, have standardized names for almost all of the neighboring flora and fauna (27, 60).

Among groups like the Siriono in which hunting and gathering predominate as the means of life and little can be stored or bartered, counting is not highly developed. The Siriono have number concepts of only 1, 2, and 3. Beyond that, quantity is indicated by "much" or "many" (27). The Tasmanians, living on an isolated island near Australia, count only to 2, all quantity after that being called "plenty." While some members of the Witoto of the Amazon jungle count to 20 using fingers and toes, 5 is the highest number word commonly used in the group. Any number over 10 is referred to as "like the hairs of my head" (72).

Such findings in different human groups point to the conclusion that different and even contrasting linguistic classifications found in various societies *are not simply arbitrary ways of "slicing" experience and objective reality. Rather, such different concepts spring from the interactions of peoples engaged in differing activities in definite environments.* It follows that concepts are not based *just* on objective features of the environment or just on the significance of these features for people dealing with them. To greater or lesser degrees, concepts embody generalizations referring both to objective realities and to their functional significance to people who deal with them.

LANGUAGE CONCEPTS AND INDIVIDUAL BEHAVIOR

Once the individual learns the words standardized in his group, he uses them in communicating with others and in dealing with those objects, situations, events, or relationships to which they refer. Certainly one of the distinctive consequences of concepts in human behavior is their *categorizing effect* on experience and behavior.

Linguistic classifications enter into the shaping of experience of relevant stimuli and reaction to them. The name or concept functions as an anchorage for classification of aspects of the physical and social world. Particular items either "belong" or do not belong in a certain verbal category. Therefore, behavior toward a particular item is influenced by the category to which that item "belongs." In an experiment, some young children were taught to call two very different objects by the same name, and some by different names. When the same name was used for two objects, other responses, like reaching for the object, were more likely to be generalized from one to the other than when different names were used (46).

Of course, experience and behavior are not determined solely by verbal factors. Man lives in a world of real objects with perceivable characteristics, of real people and real social situations. If you call a friend to see your "new car" and show him a travel-weary Model T, his perception of the car will not be significantly influenced by the label you have given it. He will see it for the battered wreck it is and drive it accordingly.

Sometimes it is concluded that the different verbal categories used in different human groups mean that the people who use them experience the world in entirely different ways. On the more practical side, we frequently hear someone say that all of our human problems are verbal problems. Such extreme conclusions are not warranted by existing findings. Experience and behavior, as we have seen, are shaped jointly by internal factors and by external stimulating conditions as these are related to one another.

At the same time, concepts learned by the individual are particularly clear-cut, organized, and lasting internal factors. In this section some experimental evidence of the categorizing effects of concepts is presented.

When individuals are shown some simple object or form, they often name it. Bartlett observed that subjects in his experiments on perceiving frequently gave names even to very simple line drawings (5).

After surveying the literature on studies of language in perceiving, Mc-Granahan concluded: "The effect of language on perception appears to be to make those features of the objective world that are represented by linguistic forms stand out in greater articulation, to give greater individuality to the object or event so represented, to cause similarities to be seen in things similarly represented, and in general to influence perception in the direction of the speech forms" (43, p. 202).

If the individual names a form or object when it is first seen, his subsequent recall of it may be definitely influenced by the name applied. This influence has limits, however. In Bartlett's experiments, a simple drawing И was called "N." Yet the name hardly ever affected subsequent reproductions of such simple patterns. The figure called "N" was correctly reproduced by every subject.

When the figure was more detailed, naming acquired much greater importance in remembering. Figure 14.5 shows one such stimulus figure and the reproductions by three different individuals. Two of them called the form a "picture frame," and their reproductions were affected by this

Stimulus Figure   Name Assigned to Stimulus Figure by Subjects

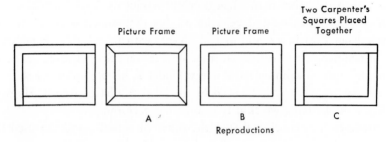

Picture Frame   Picture Frame   Two Carpenter's Squares Placed Together

A   B   C

Reproductions

FIG. 14.5. Effects of names in immediate recall of a simple drawing. (After Bartlett.)

name. The third called the figure "two carpenter's squares placed together" and reproduced the stimulus figure correctly. This example indicates that the effect of labels or names is not necessarily a distorting one but can also serve to enhance the accuracy of recall.

In experiments on remembering using the method of serial reproduction, Bartlett presented a stimulus figure to a subject, then asked him to reproduce it later. This reproduction was given to another subject, who later recalled it, and so on. He noted a pronounced tendency for these successive or chained reproductions of drawings which resembled or were named for conventional figures to progress toward the conventional forms. Thus, through the course of reproductions by 10 subjects, an extremely "primitive" drawing labeled "Portrait d'Homme" became a conventionalized representation of a human face.

Another stimulus figure presented for serial reproduction is shown in Figure 14.6. After a number of successive reproductions, it was shown to

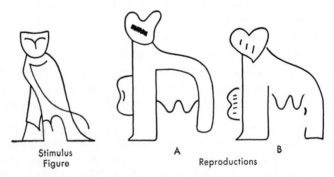

Stimulus Figure   A   B   Reproductions

FIG. 14.6. Remembering of a complex form influenced by naming of separate parts. (After Bartlett.)

a subject in the form labeled A in the figure. The subject who saw it next reported that he said to himself, "A heart at the top, then a curve and a straight post down to a little foot at the bottom. Between these two a letter W, and half a heart half-way up on the left-hand side" (5, p. 183). The subsequent reproduction by this subject is labeled B in Figure 14.6. It can be seen that this reproduction reflects the names he gave to various parts.

The tendency for recall and reproduction of forms to change in the direction of familiar objects was found by Gibson, who also noted the importance which "verbal analysis" assumed in the process (20). Carmichael, Hogan, and Walter specifically tackled the problem of the extent to which names given simple forms affected their recall (11). A set of 12 simple line drawings was prepared. Two names were assigned to each drawing. For example, some subjects were presented with the first stimulus form in Figure 14.7 and the word "bottle," while some subjects were given this same form and the word "stirrup."

The resulting reproductions were classified in five categories, depending on the extent of changes from the original drawings. The results presented are not of the typical or the most frequent changes, but rather of the most

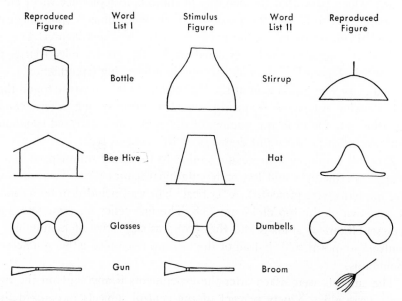

Reproduced Figure	Word List I	Stimulus Figure	Word List II	Reproduced Figure
	Bottle		Stirrup	
	Bee Hive		Hat	
	Glasses		Dumbells	
	Gun		Broom	

FIG. 14.7. Most pronounced examples of the effect of different names on reproductions of the same stimulus figure. (After Carmichael, Hogan, and Walter.)

pronounced changes. Selected examples of the most pronounced modifications in the direction of the name presented are shown in Figure 14.7.

The overall results for reproductions which showed the most pronounced changes were that an average of 74 percent of these reproductions changed in the direction of one list of names presented and 73 percent in the direction of the other list. In terms of the different stimulus forms, there was considerable variation in the effect of names given them. For example, the following percentages of reproductions showing most pronounced change were like the names given for the forms in Figure 14.7:

Word List I	Percent	Word List II	Percent
bottle	100	stirrup	69
beehive	69	hat	75
glasses	45	dumbbell	81
gun	76	broom	85

This experiment shows that names can influence recall of simple line drawings but at the same time clearly indicates that structural properties of the stimulus and other factors are also important in the recall of these figures. Aside from the rather clear-cut structural properties of the stimulus figures which permitted the majority of subjects to reproduce them fairly accurately, there is also the possibility that some subjects spontaneously named them, regardless of the name given by the experimenter. The investigators suggest a similar explanation for the greater effectiveness of "bottle" in Figure 14.7 than of "stirrup" in influencing reproduction.

In a classroom experiment at the University of Oklahoma we found that this drawing was most frequently called a bottle or jug. Considerable variation was found in the number of different names assigned spontaneously by subjects to various drawings of this general type.

Zangwill employed a procedure similar to the study summarized above using less structured and less representational figures (78). Two series of five ink blots were presented. A "critical" blot was included in both series. It is shown at the top of Figure 14.8. The first series was announced as representations of animals and the second as suggestive of mountains. A control group was told that all of the pictures resembled either animals or mountains.

The subjects were asked after the experiments if any cards in the two series were alike. Ninety percent of the control subjects recognized this fact, while only 36.7 percent of the experimental subjects noticed the presence of the critical blot in both series. The reproductions of the critical

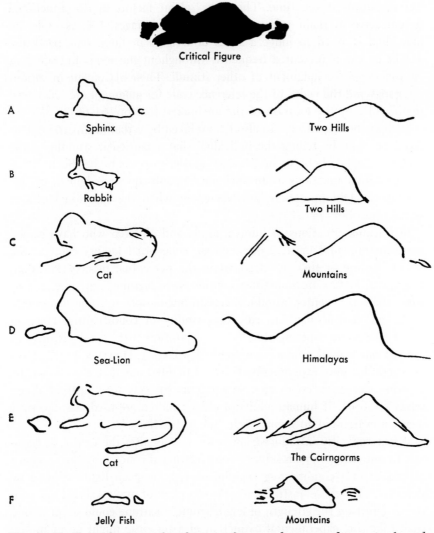

Fig. 14.8.   Reproductions of ambiguous figures when named as animals and mountains. (From O. L. Zangwill, A study of the significance of attitude in recognition, *Brit. J. Psychol.* [1938], *28*:15.)

blot in Figure 14.8 were made by six of the subjects in the experimental group who did not notice that this figure appeared in both series.

Concepts in Discriminating and Learning

As stated in Chapters 2 and 3, perceiving, judging, learning, and remembering take place within a frame of reference or system of related factors operating at the time. The more salient factors in this functional system serve as main reference points or anchorages. For example, an individual is asked to judge a series of weights or lines. One particular weight or line is presented frequently throughout the series and serves as an anchorage for judgment of other stimuli. Their placement in various categories and the width of the reference scale for judgment are influenced significantly by the location of the anchorage (see pp. 64–66).

Such anchoring effects can also be produced by verbal means (65). This could be done by telling the individual that a particular stimulus is the smallest, largest, lightest, or heaviest, as the case might be. Such verbal categorization functions as an anchorage in subsequent judgment of specific items. Discrimination becomes easier when the individual utilizes verbal categories (25).

In learning situations of human adults and children who have gained some instrumental mastery of language, conceptual factors enter at the outset because of their involvement in the perceptual process. However, conceptual factors are sometimes considered in learning experiments only when the experimenter introduces certain instructions to subjects and otherwise are uncontrolled. In surveying studies of conditioning, Hovland noted that some experimenters take the position that verbal instructions are just one way of producing a "set" (28, p. 608). However, on the basis of several learning experiments, Hovland pointed out that even when the experimenter gives no explicit instructions subjects may instruct themselves (p. 630). If human adults or older children are used as subjects, it seems unwarranted to ignore such "self-instructions."

When explicitly introduced, linguistic factors alter the course of learning. In one study, human subjects were instructed concerning the sequence of stimuli in a conditioning experiment (e.g., a green light followed by shock). With these instructions, the number of trials exerted no consistent effect on the strength of conditioning. Learning could occur in one trial. Likewise, experimental extinction of a response might occur in one trial when the subject was given verbal cues (15).

There are numerous indications that language short-cuts the long and often laborious process of learning simply through repeated perceptual-motor contact with concrete stimulus materials and situations. Learning a maze, which is classed usually as a "motor task," is considerably influenced by responses enabling the individual to follow the sequence of turns in the maze. Warden (66) found that the average number of trials needed to learn a maze by those who used words to categorize the sequence was

32.2, compared to an average of 67.9 trials by those using visual imagery and 123.9 trials by those who relied more heavily on motor aspects.

In studies of children's learning, a close relationship has been found between performance and ability to verbalize the principles involved in solving a problem (40, 41, 71). Thompson found that, in learning to assemble a mechanical puzzle, speed of learning increased as more verbalization of the procedures by the child and instructor was permitted by the experimenter (61).

As this study indicates, the child's own verbalizations are not the only linguistic influences affecting his learning. The spoken words of others also affect the process. Verbal criticism and verbal approval by an adult have been found more effective in increasing efficiency of learning discriminative tasks and motor skills than nonverbal reactions and approval (21, 67).

An experiment by Pyles demonstrates concretely how verbal categories telescope the learning of discriminations of form (50). Pyles presented a series of three-dimensional abstract forms to children from 2 to 7 years old. The children were required to learn which of these forms concealed a toy. The greatest difficulty was found when the forms were simply presented without a label. Even "nonsense" names made it easier to learn the discriminations. The number of trials was greatly reduced when the objects were given the names of animals.

However, even when no name was given and the subjects were simply shown the objects and required to learn which concealed toys, some children gave names to the forms or developed short descriptions of them. The 13 children who did this had a learning score significantly below that of all 80 subjects combined.

In summary, there is considerable impressive evidence that, once the individual functions on a conceptual level, his discriminations and learning are significantly affected by linguistic categories and relationships. Language concepts are clear-cut and organized anchorages for the learning process. Through them, trial and error is reduced or even eliminated. From a process of induction on the basis of repeated concrete contact with stimuli, learning becomes increasingly a process of deduction utilizing anchorages provided by words. This telescoping of the learning process has broad implications for human social development.

LANGUAGE IS DISTINCTLY HUMAN

In the recent history of the behavioral sciences there has been a pronounced tendency to develop principles for human behavior from laboratory findings on subhuman animals, like rats, pigeons, and chimpanzees. It has not been suggested that rats or even chimpanzees are identical with human individuals. On the contrary, it is frequently noted that to be applicable to human behavior such learning theories must make room for the stubborn fact that human beings learn and use language.

The pitfall in this line of reasoning lies in the fact that human language, communication, and conceptual functions are not just discrete factors which can be added at some future hour when it becomes convenient. As we saw in the last section, the explicit introduction of linguistic anchorages alters the learning process even for human individuals who have already mastered a language. The development of human language, learning to use language, and communicating through language make the difference between human culture and no culture, between history and no history.

Man is a member of the animal kingdom. Much can still be learned about the development and functioning of the various species through comparative study. However, comparative study necessarily implies comparison of both similarities and differences among species (53, 55, 56).

Behavior of animals lower on the evolutionary scale than man reveals "generalization" (47). For example, if a rat is trained to jump when presented a tone of 1000 cycles, he may also learn to respond to a 2000-cycle tone. Rats, raccoons, cats, monkeys, and chimpanzees have been trained to respond to various triangles as though they were equivalent. In other words, subhuman animals can be taught to respond to form *as such*.

Various animals have been studied in "delayed reaction" experiments in which the animal must wait for a period of time between perception of a goal object and actual discovery and attainment of it. Summarizing studies on chimpanzees, Yerkes and Nissen noted their dependence on spatial cues. When the experimenter eliminated the possibility of using spatial cues, delayed response became extremely difficult or impossible for most chimpanzees (77). Yerkes concluded that the difficulty was traceable to the fact that the chimpanzee lacked a "symbol or representative process" comparable to human words. A chimpanzee cannot say to himself, "The reward is under the green box," and remember this days later or weeks later, as a human subject can.

Symbols, in the limited sense of one thing "standing for" another, are not unique to human beings. Chimpanzees can be trained to use tokens to obtain food from a vending machine, and these tokens acquire reward value (16,75).

However, there are decided differences between the symbolic value of a food token for a chimpanzee and the symbolic value which similar objects acquire for human individuals. Yerkes cautioned against considering token behavior of chimpanzees as equivalent to linguistic processes of man or even as a "primary functional basis" for such processes (76). What are these differences? The token has symbolic value for the chimpanzee only by virtue of its exchange value for food (16). When no food is forthcoming for the tokens, they soon lose value for the animal.

On the other hand, human beings may collect and save objects with symbolic value (money, jewelry, precious metals) without direct regard for their immediate exchange value. Such objects acquire value for security, prestige, providing for coming generations, and other considerations which are not tied to immediate exchange value.

Symbolic Behavior and the Conceptual Level of Functioning

Typically, the symbolic behavior of subhuman animals is bound to specific and rather immediate perceptual situations. In contrast, man's capacities enable him to utilize and manipulate symbols in the absence of immediate stimuli and frequently over time spans of months or years. Man can utilize symbols apart from a specific perceptual context because of his capacity to form concepts which function as internal anchorages with an organized and enduring character.

For this reason it is useful to distinguish between symbolic reactions which are *perceptually symbolic* and those which are *conceptually symbolic*. The achievement of a conceptually symbolic level makes possible a standardized language system, an achievement which is unique to mankind among all animals. It makes possible the formation of concepts which encompass increasingly broader ranges of specific objects and situations. This vastly increased scope of generalization has been illustrated in the form of various steps from immediate stimulus situations to increasingly broader and more abstract generalizations. Figure 14.9 shows such a representation.

What accounts for the development of the conceptually symbolic level in man? It is surely not just his organs of speech. As Sapir noted, man's organs of speech are not entirely distinctive and have other physiological functions. They are employed for other ends as well as for speech (52).

Man's capacity to function on a conceptual level stems largely from the increased size and complexity of his cerebral cortex, in comparison with the higher apes (54). With the physiological difference, different processes underlie human conceptual developments and activities.

Studies of brain lesions, degeneration of cortical tissue from disease, and surgery which involves serious disturbance or removal of cortical tissue typically reveal some impairment in the ability which is ordinarily called "abstract thinking" or "abstract reasoning" (34). The implication is that the relationship between man's conceptual functioning and cortical processes is close and rather direct.

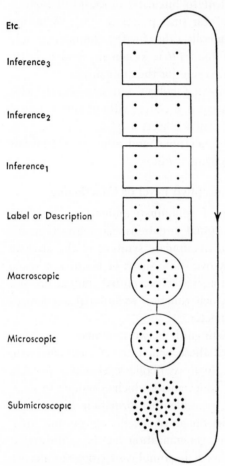

Etc.

Inference₃

Inference₂

Inference₁

Label or Description

Macroscopic

Microscopic

Submicroscopic

Fig. 14.9. Schematic diagram of the process of abstracting. (From Wendell Johnson, *People in Quandaries*. New York: Harper & Brothers, 1946. Adapted from A. Korzybski, *Science and Sanity*. Lancaster, Pa.: The Science Press, rev. ed., 1941.)

Significance of Conceptual Functioning

For nine months the Kellogs raised their own son and an infant chimpanzee together (32). Gua (the chimpanzee) developed more rapidly and surpassed the boy in many respects. Gua was ahead of Donald in learning to coöperate, to obey adults, to open doors, in toilet training, eating with a spoon, and responding to human commands. But by the time Donald was 2, he was beginning to speak and to surpass Gua in other respects with ease. In the end, Gua could only become a well-trained chimpanzee. Donald could become a socialized human adult.

If the conceptual level of functioning is treated as just "another factor" to be added to the results of animal studies, the approach to human behavior is a sort of anthropomorphism in reverse. Perhaps this approach to understanding human behavior can be typified as "zoömorphism." The heterogeneous and pervasive conceptual functions of man are reduced to symbolic responses of a rat or chimpanzee.

A chimpanzee can learn to use tools and mechanical devices. But he does not conceptualize the relationships involved in tool using. He cannot create new tools, accumulate them, and pass them on to future generations (73). This is one important example of the way in which conceptual functioning transforms the process and the significance of an organism's interaction with its environment.

Interaction among human individuals typically utilizes standardized concepts and communication with others on the basis of these common concepts. The reader is referred to Schneirla's brief and lucid summary of "social transmission" and human communication for a comparison of interaction in insect, chimpanzee, and human aggregates (57).

The vastly increased capacity of the human organism to function conceptually is basic to the standardization of language in human groups, to the development and accumulation of material and nonmaterial culture, to the transmission of these in the form of a cultural heritage from generation to generation. The cultural heritage is not transmitted biologically. The process of cultural transmission takes place on a social basis and is inconceivable without language. It makes possible the formation of a whole system of human wants and desires which are uniquely human and genuinely social motives.

LEARNING TO COMMUNICATE

A normal human infant is born with potentialities which underlie the conceptual level of functioning. There are at least two general conditions for his attainment of this conceptual level. The first apparently involves maturation of a normal central nervous system. The second involves learning through interaction in a social environment with other people who communicate through language. In this section the trends of development and learning to communicate are sketched with emphasis on their implications for socialization.

The infant's earliest sounds are primarily expressive of his affective states and needs and are directed only secondarily toward other persons. The vocalizations which adults call his "first word" usually appear within a few months before or after his first birthday. They are almost always babbling sounds which are stabilized chiefly through adult interpretations of the child's expressive use of them and by existing forms of "nursery speech" (36). From the very beginning, therefore, the child's acquisition of words is a two-way process. Both the child and older persons take part in interaction.

At first, new words are added very slowly, even though adults typically encourage the process. The acquisition of words seems to proceed at first largely on a "trial-and-error" basis. These early words are not concepts in the sense that they refer to a more or less well-defined category of objects. Rather they are categories which are broad and exceedingly flexible. They are understandable in terms of their significance to the child and may seem almost meaningless to adults.

For example, one child called all animals he saw, including cats, dogs, birds, and frogs, "see-see." This was his own version of the name of the family cat. Another child learned "bible" and applied this name to all books (48). At the age of 19 months a child learned to say "mooi" when looking at the moon. This term was later used for cakes, round marks on the window, writing on the window, writing on paper, round marks on books, tooling on book covers, faces, postmarks, and the letter O (13).

Guillaume's son learned to say "ato" (*marteau*) for hammer and soon applied the word to the following assortment of items: buttonhook, hand mirror, comb, handbag, saucepan, hairpin, wooden spade, keys, gun, box, belt, purse, ruler, puttees, basin, safety pin, candlestick, coffee mill, plate, and spoon (22). This assortment seems to have nothing in common. But to the child it did. These were all objects which he saw adults *use* to do something.

Such early words refer to items which are similar to the child in some respect (36). The similarities may be simply in terms of appearance (like "mooi" for round and curved patterns). They may be in terms of affective or motivational significance ("joos" for anything to drink or "mama" for anyone who cares for him). They may be in terms of the function which objects have in his own or his grownups' activities ("ato" for hammer, buttonhook, and so on).

At this time, words are largely an accompaniment for other forms of activity. As the child learns that his sounds make a difference to others and have consequences for his activities, his words begin to refer more clearly to definite classes of objects or situations. However, it is some time before these words acquire conventional meanings that approximate those of adults.

On one hand, conventionalization of meaning comes about under the urgency of the child's wish to bring other individuals into a situation to satisfy his desires, to secure help in some activity, or to have their company. On the other hand, conventionalization is encouraged by adults through assistance, correctives, and pressures toward this end.

"The Naming Stage"

Studies of children's vocabulary development consistently reveal a general trend (18, 42), which may be summarized as follows:

After the first year of life, words are acquired by the child rather slowly. For example, in one study, children at 1 year of age used an average of 3 words. Half a year later, the average number was 19 words. At 1 year and 9 months the average was only 22 words (59). Then toward the end of the second year or the beginning of the third, a rapid increase in vocabulary occurs. In the study mentioned above, the average vocabulary increased from 22 words at 21 months to 272 words 7 months later (Fig. 12.2). Of course, the absolute number of words varies somewhat from study to study, depending on the children and techniques used for counting words. However, the trend is consistently similar.

It is this period, roughly somewhere between 18 and 36 months, which has been called "the naming stage" (42). The child characteristically asks many "what" questions in his own style. They may consist of pointing with a primitive verbalization, like the "eh-eh-eh" which Lewis observed in his son. They may be persistent "What's dis?" and "What's dat?" which ceases only when adults give a name for the object.

The child's behavior at this time indicates the achievement of a generalization which cuts across specific sensory modalities. This can be expressed in the phrase "things have names." (Needless to say, the child himself does not ordinarily verbalize this notion during this period.)

This period of rapid development and the discovery that "everything has a name" is closely linked to the increasing acceptance and use of words as a means of motive satisfaction, of securing help, of bringing other people into his activities through communicating with them. In addition to the rather specific rewards the child achieves through the instrumental uses of words (like a cookie, a play period, a toy), his grownups grant more general satisfactions in the form of approval and attention. A child is welcomed, perhaps even pushed, into the speaking community.

From both specific and more general sources, a new striving appears in the child's motivational repertory—a striving to learn the names of things. These strivings help to keep the process of learning to communicate going; but they do not entirely account for the spurt in vocabulary development.

Why does this rapid increase occur so characteristically sometime toward the end of the second year of life in normal children? In summarizing the known behavioral facts concerning early vocabulary development, Carmichael concluded that the child's discovery "that all objects have names" is undoubtedly preceded by a period of maturation and involves some new coördination at the cortical level (10).

The significance of these developments for the socialization process can hardly be overestimated. With the discovery that "things have names," the child takes the first preliminary step away from a level in which behavior is dominated by his immediate needs and bound to immediate objects and situations. Words rapidly supplement and then replace other forms of behavior. Not only the meanings of the words acquired but the significance of language in his perception, learning, and other aspects of his psychological functioning develops and changes.

Perceptual and Conceptual Development

A child's early words are closely tied to what he has seen, handled, used, and experienced in other ways. Like his early perceptions, his first words are broad and undifferentiated. Like his perception of the world, the child's acquisition of words is selective, reflecting his desires and affective states. His earliest words are almost always names for objects or persons with motivational significance (18, 42).

Because early learning of words is tied so closely to what the child is exposed to, the vocabulary of children in restricted environments increases more slowly than that of children situated more favorably (42). Likewise, travel and new experiences may lead to accelerated vocabulary increase (7).

While learning words is at first limited and regulated by the child's perceptions, his perceptions are, in turn, reacted upon by his acquisitions of concepts. In the early period, children are most interested in persons, objects, and their uses and their words reflect this preoccupation. The definitions of words at the early age levels on standard intelligence tests are in terms of use. (An orange is "what we have for breakfast.")

Children notice and become interested in qualities and characteristics of things somewhat later. They usually begin to acquire adjectives to describe objects after they have learned a stock of names for objects (12,

42). Discrimination of qualities of things becomes more precise after some adjectives and adverbs are acquired. On intelligence tests like the Stanford-Binet, discrimination of size comes at about the 4-year-old level and discrimination of color and weight at about the 5-year-old level.

In the preschool years, however, the qualities and characteristics of objects are closely tied to the object itself. If a preschool child is persuaded to change the name of, say, "dog" to "cow," he proceeds to talk about the object (the dog) as though it really were a cow—having horns, giving milk, and so on (63). At this age a child with long hair not only appears to another child as a girl; long hair *makes* the child a girl. His language and his thinking about objects tend to be fused with his perception of them.

Under 2 years of age, a child can generalize the word "chair" to a folded chair, or "ball" to a collapsed ball (69). But this ability is confined to clearly perceivable objects. Even when he is trained by a grownup, he experiences great difficulty in learning more abstract concepts referring to classes based on some relation or quality of objects (70). A concept like "metal" appears fairly late and is used accurately only when the child's "mental age" reaches about 11 years (68).

It is significant that verbs refer at first to the immediate situations in which the child finds himself (1, 37). Anyone who has watched a young child in his early attempts to talk of past and future knows how difficult it is for him to gain any precision at all. At first, past and future refer only to the very near past and immediate future. Having no precise terms to locate distant events, one term often serves the purpose for all past and one for all future times. One of our children used "yesterday" for all past times and "next day" for any possible future time. Precise reference to past and future depends on acquiring appropriate words and, ultimately, concepts of number and time.

Implications for Socialization

Once the child attains the level of development and experience indicated by the notion that "things have names," the slow trial-and-error encounters with objects and situations which are more characteristic of subhuman animals and human infants are replaced to an increasing extent. Much learning occurs on a deductive basis. Responses to whole groups of objects and persons are acquired and differentiated by learning a name or concept.

This telescoping of the learning process makes it possible for children to learn the various aspects of their social and cultural heritage in the form of short-cut dicta. Frequently the child's concepts of objects, persons, and relationships in the social world are attained more through the pronouncements of older persons than by actual contact with specific stimulus characteristics. Such adult pronouncements embody the social norms of their group, which are special cases of concepts.

Even though young children may have little or no contact with Negroes, Hindus, or Turks, they do acquire concepts of these groups which carry value judgments of them and attribute certain characteristics to members. Without having seen an American Indian, children learn a concept of this group through books and radio. Within the space of a comparatively few years a child is able to acquire social concepts accumulated by his group over long periods of its history.

It is this acquisition of concepts about other objects, people, and relationships that enables the child to form attitudes relating himself psychologically to his social environment. By around the end of the second year of life most American children can refer to themselves by name and as "me" or "I." They can talk about things as "mine." "You" becomes a clear designation for another person. Usually last of all, during about the third year, the notion of "we" appears. The attainment of these more accurate distinctions between himself and other people permits also more definite notions of relatedness between himself and others. He forms appropriate attitudes concerning himself as a person with definite relationships to other people and with groups. Of course, this process occurs slowly. It is the process of ego formation.

Therefore, the very development of a personal identity is dependent upon the attainment of concepts and learning of language. In this fashion, a child takes the social heritage of his group as his own. Its distinctions and its values or norms are personally acquired in the process of interaction with other people and are experienced personally.

Development Without Language

Isabelle was reared by her mother, who was a deaf-mute. She and her mother were confined to a single room until she was about 6 years old, by which time she had learned no language. To the psychologists who examined her at about this time, Isabelle seemed strange—more like an infant, or even an animal, than a 6-year-old child.

Initially, it seemed that Isabelle must not have normal human capacities at all. However, the child was given training by specialists to see what could be done. In two years she not only had learned to talk but had a vocabulary of almost 2000 words. Slowly her behavior and whole manner were transformed. By the time she was 14, she had completed elementary school and acted like a "normal" child.

The case of Isabelle, which was reported by Davis (*17*), is among the more clear-cut evidence that human socialization and human "personality" development are to a large extent dependent on the acquisition of language. As we have seen, this conclusion was also indicated in tracing the development of normal children.

Lindesmith and Strauss have brought together a variety of examples of children whose opportunities to learn language were limited by lack of contact with speaking adults or, like Helen Keller, by their being both blind and deaf themselves (*39*). Such cases show changes in behavior in the direction of organized social forms following the acquisition of language, thus corroborating the trends noted in the socialization of normal children.

CONCEPTS IN FORMATION

Experiments on Concept Formation

In psychology there is a definite line of research which is identified as the study of concept formation. Experiments on concept formation have proceeded along certain definite lines using very similar methods (*64*).

Typically, an individual is shown a series of objects or drawings. Certain stimuli in the series have elements, patterns, objects, or other characteristics in common. The subject may be told that he is taking part in a memory experiment and be required to learn nonsense syllables as names for the stimulus series. Then he is shown a second series of stimuli which has something in common with the first, and is asked to name the second series correctly, using the nonsense names he has learned. Or he may simply be told to classify or sort those items which "belong" together.

The concepts which the subject is supposed to discover may be ones he already possesses in his repertory, like names of familiar objects, numbers, or forms. They may refer to some abstract or unfamiliar arrangements of lines or shapes.

Usually the individual's only source of motivation is his possible desire to do well in the task. Some studies have used children as subjects and have given concrete rewards, like candy.

The findings from this line of approach have revealed, in general, a slow trial-and-error process, development of hunches or hypotheses, and sometimes the sudden solutions usually taken as indicative of insightful learning.

Some interesting results have come from such studies. For example, Hull noted the importance of "set" produced by calling the individual's attention to elements common to various stimuli in the series (29). Heidbreder's findings in a series of experiments indicate the crucial significance of the perceptual situation. The greatest ease in concept formation was found in relation to concrete objects, as contrasted to more abstract relationships (24). It will be recalled that this general trend is found in the acquisition of conventional names by children. In addition, various situational factors, like the order of presentation of the stimulus series and the inclusion of negative as well as positive instances in the stimulus series, have been studied.

Some Neglected Characteristics of Concept Formation

The traditional line of concept-formation studies has been severely limited in its implications for concept formation in social life. Its limitations are imposed by at least three characteristics of concept formation in actual life which have been neglected in such studies:

First, after a child reaches the "naming stage" in which he discovers that "things have names," his learning of concepts is not solely on the basis of repeated exposure to stimuli whose common elements he must discover individually on an inductive basis. As we have seen, he also acquires concepts by learning a name in relation to certain stimuli and subsequently applying that name to similar objects, persons, or situations.

Second, the concept formation of both children and adults occurs first and most prominently in relation to objects or situations which have some motivational or functional significance to the individual. Once linguistic behavior achieves instrumental value to the child, he acquires concepts for use in dealing with and communicating about significant aspects of his environment.

A striking illustration of the importance of such motivational factors is provided by children who develop categories and names which are peculiar to them, based on distinctions which have meaning in their own little activities. For example, Watts (68) reported that a 16-months-old boy he observed found that certain things he used were sufficiently alike to be conveniently referred to with one name. The child called all portable objects with handles *yo-yos*. *Yo-yos* with lids were called *go-gos*.

As a corollary to the second point, concept formation in real life is typically not a strictly individual process but takes place in social interaction with other human beings. Concept formation has value to the individual not only in terms of his interests and desires but for communicating with others.

Even without adult intervention, young children sometimes standardize unique labels in interaction and use them to refer to distinctions important in their play. Jespersen (*31*) reported that twin boys 5½ years old who were frequently left to shift for themselves developed a whole set of words which only they understood. They communicated with each other using these words, even though they sounded like "gibberish" to adults.

As a matter of fact, such unique standardizations by twins are sufficiently common to be noted in standard texts on "speech defects" (*8, 62*). In one family the twins used a word *tedaden* to mean "climb upon." *Ding-a-ding* was used by the same children to mean "trade" or "you give me what you have and I'll give you what I have" (*33*).

Such childish standardizations ordinarily pass into oblivion, partly because adults encourage the use of conventional speech forms. In addition, the motivations and events crystallized by children in such unique forms are often more or less transitory and are left behind as they pass on to new interests and pursuits. Their significance for the present problem is that they represent concepts formed by interacting individuals which are developed for communicating about items and events of mutual concern in their activities.

A Study on Standardization of Names

With these characteristics of concept formation in actual life in mind, the authors carried out a study in 1948 on the formation and standardization of names by young children who had some instrumental use of language (*58*).

The following hypotheses are suggested by such characteristics:

1. If an individual attempts to deal with an unnamed object with motivational value to him in a situation requiring communication to attain the object, he will name it and will use this name consistently in referring to it.
2. When individuals interact in a group activity in relation to an unnamed object with motivational value to all of them in a situation which re-

quires communication to attain the object, the object will be named
and this name will become standardized for each individual.
3. Names stabilized by individuals and in group interaction will be used
instrumentally in communication with others.

In order to demonstrate that these hypotheses are plausible ones, preschool children were shown toys for which they had no names. In order
to get a toy, it was necessary to request it from the experimenter. No
particular kind of verbal response was required, but the situation was arranged so that the children could not point to the object or get it themselves. They received it by any request which differentiated the unnamed
toy in any way from others also available.

Twenty-two children took part individually with the experimenter.
Twenty-seven other children took part in groups of two or three. The
children were from poorer economic groups. Thus, it was possible to present highly attractive toys which they had not seen before and for which
they had no conventional names. Most children were kindergarten age
(about 5 years); a few in the individual sessions had attended the first
grade in elementary school.

A label or name was considered standardized (1) when it had been
used by the child at least three times successively without the intervention of other verbal responses in relation to the object and (2) when the
child responded to the name accurately when it was used by the experimenter afterward. In the group situations, it was required that each subject use the name at least three times and respond to it accurately.

In both individual and group situations, each child participated in
four sessions on different days. In the last session, every subject was alone
with the experimenter in order that his acceptance of the label could
be checked through his response to the adult's use of it.

RESULTS OF INDIVIDUAL SESSIONS: In the individual sessions, four unnamed toys were presented in order that at least one would appeal to
every subject. Twenty of the 22 subjects standardized a total of 44 labels
for the toys. Eighteen of these labels were names—one word used for a
toy for which they had no name at the outset. Nine of the labels were
brief descriptive phrases—a "one" or "thing" designation plus an adjective
(e.g., "wire one" or "red thing"). Seventeen were descriptive phrases of
three to five words (e.g., "all red one" or "one that winds up"). One of the
findings was that longer phrases of more than four or five words were sim-

ply not standardized. A suggestive tendency was noted for subjects to request objects they named more frequently than objects they did not name.

These findings demonstrated the tendency to stabilize names for desired but unfamiliar objects for purposes of communication and to utilize these names in referring to the objects. Once a name was stabilized, the child responded accurately to its use by the experimenter in every instance.

RESULTS OF GROUP SESSIONS: In the group situations, data pertain to one toy which was unnamed and was conducive to coöperative activities among kindergarten children. The toy was a model bucket-loader built of green metal with a black conveyor belt. It stood about 16 inches high. The toy could be loaded with sand and moved, and the sand could be caught in a receptacle and carried away. Sand and auxiliary toys were provided to make this coöperative activity possible.

The data are summarized in Table 14.1. The names adopted were all words which existed in the children's vocabulary. However, the initial reactions of different children in a group were in no case identical. Before a name was standardized for the group, there was considerable confusion and active effort in talking about the toy.

On the basis of the data at the right in the table pertaining to the subject who first used the particular label standardized and the correctives made by the children in standardizing the term, the following description is typical of the process:

One child, typically the one who most frequently initiated activity in the play situation, gave a name to the unnamed toy in his efforts to coordinate group play around it. The name for the object was useful to him in assuming a directive role in play activities. Therefore, when the other children used different words and phrases to refer to the toy, he tended to correct them verbally. For example, if one said "that big, big thing," he would respond "you mean ———," giving the label he had used. Eventually other children responded and sometimes corrected others. When a name was thus standardized, it was used consistently in play activities and in every case responded to accurately when later used by the experimenter outside of the group setting.

It should be noted that Groups 1 and 2 each standardized the same label. This occurred because subjects B (Group 1) and E (Group 2) communicated about the toy outside of the experimental situation before Group 2 participated in the experiment.

The names standardized in each group had a categorizing effect such

TABLE 14.1. Standardization of Names in Group Interaction

Group	Standardized Response (Name)	Time of Standard- ization[a] (Minutes)	No. Times Name Used by Each S	Subject First Using Name	Correctives From To No.		
1	"big green thing"	67	B—6 N—3	B	B	N	3
2	"big green thing"	64	E—8 C—3 F—3	E	E E	C F	1 1
3	"derrick"	20	G—7 J—3 M—3	G	G	J	1
4	"steps"	5	D—5 R—4 P—4	D			0
5	"erector"	30	G—7 R—4	G	G	R	3
6	"tractor"	10	A—6 L—11	A	A L	L A	6 3
7	"steamshovel"	20	M—5 V—3 A—2[b]	M	M	V	1

[a] Time of standardization was reckoned from the first exposure of the stimulus object to the exclusion of all designations for the unnamed object other than the name adopted by the group. Time from exposure to the first use of the name ultimately standardized ranged from one to five minutes.

[b] Subject A in Group 7 was present only for sessions 1, 2, and 4.

that members of different groups (except Groups 1 and 2) could not communicate about the toy. During the third session a member of Group 7 said: "J—— [in Group 3] said yesterday you didn't have no steamshovel in here when they came in to play. Didn't you?" Group 3, of which J—— was a member, called the toy a "derrick."

Thus, the group sessions demonstrated the tendency for individuals interacting in group activities to *standardize* names for novel and desired objects in order to deal with these objects and *communicate* with each other about them.

Concept Formation in Actual Life

The proposal that concept formation typically occurs in the process of interaction in response to new objects or situations which have motivational significance, and that the concepts are standardized for the purpose of communicating with others, is not new or startling. The study summarized in the last section was essentially an attempt to duplicate happenings of real life within a more restricted research setting.

Gangs of youngsters in large cities invariably standardize terms and phrases which refer to more or less unique situations and relationships they deal with. In prisons, at least a portion of the prison argot originates in the prison situation. A large share of these words pertain to prominent aspects of the prison life, notably relations between prisoners and prison officials and sexual activities in the depriving prison setting (*14*).

Lewis concluded that the development of "special languages" within the framework of a larger society is a phenomenon found throughout the history of language. "Whenever men are organized into groups for the purposes of specific action, they tend to develop a language foreign in some measure to the language of the larger society in which they move" (*38*, p. 48).

In time of war, thousands of people are faced with new objects, new problems and situations of great significance to them. Many new names and terms are standardized in group interaction and spread through the armed services. Such new terms have been noted in both the American (*19*) and the British armed services (*30*). In the British services, 240 entirely new words were reported during the early period of World War II, and in addition hundreds of existing words were put to new uses.

New editions of standard dictionaries reveal the constant additions being made to vocabulary with the introduction of new cultural elements and changed situations. The second edition of *Webster's New International Dictionary* contains examples of such new words. Some of these are illustrated in Figure 14.10. Appearing at the close of World War II, half of the new words concerned airplanes and bombing raids (*51*). New labor-management problems, new sports, and new styles of music are revealed in a number of new terms.

It is evident that the formation of concepts, like children's learning to communicate through conventionalized language, is a social process in

GREMLIN: Impish, foot-high gnome, reported by airmen

SOAP OPERA: A radio serial drama—chiefly for housewives

DIRNDL: Dress with full skirt imitative of peasant costume

JITTERBUG: Devotee of swing— impelled to wild gesticulations

JUKE BOX: Automatic player of records (Orig. Southern U.S.)

SLAP-HAPPY: (From pugilism, slang, U.S.) Witless, punch-drunk

FIG. 14.10. Examples of new words which appeared in the second edition of *Webster's International Dictionary*. (Adapted from C. D. Rice, Do you speak English?, *This Week Magazine*, December 1, 1946. Copyright, 1946, by the United Newspapers Magazine Corporation.)

which the motivations of the participants, interaction among them, and the functional use of the linguistic response in communication are essential.

CONCLUDING REMARKS

Language concepts are generalizations standardized in group interaction and shared by members of a human group for purposes of communicating with each other. In this sense, language is a distinctly human product. Man's capacity to function on a conceptually symbolic level is made possible by his biological endowment. His attainment of this level during his life history is dependent on maturation and development in a social setting and learning to communicate with others in this setting.

Both in learning a conventional language and in forming new concepts, the motivational significance of objects, situations, or events faced by individuals interacting with each other and the function of words in communication typically have crucial importance. These aspects have frequently been neglected in traditional studies of concept formation and in many accounts of language acquisition.

Early in life a human child reaches a level of development and experience in which the generalization that "things have names" is possible. This achievement is marked by a rapid acceleration in learning words. From this time it becomes possible, through acquiring new words, to reduce trial-and-error learning of concepts. Once a name is learned, particular items are subsumed under it and are attributed the characteristics denoted by the name. This short-cut learning through language permits the child to acquire major categories for the social world standardized in his group without the necessity in all cases of direct contact with the stimulus items in question. Acquiring language is basic to his socialization.

Once learned, words tend to have a categorizing effect on experience and behavior. They function as clear-cut, organized, and enduring anchorages for the individual's perceiving, judging, and other aspects of his experience and behavior.

REFERENCES

1. Adams, S. Analysis of verb forms in the speech of young children and their relation to the language learning process, *J. exper. Educat.* (1938), 7:141–144.
2. American Council on Education, *The Story of Numbers*. Washington: Achievements of Civilization, No. 2, 1932.
3. American Council on Education, *The Story of Weights and Measures*. Washington: Achievements of Civilization, No. 3, 1932.
4. American Council on Education, *Telling Time Throughout the Centuries*. Washington: Achievements of Civilization, No. 5, 1933.
5. Bartlett, F. C. *Remembering: A Study in Experimental and Social Psychology*. Cambridge: University Press, 1932.
6. Barton, R. F. *The Half Way Sun*. New York: Brewer and Warren, 1930.
7. Bean, C. H. An unusual opportunity to investigate the psychology of language, *J. genet. Psychol.* (1932), 40:181–202.
8. Berry, M. F., and Eisenson, J. *The Defective in Speech*. New York: Crofts, 1945, pp. 277–278.
9. Buck, P. H. *Ethnology of Mangarena*. Honolulu: B. P. Bishop Museum, Bull. No. 157, 1938.
10. Carmichael, L. Growth and Development, in E. G. Boring, H. S. Langfeld, and H. P. Weld (eds.), *Foundations of Psychology*. New York: Wiley, 1948.
11. Carmichael, L., Hogan, H. P., and Walter, A. A. An experimental study of the effect of language on the reproduction of visually perceived form, *J. exper. Psychol.* (1932), 15:73–86.
12. Carroll, J. B. Determining and numerating adjectives in children's speech, *Child Developm.* (1939), 10:214–229.
13. Chamberlain, A. F., and Chamberlain, I. C. Studies of a child. I. *Pedagog. Sem.* (1904), 11.
14. Clemmer, D. *The Prison Community*. Boston: Christopher, 1940.
15. Cook, S. W., and Harris, R. E. The verbal conditioning of the galvanic skin reflex, *J. exper. Psychol.* (1937), 21:202–210.

16. Cowles, J. T. Food-tokens as incentives for learning by chimpanzees, *Compar. Psychol. Monogr.* (1937), *14*, No. 5.

17. Davis, K. Final note on a case of extreme isolation, *Amer. J. Sociol.* (1947), 52:432–437.

18. Dewey, E. *Behavior Development in Infants*. New York: Columbia University Press, 1935.

19. Elkin, F. The soldier's language, *Amer. J. Sociol.* (1946), 51:414–422.

20. Gibson, J. J. The reproduction of visually perceived forms, *J. exper. Psychol.* (1929), 12:1–39.

21. Goodenough, F. L., and Brian, C. R. Certain factors underlying the acquisition of motor skill by pre-school children, *J. exper. Psychol.* (1929), 12:127–155.

22. Guillaume, P. Les débuts de la phrase chez l'enfant, *J. de Psychol.* (1927), 24.

23. Hallowell, A. I. Cultural Factors in the Structuralization of Perception, in J. H. Rohrer and M. Sherif (eds.), *Social Psychology at the Crossroads*. New York: Harper, 1951.

24. Heidbreder, E. Toward a dynamic psychology of cognition, *Psychol. Rev.* (1945), 52:1–22.

25. Hilgard, E. R., Campbell, A. A., and Sears, W. N. Development of discrimination with or without verbal report, *Amer. J. Psychol.* (1937), 49:564–580.

26. Hocart, A. M. The "psychological interpretation of language," *Brit. J. Psychol.* (1912), 5:267–279.

27. Holmberg, A. M. The Siriono: A study of the effect of hunger frustration on the culture of a semi-nomadic Bolivian Indian tribe. Doctorate dissertation, Yale University, 1946.

28. Hovland, C. I. Human Learning and Retention, in S. S. Stevens (ed.), *Handbook of Experimental Psychology*. New York: Wiley, 1951.

29. Hull, C. L. Quantitative aspects of the evolution of concepts: an experimental study, *Psychol. Monogr.* (1920), 28, No. 123.

30. Hunt, J. L., and Pringle, A. G. *Service Slang*. London, 1943; reported in M. M. Lewis (38).

31. Jespersen, O. *Language, Its Nature, Development, and Origin*. New York: Holt, 1923, pp. 185–186.

32. Kellog, W. N., and Kellog, L. A. *The Ape and the Child*. New York: McGraw-Hill, 1933.

33. Keys, John W. Personal communication from Professor Keys, director of Speech Clinic, University of Oklahoma.

34. Klebanoff, S. G., Singer, J. S., and Wilensky, H. Psychological consequences of brain lesions and ablations, *Psychol. Bull.* (1954), 51:1–41.

35. Kluckhohn, C., and Leighton, D. *The Navaho*. Cambridge: Harvard University Press, 1946.
36. Lewis, M. M. *Infant Speech*. New York: Harcourt, Brace, 1936.
37. Lewis, M. M. The beginning of reference to past and future in a child's speech, *Brit. J. educat. Psychol.* (1937), 7:39–56.
38. Lewis, M. M. *Language in Society, The Linguistic Revolution and Social Change*. New York: Social Sciences Publishers, 1948.
39. Lindesmith, A. R., and Strauss, A. L. Men Without Symbols, in *Social Psychology*. New York: Dryden, 1949.
40. Long, L., and Welch, L. Reasoning ability of young children, *J. Psychol.* (1941), 12:21–44.
41. Long, L., and Welch, L. Influence of level of abstraction on reasoning ability, *J. Psychol.* (1942), 13:41–59.
42. McCarthy, D. Language Development in Children, in L. Carmichael (ed.), *Manual of Child Psychology*. New York: Wiley, 1946; rev. ed., 1954.
43. McGranahan, D. V. The psychology of language, *Psychol. Bull.* (1936), 33:178–216.
44. Malinowski, B. The Problem of Meaning in Primitive Languages, in C. K. Ogden and I. A. Richards, *The Meaning of Meaning*. New York: Harcourt, Brace, 1930.
45. Merker, F. *Die Masai*. Berlin, 1904.
46. Miller, N. E., and Dollard, J. *Social Learning and Imitation*. New Haven: Yale University Press, 1941, p. 61.
47. Morgan, C. T. *Physiological Psychology*. New York: McGraw-Hill, 1943.
48. Morgan, J. H. B. *Child Psychology*. New York: Richard R. Smith, 1931.
49. Morris, Charles. *Language and Behavior*. New York: Prentice-Hall, 1946.
50. Pyles, M. K. Verbalization as a factor in learning, *Child Developm.* (1932), 3:108–113.
51. Rice, C. D. Do you speak English? *This Week Magazine*, December 1, 1946.
52. Sapir, E. *Language. An Introduction to the Study of Speech*. New York: Harcourt, Brace, 1921.
53. Schneirla, T. C. Problems in the biopsychology of social organization, *J. abnorm. & soc. Psychol.* (1946), 41:385–402.
54. Schneirla, T. C. Psychology, Comparative, *Encyclopaedia Britannica*, 1948.
55. Schneirla, T. C. The "Levels" Concept in the Study of Social Organization in Animals, in J. H. Rohrer and M. Sherif (eds.), *Social Psychology at the Crossroads*. New York: Harper, 1951.
56. Schneirla, T. C. A consideration of some conceptual trends in comparative psychology, *Psychol. Bull.* (1952), 49:559–597.
57. Schneirla, T. C. The Concept of Levels in the Study of Social Phenome-

na, in M. Sherif and C. W. Sherif, *Groups in Harmony and Tension*. New York: Harper, 1953.

58. Sherif, M., and Sherif, C. W. The standardization of names. A neglected problem in the study of symbolic behavior. Unpublished manuscript, 1949. A summary by M. Sherif, Social Psychological Aspects of Conceptual Functioning, in F. S. C. Northrop and H. Morgenau (eds.), *Proceedings of Stillwater Conference*. Stillwater: Oklahoma A & M College, 1950.

59. Smith, M. E. An investigation of the development of the sentence and the extent of vocabulary in young children, *University of Iowa Studies in Child Welfare* (1926), 3, No. 5.

60. Spencer, B., and Gillen, F. J. *The Arunta. A Study of a Stone Age People*. London, 1927.

61. Thompson, L. M. The role of verbalization in learning from demonstrations. Dissertation, Yale University, 1944; summarized by Hovland (28).

62. Van Riper, C. *Speech Correction. Principles and Methods*. New York: Prentice-Hall, 1947, p. 105.

63. Vigotsky, L. S. Thought and speech, *Psychiatry* (1939), 2:29–54.

64. Vinacke, W. E. The investigation of concept formation, *Psychol. Bull.* (1951), 48:1–31.

65. Volkmann, J. Scales of Judgment and Their Implications for Social Psychology, in J. H. Rohrer and M. Sherif (eds.), *Social Psychology at the Crossroads*. New York: Harper, 1951.

66. Warden, C. J. The relative economy of various modes of attack in the mastery of the stylus maze, *J. exper. Psychol.* (1924), 7:243–275.

67. Waring, E. B. *The Relation Between Early Language Habits and Early Habits of Conduct Control*. New York: Teachers College Contributions to Education, No. 260, 1927.

68. Watts, A. F. *The Language and Mental Development of Children*. London: Harrap, 1944.

69. Welch, L. The span of generalization below the two year age level, *J. genet. Psychol.* (1939), 55:269–297.

70. Welch, L., and Long, L. The higher structural phases of concept formation of children, *J. Psychol.* (1940), 9:59–95.

71. Welch, L., and Long, L. Comparison of the reasoning ability of two age groups, *J. genet. Psychol.* (1943), 62:63–76.

72. Whiffen, T. *The North-West Amazons*. London, 1915.

73. White, L. A. On the use of tools by primates, *J. compar. Psychol.* (1942), 34:369–374.

74. Whorf, B. Science and linguistics, *Technology Rev.* (1940), 42, No. 6. Cambridge: Massachusetts Institute of Technology.

75. Wolfe, J. B. Effectiveness of token-rewards for chimpanzees, *Compar. Psychol. Monogr.* (1935), 13, No. 60.

76. Yerkes, R. M. *Chimpanzees, A Laboratory Colony.* New Haven: Yale University Press, 1943.

77. Yerkes, R. M., and Nissen, H. W. Pre-linguistic sign behavior in chimpanzees, *Science* (1939), 89:585–587.

78. Zangwill, O. L. A study of the significance of attitude in recognition, *Brit. J. Psychol.* (1938), 28:12–17.

CHAPTER 15

Social Attitudes

This chapter deals with social attitudes. First, we shall gain a general picture of the topic with special emphasis on the place of attitudes in socialized man. A brief analysis of attitude and behavior conforming to a social value or norm follows. Considered as sociogenic motives, attitudes will be differentiated from other motive states and internal factors in terms of specific criteria. Finally, we shall give summary accounts of major approaches to the measurement of attitudes. One developing approach is through subtle techniques utilizing judgmental and perceptual reactions to unstructured stimulus situations which are not presented as explicitly related to the attitude under study. The other approach studies attitudes through direct verbal statements. It is represented by the Bogardus, Thurstone, and Likert scales.

The chapters to follow will be concerned with attitude formation and change and with their functioning under various circumstances.

Social Attitudes

The problem of social attitudes, whether treated under this or some other heading, is a central concern in social psychology. During the last 40 years, much more has been published on various aspects of this problem than on any other topic, both by psychologists and by sociologists. Some authors have gone so far as to equate social psychology with the study of social attitudes.

There are good reasons for this insistence on the topic. The end product of the socialization process is embodied in social attitudes of the individual and in his words and deeds reflecting these attitudes. Man's day-to-day dealings with other persons, his interaction in groups, his dealing with cultural products all end up in the formation of definite attitudes in relation to them. Psychologically, no one is born a Methodist, a Baptist, a

488

Democrat, a Republican, a defender of management or labor, an upholder of free speech, an enthusiast of an Alma Mater. In each case, he becomes one. His becoming any one of these means his forming appropriate attitudes.

Forming an attitude toward a group, an institution, a social issue is not an idle matter. It means one is no longer neutral to them; they are value laden for him in a positive or a negative way. An attitude determines a certain expectation, standard, or goal, as the case may be. Events in line with it bring about satisfaction; events and things that are contrary to the attitude-determined expectations arouse dismay or dissatisfaction proportional to the place of that attitude in the individual's scheme of things.

Desirable or forbidden food objects in many cultures do not necessarily follow their nutritional value; certain animals and plants are marked as edible and others as not edible, as determined by social attitudes (see p. 403). To an orthodox Mohammedan or an orthodox Jew, pork is forbidden, undesirable, and "dirty." If you tell a devout member of such a group that what he unknowingly ate was pork, he may vomit.

People in different cultures have definite attitudes toward what is desirable to eat in the morning and at other times of the day. There is a social attitude toward what constitutes breakfast. An average American who includes cereal, juice, or bacon and eggs in his conception of a breakfast would miss something if he were offered rolls and coffee on successive mornings, as is the custom in several European countries.

If someone utters derogatory remarks about God in the presence of a good Baptist who has a strong attitude about religion, the offender will be seen as "obnoxious" and reacted to accordingly.

Thus, we see that a social attitude important in the person's scheme has the essential earmark of a motive. Such an attitude sets the person for or against things; defines what is preferred, expected, and desired; marks off what is undesirable, what is to be avoided. In terms of its consequences in the person's behavior, an attitude is goal directed. We can, therefore, legitimately refer to social attitudes as sociogenic motives (see pp. 403–406). When we were dealing with the development of children's preferences (Chapter 12), when we were discussing the stabilization of statuses within a group (Chapter 6), when we were dealing with in-group and out-group demarcation (Chapters 5, 9), with the rise of social norms (Chapter 8), with the rise of stereotypes toward out-groups (Chapter 9), we were dealing, on the psychological side, with the formation of social attitudes in these respects.

Man's Socialization Revealed Mainly Through His Attitudes

Attitudes are formed in relation to situations, persons, or groups with which the individual comes into contact in the course of his development. Once formed, they determine that the individual react in a *characteristic* way to these or related situations, persons, or groups. This characteristic feature, which is inferred from behavior (verbal or nonverbal), denotes a functional state of readiness in relation to stimulus situations which elicit it. There is merit in the concise characterization offered by Donald T. Campbell: "A *social attitude is (or is evidenced by) consistency in response to social objects*" (11, p. 31). As a rule, of course, this consistency of response revealing a social attitude is exhibited not by one individual alone but also by other fellow members of the group or society.

For example, when we see a person or group of persons react to a flag with respect repeatedly in a consistent way, we infer that they have an attitude toward the flag. When we see millions of people observe a certain day, say the Fourth of July, with certain words and deeds, we infer that they have an attitude toward that particular day. Likewise, people's preoccupation with and struggles toward obtaining certain objects (e.g., money), emulating certain persons (a superior, leader, actress), joining certain groups, seeking certain social positions may be cited as indices of their attitudes toward these objects.

The above examples apply to social attitudes. But not all of an individual's attitudes are social. We develop attitudes in relation to any stimulus object or situation (social or nonsocial), person or group with which we come into contact repeatedly. Since this invariably occurs after some encounters, we are seldom impartial in our reactions to situations or persons. We may develop a special liking for a particular bird, a special view, a special food. We may and do develop special likes and dislikes for friends, personal enemies or rivals, for special events peculiar to ourselves and determined by our motives and individualities.

Of course, our special concern in social psychology is with social attitudes. The feature that makes certain attitudes *social* is that they are formed in relation to social stimulus situations. We saw that social stimulus situations are persons, groups, and the products of human interaction —material and nonmaterial, i.e., the man-made environment of things, technological devices, and values or norms. Attitudes formed in relation to these constitute the main body of what is socialized in man.

The major feature that makes a man a good member of his particular reference group (be it a clique, a gang, a school, a church, a union, a nation) is the attitudes he forms in relation to it. The concrete signs that give an individual the characteristic imprint of his groups and his culture are, in terms of psychological units, the attitudes he reveals in concrete situations. For they are the psychological products *par excellence* of his socialization, that is, his becoming a Frenchman, an Eskimo, a Hopi, an American, a Chinese, etc. In short, man's socialization is revealed mainly in his attitudes formed in relation to the values or norms of his reference group or groups.

Some social psychologists refer to attitudes as "conforming behavior." They represent a social attitude by a curve, the J-curve, which graphically represents the distribution of the attitude in a representative sample of the group (1). Naturally the majority of the members reveal the social atti-

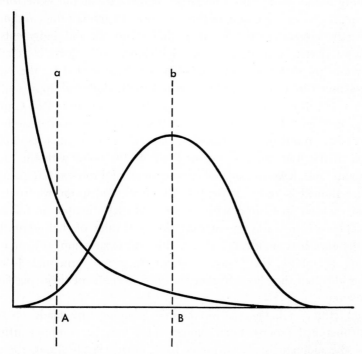

Fɪɢ. 15.1. "Two theoretical behavior distributions and their medians. Distribution A is J-shaped, distribution B is normal. The dotted lines *a* and *b* represent the medians of the two distributions." (Reprinted from *Psychology at Work*, edited by Paul S. Achilles, by permission of McGraw-Hill Book Company, Inc. Copyright, 1932, McGraw-Hill Book Company, Inc.)

tude in question and are lumped together at one end; the curve for the rest of the group tapers off to the other end, the degree of *deviation* increasing and the number of cases decreasing as the curve moves toward the opposite extremity (see Figs. 15.1 and 15.2).

The concept "conforming behavior" is itself suggestive in relation to our discussion of social stimulus situations. The characterizing word, "conforming," explicitly denotes that the behavior is so designated in relation to a standard or norm. One cannot speak of conformity if there is no standard, no norm to conform to. As social psychologists, we must make a special issue of the standard or norm of the group in question if we do not want to remain in complete confusion concerning the stimulus.

J-CURVE AND REFERENCE GROUPS: Knowledge of the stimulus *first* gives us a vantage point from which to examine the group in question and the prevailing norms in it. This knowledge prepares us, at the same time, to be aware, from the beginning, of the existence of varying values and norms in different groups. Evidence shows that standards and judgments are subject to shifts, even for the same individual, with shifts in reference groups (see pp. 624–628). The quantification represented by the J-curve acquires much more meaning after such a methodological approach.

The distributions for Catholics, Protestants, Jews, and "No Church" samples in Figure 15.2 would be much more meaningful if subjected to an analysis in terms of the reference groups of the individual respondents in each of the four samples. Let us illustrate the point with the case of Protestants and Jews. If the reference groups of Protestant respondents were ascertained in terms of Baptist, Unitarian, and so on, we would obtain for each group J-curves with the peak of each distribution falling on a particular category and representing the focal value of that group. Likewise, the Jewish respondents, who in this particular sample did not give anything resembling the J-curve distribution, would form such J-shaped distributions had they been further classified in terms of their specific reference groups.

Broad ethnic, religious, socioeconomic groupings are made up of so many functional groups. Even though there may be common attitudes among the individuals placed under these broad classifications, there are also ascertainable differences in attitudes or stands taken by different functional group units composing the larger society or strata. Frequently, it is these functional units which constitute the reference groups from which attitudes of individual members are actually derived. Analysis of an individual's conformity in attitude and behavior to social values or norms

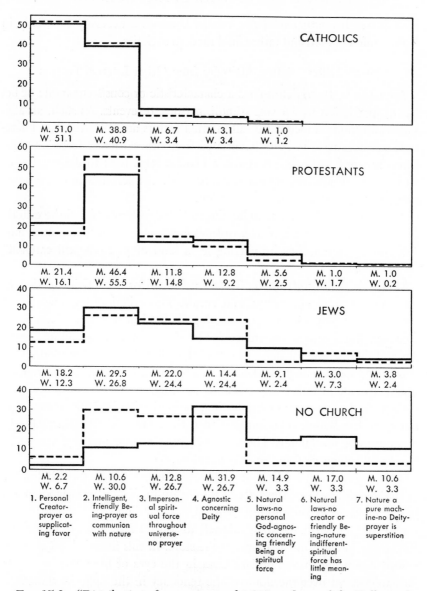

	1. Personal Creator-prayer as supplicating favor	2. Intelligent, friendly Being-prayer as communion with nature	3. Impersonal spiritual force throughout universe-no prayer	4. Agnostic concerning Deity	5. Natural laws-no personal God-agnostic concerning friendly Being or spiritual force	6. Natural laws-no creator or friendly Being-nature indifferent-spiritual force has little meaning	7. Nature a pure machine-no Deity-prayer is superstition
CATHOLICS	M. 51.0 W. 51.1	M. 38.8 W. 40.9	M. 6.7 W. 3.4	M. 3.1 W. 3.4	M. 1.0 W. 1.2		
PROTESTANTS	M. 21.4 W. 16.1	M. 46.4 W. 55.5	M. 11.8 W. 14.8	M. 12.8 W. 9.2	M. 5.6 W. 2.5	M. 1.0 W. 1.7	M. 1.0 W. 0.2
JEWS	M. 18.2 W. 12.3	M. 29.5 W. 26.8	M. 22.0 W. 24.4	M. 14.4 W. 24.4	M. 9.1 W. 2.4	M. 3.0 W. 7.3	M. 3.8 W. 2.4
NO CHURCH	M. 2.2 W. 6.7	M. 10.6 W. 30.0	M. 12.8 W. 26.7	M. 31.9 W. 26.7	M. 14.9 W. 3.3	M. 17.0 W. 3.3	M. 10.6 W. 3.3

FIG. 15.2. "Distribution of percentages of 1,219 students of the College of Liberal Arts of Syracuse University upon the question of the existence and nature of the deity." On seven opinions about the nature of the deity (specified on the abscissa), distribution of Catholics approaches most closely the J-curve of conformity. Most divergent distribution is "No Church" subjects. Men's opinions, solid lines; women's, broken lines. (From D. Katz and F. H. Allport, *Students' Attitudes*. Syracuse: The Craftsman Press.)

in terms of his actual reference groups becomes a necessity especially in highly differentiated and rather fluid modern societies.

Criteria Differentiating Attitudes from Other Internal Factors

An attitude, then, determines a characteristic or consistent mode of behavior in relation to relevant stimuli, persons, or events. As such, an attitude is an internal factor. But all internal factors are not attitudes. Therefore, attitudes have to be differentiated from other internal factors. Otherwise the word "attitude" becomes a blanket term used to denote any or all kinds of disposition, organic state, or motive. It becomes almost synonymous with the broad field of motivation.

The concept *attitude* has to be differentiated in terms of definite criteria (51) if we are to retain it as a distinct concept in social psychology and not blur its significance by making it "a kind of psychological catchall" (6, p. 611).

1. *Attitudes are not innate.* They are formed or learned in relation to given objects, persons, groups, and events. This criterion differentiates an attitude from biogenic motives. Craving for food in the state of hunger is biogenic. But a strong preference for lobster is an attitude. Some people develop such strong attitudes in eating that they do not enjoy food unless it is served in a distinguished place in a quiet atmosphere. The initial appearance of an attitude is dependent on learning.

2. *Attitudes are more or less lasting.* This criterion literally means more lasting or less lasting. The implication is that, since they are learned, attitudes are not immutable. They are subject to change under given conditions and influences (see the next chapter).

As long as an attitude lasts, its functioning is not subject (within limits) to the ups or downs of the state of the organism. When an individual has to get up early in the morning after just a few hours of sleep for some reason, he or she almost drags himself to wash, shave, put on an appearance to go to class, or the office, or the store. In this instance, his attitude toward appearing in appropriate form in the eyes of his fellow men has the upper hand over the homeostatic tendency in the opposite direction.

3. *Attitudes always imply a subject-object relationship.* In other words, attitudes are not formed in thin air. They are formed or learned in relation to an identifiable referent, be it a person, a group, an object, an institution, an issue, or an event. If it were not for these identifiable referents, the study of attitudes would not have been the central area that it has been in social psychology. The positive or negative relatedness of an individual

to a group or institution, his favorable or unfavorable stand on a political or some other issue reveals his attitudes in these matters. This subject-object relationship in formation and functioning ties up attitudes with social values or norms, institutions, groups, and issues of various sorts (political, religious, economic, and so on).

4. *The referent of an attitude may encompass a small or large number of items.* The referent may consist of one item or a large number of items falling under one classification. When members of a gang develop a negative attitude toward a rival gang and consider that gang treacherous, the six or eight individuals in that gang will be seen as treacherous. When members of a given group are handed down by their elders the dictum: "The X nation is aggressive," any individual out of millions composing the X nation is likely to be seen as aggressive. Such a stand, which encompasses millions of items, is possible on the basis of the development of generalized concepts. This implies the process of generalization, which is the essential process of concept formation.

Here again, we see the significance of the conceptual level of functioning in the acquisition of attitudes applicable to various ranges of items. Language makes generalization to an almost infinite number of stimuli possible. The generalizations in question are not simply sensory generalizations; *they cut across sensory modalities* (see Chapter 14).

5. *Attitudes have motivational-affective properties.* This criterion differentiates an attitude from other learned items in the psychological make-up of the individual. Attitude toward God or attitude toward one's clique is quite different from the habit of putting matches in the right-hand pocket of one's coat. In the sense discussed in the opening paragraphs of this chapter, an attitude is goal directed in a positive or negative way.

The affective value of an attitude is due either to the intrinsic, direct, or "instrumental" motivational appeal of the stimulus (such as food, a sex object, mother, milk bottle, a period of romance) or to the socially invested stamp of value on the stimulus. These socially invested value judgments are further expanded under item 6 below.

6. The above five criteria differentiate attitudes from other internal states or factors. These five criteria apply to both social and nonsocial attitudes. General principles underlying formation and functioning of all attitudes (social or nonsocial) are the same. They are all acquired motives in relation to given objects, events, or people.

The feature which differentiates a social attitude from other attitudes is that a social attitude is formed in relation to social stimulus situations and is shared by members of a group or of a given society. Social stimulus situations are other persons, groups, and cultural products (material and non-material). In other words, attitudes formed in interpersonal relations, in group relations (both in-group and out-groups), in relation to one's car, household furniture, utilities, in relation to group standards, values, or norms and including defined characteristic modes of behavior to them are social attitudes. Since the referents of social attitudes (individuals, groups, one's living facilities) constitute items that define an individual's vital relatedness to his surroundings, one can readily see why these attitudes are affectively charged in various degrees.

A good many social attitudes are formed in relation to one's group values or norms. Social standards or norms are usually couched in short-cut value judgments. "You shall honor your flag." "You shall be a good member" of the family or clique or organization, with all that this implies. "You shall carry on your role as leader or member," with all that this implies in the way of endowed power, rights, and responsibilities. Other examples of such socially standardized value judgments are "Nation X is fanatical," "Cleanliness is next to godliness."

The value judgments embodied in a social norm are presented with an air of finality by older or senior members to individuals who are in the process of becoming members. Except in times of rapid social transition, except in turning points in the history of groups and societies, social values or norms are upheld and transmitted to new members as imperative ingredients of their upbringing, education, and other processes of socialization. Becoming a member in no small part consists of internalizing the values or norms of the group.

Many values or norms are internalized through the formation of attitudes by new members on the basis of formula, short-cut verbal dicta, or example before they have had sufficient or (in some cases) any actual encounter with the referents of these attitudes. That is, many social attitudes are formed deductively through formula rather than through step-by-step personal experience with the objects encompassed in the value verdict of the norm.

STUDIES OF SOCIAL ATTITUDES

Various writers have recognized for many years that a social attitude determines a characteristic and consistent mode of behavior which is *selective* toward relevant stimuli. However, this selectivity has been tied to the selectivity of basic psychological processes more recently.

Consequently, theoretical, empirical, and experimental studies of social attitudes stemmed from various directions and utilized diverse concepts and modes of attack. Sociologists, psychologists, and social scientists have all contributed theoretical stands and factual bits to the thriving activity in the study of various aspects of the area. In the early sociological classic by Thomas and Znaniecki (54), who made attitudes central in their social psychology, we find the social attitude defined as "the individual counterpart of the social value" (p. 22). The data these authors used were largely letters exchanged by the people whose attitudes they studied. The experimental start made by Külpe, around the turn of the century, clearly demonstrating psychological selectivity (see p. 92) was not related to social attitudes until the middle thirties. The main bulk of techniques developed for the measurement of attitudes was not tied with the implications of judgmental-perceptual work coming from the laboratory or with sociological accounts concerning the value (norm) and attitude relationship.

On the technical side, a good many tests have been developed for assessing attitudes. In a recent survey, Donald T. Campbell classified them under four headings:

1. *Non-disguised-structured:* the classic direct attitude tests of Thurstone [55], Likert [33], *et al.*
2. *Non-disguised-non-structured:* the free response interview and questionnaire approaches, the biographical and essay studies.
3. *Disguised-non-structured:* the typical "projective" techniques.
4. *Disguised-structured:* tests which approximate the objective testing of attitudes [11, p. 15].

We shall have occasion to refer to some representative illustrations of these various tests. A good many tests attempting to achieve quantitative indices of attitudes have been of a *survey type*. The main objective in the use of survey-type tests has been to get the end product, i.e., verbal statements of "attitudes," without due regard to underlying principles and factors. A good example of this type of work is "public opinion" polling. What is attempted in "public opinion" polls is really to assess this or that attitude of the respondents. The stand of an individual on a public issue (pro or con) is an attitude.

The interest in surveys has been to reach as many people as possible in a short time, since they are usually undertaken with immediate practical considerations. On the other hand, the laboratory-type studies are more time consuming and slower in handling many people at the same time. In recent years there have been serious attempts toward developing attitude tests which embody the theoretical implications of the laboratory-type studies and, at the same time, will have the practical value of being administered to a good many people in short order.

Leads from the Laboratory for Adequate Attitude Measurement

Survey-type techniques have not yet utilized the full implications of principles and accumulating facts from the laboratory which make use in an indirect way of seemingly simple and readily quantifiable indices for assessing attitudes and other motives of the individual. The principles and relevant facts are presented in Chapters 2 and 3. Their usefulness is demonstrated in a number of experiments studying man's motives through simple, precise indices (Chapter 13).

The study of attitudes and their measurement is not a new territory. An attitude expresses the evaluative stand of the individual in relation to people, institutions, and issues, determining a characteristic, selective mode of response, like any other motive. Having a definite stand on God, the Democratic or Republican party, segregation of Negroes in one's state, or the fact that one's son or daughter is in the same class or dance hall with others of mixed ethnic origins is not an idle matter.

Any one of these attitudes determines a highly selective and characteristic mode of behavior in relevant situations, whether or not one cares to verbalize them explicitly when a pollster puts a direct question on a street corner or when an attitude tester asks him to rate his stand on a 5-point or 11-point scale. When faced with such point-blank questions, the usual tendency is to appear appropriate in terms of the currently fashionable trends. This consideration of weighing one's responses becomes much more important if the issue at hand is a highly controversial one and the respondent is not on the popular side of the fence. Under these circumstances, answers to point-blank questions or ratings are hardly the expression of his stand on the topic but are rather an expression in response to the social situation he is in (e.g., 15, 57).

After all, in the culture, one's religion, one's family affairs and expenditures, one's social aspirations are considered private affairs. The more intimate these questions are in terms of personal living, the more reticent one becomes. When faced with such a question, the individual is likely to respond in a stereotyped way. No wonder, then, that along with high reliability coefficient of test results we find reports of discrepancies between verbally expressed "attitude" and "actual behavior" of the respondents. It may be that the high reliabilities reported are often the outcome of the stereotyping effect of test situations.

Fortunately the recent experimental trend, which utilizes simple perceptual-judgmental reactions as indices of underlying motives, preoccupations, aspirations of the person, points a way for valid study of attitudes. The overall principle in this experimental trend is that when the individual is faced with relevant stimulus situations the motive or attitude in question will come in as a factor to determine the ensuing experience and action. The motive or attitude in question will be reflected even in simple judgments. The individual himself need not be aware that the psychological product is mainly determined by that particular motive or attitude.

The main requisites in such studies are (1) a stimulus situation relevant to the motive or attitude in question; (2) insuring at least some lack of objective checks or anchorages in given dimension(s) conducive to eliciting alternative reactions; and (3) presentation of the task to the subject in a way which does not appear to him directly related to his motive or attitude in question.

The last requisite, in a sense, disarms the respondent. It enables the investigator to obtain reactions in which the motive or attitude in question comes freely as a factor, hampered to a relatively lesser degree by intrusion of ego concerns which are situationally aroused in direct, point-blank questions or ratings.

In Chapter 13, various experiments utilizing this indirect or disguised approach for the study of motives were reported. Chapters 5, 6, and 9 presented experiments which studied the development and functioning of attitudes of individual members toward their in-group and toward out-groups through simple perceptual-judgmental reactions. In Campbell's survey (11) the reader will find a number of attitude studies using this indirect or disguised approach. Here we shall summarize a few experiments which illustrate this line of work.

Some Illustrative Experiments

ATTITUDES TOWARD SKIN COLOR IN SOCIAL JUDGMENTS: A study by Marks (37) neatly demonstrates how an attitude toward a preferred skin color and interpersonal attitudes of individuals bring about displacements in rating the skin colors of other individuals. Therefore, it is one of the experiments that epitomizes the modern trend in studying attitudes. It exemplifies how a simple judgment can reflect complex attitudes pertaining to interpersonal and group relations.

The problem of this experiment stemmed from the observations of the sociologist C. S. Johnson (26). Johnson observed that, at the time, the Negro youth had a preference for light-brown skin color. This preference was revealed, for example, in the way students tended to displace the actual skin color of popular school principals toward the light-brown direction and the skin color of unpopular school principals in the opposite direction.

Marks studied the relation between ratings of skin color and ratings of attractiveness, and the relation between the rater's own skin color and his ratings of others in this respect. His subjects consisted of four groups of Negro students. He had subjects in each group rate each other for six characteristics on an eight-point scale. These characteristics included "very attractive"—"very unattractive" and "very dark"—"very light" dimensions.

Marks concluded from an analysis of his results that "There is a tendency to displace the ratings of subjects considered attractive in the direction of the preferred skin color, a given subject being placed nearer this color by raters who consider her attractive than by those who consider her unattractive" (37, p. 376). Even though it was not made explicit to the subjects in the experiment, here we see the preferred skin color of the group coming in as an anchorage for judgment and thus producing these displacements.

This tendency to displace the skin color of persons considered attractive by the raters in the preferred light-brown direction was affected by two other factors: (1) the rater's own skin color and (2) the objective skin color of the person rated. In rating the skin color of fellow class members, the rater's own skin color served as a reference point or anchorage, in addition to the position of the preferred skin color. Thus, persons lighter than the rater were judged as "light" and those darker than the rater were judged as "dark." This consequently amounted to displacing one's own skin color toward a moderate color. But the objective skin colors of the rater and of the person rated "act as checks upon this tendency" and prevent a person who is very dark from rating himself as light.

ATTITUDES AS FACTORS IN THE JUDGMENT OF FUTURE EVENTS: Man is probably the only organism that is concerned with the shape of things to come as well as with the happenings of the living present. Since things that will take place in the future are relatively freer from the immediate correctives of objective checks, the relevant attitudes and other motives come in as significant factors in determining man's judgment or prediction concerning the shape of future events.

An early study demonstrating this tendency is that by McGregor (35). McGregor obtained 3500 predictions made by 400 male and female subjects in May, 1936, and relevant information concerning their attitudes, wishes, and knowledge. The subjects were students in three eastern colleges. Thirty-three of the subjects were "experts" in social science fields.

The subjects were asked to fill in a questionnaire which called for their predictions on nine social events of current interest. Among these were whether Roosevelt would be reëlected, whether there would be a war the following year, and whether business conditions would improve. After the respondents filled in this part of the questionnaire, they gave information concerning their own attitudes and wishes on these social issues. The overall finding in the study is that the attitude of the individual on the issue *does* come in as a factor in his prediction of future events in that area.

There were no significant differences between the predictions of "experts" and students who upheld the same stand on the issues. This finding is noteworthy in showing that the "experts" too are not immune to the influence of their stand on an issue.

But attitudes and other motives "do not operate in complete freedom. They are subject to external constraint" (p. 184). The more ambiguous the stimulus conditions related to the issue and the greater the importance of the outcome for the individual, the greater the influence of the attitude on the prediction. In a more exhaustive study, of course, the more idiosyncratic factors pertaining to the persons who make predictions (e.g., their optimism or pessimism, cautiousness, skepticism) have to be brought into the picture.

In a study using somewhat different procedures (e.g., inclusion of greater variety of issues, longer time span in predictions), Cantril (12) found a similar tendency in the prediction of future events. "Individuals whose attitudes favor a certain outcome for an event tend to forecast the desired outcome" (p. 387). In addition to predictions, the certainty of the predictions was obtained in this study in terms of "Very Certain," "Moderately Certain," and "Not at All." The interesting finding in this regard is that for social issues in relation to which the subjects had only few objective factors to depend on and lacked a definite stand "predictions are expressed with little certainty."

JUDGMENTS OF VARIOUS ASPECTS OF AN OBJECT ARE INTERRELATED: When an individual judges a series of weights or lines, his placement of a single stimulus is made in terms of a reference scale built up through repeated contact with the objective stimulus scale. Changing the end points or other properties of the stimulus scale leads in time to shifts in judgments of specific items (pp. 64–66).

Judgments of aspects of a situation which lack objective structure, like extent of perceived movement in the autokinetic situation, come to be regulated in terms of a reference scale or range. But in these cases, judgments are made relative to reference points which are formed by the individual (internally) in the situation itself (p. 253). Because of the uncertainty aroused in such situations, the individual is particularly prone to be influenced by external standards introduced into the situation, like the judgments of other persons or the standards of a group.

What if the stimulus objects being judged are relevant to an individual's attitudes? Will judgments of various dimensions of such objects be affected by the attitude in question? If so, what will be the effects of different attitudes with slight or considerable significance to the individual?

In a series of experiments, Asch and his co-workers (3, 4) investigated the role of attitudes in judgments of photographs, professions, political slogans, and political figures. In relation to each, judgments were made along several dimensions, like "intelligence" and "honesty" for persons in the pictures, "intelligence" and "social usefulness" of professions, "compellingness to action" and "social significance" of slogans, and "intellectual power" and "physical attractiveness" of political leaders. The results were analyzed chiefly in terms of the relationships (rank-difference correlations) between average rankings for the subject sample.

For our present discussion, the types of judgments required and the relative significance of the various stimulus objects to subjects need to be made explicit. The stimulus material presented was all well structured objectively. However, the specific dimensions to be judged (like "intelligence," "idealism," "literary value," and so on) were ones for which subjects had few objective guides. Such rankings were likely to be guided by the generally favorable or unfavorable stand taken by the subject toward the object in question.

Following Asch, we can say that the subjects had no established attitudes toward the persons in the photographs, although they apparently had personal preferences for certain features and characteristics. As numerous studies have shown, individuals in any particular social group are likely to have attitudes toward various professions in terms of which they can rank them as to general desirability, prestige, and the like. Well-known slogans and political leaders are objects of distinct and intensely held attitudes, as the results indicate.

Judgments of various characteristics of unknown individuals in photographs tended to be related to one another, though not highly correlated. (The mean correlation between ratings of honesty and intelligence was .35.) It was concluded that specific ratings were made in terms of a generally favorable or unfavorable impression of the person pictured.

On the other hand, relationships between judgments on specific dimensions for the professions tended to be higher. Highest relationships between ratings of various characteristics were found, on the whole, for the political figures. For example, the correlation between average ranks of "intellectual power" and "honesty" was .80. In these cases, a clear-cut tendency was noted to rate particular characteristics for a given individual high or low in terms of intensely favorable or unfavorable attitudes toward them. Ratings of political slogans likewise were closely related in terms of well-defined positive or negative stands toward the slogan and the political viewpoint it represented. This tendency for judgments of specific characteristics to be related to the underlying positive or negative attitudes toward the object or person is illustrated in Figure 15.3, which shows the frequency distribution of rankings of Roosevelt and Hitler for "intellectual power" and "physical attractiveness."

As might be expected, the experimental introduction of standards for judgment was most effective for stimuli which were not objects of established attitudes. The judgments of slogans were not markedly affected by such introduced standards; on the contrary, the subjects tended to interpret the standards in terms congruent with their own attitudes toward the slogans. For stimuli which were objects of less intense attitudes, experimentally introduced standards attributed to reference groups of the subject tended to be most effective. Standards imputed to an out-group toward whom subjects had a strongly unfavorable attitude were rejected as guides for judgment.

Attitude as a Factor in What We See and Hear First: In one glance, we pick up from many possible stimulus objects only a circumscribed number of items within the limits of the span of experience. What we pick up first is determined by the particular set of external and internal factors operative at the time (pp. 85–97).

An experiment by Postman, Bruner, and McGinnies (45) exemplifies studies which demonstrate that attitude is a determinant of psychological

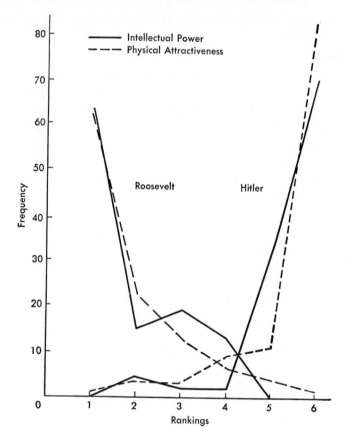

FIG. 15.3. Frequency of rankings for two political figures from favorable (represented by 1) to unfavorable (represented by 6) on "intellectual power" and "physical attractiveness." (After Asch.)

selectivity. The investigators first got an index of the dominant values of their subjects through the Allport-Vernon test of values. They presented 36 words, each word representing one of the six values included in the test. The initial exposure of each word was too brief for it to be recognized. They increased exposure time in gradations until each word was recognized. The finding was that the greater the value of the word in the eyes of the subject, the shorter was the time needed to recognize it. Similar results were obtained by Vanderplas and Blake (59) using auditory presentation of words. The audibility threshold was lower for words that corresponded to the dominant value or attitude of the individual. As pointed out in more recent experiments, such selectivity may occur for motivational relevant items toward which subjects have either positive or negative stands (see pp. 432–433).

One of the fertile areas for the study of the effect of attitudes is the way and speed with which figure-ground delineations are made. Following the lead provided by Murphy and his associates (39, 50), a demonstration experiment showing the effect of attitude on figure-ground delineation was included in our experimental course on sociogenic motives at the University of Oklahoma in the spring semesters of 1954 and 1955 (58). In both demonstrations two campus groups were chosen who had strong, differentiated views on a political issue. The members of each group separately were presented with two communications from opposing points of view which came through loud-speakers simultaneously, but with approximately the same loudness. The overall finding in these studies is the tendency for opinionated individuals to hear the motivationally relevant communication as the figure and the other as the ground. On the other hand, the control subjects in the 1954 demonstration were almost equally divided in hearing one or the other communication as figure.

Examples of Indirect Attitude Measurement

The illustrative experiments, chosen from others which might have been mentioned, are sufficient to drive home the point that, under conditions specified previously (p. 499), attitudes can be effectively studied through seemingly simple judgmental-perceptual reactions. For systematic variations in these reactions reflect the stand of the person and the intensity of the stand.

Effective use is being made of these perceptual-judgmental reactions in studying personality characteristics of the individual, even though the underlying theory and practical criteria for their use are not wholly clarified. The basic assumption of all the "projective" techniques so widely used in clinical work today is that if the stimulus material embodies alternatives in given dimensions the individual will reveal something about himself (his attitudes, motives, and concerns) through his judgments, his perceptions, or the way he handles and arranges stimulus objects. This basic assumption underlies all the available projective techniques, whether it is explicitly stated or not. The word-association test of Kent-Rosanoff (29), Rorschach ink blots (48), the Thematic Apperception Test (56), the World Test, in which miniature objects are available for possible construction of a "town, village, farm, or zoo" (10), and the Rosenzweig Picture-

Frustration test, in which the subject can supply his own descriptive re-action to remarks made by one of the persons in the picture (49), are outstanding examples of these tests.

In recent years, attempts have been made toward constructing indirect, disguised tests for the measurement of social attitudes. Here we shall de-scribe briefly only two of them. The first is along the traditional lines of "projective" tests; the second is along the lines of judgmental studies.

"Loafer" or "Forgotten Man": In 1943, Proshansky (46) devised a "projective method for the study of attitudes." He correctly advanced the hypothesis that "extreme groups, i.e. those inclining towards strongly pro-labor or anti-labor attitudes, would reveal their social orientation through their manner of reporting upon pictures of social conflict situations" (p. 393). Accordingly, he exposed his subjects, who had pro and con stands on the issue, to relevant pictures and asked them to give brief interpretive descriptions for each picture. He found considerable agreement between the attitude and the picture responses "as evaluated by three judges."

Probably anyone will agree that the subject who gave the following de-scription of the picture is *pro*labor in his attitude:

"Home of a man on relief—shabby—dresses poorly. Scene is probably in a shack down South. Also, might be the home of some unemployed la-borer. Horrible housing conditions. Why don't the government provide for these people? The ordinary worker is always forgotten and allowed to rot."

The reader will probably agree that the following description given by another subject to the same picture reveals an *anti*labor attitude:

"Picture of one room, very messy, stove in the center, woman on the left, man standing next to stove, couple of children near them. This is a room of what we call 'poor people.' They seem to be messy, sloppy people, who seem to enjoy dwelling in their own trash" (p. 394).

The two descriptions above reveal rather clearly the stands of the writ-ers. But all descriptions cannot be as clear as these. There are all kinds of possible gradations. This creates serious scoring difficulties and the use of three or more judges for evaluation of results is no sure remedy for them. Judges too have their biases. The objective remedy lies in using stimulus material and securing reactions in which responses can be scored directly by anyone who can count. The following construction of an indirect atti-tude measurement technique is one of the successful attempts in this di-rection.

Attitude Determines Which Alternative Is Chosen: In 1948, Hammond (22) reported two experiments which are full of implications for the theory and methodology of attitude measurement. In the first experiment he demonstrated how attitudes can be measured in a "disguised" or indirect way, that is, without the individuals' being aware that their attitudes were under investigation. He called this the "Error Choice Technique." In the second experiment, Hammond definitely established that it *does* make a difference whether or not individuals are aware that their attitudes are under investigation.

1. In the first experiment, Hammond studied attitudes toward labor and toward Russia. In the labor test, he had a number of items which allowed two alternatives, one of which had to be chosen as correct by the subject. (Example: Average weekly wage of the war worker in 1945 was [a] $37 [b] $57.) Both of these figures were actually wrong. They deviated equally from the actual average, but in opposite directions. Similarly, on the Russia test, two alternatives were given in each item, one of which was to be checked by the subject. (Example: Russia's removal of heavy industry from Austria was [a] legal, [b] illegal.) For items like the last example, "the facts were indeterminable" and hence the checking of "legal" or of "illegal" depended largely on the subject's attitude. The systematic errors in one direction or another in checking alternatives were taken as the measure of the attitude of the individual on the issue.

Both tests were administered under the guise of "information" tests. In order to make this guise more plausible, an equal number of items with factual alternatives were embedded in each test. In these factual items, correct alternatives could be checked rather easily.

The subjects were a group of businessmen (employers and younger businessmen) and a group of men employed in a labor union. The hypothesis was supported. The "mean errors in each group were found to be significantly different in the direction predicted." The difference was sufficiently great so that one can be justified in speaking of "a positive systematic error for one group as against a negative systematic error for the other."

2. In the second experiment, the same "nonfactual" items used in the first experiment were given to the subjects under two different instructions. To one group of subjects, the test was given as an "information" test (Info-form). To the second group of subjects the test was given as an "attitude" test (Att-Info-form). In the latter case the attitude-measurement aspect of the study was accentuated in the instructions. The results are instructive for attitude theory and measurement. In the labor test, one-

third of the responses by the two groups were significantly different from one another (at the 5 percent level). On the Russia questionnaire, the differences in responses obtained under two differing instructions were still more marked. This finding indicates that it *does* make a difference whether subjects are *aware* or not that their attitude on an issue is under study. As seen in the above demonstration, the weight of this awareness as a factor increases as the attitude under study is more consequential under the circumstances.

The "error-choice" technique has been tried on several other issues. One of the clear-cut studies was conducted by Kubany (30) on the issue of National Health Insurance. This study used definite criteria for subject selection which are necessary in devising a valid technique for measurement. (1) Two samples were selected from groups with known stands on the issue in question. In this case, the two groups were graduate social work students, who were known to be favorable, and third-year medical students, who were known to be opposed on the whole. (2) After administering the error-choice items, a direct question was asked concerning whether the subject favored or opposed "some form" of National Health Insurance. Four social work students and 10 medical students were then eliminated from the validation groups because they gave answers to this general question which were different from others in their respective groups. In this way, the investigator obtained samples with definite and opposing stands on an issue important to each group.

Fifty items were administered to these subjects. Twenty-two were genuine information items and the remainder were "error-choice items." Analysis revealed little relationship between correct scores on the actual information items and "systematic bias" on the error-choice items. Since the criteria used in subject selection insured two samples with definite and opposing attitudes, the investigator had a valid basis for eliminating those items with little relationship to the overall stands taken by the subjects.

The responses to the 18 error-choice items which remained after the item analysis differentiated clearly between the two subject samples. Of these 18, the average number of errors in the pro direction for social workers was 14.64, while the average in the pro direction for medical students was only 5.93. The overall average for all subjects combined was 9.55. As Figure 15.4 shows, this overall average is a cutting point differentiating almost all individuals in the two samples. Since the stands on the issue taken by subjects in the two samples were known and also checked directly, Kubany's study indicates that this indirect technique for measuring attitudes can be used to make valid distinctions between individuals' attitudes in terms of their "systematic" bias. The frequency distribution of total items answered with a favorable (pro) bias for the two samples reveals two distinct distributions with only the "slightest overlap" (Fig. 15.4).

As Hammond pointed out, the usefulness of this error-choice technique can be extended by increasing the number of alternatives available from

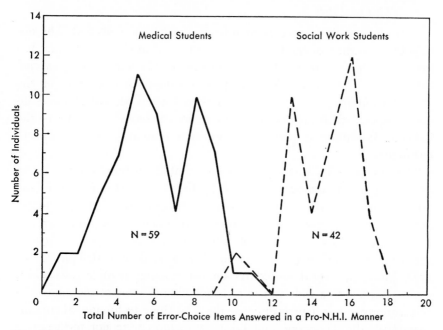

FIG. 15.4. Graph illustrating the nature of two populations as determined by their scores on the 18 error-choice items. (From A. J. Kubany, A validation study of the error-choice technique using attitudes on national health insurance, *Educat. and Psychol. Measurem.* [1953], *13*:157–163.)

two to three, five, or more. When thus extended, its differentiating value may be sharpened, to the extent of indicating the intensity of the attitude in question. Of course, it is perfectly feasible not to restrict reactions of subjects to alternatives that are altogether indeterminate or "nonfactual." We have already summarized experiments in previous chapters in which the subjects were not restricted in their response to a predetermined number of alternatives (pp. 202–206; pp. 312–316). In these experiments on group structure and intergroup relations, the subjects were given opportunity to approximate an objectively correct response in their judgments as well as to vary from an objectively correct response in various degrees, in directions determined by their attitudes.

Another indirect technique for the assessment of the direction and intensity of the attitude of an individual on a given issue is described later in this chapter (pp. 530–531).

DIRECT TECHNIQUES FOR MEASURING ATTITUDES

Attitudes are all inferred from behavior, verbal or nonverbal. The distinguishing feature of the techniques summarized in the sections that follow is that they all attempt to secure a measure of attitudes through verbal behavior in situations in which the person is *aware* that his views on the issue at hand are being investigated. In other words, these techniques do not "disguise" their aim, which is to secure responses pertaining to the individual's attitude. In terms of the subject's awareness, they are "direct" techniques.

The earliest widely used device for investigating attitudes through direct or undisguised means was developed by the sociologist Bogardus in the mid-twenties to study "social distance" among various ethnic groups. Shortly thereafter, Thurstone proposed a technique for devising scales to measure attitudes on a variety of issues through the method of "equal-appearing intervals" adapted from the classical work on psychophysics. In 1932, Likert developed procedures for constructing attitude tests which were applicable to a wide variety of issues without some of the more difficult assumptions and procedures of the Thurstone technique. Significant changes in the Thurstone and Likert procedures were not forthcoming until World War II, when a large number of social scientists and psychologists participated in massive research projects designed to contribute as much as possible to the war effort.

After the middle thirties, however, the measurement of social attitudes had been significantly affected by a development which occurred essentially outside of academic and scientific circles, in spite of its reliance on already established techniques. This was the appearance of "public opinion polls" or surveys, at first in the fields of journalism (e.g., Gallup and Roper polls) and immediately thereafter in advertising, commerce, industry, and government. Since the turn of the century, social surveys of various kinds had been conducted by social scientists, magazines and newspapers had conducted "straw polls," and statistical procedures for selecting samples of people representing a population were developed. Nevertheless, the modern success story of "public opinion" polls in America started in the thirties, and there can be no doubt that the area of attitude measurement has been colored ever since by their popular and practical vogue.

In the following pages there will be little space to mention the numerous variations and adaptations of the techniques presented. Nor have we mentioned such well-known devices as "self-rating" (in which the individual places his own position along some continuum), a technique which is often useful in conjunction with others but is seldom adequate by itself. Finally, no mention is made of techniques derived from clinical psychology and social research which can be utilized with great profit in certain research problems and do not even require the individual's presence. For example, personal documents (letters, autobiographies, diaries, public utterances, and the like) can be analyzed. The interested reader is referred to Gordon Allport's paper on the use of personal documents (2) and to Berelson's treatment of "content analysis" (5).

"Public Opinion" Surveys

Of the techniques which social scientists have used in attempting to tap attitudes of groups, surveys of "public opinion" are the most widely known. Reports of such surveys are published in daily papers and magazines, broadcast over the radio, circulated privately to interested organizations or paying customers, and quoted by business executives, advertising agencies, political commentators, and members of Congress.

The techniques can be discussed as they are used typically by commercial organizations with deadlines to meet or as they have been employed occasionally by social scientists to study well-defined problems with theoretical as well as practical significance. Data obtained can be evaluated in terms of their use and influence in modern life or in terms of their contribution to our understanding of social attitudes.

On the whole, substantial contributions to an understanding of social attitudes through these questionnaires constitute only a tiny fraction of the massive results. Throughout this brief discussion, the reader should be aware that in some cases these techniques have been used in coördinated investigations which have minimized many of their shortcomings. Selected readings on significant aspects of "public opinion" work are indicated in context.

All surveys are not studies of "opinion." Surveys are also undertaken to determine factual questions, like family income, religious affiliations, number of children in the family, employment, property ownership, or the use of various commercial products. Of course, studies of "opinion" also require securing at least a minimum of factual data about the persons studied.

One assumption underlying the conception and use of "public opinion" surveys is that attitudes of individuals can be tapped by asking direct and relevant questions. Traditionally and in practice, an "opinion" is considered a verbal response which is taken to indicate the individual's positive or negative attitude on the topic in question.

The greatest appeal and potential significance of survey techniques are that they attempt to obtain results representative of large groups in the population or even the total adult population. This distinctive feature is also the source of greatest difficulties, largely because practical and financial problems usually necessitate obtaining results from any single individual as expeditiously as possible.

The "public" studied may be qualified voters, all adults over a certain age, heads of families, persons with radios, persons in certain localities or strata of the population, depending on the problem under investigation. The particular population chosen is studied by selecting a representative sample or cross section. Although certain sampling problems are more or less peculiar to "opinion" research, the criteria and methods of sample selection are in general common to all surveys. Discussions of different sampling techniques and problems may be found in Stock (13, pp. 127–142), McNemar (36, pp. 331–338), and in more detail in Parten (42, chaps. IV, VII, VIII, IX).

Here only one point concerning sampling will be considered because it is particularly significant for all opinion-attitude research and because it is only beginning to be considered in research utilizing survey techniques. The most widely used sampling technique is some form of "stratified sampling." Cases are selected to represent various strata of the population being studied. For example, cases may be selected to represent persons of different sex, age groupings, color or ethnic groups, living in different regions of the country, in rural areas and cities of various sizes, and with different income levels or standards of living (based on income, owning property of various kinds, a telephone, occupation, and the like). Such strata are important sociological categories and may be adequate for analyzing certain types of data.

However, when surveys aim at studying social attitudes, placement of individuals in such broad strata may be insufficient for significant analysis of results. As we have noted, social attitudes are formed by individuals in relation to developing trends and prevailing norms of groups to which they relate themselves psychologically as members or as aspirants. Such reference groups need not coincide with those in which the individual is a registered or apparent member. The categories ordinarily used in selecting a stratified sample permit only broad and general inferences concerning the reference groups of individuals sampled.

Investigations utilizing the concept *reference groups* in the study design and analysis of data obtained by survey techniques are beginning to appear in the literature. Significant future developments in opinion research, as well as investigation of social attitudes in general, can be anticipated through this approach (see Chapter 18).

TECHNIQUES FOR OBTAINING DATA: As noted above, the data in opinion surveys is obtained typically through direct questions which require the individual to state a positive or a negative stand on the issue. For example, in 1948, samples in nine countries ranging in sample size from 945 to 1195 persons per sample were asked the following question:

"Do you believe that it will be possible for all countries to live together at peace with each other?"

The results for each country are listed below in terms of percentage of the particular sample replying "yes," "no," or "don't know" (9, p. 62). (The samples in various countries differed somewhat both in size and in the strata of the population represented.)

	Possible	Not Possible	Don't Know
	%	%	%
Australia	42	54	4
Britain	47	44	9
France	47	41	12
(West) Germany	58	35	7
Italy	30	59	11
Mexico	18	74	8
Netherlands	46	49	5
Norway	43	52	5
United States	49	45	6

The difficulties in planning the question, selecting respondents, and interpreting results obtained in response to a *single question* through survey techniques can be seen by comparing the replies to a slightly different question pertaining to the same topic obtained by affiliates of the Gallup organizations in five of these nine countries at about the same time as the above results (9, p. 62). This question and the results were as follows:

"Do you think there will be another big war within the next ten years?"

	Will	Will Not	No Opinion
	%	%	%
Italy	58	26	16
United States	57	26	17
Norway	53	27	20
Netherlands	52	34	14
England	35	36	29

Quite aside from the problem of adequate sampling, it has been demonstrated that answers to single questions on the same topic vary with the manner in which the question is worded, the order of the questions on the "ballot" or questionnaire, the manner in which they are asked, the respective status or group affiliation of the interviewer and the person responding. For example, substantially different results are obtained when Negro interviewers or white interviewers question Negro respondents, when interviewers identified as Jews or not so identified question non-Jewish individuals, and when middle-class or working-class interviewers question working people. There is also indication that interviewers tend to obtain disproportionately high frequency of answers which are in line with their own opinions. The reader interested in these findings and related problems can consult Rugg and Cantril (13), Doob's lucid summary of "the mechanics of polling" (16, chap. 2), and Parten (42, chap. 6).

Rather than requiring a "yes" or "no" answer, questions sometimes include a limited number of choices. The following results were obtained in surveys on the same date by the American Institute of Public Opinion (Gallup) using two sets of alternatives which are identical except for the use of "working class" in the first set and "laboring class" in the second (9, p. 115):

If you were asked to use one of these four names for your social class, which would you say you belong in: the middle class, lower class, working (or laboring) class, or upper class?

	Form A	Form B
	%	%
Upper	3	4
Middle	38	53
Lower	3	4
Working (A)	52	
Laboring (B)		35
Don't Know	4	4

Another type of question used is the "open-ended" question. Example: What do you think about a federal sales tax? Responses to this kind of question must be classified or coded, either by the interviewer or by analysts. This procedure involves the possibility of considerable error unless the coders are highly trained and qualified, and of variations even if they are. The most useful function of such questions in practice is in exploratory investigations.

Rating devices have been employed, usually with the attempt to get at the intensity with which a person upholds or opposes a certain stand on an issue. In addition, techniques derived from "attitude scales" summarized in succeeding sections have been tried out in a more limited fashion.

While the commercial polling organizations release results from single questions, the substantial investigations of a problem through survey techniques have used several different types of questions, sometimes starting with general, open-ended questions and funneling down to more specific questions.

Survey work has also been carried out with "open-ended interviews," which do not utilize fixed questions requiring "yes" or "no" answers but attempt to stimulate the individual to discuss a topic in a "non-directive" manner. The problem of evaluating such data for analysis is difficult. Some advantages and disadvantages of such interviews were discussed cogently by Lazarsfeld, who wisely concluded that survey research often requires a combination of the methods available (*31*).

"Opinions" and Attitudes: Obviously the value of these techniques for studying attitudes depends on whether or not individuals reveal their attitudes on the issue being investigated in their responses to a direct question.

The most common justification used in support of their validity by professional pollsters has been that these techniques have been used to predict the winner in a good many elections. Even if the major commercial polls had not had the misfortune to predict the wrong winner in the 1948 presidential election, this is hardly a substantial justification. (The reader who is particularly interested in post-election analyses of these preëlection surveys can consult Mosteller et al. [38] and the files of the *Public Opinion Quarterly* and the *International Journal of Opinion and Attitude Research* during the year following.)

Response to a question about a presidential election when it is the center of public attention and public discussion is not necessarily a "typical" response. For one thing, just before a national election one can be relatively confident that *most* people know something about the issues and have at least a preference for one candidate or another. (However, not all do, and perhaps others do not care to state it.) For another, at this time the majority of people probably express their preferences *relatively* freely.

As Doob has pointed out, commercial organizations that make election predictions mobilize all of their efforts at that time, make many more surveys, and expend more time and money than on ordinary issues which are not to be compared to outcomes as concrete as election results. In relation to other public issues, it is by no means equally probable that a particular individual has an attitude on the issue or that he will reveal it in response to a direct question put to him on a street corner, at his doorstep, or even in his living room. Assuredly there is no apparent basis for the sweeping contention of some commercial pollsters that surveys on public "issues" involve "fewer technical problems and less likelihood of error" than election polls (quoted by Myers [40]).

In public opinion surveys as ordinarily executed, an individual is approached by an interviewer who asks him to respond to some question. Many people, for one reason or another, refuse the request, even as many as 14 percent of those approached (13). Some who are interviewed may express "opinions" on topics they have never heard of, and these "opinions" are included in the analysis unless some careful factual checks are made. Myers (40) mentions a case in which 70 percent of the persons interviewed expressed an "opinion" on a piece of nonexistent legislation. Contrariwise, the interviewee may say he has no opinion or give a misleading response when he has a definite attitude on the issue, because of the way he has "sized up" the interviewer and the situation.

In relation to issues which do concern him, the individual may or may not respond truthfully, and he may or may not be aware of a selective process in his responses. His behavior may reveal his attitudes, but not those which the questions are designed to tap. In short, the interview may situationally arouse attitudes pertaining to the individual's status concerns and other personal matters. In relation to issues involving his social prestige or social approval, the person may respond one way if he believes his response is "secret" and another if directly questioned (13).

In several cases, when poll results have been checked for their truthfulness against outside criteria, considerable falsification has been found even for factual questions, as Hyman demonstrated on the question of whether or not people had cashed any war bonds (25). Through poor recall or through attitudes related to the interviewing situation, people may give quite inaccurate accounts about certain merchandise they have purchased (see *16*, pp. 149–151). Unless results on "opinions" can be checked against some other behavior of consequence, like purchases, supporting some cause in word or deed, attending some public event, protesting some decision, or casting a vote, there is, in fact, no way of deciding whether or not relevant attitudes are tapped by these techniques. This is the question of validity.

Despite the continuing improvement of techniques and the understandable enthusiasm of their users, considered judgment requires agreement with Doob's conclusion that with a few exceptions the validity of a poll should be viewed with "extreme skepticism" (*16*, p. 150). On the basis of large groups, opinion surveys may reveal significant trends. But when this is accomplished by canceling out known sources of error with other sources of error in the opposite direction, very little can be claimed for the technique itself in the way of valid measurement of underlying attitudes and group processes.

"Public opinion" techniques are frequently used in social science. In terms of understanding social attitudes, those studies which have made a substantial contribution have utilized a combination of available techniques for a truly intensive study of a specific problem, in contrast to "single question" or even "single questionnaire" surveys. *The People's Choice*, by Lazarsfeld, Berelson and Gaudet (*32*), is an early and notable example. From this intensive study in Erie County, Ohio, the serious reader can learn more about attitudes relevant to voting for political candidates and factors influencing them than from the accumulated bulk of polls since 1936. One interesting finding of this investigation was that it was the people who were "undecided" who were affected most by persuasion in personal relations and by propaganda from mass media.

The reader seriously concerned with the question of validity of the techniques discussed so briefly in this section and with the significance of "public opinion polls" in modern social life is referred to Katz's article on the interpretation of survey results (*27*), Cartwright's discussion of public opinion polls and democratic leadership (*14*), and Doob's comprehensive account of problems of validity and the practical importance and influence of poll results (*16*, chap. 8).

Measuring Social Distance: Bogardus Scale

The concept of "social distance" was utilized by the sociologist Park in dealing with the observed fact that the relative intimacy and understanding between members of a given group and members of other groups vary (*41*). On this basis, Bogardus began a series of studies on the degrees of intimacy or distance (prejudice) members of a group preferred in relation to various out-groups and their rationale or "reasons" for these preferences. In these studies he developed a test for measuring social distance which is still widely used in substantially the form it was proposed.

First, Bogardus found that individuals could rank various national and ethnic groups in terms of the friendliness or antipathy they felt toward them and that their statements concerning these preferences expressed highly generalized attitudes, rather than specific affection or antipathy stemming from concrete experiences with specific individuals (7). Then he devised a list of statements representing varying degrees of social intimacy or distance and asked subjects to mark those classifications to which they would willingly admit members of a given group (8). These statements were:

1. To close kinship by marriage.
2. To my club as personal chums.
3. To my street as neighbors.
4. To employment in my occupation.
5. To citizenship in my country.
6. As visitors only to my country.
7. Would exclude from my country.

These categories were listed across the top of the form. Down one side, the names of 39 national and ethnic groups were listed. The subject's task was to mark the statement(s) he considered appropriate for each group.

The ratings made in this manner by members of a given group can be ranked in descending order to give a picture of the scale of social distance for that group toward various out-groups. Social scientists have been using the social-distance test to check the established social distance-scale and hence attitudes of friendship and prejudice toward various groups for over 25 years. Results obtained by this means are summarized in Chapter 19, which deals with group prejudice.

On the whole, the social-distance scale has been one of the most useful direct devices for tapping attitudes toward various out-groups. It is simple and easy to administer. Probably the main reason for its adequacy and continued use is that it was devised on the basis of empirical observation of group relations and the role of group norms in shaping the attitudes of members toward various out-groups. Of course, its applicability is limited to problems concerning attitudes toward out-groups and their members.

Likert Technique for Measuring Attitudes

As part of a larger investigation on social attitudes undertaken by Gardner Murphy in 1929, Likert (33) developed a technique for measuring attitudes which has been widely used for studying many issues, including quite broad topics like "internationalism," "morale," "conservatism," and "progressivism." The following are 4 items of the 18 statements included in the "Negro Scale" in Likert's original study:

No negro should be deprived of the franchise except for reasons which would also disfranchise a white man.

Strongly Approve	Approve	Undecided	Disapprove	Strongly Disapprove
(5)	(4)	(3)	(2)	(1)

Negro homes should be segregated from those of white people.

Strongly Approve	Approve	Undecided	Disapprove	Strongly Disapprove
(1)	(2)	(3)	(4)	(5)

If the same preparation is required, the negro teacher should receive the same salary as the white.

Strongly Approve	Approve	Undecided	Disapprove	Strongly Disapprove
(5)	(4)	(3)	(2)	(1)

All negroes belong in one class and should be treated in about the same way.

Strongly Approve	Approve	Undecided	Disapprove	Strongly Disapprove
(1)	(2)	(3)	(4)	(5)

The subject is asked to choose one alternative (e.g., from "Strongly Approve" to "Strongly Disapprove" above) for each statement. Thus, each item in the test is a rating device designed to reveal both the direction of the individual's stand on the issue and the intensity with which he holds it. The number in parentheses below each alternative is the score value for that choice. On this scale the higher value indicates a pro stand and the low value indicates an anti stand. These score values are assigned by the investigator.

An overall test score is obtained by finding the sum of the numerical scores for the alternatives an individual checks on the various items. This overall individual score can be interpreted only in relation to the distribution of scores made by other persons. In other words, like the scores for a good many achievement and educational tests, the scores made by subjects who have actually taken the test are the basis for evaluating an individual's score.

Typically a high score on a Likert-type test is taken as indicative of a stand toward one extreme on an issue and a low score as a stand toward the opposite extreme. For example, suppose that the "Negro Scale" had 10 items like those above. The highest possible total score would be 50 and would be obtained by a person who chose categories with the score value of 5 for all 10 statements. This would represent the most pro stand on the test. The lowest possible score for 10 items would be 10 (anti stand). Scores in the middle range can be obtained either by checking the "undecided" category fairly consistently or by checking some statements in the pro and some in the anti direction for the issue in question. Such scores are more difficult to interpret.

The statements included on such tests are chosen from a large number collected from other tests, current periodicals, and books and formulated on the basis of empirical observation of different viewpoints on the issue in question. Items are selected to be clear-cut and unambiguous statements on the issue which represent definite favorable or unfavorable stands. Preferably an equal number of pro and con statements are included. Statements for any one scale should pertain to only a single issue, but should not include statements on which all persons in a population will agree or disagree. All items are statements pertaining to desirable or undesirable behavior or courses of action, and are not statements of fact.

Final statements are selected after the preliminary test has been administered to a large number of subjects. The results of this preliminary testing are analyzed to cull out items which do not differentiate between subjects who have high and low total scores on the test and are not highly correlated with total test scores. In practice it is possible to present such tests on several issues at the same time by mixing up the items from the various tests and then scoring them separately.

"Scalability" of Test Items: Guttman Technique

On the Bogardus test, an individual's stand toward various groups can be placed in relation to a series of statements representing varying degrees of social distance. Occasionally an individual will check the scale in rather inconsistent fashion, expressing, for example, willingness to live on the same street with members of a group but not to admit them to employment in the same occupation. By and large, however, when most individuals check, say, "To close kinship by marriage," they also indicate willingness to admit the group to all other types of contact represented on the test. Conversely, if they check "Would exclude from my country," they are highly unlikely to indicate willingness for closer degrees of social contact.

Furthermore, it has been found that a given population ranks groups in terms of social distance rather characteristically. If we know how a person ranks, say, English, Italians, and Turks, it is possible to predict with considerable accuracy how he ranks Canadians, Spaniards, and Hindus.

Likert-type tests are advantageous in that they can be devised for a large number of issues other than social distance. They are not "scales" in the same sense that the Bogardus social-distance test is. The total score does not necessarily indicate a stand on the issue which can be predicted with assurance without inspecting the choices made on specific statements, unless it lies at one or the other extreme of possible total scores. The total score represents a sum of values assigned so that alternatives on one side of the issue (for example, pro) carry relatively more weight than alternatives on the other side (con in this instance). In research practice, they have often shown considerable utility when applied to a significant problem, as for example in Newcomb's Bennington study on attitude change (see the next chapter, pp. 541–543).

During World War II a research project of monumental scope was undertaken to measure soldiers' opinions (53). It was necessary to devise techniques to find out a good many things about large numbers of men in short order, and to be able to say something useful about the findings. Some of these problems were related to the men's attitudes, like the enlisted man's evaluation of officers. These research projects concentrated on utilizing a small number of items and improving techniques for selecting and scoring items so that conclusions could be stated concerning results obtained with some definiteness.

One of the developments during this project was carried out by Guttman and his associates (53, chaps. 1–9). This work has been called "scalogram analysis" and "scale analysis." The technique starts after the investigator has chosen the issue to be studied, decided to utilize an undisguised verbal test form, and chosen a preliminary list of items, as in the Likert-type construction or with the aid of "judges." The items chosen have been similar to items on a Likert-type test, usually with five alternative responses to each item (e.g., "Strongly Agree" to "Strongly Disagree").

The analysis is aimed at discovering whether or not the issue in question is "scalable" for the people being studied. In order to do this, the items are first administered to a sample of this population, as they are in the Likert technique. The issue in question is said to be "scalable" for the population being studied (1) if "it is possible to rank the people from high to low in such a fashion that from a person's rank alone we can reproduce his response to each of the items in a simple fashion" and (2) if the errors which prevent perfect "reproducibility" as defined above in (1) are not distributed systematically. In addition, Guttman included several related qualifications concerning "scalability" which pertain to the type of items used. For example, the required results might be obtained by including only items which about everyone in the population would check in one way, or by using too few items, especially those evoking stereotyped agreement or disagreement, or by scoring on the basis of too few alternatives for single items. If a test is found scalable by the criteria of (1) "reproducibility" and (2) distribution of error but contains items with these characteristics, the conclusion that a scale can be made is not justified (53, pp. 78–80).

In practice, of course, no perfect scales are found. The analysis proceeds on an empirical and trial-and-error basis to rank individuals in terms of total scores and then to try to combine the response alternatives for the various items in such a way that the errors in reproducibility are reduced.

If an issue for a given population is not found to be "scalable" through this mode of analysis, Guttman notes that it is still possible to devise tests in terms of which individuals can be ranked "efficiently" and these ranks related to their positions in respects other than the issue in question. He called such tests "quasi-scales." The distinction is probably a useful one. It does not clarify our understanding of measurement techniques to call every test a "scale." Guttman has pointed out one possible way to attempt to arrive at a "scale," if a scale is defined for social research through analogy with physical scales.

Guttman has given a lucid account of this technique using a simple example (21). The technique is limited in practice by the problems of validity which plague all direct techniques. In actual use, the cautions mentioned above concerning the type of items used should be strongly emphasized, in order to avoid securing high reliability coefficients at the expense of securing a scalable series of stereotyped responses. A number of comments and critiques have been made on this technique (18; 20; 34; 36, pp. 311–312).

The Thurstone Scales

The Thurstone scales are probably the most elaborately constructed of the attitude-measurement techniques that have been in wide use during the last quarter of a century. Following procedures devised by Thurstone and his associates, a good many scales have come into use to measure the attitudes of the individual toward the church, Chinese, war, crime, punishment, prohibition, and so on.

A number of statements ranging from the most favorable to the most unfavorable stand on the issue are presented to the subjects on a form. The scale values of the statements are established beforehand, as we shall see presently. These scale values range from 0.0 (which represents one extreme) to 11 (which represents the opposite extreme). For illustrative purposes only, 11 statements chosen from 32 actually used in a study of attitude toward war (43) are presented below. These 32 statements were used in a study of attitude change. The scale value of each statement is given on the left. In this case, 0.0 is the most antiwar end and 11 is the most prowar end. In actual administration of the test, of course, these scale values do not appear on the form, and the statements are presented in mixed order to avoid a directional set. For the reader's convenience, the statements are ordered here from the most anti- to the most pro-war statements. It will be noted that scale values from statement to statement are rather evenly graduated.

(0.2) There is no conceivable justification for war.
(1.4) War is a futile struggle resulting in self destruction.
(2.4) War is an unnecessary waste of human life.
(3.2) The benefits of war are not worth its misery and suffering.
(4.5) We want no more war if it can be avoided without dishonor.
(5.5) It is hard to decide whether wars do more harm than good.
(6.6) There are some arguments in favor of war.
(7.5) Under some conditions, war is necessary to maintain justice.
(8.5) War is a satisfactory way to solve international difficulties.
(9.8) War stimulates men to their noblest efforts.
(10.8) The highest duty of man is to fight for the power and glory of his nation.

Preceding these statements in the form are the instructions, which include "Put a check mark if you agree with the statement." The stand (attitude) of the individual on the issue is taken to be the average of all the scale values for the statements with which he agrees.

How Statements Are Chosen and Scale Values Determined: The main points involved in determining the choice of final statements and their scale values may be summarized by following the essential procedures used by Thurstone and Chave in their construction of a scale for measuring attitude toward the church (55). The procedures used by them in 1929 served as the model for the construction of numerous other scales.

Out of several hundred statements expressing an opinion on the church, 130 brief and relevant ones were retained and edited in accordance with clearly stated criteria. These 130 statements covered a whole range of pro to con gradations on the issue. The statements were mimeographed on small slips with a code number on each. Then 341 judges were asked to sort them into 11 piles. The statements expressing highest appreciation of the church were to be put in the first pile (designated as A) and those expressing the strongest depreciation of the church in the eleventh pile (pile K). Other statements were to be sorted in the appropriate piles in between. The sixth pile (pile F) was to contain statements that expressed a neutral stand toward the church.

The sorting by any judge who put 30 or more of the 130 statements into any one of the 11 piles was excluded from computation. Forty-one judges were thus eliminated. The sortings of each statement were then tabulated in the form of cumulative frequencies. For example, the statement with the code number 51 (viz., "I feel I can worship God better out of doors than in the church and I can get more inspiration there.") was not put in category 1 by any subject. The cumulative frequency, scale value, and Q of this particular statement are shown in the following tabulation:

Scale Value	Q	A	B	C	D	E	F	G	H	I	J	K
		0–1	1–2	2–3	3–4	4–5	5–6	6–7	7–8	8–9	9–10	10–11
6.9	1.7	0%	1%	1%	3%	8%	21%	54%	76%	91%	98%	100%

The scale value of a statement is the mid-point of the cumulative frequency; that is, half of the sortings lie above it and half below it. In the example above, it can be seen that this point lies somewhere between 6 and 7, the scale value actually being 6.9. The scale value of a statement can also be shown graphically. If we draw a horizontal line from the point on the ordinate where the cumulative frequency includes 50 percent of the judgments and then drop a line from the point where it crosses the eumulative frequency curve (ogive), the vertical line touches the abscissa at the point chosen to represent the scale value for the statement (see Fig. 15.5).

In addition to securing statements representing different scale values, two major criteria used for inclusion in the final scale were (1) the "criterion of ambiguity" and (2) the "criterion of irrelevance." The criterion of ambiguity concerns the relative spread of judgments made over so many

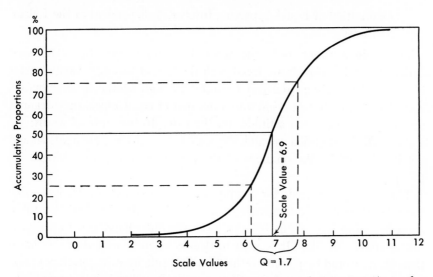

Fɪɢ. 15.5. Accumulative proportions (ogive) curve of statement 51 in the construction of Thurstone's scale for the measurement of attitude toward the Church. The scale value of the statement and the Q of the distribution are indicated graphically. (Adapted from L. L. Thurstone and E. J. Chave, *The Measurement of Attitude.* Chicago: University of Chicago Press, 1929, p. 38, Fig. 3.)

categories (piles). If the judges spread their placements of a statement over a wide range covering practically all of the categories, that statement was considered ambiguous and undifferentiating. Such statements were excluded from the final list. The measure used for this criterion was Q, or the range between the 25th and 75th percentile points of the frequency distribution. Accordingly, statements with large Q values were discarded and those with small Q values retained for consideration.

The criterion of "irrelevance" concerns the consistency of endorsements by individuals. To check the consistency, the 130 original statements were given to each subject with the instructions to check the items with which he agreed. If a subject whose agreements centered around statements with scale values in the neighborhood of 2 checked a statement with a scale value of 9, such a statement was lacking in internal consistency. In concrete terms, if individuals who had a high regard for the church as shown by their endorsement of items with scale values from 1 to 3 would check a statement with a scale value of 9 or 10 which depreciated the church, such items with out-of-place endorsements were discarded.

Assumption of Equal-Appearing Intervals Independent of the Judges' Attitudes

The main assumption in the construction of a Thurstone-type scale is that, when individuals are faced with the task of sorting a large number of statements ranging from very favorable through neutral to unfavorable, they will be able to sort them into a number of equal-appearing categories unaffected by their own attitudes on the issue. In the authors' words: "If a scale is to be regarded as valid, the scale values of the statements should not be affected by the opinions of the people who help to construct it" (55, p. 92).

This assumption holds for sharply defined statements on an issue, like the one "War stimulates men to their noblest efforts," or "War is a futile struggle resulting in self destruction." On the other hand, one can suspect that a statement like "It is hard to decide whether wars do more harm than good" would be placed on the "warlike" side by strong pacificists and on the "pacifist" side by those who are strongly militaristic.

To drive home the implication of the problem involved here, try a little experiment yourself. Find a few highly devout and religious persons and/or a few staunch atheists. Give them the following statement: "The advantage or disadvantage of faith in God is a debatable question." Ask them to indicate the place of this statement on a graphic scale. You can do that by drawing a six-inch line on a piece of paper and marking one end "most favorable" and the opposite end "most unfavorable." Statements like this which seem "in between" or "neutral" to many people are often interpreted quite differently by adherents of an extreme viewpoint on the issue. This can be demonstrated for other issues on which persons are intensely committed to a stand at one extreme or the other.

Is the judgment of a statement independent of the rater's attitude on the issue? The assumption that an individual will be unaffected in his judgment or rating of items on an issue for which he has a strong attitude is in sharp contradiction to the indications of findings in judgment and perception. For example, as reported earlier, judgment of lines of intermediary length is displaced in the direction of longer lines which have been associated earlier with reward (47).

The resolution of this contradiction will bring into line the recent work on judgment and a basic assumption in attitude measurement. This consideration is important since several investigators did report a high degree of correspondence between the placement of items made by individuals representing different stands on an issue (19, 44).

The first attempt to validate the assumption that the placement of items would be independent of the judges' attitudes on an issue was carried out by Hinckley (23). In this experiment, 114 statements ranging in all gradations from very unfavorable to very favorable views on the social position of Negroes were sorted into 11 categories by two white groups differing in their attitudes toward the issue and by a number of Negro subjects. The procedures, instructions, and determination of scale values were essentially the same as those used by Thurstone and Chave (see above). High degrees of correspondence were found between the scale values of the items as judged by two white groups ($r = .98$) and those based on judgments of anti-Negro white judges and Negro judges ($r = .93$).

Hinckley also followed the procedure of eliminating the sortings of all subjects who placed 30 or more statements in any one category or pile. However, this procedure involves the danger that, on the assumption that judges who did this were "careless," the individuals who had the strongest and most extreme attitudes on the issue were eliminated.

An observation by Hinckley is highly suggestive in this respect. Hinckley reported that "One tendency which revealed itself in the sorting of the subjects was the bunching of statements in one or more piles to the apparent detriment of other piles. This phenomenon of bunching at the extremes was noticed in the cases of *certain* of the white subjects, but was *especially noticeable* in the Negro subjects" (p. 283, italics ours).

A point made by Edwards (17) concerning the spread of judgments on "neutral items," that is, intermediary items which are not clearly anti or pro on the issue, is also suggestive. Edwards indicated that the spread of "neutral items," over so many categories in the scale is larger than the spread of sharply defined statements at the ends of the scale.

It is precisely these "neutral" ambiguous statements which would be subject to displacements in the judgments of persons with a strong pro or con attitude. It seemed possible that these very displacements due to the judge's strong attitude on the issue were being thrown out by the procedure that eliminated judges who "bunched" their judgments in a few piles and neglected others.

EXPERIMENTAL CHECK WITH IMPLICATIONS FOR ATTITUDE MEASUREMENT

In order to test the hunches summarized in the last section, a replication study was carried out and additional procedures were introduced to cross-check the results (24, 52). The same 114 statements used by Hinckley were sorted by various groups of judges under two conditions. The judges were (1) Negro graduate and undergraduate students, (2) pro-Negro white students whose stand on the issue was indicated by their activities, (3) undifferentiated white students, and (4) a number of anti-Negro white students differentiated from the others on the basis of a Likert attitude test.

The sortings were done under two conditions:

1. *Imposed categories:* Under this procedure, the same number of categories (11) for sorting was used with very much the same instructions as those used by Thurstone and Chave and by Hinckley.

2. *Own categories:* In this procedure the same 114 statements were used; but instead of being asked to use 11 categories, the judges were instructed to sort the statements into as many or as few categories as they thought necessary to differentiate the stand expressed in one pile from the stand expressed in another. The most unfavorable pile was designated as 1 and the last pile which the judge might choose (3rd, 4th, 5th . . . 12th, as the case might be) was to be the most favorable.

To reduce the memory effect of the first sorting of the 114 statements, there was an interval of two weeks between judgments made under these two conditions. The "Imposed categories" condition came first for 151 subjects. Thirty subjects sorted first under "Own categories" condition. An additional 61 subjects sorted only under the "Own categories" condition.

The results relevant to the hypotheses formulated for the study may be summarized as follows:

1. Individuals with strong attitudes or personal involvement on the Negro issue showed a marked tendency to bunch together a disproportionately large number of statements in the extreme (very favorable or very unfavorable) categories of the scale. This tendency to bunch together statements was especially striking among the Negro graduate students, who had a sense of mission concerning the social status of Negroes at the time. It was the first year of their attendance at a southwestern university

on a desegregated basis. When these individuals with strong attitudes on the issue, who frequently put more than 30 statements into one pile, are excluded from the analysis, the frequency distributions for the judgments obtained are much like those obtained by Hinckley.

2. Not all statements were subject to displacement. Statements which were rather indefinite—the "neutral" and ambiguous items in the middle of the scale—were subject to greatest displacements. For example, a statement which expressed a noncommittal stand on the merits of social equality was placed toward the anti end of the scale by the strongly involved Negro and pro-Negro white individuals, while it was placed nearer the middle by individuals with less intense attitudes. This fact lends further support to the principle that it is the unstructured, more ambiguous stimulus situation that is most subject to being recast or shaped by the attitude of the individual.

3. The direction of displacements or bunching together of items in categories (piles) at one or the other end of the scale is predictable. Those individuals who have strong pro attitudes on the issue place ambiguous or "neutral" items in categories toward the end of the scale *away* from their own stand, and *toward* the anti end of their scale. Individuals with anti attitudes on the issue tend to displace items in the opposite direction, that is, toward the pro segment of their scale.

This tendency is reminiscent of the typical reactions of intensely involved individuals facing relevant and significant situations. Commitments and affiliations from others without reservation are desired by these people. "Those who are not for us are against us." Consequently, they are more "choosy" in accepting statements or followers on their side. In more technical language, for persons highly involved in an issue the *threshold of acceptance* for relevant stimuli is heightened and the *threshold of rejection* is lowered, probably proportional to the degree of their involvement or commitment to the issue and their individual intensity.

4. It was also predicted in the hypothesis that individuals with strong attitudes on the issue would sort the statements into fewer categories or piles, while individuals who are not so involved would use a larger number of categories and shadings of opinion. A person strongly involved in an issue tends to see relevant situations in terms of black and white. Gradations in between have little appeal in his selectivity. The data relevant to testing this hypothesis were obtained under the "Own categories" condition.

It was found that individuals with strong involvement on the issue used only a few categories for sorting the 114 statements. When allowed to choose their own categories, they found four or fewer piles sufficient for differentiating this large number of statements. As under the "Imposed categories" condition, they lumped together a disproportionately large number of statements at the end of the scale opposite to the end that represented their stand on the issue, thus revealing again a raised *threshold of acceptance* and a lowered *threshold of rejection*.

"OWN CATEGORIES" PROCEDURE AS ATTITUDE-MEASUREMENT TECHNIQUE: This method of placing statements on a given issue using the individual's "own categories" may be advantageously used as an indirect, disguised, or "projective" technique for the assessment of various attitudes.

1. The task is given as a sorting or discrimination task. Therefore, the individual is not put on his guard with the awareness that a personal stand or characteristic of his is under investigation.

2. The number of "own categories" he uses and consequently the magnitude of the *own scale* he employs (whether it is constricted or extended) may be used as indicators of the intensity of his attitude. It may be possible to tap the rigidity or flexibility of the person in regard to a large number of issues through the use of this technique.

3. The intensity index obtained from the magnitude of the person's own scale and own categories can be checked against the amount of displacement of items to a few categories. This displacement can be expressed in terms of the proportion of judgments in the category with the highest frequency, in the category with second highest frequency, and so on.

4. The pro or con direction of the person's attitude is indicated by the location of the categories with highest frequencies at the extreme segments. When there are a good many ambiguous, "neutral" items, the tendency is to displace these items in a characteristic way so that the peak frequency of judgments is located in the segment of the scale opposite to one's own preferred stand.

Now we can turn to the implication of the findings of these studies for the assumption of the independence of placement (discrimination) of items from the attitude of the individual judging them. The placement of items in given categories is independent of intense attitudes when the procedure used is the "equal-appearing intervals" technique to the extent that items are clear-cut, definite, or structured. Judgment of items is affected by the individual's attitude to the extent that items are indefinite, vague, or ambiguous. The results obtained do not indicate that this relationship is the result of "carelessness" of the individuals. The relevant results in this connection are that those individuals who piled together "neutral" statements in a systematic way toward the ends of the scale also lumped them at the same end two weeks later, and also constricted their "own scale" by using fewer categories. It is highly unlikely that this characteristic mode of sorting results from remembering how the 114 statements were sorted on the first occasion. Subjects were not told they would sort the statements twice under different instructions. Furthermore, any memory effect weakens the explanation of "carelessness," for one cannot remember placement of over a hundred items if it was done carelessly in the first place.

Reduction of Attitudinal Influence Using the Method of Paired Comparisons

In spite of this evidence concerning the effect of attitude on the placement of relevant items, it might be argued that perhaps these individuals lacked in discriminatory ability. This possibility was ruled out in an experiment by Kelley, Hovland, Schwartz, and Abelson (28). In brief, this experiment used the method of paired comparisons and showed that when the individual is presented with two statements side by side with instructions to check one as the *more favorable* of the two, more discriminating comparisons are made and displacements due to the influence of the individual's attitude are highly reduced, though not altogether absent.

The investigators chose 20 statements from the 114 on the Hinckley list. The scale values of these statements covered the range of scale values. The 20 items were paired in all possible combinations and the 190 pairs of statements thus obtained were mimeographed in booklet form. The subject's task was to check which one of the two statements in each pair was more favorable to the Negro. Every one of 20 statements was compared to every other statement in terms of its favorableness.

The subject who is most consistent in his comparisons will judge the statement at the extremely favorable end of the scale as "more favorable" more frequently (viz., 19 times) than any other, the statement next 18 times, and so on. That statement that is located at the extremely unfavorable end will not be judged as "more favorable" at any time.

Subjects were obtained from the same populations as in the experiment previously reported. They were Negro students and white students from the same state. Seventy-one Negro and 78 white subjects were included in the final analysis of data.

The results show that under the stimulus conditions presented by the paired comparisons technique there is a high degree of correspondence between the comparisons of Negro and white subjects. This means, of course, that displacement of items causing disproportionate bunching at the extremes, which was found when the equal-appearing intervals technique was used, is not due to lack of discriminating ability of the subjects.

However, even with this technique significant differences were found between the judgments of white and Negro subjects for four of the 20 statements. For example, the statement "Negroes must undergo many years of civilization before they may be said to reach the social level of the whites" was judged more favorable with significantly greater frequency by the white subjects. The statement "I believe the Negro is entitled to the same social privileges as the white man" was judged as more favorable significantly more times by the Negro subjects as compared with judgments of white subjects.

Illustrative Comparison of Methods for Attitude Measurement

The methods of "equal-appearing intervals" and "paired comparisons" can profitably be compared to clarify the problem of stimulus conditions in attitude assessment. The points brought forth here can be used in appraising other methods and the functioning of attitudes or some other motive within the particular stimulus conditions they present.

If the investigation is concerned with the discriminating ability of a person in some respect (comparison of length, size, and the like), the method of paired comparisons is certainly superior. Here two items are presented side by side or in close temporal sequence. One member of a pair is compared against the other member, which is immediately and objectively available for comparison. Under this condition, when two items are perceptually present for comparison, the objective stimulus factors are circumscribed for the individual within an easy range for perception or discrimination and, therefore, the objective factors are given the upper hand or greater weight. Assuming an individual with normal capacities, the resulting judgment or perception is largely determined by the objective properties of the two stimulus objects. Consequently, the effect of attitude or some other internal factor(s) is reduced to a minimum.

On the other hand, if we are interested in studying attitudes and differentiating between individuals or groups of individuals in terms of their stands on an issue, the method of equal-appearing intervals is more suitable. (It should be noted that this discussion is not concerned with selecting items for test construction, but with the method of judgment itself.)

In the application presented in the Thurstone procedure, the individual judges each item one at a time within a rather wide range consisting of a number of categories. (Eleven categories were used in the studies reported above.) If an experimentally imposed number of categories is used, the end categories come in as definite anchorages which determine to a great extent the positions of other items relative to them.

However, if the items to be placed or judged are somewhat ambiguous verbal items and the individual is personally involved in the issue, his attitude comes into the picture as a weighty factor or anchorage. As a consequence, his threshold of acceptance for items in categories close to his own position is raised. His threshold of rejection is lowered, and items incongruent with his own position are thrust toward the opposite end of the scale. Thus, his attitude and its intensity determine the *latitude of acceptance* which is tolerable to him for items placed around his own stand on the issue. Within the limits of this latitude of acceptance, items will be assigned relative places within this segment of the scale, which is positive in terms of his attitude.

But beyond the limits of his latitude of acceptance, items will be lumped together as undesirable, rejected items with relatively few discriminations made among them. It seems likely that, the more intense a person is in his identification with a group and in his commitment to an issue, the smaller will be his tolerance to cases of deviation from that area which constitutes his latitude of acceptance.

One of the best ways to test this proposition is through using the "Own categories" procedure. Give a man strongly devoted to an issue a number of relevant statements. Let them be *logically* well differentiated from positive to negative stands on the issue, but with a good number of items which are ambiguous in the sense that they are open to alternative interpretations. Ask him to choose the statement that comes closest to his stand for the first category and to differentiate others into as many categories as he deems necessary. In other words, specify only his own position as the starting point and request him to extend possible acceptable alternatives and unacceptable alternatives. You may find that the range of acceptable alternatives will reflect his stand and its intensity.

This analysis is given as illustrative and is applicable to stimulus conditions implied in various attitude assessment techniques. When the particular technique appears to the individual related to his personal concerns, situationally aroused attitudes may become the decisive anchorages in terms of which response is shaped.

REFERENCES

1. Allport, F. H. The J-curve hypothesis of conforming behavior, *J. soc. Psychol.* (1934), 5:141–183.
2. Allport, G. W. *The Use of Personal Documents in Psychological Science.* New York: Social Science Research Council, Bull. 49, 1942.
3. Asch, S. E. Studies in the principles of judgments and attitudes. II. Determination of judgments by group and by ego standards, *J. soc. Psychol.* (1940), 12:433–465.
4. Asch, S. E., Block, H., and Hertzman, M. Studies in the principles of judgments and attitudes. I. Two basic principles of judgment, *J. Psychol.* (1938), 5:219–251.
5. Berelson, B. *Content Analysis in Communication Research.* Glencoe, Ill.: Free Press, 1952.
6. Blumer, H. *An Appraisal of Thomas and Znaniecki's The Polish Peasant in Europe and America.* New York: Social Science Research Council, Bull. 44, 1939.
7. Bogardus, E. S. Social distance and its origins, *J. appl. Sociol.* (1924–25), 9:216–226.
8. Bogardus, E. S. Measuring social distances, *J. appl. Sociol.* (1924–25), 9:229–308.
9. Buchanan, W., and Cantril, H. *How Nations See Each Other: A Study in Public Opinion.* Urbana: University of Illinois, 1953.
10. Buehler, C., and Kelly, G. *Manual for the World Test.* New York: Psychological Corporation, 1941.
11. Campbell, Donald T. The indirect assessment of social attitudes, *Psychol. Bull.* (1950), 47:15–38.
12. Cantril, H. The prediction of social events, *J. abnorm. & soc. Psychol.* (1938), 33:364–389.
13. Cantril, H. *Gauging Public Opinion.* Princeton: Princeton University Press, 1944.
14. Cartwright, D. Public opinion polls and democratic leadership, *J. soc. Issues* (1946), 2:23–32.
15. Corey, S. M. Professed attitudes and actual behavior, *J. educat. Psychol.* (1937), 28:271–280.
16. Doob, L. W. *Public Opinion and Propaganda.* New York: Holt, 1948.
17. Edwards, A. L. A critique of "neutral" items in attitude scales constructed by the method of equal appearing intervals, *Psychol. Rev.* (1946), 53:159–169.
18. Edwards, A. L., and Kilpatrick, P. Scale analysis and the measurement of social attitudes, *Psychometrika* (1948), 13:99–114.

19. Ferguson, L. W. The influence of individual attitudes on construction of an attitude scale, *J. soc. Psychol.* (1935), 6:115–117.
20. Festinger, L. The treatment of qualitative data by scale analysis, *Psychol. Bull.* (1947), 44:149–161.
21. Guttman, L. The Cornell technique for scale construction, *Educat. & psychol. Measurem.* (1947), 7:247–280; excerpt in R. W. O'Brien, C. C. Schrag, and W. T. Martin (eds.), *Readings in General Sociology*. Boston: Houghton Mifflin, 1951.
22. Hammond, K. R. Measuring attitudes by error choice: An indirect method, *J. abnorm. & soc. Psychol.* (1948), 43:38–48.
23. Hinckley, E. D. The influence of individual opinion on construction of an attitude scale, *J. soc. Psychol.* (1932), 37:283–296.
24. Hovland, C. I., and Sherif, M. Judgmental phenomena and scales of attitude measurement: Item displacement in Thurstone scales, *J. abnorm. & soc. Psychol.* (1952), 47:822–832.
25. Hyman, H. H. Do they tell the truth? *Publ. Opin. Quart.* (1944), 8:557–559.
26. Johnson, C. S. *Growing Up in the Black Belt*. Washington: American Council on Education, 1941.
27. Katz, D. The interpretation of survey findings, *J. soc. Issues* (1946), 2:33–44.
28. Kelley, H. H., Hovland, C. I., Schwartz, M., and Abelson, R. P. The influence of judges' attitudes in three methods of attitude scaling. Yale Communications Research Program, New Haven, 1953 (mimeographed).
29. Kent, G. H., and Rosanoff, A. J. A study of association in insanity, *Amer. J. Insanity* (1910), 67:37–96, 317–390.
30. Kubany, A. J. A validation study of the error-choice technique using attitudes on national health insurance, *Educat. & psychol. Measurem.* (1953), 13:157–163.
31. Lazarsfeld, P. F. The controversy over detailed interviews—An offer for negotiation, *Publ. Opin. Quart.* (1944), 8:38–60.
32. Lazarsfeld, P. F., Berelson, B., and Gaudet, H. *The People's Choice*. New York: Duell, Sloan and Pearce, 1944.
33. Likert, R. A technique for the measurement of attitudes, *Arch. Psychol.* (1932), No. 140.
34. McCarthy, P. J. A special review of *The American Soldier*, Vol. IV, *Psychometrika* (1951), 16:247–269.
35. McGregor, D. The major determinants of the prediction of social events, *J. abnorm. & soc. Psychol.* (1938), 33:179–204.
36. McNemar, Q. Opinion-attitude methodology, *Psychol. Bull.* (1946), 43:289–374.

37. Marks, E. S. Skin color judgments of Negro college students, *J. abnorm. & soc. Psychol.* (1943), 38:370–376.

38. Mosteller, F., et al. *Report to the Committee on Analysis of Pre-election Polls and Forecasts of 1948.* New York: Social Science Research Council, 1949.

39. Murphy, G. Two outrageous hypotheses about learning. Presidential address, Southwestern Psychological Assoc., Oklahoma City, December, 1954 (mimeographed).

40. Myers, R. C. Vital part of the poll question, *New York Times Magazine,* January 2, 1949, p. 8.

41. Park, R. E. The concept of social distance, *J. appl. Sociol.* (1923–24), 8:339–344.

42. Parten, M. *Surveys, Polls and Samples: Practical Procedures.* New York: Harper, 1950.

43. Peterson, R. C., and Thurstone, L. L. *Motion Pictures and Social Attitudes of Children.* New York: Macmillan, 1933, pp. 24–25.

44. Pintner, R., and Forlano, G. The influence of attitude upon scaling of attitude items, *J. soc. Psychol.* (1937), 8:39–45.

45. Postman, L., Bruner, J. S., and McGinnies, E. Personal values as selective factors in perception, *J. abnorm. & soc. Psychol.* (1948), 43:142–154.

46. Proshansky, H. A projective method for the study of attitudes, *J. abnorm. & soc. Psychol.* (1943), 38:393–395.

47. Proshansky, H., and Murphy, G. The effect of reward and punishment on perception, *J. Psychol.* (1942), 13:295–305.

48. Rorschach, H. *Psychodiagnostics.* New York: Grune and Stratton, 1942.

49. Rosenzweig, S. The picture-association method and its application in a study of reactions to frustration, *J. Personal.* (1945), 14:3–23.

50. Schafer, R., and Murphy, G. The role of autism in a visual figure-ground relationship, *J. exper. Psychol.* (1943), 32:335–343.

51. Sherif, M., and Cantril, H. *The Psychology of Ego-Involvements.* New York: Wiley, 1947.

52. Sherif, M., and Hovland, C. I. Judgmental phenomena and scales of attitude measurement: Placement of items with individual choice of number of categories, *J. abnorm. & soc. Psychol.* (1953), 48:135–141.

53. Stouffer, S. A., et al. *Measurement and Prediction.* Vol. IV. *Studies in Social Psychology in World War II.* Princeton: Princeton University Press, 1950.

54. Thomas, W. I., and Znaniecki, F. *The Polish Peasant in Europe and America.* Boston: Badger, 1918.

55. Thurstone, L. L., and Chave, E. J. *The Measurement of Attitude.* Chicago: University of Chicago Press, 1929.

56. Tomkins, S. S. *The Thematic Apperception Test.* New York: Grune and Stratton, 1947.
57. Travers, R. M. W. *Educational Measurement.* New York: Macmillan, 1955, p. 257.
58. Unpublished experimental reports directed by M. Sherif, University of Oklahoma. Demonstrations in 1954 by W. Prado and I. J. Rosenfeld and in 1955 by B. J. Murfett and R. E. Parrish.
59. Vanderplas, J. M., and Blake, R. R. Selective sensitization in auditory perception, *J. Personal.* (1949), 4:252–266.

CHAPTER 16

Attitude Formation and Change

Interest in the area of attitude change is active and widespread. Psychologists, social scientists, "public relations" offices, action agencies, and government agencies of different nations are engaged in attempts to change or form attitudes. The attitudes in question range through the gamut of human activities: financial, economic, political, religious. They concern man's relation to man within nations and between nations. They pertain to ways of living in different human groupings.

The accelerated rate of social transition in our times and the increased interdependence that prevails within nations and across national frontiers may be at the basis of this widespread interest in attitude change. The rapid rate of social transition has brought about unbearable gaps between what is new and emerging, on one hand, and what are old, traditional, and "established" ways of looking at things, on the other. At the same time, advances in industrial development, in means of transportation and communication, and developments in the proportions and crushing destructiveness of modern warfare have rendered human groups so interdependent that the outlook and stand of one group becomes the vital concern of others.

Problem of Attitude Change

Before discussing studies of attitude change, the main features of the problem should be specified. As we have seen in the last chapter, an attitude is inferred from an individual's positive or negative stand toward its referents. It determines a consistent, characteristic mode of reaction in relevant situations, which may involve people, an issue, an institution, an object or value.

Attitude change means change of the individual's stand on a given issue.

538

How can we know that a person's attitude on some issue has changed? We know and measure a change of attitude by the same means used to assess its existence. An attitude is revealed and measured through a characteristic mode of behavior, verbal or nonverbal. A change of this attitude is assessed through significant changes in this characteristic mode of behavior. Since an attitude denotes an existing stand or partiality toward its referent, a change in attitude denotes a change in the direction and/or degree of this stand or partiality. Attitude change seldom implies a reduction to a state of neutrality. It usually means a change from one stand to another stand on an issue. On the whole, attitudes are formed in relation to groups, institutions, and issues toward which a person cannot stay neutral. Attitude change, therefore, usually means taking a new stand in place of an existing stand on an issue.

FACTORS IN FORMATION AND CHANGE OF ATTITUDES

Formation or change of an attitude is not self-generating. An attitude is not formed in thin air. It is formed in relation to an object, a person, a group, an institution, an issue, a value or norm through exposure to them in interpersonal relations, in group relations, in communication from newspaper, book, poster, radio, television, and the like. However, these outside influences alone are not sufficient to account for the formation or change of an attitude. The individual's own selectivity, largely determined by his existing motives and attitudes, has to be considered as well.

In attitude formation and change, we have to study both (1) internal factors and (2) external factors in an interrelated way. Among the internal factors are existing attitudes and other motives relevant to the object, person, issue, or communication to which the individual is exposed or exposes himself. One important question here is: How does the point of view presented through personal contact or some medium of communication fit into the person's attitudinal pattern as formed at the time? Is it readily assimilable? Or does it appear to him too distant, too hard, or even too outrageous to swallow?

The following external factors are among those that have to be specified for analysis: the point of view or stand represented in the stimulus material, the initiator of the point of view (who sponsors it), who presents it, the form of presentation, the medium through which it is presented, the social context at the time (e.g., group interaction, audience, alone).

Adequate understanding of attitude formation and change requires analysis of such internal and external factors as they are related to one another. The interrelation of external and internal factors is reflected in the way the individual perceives, judges, or appraises external influences. His perception and appraisal of external stimulus situations are always affected by his existing attitudes and other motives which are operative at the time (Chapter 15).

Techniques for Attitude Change: One-Way Exposure and Group Interaction

A traditional technique in studying attitude formation and change, which is still widely used, has been to expose the individual to an external influence embodying the stand intended by the experimenter. The external influence is typically some form of communication. Before and after the individual has been exposed to the stimulus material, he is asked to respond to attitude tests, questions, or check lists. His responses are used to assess the influence of the stimulus material presented. In some studies this assessment is repeated at appropriate intervals to check the effects over a time span.

In the interaction technique, exposure to a certain stand is not solely through a one-way influence. The individual is placed in a social setting and is given opportunity to participate in give-and-take relations with others. The modern trend in attempts to produce attitudes and to change attitudes in given directions is toward increased emphasis on interaction techniques.

Studies in which attitudes or attitude changes are produced through interaction may be classified under two headings: (1) interaction situations in which individuals actively participate around an issue toward a common goal of high appeal to them; (2) interaction situations which lack active participation toward a common goal. Many studies of intergroup "contact" have concerned the latter type of interaction.

In this chapter we will first report some representative studies on attitude change in *interaction situations involving active participation* by individuals. Then studies illustrating research on *"contact" situations* will be discussed. This background on effects of interaction will lead us to some *experiments on attitude formation* in lifelike interaction and in the laboratory. The second part of the chapter will be devoted to experiments dealing with the effects of one-way exposure to various types of *communication* or *propaganda*. Finally, we shall take up the effects of propaganda through *mass media of communication*.

ATTITUDE CHANGE WITH SHIFTS OF REFERENCE GROUPS

Newcomb's Bennington Study

One of the most impressive investigations of attitude change is Newcomb's Bennington study (39, 40). The data in this study pertain to college students' attitudes on specific social issues when these students started as freshmen and as they progressed through sophomore, junior, and senior years in an educational setting where rather definite stands on these social issues prevailed. Two of the chief merits of the Bennington study are that interaction took place within a real-life social setting whose general atmosphere was conducive to definite stands on the social issues studied and that the same individuals' attitudes on these issues were assessed yearly over a four-year period. This kind of field study is a useful bridge between experiments with stricter controls, but more limited scope, and observational reports on actual groups.

In Chapters 5 and 6 we saw that as groups form with definite status and role structures and with norms, these groups become reference groups for the individual members. For the individual, the process through which a group becomes a reference group means forming attitudes derived from the prevailing values, norms, and practices of the group.

Bennington College for women started in the thirties. Investigation of attitudes started during the first year there was a senior class. The campus afforded a rather self-sufficient community life for its 250 students. It was rather isolated geographically and was exposed to fewer immediate outside influences than colleges closer to town or city life. At the time, the average student spent only one week end per month away from the campus. The campus included facilities for meals and living, a coöperative store, post office, telegraph service, gasoline station, and a wide range of recreational possibilities.

On the whole, the college and faculty upheld liberal stands on social and political issues in a "depression-torn America and a war threatened world." The faculty felt that it was their educational duty to make students aware of social issues. The small student body was unusually homogeneous, the large majority coming "from urban, economically privileged families whose social attitudes were conservative." The whole college atmosphere represented a liberal trend along the lines of progressive education, in which participation in project units rather than formal lectures and discipline constituted the main method.

Each year for a four-year period the students' attitudes on nine social issues were measured by attitude scales and through interviews. Among these issues were unemployment, public relief, and the rights of organized labor. The trend in attitude change on the nine issues as the students progressed from the freshman year through the senior year is best shown by a Likert-type scale called PEP (Political and Economic Progressivism Scale).

For a great majority of the students the college community with its liberal atmosphere became, in time, their reference group. Accordingly, this great majority shifted from the rather conservative stands they held during their freshman year to liberal stands by their senior year four years later. The differences on six of the nine social issues were statistically reliable. Prestige and leadership in this community were acquired by students who kept pace with the liberal atmosphere of the social setting.

However, attitude changes in the liberal direction were by no means universal. All of the 250 persons could hardly be expected to change from conservative stands to liberal stands, especially because of the following facts: (1) Most individuals initially had attitudes harmonious with their conservative background. (2) Influences from this background were toward perpetuating these attitudes. (3) Interaction among the subjects in the college community was not focused on the nine issues studied. In spite of the attitude change by the majority of subjects, there were some who did not change appreciably and a few who actively resisted the dominant stand in the community.

As Newcomb stated, both the changed attitudes of the great majority and the strong resistance to change by a few can be explained in terms of the *reference-group* concept. For the great majority who did change, the campus collectivity became their reference group. For those who resisted change, groups outside of the campus (family or friends) continued to be their reference groups. The college community did not become a reference group for these individuals.

The finding that attitudes changed when individuals took the college community as their reference group and did not change when individuals maintained their reference groups elsewhere is significant. There is still the problem: Why did the college community become a reference group for many individuals and not for others? From a theoretical viewpoint, functional analysis of factors which outweighed influences toward change for some subjects is just as important as understanding what factors were dominant in producing attitude change for the majority of subjects. This functional analysis is possible in part through investigating the relative significance which the college community and other groups (family, cliques, and the like) acquired for the student, as determined by the intensity of identifications and other personal idiosyncrasies.

For the majority of individuals, the college community was effective in providing a sense of belongingness, a sense of status and achievement during the living present of their college years. Thus, they were "absorbed in college community affairs" and "influenced by community expectations regarding codes, standards, etc." For many individuals who did not change, the college life did not provide these anchorages. Their anchorages remained elsewhere, or they were groping as a result of a conflict between anchorages. Hence, they were "indifferent to activities of student committees" and "resistant to community expectations."

The conflict between home identification and active participation in college life is reflected in the following statement by one subject who did not change: "*I am all my mother has in the world. It's considered intellectually superior here to be liberal or radical. This puts me on the defensive,* as I refuse to consider my mother beneath me intellectually, as many other students do" (40, p. 147). A similar influence is expressed by another girl who did not change her attitudes: "Family against faculty has been my struggle here."

Of course, these are only a few hints. For a full analysis of personal variations, we would have to have (1) an intensive study of each individual's life history, (2) analysis of situational factors like personal rivalries and their resulting victories and defeats, and (3) analysis of informal cliques, their relations to each other and to the general run of activities in the larger setting. Analysis of small groupings would be particularly important in a study of interaction involving such a large number of individuals.

Influences Conducive to Lasting Changes

In a later chapter we shall have occasion to discuss other cases of attitude change with shifts in reference groups and to relate them to ego functioning (Chapter 18). In this section we will take up the implications of findings reported by Newcomb in following up the Bennington study.

In 1939 Newcomb sent questionnaires to 1936, 1937, and 1938 graduates of Bennington with the objective of checking the persistence or nonpersistence of attitudes developed during the period of college residence. The overall findings were that, the longer the residence in this "closely knit, integrated community," the greater was the change in the liberal direction and the greater was the persistence of the changed attitudes (41, p. 206).

A study by Brophy (2) investigating the relative weights of various factors in changes of intergroup attitudes (prejudices) lends support to Newcomb's finding. This study shows that prolonged interaction with individuals belonging to a discriminated minority in circumscribed situations which are relatively uninfluenced by immediate outside influences is conducive to attitude change in favorable directions.

Brophy found that the number of times white merchant seamen had shipped with Negroes as fellow crew members was closely related to reduced prejudice. A contributing factor to this reduced prejudice was the experience of sharing common dangers while being bombed and strafed in the South Pacific. However, whether or not they were exposed to such common danger, joint participation in responsibilities on deck and sharing hardships of the isolated shipboard life were in themselves sufficient to produce common ties among the white and Negro crew members. This conclusion gains support from another finding. Brophy reported that when prejudice indices for various occupational groups (deck, engine, galley) were assessed, the deck crew exhibited the least prejudice toward Negroes.

It is on deck that white and Negro personnel have greatest opportunity for interaction. Especially during give-and-take activities on deck in the open seas, emergence of a delineated group whose membership cuts across color lines is more likely. In such situations, the values that come to the foreground are the values of fellow group members. In other words, white and Negro share the same reference-group values. In Brophy's study, common reference-group values were further strengthened by the active non-segregation policy of the union to which many white seamen belonged. In this case, the values of emerging groups were strengthened by the outside parent organization, which also served as a potent reference group for many members.

NORMS EMERGING IN DECISIONS BY A GROUP ARE BINDING

Studies of Group Decision

One of the most effective methods of changing attitude and behavior on a given issue was devised by Kurt Lewin and his associates during World War II. The series of experiments utilizing this method constitutes a landmark in the area of attitude change. The first series of experiments and the theoretical basis were summarized in convenient form by Lewin (30, 31).

This series of experiments places the problem of attitude change, with attendant changes in behavior, in proper focus. Man's directive attitudes are derived from standards or norms of a group to which the individual relates himself. They are formed by the individual as a result of his active participation in a group setting. It stands to reason, therefore, that a person's social attitudes will be resistant to changes attempted by merely exposing him in a passive role to a lecture or exhortations contrary to what he and his like stand for. These socially derived stands become very much a part of the person. A change in his social attitudes amounts, indeed, to changing a bit of himself. As Cartwright and Zander stated: "Although group standards can change, the more striking characteristic about them is their enduring quality" (5, p. 145). They summarize the rationale of the group-decision experiments as follows: "The logic behind these studies is that a group norm is the property of the group as a whole. If one is to change this norm and thus the behavior of the individuals, it can best be done by having the entire group participate in the decision to make the change" (5, p. 149).

The first experiment was carried out during World War II with the objective of changing food habits to include items not usually found desirable by American families, viz., sweetbreads, beef hearts and kidneys. The subjects consisted of six Red Cross groups of volunteers. There were 13–17 individuals in each group. For three groups a "lecture method" and for the remaining three groups a "discussion method" were used in the attempt to produce changes toward including the meats in family meals. In both methods, 45 minutes were available.

In the "lecture" groups, attractive lectures were given exhorting the audience to use the neglected cuts of meat. The lecture was linked to an appeal to save usual meat cuts for the war effort. The vitamin and mineral values of the neglected meats were elaborated. The health value and economy that could be achieved through using them were stressed. Information on ways to prepare them attractively was provided. Mimeographed recipes were distributed.

In the "discussion" groups, Alex Bavelas introduced the problem, linking it with the war effort and general health. Then the problem was left to the subjects to "see whether housewives could be induced to participate in a program of change without attempting any high-pressure salesmanship." The discussion turned to obstacles to using the meats, the possible objections by the husband, the odor during cooking. After discussion was carried on by the participants themselves, the nutrition expert provided the same preparation techniques that were given to the lecture groups. At the end of the period, a group decision was requested by show of hands.

Some time later the subjects were checked to find out whether they had included the food items in their meals. The difference in changes brought about by the lecture method and by the discussion method is impressive. Only 3 percent of the individuals exposed to the lectures were sufficiently influenced to include any food items which they had not used before. On the other hand, 32 percent of the individuals in the discussion group started using new food items. This experiment served as the model for other studies of attitude and behavior change.

In the experiment just summarized, the lecturer and the leader of the discussion groups were different persons. It was possible, therefore, that the impressive differences obtained were due to the personalities conducting the sessions. To rule out this alternative, Lewin had Dana Klisurich, under the direction of M. Radke, conduct both the "lecture method" and the "discussion method" sessions in a second experiment.

The subjects consisted of housewives. In each session, six to nine individuals participated. Half of the sessions used the "lecture method" and the other half used the "discussion method." Two checkups were made: one after a two-week interval and the second after a four-week interval. Again, the discussion method produced decisively greater change in the desired direction, and the effects were retained after an interval of four weeks.

Therefore, it can be safely concluded that the results obtained, within this social setting, were due not primarily to the personalities of investigators conducting the sessions but largely to the effectiveness of active participation in a discussion situation in contrast to passive reception of a lecture.

The technique of getting individuals personally involved in an issue by having them actively participate toward changing attitude and behavior has been utilized in various studies and applied to a number of practical problems. A recent confirmation of the more binding character of group decision over influence through a lecture was reported by Levine and Butler (29). In the experiments summarized above, only the individuals participating in the "group decision" sessions were told that there would be a subsequent check on their behavior in the matter studied. The subjects who heard lectures were not given this prior warning. Levine and

Butler checked on the possible effect of this forewarning by eliminating it for all groups.

The experiment was carried out in an industrial plant. Subjects were 29 supervisors. Part of their job was to rate the work done by men under their supervision. Three different hourly wage rates prevailed. The supervisors' usual tendency was to overrate men in higher job grades and underrate those doing lower-grade jobs. This resulted in a biased rating on the part of supervisors in favor of men in higher-grade jobs. The problem was to change this biasing tendency.

The 29 subjects were divided into three groupings. One was exposed to a lecture giving detailed information on how to correct errors in rating. In the second, the "group decision" technique was applied. The third served as a control. The individuals who participated in the discussion and reached a common decision to eliminate the biased rating subsequently showed marked improvement, while those who listened to the lecture and those in the control sample did not. It can be concluded, then, that the greater effectiveness of the discussion technique cannot be attributed to the forewarning concerning the subsequent checkup.

Discussion Method and Its Cultural Setting

As we have seen, the crucial step in attempting to bring about an effective change in attitudes is getting the individual personally involved (ego-involved) in the issue at hand. Getting an individual personally involved means arousing related ego-attitudes. Such personal involvement is enhanced in the give-and-take process of social interaction. (Ego-involvement is discussed in some detail in the next chapter.)

One of the main reasons for the ineffectiveness of attempts to change attitudes through information or logical argument alone is that the change often implies to the individual a break from the security of cherished group ties. However, if social interaction focused on an issue of considerable significance takes place among members of a group, the individual participant can safely move with the developing trend toward crystallization of a group decision or norm. In these circumstances, the new group norm becomes the individual's autonomous norm. It is subsequently binding for him whether he is acting in the actual presence of his group or away from his fellow group members. If the individual member deviates from the range of a decision or norm thus reached, he *autonomously* feels that he is violating his own values. In other words, the pressures to follow the decision do not stem from outside correctives alone, but from within himself.

The individual's personal involvement in the group decision leads, therefore, to effective change in attitude and behavior. However, in extending the implications of this finding to formulate techniques for attitude change, a caution is necessary. The mode of arousing ego-involvements of individuals in different cultures may vary. As we will see in the next chapter, situations in which ego-involvements are aroused are defined to an important extent by the status and role relations and the dominant norms of a culture concerning approved and disapproved actions.

A recent study carried out in India illustrates the point (36). In an attempt to change caste attitudes among secondary-school students in India using various methods, the greatest changes arose as a result of a lecture using emotional appeals. The experimenter wrote: "Contrary to our original expectation and hypothesis, these young boys do not seem to be in a position to exploit fully the discussion technique, in bettering their social relationships. Does it indicate that our boys have got to be used to democratic ways of discussion and at present prefer to be told what are the right attitudes rather than to be allowed to talk them out?" (36, pp. 114–115).

Within a social organization whose values clearly encourage dependence on authority and discourage settling issues on a give-and-take basis in small subunits, particular dependencies may become so much a part of the individual's ego system that group discussion methods for attitude change used in American studies may be less effective than methods more in harmony with the social organization. The published reports on attempts to introduce free discussion methods among the German youth right after World War II were instructive in this respect. The general tendency in such discussions was revealed in expectations that someone should take the lead and pave the way for a course of action.

CONDITIONS IN WHICH "CONTACT" IS CONDUCIVE TO ATTITUDE CHANGE

Contact among members of unfriendly groups has been proposed as the key to settling social problems and changing their attitudes toward each other. Certainly there has to be some sort of contact among contending or inimical parties, some exchange of views, some give-and-take between them before their attitudes toward each other can change. But not infrequently the word "contact" is used in an indiscriminate way (57).

"Contact" implies some sort of interaction among people. But what kind of interaction, under what circumstances, under whose auspices, and in relation to what kind of goals? In studies dealing with the effect of contact in changing attitudes, these and other crucial specifications are frequently neglected. A variety of interaction situations are lumped together as "contact situations." They range from a tea party planned by outsiders not thoroughly familiar with the issues between groups to group interaction dedicated to attaining a common goal. Studies of the effect of "contact" become meaningful only in terms of the specific character of the interaction situation studied.

Some of the specifications that determine the character of a particular contact situation were mentioned above. In studying contact situations, assessment of the way participants perceive the sponsors (as patronizing, as understanding, as neutral or partial) and the other participants is particularly important for explaining the positive or negative results obtained.

The effects of contacts between unfriendly groups are discussed further in Chapter 19. Here we shall mention a few representative studies to make the problem concrete. One of the early studies in this area by S. C. Dodd (9) was carried out in the Near East. Students coming from antagonistic ethnic groups were given lectures on the virtues of beliefs upheld by each group. They were taken to visit each others' religious edifices. When these students were retested after these experiences, they showed rather insignificant shifts from their original stands toward each other. If anything, their attachment to the values of their own groups was intensified.

On the other hand, F. T. Smith (53) obtained a definite, favorable shift in attitudes of 46 graduate students who spent two week ends in Harlem (New York) meeting prominent Negroes (an editor, a poet, an artist) and attending a party at a "distinguished Negro home."

In a more recent study, Festinger and Kelley (13) devised social contacts among white residents of a new housing project. These people were somewhat isolated from one another socially and did not have very favorable attitudes toward fellow residents or toward residents of the town at large. The overall result of the contact situations was that those individuals who were initially favorable toward the experimental project changed in a positive direction; those who were unfavorably disposed initially did not show positive change. In some cases, their unfavorable attitudes became sharpened.

Mussen (38) studied the effect of a four-weeks contact between white and Negro boys in an unsegregated summer camp. At the end of the camp period, about 25 percent of the 106 white boys showed more prejudice, and just about the same proportion became less prejudiced. Through functional analysis of factors from the setting and factors pertaining to individual participants, it was possible to explain cases of change, no change, and change in the negative direction. The boys who became less prejudiced were those who enjoyed their stay at the camp more and who made better social adjustments in the camp setting. On the other hand, the boys who became more prejudiced exhibited in their test responses "great needs to defy authority, and strong aggressive feelings." In these results, we see both social interaction and personality factors at work to produce differential reactions under these particular conditions and for this time period.

From research on social interaction and on "personality" factors we know that neither the characteristics of interaction nor individual characteristics are fixed entities. We should think that it would be possible to organize camp activities in a manner that would insure greater participation and personal involvement of those individuals who showed "great needs to defy authority and strong aggressive feelings." It is possible that with greater personal involvement and greater feelings of responsibility in the ongoing activities, a larger proportion of these resistant individuals would be influenced in a positive direction.

There is need of carefully designed experiments on interaction among small numbers of individuals in groups having positive and negative relationships. If the groups themselves and relations between them are produced experimentally, we can have a clear notion of the factors involved when they meet and interact. The reader will recall that this was the procedure in the experiment on intergroup relations at Robbers Cave reported earlier (Chapter 9). It was found there that when groups were antagonistic toward each other it was not sufficient to bring them into contact, even when the activities in the contact situations were satisfying in themselves (like meals in the same hall or watching a movie together). Such contact situations were utilized for further expressions of intergroup conflict. It was only in situations with superordinate goals of high appeal value to both groups that they coöperated across group lines. This intergroup coöperation followed the realization that goals could not be attained through the energy and resources of one group without the other (pp. 316–330).

In meetings between members of unfriendly groups in actual life, there is a further problem. This problem concerns persistence of the effects produced by contact after the participants return to their own group settings. It frequently happens that the changes effected in the contact situation are at variance with the norms of the person's own group. The individual participant must deal with members of his own group after he leaves the contact situation. Will he maintain his change in the face of correctives applied by his own group? In discussing this problem, Vosk noted the "disheartening evidence of indifference, of relapse into former patterns, even of occasional 'boomerang' effects when the returning idealist finds himself at too great odds with his home-town group or his factory associates" (57, p. 16). Because of such "relapses" by single individuals when they return to the influence of their own groups, it has become common practice for human relations workshops to request "teams" from communities, schools, or industrial plants, rather than single individuals. In this way, returning teams whose attitudes have undergone change in the workshops can form a nucleus for maintenance of their new attitudes on the issue.

STUDYING ATTITUDES IN THE PROCESS OF FORMATION AND CHANGE

An attitude is a complex product revealed in a characteristic stand taken by a person toward its referent. Motivational and cognitive factors enter jointly into its formation and its change. If we can follow attitude formation and change step by step, we will be in a better position to single out factors conducive to attitude formation and attitude change and to relate them to each other in a functional way.

The experiments on group formation, delineation of an in-group and an out-group, and production of negative and positive intergroup relations reported in Chapters 6 and 9 were carried out with the aim of studying attitudes in the process of formation and change. In these experiments, attitude formation could be studied "from scratch." It was possible to follow the formation of attitudes as individuals became members of a newly formed group. We saw the development of attitudes in relation to emerging group norms. We watched the rise of negative attitudes and stereotypes toward an out-group under specified conditions of interaction between groups. Then we followed the change from negative intergroup attitudes to attitudes of coöperation and friendship toward the out-group under conditions that embodied compelling superordinate goals for both groups (see pp. 324–328).

If some of the essential features of such lifelike interaction can be extracted, formation and changes of an attitude can be demonstrated under the more precisely controlled conditions of the laboratory. The great advantage of laboratory experiments on attitude formation lies in the possibility of controlled variation of specific factors. To the extent that factors included are important in attitude formation in real life, laboratory studies elucidate psychological processes involved. On this experimental basis, study of attitude formation and change in less restricted and more naturalistic settings can become more coördinated and analytical.

An experiment demonstrating attitude formation in the laboratory was undertaken in 1937 (49). The autokinetic situation was utilized (see pp. 250–252). It will be recalled that when an individual reports the extent of autokinetic movement by himself (*alone*) for so many successive trials (e.g., 50 or 100), he establishes his own range (scale) of perceived movement and a unique modal point within that range. When two or three individuals face this situation for the first time together, they establish a common range (scale) and a common standard within that range as they give their judgments aloud on trial after trial. After taking part in interaction with others, the individual tends to stick to the common range and norm when he subsequently faces the autokinetic situation alone.

In the present study, the problem was to *pre*determine a common range and standard for the individual. If a predetermined range and norm can be developed in a social situation and if the individual subsequently carries that norm to an *alone* situation in which there is no external social pressure, then it can be said that a characteristic and consistent mode of behavior (i.e., attitude) is produced in an elementary form. This was the aim of the experiment.

There were seven pairs of subjects. All were male college students who were not acquainted with one another prior to the experiment. In each pair, one person was a "planted" subject who was instructed beforehand to distribute his announced judgments in a certain fashion in the presence of the other subject, who was "naïve." In all pairs, the "planted" subject was the same person, in order that voice, appearance, and manner of the influencing person would be constant in each case.

The range (scale) and the standard prescribed for each pair of subjects were different. For the first pair, the prescribed range was 1–3 inches, 2 inches being the prescribed norm. The "planted" subject was to give the judgment of "2 inches" 50 percent of the time. For the second pair, the range was prescribed as 2–4 inches with a norm of 3 inches, and so on to the seventh pair, whose prescribed range was 7–9 inches and whose norm was 8 inches.

Each "naïve" subject took part in two experimental sessions on different days. In the first session he participated with the "planted" subject. Each subject of the pair gave 50 judgments. After every exposure of the light (for 2 seconds), the subjects gave their judgments aloud. The planted subject was told to let the other (naïve) subject give his judgment first at least half of the time, in order that the factor of *primacy* not be stressed. In the second session on the following day, 50 additional judgments were obtained from the naïve subject under the same experimental procedures. But in the second session the naïve subject was *alone*, i.e., the social influence being studied was not present in the situation. The problem was to determine how much of the consistency or conformity that was developed in the initial social situation was carried over by the individual when he was *alone*.

As judgments were given aloud time after time, the naïve subject converged toward the prescribed range and norm adopted by the planted subject. However, this convergence toward a common range and norm was not without some hesitancy or resistance. At first, when his judgments diverged from the planted subject's considerably, there was uneasiness and resistance on the part of the naïve subject. But since he did not have objective gauges to give him support against the consistent, steady judgments by the planted subject (who of course showed no difficulty in giving judgments), the naïve subject moved, in time, toward the scale and norm of the planted subject.

The naïve subject's adoption of the predetermined standard takes place in this experimental condition because, within limits, he does not have objective anchorages to check the truth or falsehood of the planted subject's pronouncements. If objective anchorages are available and clear-cut, the individual may be temporarily influenced because of immediate social pressures but is highly unlikely to carry over a predetermined standard when he faces the situation alone. In other words, he will not form an attitude in the predetermined direction (see pp. 97–106). In actual life there are many situations in which objective anchorages are not available to the individual. One counterpart is the situation in which a demogogue makes pronouncements and slogans on matters which his public cannot easily check.

One of the interesting findings in the experiment was that convergence toward the prescribed norm did not disappear in the second, alone session when the immediate social influence was no longer present. In fact, on the whole, convergence toward the prescribed norm was greater in the *alone* session than in the initial session when the social influence was present. Convergence was particularly striking in the alone session by the only subject who had put definite resistance in the initial social situation. In the first (together) session, only 34 percent of his judgments were within the prescribed range. His median was 7.40, while the norm prescribed for this pair was 8 inches. On the following day, when this subject made his judgments alone, 80 percent of his judgments were within the prescribed range and his median (7.83) approached the prescribed norm of 8 inches more closely.

It seems that the psychological process involved here has implications for reactions to influences from other people in unstructured stimulus situations. It is not a rare occurrence in everyday life to react negatively or hesitatingly to a suggestion by a person while in his presence but to respond positively when he is gone. Perhaps there is a disinclination to accept suggestions readily unless its source has strong prestige or the individual experiences pressing demands. To appear to yield easily is not pleasant for one's ego.

Attitude Formation Due to Institutional Preference

In the experiment reported in the last section, the source of influence was a planted subject who did not have established value in the eyes of those exposed to his predetermined pronouncements. He was a stranger who gave judgments in an assured and definite fashion. The motivational aspect in this situation came from the individual himself. It stemmed from the strain of being uncertain about the dimension in which he had to pass judgments without a tangible basis. We know from various studies that, the more uncertain the situation, the more difficult it is to make discriminations. The basis for objective comparisons is lacking. The individual experiences strain and his judgments and judgment time become more variable. Under this strain of uncertainty, the stability and certainty of the pronouncements by his fellow participant became the factors most conducive to stabilizing his own judgments.

Recently, an experiment was carried out by Norman Walter (58) utilizing the autokinetic technique with the following objectives: (1) producing shifts from personally established standards by introducing anchorages attributed to highly valued institutions and (2) subsequently breaking down these experimentally produced attitudes as a consequence of discrediting the institutional anchorages.

The subjects were college students. The experimental subjects took part in four autokinetic sessions *alone* on separate days with four different sets of instructions. In the first session, the subjects judged the extent of autokinetic movement with standard instructions. Each established his own unique range and norm. The control subjects repeated this same procedure at the three additional sessions on different days.

Just before the second session, the experimental subject was given a norm which differed significantly from his individual norm. This new norm was planted by the experimenter in an informal way. He mentioned it as the average judgment of students in an institution which had high prestige in the subject's eyes. (The relative prestige of institutions for the subjects was ascertained prior to the experiment.) In the experimenter's words: "Eighty per cent of the cases in the experimental group showed significant norm changes from the first to the second session as compared to only 10 per cent such changes in the control group. The reduction in variability in the experimental group in session II as compared to session I was significant at below .01 level of confidence."

In the subsequent two sessions, the norms for experimental subjects were broken down by introducing information which conflicted and discredited the institutional norms previously introduced. As a consequence, variability of judgments increased greatly. The breakdown in norms and highly variable judgments are reminiscent of the sort of floundering about which often follows disillusionment. On the other hand, the control subjects, who simply continued to give judgments alone throughout the four sessions, showed continued decrease in variability of judgments.

CHANGING ATTITUDES THROUGH COMMUNICATION

In highly complicated modern societies, many individuals and groups attempt to shape attitudes through various forms of communication. Newspapers, magazines, books, radio, and television are filled with direct and indirect efforts to influence people. Pamphlets flood the mail. Handbills are distributed. Signs crowd the highways. Speakers reason and exhort in auditoriums and on street corners. Educators are interested in bringing the attitudes of the young people they teach into line with scientific findings and often with their views on other matters as well.

Many writers who have surveyed studies on changing attitudes through communication have justly commented on the scarcity of well-planned experiments in the bulk of research reports. The research has other shortcomings. Lacking contemporary emphasis on the intimate relationship between attitudes and group processes, many early studies tried to measure the discrete effect of some form of communication on some people, without specifying their relationships to each other, to the communication, its source, the situation in which it was presented, or other prevailing influences. As a result, studies with similar problems and designs often yielded quite different results. Representative early experiments and some significant leads derived from them are summarized in the next section.

Experiments Finding Change, No Change, and Unexpected Change

Experiments using communication to change attitudes have presented speeches, written material in factual or "emotional" form, debates, discussions, motion pictures, and entire courses of study.

The more carefully planned experiments use at least two samples of subjects. While random selection of the samples from a population or "matching" samples in terms of age, sex, educational level, and the like is desirable in such research, the usual samples are rather similar, intact groups, usually school classes. Both samples are given a standard attitude test, say a Thurstone- or Likert-type test, on the issue being studied. Then the experimental sample receives the communication, while the control sample receives no communication or an irrelevant communication. Change due to the communication is inferred by comparing the pretest scores of the experimental and control samples with their scores on an equivalent form or the same form of the test administered after the communication. Some studies have eliminated the pretest by using large numbers of subjects whose initial selection was "random" and matching the control and experimental samples. Others have yielded suggestive results by presenting communication with opposing contents to two similar samples. If only pretest and posttest scores for one group receiving communication are presented, it is difficult to attribute shifts in scores to the communication. There is no way of showing that two administrations of the test in themselves would not have resulted in such shifts, or that some other influence operating at the time did not produce a shift.

Surveys like Murphy, Murphy, and Newcomb's comprehensive summary in 1937 (37) and Williams' summary on attitudes toward out-groups (60) show that most studies report some shifts of average test scores in the direction intended by the communication. Other experiments have reported no changes or unreliable shifts. In some studies, changes toward the stand in the communication were found for some subjects and changes in the opposite direction were found for others.

SHIFTS TOWARD THE COMMUNICATION: Murphy, Murphy, and Newcomb (37) noted that one frequent finding in studies reporting shifts in attitude scores following communication was that the most prominent changes were made by individuals whose initial test scores were "neutral" or "undecided." The implication is that communication may be more effective when an individual has no clear-cut stand on the issue initially. Since most studies present overall results for a sample, it is often not possible to state whether shifts reported represent crystallization of a stand by some individuals who were initially neutral or whether many individuals actually changed from one stand on the issue to another.

Schlorff studied the effect of weekly classes throughout a semester concerning the history and status of Negroes on the way ninth-graders ranked various groups (48). A significant upward shift in rank for Negroes was found for the experimental group at the end of this special curriculum, while the rank assigned to Negroes by the control group remained the same. However, the rank assigned to Negroes by experimental subjects was still at the low end of the scale.

Cherrington and Miller (in 37) compared the effects of a speech and a pamphlet, both by the same well-known pacifist, on attitudes of college students toward war. This study took place during peacetime between the two world wars. A Thurstone Scale of Attitude Toward War was given prior to the communications and an alternate form was given following the communications. Available subjects were tested again six months later. The control group, which neither heard the speech nor read the pamphlet, showed considerable shifting in scores from the pretest to the posttest, so the results are not entirely clear-cut. However, the test scores of both experimental groups shifted considerably more in the antiwar direction than the control scores, and this change was still evident for those subjects tested six months later.

In a series of investigations, Peterson and Thurstone (44) studied the effects of motion pictures on attitudes of school children. The general plan was to measure attitudes by a Thurstone scale or by paired comparisons, to present a motion picture from one to three weeks later, and then to administer the test again. At intervals from 10 weeks to 19 months after the movie, the attitude tests were administered a third time. Rather dramatic shifts in the distribution of test scores on attitudes toward Negroes were found following *The Birth of a Nation*, the shifts being in the less favorable direction. Smaller shifts were found for scores on attitude toward Chinese and Germans following films which presented those groups in a sympathetic fashion. Two films about war (*All Quiet on the Western Front* and *Journey's End*) had differing effects. The former resulted in shifts toward pacifism, and the latter produced no effect on one group but a slight shift for another. Pictures pertaining to capital punishment and prohibition had no effect on scores for tests on those issues. When a substantial shift in test scores followed the movie, some carry-over effect was still evident on the retests from 10 weeks to 19 months later.

No Change Following Communication: In the Peterson and Thurstone studies on motion pictures, it was found that while some single picture had no effect on attitude test scores, two or three films on the same topic might produce significant effects. It is not possible to specify what factors produced this cumulative effect. Length, frequency, and repetition of propaganda representing a certain stand are important factors which have yet to be adequately studied.

A number of experiments indicate that presenting communication designed to influence people's attitudes regularly over a time period does not guarantee attitude change. An entire course on race relations resulted in no significant shifts in ranking various out-groups (62). A course on the Negro in a college curriculum produced no reliable gain in scores on the Hinckley scale (10). Eighteen weeks of high-school classes emphasizing antiwar material and respect for other nations had no significant effect on scores for tests of relevant attitudes (3).

Changes in the "Wrong" Direction—"Boomerang Effect": The finding that communications may sometimes produce shifts in the distribution of test scores toward the stand presented is significant. Of equal interest, however, is the finding that a communication sometimes produces the opposite effect. In some studies, shifts were found in the "wrong" direction, that is, away from the stand presented. The propaganda "boomeranged" on its originator.

For example, Manske studied the effects of 10 lessons on the Negro in 22 high-school classes (33). Test scores on the Hinckley scale for two classes shifted in the direction of their teachers' stands on the topic. Test scores in eight classes shifted in the direction opposed to the teachers' stand on the topic.

During Wilke's experiment on the effects of propaganda on four different issues to college students at New York University, some "real-life" propaganda activity concerning one of the issues aroused large numbers of the student body. This was an actual antiwar campaign "which culminated in an anti-war conference to which delegates from all classes had been elected . . ." (59, p. 12). The student body became sharply divided on this issue. After the experimental presentation, strong counterpropaganda was presented by some of the subjects. While the experimental communication (like the real-life propaganda efforts) produced stronger antiwar stands in some subjects, other subjects reacted negatively to it.

Here Murphy's insightful comments on propaganda effects are to the point. As noted above, in some cases the entire distribution of test scores shifts toward the communication. At times, however, response to propaganda takes on an "all-or-none character." People either "side with the speaker or against him. He puts his appeal over to the hearer, or if he fails by a hair's breadth, he may fail altogether and create against his position feelings which he never suspected" (37, p. 875).

Recent Experiments on Reaction to Propaganda

By studying trends over a period of time, it has been demonstrated that people's attitudes do change under the impact of events and the resulting shifts in communication content. For example, the attitudes of college students toward war shifted dramatically away from neutrality and toward active participation in the months following Pearl Harbor (55). At the same time, attitudes toward other peoples who became the enemy become more unfavorable (56). The great advantage of the experimental approach is the possibility of specifying more precisely the factors which produce such changes. The somewhat confusing bulk of experiments on attempts to change attitudes through specific communications led to increased emphasis on well-designed experiments which varied factors other than the content and style of communication.

An outstanding effort toward a coördinated research on reaction to propaganda was initiated after World War II by Carl I. Hovland and his associates in the Yale Communication Research Program. A summary of the earlier experiments in this research program and underlying theoretical considerations were presented by Hovland (17). The studies and approaches up to 1953 are presented in *Communication and Persuasion*, by Hovland, Janis, and Kelley (18). Most of the experiments cited in this section were carried out as a part of this program. Typically, classroom audiences were used in the experiments. An attempt was made to investigate effects of persuasive communications as they are affected by the nature of the communicator, the communication, and the audience to which it is presented.

By varying the source of the communication, Hovland and Weiss (21) found that an identical communication has greater effect when its source is regarded by subjects as trustworthy and reliable than when the source seems generally untrustworthy to them. The audience learned what was presented about equally well regardless of the source; but they were influenced more by the "high credibility" sources. Thus, attitudes toward the content of communication are not the only internal factors which affect reaction to it. Individuals' attitudes toward the source of the communication also take part in patterning their perception of the content. In this study the issues presented were unlikely to be objects of well-established attitudes (e.g., antihistamine drugs, the development of atomic submarines, steel shortages, future of movie theaters). If the communications presented topics on which subjects had an entrenched and strong stand initially, the contrast produced by varying the source might be even more pronounced. In Asch's experiments summarized in the last chapter, verbal material pertaining to more definite attitudes tended to influence judgments when attributed to a congenial source (reference group), while standards attributed to an antagonistic source (like the Nazis) were usually rejected altogether as a basis for evaluation (pp. 501–503).

Should propaganda draw a conclusion for the audience or let the audience draw conclusions? Hovland and Mandell's experiment (20) indicates that when the content presented is (1) "complex," hence not clearly structured, and (2) not intimately related to intense attitudes, drawing a conclusion is more effective than leaving the issue up in the air. As Hovland, Janis, and Kelley (18) suggest, however, this finding might well be reversed if the topic of communication produces ego-involvement, that is, arouses definite and personally experienced attitudes held by the subjects.

Should propaganda present more than one side of an issue? In this connection, a word of caution is needed. Considerable research indicates that when two sides of a question which is important to the audience are presented by two sources perceived to be about equally reliable, the usual result is that individuals line up on the side of their original stand on the issue. Maintenance of original stands was reported by Knower (26), who presented two opposing written arguments on prohibition, and was demonstrated in reactions to debates on "social security" by Millson (35) and on the relative "value" of men and women by Jarrett and Sheriffs (24). Those who were substantially influenced by either side were usually individuals who had been "undecided," that is, had not had definite attitudes on the issue.

On the other hand, if the issue at hand is problematical, there may be advantages in propaganda which takes cognizance of the "other side" of the question as well as the one being advanced. In an experiment by Lumsdaine and Janis (32), one sample of high-school students was given a one-sided communication concluding that Russia could not produce atomic bombs in quantity for at least five years. Another sample was presented a communication giving the same conclusion, but including arguments on the other side of the question. Both communications were about equally effective in influencing the audiences. However, following a second communication in which "counterpropaganda" presented the opposing argument (viz., atomic bombs would be produced in quantity in less than five years), those persons who had heard only one side in the first place were more likely to be influenced by the counterpropaganda. People who had already heard the "two sides" were less likely to be influenced by the subsequent exposure to the opposing argument.

When the President of the United States unexpectedly announced that an atomic explosion had occurred in Russia, Janis, Lumsdaine, and Gladstone (23) retested subjects who had received a one-sided communication initially. Their reactions to the President's announcement were compared to those of a control group who had not received any preparatory communication. The control subjects were more inclined to believe that Russia would soon have a large supply of bombs than subjects who had previously heard the one-sided presentation giving reasons why a large supply of bombs would not be available soon.

Suppose the propaganda runs counter to the norms of a group. Which members of the group, if any, are likely to be affected by the communication? Kelley and Volkart (25) attacked this significant problem by presenting propaganda to Boy Scout troops which recommended reduced emphasis on the traditional scouting activities, like camping and woodcraft, and more activities in the city where the boys lived. Those Scouts who indicated that they valued Scout membership most highly were least influenced by the communication. As the authors noted, the communication was presented to the boys with the consent and in the presence of the Scout authorities. Otherwise, some good members who valued their group and its norms highly might even have rejected the communication as outrageous.

More research is needed specifically relating the individual's group reference and the direction and intensity of his attitude to his reactions to relevant communication. There is some experimental evidence that when an individual's stand is opposed to the content of communication (*19,*

42), or to its source (21), he is likely to perceive the communication as "propagandistic," as "unfair" and "biased," and not to be greatly influenced by it.

Experiments by Janis and King reported in *Communication and Persuasion* (18, Chap. 7) are relevant for understanding something about the reactions of those who transmit propaganda, in contrast to its originators. In these experiments, subjects themselves delivered a communication prepared to put forth a certain point of view. The significant finding was that when the communication was not "set" in printed form, but required the subject to improvise supporting arguments for a prepared outline, the individual was more likely to be influenced in the direction of the argument outlined. In the process of "putting over" a point of view set forth for him in the communication, the individual actively formulated supporting points and then became personally involved in these points and in the stand itself.

MASS MEDIA OF COMMUNICATION IN PERPETUATING AND CHANGING ATTITUDES

During the summer of 1955, an investigator would have had to look far and wide for an American child over the age of 2 or an adult who had not heard of Davy Crockett. Besides knowing that Davy Crockett was a frontiersman who "killed him a b'ar when he was only three," children knew that he was a hero. A parent did not use the name of Davy Crockett lightly or smile too broadly at a fur cap perched on a small head perspiring in the summer heat.

Davy Crockett was certainly not unknown prior to that time. But his rapid rise to fame in 1955 can be traced directly to the mass media of communication. In particular, the television, radio, and motion picture carried communication in word, music, and pictures which could be grasped immediately by millions of people at all age levels.

Two characteristics of the mass media are particularly significant for social psychology (51):

1. The mass media of communication have acquired importance as social stimuli and have replaced many functions of personal contacts (face-to-face relations) in shaping attitudes, including those defining the individual's psychological relatedness and social aspirations.

2. The mass media of communication (e.g., newspapers, magazines, radio, television, motion pictures) reach millions of people simultaneously or within very brief periods of time.

Through the mass media, communication can be presented to an entire populace or even a world-wide audience within a few hours. This presentation is prepared by individuals. But the presentation is not through personal contact. The mass media of communication represent social stimulus situations with distinctive properties. The flexibility and intimate nuances of face-to-face relations are sharply reduced. In their place, however, are the prestige and authority of an institution. In addition, each of the means of mass communication has special properties. These are reflected in the compellingness of the printed newspaper headline, the ubiquity of the radio voice which follows one from house to car and to the beach, the halo of the movie screen and the darkened theater, the more "intimate" message from television which is readily apparent to baby sister and grandmother alike.

Those who receive communications from newspapers, magazines, radio, movies, television constitute a "mass audience" in the sense that millions can and do receive them within astonishingly brief times. Compare this rapid dissemination to the spread of news in the days of runners, pony express, or even in the days before radio. In terms of the context in which communication is received, however, reception is not by a "mass" but by individuals alone or in small groups, families, or audiences in a theater. Communication from the mass media comes to people who are in social situations or who later renew their participation in interaction situations. In one study it was found that school children watch television and movies most frequently in the company of age-mates or their family groups (15). Response to communication is necessarily related to the interaction situations in which the individual receives it and customarily moves, the settings in which he functions as a member with established attitudes and personal identifications.

In this age of mass communication, it is equally true that the interaction settings in which an individual moves cannot remain immune to the outpourings of the mass media. At the very least, these outpourings cause reverberations in the family and group setting in which they are received. Communications are sifted, rehashed, and sized up by individuals in social situations. However, their compellingness is conducive to shaping activities, values, and goals in the settings as well. Riley and Flowerman (46) report that school children who are highly oriented toward their age-mate groups tend to perceive and evaluate the content of mass media in terms of its utility in their age-mate activities.

Further analysis by Riley and Riley (47) indicated, in turn, that children's responses to the content of mass media (comics, television, and so on) differ depending on whether the child's family or age-mates are his dominant reference group, and particularly whether there is a discrepancy between psychological reference to age-mates and actual membership in age-mate groups. Such findings have implications for adults as well as children. They point to the need for studying reactions to mass media as they are affected by the individual's attitudes deriving from his reference groups and, reciprocally, to the influence of the mass media on interaction processes and values within these groups.

Sources of Mass Communication

Communication in radio broadcasts, newspaper columns, or television programs does not fall on uniform members of an abstract "mass." The mass media contain no guarantee that stimuli will reach individuals for whom they are intended. People do change stations on their radio and television sets. They do stay away or walk out of theaters. They do skip over newspaper items. As we shall see later, there is considerable latitude for the individual to be *selective* in both his choice of and his response to mass communications.

But selective choice and response to communication from mass media by recipients are only a part of the picture. Limits to the selectivity of individuals on the receiving end are set by the content available to them. A person whose selectivity was directed exclusively to geological formations in the Andes, to oboe music or Indian wrestling would have a long wait between presentations from the mass media.

The content of communication, which sets limits for the selectivity of individual listeners, is not chosen solely on the basis of intrinsic significance, news value, truth, or beauty. It is chosen selectively by its sources or originators. For this reason, comprehensive analysis of the effects of mass communication on individuals and groups must start with the selectivity of the initiators of stimuli pouring from mass media in increasing volume (51). The prominent emphasis until recent years has been on the selectivity of the recipient alone. But the selectivities of recipients and initiators are not unrelated. They act and react on one another under varying conditions to an extent which is yet to be determined empirically.

Fearing's theoretical analysis of communication is relevant in this connection (12). He pointed out that frequently the "communicator" is to be distinguished from those who present the communication. A communicator is distinguished by his function in producing or controlling the production of communication which is intended to influence certain people ("interpreters"). In producing communication material, the originator always proceeds on certain assumptions concerning the interests, desires, and attitudes of the audience he intends to reach. In terms of these assumptions and his intentions, he plans the communication and its presentation, including the persons who deliver it. Fearing calls those who deliver communication originated by others "pseudo-communicators."

In this analysis, Fearing notes that the "intent" of the communicator varies considerably in terms of how specific his intentions are and of how much the resulting efforts are planned. He suggests that "the intent-pattern of the communicator may bear a significant relation to his role in the power-structure of the groups, subcultures, or class in which he has membership" (12, p. 77). Those factors pertaining to the communicator's social status and role, especially in terms of the power structure of his groups, are significantly related to "high specificity of intent" (p. 81).

Advertisers, publicity men, "public relations" experts of various kinds have highly specific intentions clearly set on "selling" a product, a person with some talent or ability, or some event. Intentions of other originators are not always easy to infer. Analysis of the selectivity of communicators has to rely largely on inferences from "(a) statements by or information about communicators, and (b) content analyses made for the purpose of inferring the character of the communicator's intent" (12, p. 80).

The mass media of communication are products of revolutionary technological developments of modern times. The technological and organizational changes which brought about mass production and transportation were conducive also to the development of mass communication. These have produced tremendous concentrations of wealth and power in the form of giant industrial and business enterprises. The trend in communications "industries" is similar. For example, in 1920 the largest 25 cities in the United States were served by 125 different major newspapers with 104 different ownerships. By 1950, these same 25 cities had 86 major newspapers with no more than 46 ownerships. Circulation of newspapers in these cities during the same period increased by almost 11 million. During these years, the proportion of all cities in the United States with competing daily papers shrank from 42.5 percent to 6.8 percent of the total (28).

Similar concentration is found in radio broadcasting. In 1943, out of 900 "independent" radio stations, "about six hundred of these, together using 95 per cent of the nighttime broadcasting hours of the entire country, bind themselves by contract to four national networks; the four national networks receive over 74 per cent of their revenue from four national industries" (*11*, p. 282).

Such information tells us little about the particular "intent" of a specific originator of mass communication, but it does help to place many originators in the social organization. Owners of mass media with ultimate control over their output are largely at the top of huge business enterprises and possibly of other business and financial organizations as well. William Allen White, a newspaperman himself, reported: "Too often the publisher of an American newspaper has made his money in some other calling than journalism. He is a rich man seeking power and prestige. He has the country club complex. The business manager of this absentee owner quickly is afflicted with the country club point of view" (*7*, pp. 59–60).

Beyond such sociological information and possibly biographical material, data concerning originators of mass communication and their selectivity are secured by inference from the communications presented. Of course, precise analysis of specific communications would take into account as much data as possible concerning both differences and similarities in selectivity of their originators.

Content of Mass Communication

Through detailed analysis of communication content, information has accumulated concerning values typically emphasized through mass media. An overall view of shifts in values and lines of action presented would require a continuing analysis of material over a period of years. It is possible only to convey in a general fashion the sort of values frequently presented. Most of these are derived from contents of "entertainment" rather than from "news" presentations. Content analyses show that, to an overwhelming extent, concepts and values presented are conducive to perpetuation of existing values and traditional stereotypes. Let us take a few examples.

Berelson and Salter (*1*) studied short stories in widely circulated American magazines and found that "nice people," heroes and heroines, were almost synonymous with white, English-speaking Protestants. Negroes, for example, were typically presented as members of the lowest occupational and social groups. Shuey (*52*) compared the proportions of magazine pictures showing Negroes and whites in various social roles and occupations with the actual proportions in the population according to census figures. The finding was that pictures in advertisements "vigorously preserved" the stereotype of the Negro as a servant, while non-advertising and news pictures concentrated disproportionately on Negroes as "primitives," athletes, or entertainers.

Recent analysis of "reality as presented by television" by Smythe (54) comes to similar conclusions. Four out of five characters in television dramas were white Americans. Europeans provided 10 percent of the heroes but 24 percent of all villains. Only 44 percent of the Italian characters were "law-abiding." The life reflected in these dramas was one which values "managerial and service activities" and depreciates "physical production work." The personal characters of the heroes were stereotyped versions of dominant values in the culture. American women were portrayed as somewhat less "honest," "clean," and "fair" than the men, but more "kind," "strong," "sharp," "hard," and "quick." Household workers or domestic help were depicted as deviating from ideal patterns and were distinguished as "dull" and "soft."

How may these traditional values and stereotypes be utilized in communication designed to persuade people to form certain attitudes or take specific actions? In a study by the Bureau of Applied Social Research at Columbia University, it was found that such values were deliberately used in advertising to sell products. One advertising man was quoted to this effect: " 'You want to sell the greatest number of people. Therefore, in your advertisement you present someone whom they will want to emulate.' This man had actually conducted research of his own to determine what particular Anglo-Saxon names possessed the greatest power to suggest high social and economic status—in other words maximum snob appeal" (61, p. 11).

Surveys or polls are conducted for advertising, radio, and motion-picture agencies in planning sales approaches, choice of characters, story themes, and the like. Conducted under the misleading banner of "giving the public what it wants," such surveys have, on the whole, the effect of perpetuating and conserving values and concepts.

Pearlin and Rosenberg (43) studied techniques used in "institutional advertising." Such communications do not try to sell a product, but try to "sell" their sponsors (e.g., United States Steel, Standard Oil, Association of American Railroads). Emphasis is placed on the more general and traditional values in the culture and on the role played by the organization in question in maintaining these values. The organizations are presented in terms comparable to the intimate groups in which the recipients usually move: "The Industrial Family that serves the Nation"; ". . . this Railroad Hour family says to you and your family. . . ." The recipient is associated with the organization as intimately as possible. For example: "People all over the country have invested their money in the ownership of the [U.S. Steel] Corporation. You yourself probably have an interest, either directly or because your insurance company, your hospital or your local college may well own stock in United States Steel" (43, p. 21).

The attempt is made to create a unity of interest and values with the recipient, to involve him personally in the way that he is involved in his own face-to-face groups. This ego-involvement produced by the modern mass media presents broad opportunities to shape attitudes and decisions of individuals.

Merton analyzed striking cases of personal involvement and subsequent action produced through communication broadcast over the radio during World War II (34). On September 21, 1943, the Columbia Broadcasting System had its War Bond Day. From eight that morning until two the next morning, a radio star, Kate Smith, broadcast spot appeals at repeated intervals. At that time, it was estimated that Kate Smith's regular daytime programs drew a weekly audience of about 23 million and that approximately 21 million listened to her weekly evening program.

As a result of the "Marathon" war drive, 39 million dollars of bond pledges were made in one day. The appeals that Kate Smith used were largely concerned with "sacrifice themes" (appealing to people to do *their share*) and "participation themes" (asking for their personal participation). Such themes constituted about 70 percent of those presented. A concrete illustration of a "sacrifice theme" will show how it demanded personal involvement and direct action from listeners: "Could you say to Mrs. Viola Buckley—*Mrs. Viola Buckley whose son Donald was killed in action*—that you are doing everything you can to shorten the war . . . that you are backing up her son to the limit of your abilities?"

The comments by listeners indicate that attempts to involve them personally in the values and line of action suggested were successful:

"Well, Dad, we *did* something. I was part of the show."

"*We felt that others had been impressed and bought a bond*. And the fact that so many people felt the same way made me feel right—that I was in the right channel."

Such are the potentialities of influencing the attitudes and actions of people through mass media of communication. In the next section we will consider some of the obstacles in utilizing mass media for changing attitudes pertaining to human relations.

Selectivity of the Recipients of Mass Communication

It was once a popular belief among action groups and educators interested in attitude change that attitudes with harmful consequences are the result of "false information" and that the antidote consists of disseminating the "facts." No one will deny the importance of the widest possible dissemination of factual information and scientific findings. However, some difficulties in this approach as a basis for attitude change are now realized.

One of these was implied in the last section. For every presentation over the mass media designed to bring a factual or representative picture of human relations, there are thousands presenting stereotyped conceptions. For each specific factual account or representative dramatization, there are a hundred short stories, a thousand advertisements, soap operas, dramatic sketches, and movies with contrary emphasis.

Another facet of the problem was suggested by Flowerman (*14*). He noted that it is one thing to influence people to use a certain brand of soap when the value of cleanliness is already a norm in their group and quite another to attempt to influence them to do something that is clearly opposed to the norms of their group. Frequently, information which is in line with the "facts" or scientific findings runs counter to well-established norms of groups in which the recipients are members. The selectivity of recipients is influenced by social attitudes derived from norms of groups in which they live, work, and find lasting belongingness.

The individual's attitudes direct him selectively toward certain stimulus situations and away from others. Thus, people who attended a wartime documentary film which was widely advertised and presented free of charge to inform civilians how they could best aid in the war effort were largely those who were already doing more of the things which the movie encouraged (*4*).

Lazarsfeld, Berelson, and Gaudet (*27*) concluded that during a political campaign people who have a definite stand on an issue or candidate tend to read newspapers and listen to speeches which are in harmony with that stand. The possibility of their being influenced by the opposing side is reduced by their selective choice of communication.

Hyman and Sheatsley (*22*) analyzed the results of a number of surveys concerning interest in and information about public issues. They reported considerable lack of interest in some issues and relatively great interest in others. However, only about 37 percent of the people expressed "high interest" in at least six of the eight issues mentioned. Information about these issues went hand in hand with interest in them. Since the issues were all widely discussed in various mass media at the time, the implications were clear. When a person's selectivity is not directed toward an issue, the current of information concerning it flows around him, not to him.

When information reaches a person with a definite attitude on the topic, his perception of it may be affected significantly by his attitude. For instance, during World War II a leaflet was shown to German war prisoners in Italy depicting life in Allied prison camps in America (16). The pictures were actual photographs taken in Allied camps. One showed prisoners eating eggs for breakfast. This item proved to be so far removed from the German soldiers' attitudes concerning treatment which might reasonably be expected that they simply laughed at it. Even though the pictures were factual, the leaflet was withdrawn.

When the content of communication is less clear-cut and more complex than a photograph or an information item, the alternatives for perceiving it are increased. Rather than ignoring the communication opposed to his own attitude or rejecting it as absurd, the individual may perceive it in a way which the communicator did not anticipate. Cooper and Jahoda (8) found such "distortions" of cartoons portraying a "Mr. Bigott." He was drawn to show prejudiced people the absurdity of holding social prejudices against minority groups. People with intense prejudices who looked at these cartoons simply did not "get the point" which their creator had attempted to convey. In their eyes, Mr. Bigott became simply a ridiculous figure, a pretentious upstart, a person of low intellectual and social status, but not a person whose views were like their own. Some prejudiced people even saw Mr. Bigott as a foreigner or a Jew. Motion pictures and radio broadcasts dealing with issues relevant to intensely held attitudes have also been misinterpreted by members of the audience with attitudes contrary to the message.

When a communication presents a clear-cut content which is contrary to a person's attitude, there is less possibility that he can interpret it in a way harmonious with his stand. Rather than being influenced in the direction suggested by the communication, he may react against the communication and move further in the direction of his own stand.

RELATING INTERNAL FACTORS AND EXTERNAL FACTORS IN ATTITUDE CHANGE

The results of attitude-change studies using different techniques often seem inconclusive and even contradictory. We find results showing that "contact" is effective; others indicate little positive change with contact or even report changes in a negative direction. Similar confusion results if we try to come to general conclusions about effects of "communication."

One reason for a lack of coherence in research findings is that often different investigations of "contact" or of "communication" have studied quite different situations. "Contact," for example, has been used in experiments and research summaries to cover a wide range of interaction situations. "Communication" has covered everything from a 10-minute factual lecture to a dramatic motion picture and an entire course of study at the college level.

In summarizing illustrative research, we have tried to emphasize that the nature of external influences (like contact or communication) has to be specified in relation to a context of external factors and the relevant attitudes and other internal factors operative at the time. The effects of a contact situation become comprehensible when it is possible to analyze the nature of interaction, the individuals who participate, the sponsors, the setting, and the stand represented. We suggest that "contact situations" can be effectively analyzed in the same terms as interaction situations in general. They may range from transitory togetherness situations to interaction focused on a common problem which leads to stabilization of a group (see Chapters 5 and 6). Research on "contact situations" would, therefore, become a study of interaction situations with special problems produced by participants belonging to different groups, by their established attitudes toward each other, and by their perception of the sponsors of the event and of the purpose of the interaction situation.

The attitudes of individuals exposed to interaction situations or to communication have often been reported only in averages and a range of test scores or questionnaire responses. In some studies it is difficult to ascertain whether or not individuals had a definite attitude on the issue prior to the experiment.

In studying attitude change, a substantial step forward may be made by more concentrated attention to the psychological processes involved and the precise nature of external influences presented. An established attitude implies a characteristic stand toward its referent. When an attitude is situationally aroused, the individual's perception and reaction to relevant objects, persons, and situations are affected by the attitude. To understand his perception of the external situation, the relationships between his attitude and the relevant external factors have to be ascertained. (See Chapter 3, pp. 82–83.)

We may consider reaction to external factors designed to influence a person's attitudes as an evaluation or judgment. Therefore, some general principles of perception and judgment can be used to deal with the patterning of internal and external factors which produces a particular reaction.

In Chapter 2 we learned that judgment of any particular stimulus is affected by its relationship within a reference scale formed through contact with a series of stimuli (pp. 46–51). It will be recalled that the introduction of one stimulus repeatedly as an anchorage affects judgments of the entire series. If the anchorage is carried outside of the stimulus scale, it tends to be assimilated as a part of the reference scale, with the result that the scale itself is extended. Such assimilation of anchoring stimuli was found in experiments by Volkmann, Rogers, and McGarvey (p. 65).

However, if an anchoring stimulus is carried too far beyond the end points of the stimulus scale, the *assimilation effect* breaks down. It has been shown that when carried step by step away from the scale, the anchorage causes the scale to contract or shrink. That is, when the anchorage is too distant, a *contrast effect* is produced (p. 66).

An experiment by Edwin Cohen (6) demonstrates contrast effects in judgments reached by consensus. Contrast was produced by introducing anchorages at great distance from the position of items previously judged. This study followed leads derived from the experiments by Volkmann, Rogers, and McGarvey already mentioned. Pairs of subjects were asked to agree on ratings (judgments) of 30 statements representing somewhat undesirable behavior, like "fishing without a license." These 30 statements were presented a second time, but this time were mixed in with 14 statements representing *very* undesirable behaviors, like "kidnapping a baby for ransom." These extremely undesirable behaviors served as anchorages which were far removed from the moderately undesirable behaviors. Therefore, the second consensus reached in rating the moderate statements shifted significantly. The somewhat undesirable statements now seemed *less* serious than when they were judged without the very undesirable statements. Consensus was reached in both cases, but consensus with the extreme anchorages differed significantly from consensus without the extreme anchorages. Since the shift in judgments produced by the extreme anchorages was away from the anchorage, the effect of the extreme anchorages was a contrast effect. Judgments by control subjects showed that the shifts did not result simply from the repetition of the ratings. They occurred only in the experimental sample when the extreme anchorages were introduced.

In earlier chapters we have seen that attitudes and other internal factors can also function as anchorages (e.g., see Marks study in the last chapter, pp. 499–500). When an individual with a definite attitude is presented with some stimulus situation or communication, both his own attitude and the stand represented may function as anchorages in structuring his perception and evaluation. We may be able to analyze reactions to a given stimulus (communication) in terms of the reciprocal relationships between these anchorages and the reference scale of existing stands on the issue.

The individual's stand on an issue and the contents of stimulus material presented do not usually represent single points on a scale. Rather, each covers a segment on a scale, which may be defined more or less clearly in different cases. As suggested in the last chapter (p. 533), the individual has a *latitude of acceptance* for positions or stands near his own. The magnitude of his latitude of acceptance is likely to be related to the intensity with which he upholds his own stand on the issue. The narrower his latitude of acceptance, the less his tolerance for other positions on the issue and the more intensely he rejects them.

In order to assess the individual's reaction to stimuli relevant to his attitude, we would need to know his own latitude of acceptance, the range of positions presented to him, and, in addition, *the distance between his own stand and the stand presented.*

On the basis of judgment experiments, we would predict that, the closer the presented stand is to the individual's own stand on the issue, the greater is the likelihood of an assimilation effect. The result may be that his latitude of acceptance is extended to include the stand presented, implying a shift in his attitude on the issue.

On the other hand, if the distance between his own stand and the stand presented is too great, the individual is likely to reject the stand presented to him. He may even react in *contrast* to the stimulus presented by shifting his own stand in the opposite direction still further away from the stand presented. This seems to be what happens in the "boomerang" effects noted in "contact" and "communication" studies. In terms of this analysis, this would occur at the point where stimuli presented cease to cause his own scale to expand and result instead in withdrawal and reaffirmation of his own stand.

The stand presented in the external situation is not the only factor which may become an anchorage. Among those external factors which are frequently critical is the originator of the stand presented. An originator who has prestige for the individual may be more effective in extending the range of positions tolerable to him. He may reject a somewhat distant stand less readily if the person who presents it is significant in his eyes. Conversely, he may reject a stand much closer to his own if its source is insignificant or inimical to him.

In closing this discussion, we may ask a few questions that need to be answered in the analysis of attitude change. These questions all pertain to the *reciprocal effects of reference scales and anchorages* in judgmental reactions (50):

What will be the effects of varying the distance between anchorages and the reference scale if the magnitude of the reference scale itself is increased or decreased? We should think that the effect of anchorages is a function of the magnitude (range) of the scale, as well as the position of the anchorages relative to the scale (see pp. 64–66).

What will be the effect of an anchorage when carried so far beyond the bounds of the scale that it appears only faintly related to the individual's reference scale? Will his judgments of stimuli within the scale be made as though no anchorage is presented?

What will be the effect of varying degrees of exposure to the same scale (e.g., practice) on subsequent judgments of similar stimuli? Research on this problem will link the work on reference scales and anchorages to a central problem in psychology, viz., learning. (See the experimental work surveyed earlier, pp. 48–50.) A related question is: What will be the effect of varying kinds of exposure to the same scale (e.g., with and without ego-involvement) on subsequent judgments of similar stimuli?

Technological Changes as Factors in Attitude Change

One of the neglected areas in studying attitude change in social psychology is technological change. It is well known that technological changes bring about changed relations between men and between groups. The grim consequences of the development of atomic and hydrogen bombs are already producing changes in attitudes toward war in various parts of the world. The differences in family attitudes in urban and rural areas, documented by sociologists, are attributed in no small part to the differences in human relationships produced by means of production, transportation and communication. Convincing evidence of this explanation is found in the tendency for rural and urban attitudes to become more similar as the rural areas are exposed more and more to mechanization and to modern means of transportation and communication. The topic of technological changes and their effects on social relations, concepts, and attitudes is treated in Chapter 20.

REFERENCES

1. Berelson, B., and Salter, P. J. Majority and minority Americans: An analysis of magazine fiction, *Publ. Opin. Quart.* (1946), 10:168–190.
2. Brophy, I. N. The luxury of anti-Negro prejudice, *Publ. Opin. Quart.* (1946), 10:456–466.
3. Campbell, D. W., and Stover, G. F. Teaching international-mindedness in the social studies, *J. educat. Sociol.* (1933), 7:244–248.
4. Cartwright, D. Some principles of mass persuasion, *Human Relat.* (1949), 2:253–267.
5. Cartwright, D., and Zander, A. (eds.). *Group Dynamics: Research and Theory.* Evanston, Ill.: Row, Peterson, 1953.
6. Cohen, E. Stimulus conditions as factors in social change. Doctorate dissertation, University of Oklahoma, 1955.
7. Commission on Freedom of the Press, A *Free and Responsible Press.* Chicago: University of Chicago Press, 1947.
8. Cooper, E., and Jahoda, M. The evasion of propaganda: How prejudiced people respond to anti-prejudice propaganda, *J. Psychol.* (1947), 23:15–25.
9. Dodd, S. C. A social distance test in the Near East, *Amer. J. Sociol.* (1935), 41:194–204.
10. Droba, D. D. Education and Negro attitudes, *Sociol. and soc. Res.* (1932), 17:137–141.
11. Durr, C. J. Freedom of Speech for Whom? in D. Katz, D. Cartwright, S. Eldersveld, and A. M. Lee (eds.), *Public Opinion and Propaganda.* New York: Dryden, 1954.
12. Fearing, Franklin. Toward a psychological theory of human communication, *J. Personal.* (1953), 22:71–88.
13. Festinger, L., and Kelley, H. H. *Changing Attitudes Through Social Contact.* Ann Arbor: University of Michigan, Research Center for Group Dynamics, 1951.
14. Flowerman, S. The use of propaganda to reduce prejudice: A refutation, *Internat. J. Opin. & Attit. Res.* (1949), 3:99–108.
15. Freidson, E. The relation of the social situation of contact to the media of mass communication, *Publ. Opin. Quart.* (1953–54), 17:230–238.
16. Herz, M. F. Some psychological lessons from leaflet propaganda in World War II, *Publ. Opin. Quart.* (1949), 13:471–486.
17. Hovland, C. I. Changes in attitude through communication, *J. abnorm. & soc. Psychol.* (1951), 46:424–437.

18. Hovland, C. I., Janis, I. L., and Kelley, H. H. *Communication and Persuasion: Psychological Studies of Opinion Change.* New Haven: Yale University Press, 1953.
19. Hovland, C. I., Lumsdaine, A. A., and Sheffield, F. J. *Experiments on Mass Communication.* Princeton: Princeton University Press, 1949.
20. Hovland, C. I., and Mandell, W. An experimental comparison of conclusion-drawing by the communicator and by the audience, *J. abnorm. & soc. Psychol.* (1952), 47:581–588.
21. Hovland, C. I., and Weiss, W. The influence of source credibility in communication effectiveness, *Publ. Opin. Quart.* (1951), 15:633–650.
22. Hyman, H. H., and Sheatsley, P. B. Some reasons why information campaigns fail, *Publ. Opin. Quart.* (1947), 11:412–423.
23. Janis, I. L., Lumsdaine, A. A., and Gladstone, A. I. Effects of preparatory communications on reactions to a subsequent news event, *Publ. Opin. Quart.* (1951), 15:487–518.
24. Jarrett, R. F., and Sherriffs, A. C. Propaganda, debate and impartial presentation as determiners of attitude change, *J. abnorm. & soc. Psychol.* (1953), 48:33–41.
25. Kelley, H. H., and Volkart, E. H. The resistance to change of group-anchored attitudes, *Amer. sociol. Rev.* (1952), 17:453–465.
26. Knower, F. H. Experimental studies in changes in attitudes: II. A study of the effect of printed argument on changes in attitude, *J. abnorm. & soc. Psychol.* (1936), 30:522–532.
27. Lazarsfeld, P. F., Berelson, B., and Gaudet, H. *The People's Choice.* New York: Duell, Sloan and Pearce, 1944.
28. Lee, A. M. Freedom of the Press, in D. Katz, D. Cartwright, S. Eldersveld, and A. M. Lee (eds.), *Public Opinion and Propaganda.* New York: Dryden, 1954.
29. Levine, J., and Butler, J. Lecture vs. Group Decision in Changing Behavior, in D. Cartwright and A. Zander (eds.), *Group Dynamics: Research and Theory.* Evanston, Ill.: Row, Peterson, 1953.
30. Lewin, K. Group Decision and Social Change, in G. Swanson, T. M. Newcomb, and E. L. Hartley (eds.), *Readings in Social Psychology.* New York: Holt, rev. ed., 1952.
31. Lewin, K. Studies in Group Decision, in D. Cartwright and A. Zander (eds.), *Group Dynamics: Research and Theory.* Evanston, Ill.: Row, Peterson, 1953.
32. Lumsdaine, A. A., and Janis, I. L. Resistance to "counterpropaganda" produced by one-sided and two-sided "propaganda" presentations, *Publ. Opin. Quart.* (1953), 17:311–318.
33. Manske, A. J. The reflection of teachers' attitudes in the attitudes of their

pupils. Doctorate dissertation, Teachers College, Columbia University, 1935; see Murphy, Murphy, and Newcomb (37), p. 950.

34. Merton, R. K. *Mass Persuasion: The Social Psychology of a War Bond Drive*. New York: Harper, 1946.

35. Millson, W. A. D. Problems in measuring audience reaction, *Quart. J. Speech* (1932), 18:621–637.

36. Murphy, G. *In the Minds of Men*. New York: Basic Books, 1953.

37. Murphy, G., Murphy, L. B., and Newcomb, T. M. *Experimental Social Psychology*. New York: Harper, 1937.

38. Mussen, P. Some personality and social factors related to changes in children's attitudes towards Negroes, *J. abnorm. & soc. Psychol.* (1950), 45:423–441.

39. Newcomb, T. M. *Personality and Social Change*. New York: Dryden, 1943.

40. Newcomb, T. M. Attitude Development as a Function of Reference Groups, in M. Sherif, *An Outline of Social Psychology*. New York: Harper, 1948.

41. Newcomb, T. M. *Social Psychology*. New York: Dryden, 1950.

42. Parrish, J. A., and Campbell, D. T. Measuring propaganda effects with direct and indirect attitude tests, *J. abnorm. & soc. Psychol.* (1953), 48:3–9.

43. Pearlin, L. I., and Rosenberg, M. Propaganda techniques in institutional advertising, *Publ. Opin. Quart.* (1952), 16:5–26.

44. Peterson, R. C., and Thurstone, L. L. *Motion Pictures and the Social Attitudes of Children*. New York: Macmillan, 1933.

45. Ram, P., and Murphy, G. Recent investigations of Hindu-Muslim relations in India, *Human Organiz.* (1952), 11:13–16.

46. Riley, M. W., and Flowerman, S. Group relations as a variable in communications research, *Amer. sociol. Rev.* (1951), 16:174–180.

47. Riley, M. W., and Riley, J. W., Jr. A sociological approach to communications research, *Publ. Opin. Quart.* (1951), 15:445–460.

48. Schlorff, P. W. An experiment in the measurement and modification of racial attitudes in school children. Doctorate dissertation, New York University, 1930; reported by Murphy, Murphy, and Newcomb (37), pp. 947, 950.

49. Sherif, M. An experimental approach to the study of attitudes, *Sociometry* (1937), 1:90–98.

50. Sherif, M. Some methodological remarks related to experimentation in social psychology, *Internat. J. Opin. & Attit. Res.* (1947), 1:70–93.

51. Sherif, M., and Sargent, S. S. Ego-involvement and the mass media, *J. soc. Issues* (1947), 3:8–16.

52. Shuey, A. M. Stereotyping of Negroes and whites: An analysis of magazine pictures, *Publ. Opin. Quart.* (1953), 17:281–287.
53. Smith, F. T. An experiment in modifying attitudes toward the Negro, reported in Murphy, Murphy and Newcomb (37) pp. 972–973.
54. Smythe, D. W. Reality as presented by television, *Publ. Opin. Quart.* (1954), 18:143–156.
55. Stagner, R. Studies of aggressive social attitudes: II. Changes from peace to war, *J. soc. Psychol.* (1944), 20:121–128.
56. Stagner, R., and Osgood, C. E. Impact of war on a nationalistic frame of reference. I. Changes in general approval and qualitative patterning of certain stereotypes, *J. soc. Psychol.* (1946), 24:187–215.
57. Vosk, Marc. Assessing techniques for change: Mass media, group process and intergroup contact. Paper given at the Second Conference on Research in Intergroup Relations, National Association of Intergroup Relations Officials, Chicago, December 30, 1953 (mimeographed).
58. Walter, Norman. A study of the effects of conflicting suggestions upon judgment in the autokinetic situation, *Sociometry* (1955), 18:138–146; fuller text, doctorate dissertation, University of Oklahoma, 1952.
59. Wilke, W. H. An experimental comparison of the speech, the radio, and the printed page as propaganda devices, *Arch. Psychol.* (1934), No. 169.
60. Williams, R. M., Jr. *The Reduction of Intergroup Tensions: A Survey of Research on Problems of Ethnic, Racial, and Religious Group Relations.* New York: Social Science Research Council, Bull. 57, 1947.
61. Writers' War Board. How Writers Perpetuate Stereotypes. New York, 1945.
62. Young, D. Some effects of a course in American race problems on the race prejudice of 450 undergraduates at the University of Pennsylvania, *J. abnorm. & soc. Psychol.* (1927), 22:235–242.

CHAPTER 17

Ego-Involvements

Now we have come to the most distinctive psychological formation of the human individual—the ego. As a systematic area of empirical and experimental study, the topic is relatively new. Ego or self problems have come to the foreground for psychologists and sociologists because of the necessity for integrating concepts to deal with the individual's experience and behavior in his day-to-day activities.

The concept of self or ego is proving to be one of these integrating concepts. Without such a concept, it is impossible to account for the *consistency* of the person and the day-to-day *continuity* of this consistency in his social and other relations. The degree of consistency a person achieves in various aspects of his life is proportional, on the whole, to the integration of the ego in so many respects. In Murphy's words, "Indeed, the self-picture has all the strength of other perceptual stereotypes and in addition serves as the chart by which the individual navigates. If it is lost, he can make only impulsive runs in fair weather; the ship drifts helplessly whenever storms arise" (48, p. 715).

The main objectives of the present chapter are (1) to gain an understanding of the *consistency* of the normal human individual in his daily social dealings in terms of his ego-involvements, (2) to give a brief picture of the developmental formation of the ego system, (3) to present a glimpse of the rudderless-like floundering which the individual undergoes when relevant ego anchorages are disrupted, and (4) to demonstrate some effects of ego-involvements in social relationships.

The problems with which we are primarily concerned are the individual's achievement of stable modes of relatedness to persons, objects, groups, institutions, values, or norms and his maintenance of these modes of relatedness. In personal and group relations, the mode of his relatedness

579

is revealed through status and role expectations. Fulfillment of these expectations arouses satisfaction and, in extraordinary cases, joy. Lack of fulfillment and reversals arouse disappointment, disillusionment, and, in extraordinary cases, insecurity and anxiety. In the performance of given tasks, ego-involvement is revealed in striving toward attainment of a performance level which the individual sets in the situation. Attaining the level aimed at produces feelings of success and a rise in the person's self-esteem, as repeatedly pointed out in the literature (33, 41).

PERSONAL CONSISTENCY LARGELY A MATTER OF EGO-INVOLVEMENTS

In the preceding chapters we characterized an attitude in terms of the consistency of behavior in regard to given stimuli. As we have seen, an attitude denotes a person's stand toward its referents and determines a highly selective and characteristic mode of response. An individual's stands in regard to various issues, other individuals, and groups are *not unrelated*. In other words, an individual's major attitudes are not so many discrete items in his psychological make-up.

We can demonstrate the interrelatedness of a person's major attitudes by the way he expresses them in his day-to-day relations. He does not say, "I have an attitude toward religion, toward a flag, toward a country, toward a club, toward a profession to such and such a degree." He puts it in personal terms. He speaks of "my religion, my flag, my country, my club, my job." He ordinarily expresses his attachment and its intensity in colorful forms: "My love for my country or family . . ."; "My devotion to my religion . . ."; "My club is the best. . . ." Such stands are put in other personal forms: "I *am* American," "I *am* Italian," "I *am* a lady," "I *am* a Republican," or "I *am* a Democrat." We shall refer to these stands expressed and experienced in personal terms as *ego-attitudes*. What the person considers *himself* consists of interrelated ego-attitudes. His personal goals, aspirations, expectations stem from his ego-attitudes. (To express the same thing in different words, we could have said that the person's identity consists of interrelated "selves" instead of ego-attitudes.)

When we speak of the identity of the individual in terms of a system of interrelated ego-attitudes, we have in mind much the same thing as Murphy wrote about: "Empirically the organism's *wants*, and therefore its *attitudes*, are legion; and its awareness of these, whether vague or clear, is an awareness of a cluster of selves, spatially and temporally overlapping and fusing with one another, dropping old phases, adding new ones" (48,

p. 489). The present conception of the psychological identity of the person has much in common with that of Snygg and Combs when they come closest to defining the nature of the self: "Although we speak of the phenomenal self in the singular it should *not* be supposed that the phenomenal self is a *unit function*. . . . It is composed of all meanings which the individual has about himself and his relation to the world around him. Arising from all of the experiences of the individual, it must of course be defined in many exceedingly complex and intricate ways" (68, p. 78, italics ours).

Definition of Ego

The characterization of ego presented here is based on empirical and experimental material. It will become more meaningful as it is used in functional analysis of the day-to-day dealings of human beings, in handling experimental results revealing the effects of ego-involvements, in understanding cultural variations in personal identity, and in accounting for its formation and breakdowns.

Ego or self is a developmental formation (a "subsystem") in the psychological make-up of the individual consisting of interrelated attitudes which are acquired in relation to his own body, to objects, family, persons, groups, social values, and institutions and which define and regulate his relatedness to them in concrete situations.

As we shall see, this conception of ego or self is conducive to experimental analysis and testing in terms of various interrelated dimensions. It avoids the reification of the ego or self, which easily ends up (as Ausubel put it) in "homuncular" entities. With its emphasis that ego or self is a developmental product of *interaction* in given situations, the present conception makes place for cultural variations. Yet, by approaching the study of this biosocial product in terms of general principles applied to the study of attitudes in general, cultural variations in ego functioning become special cases to which the same general principles can be applied. These general principles were presented in Chapters 2 and 3 and were applied to the problem of attitudes and attitude change in Chapters 15 and 16.

This conception of the person's psychological identity as consisting of interrelated ego-attitudes needs some elaboration before we apply it to specific problems.

1. When one gets down to empirical and experimental studies of self or ego, in the last analysis, various ego problems are always studied in terms of a person's stands or attitudes toward given events (past or pres-

ent), persons, groups, and situations, as they are revealed in his words, deeds, or expressions. The conception of an ego system in which ego-attitudes are unit parts lends itself to analysis in given dimensions. In this analysis we can utilize the developing attitude-assessment techniques to good advantage. A few of these developing techniques were presented in Chapter 15.

2. Ego is a *subsystem* in the individual's psychological make-up. The interrelated constellation of ego-attitudes which constitutes the ego or self is not coextensive with the psychological make-up of the individual. As the Gestalt psychologists Koffka (36), Köhler (37) and Lewin (40) pointed out, it is a subsystem in the total psychological make-up of the person. When component ego-attitudes are aroused owing to their relevance to the ongoing activity or situation at hand, they participate as internal factors within the frame of reference operative at the time. The criteria differentiating attitudes from other internal factors also apply to ego-attitudes (pp. 494–496).

3. The subsystem designated as ego or self is a *developmental* formation which is not present at birth. It develops as one's body and its parts are differentiated from the environment and as attitudes are formed defining one's modes of relatedness to objects (including his own body), persons, groups, values, or norms in his setting. We shall elaborate this point later in the chapter (pp. 594–598).

4. Even though constituent parts (ego-attitudes) are functionally interrelated, ego formation is not a unitary structure. Interrelationship need not imply integration. Because of the interrelatedness of ego-attitudes, there may be conflicts between component parts of the ego, especially in social settings with contradictory values or norms (32, 43). The plight of the modern professional woman (engineer, doctor), who is sometimes caught in a situation requiring her to act in the same breath in terms of her attitudes as a professional person and as a woman, is a good example of conflict among component parts of the ego. The conflict of the "marginal man," who is pulled apart by two antagonistic reference groups, will further clarify the point (see the next chapter, pp. 635–637).

What Is Ego-Involvement?

An individual is ego-involved when one or more ego-attitudes participate as factors in determining his experience and behavior. Ego-attitudes become operative as internal factors within the frame of reference at a given time because of their relevance to the ongoing psychological activity or their relevance to external stimulus factors. (The relations involved here will be clearer if the general scheme of psychological functioning presented on pages 77–86 is kept in mind.)

Ego-involved activity (i.e., activity in which ego-attitudes participate) is goal directed. Like any other motive, an ego-attitude implies specific expectations toward a certain goal, ideal, or value. Whether the individual is explicitly aware of the fact or not, ego-involved activity produces differential effects on his experience and behavior. When he is ego-involved, his reactions are no longer neutral; they are not haphazardly distributed around an indifference point. His reactions in perceiving, judging, remembering are heavily loaded by the goal-directed nature of the involvement.

Like any other motivated activity, ego-involved activity characteristically reveals heightened selectivity, increased effectiveness of the person's perception, judgment, memory, and action. In functional terms, the *consistency* revealed in ego-involved behavior is the outcome of this heightened selectivity and sensitized psychological processes concentrating on the relevant aspect of the stimulus field or on the ongoing psychological activity. This is why the more integrated, the more single-mindedly devoted of our fellow men, like Beethoven, Tolstoi, Van Gogh, and Gandhi, are those who become almost deaf and dumb to some of the ordinary details in their surroundings that are noticed by others not so intensely preoccupied. From the viewpoint of single-minded preoccupation, some items become irrelevant and even unintelligible. An incident from Beethoven's life will illustrate the point. One morning Beethoven was changing his clothes before an open window while preoccupied with an ongoing composition. Seeing him undressing, some children in the street made fun of him in loud tones. Beethoven was so absorbed that he simply could not understand what was so out-of-the-ordinary to arouse this fun making. To him, their behavior had no point.

Ego-Involvement Affects Perception of Our Own Acts: In a description of the great conductor Toscanini by one of the musicians in his orchestra, we see that a person can become so personally involved with his work that he even fails to recognize behavior he is actually carrying out *as his.* Toscanini has an "unconscious habit" of singing while he conducts. He usually tries to do so, according to this musician, an octave above the instrument playing the "lead," whether it is a piccolo or a bassoon. Although he stops a rehearsal with fury if even one false note is played by some instrument, he simply does not hear his own voice. In one instance, he did hear a voice but was so involved in the music that he had no idea it was his own. As this musician tells the story: "Once, in Salzburg, the Maestro was putting the orchestra through a tense dress rehearsal. His own siren vocalizing soared out above the instruments. Suddenly his face clouded over with a look of impending storm. His baton, descending with a swish against his desk, halted the orchestra.

" 'Silence,' he roared. 'Who is singing here?' He waited for the culprit to identify himself. 'Well, whoever it is will now kindly shut up!'

"With a contemptuous look of warning for all, the guilty one resumed his conducting" (72, p. 20).

We Attend to Other Motives with Relevant Ego Concerns

Hunger, sex, and sleep are motives that we have to satisfy, at least to a minimum degree. They produce differential effects in experience and behavior when they are operative as factors in the frame of reference at a given time. But hunger, sex, and sleep do not function in insulated ways. They are the hunger, sex desires, or sleepiness of the organism of a person who has claims to be "a man of good taste," "an honorable man," one who is in dead earnest to maintain his standing in life, to raise the value of his good name in the eyes of his fellow man and in his own eyes.

Ego-attitudes, like trying to be and remain "an honorable man," are motives too. Proportional to their intensity, these ego-attitudes also come in as factors to determine the course, the ways, the means of satisfying our hunger, our sex desires, and so on. When we are hungry, we want to eat. Relevant ego-attitudes enter the picture too. Our ego-involvements give generality to our eating behavior. We want to eat in certain places and with certain people. We actively strive to satisfy our sexual desires with as socially desirable a person as we can under the circumstances. In short, almost always, relevant ego-attitudes come in as factors, no matter what other goal we may be pursuing, what other tasks we may be engaged in. If we, as respectable citizens of society, discover that we have landed in a disreputable hotel, we want to move to a reputable one, even if we are very tired, our bed is comfortable, and the hotel is quiet and relatively inexpensive.

The consistent regulation of behavior directed toward food or sex objects in terms of the pattern of our ego-involvements is ordinarily not a hypocritical matter of just yielding to external social pressures for conformity. Ego-attitudes are also motives that have to be satisfied. When we satisfy our hunger or our sexual desires in ways or directions which are out of step with our ego-attitudes, we are caught in *conflict*. We feel *ashamed* and *guilty*. When we postpone the satisfaction of a biogenic motive because it is out of step with our ego-involvements, we are simply behaving in terms of one set of motives (ego-attitudes in this case) rather than the other motive operative at the time. This is not always easy. But, except in cases of extreme deprivation or ego breakdown, the normal human adult usually regulates the satisfaction of his other motives in terms of his ego-involvements (see pp. 403–410). What he considers *himself* consists of the particular pattern of his ego-attitudes. This is what gives consistency to his person from day to day.

In this connection, an important temporal matter should be noted. The person is not hungry, thirsty, or sleepy 24 hours a day. After a good meal, after a good night's sleep, he is satiated in regard to hunger or sleep. This periodicity is not the case with ego-attitudes. Whatever his dominant ego values (ego-attitudes) are, they are with him most of the time. There is no periodicity about them. Within limits, they are not subject to satiation. They are generalized and ever-present anchorages in him. They are ever ready for arousal, with very low thresholds, in relevant situations. One of the proofs of the low thresholds for arousal of ego-attitudes is that the highly successful studies tapping attitudes with indirect methods do not mention to the subjects that their attitudes are being studied. Relevant stimulus material on an issue is sufficient to activate the particular stand or ego-involvement.

Personal Consistency in Laboratory Experiments

During the past two decades the effects of ego-involvements on judgment, perception, memory, and other processes have been studied in the laboratory and expressed in quantitative terms. The reader will remember the Marks experiment showing displacements of skin color ratings as a function of the rater's own shading and personal friendship preferences for others (pp. 499–500). Another good illustration is Hammond's study in which the subjects piled up errors consistently in one direction rather than in the other possible direction, as determined by their own cherished stands on the issue (pp. 506–508). We also remember that, the more intensely individuals are involved in their stand concerning the social position of their own group or another group, (1) the more constricted the scale on which they distribute their ratings of statements on the subject and (2) the greater the tendency to lump together statements at one or the other extreme categories, depending on the location of their own stand (pp. 528–531).

Such differential effects of ego-involvement have been shown in remembering by Seeleman (62), Edwards (13), and Wallen (73); in learning and retention by Clark (9), Levine and Murphy (39), Tresselt and Levy (71), and Kalish et al. (34). The upshot of these and other experiments is that, when subjects are ego-involved, learning and retention are selective. The selectivity is revealed whether retention is measured through recall, recognition, or some other procedure. Selectivity in these cases is guided by relevant ego-attitudes. Experiments dealing with the differential effects of ego-involvements in various activities were surveyed in Sherif and Cantril (65, 1947).

An interesting study was reported more recently by Higham (28). Following the research of Bartlett and of Allport and Postman, Higham carried out an experiment dealing with the transmission of rumor. The general procedure in this line of research is to present the stimulus material to the first subject, who relays what he retains of it to the second subject, who relays it to a third subject, and so on to the last subject. The objective is to assess changes (distortions, transformations) as the stimulus material is relayed from subject to subject.

Higham compared the percentages of details correctly retained from four different stories in successive reproductions. One of the stories was definitely ego-involving for the subjects in this experiment. It dealt with a conversation between the professor and his Senior Lecturer concerning the nature of the examination that the subjects were to take three weeks later. Obviously, the subjects were ego-involved in this stimulus material. The percentage of items correctly retained from this particular passage was significantly greater than that retained from the other, more "neutral" passages (see Fig. 17.1).

Continuity of Personal Consistency

SPECIFICITY OR GENERALITY OF CONSISTENCY FROM SITUATION TO SITUATION: Is a person who is honest in one situation also honest in other situations? This is a specific instance of the more general question: Is a personal characteristic or "trait" specific to a given situation or is it general in various situations? This long-standing controversy seems to be resolved in terms of the ego-involvements of the person.

As we have noted, ego-attitudes function as generalized anchorages. When relevant ego-attitudes are aroused, behavior becomes more consistent. As G. W. Allport (1) concluded, a person is consistent in his behavior from one situation to others if he is ego-involved in them. When ego-involved, the individual is less *stimulus-bound*. On the other hand, if he is not ego-involved in various situations, he becomes more stimulus-bound. His behavior is more heavily determined by the properties of the stimulus situation (e.g., difficulty, complexity, duration, relevance for other motives).

The principle was well demonstrated by Klein and Schoenfeld (35) for

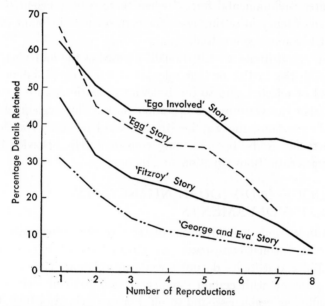

Fig. 17.1. Number of reproductions. (From T. M. Higham, The experimental study of the transmission of rumor, *Brit. J. Psychol.* [general section] [1951], 42:42–55).

experiences of confidence. These investigators studied the effect of personal involvement upon confidence ratings in different situations. Confidence ratings in a number of paper-and-pencil tasks were compared under two conditions: a "stress" or ego-involvement condition and a more neutral condition. To arouse ego-involvement in the first condition, the subjects were told that the tasks were to assess their intelligence and that the results would be sent to the personnel office of the university. Under the neutral condition, the tests were given as a matter of routine. The main finding was that the intercorrelations between confidence ratings made by the subjects on various tasks were significantly higher when the subjects were ego-involved than when they were not ego-involved. Confidence ratings by the subjects under neutral conditions were more affected by the intrinsic difficulty of the tasks and consequently differed more from one another.

Similar findings were obtained by Holt (31) in a study on setting of goals or aspiration levels for performance in different tasks. Setting goals for one's own performances "is more specific, more peripheral and responsive to outer environmental forces" when there is little ego-involvement. Personal consistency in setting goals for performances is found when the individual becomes ego-involved.

In short, ego-attitudes are situationally aroused as the individual participates in activities in this or that role—as superior, equal, inferior, as he is accepted or rejected, and so on. Relevant ego-attitudes are involved as he undertakes the performance of various tasks. Thus, ego-involved, the individual's reactions, the way he strives toward the goal, the degree of effectiveness he exerts, become more consistent. His behavior becomes more characteristic from situation to situation.

UNIQUE INDIVIDUAL NUANCES IN EGO-INVOLVEMENTS

Ego-attitudes and their involvements give to the individual's behavior a pattern of personal consistency and day-to-day continuity of his consistency. But ego-attitudes do not operate in isolation. They are ego-attitudes of a person with certain intelligence, temperament, wit, outgoingness, joviality, agreeableness, and so on. For example, even though an individual's confidence ratings, or the level of his future goals, are determined mainly by his ego-attitudes, the style with which tasks are executed and the expressions revealed constitute a unique pattern reflecting subtle personal nuances. These unique nuances constitute an important area of study for those primarily interested in variations of personality expression.

Despite the uniqueness of individual patterns of expression, the literature is inconclusive in providing a sound basis for classifying individuals into distinct types according to those personal nuances referred to under some title like personality "traits" (2). As Murphy concluded after surveying the relevant material: "It must be conceded that the majority of these types as currently applied in psychology have not as yet been validated in terms of either empirical or rational definitions of points of cleavage. For example, with extroversion-introversion, or ascendance-submission, or superego vs. id orientation, or adjustment vs. maladjustment, or aggressiveness vs. shyness, the distribution curves are smooth—indeed, usually normal—with not even that suggestive trace of bimodality which might warrant the belief that a fundamental discontinuity has been smothered by accidental factors" (48, p. 740).

The clear implication of such findings is that classifying individuals into distinct "types" in terms of personal "traits" has not been feasible. When individuals are rated in terms of variations exhibited in given personal "traits," they do not fall into bimodal or multimodal distributions indicative of types. Rather, they occupy relative positions within a distribution that represents continuity from *more* to *less*, with most cases falling in between. The distribution obtained reveals personal variations in traits that can be represented along the same reference scale.

Ego-Attitudes Integrating Distinct Personal Consistency

Yet, when we look around us at different individuals, when we observe people in different cultures, we find cases of distinctly differentiated consistencies in outlook on life, in responsiveness to different aspects of interpersonal and social surroundings. We see a person set on attaining a powerful office, for whom only those aspects of the stimulus field stand out which are of service in attaining that office. We see persons who are dead set to prove to themselves and others that they can outstrip others in accumulating wealth. When a person's whole being is dazzled with the picture of an office, of wealth or fame, of the image of himself as the creator of an outstanding composition or book, his selectivity is focused on relevant aspects of the social and material surroundings. What is a supreme object of attention for one person becomes an insignificant detail for another. The person possessed by a major ego value experiences the world around him in a highly selective way. He reacts to his surroundings with characteristic consistencies from day to day, and not in a stimulus-bound fashion, just adapting himself to every up and down of his external circumstances.

It is possible to differentiate persons into types in terms of the distinctiveness of their major ego-involvements. This manner of approaching personal distinctiveness is through the integrating function of dominant ego-attitudes, rather than separate personality "traits" or attributes. As Murphy put it, "Any typology derived from less central characteristics will be broken down almost as fast as it is formulated" (48, p. 742).

The advantage of viewing personal distinctiveness in terms of dominant ego-attitudes becomes clear if the implications of ego-involvement experiments are drawn at this point. When the individual is ego-involved, he "tightens up"; he becomes less subject to variations in the stimulus field; he deals with situations and tasks more in terms of his own claims and pretensions. This generalization pertaining to ego-involvement, in turn, can be handled as a specific instance of some general principles presented in Chapter 3. Applied to our present problem, these general principles lead us to regard the person's dominant ego-attitude(s) as a major anchor which determines the striking features of experience and behavior. As a major anchor, his dominant ego-attitude(s) becomes the weighty determinant of what aspects of the stimulus field he attends to and what he ignores. The properties of less conspicuous parts of the frame of reference are colored by the major anchor (ego-attitude).

Ego-attitudes are not transitory affairs. They are what we are and what we want to be. When a person is on the way to becoming a successful student, a good family man, a popular social mixer, a doctor, a soldier, or a writer, the ego-attitudes implied in these images require long-range adjustments in experience and behavior year in and year out.

The most readily identifiable kinds of ego-attitudes are derived from the dominant values or norms of one's groups and sociocultural differentiations along professional and class lines. Our claims for proving our self-esteem, our achievement of a status and its improvement, our being accepted as a popular person, as honorable, as talented, as outstanding are always in relation to other people in given settings. In given social settings there are definite and established lines of success, line of professions, avenues for achievement. If one decides to choose the army for a profession, one has to prove bravery and daring to get ahead, and not just once but consistently. These are not merely matters for dead, mechanical conformity. They require onward moves of a person who is set to get ahead.

There are culturally defined spheres of behavior, socially differentiated groupings each with its own reference scales. Individual variations in any dimension (e.g., speed of reaction, sociability, outgoingness, self-composure) can be studied properly only when individuals are placed in their own reference scales. It would be meaningless, for example, to take a random sample of Frenchmen and a random sample of Englishmen and to compare the expressiveness of individuals without regard to their national membership. The two samples belong to two reference scales which are distinct and probably discontinuous. The relative stand of any one person makes sense only when his expressiveness is put on his appropriate reference scale. Such culturally defined reference scales give a sound basis for distinct groupings, for multimodalities or discontinuities.

An observation by Murphy makes the point concrete: "As one takes the short, choppy trip from Dover to Calais, he moves almost from one world to another, from stolid, casual, pipe-smoking British tars and longshoremen to the animated and confused bustle of excitable, irritable, nervously intent French sailors, baggagemen and porters. The life of the whole city of Dover and the whole city of Calais accentuates the contrast" (48, p. 763). We can see from this description that the degree of expressiveness that falls within the middle segment of the French scale would be in the "over-expressive" segment of the British reference scale.

CULTURAL VARIATIONS IN EGO-RELEVANT BEHAVIOR

Unless a cultural group is in a state of disintegration or undergoing rapid change, the modal behavior of good members of the group centers around that segment of their reference scale representing the prevailing values or norms. A social value or norm, it will be recalled, defines the expected, even the ideal behavior in a given setting.

Since being an accepted, responsible member in good standing means interiorizing and cherishing at least the central norms of the group, the behavior of a great many individual members will center around the group norms. In fact, *the frequency of members exhibiting behavior close to the central norms may be a good operational index of the solidarity in the group.* The greater the solidarity in the group, the greater the likelihood that individual members will observe its norms without the necessity of external pressures. Individuals cherishing the same norm will exhibit variations in behavior within the same continuous reference scale. The more divergent the norms of different groups in given dimensions, the more discontinuous the reference scales within which behaviors of their respective members will be distributed.

By way of illustration, we shall present some cultural variations in ego-relevant behaviors. Behavior pertaining to such matters as the line of work put at a premium, coöperation-competition, conceptions of the ideal male and female, kinship ties and responsibilities are examples of ego-relevant behavior. Ethnologists have accumulated a great many cases of such variations. Here we can present only a few. The implication is not that people who exhibit them function in terms of bizarre psychological principles. On the contrary, these behaviors are exhibited because of identical, universal principles. If we had sufficient information concerning the interaction processes that gave rise to the particular norms, we could single out in each case the precise factors responsible for these behavioral variations.

Different virtues may be emphasized in different social settings. The ideal man of the Middle Ages is not among the ideal types today. In contemporary America, for example, perhaps the great banker or industrialist has the prestige of being a great man. Prize fighters and successful football players and coaches seem to have as much glamour as scientists or artists. On the other hand, the Trobriander "wants, if he is a *man*, to achieve social distinction as a good gardener and a good worker in general" (*45*, p. 62). In a study carried out in the twenties, children in the Soviet Union ranked laborers considerably higher than bankers and lawyers (*10*).

It would appear out-of-the-ordinary if we learned that in some locality marriage proposals were consistently being made by women rather than men. In more usual practice, the man makes the *marriage proposal*. When a woman makes the proposal, she does it after going through quite a bit psychologically, until desire for the particular man overwhelms her ego concerns. But initiative in marriage proposals by women has been reported to be the expected behavior in at least one culture by the anthropologist Rivers (*60*). Among the Eddystone Islanders, "the initiative in proposing marriage seems often to come from the women. If a girl takes a fancy to a man, she will carry off his basket and run with it to the bush, a custom evidently closely associated with that of the *tugele*, which is connected with warfare. Carrying off the basket is a definite sign of preference and, if the man is willing, he will begin negotiating with the parents of the girl" (p. 80).

As we grow up, many social ties and many important experiences are associated with our personal names. As McDougall observed, one's *name* "becomes a handle by aid of which he gets hold of himself as an agent, a striver, a desirer, a refuser." In some cultures, important changes in the individual's life are marked by a change of names. In our own culture, a woman usually takes her husband's family name when she is married. The Andamanese girl gets a new name at the time of first menstruation. This is called the "flower name" (*57*, p. 119). Likewise, in one of the Melanesian groups, "on marriage both man and woman change their names and assume a common name" (*59*, p. 347).

Competitive or coöperative behavior in human relations is a readily observable manifestation of ego-attitudes. Reference scales for competition and coöperation show marked variations from culture to culture. In a series of coördinated studies by Margaret Mead and her associates (*47*) comparing coöperative and competitive behavior in different cultures, it was found that modal behaviors in these respects varied significantly, depending on the dominant values of the setting. Thus, the modal behavior in human relations among the Manus, Kwakiutl, and Ifugao is competitive. In varying degrees, behavior among the Iroquois, Samoans, Zuni, Bathonga, Dakota, and Maori is rather coöperative. Among the Zuni, for example, "in the economic as well as the ceremonial field the aggressive, competitive, non-cooperative individual is regarded as the aberrant type" (20).

The reciprocal relations, personal ties, mutual affection, and responsibilities implied in *kinship* are certainly among the more intimate of human ego-involvements. Yet the range (the number of persons included), the degrees of intimacy, the particular roles and responsibilities, the bases for kinship arrangements exhibit enormous variations from culture to culture. As the anthropologist Radcliffe-Brown (58) expressed it: "If you will take time to study two or three hundred kinship systems from all parts of the world you will be impressed, I think, by the great diversity they exhibit" (p. 17).

Each one of these diverse kinship systems is based on a unique set of criteria, which may include religious beliefs, age, consanguinuity, and many others. Biological consanguinuity is only one of these criteria. In the words of Davis and Warner: "Every concrete system of sociologically related kin diverges from the biological distances, sometimes moderately and sometimes radically" (*11*, p. 296). According to the particular criteria employed in different cultures, mutual responsibilities, authority in child rearing, lineage, and place of habitation vary.

In relatively more "primitive," industrially undeveloped groupings, kinship reciprocities seem to be the main basis of orderly human relations. Thus, Lowie stated that "a native may be at a complete loss how to treat a stranger who falls outside of the established rubrics" of kinship (*42*, p. 8). Sociologists have presented a great deal of evidence pertaining to the narrowing range of effective kinship ties under conditions created by modern industrial growth, especially in great cities. Radcliffe-Brown (58), for example, makes a special note of the narrowed scope of British kinship ties during recent centuries. (See Chapter 20 for further discussion of this general point.)

Our *conceptions of ourselves as men or women* with given qualities are derived largely from group values or norms. The values or norms pertaining to masculine or feminine characteristics and functions vary in different historical periods, as well as from culture to culture. In the United States, for example, the changing conception, rights, status, education, and privileges of women have certainly affected reciprocal expectations, courtship, and responsibilities in marital and love relationships. It is a rare person in a university town of America today who is not acquainted with at least one woman putting her husband through college. This modern commonplace event is in striking contrast with the conception of the seventeenth-century American woman depicted in the following description of that period:

> The dutie of the husband is to travel abroad to seeke living: and the wives dutie is to keepe the house. The dutie of the husband is to get money and provision; and of the wives, not vainly to spend it. The dutie of the husband is to deale with many men: and of the wives, to talke with few. The dutie of the husband is, to be entermedling: and of the wife, to be solitarie and withdrawne. The dutie of the man is, to be skilfull in talke: and of the wife, to boast of silence. The dutie of the husband is, to be a giver: and of the wife, to be a saver. . . . Now where the husband and wife performeth the duties in their house we may call it College of Qyietness: the house wherein they are neglected we may term it a hell [69, p. 203].

EGO IS A DEVELOPMENTAL PRODUCT

The ego system of a modern adult reveals complicated and at times contradictory features. One of the best ways of gaining a clear picture of ego or self is through a developmental account of its formation and functioning in the individual. The findings of investigations over a good many decades are beginning to give a rather coherent picture of the development and functoning of the ego system. Here we shall present briefly some essentials of this composite picture. Detailed developmental accounts with emphasis at different points are given in the works of Freud (16, 17), George Herbert Mead (46), Piaget (53, 54, 55), Wallon (74), Koffka (36), Gesell (18, 19), Murphy (48), R. Faris (15), and Ausubel (4, 5). A survey of various approaches and empirical findings up to 1947 is presented in Sherif and Cantril (65, chap. 7-9). One cannot help drawing a few overall conclusions from this extensive literature.

The ego or self is not innate. Nor would it develop merely through maturation of the organism apart from a social environment. In Ausubel's words, "Ego development is the outcome of continuous biosocial interaction. There is no predetermined course or sequence of events which reflects the unfolding of a detailed blueprint designed by inner impulses" (4, p. 44).

During the earliest phase of his life, the infant lives in a state which Piaget called an "undifferentiated absolute." His momentary needs and wishes reign supreme. The boundaries between what is subjective in him (his wish, his whim) and what is objective and external to him are not differentiated. Even his own body and its parts have to be differentiated psychologically as *his* in the course of interaction: through manipulation, through painful experiences stemming from various parts of the body, through contact and even collision between his body and its parts and other objects. The infant discovers in time, for example, that it is one thing to hit or bite external objects and quite another to hit or bite parts of his own body. The "double sensations" connected with touching one's body and hearing one's voice were noted by Gesell, as well as early observers like Preyer (56) and Shinn (67).

Differentiation of one's own body from surrounding objects is not achieved overnight. "Visual perception of the various parts of the body, auditory perception of the voice, and the experiences of touch, pain, striped-muscle strains, etc. are evidently differentiated out of the original matrix *before* they are articulated within a single going concern. It is only because these various components are experienced together, and in their interaction that they come to make up a perceived whole rather than a conglomeration" (48, p. 481). As this summary statement by Murphy indicates, one's own body is differentiated from all other objects through many different experiences and comes to be perceived in a unitary way with all the affective tones that became involved in its formation. With this achievement, the position of one's own body serves as a main anchorage for experience and localization of other objects. But the stability of this anchorage is not independent of the stability of other objects in space.

Individuals who care for the child, who are responsible for his major gratifications and frustrations, begin to stand out from the rest of the surroundings. Differential treatments, facilitation and resistances which the infant receives from significant persons in his environment and, in time, the experiences of being warmly received, of being ignored, of being rejected serve as landmarks for the developing ego. All of these experiences are interrelated; but they are not simply of one piece. The resulting products are formed in many specific situations in time and are incorporated as the individual's ego-attitudes in so many capacities. For example, around the age of 2 or so the child learns his sex and finds out through example, verdict, and correctives of grownups and age-mates that certain attributes and activities go with being a boy or a girl.

With the learning of *communicable language,* ego development acquires an accelerated pace. The child becomes able to place himself and others in certain categories with all the adjectives (values) and stereotypes that accompany them. Things related to him, to his toys, his clothes, his family, his school are endowed in time with definite values (adjectives). Language makes it possible for the developing child to extend his relatedness to objects, persons, groups, values beyond those immediately present in his experience. The categorizations made possible through the use of linguistic concepts are crucial to the formation of more abstract ego-attitudes, like those related to one's family, religion, feminine or masculine qualities, professional virtues.

One of the important steps in developing personal consistency in day-to-day activities is gaining continuity of ego-attitudes embodying future goals. Through such continuity the individual forms a more or less clear picture of what he wants to be, what kind of man or woman, what he wants to achieve over a period of time. Gesell's observations established that the child does not set consistent standards for himself until around the age of 6. Of course, the exact age when such consistency becomes marked will vary, depending on the circumstances of his upbringing in his particular cultural setting. Consistent standards emerge slowly because setting goals for the future in terms of months or years requires a degree of conceptual development permitting anticipation of the future shape of things. As Goodenough stated: "Goals are not clearly realized until after the crystallizing effect of verbal formulation has taken place and the distinction between self and not self has become sufficiently advanced to give form and pattern to a child's social attitudes . . ." (23, p. 423).

Developmental findings pertaining to the rise of ego-attitudes as a result of participating in *age-mate and other group situations* provide a basis for understanding more recent data on the formation and change of attitudes in group interaction (Chapters 6, 8, 9). Among the developmental studies, the extensive work by Piaget and his collaborators (53, 54, 55) is outstanding. The upshot of a series of coördinated research is that *rules and standards* (of language, logic, and social relations, including the rules of children's games) are *first* external to any individual child. Moral rules or norms, for example, are passed to the child by others through example, verdict, and various correctives. In other words, standards or norms pertaining to group relations, including morality, are first handed down from those in authority (*heteronomy* in the observance of norms). Even though the child comes to abide by them because of the authority of grownups and older children, he lapses from them easily, giving in to his desires when he is not exposed to external social pressures and authority. These externally applied standards or norms have not yet become his own standards or norms; they are not yet interiorized as ego-attitudes.

Especially through participation in games and other activities with age-mate groups, the child develops a grasp of reciprocal human relationships —role and status reciprocities. He comes to see his own viewpoint and the viewpoints of others as give-and-take affairs in a consistent way. In Piaget's words: "From the moment that children really begin to submit to rules and to apply them in a spirit of genuine cooperation, they acquire a new conception of these rules" (55, p. 89). Through coöperative participation, the child comes to accept group norms as his own and to develop inner loyalties and responsibilities toward the group and its norms. The interiorization of standards or norms is a major step toward the *autonomy* of his behavior in group relations. This conclusion stemming from Piaget's work is in line with findings by other investigators, like Berne (7), Parten (51, 52), Salusky (61), Beaver (6), Green (24), Bridges (8), and L. B. Murphy (50).

The relationships involved in competing or coöperating with others, in experiencing sympathy with others, in setting consistent goals in relation to others are beyond the grasp of younger children. For example, genuine competition involves experience of the child's own performance, the performance of others, and his relations to them as aspects of a single pattern. To set consistent goals which are not subject to change at the whim of the moment, the child has to forecast himself and his activities into the future. Such experiences require the participation of conceptual functions which develop only in time. This explains why ego-attitudes pertaining to competition (25, 38), coöperation (7), sympathy (50), and setting consistent goals or aspiration levels (18, 23) come to operate effectively as the child develops in years, as he becomes more adept in group interaction.

Greenberg (25) and Leuba (38) found that younger children do not exhibit consistent patterns of competitiveness until around the age of 4. This finding was substantiated by Hirota (30) in a recent study of Japanese children. More recently, these results were corroborated in studies by Harry and Sarah Allison (1954) and by Stanley Mahoney (1955) at the University of Oklahoma. Piaget's research, investigations by Berne (7) and Hirota indicate that coöperative behavior and responsibility for self and others increase significantly with age as a child participates in group activities. An age trend for the appearance of sympathetic responses to the distress of others was found by L. B. Murphy (50). Experiencing sympathy depends to a large extent upon a concept of reciprocity involved in putting oneself in another person's shoes.

As an overall summary, we may follow the general picture drawn by Gardner Murphy (48). The earliest ego-attitudes are formed in relation to motive-relevant *objects:* one's own body, its parts, and significant others. All these and other items incorporated in the ego are endowed with affective *qualities* and *adjectives* (stereotypes) which become more abstract in nature through language development. With advances in conceptual development, ego-attitudes pertaining to family, school, clique, church, club, professional memberships, and *in-group and out-group delineations* are formed, depending on the particular life history of the individual in a given setting. All of these delineations are endowed with given positive and negative values. When involved in psychological functioning, these various ego-attitudes come in as integrating factors in relevant activities to give a characteristic consistency to the person's behavior in various situations from day to day.

Regressions and Breakdowns of the Ego

The ego, then, is a developmental product consisting of interrelated attitudes which define the value of one's own body, its parts, objects, tasks, persons, and groups in one's scheme of living. These ego-attitudes constitute the individual's particular mode of relatedness to given situations in so many capacities or roles. His unique consistency from day to day and from situation to situation is determined by the continuity of these stabilized modes of relatedness (ego-attitudes). When they are disrupted, either through internal states or through loss or failure of external referents, the organizing balance of his behavior is seriously disturbed. Behavior then becomes more variable, more floundering.

The conceptual level of functioning makes it possible for the human individual to live in both present and future, to make his adjustments in terms of goals set for the years to come. With the lowering of this conceptual level, the individual becomes more distractible, more stimulus-bound, more subject to the ups and downs of his momentary whims. This state of behavior is referred to as regression to a more childlike or a more primitive level. Such ego breakdowns may be due to the effects of alcohol, to serious brain injury, to the onslaught of great passion in conflict with central ego-attitudes, to great disillusionment. Later in the chapter we shall present an experimental demonstration of floundering and variable behavior resulting from elimination of stable environmental anchorages (pp. 602–606).

Here a few illustrations will make the implications of ego breakdowns more concrete. In Chapter 13 we saw several examples of ego breakdowns. The starving conscientous objectors cared not a whit about appearing like gentlemen. They even licked their plates in the presence of others. General Wainwright and his fellow prisoners dropped their self-respect as Allied officers to do odd jobs when offered a little more "work rice." Starving mothers in several countries of postwar Europe not only engaged in prostitution but sent their own children on the streets to solicit a little more food. When the organism's balance is impaired in a prolonged way through powerful onslaughts of physiological requirements, sociogenic motives which are parts of the ego system tend to become subordinate for the time being. To be sure, there are unique individuals who can uphold their ego values to the bitter end. But these heroic people are few.

During the depression years of the early thirties, suicides occurred not only among unemployed people but also among people who had lost title to their business or enough of their wealth so that they could not endure the prospect of living in a manner which they had long considered beneath their level. The psychological effects of prolonged unemployment have been found to include breakdowns of some ego-attitudes, a narrowing or even collapse of ego formation. If unemployment is prolonged, the unemployed person may come to feel that he is useless, superfluous. Eisenberg and Lazarsfeld found that "the last stage of unemployment consists of a general narrowing of wants and needs. Yet there is a limit beyond which this narrowing cannot go; otherwise, a collapse occurs" (*14*, p. 378).

The consequences of brain injury and psychosurgery (in which various portions of the frontal lobes are removed or the fibers connecting the frontal lobes with the rest of the brain are severed) have crucial implications for a clear conception of ego formation and breakdown. Goldstein (*21, 22*) and others have presented cases of brain-injured persons who regressed from the usual abstract level to a more concrete level in their reactions, thus becoming more distractable by external stimuli and less consistent in their behavior (*75*, pp. 469–475). According to Goldstein and Scheerer, the abstract attitude is at the "basis for the *conscious* and *volitional* modes of behavior." Among such modes of behavior are the following: "To account for acts to oneself; to verbalize the account . . ."; "To hold in mind simultaneously various aspects . . ."; "To plan ahead ideationally; to assume an attitude towards 'mere possible' and to think and perform symbolically" (22, p. 4). On the other hand, the "concrete attitude" is characterized as follows: "We surrended to experiences of an unreflected character; we are confined to the immediate apprehension of the given thing or situation in its particular uniqueness" (22, p. 2).

For us, simply from the theoretical point of view, the effects of psycho-surgery on ego functioning afford evidence with interesting implications. Evaluation of the available evidence is still a subject of controversy.

MOTIVATIONAL CHARACTER OF EGO-ATTITUDES

In specific contexts, we have stressed the motivational character of the ego or self. This motivational character is crucial in understanding what-ever integration the person achieves and whatever letdowns of integration he undergoes, whether momentary or lasting.

Having an attitude implies certain definite expectations toward its referent, which may be an object, a person, a group, an issue. To any such referent we are no longer impartial. We are partial in a positive or nega-tive way. In interpersonal relations, the expectations generated by our atti-tudes are revealed in specific types of behavior. Referents of an attitude are objects of value for the person, positive or negative. As such, behavior toward referents of an attitude has a characteristic, a consistent pattern (pp. 490–496). In other words, like all motives, attitudes are goal directed.

As we have seen, the very differentiation of one's own body from sur-rounding objects is the outcome of many varied experiences which are heavily charged with affective qualities. In time, the body becomes a cen-tral anchorage for experiencing other things. Achieving this psychological relatedness implies that oneself becomes part of an ordered time and space. There is satisfaction in this orderliness. When it is disrupted, we feel lost in both a physical and a psychological sense. Because of all the affectively charged experiences which culminate in a differentiated bodily self, the body inevitably becomes an object of value (49, p. 211). Herein may lie the basis of self-love, which is often treated under the title of "narcissism."

What is true of our attitudes toward our body and its parts is true also of other ego-attitudes. As established modes of relatedness are formed to other persons, groups, values, institutions in the social world, relevant ego-attitudes become functioning parts of the ego system. As such they func-tion as anchorages for experience in relevant situations, lending to behav-ior a sustained directionality.

When we are hungry, it is with the hunger of a person who has self-respect to maintain in the place he eats, who has definite conceptions regarding the kind of person he eats with and how the food should be served. It falls short of the mark to say simply that we are conditioned to certain trimmings. Indeed, there are occasions when the significance of the trimmings may change. When the occasion means an uplift for our status concerns, we are not so sensitive to the trimmings. The problem involved, then, is not that of a mechanical habit.

The way we tackle a given task is determined not simply by the objective difficulty or importance of the task but to a great extent by ego-attitudes which are involved. Whatever other goals we may be pursuing, whatever tasks we may engage in, our behavior *is* affected by concerns related to ego-involvements operative at the time. These involvements constitute an integrating basis that lends the characteristic consistency to a person's behavior. When these involvements cease to operate or change in character, the general character of behavior changes.

The sustained directionality that ego-attitudes give to the person becomes strikingly evident when the stability of relevant ego components is disrupted for some reason. The consequences of such disruption help us to understand the motivational character of ego-attitudes.

Loss of Stable Anchorages: It is helpful at this point to recall the general functional scheme presented in Chapter 3. Perceiving, judging, appraising, behaving take place within definite reference frames. Even in cases of rather simple events, ambiguity or unstructuredness of the stimulus field delays judgment time and renders ongoing activity rather tense and difficult. At its simplest level, this is not a pleasant experience. The ego is no exception in regard to this general tendency. Once it is formed, with all its diverse relatedness to objects, persons, and groups with varying affective ties, the ego tends to be anchored safely in so many capacities. When these ties to the social environment are disrupted, we experience insecurity. In fact, the feeling of personal security consists mainly of the stability of our relatedness in various capacities.

It is not coincidence that our main concern, when we are confused and feel "left out," becomes to *belong*, and to belong at any cost. The experiences of being left out or marginal in situations to which we are psychologically related are painful and lead to unfortunate consequences. Belongingness in personal and group situations becomes a major goal of our strivings.

One telling piece of evidence pertaining to the sources of personal security is that the experience of *anxiety* (as distinguished from simple fear) appears only after ego formation has advanced to a degree where some stability of psychological relatedness is possible. In Sullivan's words: "With the appearance of the self system or the self-dynamism, the child picks up a new piece of equipment which we technically call anxiety. Of the very unpleasant experiences which the infant can have we may say that there are generically two, pain and fear. Now comes the third [anxiety]" (70, p. 9).

When the stability of relatedness defined by ego-attitudes is disrupted, the consequence is ego-tension, the degree and consequences of which vary from case to case. We use *ego-tension* here as a generic term referring to painful, unpleasant experiences, like anxiety, insecurity, personal inadequacy, aloneness, shame, which can be accounted for only with reference to the ego system. When ego-tension is caused by failure or potential failure threatening our sense of adequacy, our sense of self-esteem, or by blockage of our ego-involved goals, the appropriate designation may be *anxiety*. When the ego-tension arises from disruption of the stability of our relatedness or belongingness in the physical or social surroundings, when it is a consequence of blows to our status strivings, a more appropriate term may be *insecurity*. When ego-tension is due to physical or psychological isolation from individuals or groups we are identified with (viz., reference groups), the appropriate term may be *aloneness*. When ego-tension is aroused by a serious discrepancy between our actions and the level of our ego values, the resulting product may be referred to as *shame*. In those cases in which the deviation is related to our few most central, fundamental ego values, the resulting ego-tension may be termed the experience of *guilt* (66).

Ego-tensions also arise through conflicts between different ego-attitudes. For example, ego-tensions result when we are caught in a situation which demands that we function simultaneously in contradictory roles. Ego-tensions of this kind are frequently encountered in "casually patterned" societies with contradictory values existing side by side. They have been treated extensively by sociologists, psychologists, and novelists who are seriously concerned with the plight of modern man.

An Experimental Demonstration of Insecurity

Proceeding from the concepts and theoretical formulation summarized in this chapter, Sherif and Harvey (66) experimentally produced situational insecurity by eliminating external anchorages in the situation surrounding the subjects. The general hypothesis of the experiment was that the performance of a task under conditions which lacked stable external anchorages would result in increased variability in behavior, like the floundering frequently observed when ego ties are disrupted. Specifically, the study investigated the effects of situational uncertainty on ego functioning.

The basic assumption was that the individual's ego, which implies his characteristic relatedness to his surroundings and is reflected in his characteristic reactions, is built up in relation to physical and social anchorages from childhood on. The stability of his ego, hence the consistency of his reactions, is dependent upon the stability of these physical and social anchorages. If the physical and social anchorages become uncertain or unstable, the individual's personal bearings become uncertain or unstable. The condition of uncertainty is at the basis of the experience of insecurity. Psychological states of anxiety or insecurity always involve ego reference.

At least initially, the psychological consequences of the experienced loss of physical and social bearings are increased fluctuations, variations in reactions, floundering about in search of something to hold on to, strivings to reëstablish some level of stability through available anchorages.

In this study the problem was to produce situational insecurity through elimination of spatial anchorages, thus affecting the stability of some of the earliest ego relationships, namely, spatial anchoring of the self. Variability of behavior was tapped through simple judgmental reactions, with the assumption that even complicated motivational states are reflected in such reactions when the stimulus situation lacks objective structure.

In line with leads derived from our previous work, the autokinetic situation was utilized (see pp. 250–252). Through preliminary trials, three conditions representing three degrees of situational uncertainty were chosen. Under condition A, the subjects were taken to their seats in an ordinary experimental room whose proportions they glimpsed briefly. Then 50 judgments of extent of autokinetic movement were obtained from each subject. Under conditions B and C, judgments were obtained after the subjects had carried out the rather difficult task of locating their seats in a large hall in pitch-black darkness. In condition C, all possible anchorages were eliminated. In fact, obstacles were introduced that hindered the subject's smooth orientation of himself. (See Figure 17.2 for the experimental setup in condition C.) He had to proceed from the door, mount and descend stair-steps, and continue at an angle to his seat entirely on the basis of verbal instructions. The experimenter did not even speak to him after he entered the room. These procedures were so effective in eliminating anchorages under condition C that some individuals became

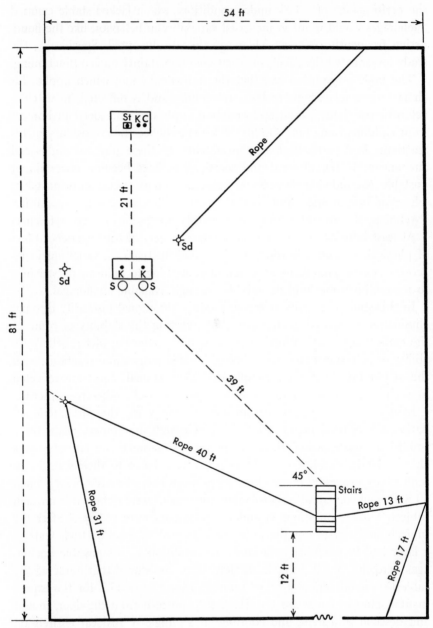

Fig. 17.2. Disposition of the experimental setup for condition C. (Adapted from M. Sherif and O. J. Harvey, A study in ego functioning: Elimination of stable anchorages in individual and group situations, *Sociometry* [1952], 15:272–305.)

thoroughly disoriented. They reported walking west while they were actually moving south. A few even thought they were moving west while they were actually moving east. Their verbal reactions revealed this disorientation and uncertainty: "Felt helpless and ill at ease—was very puzzled." "Completely confused. Lost as heck." Condition B was intermediary between A and C in availability of anchorages for orientation before the autokinetic sessions started.

Sixty subjects took part in the experiment. All were normal university students who were not previously acquainted with the autokinetic situation or with one another. Under all three experimental conditions, each subject took part first in an individual session and later in a group session with another subject. There were 10 pairs of subjects under each of the three experimental conditions.

In line with the hypotheses, the results revealed that:

1. The more uncertain the situation, the greater the scale within which judgmental reactions were scattered, that is, the greater the variability of behavior (see Fig. 17.3).

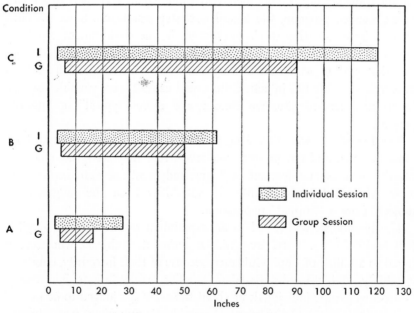

FIG. 17.3. Spread of individual judgment ranges under conditions A, B, and C in individual and group situations. (Adapted from M. Sherif and O. J. Harvey, A study in ego functioning: Elimination of stable anchorages in individual and group situations, *Sociometry* [1952], *15*:272–305.)

2. The more uncertain the situation, the greater the magnitude of the norm or standard around which judgments were distributed.
3. The more uncertain the situation, the larger the differences between the scales and norms of judgment for different individuals; that is, individual differences were more pronounced.
4. The more uncertain the situation, the greater the tendency, on the whole, toward convergence of judgments in the social situation (p. 257).

The tendency under (4) is stated with qualifications due to the nature of specific procedures in the present study and the perceived relationships between the subjects. It would be expected that if the subject pairs had established reciprocal relationships or if the experimental situation produced pronounced mutual dependencies, the tendency observed would be more pronounced.

TAPPING PERSISTENT PERSONAL INSECURITY THROUGH VARIABILITY OF REACTIONS: In the experiment just reported, it was established that judgments and other reactions under experimentally created conditions of situational uncertainty become markedly more variable. As part of a coördinated research program, the logical next step was taken. Since insecurity aroused by eliminating stable anchorages in the environment can be assessed through increased variability of judgments, it was reasonable to predict that persons who were already persistently insecure and floundering in search of stable ties in actual life would exhibit more variable reactions to an unstructured situation than would more "typical" or "normal" persons.

The hypothesis was, therefore, that individuals whose social and personal behavior and test performance reveal that they are rather characteristically anxious and insecure will give judgments of autokinetic movement which differ significantly in variability from the judgments of subjects from a "normal" population.

The hypothesis was tested in an experiment carried out by Virgil T. Hill in 1952 (29). There were nine experimental subjects, who were referred to a Clinic of Pupil Guidance because of their insecurity, emotional instability, and other disordered personality manifestations. The control subjects were nine individuals of about the same age judged to be normal. Ninety-eight judgments of extent of autokinetic movement were obtained from each subject in two alone sessions.

The results showed strikingly greater variability in the judgments of the "insecure" (experimental) subjects than in those of the "normal" (control) subjects. The smallest variability shown by the experimental (insecure) subjects was far greater than the largest variability shown by the control (normal) subjects. In other words, the results gave distinct distributions of behavioral variability. The quantitative results gained further support from the more uneasy and protesting behavior manifested by the insecure subjects under the uncertainty of the autokinetic situation. Several of the insecure subjects did not show up voluntarily for the second session of the experiment, so new subjects had to be procured and escorted personally to the experiment by the investigator.

EGO-INVOLVEMENTS IN SOCIAL RELATIONSHIPS

The objects, persons, and other concrete and abstract referents to which the human individual relates himself in some capacity and, as a consequence, endows with friendly or unfriendly values are legion. These referents of his intense or mild personal involvements range in degree of concreteness from his clothing, his souvenirs, members of his family all the way to referents too large or too abstract to be grasped in immediate perceptual (contact) terms. The nation with which he identifies himself, his great-grandparents and other ancestors whose good name he strives to uphold, the God he worships are just a few of his serious involvements. Ethnology books are full of cases in which man *conceived* a commonality of essence between himself and certain animals or plants. This conceptual relatedness, in many cases, puts the given animals and plants in a category apart from ordinary, edible objects (e.g., 12, 27).

In discussing the referents of ego-involvements, we have to restrict ourselves to social relationships which are immediate and pressing today. Accordingly, ego-involvements in personal relationships will be discussed briefly in this chapter. The next chapter is devoted to involvements in group relations.

Ego-Involvements in Interpersonal Relations

FORMING IMPRESSIONS OF OTHER PERSONS: The impressions we form of the physical appearance and personal characteristics of other individuals tend to be immediate, like any perception. We do not form such impressions by adding up so many discrete items (physical or psychological "traits") and arriving at a total. Rather, our immediate impression constitutes a definite structure which is the outcome of functional relationships among constituent parts. One or a few constituent parts participate in the structuring with greater weight than others: they are anchorages which determine the salient characteristics of the whole impression.

These conclusions are supported in an experiment by Asch (3). A number of discrete characteristics attributed to a person were read to the subject with instructions to describe the impression formed of the person. For example, "energetic—assured—talkative—cold—ironical—inquisitive —persuasive" were among the characteristics presented. Preliminary work had revealed that in some manner individuals arrived at a consistent impression of a person, even though they heard only a sequence of discrete terms.

In subsequent units of the study, the subject was asked to select from a check list of paired traits those "most in accordance with the view he had formed." The traits on the check lists were not the same ones read to the subject, but different traits (e.g., popular-unpopular, strong-weak). Results obtained from these check lists were supplemented by the subjects' written reports of their impressions. It was found that some characteristics had special importance in causing a conception of a person to be formed.

The conclusion drawn from these and other units was that: "A given quality derives its full concrete content from its place within the system formed by the relations of the qualities. . . . In the extreme case, the same quality in two persons will have different, even opposed, meanings, while two opposed qualities will have the same function within their respective structure" (p. 283).

Another of Asch's findings with far-reaching implications is that centrality-peripherality of trait qualities is by no means absolute. Thus, the characteristic of "warmth" becomes relatively insignificant when included in a list containing characteristics like "obedient—weak—shallow . . . vain," but it may be a major reference point when included in another list.

APPRAISALS OF OTHERS IN EGO-INVOLVED RELATIONS: In the Asch experiment briefly reported above, the structure of the impression was formed through relationships among various *external* items. Each attribute contributed to the total impression according to its relative weight in the particular system of relationships among external attributes.

Our impressions of other persons, our appraisals of them are determined mainly on the basis of interrelated objective attributes (qualities) if we are *neutral* to the person. However, in actual life, the impressions we form, the appraisals we make are frequently of people with whom we stand in definite relationships: as friends, as enemies, as admired or detested figures, as coöperating or competing persons. In the formation of impressions or appraisals of other persons, these personal involvements become weighty factors determining the structure.

At times, the nature of established human relationships determines the whole color of the impression. Thus, positive or negative ego-involvement may be the dominant factor in transforming the impression. The steady behavior of the same person is judged "consistent" if we admire him; it is seen as "stubborn" if we detest him. The same behavioral feat is condemned as "fanatic" when exhibited by our enemy; it is lauded as "heroic" when engaged in by a man on our side. When we interact with other people, we do not long remain neutral to them. The relationship tends to be stabilized in some (positive or negative) way. Changes in the relationship are reflected in changed appraisals of their attributes. What was judged as "cute" and "irrepressible" in the sweetheart in days of romance is seen as "infantile" and "unbearable" when the romance cools off.

In structuring impressions and appraisals of other persons, neither neutrality, nor friendship, nor enmity should be taken as the "typical" case. Each is one of many possible cases. In each instance the ensuing experience and, hence, reaction are determined by the particular constellation of internal and external factors.

Indirect Experimental Assessment of Interpersonal Attitudes

One of the recent developments in studying attitudes in interpersonal and group relations has been their assessment through "indirect" indices. The general procedure in these experiments is to place the subject(s) in a situation lacking in structure in some dimension and to obtain reactions which serve, without his being aware of it, as indices of his involvement with other persons in the situation.

An early demonstration of this experimental approach utilizing the autokinetic technique was performed in 1937 (64). In this case, a planted subject (one coöperating with the experimenter) had considerable prestige in the eyes of the naïve subject. The following is a verbatim report by the coöperating subject:

Miss X and I [Assistant in Psychology, Columbia University] were subjects for Dr. Sherif. I was well acquainted with the experiment but Miss X knew nothing whatsoever about it. Since she was a close friend of mine, and I carried some prestige with her, Dr. Sherif suggested that it would be interesting to see if we could predetermine her judgments. It was agreed beforehand that I was to give no judgments until she had set her own standard. After a few stimulations it was quite clear that her judgments were going to vary around five inches. At the next appropriate stimulation, I made a judgment of twelve inches. Miss X's next judgment was eight inches. I varied my judgments around twelve inches and she did the same. Then I changed my judgment to three inches, suggesting to Dr. Sherif that he had changed it. She gradually came down to my standard, but not without some apparent resistance. When it was clear that she had accepted this new standard, Dr. Sherif suggested that I make no more judgments lest I might influence hers. He then informed her on a subsequent stimulation that she was underestimating the distance which the point moved. Immediately her judgments were made larger and she established a new standard. However, she was a little uneasy with it all, and before the experiment had progressed much farther whispered to me, "Get me out of here."

When we were again in my office, I told her that the point had not moved at all during the experiment. She seemed quite disturbed about it, and was very much embarrassed to know that we had been deceiving her. Noting her perturbation, I turned the conversation to other matters. However, several times during our conversation she came back to the subject, saying, "I don't like that man" (referring to Dr. Sherif) and similar statements indicating her displeasure with the experience. It was not until some weeks later when she was again in my office that I discovered the full extent of her aversion. I asked her to serve as a subject for me in an experiment and immediately she exclaimed, "Not down in *that* room," pointing to Dr. Sherif's experimental room.

In 1946, Zeaman (76) demonstrated the regulation of reaction as determined by ego-involvements with other persons. In this demonstration, two coöperating subjects were used, one for whom the naïve subject felt a good deal of affection and one for whom he tended to feel antagonism. In Zeaman's words:

One male graduate student of the Anthropology Department at Columbia was used as subject. He was cooperative, and intelligent, but entirely naïve about the experiment procedure and apparatus, and about the autokinetic effect. The relationship between the observer and the two experimenters was primarily that of very close friendship although after a period of sharing an apartment for one year, different modes of behavior had set in on the part of the subject with respect to the male and female experimenter. It is . . . this difference in relationship that forms the independent variable in this experiment. The relationship between the subject and the female experimenter was a non-competitive, pleasantly affectional relationship. . . . Between the subject and the male experimenter, on the other hand, there existed a relationship characterized by mutual striving for ascendancy, aggression . . . and a consequent tendency to deprecate the judgments of the other person. Over a period of many months, these relationships had proved relatively invariable.

First the naïve subject gave his judgments alone. Then 35 judgments apiece were obtained for the subject with the female experimenter, who

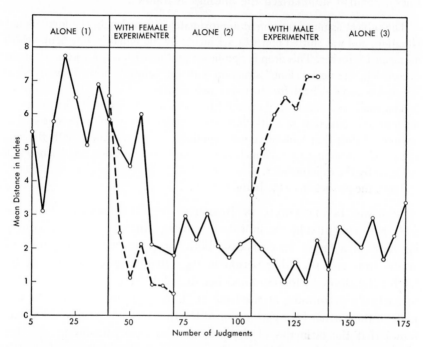

FIG. 17.4. The effects of positive and negative personal involvements on judgment. The means of each five successive judgments of distance of autokinetic movement are indicated on the unbroken line. The two experimenters' "planted" judgments are shown on the broken lines. The five situations are specified at the top of the figure. (Courtesy of D. Zeaman.)

deliberately began making judgments around the subject's "alone" mean and then lowered them considerably (see Fig. 17.4). After a brief rest, 35 additional "alone" judgments were taken, and after that 35 judgments together with the male experimenter, whose judgments were considerably greater than the subject's. Finally, another alone session was given.

Zeaman had predicted that the subject's positive and negative attitudes toward the female and male "experimenters" would be revealed in his judgments of the extent of autokinetic movement. "Specifically it was predicted that the female experimenter would be able to shift the subject's norm in the direction of her judgments, while the effect of the male experimenter's judgments would be to shift the subject's norm in a direction away from the norm assumed by the male experimenter."

Figure 17.4 shows the mean of each five successive judgments by the naïve subject (the solid line) and the two coöperating subjects (dotted lines). Zeaman summarized the findings as follows:

The subject assumed a norm at approximately 5.9 inches in the first "alone" situation, and was shifted down to 3.4 inches by the female's judgments which averaged 1.9 inches. This drop is significant on the .01 level. A further decrease occurred in the next "alone" situation with the subject's norm leveling off at 2.4 inches as an average for thirty-five judgments.

The male experimenter then set his norm at 5.9 inches to discover the amount and direction of shift that would occur in the subject's norm. The amount of shift that took place was significant on the .05 level, with the subject's norm dropping to 1.57 inches, this time in a direction away from that assumed by the experimenter.

Thus, the predictions were borne out. . . .

PERSONAL INVOLVEMENTS IN JUDGMENT OF PERFORMANCE: McGehee (44) had pairs of subjects, in a dart-throwing situation, take turns throwing darts at a target. In each case, both the person performing the task at the time and the other person in the situation gave estimates of the hit for the throw to follow. McGehee designated the estimate of the person actually performing at the time as "level of aspiration" and the estimate of the partner (not performing at the time) as "judgment." McGehee found that the estimates of the persons who were performing were less variable, that is, less subject to the ups and downs of their own actual performance. The judgments of future performance made by the onlooker were more variable, that is, more influenced by actual variations in the other person's performance. He explained the difference obtained under the two conditions as due to the "fact that ego-levels of the subjects are more involved in the erection of levels of aspiration than in making a judgment." In McGehee's experiment, no point was made of the nature of personal relationships between the subjects in the pairs.

At this point a relevant question was raised by C. Sherif (63): How will the judgments of the onlooker of the performance be affected if there is an established personal relationship between him and the performer? Will the estimates of the onlooker still be more variable if he is personally involved with the performer? Her experiment followed closely the design used by McGehee. Each subject participated with another person in a dart-throwing performance, which they were told was a test of eye-hand coördination. Each pair of subjects in the first unit consisted of a parent and his or her child. The pairs in the second unit were husbands and wives. After a few practice trials by one member of the pair, the second member wrote an estimate of the first member's next score, keeping his estimate a secret. The subject who was throwing darts at the time then estimated aloud the score he expected to make on that trial. This procedure was followed for a series of 25 trials. Then the subjects changed places, the second member of the pair becoming the thrower and estimating his own performance. The identical procedure was followed with the second subject. Each subject thus made a series of 25 judgments of his own future performance and 25 judgments of his partner's future performance.

In this situation, the subjects tended to be as ego-involved with their partner's (parent, child, husband, or wife) performance as with their own. (In some cases, more ego-involvement was revealed in reactions to the partner's performance.) As a result, the judgments of their own and the partner's future performance tended, on the average, to resemble each other in many respects, such as accuracy, "rigidity" (or tendency to hold the level of judgments constant), and the tendency toward shifts in judgment as performance improved or deteriorated. The spontaneous remarks and reactions of the partners in this study substantiated these findings in a crucial way. Many of the subjects were considerably more loquacious, more tense, and more pleased with the performance of their child, or parent, or mate than with their own. The records of the spontaneous remarks by the subjects during the experiment reveal reactions indicative of ego-involvement both when they judged their partner's performance and when they judged their own.

The subjects quite frequently gave spontaneous suggestions to their partners on the best techniques of holding and throwing darts. Of course, nothing in the instructions requested such advice. The subject who was throwing was often advised by his partner: "Don't tighten up"; "Take it easy"; "Get a good grip on the dart"; "You're taking it too casually, dear"; and the like.

Every subject made encouraging remarks to his partner. For example, a mother said to her son: "Get that yellow, S——! Get it for Daddy!" All were generous with praise of the partner's successes. Some offered excuses for their partner's "failures" (that is, when the performance did not meet their expectations). For example, one husband explained that his wife had not felt well that day, but the explanation came only after a long series of low scores on her part. One daughter hid her face in her hands and groaned, or giggled nervously when her mother missed the target, a reaction quite similar to her reactions to her own "failures."

The findings of this study were substantiated and extended in an experiment by O. J. Harvey and M. Sherif (26). The extension in that study was the inclusion of subject pairs who had negative interpersonal relationships with one another. Four kinds of subject pairs were utilized: (1) pairs of college students positively involved with each other as sweethearts; (2) pairs of high-school students positively involved as "steadies"; (3) pairs of high-school students positively involved as friends; (4) pairs of high-school students who were *negatively* involved with one another rather strongly—these negatively involved pairs were individuals who had recently had a fight with each other or who were competing for the attentions of the same boy or girl.

In line with the previous experiment, it was found that when individuals are positively involved with one another there is no significant difference in judgments of one's own future performance and one's partner's future performance. Thus, the greater variability shown in judging a "neutral" person's future performance disappears when judgment pertains to the future performance of a beloved person. The findings further indicated that the consistency of judgment of another person's performance decreases as the degree of personal involvement in the partner decreases. Finally, when the partners in the situation are *negatively* involved with one another, there is a significant difference between judgment of one's own future performance and judgment of his antagonist's future performance.

The spontaneous remarks by subjects who are highly involved with one another in a positive way were reminiscent of the remarks cited in the experiment reported before. Words of satisfaction were expressed at the partner's successful performance. Encouragement and advice were extended as the occasion called for them. Typical examples are: "Get me a bull's-eye." "Goodness, you're as good as I think you are." "Honey, you're disappointing me. Now slow down; you can beat that."

As a theoretical conclusion, it can be advanced that setting future goals is a special case of judgmental activity in which ego-involvements operate as factors. It is the ego-involvement and its degree that give to behavior its characteristic consistency from day to day.

We can now proceed to ego-involvements in group relations—a central topic for social psychology. This necessarily leads us to take up the concept of reference groups and its implications in the modern scene.

REFERENCES

1. Allport, G. W. The ego in contemporary psychology, *Psychol. Rev.* (1943), 50:451–478.
2. Anastasi, A. The nature of psychological traits, *Psychol. Rev.* (1948), 55:127–138.
3. Asch, S. E. Forming impressions of personality, *J. abnorm. & soc. Psychol.* (1946), 41:258–290.
4. Ausubel, D. P. *Ego Development and the Personality Disorders.* New York: Grune and Stratton, 1952.
5. Ausubel, D. P. *Theory and Problems of Adolescent Development.* New York: Grune and Stratton, 1954.
6. Beaver, A. P. The initiation of social contacts by preschool children, *Child Development Monogr.* (1932), 7.
7. Berne, E. V. C. An experimental investigation of social behavior patterns in young children, *University of Iowa Studies in Child Welfare* (1930), 4, No. 3.
8. Bridges, K. M. B. *The Social and Emotional Development of the Preschool Child.* London: Trench, Trubner, 1931.
9. Clark, K. B. Some factors influencing the remembering of prose material, *Arch. Psychol.* (1940), No. 253.
10. Davis, J. Testing the social attitudes of children in the government schools in Russia, *Amer. J. Sociol.* (1927), 32:947–952.
11. Davis, K., and Warner, W. L. Structural analysis of kinship, *Amer. Anthropol.* (1937), 39:291–313.
12. Durkheim, E. *The Elementary Forms of the Religious Life* (trans.). New York: Macmillan, 1915.
13. Edwards, A. L. Political frames of reference as a factor influencing recognition, *J. abnorm. & soc. Psychol.* (1941), 36:34–50.
14. Eisenberg, P., and Lazarsfeld, P. F. The psychological effects of unemployment, *Psychol. Bull.* (1938), 35:358–390.
15. Faris, R. E. L. *Social Psychology.* New York: Ronald, 1952.
16. Freud, S. *Group Psychology and the Analysis of the Ego.* London: Hogarth, 1922.
17. Freud, S. *The Ego and the Id.* London: Hogarth, 1927.
18. Gesell, A., and Ilg, F. L. *Infant and Child in the Culture of Today.* New York: Harper, 1943.

19. Gesell, A., and Thompson, H. *The Psychology of Early Growth.* New York: Macmillan, 1938.
20. Goldman, I. Competitive and Cooperative Habits Among the Zuni Indians of New Mexico, in M. Mead (ed.), *Cooperation and Competition Among Primitive Peoples.* New York: McGraw-Hill, 1937.
21. Goldstein, K. *The Organism.* New York: American Book, 1939.
22. Goldstein, K., and Scheerer, M. Abstract and concrete behavior: an experimental study with special tests, *Psychol. Monogr.* (1941), 53:1–31.
23. Goodenough, F. L. *Developmental Psychology.* New York: Appleton-Century, 2nd ed., 1945.
24. Green, E. H. Group playing and quarreling among pre-school children, *Child Developm.* (1933), 4:302–307.
25. Greenberg, P. J. Competition in children: an experimental study, *Amer. J. Psychol.* (1932), 44:221–248.
26. Harvey, O. J., and Sherif, M. Level of aspiration as a case of judgmental activity in which ego-involvements operate as factors, *Sociometry* (1951), 14:121–147.
27. Herskovits, M. *Man and His Works.* New York: Knopf, 1950.
28. Higham, T. M. The experimental study of the transmission of rumor, *Brit. J. Psychol.* (general section) (1951), 42:42–55.
29. Hill, V. T. The spread of reaction of insecure and "normal" individuals in the autokinetic situation, University of Oklahoma, 1952.
30. Hirota, K. Experimental studies of competition, *Jap. J. Psychol.* (1951), 21:70–81. Abstracted in *Psychological Abstracts* (1953), 27:351.
31. Holt, R. R. Effects of ego-involvement upon levels of aspiration, *Psychiatry* (1945), 3:299–317.
32. Hughes, E. C. Dilemmas and contradictions of status, *Amer. J. Sociol.* (1945), 50:353–359.
33. James, W. *The Principles of Psychology.* New York: Holt, 1890.
34. Kalish, H. I., Bleke, R. C., Garmezy, N., and Rodnick, E. H. Effects of anxiety and experimentally induced stress upon verbal learning, *Amer. Psychologist* (1954), 9:402 (abstract).
35. Klein, G. S., and Schoenfeld, N. The influence of ego-involvement on confidence, *J. abnorm. & soc. Psychol.* (1941), 36:249–258.
36. Koffka, K. *Principles of Gestalt Psychology.* New York: Harcourt, Brace, 1935.
37. Köhler, W. *Gestalt Psychology.* New York: Liveright, 1929.
38. Leuba, C. J. An experimental study of rivalry in young children, *J. comp. Psychol.* (1933), 16:367–378.
39. Levine, J. M., and Murphy, G. The learning and forgetting of controversial material, *J. abnorm. & soc. Psychol.* (1943), 38:507–517.

40. Lewin, K. *Dynamic Theory of Personality*. New York: McGraw-Hill, 1935.
41. Lewin, K., Dembo, T., Festinger, L., and Sears, P. S. Level of Aspiration, in J. McV. Hunt (ed.), *Personality and the Behavior Disorders*. New York: Ronald, 1944.
42. Lowie, R. H. *Primitive Society*. New York: Boni and Liveright, 1925.
43. Lynd, R. S., and Lynd, H. M. *Middletown in Transition*. New York: Harcourt, Brace, 1937.
44. McGehee, W. Judgment and the level of aspiration, *J. gen. Psychol.* (1940), 22:3–15.
45. Malinowski, B. *Argonauts of the Western Pacific*. London: Routledge, 1922.
46. Mead, G. H. *Mind, Self, and Society*. Chicago: University of Chicago Press, 1934.
47. Mead, M. (ed.). *Cooperation and Competition Among Primitive Peoples*. New York: McGraw-Hill, 1937.
48. Murphy, G. *Personality: A Biosocial Approach to Origins and Structure*. New York: Harper, 1947.
49. Murphy, G., Murphy, L. B., and Newcomb, T. M. *Experimental Social Psychology*. New York: Harper, 1937.
50. Murphy, L. B. *Social Behavior and Child Personality*. New York: Columbia University Press, 1937.
51. Parten, M. B. Social participation among pre-school children, *J. abnorm. & soc. Psychol.* (1932), 27:243–269.
52. Parten, M. B. Social play among pre-school children, *J. abnorm. & soc. Psychol.* (1933), 28:136–147.
53. Piaget, J. *Judgment and Reasoning in the Child*. New York: Harcourt, Brace, 1928.
54. Piaget, J. *The Child's Conception of Physical Causality*. New York: Harcourt, Brace, 1930.
55. Piaget, J. *The Moral Judgment of the Child*. London: Kegan Paul, 1932.
56. Preyer, W. *The Mind of the Child* (trans.), Part II, *The Development of the Intellect*. New York: Appleton, 1890.
57. Radcliffe-Brown, A. *Andaman Islanders*. Cambridge, England: Cambridge University Press, 1922.
58. Radcliffe-Brown, A. R. The study of kinship systems. Presidential Address, *J. Royal Anthropol. Inst. of Great Britain and Ireland* (1941), 71, parts I and II.
59. Rivers, W. H. R. *History of Melanesian Society*. Cambridge, England: Cambridge University Press, 1924, Vol. I.
60. Rivers, W. H. R. *Psychology and Ethnology*. London: Kegan Paul, 1926.

61. Salusky, A. S. Collective behavior of children at a preschool age, *J. soc. Psychol.* (1930), 1:367–378.
62. Seeleman, V. The influence of attitude upon remembering of pictorial material, *Arch. Psychol.* (1940), No. 258.
63. Sherif, C. Variations in judgment as a function of ego-involvements. Paper presented at the Eastern Psychological Association meeting, Atlantic City, New Jersey, April 26, 1947.
64. Sherif, M. An experimental approach to the study of attitudes, *Sociometry* (1937), 1:90–98.
65. Sherif, M., and Cantril, H. *The Psychology of Ego-Involvements.* New York: Wiley, 1947.
66. Sherif, M., and Harvey, O. J. A study in ego functioning: Elimination of stable anchorages in individual and group situations, *Sociometry* (1952), 15:272–305.
67. Shinn, M. W. *Notes on the Development of a Child.* Berkeley: University of California Press, Vol. I, 1899; Vol. II, 1907.
68. Snygg, D., and Combs, A. W. *Individual Behavior: A New Frame of Reference for Psychology.* New York: Harper, 1949.
69. Stern, B. J. From the original document quoted by Stern in The family and cultural change, *Amer. sociol. Rev.* (1939), 4.
70. Sullivan, H. S. *Conceptions of Modern Psychiatry.* Washington: William A. White Psychiatric Foundation, 2nd ed., 1947.
71. Tresselt, M. E., and Levy, B. Recognition for ego involved material, *J. Psychol.* (1949), 27:73–78.
72. Unsigned article, I Play for Toscanini, *This Week Magazine*, New York *Herald Tribune*, March 16, 1947.
73. Wallen, R. W. Ego-involvement as a determinant of selective forgetting, *J. abnorm. & soc. Psychol.* (1942), 37:20–39.
74. Wallon, H. *Les Origines du Caractère chez l'Enfant.* Paris: Presses Universitaries de France, 1933.
75. White, R. W. *The Abnormal Personality.* New York: Ronald, 1948.
76. Zeaman, D. The account of the demonstration contributed by Dr. David Zeaman (1946).

CHAPTER **18**

Ego-Involvements and Reference Groups

Man's experience of being accepted or rejected, his status and prestige concerns have very little meaning apart from his claims and aspirations in given group settings. The continuity of man's personal identity consists, in no small measure, of his group ties and strivings for such ties. His belongingness in groups, his upholding the group values or norms are not due only to external social pressures, as we have seen in various contexts. Becoming a member of a group or aspiring to become one generates a sense of inner urgency to cherish and uphold his group values. For he experiences these values or norms *as his.*

These overall statements are based on conclusions derived from our discussion of the properties and functioning of groups (Chapters 5–9). The development of the *autonomy* of a person's relations with other individuals is an outcome of his give-and-take activities in play, work, and other vital matters.

In modern societies, groups with which the human adult is ego-involved extend far beyond the immediate limits of his actual contacts in given space and time. His group relatedness or aspirations for relatedness, the standards by which he gauges his personal accomplishments at times lie far beyond his perceptual range. One impact of this state of affairs is the growing interest in studying a variety of behaviors governed by *reference group* values or standards.

EGO-INVOLVEMENTS IN GROUP RELATIONS

Every adult has a *place* in his particular pattern of reciprocities. He does not just happen to be in that place. It is attained and even achieved in the course of interaction. As we have noted, the individual's sustained experience of a pattern of reciprocities (status and role relations in the family,

619

play, or work group) is the outcome of considerable psychological development reached through prolonged give-and-take processes.

Definite reciprocal expectations necessarily go with being a part of a given pattern of human relations. Not living up to these expectations may render the very belongingness in that pattern shaky. Certain attributes which have to be lived up to accompany every status, every role, every brand of membership in any group or profession. Every professor, no matter where he is, has to utter a word of wisdom once in a while. Every administrator has to convey in a subtle or crass manner some signs of power every so often.

In order to move on from the social place we are in, and even to maintain it, we will strive to exhibit the necessary qualities, skills, and accomplishments. This striving is not just the result of external pressures. Fear of failure in examinations is not the whole story for many students. There is also the satisfaction derived from a high relative standing for one's self-esteem, as well as from standing high in the eyes of those who are in the same boat. The attainment of some standing, being and having things that "our kind" have are very much in the functioning of our ego. All these can be expressed in terms of anchorages provided by our groups and reference scales defined by them.

The American values of "amounting to something," or "cleanliness is next to godliness" are not sought after only because of external pressures. Strivings along these dimensions become so much a part of us that we tend to think of them only in terms of our personal values. In recent years some authors have emphasized a dichotomy between the "real self" of the individual and social pressures from the group. Therefore, this social context of man's directive personal strivings has to be stressed in order to keep things in proper perspective.

WHO RATES THE RUGS AND WHEN: The perspective of seeing man's unique strivings in the light of their appropriate reference scales, and seeing the reference scales in the light of concrete behaviors of individuals within their bounds can be applied to many phases of life. Let us see its application in the case of business executives:

In the hierarchy of U.S. business, a big problem is the question of executive prerogatives. Who eats in the executive dining room? Who gets the best offices? And when does a man rise high enough to rate a rug on his floor? The scramble for the prerequisites of rank is the butt of a thousand jokes, often leads to ludicrous situations. But to corporations themselves, the scramble is no joke. . . .

In many companies executives continuously play the game of "one-up-manship," the gentle art of being a jump ahead of colleagues in acquiring everything from better ashtrays to air conditioners. In general, the president and board chairman, who get the best of everything anyway, are rarely involved; the struggle takes place among the vice presidents, and below. A few years ago, a Dallas company set up a new subsidiary with five brand-new vice presidents installed in identical offices. Everything was peaceful until one used his expense account to replace his single-pen set with a two-pen set. Within four days all five worked their way up to three-pen sets. . . . A big Chicago oil company caused a major crisis a few years ago when it bought a new type of posture chair to test on a few of its executives. Those left out were so miserable that one man, to save face, bought a chair with his own money and smuggled it into the office [47, p. 80].

In the reciprocally aroused strivings for upward mobility of these individuals within a given set, we see a neat demonstration of setting personal goals in terms of one's reference scale. The executive who, with greater zeal than the rest, went so far as to buy the coveted chair for his office with his own money illustrates the personal variations of strivings within a given reference scale.

We all have our "Joneses" whom we want to keep up with and to excel, if possible, in many phases of life. In every culture, people are sensitive and, within the bounds of tolerable variations, responsive to their particular Joneses. The particular Joneses in different settings give the differences in direction and goals.

One of the behavioral indices of an individual's ego-involvements in group demarcations manifests itself when he answers the question: "Who am I?" This was recently demonstrated quantitatively in a study by Kuhn and McPartland (22). These investigators requested their 228 subjects to fill in twenty blanks on one sheet with "answers to the simple question 'Who am I.'" The subjects were to give their answers as if responding to their own question, and not to somebody else. The investigators' assumption was that "the ordering of responses is a reflection of the make-up of the self-conception." In line with this assumption they found that: "First, from the ordering of responses on the page it was evident that *respondents tended to exhaust all the consensual references they would make before they made (if at all) any subconsensual ones.* . . . This ordering of responses held whether a respondent made as many as nineteen consensual references or as few as one" (p. 70, italics in original).

"Girl," "husband," "Baptist," "pre-med," "daughter" are examples of "consensual" responses. "Happy," "bored," "pretty good student" are examples of sub-consensual responses. This demonstration lends additional support to the conclusion that people do think of themselves in terms of social demarcations. Sub-consensual responses like "good student" or "good wife" specify unique individual variations within social demarcations.

Status and Ego-Involvements

The formation of ego-attitudes and the subsequent shaping of reactions through their situationally aroused involvements remain subjective phenomena if they are not related to appropriate social situations. In this connection, we have to remember that formally or informally organized groups of any kind are necessarily hierarchical in some respect with their peculiar status and prestige scales (Chapter 5, pp. 162–170). This hierarchical property of group structure is reflected in the particular kind of "Joneses" to whom people in different group settings are responsive. Family, church, gang, professional organization, union, club, university—all have their own status scales. As we trace the division and increase of functions from relatively simple, primitive societies to highly differentiated modern societies, the groups that the individual belongs to increase both in number and in complexity. The fact is referred to as *multiple group* affiliations of individuals in differentiated societies. The status and prestige standards of individual members exist within the bounds of reference scales prevailing in his various groups.

Status is a sociological denotation. Status is a standardized position in the group. As the anthropologist Linton stated, "In all societies certain things are selected as reference points for the ascription of status" (26, p. 215). The scale of status positions is on the stimulus side for the would-be member; hence, the status positions of a group are data of sociology. The individual learns them as he comes to belong *psychologically* and to participate in his groups. In its main features his ego consists of a series of belongingnesses. Social psychologists must learn a great deal from the social scientists about these status positions, for they can also be studied sociologically on their own level without reference to this or that individual. For example, the relative roles of father and mother, and the range and particular roles of kinship relations can be studied without reference to particular individuals in those particular roles. As clearly pointed out by Piaget, at first the family is a perceptual pattern to the child and a place of satisfaction of his needs. It is only after a certain degree of ego development that he grasps the significance of reciprocal roles in the family as they are standardized in the particular social setting.

Therefore, it becomes imperative for the social psychologist to learn something about the sociology of *status* if he wants a proper perspective toward the stimulus situations individuals face. We shall restrict our discussion to a few relevant points derived from Benoit-Smullyan's concise discussion of status types and status interrelations (2). Everywhere, group organizations are hierarchical affairs. The hierarchies may be based on diverse criteria, of which economic and political power are major. In lesser organized groups other criteria may determine status. For example, in a schoolroom a hierarchy is established among the pupils according to the degree of success in school subjects. Status may be defined "as relative position within a hierarchy" (2, p. 155).

By a hierarchy we mean a number of individuals ordered on an inferiority-superiority scale with respect to the comparative degree to which they possess or embody some socially approved or generally desired attribute or characteristic. A hierarchical position is thus always a position in which one individual is identified with others with regard to the possession or embodiment of some common characteristic, but differentiated from these others in the *degree*, or *measure*, to which the characteristic is possessed or embodied. The three chief hierarchies with which we will be concerned are: the economic hierarchy, the political hierarchy, and the prestige hierarchy. Relative position within these hierarchies constitutes economic status, political status, and prestige status respectively [2, pp. 151–152].

Economic status, political status, and prestige status are the three primary or basic types of social status. The individual's position may not be on the same level in these three major types of status. For example, he may be high in prestige status and not so high in economic status. After pointing to certain concrete cases of such discrepancies, Benoit-Smullyan comes, however, to the conclusion that "in fact, *the data suggest that economic status has been the dominating element in our own* [American] *recent history . . .*" (2, p. 151, italics ours). "Wealth is frequently 'converted' into power by direct or indirect bribery, by purchasing posts of command or weapons of coercion, by hiring the services of guards or soldiers or propagandists" (2, p. 159).

In a society dominated by private property relationships, all prestige sooner or later has to be regulated largely by economic status. "It is significant that the dispossessed aristocrat does not indefinitely retain his prestige unless he is sooner or later able to win back his power. Similarly, the *nouveaux riches,* though snubbed persistently, do sooner or later gain in prestige status providing they retain their money. We have to do here with one phase of an interesting social process which we may name 'status conversion' " (2, p. 159).

Particularly significant for the social psychologist is the concept of *status equilibration* that Benoit-Smullyan introduces. He characterizes the concept as follows: "As a result of status conversion processes which are normally at work in every [capitalist] society, there exists a real tendency for the different types of status to reach a common level, i.e., for a man's position in the economic hierarchy to match his position in the political hierarchy of prestige, etc." (2, p. 160). We shall have occasion later to note an important implication of the status equilibration hypothesis for human relations (see p. 639).

Reference-Group Standards Determine Level of Personal Goals

When individuals face a task in which they do not have an established level of achievement but are given the achievement level of groups who are consistently established (in their eyes) as superior or inferior, the position of their own group provides the main anchorage in setting a goal for performance. This was neatly demonstrated by Chapman and Volkmann (6) in an experiment carried out in 1939. Their experiment served as a model for numerous other studies.

Chapman and Volkmann started by calling attention to the principle that "conditions which govern the setting of a level of aspiration (Anspruchsniveau), in the sense of an estimate of one's future performance in a given task, may be regarded as a special case of the effect upon a judgment of the frame of reference within which it is executed" (p. 225). The subjects were asked to predict their future performance on a literary test, which was described and illustrated with an example. The subjects (college students) did not have sufficient objective criteria on which to base their level of performance. They were provided, however, with statements of the alleged performances of other groups which stood in different positions relative to the subjects' reference group. One standard was attributed to literary critics (higher than the college reference group) and one to WPA workers (lower than the college reference group). The subjects who compared themselves to the "superior" standard (literary critics) *lowered* their goals for performance. On the other hand, the "inferior" standard introduced for other subjects had the effect of raising the level of their goals.

One procedural point in this study clarifies the functioning of the anchorages involved and deserves special emphasis. The instructions in the study reported specified only the achievement level of another group on the task. No mention was made to the subjects of the standing of their own group. The subjects raised or lowered their estimates of their performance by spontaneously *using their own group as the main anchorage* and regulating estimates of their own performance according to the position of their own group relative to those groups whose alleged performance was given them. These findings were later substantiated with different stimulus material (tasks) and for subjects with different reference groups.

In the second part of their experiment, Chapman and Volkmann found that, when the subject had previously established standards for his own performance on a task, the introduction of standards attributed to various groups produced practically no shifts in his level of aspiration. In this case, the erection of goals was regulated in terms of the subjects' established personal levels of achievement.

Another comprehensive formulation of the regulation of personal goals relative to the standards of one's own reference group was offered by P. Sears (36) in her work on the level of aspiration of academically successful and unsuccessful school children. Sears' experiment is especially significant in that she utilized a hierarchy of success and failure established in a school situation. She showed how relative standing established in a success-failure hierarchy in the school group influences the standard for performance on a subsequent occasion. Sears, then, created experimental "success" and "failure" for the children's performances. She found that even in such experimentally created situations the children set their goals in accordance with what they believed to be their position relative to the social norms for performance they had accepted. In explaining the findings pertaining to different characteristics of the aspiration levels of successful and unsuccessful children, Sears concluded: "The cultural pressure to excel and to keep the performance improving, plus the cognizance of the position of the self relative to social norms, seems to account for most of the results obtained in the present investigation" (p. 528).

A concise statement of the principle that appears in these and similar studies was made by Lewin, Dembo, Festinger, and Sears (24) in surveying studies on "level of aspiration." In line with the previous formulations mentioned above, they concluded that influences like standards of one's own groups, introduced standards from other groups, and temporary situational factors which similarly affect setting a level of aspiration "may be conceived of as frames, involving a scale of values, within which the individual makes his decision as to a goal" (p. 337).

In Hyman's study of psychological aspects of status (15) we find a demonstration of the fact that the standards people set for themselves are determined by the standards of groups to which they relate themselves. It was Hyman in this study who first used the term "reference group." Hyman conducted intensive interviews to discover the individual's dimensions of status, his reference groups, the genesis, criteria, and values of his status conceptions, and his satisfaction with his status.

Among the interesting findings was the "rare occurrence of the total population as a reference group and the great frequency of more intimate reference groups. . . . Individuals operate for the most part in small groups within the total society, and the total population may have little relevance for them. Far more important are their friends, people they work with. Consequently, objective measures of status will very likely differ from subjective measures if total population is the basis for the determination of objective status" (p. 24). This finding illustrates a point made earlier. In accounting for the social influences on the individual, terms like "culture," "society," or even "subculture" are too general. Concepts like membership group and reference groups permit us to specify the sources of social influences in terms of concrete social stimulus situations (including conceptual classifications) which actually operate in the patterning of given individual behaviors.

Hyman then constructed scales to measure "subjective status" in several respects, e.g., economic, intellectual, cultural, social, and the like. He showed how an individual's judgments of his own status shifted when related to different groups. He found that "striving for status is generally directed in the channel of the most valued status," that is, toward that status highest in the hierarchy. Dissatisfaction with status was found to vary "inversely with the level of status." This finding also illustrates how one's position on a status scale may influence his aspirations and strivings.

The results pertaining to individuals who were comparatively unconcerned with status problems are revealing. Lack of concern with status was found among (1) those individuals whose status conception was similar to the status of their reference group; (2) those individuals who maintained a status in a group high in the hierarchy and took their position for granted; and (3) those individuals who rejected the scale of status established in the social order around them as a basis for judging their own status. Hyman concluded that "the values of an individual are set into operation by certain reference groups, in which case specific statuses contribute to general status in accordance with their value" (p. 91).

Regulation of Individual Performance by Reference-Group Standards

In earlier chapters we referred to the frequent finding reported by Roethlisberger and Dickson and by others pertaining to "rate setting" by informal work groups in industrial plants (pp. 172–173). Once a group norm for production output is established, members of the informal group apply *sanctions* to those in their midst who deviate from it. These sanctions are applied to deviates because of inner irritation experienced by group members with those who violate the norm. These inner feelings of irritation stem from the interiorization of group norms by the individual member.

Individuals who regulate their output in accordance with group norms and apply sanctions to deviates have taken the informal work group as their reference group. This conclusion was substantiated in a study by M. Dalton. He studied a department in an industrial plant where 100 men worked under a piece-rate system. Under this system they received a bonus for production over 66 percent. However, through interactions within the group, a "well recognized rule" was established that no worker must produce over 150 percent on any job. A majority of the men consistently made a bonus, but were careful not to exceed the 150 percent mark. Ten men disregarded the rule and averaged between 150 and 200 percent. On the other hand, 18 men averaged below 100 percent. After finding that *skill* alone did not account for this range of performance, M. Dalton demonstrated that it could be fully accounted for in terms of (1) the social backgrounds and (2) present social activities of the individuals with differential outputs. The findings were summarized by Whyte (53) as follows:

1. "Most of the bottom production group grew up in large cities where for years they had been active in boys' gangs. Such activity tends to build loyalty to one's own group and opposition to authority—whether from parents or management. The rate busters all grew up on farms or in small towns where they lived under the close supervision of parental authority and had little time or opportunity to develop gang activities and the accompanying loyalty to the gang."

In other words, the "rate busters" and "restricters" (who averaged below 100 percent) had differing life histories in terms of group interaction and differing ego-attitudes as a consequence.

2. "In terms of present social participation, the restricters are the men

who lead an active social life *in the shop*. Furthermore, they lead a highly active group life outside of work" (italics ours). Those who averaged below 100 percent were the men who were good and active members of the informal group.

On the other hand, the rate buster "is either a lone wolf in factory and community or else an individual with a strong drive toward social mobility, who, thus, cuts himself off from others on the same level and seeks association with those of superior status." That is, the rate busters tended to be individuals whose psychological relatedness was elsewhere than in their immediate factory and community groups. These conclusions were substantiated by other behavioral indices. For example, the restricters were the most generous in giving contributions to group charities, while the rate busters were the most stingy.

THE EGO OF THE INDIVIDUAL AND REFERENCE GROUPS

As we recall, *reference groups are those groups to which the individual relates himself as a part or to which he aspires to relate himself psychologically*. Obviously, the definition of reference group is in ego terms, that is, in terms of the individual's psychological relatedness. This psychological relatedness to reference groups may or may not coincide with actual associations with groups as recorded by objective criteria. The individual's psychological relatedness to groups may or may not coincide with the actual group settings in which he carries out his daily activities. Elaboration of this point provides the crux of the usefulness of the reference-group concept.

One of the cardinal points emphasized repeatedly throughout this book has been the effect of reference groups in the formation and change of the individual's directive attitudes. His directive attitudes derived from reference groups pertain to his central concerns: to having some place in the scheme of human relations, being accepted, being somebody who counts, setting goals for achievement. Expressing the same idea in more technical language, reference groups provide the main anchorings in the formation and change of ego-attitudes, in the erection of future goals. When these anchorings come in as factors in given situations, we say the individual is ego-involved. And when he is ego-involved, the result is a characteristic consistency of the person's behavior. In this sense, it can be said that the consistency or inconsistency of a person is, to a large extent, a function of his reference groups. This point will receive factual support when we make specific applications of the concept later in the chapter (pp. 637–639).

Two Conditions Necessitated the Concept of Reference Groups

Two conditions have been primarily responsible for bringing reference-group problems to the foreground. We will discuss each briefly.

1. The first condition arises from the diverse alternatives that *modern* man encounters in his surroundings as a result of multiple groups, diverse values, and possibilities afforded by vertical mobility. (a) For men who live in relatively undifferentiated cultures in which an integrated kinship system is the only or dominant basis of belongingness, status, and role attribution, and for attendant matters of loyalty, privilege, and responsibility, their membership group is at the same time their reference group. If vertical mobility is also of a very low degree, there are hardly any alternatives in such cultures for other membership or aspirations for membership, for different values or ideologies. In such cultures, the classificatory scheme of relatedness, which the child's ego system becomes as he acquires language, develops through adolescence to adulthood in accordance with well-established social ties and expectations in various phases of living. (b) On the other hand, in highly differentiated modern societies with considerable vertical mobility, the developing child faces multiple groups and diverse values which are integrated or conflicting in varying degrees. Of course, the integration or conflict of the alternatives he faces varies according to his particular life circumstances as well as according to the overall relationships among parts in the social organization. Conflict between alternatives presented by multiple groups and competing values is sharpened for individuals living in modern societies with a high rate of social change and a high degree of vertical mobility. By a high degree of vertical mobility we mean a fluid state of opportunities for changing one's social class and climbing up the social ladder.

2. The second condition stems from man's psychological capacity to relate himself to groups, values, and goals beyond the limits of immediate surroundings within his perceptual range, and beyond the limits of the living present into the future. No matter how dissatisfied or frustrated a cat may be in a given household, one cannot imagine his aspiring to be appropriated by another family in another town. Such aspirations beyond immediate situations are distinctive to man. What is true of the expansion of man's relatedness beyond immediate surroundings is true also of the

temporal scope of his relatedness. Man sets goals that go far beyond the living present and into the future. This expansion of man's ego far beyond immediate perceptual surroundings and into future time makes it possible for him to relate himself to groups of which he is not an actual member. Reference-group problems are, therefore, distinctly human problems which have come into sharp focus in modern times. These problems are not encountered at the subhuman level. As Scott (35), an authority in the area of animal behavior, commented: ". . . The typical animal under natural conditions tends to be a part of one primary group throughout life and there are no verbal standards for such groups" (p. 69).

Thus, the concept of reference groups is needed because of man's capacity to relate himself to groups other than those in which he moves at a given place and time, and because of the increased complexity of social organization in modern societies.

Membership and Other Reference Groups

A central portion of the individual's sense of personal identity, his ego-attitudes defining his status and role relations with others, his prestige concerns, the level of his future goals is derived from groups of which he is a part or aspires to be a part. In order that the concept have a distinct meaning, only such groups should be designated as "reference groups" of the individual. When we speak of a *reference* group, we are specifying it from the point of view of given individuals (40).

The reference-group concept is not used to study any group in its own right. If the term is used to refer to any group being studied, it loses its differentiating denotation as a concept. Then the concepts "group" and "reference group" become synonyms. In this case no useful purpose is served by cluttering terminology with the addition of the extra word "reference" to "group" (see pp. 144–145).

A reference group of an individual is the group that provides his specific anchorings in attitude formation and attitude change. It is the position of these reference-group anchors that defines for that individual the relative positions (proximity or distance) of other groups. If the position of a given group along the social-distance scale prevailing in his reference group is low, this is reflected in his negative attitude toward that group. If the position represented in propaganda material is too far from the stand prevailing in his reference group on the issue, the individual reacts to it with irritation. If its position is close to the stand in his reference group, the individual may assimilate it (p. 573).

MEMBERSHIP AND REFERENCE GROUPS NEED NOT BE THE SAME: The rationale for having the concept in the prefaced form *reference group* lies in the observed cases of disparity between membership and reference groups. When the group with which the individual is actually associating is also the group with which he identifies himself, interiorizing its values and norms as his own attitudes, then his membership and reference groups are one and the same. As a rule, in cultures that are stable, that are not going through rapid social change, that do not offer diverse opportunities for vertical mobility, the individual's membership groups are at the same time his reference groups. Also, in a differentiated but highly integrated society, the same will be true.

But in highly differentiated societies with multiple groups representing diverse viewpoints and interests, there are many individuals whose reference groups are not the groups with which they are actually associating in day-to-day living. There are lower-class individuals who "see" themselves in the middle class and regulate their attitudes and behavior in terms of middle-class values or norms. There are middle-class individuals who fancy themselves in a higher class and exhibit this kind of psychological relatedness in their actual behavior, in choice of a residence on the "right" side of the tracks, of a family car appropriate for that higher level, in the choice of a college for their son or daughter which is attended by offspring of the aspired set.

Cases of discrepancy between actual group membership and psychological relatedness are not infrequent in the United States, which is a good example of a highly differentiated society with possibilities of vertical mobility.

Vertical mobility, which is deduced from the moves of individuals to launch themselves in the socioeconomic class higher than their actual class, is due (1) to the existence of hierarchical class demarcations of society and (2) to the pregnability of class lines for the individuals dead set in their upward move. The demarcation lines between classes are drawn mainly on the basis of socioeconomic functions of individuals in the scheme of society. But how people place themselves and others in a class structure in the community does not correspond strictly to the objective economic class to which they actually belong.

Especially in societies in which class lines are not altogether impregnable, there is sometimes a discrepancy between objective socioeconomic placement and psychological placement of individuals. Lloyd Warner and his associates built up a classificatory scheme of social-class placements in

America mainly on the basis of evaluations of people living in the community (50). In the words of Warner and Lunt, "In the final analysis, however, individuals were placed by the evaluations of the members of Yankee City itself, e.g. by such explicit statements as 'she does not belong' or 'they belong to our club' " (50, p. 90). According to this extensive work, Warner and associates placed the people in the city in six status classes: "Upper upper," "Lower upper," "Upper middle," "Lower middle," "Upper lower," "Lower lower" (see Fig. 18.1).

Centers (5) studied the class identifications of a cross section of white

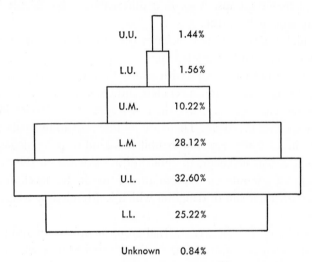

U.U.   1.44%

L.U.   1.56%

U.M.   10.22%

L.M.   28.12%

U.L.   32.60%

L.L.   25.22%

Unknown   0.84%

FIG. 18.1.   Representation of class demarcations and hierarchy in Yankee City. (After Warner and Lunt.)

adult males and related these reference groups to actual occupational groupings and to political attitudes. He found that about three-fourths of the people in business, management, professional, and white-collar occupations identified themselves as members of the "middle class." About 79 percent of persons occupied in some form of manual labor identified themselves as "working class." The remainder in these occupational strata identified themselves with other classes.

For our present discussion, Centers' significant finding was that individuals in a given occupational stratum who differed from others in their class identification also tended to differ in attitudes toward social-political issues. In Centers' words: "*If people's class identifications are the same, their attitudes tend to be similar even though their objective occupational positions are different"* (p. 308, italics in original).

There was the possibility that if a workingman related himself to a "middle class" he might have a different conception of that classification from that of a businessman who identified himself as "middle class." Centers checked this point by having individuals choose the occupational groups included in the class they identified with. He found that an individual with a discrepancy between occupational membership and class identification included about the same occupations in the class he identified with as a person whose occupation and class identification coincided. The result was that "Manual workers who affiliate with the middle class are identifying themselves with primarily nonmanual occupational strata" (p. 311).

It is not coincidental that the fashionable women's colleges started to come into existence after the breath-taking industrial development of America got well under way in the second half of the nineteenth century. It is not coincidental that Veblen's incisive analysis (49) concerning the decisive effect of higher-class values and practices in shaping the aspirations and practices of people in other classes appeared around the turn of the century when vertical mobility acquired fluidity. The reader who is interested in problems of vertical mobility may consult the recent concise discussion by Kurt Mayer (27, especially Chapters 7–8) and more extended treatments of specific topics in Bendix and Lipset (1, especially Part IV).

The recent redrawing of political boundaries after the two world wars created disparities between behavior regulated by reference-group attitudes and the actualities of demarcation lines. One interesting case of this kind was reported in the newspapers in connection with Prince Esterhazy's trial for smuggling checks across the national borders of Hungary. Prince Paul Esterhazy is "the head of one of Europe's greatest families." The great days for the Esterhazy family were those in the splendor of the Austro-Hungarian Empire and their association in the glitter around the imperial family. A telling reaction from the prince indicates that psychologically he is still living in the entirety of the empire rather than regulating the boundaries of his relatedness in terms of existing boundaries. "In the court he saw his world falling about him, as he described the loss of his wealth and estates since the war's end. But in his mind the prince still lives in the days of the Austro-Hungarian Empire. When one of his administrators was asking why he had smuggled checks abroad, he replied: 'We did not send them abroad. We sent them to *Austria*'" (*30*, p. 7, italics ours).

Growing Interest in the Concept of Reference Group

In spite of its recent history, the term "reference groups" has come to be widely used. It is frequently pointed to as an effective conceptual tool in handling problems pertaining to man's group relations and the formation and change of attitudes. Many cases of observed inconsistency in behavior, of contradictions in behavioral adjustments, of setting goals in an out-of-step fashion with actualities in given dimensions acquire a coherent meaning when analyzed in terms of the principles which led to the formulation of the reference-group concept. Presenting a highly differentiated social pattern, encompassing diverse professional, regional, rural-urban, ethnic demarcations as it does, the United States has been the most fertile soil for the development of theoretical and empirical contributions utilizing this concept. In less diversified societies, in societies with less fluidity in vertical mobility, the application of the concept may not come to the foreground in such a striking way (cf. *43*, pp. 214–217).

The term "reference group" was first used in 1942 by Hyman (*15*) in his study of status. It was found useful in Sherif and Cantril's survey (*41*) of ego-involvements in group relations. In accounting for "membership and other reference groups" in the 1948 edition of this book (Chapter 6), the concept proved to be a most integrating one. Similarly, the concept was found valuable in the works of Lindesmith and Strauss (*25*), Newcomb (*31*), Merton and Kitt (*29*), Killian (*19, 20*), Hartley and Hartley (*10*), Jahoda, Deutsch, and Cook (*16*), and others. Among the more recent significant contributions are those of Kelley (*18*) and Shibutani (*42*). Some of the analyses and empirical studies illustrating the usefulness of the concept for specific problems will be reported in the next section.

ATTITUDES DERIVED FROM REFERENCE GROUPS ARE MANIFOLD: An attitude derived from a reference group does not stand alone. It is one of many attitudes thus derived. The simple reason for this is that the group with which a person identifies himself appeals to various aspects of the individual's relatedness. It is in relation to his reference group that the individual has his sense of belongingness, his claims for some status and prestige. It is in terms of its reference scales in many phases of his life (professional, domestic, political, and so on) that the individual sets his goals and experiences, his successes and failures.

In our discussion of groups we emphasized that it is the values and norms of the reference group that become interiorized and binding for the individual, whether or not external social pressures are operative. A recent illustration of this general fact was provided by Breed (4) in his analysis of "social control in the newsroom." Breed shows convincingly how the new staff member reflects the policy laid down by the editors in the choice of his reporting, not primarily owing to coercion exerted, but rather to the new man's appropriation of the newsroom people as his reference group. The aspirations for status, for having an edge on other papers, the prestige of the editors, the pleasant nature of the activity, the integrated character of allegiance to policy in the newsroom are among the factors contributing to conformity in reporting by the new staff member.

REFERENCE-GROUP CONCEPT APPLIED TO SPECIFIC PROBLEMS

The usefulness of the concept of reference groups, as we have seen, stems from the fact that it is attained on the basis of a host of facts which reveal the regulation of experience and behavior by their appropriate anchorages (Chapters 2 and 3). Whenever *conflict* of anchorages arises, or whenever status anchorages are disproportionately high or low in relation to one another, we face significant psychological problems. Reduced to its bare essentials, *marginality* is the condition of being caught between two conflicting reference groups, or being caught between one's reference group and a group which is capable of exerting pressures, putting demands on him, and requiring conformity of him. Again, in bare outline, at least some cases of *inconsistency* revealed by the individual in intergroup relations are due to the fact that, as the individual goes through various situations, different roles prescribed by contradictory norms of his multiple reference-group affiliations are activated. Having attained a high status in some dimension of human relations, one finds that being still in low status in some other respect becomes insufferable; hence some of the comedies and tragedies that accompany the efforts for *status equilibration.*

Marginality in Human Relations

Personal conflict, uncertainty, or insecurity follows lack of stability of anchorings in reference groups. These situations have been extensively studied by sociologists—notably Park and Stonequist—as *marginality* (45).

The state of marginality gives us a good opportunity to emphasize certain points which we could touch upon only briefly in the course of this discussion. Since our task in this chapter is the clarification of the reference-group concept, the emphasis has been on instances in which the groups are not face to face, or which are not within the perceptual range of the individual. However, such emphasis should *not* imply that immediate face-to-face group situations, in which the membership group is not a reference group, do not have some effect on the individual. On the contrary, even in cases in which a sharp cleavage exists between the group in which he is registered or taken for granted and his reference group, he is bound to feel the immediate pressures and demands for conformity of the group situation he moves in. In such cases, he will be pushed in one direction by his actual membership group, pulled in the opposite direction by his reference group.

In cases of marginality, however, the situation is ordinarily one of *lack of stability in reference-group ties*. The individual cannot relate himself in a consistent way to either group. Both groups, at times, are reference groups for him, however unstable his ties with one group. The degrees to which he is ego-involved with the value scales of one or the other may vary.

The most common example of marginality is that of individuals belonging to an ethnic group, religious group, or color group in a minority position who, because of their inability to be accepted in the larger society and their tendency to reject standards or position of their own group, feel insecure in their reference-group affiliations in a major way.

Among psychologists, Kurt Lewin has written on these problems (23), and Hartley and his associates carried out interesting studies with children on the conflicting values of groups to which they relate themselves (11).

Marginality is not confined to members of minority groups. The *foreman* in industrial life is often in a similar position. Ordinarily, of course, the foreman rises out of the rank and file of workers. But as a foreman he is betwixt and between management and the workers. He cannot consistently relate himself to management, partly because of his origins and his economic situation, and because he does not actually take part in making policy decisions but just carries out the directives of management. Roethlisberger (33) pointed out that management calls the foreman the "grass roots level of management" or "front-line personnel man." But the foreman calls himself a "go-betweener." He has to uphold management's standards and regulations and at the same time try to get workers to conform to them spontaneously. "Again and again he is put in a position of either getting the worker's cooperation and being 'disloyal' to management or of incurring the resentment and overt opposition of his subordinates" (p. 290).

The workers, in turn, think of the foreman as "the boss." In an interview from a study by Whyte and Gardner (54), one worker said: "You can't talk about this sort of thing with the boss. After all, he's part of management and you couldn't expect him to see things as we do. He's a good guy, as far as that goes, but he's a management man" (p. 19).

The foreman thus is unable to take either management or the workers as his reference group in a consistent way. The result may be, in the words of one foreman: "You don't know where you stand. It's a hell of a situation because I get on edge and blow my top and say things that I really didn't mean to say" (p. 20).

In the American Soldier Studies of World War II, Stouffer and associates apply a similar analysis to the conflicting situation of the *noncommissioned officer* (46). Here the "noncom finds himself in a conflict situation involving official responsibility to his officers on one hand and unofficial obligations to the other enlisted men on the other hand" (p. 410).

Inconsistency in Intergroup Relations

We have mentioned the relative consistency and continuity of the individual's identity (pp. 580–588). However, especially in modern complex societies, his behavior may appear highly contradictory and inconsistent in various situations. As an example, M. Jahoda takes the case of some union members who actively participated in the Detroit race riots of 1943 even though in their union they were taught and practiced nonsegregation. Now if these union members had been nothing but good and stanch union members, they would not have participated in the riots. But they were also members of families, neighborhood groups, churches, ethnic groups, and, as they have been reminded in so many ways from childhood on, a "white" group, which, they have learned, stands at definite distances from other groups. These groups were major reference groups long before these individuals became members of a union with an antidiscrimination policy. It is not surprising that, in a situation in which they could act either as a "regular person" in terms of their major reference groups of neighborhood, color, etc., or as good union members, many of them—probably with no thought of doing otherwise—acted contrary to their union's practices (39).

To be sure, behavior of individuals may be inconsistent for a number of reasons, perhaps idiosyncratic ones related to continual thwarting of biogenic motives or persistent conflict situations of a personal nature. However, a large proportion of instances of inconsistencies in social behavior can be understood in relation to *conflicting norms of various reference groups* which have been internalized and may be situationally aroused. Charters and Newcomb (31) showed that when Catholic subjects are situationally ego-involved as Catholics, their reactions to general statements are substantially different from their reactions to the same items when Catholic group reference is not activated.

When an individual has multiple reference groups, the norms of which conflict in various areas, he will sooner or later find himself in a situation where the norms of different reference groups point in different, even opposite, directions. Consider the situation of the modern professional woman (14). In her work, of course, her professional group is the major reference group; in social life, perhaps the ladies of the community; in her home, her family. It is not unusual for her to find herself in a situation where the norms of two or more of these reference groups are in conflict. Of course, she will probably react in terms of one or the other. She may even be aware of the source of her dilemma, feeling resentment toward one or the other of her reference groups responsible for the conflict in this area.

Killian (20), of Florida State University, made an interesting analysis of "the conflict of civilian and army norms in a military railway service." Although the men studied were all in the army and subject to all rules and customs of "military courtesy," the usual behavior between them, whether officers or enlisted men, was in terms of status in civilian railroad groups. In spite of "constant pressure from the general headquarters for compliance with traditional military practice," the railroad group and its norms persisted as the major anchorages and resulted in behavior quite inconsistent with the army situation.

In an analysis of the significance of multiple group membership in a disaster situation in four southwestern communities, Killian (19) studied the reactions of individuals to a situation where, by necessity, a choice in reference groups had to be made. For example, frequent conflict was found between loyalty to family or friends and loyalty to occupational groups. An example of apparently inconsistent behavior in the eyes of those who watched was that of the state trooper who decided after a tornado struck that as a patrolman his job was to drive to the next town for help. But to the friends and acquaintances who called for his help as he drove out of town his action must have seemed inconsistent, even heartless. He stated that this was "one of the hardest things I ever had to do."

The behavior of telephone workers in two disaster communities who were on strike at the time reveals the conflict between reference groups within the community and those outside of the community. "In both communities, the striking workers were allowed to return to duty by union leaders, but were ordered to walk out again a few days later. In both cases the union officials considered the emergency to be over sooner than did the townspeople of the stricken communities. In one town the workers obeyed the union's orders only to find themselves subjected to harsh criticism by their fellow-townsmen. In the other community the workers resigned from the union rather than forsake their loyalty to their other membership group" (p. 313).

Status Equilibration

To the degree that the individual has interiorized the norms of his various reference groups, conflict or contradictions of these norms will be experienced as personal conflict or insecurity. This relationship becomes more precise when individuals' statuses in their various reference groups are specified. Groups are necessarily hierarchical along some dimensions. Status denotes the relative position of each member in these respects. Of course, to have a relative position, the individual must in some degree relate himself or belong to the group. This relatedness implies experience of the hierarchy of the group and ego-involvement with it. Once he is a member, his aspirations for status and standards of attainment are determined in terms of this scale.

Now what happens when the individual's status in various reference groups differs? In delineating the concept of status equilibration, the sociologist Benoit-Smullyan suggests that "there is a real tendency for the different types of status to reach a common level" (2, p. 160). For example, a millionaire who finds himself admired only for his money teams up with a college professor or public relations expert, or endows a research foundation, in the effort to attain prestige socially commensurate with his financial status. Or a lady newly arrived in a financial sense may indulge in literature or the arts, or psychology, in order to bring her social status in the community to the level of her financial status. In the process of striving, she may be a little ashamed of her associates on the wrong side of the tracks and try to minimize or even break off her relationship with them. As Hartley suggests, another way the individual may seek to adjust his statuses is by trying to raise the prestige of one of his reference groups to the level of the higher group. Hartley's study with Fenchel and Monderer on college students' status and status strivings in five significant reference groups found the tendency to be expected from the notion of status equilibration (9). Striving for status was significantly greater in reference groups in which status was lower. "The results indicate a definite tendency for the status ratings to approach a common high anchorage level within the individual's status structure, as defined by his different reference groups" (p. 477). The explanation for this, we should think, lies in the ego-involvement in these anchorages defined by reference groups, and in the personal uneasiness at being exposed to situations of conflict and contradiction.

STATUS EQUILIBRATION IN INTERGROUP RELATIONS: The personal problems that are produced by concern over equilibration at the highest attained status have their serious counterparts in intergroup adjustments of individuals, especially those who are members of minority groups in a country with heterogeneous ethnic composition.

Minority group members, at the same time, are citizens of the larger society. The tendency for the general run of minority group members is to internalize the social-distance scale that exists in the country as a whole, putting various groups at various positions on the hierarchy of social distance standardized from the point of view of the group on top of the scale (Chapter 19). Having accepted the social-distance scale with its relative positions for various groups, they tend subjectively to place their own group close to the highest position and to keep the rest of the social-distance scale intact. In the last analysis this tendency reflects an attitude which means that the minority group members in question reject discrimination against their own particular group but at the same time accept discrimination applied to other minority groups.

Probably this subjective placement would not have been made if the upward move had been perceived as impossible, as it is considered by members of the low caste in a country where lines between hierarchical positions are more sharply drawn and more or less frozen—e.g., until a few decades ago, in India. But in a society in which there is a greater degree of *fluidity*, a greater degree of give-and-take in a greater number of social functions (business, education, social intercourse, and so forth) between groups high and low on the social-distance scale, special complications arise. Here we shall cite only two important cases.

1. Some members of the minority groups not high on the social-distance scale do actually arrive at topmost status in business, education, art, or some other area of social life through their personal achievements. There are some among these individuals who have attained topmost status in some respect who strive to equilibrate their statuses in other areas to this highest one. The consequence of such strivings is reflected in pulling away from the norms of their original group even to the point of depreciation of the group from which they stem. This phenomenon is described as *self-hatred* of one's own group by Lewin (23) and others. Whether a person in this situation will turn against his own group or instead stand with his own group involves intricate personality problems which we cannot consider here. The important point in this connection is to note the occurrence of such cases due to the intergroup relations mentioned above.

2. The depreciation of the group from which one stems may be due to the unsatisfactory nature of one's belongingness and status in his own group. The anchorages in one's own group having become precarious through the lack of motivational support, the aspiration to belong to a higher group determines his subjective acceptance of the anchorages related to the higher group. Usually in such cases there is a wide gap between actualities of real belongingness and statuses and subjectively desired belongingness and statuses. This gap between actual belongingness and status on the one hand and fantasied identification and status on the other becomes the source of personal conflicts, insecurities, and painful experiences in social adjustments.

Adolescent Attitudes and Practices

In modern societies the dramatic period of adolescence, which is the period of transition from childhood to adulthood, is marked with the appearance of new interests, new attitudes and practices. Works on adolescence are replete with descriptions and inventories of such changes in the adolescent generation (12, 13, 21). Especially parents brought up in the genteel tradition may simply be unable to understand why their teenage daughter insists on wearing those unladylike, unbecoming blue jeans just below knee level or spends a great part of her life by the telephone. A great many of the changes in adolescent attitudes, interests, and conception of self acquire functional coherence when considered in terms of the youngsters' reference-group ties.

Of course, bodily and sexual maturation during adolescence in itself has dramatic effects. The changes in the adolescent's body, his desires, the way he sees himself, demand changes in relation to other persons in general and the opposite sex in particular. The adolescent must step from his "childish" relationships. He gets specific ideas and values of becoming a full-fledged man or woman in his society. And at this stage he ardently desires to fulfill them.

On the other hand, parents, grownups, and the social organization and its norms have very definite and, in complicated societies, often conflicting ideas or norms of how the transition from childhood to adulthood should be made.

In less differentiated societies the young person settles down in his appropriate adult role shortly after puberty with a definite sexual role, a definite work role, and other roles. This may occur in a dramatic, even abrupt fashion, through "transition" ceremonies and rites, which often involve prescribed trials of various degrees of severity—as illustrated in the works of Mead (28), Van Gennep (48), Webster (51), Radin (32), and others.

But in more complex societies, e.g., America today, settling down is a delayed, prolonged process. During this period the fulfillment of the adolescent's desires and his dreams must be postponed in many instances. At the same time, although he is no longer a child, he is *not consistently treated or accepted as an adult*. Consequently, the youth and his parents and other grownups, whose job it is to help carry through these restrictions, are in conflict. As Kingsley Davis (8) writes, this is especially true in countries where the values of adults and adolescents by virtue of a rapid rate of social change are miles apart, as in China or Turkey or many other countries today.

In this state of instability and conflict the adolescent tries to belong some place at any rate. In a setting where social mixing of various groups is not encouraged, these attempts to become somebody may be through daydreams and fantasy. But in most modern societies, on the whole, adolescents gravitate toward one another.

Thus arises a "peer culture" or "adolescent culture," as Blos (3), Zachry (55), Harold Jones (17), and other writers on the subject have called it, which is peculiar to the adolescents, at least in some dimensions of their lives. Frequently it is peculiar to a particular group of youngsters.

Although adolescents of course know perfectly well what grownups want them to learn, they are, in this state of transition, centered in their own group of adolescents. For the time being at least it becomes the dominant reference group which regulates their attitudes and interests, their activities and aspirations to a considerable degree. In this setting, parents and adults may simply constitute annoyances in so many aspects of living important to them. One high-school girl in California, peeved by her parents' interferences in her activities, remarked: "I am afraid my friends will think I have no control over my parents" (*44*, p. 4).

Conflict situations arise when practices and values sanctioned by the family and those sanctioned by the adolescent's peer group on the same issues pull in *opposite* directions. In such situations, the boy or girl faces a choice of contradictory alternatives, with considerable wear and tear as a consequence. The relative strengths of the reference groups will determine which alternative will be followed. A recent substantiation of this dilemma is provided by Rosen (*34*). He found that, for the youngsters he studied, the peer group tended to be more influential in the choice: "More often than not in cases where parent-peer groups have conflicting attitudes on the issue examined in this study adolescents agreed with their peers rather than their parents" (p. 160).

In more stable strata of society, adolescents may keep the major norms of the family reference group intact. Depending on the youngsters they associate with, many of these norms may not even bring up questions of great importance to them. For example, questions relating to political or social norms may be of very little importance to a group of upper-class adolescents.

It should be noted, of course, that this period of resistance to adults and preoccupation with age-mate reference groups, in some cases to the point of rebellion, is usually transitory.

Ordinarily, within an age range considered acceptable by society, the adolescent does "settle down," taking on economic and social roles in the adult society, including those of husband and wife. With these events, his reference group ordinarily becomes the adult group or groups in which he functions and moves, and the interests, attitudes, and values of his youthful adolescent group appear even to him as silly youthful adventure.

Whenever individuals cannot consistently relate themselves to the scale of values of the groups within which they move and function, there is a tendency for these individuals to gravitate toward one another and to form informal reference groups, from which, at least for the time being, they derive their major self-identity, aspirations, and values (see pp. 146–151).

Another excellent example of this tendency is found in "interstitial areas"—slum areas of large cities. The children and young people in such areas are very frequently in the position of being rejected by society at large and hence are unable to identify with society; at the same time they reject the values of their families (7). These family values, which are often carry-overs of Old World norms, are unacceptable to children in constant contact with the established American setting. Interstitial areas and their conflicts and problems have been rather extensively studied by a number of sociologists.

Such interstitial areas may appear from the outside to be "disorganized," but as William Whyte pointed out, there is actually a high state of organization on an informal basis.

Informal reference groups may become so all-important that their standards may counteract chances to improve in status or to have contacts with the opposite sex. For example, Whyte found (52) that one group of young men broke off contact with a group of attractive girls when these contacts threatened to be a disruptive influence to the solidarity and integrity of the group.

Clifford Shaw's Jack-Roller (37) ran away from the opportunity to become a member of a well-to-do family. The husband in this childless family was the vice-president of a company and an influential man in the community. In this case, the boy's major identification was with a reference group which, in the eyes of society, was delinquent. But he had come from a slum area which the rest of society looked down upon, and he found no secure identification with his family group. When he became a member of a neighborhood gang as a young boy, he began to feel he was somebody in his own right—a person with a place in life. The informal groups of boys in which he functioned at various times in his development were the ones that gave him a sense of personal identity; they were his reference groups in everything that counted for him.

The knowledge of how he was supposed to behave and the opportunity to do so in a life of comparative ease were not enough for him. The norms of society were not the norms of his reference group and, hence, were not his norms.

This means that one has to analyze goals, standards, and the like in relation to those of the individual's reference groups.

For example, ordinarily we think of a person who gives information to authorities as "repentant"—they have "seen the light" and are on their way to being reformed. But that is not the way these fellows view these events. In the Jack-Roller's words: "To squawk on a fellow-prisoner is an unpardonable sin and only the lowest characters will squawk. . . . They are not fit to be associated with decent boys."

REFERENCES

1. Bendix, R., and Lipset, S. M. (eds.). *Class, Status and Power.* Glencoe, Ill.: Free Press, 1953.
2. Benoit-Smullyan, E. Status, status types and status interrelations, *Amer. sociol. Rev.* (1944), 9:151–161.
3. Blos, P. *The Adolescent Personality.* New York: Appleton-Century, 1941.
4. Breed, Warren. Social control in the newsroom: a functional analysis. *Soc. Forces* (1955), 33:326–335.
5. Centers, R. The American Class Structure: A Psychological Analysis, in G. E. Swanson, T. M. Newcomb, and E. L. Hartley (eds.), *Readings in Social Psychology.* New York: Holt, 1952.
6. Chapman, D. W., and Volkmann, J. A social determinant of the level of aspiration, *J. abnorm. & soc. Psychol.* (1939), 34:225–238.
7. Child, I. L. *Italian or American? The Second Generation in Conflict.* New Haven: Yale University Press, 1943.
8. Davis, K. The sociology of parent-youth conflict, *Amer. sociol. Rev.* (1940), 5:523–535.
9. Fenchel, G. H., Monderer, J. H., and Hartley, E. L. Subjective status and the equilibration hypothesis, *J. abnorm. & soc. Psychol.* (1951), 46:476–479.
10. Hartley, E. L., and Hartley, R. E. *Fundamentals of Social Psychology.* New York: Knopf, 1952.
11. Hartley, E. L., Rosenbaum, M., and Schwartz, S. Children's use of ethnic frames of reference: an exploratory study of children's conceptualizations of multiple ethnic group membership, *J. Psychol.* (1948), 26:367–386; Children's perception of their ethnic group membership, *ibid.,* 387–398; Note on children's role perception, *ibid.,* 399–405.
12. Hollingworth, L. *The Psychology of the Adolescent.* New York: Appleton, 1928.
13. Horrocks, J. E. *The Psychology of Adolescence.* Boston: Houghton Mifflin, 1951.
14. Hughes, E. C. Dilemmas and contradictions of status, *Amer. J. Sociol.* (1945), 50:353–359.
15. Hyman, H. H. The psychology of status, *Arch. Psychol.* (1942), No. 269.
16. Jahoda, M., Deutsch, M., and Cook, S. W. *Research Methods in Social Relations.* New York: Dryden, 1951.
17. Jones, H. E. *Development in Adolescence.* New York: Appleton-Century, 1943.
18. Kelley, H. H. Two Functions of Reference Groups, in G. E. Swanson, T. M. Newcomb, and E. L. Hartley (eds.), *Readings in Social Psychology.* New York: Holt, rev. ed., 1952.

19. Killian, L. M. The significance of multiple group membership in disaster, *Amer. J. Sociol.* (1952), 57:309–314.
20. Killian, L. M. The conflict of civilian and military norms in a military railway service. Manuscript kindly made available by the author (1953).
21. Kuhlen, R. G. *The Psychology of Adolescent Development.* New York: Harper, 1952.
22. Kuhn, M. H., and McPartland, T. S. An empirical investigation of self-attitudes, *Amer. sociol. Rev.* (1954), 19:68–76.
23. Lewin, K. *Resolving Social Conflicts.* New York: Harper, 1948.
24. Lewin, K., Dembo, T., Festinger, L., and Sears, P. Level of Aspiration, in J. McV. Hunt (ed.), *Personality and the Behavior Disorders.* New York: Ronald, 1944, Vol. I.
25. Lindesmith, A. R., and Strauss, A. L. *Social Psychology.* New York: Dryden, 1949.
26. Linton, R. *The Study of Man: An Introduction.* New York: Appleton-Century, 1936.
27. Mayer, K. B. *Class and Society.* New York: Doubleday, 1955.
28. Mead, M. *From the South Seas, Studies of Adolescence and Sex in Primitive Societies.* New York: Morrow, 1939.
29. Merton, R. K., and Kitt, A. S. Contributions to the Theory of Reference Group Behavior, in R. K. Merton and P. F. Lazarsfeld (eds.), *Continuities in Social Research: Studies in the Scope and Method of the American Soldier.* Glencoe, Ill.: Free Press, 1950.
30. New York *Herald Tribune,* February 10, 1949.
31. Newcomb, T. M. *Social Psychology.* New York: Dryden, 1950.
32. Radin, P. *Primitive Religion, Its Nature and Origin.* New York: Viking, 1937.
33. Roethlisberger, F. J. The foreman: master and victim of double talk, *Harvard Bus. Rev.* (1945), 23:283–298.
34. Rosen, B. C. Conflicting group membership: A study of parent-peer group cross-pressures, *Amer. sociol. Rev.* (1955), 20:155–161.
35. Scott, J. P. Implications of Infra-human Social Behavior for Problems of Human Relations, in M. Sherif and M. O. Wilson (eds.), *Group Relations at the Crossroads.* New York: Harper, 1953.
36. Sears, P. S. Levels of aspiration in academically successful and unsuccessful school children, *J. abnorm. & soc. Psychol.* (1940), 35:498–536.
37. Shaw, C. *The Jack-Roller.* Chicago: University of Chicago Press, 1930.
38. Sherif, M. *An Outline of Social Psychology.* New York: Harper, 1948.
39. Sherif, M. The problem of inconsistency in intergroup relations, *J. soc. Issues* (1949), 5:32–37.
40. Sherif, M. The Concept of Reference Groups in Human Relations, in M.

Sherif and M. O. Wilson (eds.), *Group Relations at the Crossroads*. New York: Harper, 1953.

41. Sherif, M., and Cantril, H. *The Psychology of Ego-involvements*. New York: Wiley, 1947.
42. Shibutani, T. Reference groups as perspectives, *Amer. J. Sociol.* (1955), 60:562–569.
43. Stern, E., and Keller, S. Spontaneous group reference in France, *Publ. Opin. Quart.* (1953), 17:208–217.
44. Stolz, H. R., Jones, M. C., and Chaffey, J. The junior high school age, *Univ. High School J.* (1937), 15.
45. Stonequist, E. V. *The Marginal Man*. New York: Scribner, 1937.
46. Stouffer, S. A., et al. *Studies in Social Psychology in World War II, The American Soldier, Combat and Its Aftermath*. Princeton: Princeton University Press, 1949.
47. *Time*, January 24, 1955.
48. Van Gennep, A. *Les Rites de passage*. Paris, 1909.
49. Veblen, T. *The Theory of the Leisure Class*. New York: Macmillan, 1899.
50. Warner, W. L., and Lunt, P. S. *The Social Life of a Modern Community*. New Haven: Yale University Press, 1941.
51. Webster, H. *Taboo, A Sociological Study*. Stanford: Stanford University Press, 1942.
52. Whyte, W. F. *Street Corner Society*. Chicago: University of Chicago Press, 1943.
53. Whyte, W. F. Economics and human relations in industry, 1947. Mimeographed paper made available by the author.
54. Whyte, W. F., and Gardner, B. Problems of the foreman, *J. appl. Anthrop.*, Special Issue, Spring, 1945.
55. Zachry, C. *Emotion and Conduct in Adolescence*. New York: Appleton-Century, 1940.

CHAPTER **19**

Group Prejudice

In this chapter we shall discuss a vital problem in intergroup relations. This problem is *group prejudice*, that is, the prejudice shown by members of a group toward other groups and their members. In the literature on this topic, "prejudice" refers to an unfavorable stand toward the out-group(s). It is revealed in the *social distance* at which members of a prejudiced group hold another group and its members.

In Chapter 9 we learned that social distance is great when relations between groups are unfriendly or hostile. When unfriendly interaction continues over a time span, this social distance is established as a group norm. Norms of social distance are lasting end products of particular kinds of intergroup relations.

Group prejudice may be defined as the negative attitudes of group members, derived from their established norms, toward another group and its members. Since prejudice refers to attitudes derived from group norms, it may be differentiated from entirely personal dislikes resulting from actual daily contacts. However, like other attitudes an individual forms in relation to norms of his reference group, prejudice toward an out-group may become so much a part of his ego system that he experiences it as a personal preference.

Using the Bogardus social-distance scale and variations of it, the social distance at which one group places others is indicated satisfactorily. This measuring technique was discussed on pages 517–519. When members of a group are asked to rate their willingness to accept other groups, we find that the social distance at which other groups are placed varies. Some groups are welcome to the intimacy of "close kinship by marriage." Others are rated unacceptable as "chums" or "neighbors" and are kept at the distance implied by "employment in my occupation in my country." Still

648

others are seen across such a gap that they are rated permissible as "visitors only to my country" or even are altogether inadmissible.

When these groups are arranged in descending order, starting with those accepted to intimate relationships and going down to those kept at the greatest social distance, we have a fairly reliable picture of the social-distance scale established in the group which made the ratings. In the United States, social scientists have checked the established scales of social distance for 30 years. There are fewer test results from other countries. However, enough data are available to indicate that established social distances are not unique to one country.

In the next section we will gain an overall view of established social distances in the United States and compare them with those obtained in some other countries for illustrative purposes.

NORMS OF SOCIAL DISTANCE

One index of a social norm is the striking similarity in responses of group members (p. 172). If members rank out-groups on a social-distance scale in a similar fashion, we may say that the social distances are norms for the group. A survey of group norms gives us a static picture. But it is a necessary procedure before we can understand the attitudes of members. To the single individual, norms are at first external. Initially they are social stimuli embodied in the practices, examples, and words of others.

A remarkably similar picture of social distances for national and ethnic groups in the United States is found in different strata of the population and different regions. In spite of rapid change and earth-shaking events, social distances have remained consistent over a period of time.

Table 19.1 shows two lists of groups. The first was obtained by Bogardus in 1926 and the second in 1946 after a 20-year interval (14). Both lists are based on the rankings of a "roughly defined" stratified sample. Persons from 18 to 35 years old with at least a high-school education and those from skilled or professional groups are somewhat overrepresented. There are shifts in positions of a few groups. But the most striking feature of the lists is their remarkable correspondence. In Bogardus' words: "The population groups to which the greatest nearness was expressed in 1926 . . . maintained this role for the most part in 1946. . . . Likewise the groups which were placed at the greatest distance in 1926 maintained this position with only one major exception, the Chinese, in 1946. It is likewise true that the groups which occupied middle positions on the scale in 1926 were accorded similar positions in 1946" (p. 56).

TABLE 19.1.   Social Distance in the United States in 1926 and 1946.

Groups	Rank 1926	Groups	Rank 1946
English	1	Amer. (nat. white)	1
Amer. (nat. white)	2	Canadians	2
Canadians	3	English	3
Scotch	4	Irish	4
Irish	5	Scotch	5
French	6	French	6
Germans	7	Norwegians	7
Swedes	8	Hollanders	8
Hollanders	9	Swedes	9
Norwegians	10	Danes	10
Danes	11	Germans	11
Spanish	12	Finns	12
Finns	13	Czechs	13
Russians	14	Russians	14
Italians	15	Poles	15
Portuguese	16	Spanish	16
Poles	17	Romanians	17
Romanians	18	Bulgarians	18
Armenians	19	Italians	19
Czechs	20	Armenians	20
Indians (Amer.)	21	Greeks	21
Jews	22	Portuguese	22
Bulgarians	23	Jews	23
Greeks	24	Indians (Amer.)	24
Syrians	25	Chinese	25
Mexican Amer.	—	Mexican Amer.	26
Mexicans	27	Syrians	27
Japanese Amer.	—	Filipinos	28
Japanese	29	Mexicans	29
Filipinos	30	Turks	30
Negroes	31	Japanese Amer.	31
Turks	32	Koreans	32
Chinese	33	Mulattoes	33
Mulattoes	34	Indians (East)	34
Koreans	35	Negroes	35
Indians (East)	36	Japanese	36

SOURCE: Reprinted from E. S. Bogardus, Changes in racial distances, *Internat. J. Opin. & Attit. Res.* (1947), 1:58.

In 1938, college students at such different colleges and universities as Bennington, Columbia, Howard (a Negro university), Princeton, and the City College of New York ranked ethnic and national groups in much the same way (35).

Very similar ratings have been found in far-flung parts of the country —Florida, New York, Illinois, Kansas, Nebraska, and Washington (32). High relationships were noted between the social-distance scales of school children in low, middle, and upper social classes in St. Louis, of different religious groups, and even of Negro and white college groups (35, 58, 78).

Of course, social-distance scales vary somewhat from one region to another in the United States. The variations are relative, however, with few if any reversals from the lower to upper parts of the scale in rankings made by members of majority groups.

Members of minority groups in the United States make rankings strikingly similar to those of majority group members. There is one important difference. The minority group retains the established scale but moves its own group from its lower position to a rank near or at the top.

There are differences in the placements of various groups from individual to individual and in the general degree of social distance maintained by different individuals. The technique used to obtain data permits the individual to record degrees of acceptance or rejection. But only a small proportion of the individuals are found willing to accept members of all groups to close relationships. Probably such individuals reject the existing social-distance scale and the concept of such a scale.

By and large, however, evidence available for the last 30 years indicates that the overwhelming majority of people in the United States accepts the established social-distance scale in some degree. In other words, the norms of social distance are established throughout the country. This conclusion does not imply that they are rigid or unchanging.

To say that a social-distance scale is established in the United States does not mean that it represents "natural" preferences or aversions. In other countries, different preferences and aversions are established as "natural." In 1928, LaPiere (49) reported very little prejudice against Negroes among the French middle and lower classes. According to newspaper reports, American Negro soldiers in Italy were accorded friendly treatment by at least some sections of the populace.

In Brazil, the native Indians, Portuguese settlers, and Negroes intermarried to such an extent that group identification by color is sometimes difficult. Apparently, in this case, social distance follows class lines more than color lines. The upper class is predominantly light in color and the lower class predominantly black (64). Willems (75) and Freyre (28) both report that prejudice toward persons of darker coloring exists, but to a lesser degree than in the United States. It is interesting that Germans are placed at greater distance than in the United States, but Italians (who are rather low on the United States scale) are assimilated into Brazilian life (47).

In the Hawaiian Islands, the population includes persons of American, British, Norwegian, German, Spanish, Puerto Rican, Portuguese, Negro, Chinese, Korean, Japanese, Filipino, Hindu, Danish, Micronesian, and Polynesian derivation and about every possible combination of these. For most of the population, intermarriage has been the rule (1). In general, the social-distance level is probably lower than in the United States. However, the upper class is largely white, and a lighter complexion is helpful in obtaining employment offering good status and income. Orientals are ranked somewhat higher than, say, in California. The Japanese are one of the larger minorities. Their rankings of the other groups follow about the same order as those made by white groups, except that their own group is ranked first and greater preference is indicated for fellow Orientals (56).

Still different pictures of social distances are found in other parts of the world. In 1935, Dodd (25) reported results of a modified Bogardus scale administered in the Near East. This scale was repeated about 15 years later by Prothro and Melikian (65) in the same area. Similar rankings of national groups were made by Moslem and Christian subjects in the recent study. Syrians, Lebanese, and Egyptians, who were most like the subjects, were ranked first. Various technologically advanced countries, like America, France, Japan, followed. Next were "more backward people or those with backward governments: Chinese, Saudi Arabs, Iraqi, and Sudanese." Last came the Turks, "whose government and soldiers dominated the Arab world for many years."

Probably the most interesting comparison in these two Near Eastern studies is the relative importance of religious and national groups. In 1935, Dodd concluded that greatest social distances prevailed between religious groupings. Prothro and Melikian found instead that social distances were greater between national groups. They attribute this shift to the strong surge of nationalist sentiment and activity in the years since 1935.

Even in the United States, where the social-distance scale has exhibited a remarkable stability, some shifts in relative rank are found. In Table 19.1 it is evident that those groups which were shifted upward substantially were allies or victims in World War II (e.g., Czechs, Chinese) while most of those which were dropped considerably were Axis nations (e.g., Germans, Italians, Japanese). It is possible that further shifts have occurred since then, but it is not probable that they have changed the general character of the scale.

Stereotypes Support Prevailing Social Distances

When groups are placed at considerable social distance, unfavorable characteristics or "traits" are attributed to their members. We saw the rise of stereotypes in the Robbers Cave study on intergroup relations (Chapter 9). Stereotypes concerning the essential nature of a group and its members accompany social-distance norms. In fact, stereotypes can be taken as one index of social distance. In the United States, those peoples ranked high on the scale, like the English, are attributed characteristics acceptable to American values, even though some critical traits are included. On the other hand, the fundamental natures of peoples low on the scale (Negroes, Japanese) are characterized in terms alien to American values (30). In a context of unfavorable traits, even apparently desirable characteristics take on a negative connotation. In 1936, both Japanese and Americans considered the Japanese "suave"; but we would expect that "suave" meant something different to the Americans, who even then placed the Japanese fairly low on the social-distance scale (48). The favorableness or unfavorableness of stereotypes attributed to different groups varies in terms of their position on the social-distance scale.

Once established in a group, stereotypes tend to persist. In 1932, Katz and Braly (45) found that Princeton students assigned stereotypes with a high degree of consistency. A repetition of this study in 1950 found that the characteristics most frequently checked in 1932 were also most frequently checked in 1950 (29). As would be expected from the social-distance comparisons by Bogardus reported in the last section, stereotypes of Germans and Japanese had changed in a negative direction.

Like the social-distance scale, stereotypes of national and ethnic groups are widely accepted by most people in the United States. They are even accepted by some members of groups who suffer discrimination because of the prevailing stereotypes. Similar stereotypes of various groups have been reported for Negro and white college students (9, 57). In a study carried out in 1935 and repeated in 1942 by Meenes (57), Negro college students by and large accepted the generally unfavorable stereotypes of Negroes (e.g., "superstitious, happy-go-lucky, loud, lazy"). These young people said that the stereotypes applied to "Negroes in general," but not to themselves. Being serious-minded students, they could not picture themselves as superstitious, happy-go-lucky, or lazy; but they seemed to accept this picture of most Negroes.

Allowing for exceptions to the "general rule" is typical of the use of stereotypes. It is a general characteristic of categorical thinking that contrary cases are taken as accidental exceptions, rather than as evidence to weaken the stereotype. Members of minority groups who have made achievements in public life or who are observed to differ from the stereotyped traits assigned their group may be exempt from one or more of these traits by the prejudiced person.

Are group stereotypes true or false? Many people regard them as characteristics which a group actually possesses, or did possess at one time. Such an unqualified stand merely justifies existing stereotypes. On the other hand, many people of good will who desire to see group prejudice and stereotypes eliminated hold that stereotypes never have any relation to characteristics which could be observed in members of the groups in question. It seems that putting the question in this two-sided form hinders our understanding of stereotypes.

The personal and emotional characteristics typically included in stereotypes are so inclusive and widely distributed that we could surely find them in some individuals of almost any group. In any one group, individuals vary sufficiently so that it is not meaningful from a scientific point of view to characterize all of them as good, bad, cruel, kind, etc. On the other hand, it is true that the structure of relations, ways of life, social norms, treatments in a group have consequences for the lives of individual members. Investigations of similarities among group members may be useful in understanding stereotypes. However, such inquiries cannot teach us why stereotypes develop, why they are maintained, why certain characteristics are chosen while others are excluded, and cannot clarify their relationships to established social distances.

In Chapter 9 we saw that unflattering stereotypes can arise in relation to an out-group whose members cannot be readily differentiated from the members of the in-group in terms of personal characteristics and social backgrounds. This experiment supported the hypothesis that group stereotypes are standardized in harmony with the nature of relationships between groups. Avigdor (8) proposed that when groups come into conflict certain traits which are displayed in the situation by at least some members of the group are selected for emphasis by the other group precisely because these traits serve their interests in the conflict situation. When groups are engaged in harmonious interaction, other traits are selected which further the relationships between them. Her experimental study of children's groups in conflict and coöperation supported this view (pp. 300–301).

Since stereotypes are linguistic categories, there is a tendency to perceive and respond to out-group members as though each possessed the traits subsumed in the stereotype. This categorizing tendency was noted for language concepts with less emotional value than group stereotypes (pp. 458–462). Once established, stereotyped traits may be generalized from one out-group to others with comparable positions on the social-distance scale.

Group stereotypes are not, however, inevitable products of language. Recent studies in the United States and England reported that a number of people either refused to attribute "traits" to other groups or indicated that they were aware that the only basis for doing so was group stereotypes (29, 27). We cannot be sure that all individuals who indicate awareness of group stereotypes in an experiment do not fall back on them in their daily social reactions. Some may be expressing sophistication derived from lectures or reading which is not reflected in their daily behavior. In any case, the use of language does not require the sort of thinking which results from acceptance of group stereotypes.

Group stereotypes refer to qualities which are presumed to inhere in this or that group. This tendency to account for events in terms of their essence or nature can be described as a *substantive* mode of thinking. Men and women are thought to have fundamentally different *natures,* even though these natures have changed a good deal in the last 50 years. Italians, according to this substantive mentality, are just naturally a bunch of easygoing, talkative people who spend a large part of their time singing opera in the streets. Not all problems are dealt with in this fashion. Very few people in the United States would seriously suggest that it was in the essence or nature of their cars to backfire. In this case, we want to know what causes the difficulty. We take the car to a mechanic or work on it ourselves to find out. This procedure represents a *process analysis* of events. We recognize that certain factors contribute in a related way to produce a certain result. The concepts used in this process analysis are not taken as essences. The blinding effects of group stereotypes can be reduced and eventually eliminated when the process analysis is utilized in dealing with social problems as well as in mechanics and other applied sciences.

Group Superiority Doctrines

The problem of group prejudice is not simply psychological. Gordon Allport (4) concluded in his comprehensive survey of the topic that the problem is "truly many-sided." In order to understand manifestations of prejudice, the conditions in which norms of social distance arise and the conditions in which individuals are exposed to them must be comprehended. As Allport noted, "a multiple approach is required." Understanding the formation of social-distance norms requires historical analysis. Their maintenance and functioning is a problem at the sociological or sociocultural level of analysis. Some analysis of the background and social stimulus settings is essential for a balanced understanding of the formation of attitudes of prejudice by individuals. Without knowledge of the stimulating conditions, analysis at the level of single individuals becomes mere description or substantive attribution of traits.

Accordingly, we will glance at a few periods in which social-distance scales developed, focusing on common features in the conditions of contact which led to the particular social distances standardized. This aim forces us to neglect variations in group customs and values, which frequently are weighty factors in determining the particular end products of intergroup contact. In order to bring all of the cultural, religious, economic, military, and individual factors into the picture for even one instance, an entire book would be necessary.

Probably within small, homogeneous societies, like tribes subsisting on cultivation, social distances are not found. Such relatively small and homogeneous societies do develop social distances toward other groups with which they come into contact. Allport (3) observed that social distances within a society are found only in heterogeneous organizations in which different groups of people have different functions and interests.

Aristotle, Vitruvius, Ibn-Khaldun, Bodin are but a few of those who recorded for history their belief in the superiority of their own group and the peculiarity and inferiority of other peoples. In their times, group superiority was not based so often on notions of inherent group differences. It was attributed to the influence of external forces like geography or climate or astrological influences. Notions of group superiority have also been based on acceptance of religious faith—Christian and heathen, Moslem and infidel. In the name of these superiorities, men suffered and died.

Race doctrines, which have been the common basis for group superiority notions in modern times, are more recent in origin. Historians have noted few arguments for superiority or inferiority of human groupings based on alleged hereditary differences before the seventeenth century (*10, 11, 55*). In 1738 Linnaeus, the great classifier of plants and animals, assigned mankind to one species subdivided into four varieties. The use of such attempts to classify human groupings in terms of physical characteristics to support superiority doctrines cannot be laid on the shoulders of scientists, however.

A characteristic common to the major group-superiority doctrines is that they were promulgated in groups seeking to rise above or to maintain ascendance over other groups. Regardless of their content, superiority doctrines have been products of group conflict. Ruth Benedict wrote: "The first lesson of history in this respect is that when any group in power wishes to persecute or expropriate another group it uses as justification reasons which are familiar and easily acceptable at the time" (*10*, p. 41).

When early European explorers came into contact with the peoples inhabiting the African, Asian, and American continents, they felt and expressed their own superiority. But their reactions were based to a considerable extent on the fact that the newly found peoples were not Christians and that often the new societies were less developed technologically. Classifications of human groups in terms of "races" were being made in the period when exploration of the new geographical areas turned more and more to expropriation of their wealth (*10, 11, 26, 55*).

Doctrines of "race" superiority have advantages over other justifications for group superiority which may account for their spread and perpetuation. Unlike justifications based on differences in environmental forces or religious beliefs, race doctrine places groups in relative positions of privilege on the basis of characteristics which are presumed to be *unchanging*. The differences are said to inhere in the biological make-up of every individual in the respective groups. Ideally, race doctrines picture a world in which "superior" groups rule forever and "inferior" groups remain forever subordinate. The biologists Dunn and Dobzhansky stated: "Many people declare it to be the 'white man's burden' to rule men of all other colors. And so anxious have some white men been to lay this burden upon themselves that they used their superior weapons to fight and kill colored people, and incidentally other whites, for this privilege" (*26*, p. 108).

Race doctrines have been supported by certain "men of science." In an age of wonders wrought by science, such explicit or tacit support has been another advantage for promulgators of race doctrines. However, it is misleading to suppose that race doctrines have been squarely based on biology. Certainly Count de Gobineau's *Essay on the Inequality of Human Races* (1853–57) was not an exposition of the biology of his time but a passionate plea for the dominance and "purity" of European aristocrats. In the race doctrine of Houston Chamberlain, espoused in the rising tide of German nationalism, race was based on ideas and character, not biology. Those who followed the Leadership Principle were incorporated into the Chosen Race. Nazi race doctrine exposed the common basis of all such doctrines in its most naked form.

Race is a biological concept. Geneticists and other biologists agree that there are no "pure" races (26, 42). On July 18, 1950, a group of geneticists and anthropologists from various countries issued a statement on the nature of race and racial differences. This statement has been published in book form with additional explanation by Montagu (60). The eminent scientists agree that the concept of race is a statistical category based on characteristics which are *superficial* in the biological make-up and adaptability of the organism. There are several different racial classifications. None has been found which does not result in overlapping among different groups. The classifications result in inconsistencies when more than one criterion characteristic is used. For example, dark-skinned Hindus are classified most frequently in the same general category as white-skinned Europeans.

The statement notes that cultural traits and achievements have no demonstrated genetic connection with racial traits (60). Racial classifications made in science need not coincide with national, religious, geographic, linguistic, and cultural groups. Perhaps most crucial for social psychology is the following statement: "Whatever classifications the anthropologist makes of man, he never includes mental characteristics as part of the classifications" (60, p. 14).

Certainly in the field of psychology there is enough evidence for some definitive statements concerning group differences in behavior and race. Following an unusually extensive and careful survey, Anastasi and Foley (7) concluded that it is misleading to state that investigators have merely failed to prove race differences in behavior:

It is a fact that there are *group differences in behavior*, but not that such differences are racial or biological in origin. There is a considerable body of data, both in racial studies and in other more general investigations on the origins of individual differences in behavior, to show the influence of environmental factors in behavior development. But no study has conclusively demonstrated a necessary association between behavior characteristics and race as such. (pp. 782–783).

Social-Distance Scales in Formation

A traditional explanation of the origin of social distances suggests that group conflict inevitably develops from the ethnocentrisms of culturally different groups. There is a tendency for members of a group to evaluate other groups in terms of the norms or values developed within their own group. While cultural differences may become a very important factor in intergroup conflict, they are not sufficient to account for intergroup conflicts or norms of social distance. First, there are instances of groups with different cultures existing peacefully side by side with comparatively little social distance (e.g., 52). Second, some intense intergroup conflicts and definite social distances have arisen between groups which were culturally homogeneous. The bitterness and estrangement of the American colonists during the Revolutionary conflict with their mother country constitute one example.

When examining conditions of contact and the rise of social-distance norms for culturally different out-groups, a common finding is that one group attempted to gain cultural, socioeconomic, or military control over the other. The particular nature of relations established between groups and the resulting social distances can be understood through the interests and characteristics of the more developed group on the one hand and the vital interests and established ways of the less developed group on the other (*11*).

In the United States, Negro slaves were brought in as the demand for plantation workers exceeded the available supply of indentured white and Indian slaves (*30*). There is not space in this volume to present even a condensation of white-Negro relationships. Some background of this history, like that presented by Arnold Rose (*68*), should be required reading for serious students of social distances in the United States. Even a glimpse of this background is sufficient to eliminate the prevalent notion that relations between the groups and social-distance norms today are nothing but a lingering reflection of conditions which prevailed 100 years ago.

Goldstein (*30*) traced Negro-white relations and the changing stereotypes of Negroes in fascinating detail through analysis of documents, literature, songs, and cartoons. She found that the stereotype of the happy Negro slave developed after 1820 when slavery began to face some real opposition. This stereotype of the happy, contented servant was current during the period (1826–1860) in which there were 200 slave revolts or uprisings on relatively small scale, in addition to frequent sabotage, escape, and malingering (68).

Prior to the Civil War, contacts and intimacy between slave and owner were restricted, of course. But total segregation was not seen as the pressing issue that it became later. In Georgia, Negro and white workers toiled side by side in a cotton mill in 1842 (30). After the Civil War, the stereotype of the "brute Negro" emerged full blown. Until he was freed, the stereotyped Negro was a gentle enough fellow. The animal-like creature with uncontrollable passions was the one who must be completely segregated. Another addition to Negro stereotypes was the comical figure who tried to emulate "white folks" in crude displays of flashy clothes, gold teeth, and, more recently, fancy cars.

Understanding social-distance norms seems to require analysis of the particular relationships between groups pursuing their vital interests over a period of time. The value of studying this background and its relevance for understanding social-distance norms is demonstrated in MacCrone's intensive historical study of race relations in South Africa and his studies of the social distances among various groups in South Africa in 1937 (55). The original European traders and settlers in South Africa regarded the natives as cultural inferiors but admitted them to their community as they became Christians. MacCrone traces the alterations in relationships between white settlers and native groups as the white settlers increased, as native groups resisted their encroachments, as new groups of more docile colored labor were brought in as slaves. By the end of the eighteenth century the Christian-heathen dichotomy was no longer emphasized. The picture of the "white man and his civilization" was clarified as the justification for his dominance. MacCrone found that the social distances that existed at the beginning of the nineteenth century were widely accepted in 1937 in much the same form by English-speaking students, Afrikaans, Jews, and even some Bantu (native) subjects who were trying to "improve" themselves.

Since 1948, the *apartheid* doctrine has been systematically applied in South Africa. According to a United Nations Commission Report: "The doctrine is based on the theory that the White race, as the heir to Western Christian civilization, is in duty bound to maintain inviolate and to perpetuate its position in Western Christian civilization, and must at any cost, although in a numerical minority, maintain its dominating position over the coloured races" (74, p. 115). This report lists the detailed and specific restrictions placed on all persons of colored complexion and notes that the policy is opposed by all educated members of subordinate groups. As indicated in the report, this policy of complete segregation followed the beginnings of some organization among minority peoples to improve their lot.

When studied over a time span, it can be seen that the classifications of social distance which come to prevail are those of majority groups, and not those of minority groups. Initially, social-distance norms and stereo-types flow from powerful dominant groups and are defined in terms of their particular status and point of view. Subordinate groups may, in their strivings to be accepted by the dominant group, adopt the social-distance scale of the more powerful group. As objects of low placement and discrimination, individual members of minority groups may carry hostilities toward the dominant group. Such hostilities are usually hidden in the face of overwhelming odds against their expression. They cannot prevail in society at large. They are not even norms in the subordinate group until they are experienced by members of that group as a cause for *group* concern. When such hostilities become group concern, they may be the focus for a developing in-group organization (76).

These quick glances at the backgrounds of social-distance norms give us perspective on the nature of the stimulating conditions in the formation of prejudiced attitudes. Attitudes of prejudice cannot be studied adequately without reference to the social-distance norms prevailing in the groups in which the individual functions in some capacity. Their formation can be understood in terms of the psychological processes through which the individual relates himself to groups possessing these norms.

FORMATION OF ATTITUDES OF PREJUDICE

Since the content of group prejudice is derived from existing social norms, an insight into prejudiced attitudes requires understanding how an individual becomes a group member and accepts group norms as his own standards. There are variations from individual to individual in any psychological process. But it must be emphasized that typically the formation of prejudiced attitudes is not a product of "distorted" personality development. Prejudiced attitudes are formed through the same processes as other attitudes derived from group norms. The main problem in attitude formation toward out-groups is that of internalization of group norms. Individual variations are discussed briefly in the next section.

Research on the appearance of prejudice in children has reported its beginnings at an early age (38, 50). For most children in the United States, prejudice appears during the preschool years. These initial signs of prejudice are not simply the awareness of differences in physical appearance. Obviously members of some groups placed at considerable social distance do not possess distinguishing physical features. Children begin to notice differences in skin color even before prejudiced attitudes are formed in any clear fashion (19, 20, 41).

Social definitions of group membership and significance of perceived differences are not long in coming. The child learns labels for out-groups even before he can identify members consistently, and he senses their emotional and affective value (36, 66). At this stage, roughly school age and under, children's attitudes toward various groups tend to be somewhat unintegrated aspects of their psychological make-up. Meltzer (58) reported low intercorrelations between tests of preference for children. Hartley (39) found that young children's scores on tests of attitude toward Negroes were not closely related to each other.

An anecdote related by Ruth Hartley (41) in her study on racial aspects of self-identification in nursery-school children illustrates the lack of integration in youngsters' attitudes. The oldest white girl in this study had expressed "well crystallized" prejudice against Negroes. She was asked to show the experimenter which child in pictures of Negro and white school children was like herself. In spite of consistent identification with the white child in other pictures, she chose a Negro girl in one picture. In this picture, the Negro girl had curls. She also had curls which were her "pride and joy." "Although accurately perceiving the racial nature of all the other pictures, she denied that this one was of a Negro child."

The preschool child is just learning "what he is." His ego is more fluctuating, more variable, inconsistent, and more specific to situations he has encountered than an adult's (see pp. 594–598). He is a "big boy," a "good girl," a "pretty girl," a "naughty boy." If a 4-year-old is asked, "What are you?" he is not very likely to answer in terms of ethnic or religious group membership (36). He has learned some group labels; and if these include "nigger," "kike" or other derogatory epithets, he is likely to be aware that they are words to say when one is angry or acting "nasty" (66). He may associate these labels with physical differences he observes. His recognition of group membership is likely to be based only on such obvious signs as skin color or dress. For example, a preschool child who had been exposed to the cowboy and Indian game, the "ten little Indians," and the popular moving pictures conceived of Indians as people who wore feathers and were bare to the waist. When a small gathering of Oklahoma citizens of Indian descent was pointed out to her, she completely rejected the possibility that these were Indians: "They couldn't be. They have shirts on!"

The child comes to know that he belongs to the Smith family, that as a child in that family he does not play with "bad children," with "dirty children," and with "Negro children." Under about the third grade, children may acknowledge that they choose white children as playmates because their parents have told them not to play with Negro children. In one southern community some years ago, the most frequent cause of punishment was playing with Negro children (40). The child at this time is finding that he is a member of a number of groups—a Sunday school, a school, a play group.

Through achieving clear-cut identifications with groups, the child begins to be aware that he has certain appropriate "places" and standards in life. His developing ego consists of "what I am not" as well as "what I am." He has notions about "how I act with my kind" and "how I act toward *others*." Age-mate association becomes very important to children, usually before they start to elementary school. At times, the examples and labels used by other children are learned as well or better than the short-cut dicta concerning behavior enunciated by parents. Older children are aware of pressures from their age-mate groups (40). One boy told an investigator: "I represent a room in safety council which has many Negroes. They say their safety laws to me. When I meet them in the hall I say hello to them. All the other children look at me like it would be a crime to be sociable with them" (79).

In her study of age-mate groupings in New York public schools with sizable Negro enrollments, Criswell (21) found that the fifth-grade level was the point where "mutual withdrawal" between Negro and white children was crystallized. From this point, white children clustered around their most popular members almost exclusively. And this cluster of popular white children was "farthest withdrawn from the other race." Personal preference, satisfaction, and prestige were found in one's own color group.

In communities where the urgency and generality of the lesson of associating with one's "own kind" is greatly emphasized, children not only withdraw earlier but may regard the out-groups as undesirable in an absolute fashion. In one southern community, children in the fourth and fifth grades were inclined to attribute only unfavorable traits to Negroes (13). Even the few favorable traits usually accorded by adults (e.g., "musical") were neglected.

By the time they reach high school, children's stereotypes approximate those of the adult community. Older children are likely to forget the role of parents and age-mates in transmitting the social-distance norms. The high-school student or adult feels that his attitudes are his own and have always been his. He feels his desire to associate with his own group is a purely *personal* preference. Usually, it is when he is exposed to contradictory influences, parents or other adults urging one way and age-mates taking another direction, that he becomes aware of external pressures. But if the social-distance norms are presented to him from all sides (family, age-mates, mass media utilizing traditional stereotypes), the child forms appropriate attitudes which define for him his "place" in his social world. These attitudes are functioning parts of his ego constellation. It is small wonder that they are experienced as a "natural" part of himself.

Once a part of the ego, attitudes of prejudice are factors regulating behavior in situations related to out-groups and their members. It must be emphasized that they are not the only attitudes in the ego constellation, and that behavior is always an outcome of both internal and external influences. Even grownups do not always behave in a consistent way, if by consistency we mean always behaving simply in terms of attitudes of social distance. In order to analyze the behavior of a single prejudiced individual in a situation involving out-groups or their members, one must know something about his other attitudes, their organization in his ego system, and the demands of the particular situation.

INDIVIDUALS AND THE SOCIAL-DISTANCE SCALE

In his study of children's attitudes, Hartley (38) concluded that children's prejudices arise through contact with prevailing social norms rather than through individual contacts with members of the out-groups in question. Hartley found that children in an all-white school and in a mixed school in New York City and in schools in urban Tennessee and urban and rural Georgia gave remarkably similar reactions toward Negroes. Individuals in Florida, New York, Illinois, Washington, Vermont surely have very different opportunities for contact with Negroes. Yet the social-distance scale is similar in those states. Katz and Braly (45) found that students assigned "typical traits" to 10 ethnic groups with remarkable consistency even when these groups were personally unknown to them.

Once an individual accepts a social-distance scale, with his own group at the top and other groups ranked downward, prejudice toward out-groups tends to be generalized. Hartley demonstrated such generalization by including three nonexistent groups in a list of groups to be rated (35). He simply made up names for these three: Danirean, Pirenean, Wallonian. Of course, the subjects could have had no knowledge or contact with them. The result was that correlations from .78 to .85 were found between the average social-distance ratings of these fictitious groups and the average social-distance ratings of actual out-groups. People who were less prejudiced accepted these nonexistent groups to rather close proximity—closer than implied in the statement "To my school as classmates."

The degree of prejudice, as measured by scores on an attitude test, has been found to vary in different regions. For example, scores on a test of prejudice were higher in a southwestern city than in California (17). As noted earlier, it has been observed that the general level of prejudice in some countries, like Brazil, is less than in the United States.

Within a group where social-distance norms prevail, it is the individual who conforms to the group most closely who is likely to be the most prejudiced. This seems to be the implication of findings that individuals who express higher degrees of patriotism tend to be more prejudiced than those whose expressions are more tempered (61). Greater prejudice is manifested by regular churchgoers than by those who attend irregularly or not at all (5, 44, 70). Since churchgoers hear regular messages that all are equal in the eyes of God, the implication is that regular church attendance is more symptomatic of conformist tendencies than serious concern with the text of the service. In a recent study, scores on a test of attitudes toward certain social, moral, and religious stands of the Catholic Church and scores on tests of attitudes toward Jews and Negroes obtained from Catholic college students were analyzed (63). A "very significant" tendency was found for those scoring high on the religion scale to be less favorable toward Jews and Negroes and to favor the segregation of Negroes in church. Those with low scores on the religion scale were significantly less prejudiced and were opposed to segregation. The implication is that those who conformed more rigidly to official teachings tended to be more prejudiced. It would be interesting to know whether this finding would continue to operate over a period of time after the Church had taken a firm public stand against segregation.

Conversely, in a society where social-distance norms prevail, lack of prejudice implies nonconformity. The person who is not prejudiced tends to be one who is rebellious against at least some of the major norms of society. He is dissatisfied with things as they are; he is a dissenter (39, 62, 73). As Hartley pointed out in his survey, the individual who is a "dissenter" or nonconformist to these norms need not be a rebellious spirit at loose ends. His rejection of the social-distance scale prevalent in the larger society may represent conformity to a smaller group within society. In fact, studies on changes of reference groups would indicate that in many cases rejection of the social-distance scale may be contingent upon participation in the trend of a new group and identification with it (see pp. 541–544).

INDIVIDUAL VARIATIONS IN PREJUDICE: In emphasizing the primary importance of membership in groups possessing social-distance norms for the formation of prejudiced attitudes, we had to postpone the discussion of the obvious fact that even in the same group individuals vary considerably in the intensity and the particular manner in which they reveal their prejudices. Once the fact of membership in groups possessing social-distance norms is recognized as the essential condition for forming prejudiced attitudes, individual variations in conforming to these norms can be analyzed meaningfully.

A rather typical procedure in research on attitudes of prejudice has been to make intensive studies of persons who make extremely high scores on tests of prejudice and those who make low scores on the same test (3, 54). The aim has sometimes been to construct polar personality "types" of the "prejudiced" and the "unprejudiced" personality based on various tests and interviews. At best, such studies result in descriptions of personal characteristics associated with extreme prejudice or low prejudice. At worst, they place descriptive labels on prejudiced people and lend support to the erroneous notion that prejudiced attitudes stem *primarily* from a few individual factors, like personal frustrations or insecurities. The difficulty in interpreting such research is that factors which may be associated with high or low scores on the test cannot be legitimately used to explain the presence or absence of prejudice. In order to do this, it would be necessary to show that some subjects were prejudiced and some were *not* prejudiced. This is seldom the case. For example, in a study of veterans of World War II, even those individuals who were designated as most tolerant toward Jews expressed stereotypes from time to time, and many of them were anti-Negro (12).

Recent large-scale studies in California found close relationships between high scores on tests of ethnocentrism and tests of prejudice (2). These results have been interpreted by various authors in rather different ways. To some, their implication is simply that more prejudiced individuals tend to conform more closely to their family and other groups than do those with less prejudice. Others find in the results evidence for the role of particular kinds of personal experiences in producing high levels of prejudice. The interpretations given have been criticized for neglecting the relationship between group membership and individual attitudes to the point of ignoring the stimulus conditions in which individual attitudes are formed (e.g., 16, 43).

When studies of individual variations in prejudice start with analysis of group identifications, status in various groups, and situations to which the individual is exposed and relate these systematically to differences in life history and personal characteristics and capacities, some interesting relations may be found between personal factors and degree of prejudice. It seems likely that *degrees* of prejudice within the same social group may be related to differences in frustrations, insecurities, status changes experienced, personal intensity, intelligence, and the like. But it is well to keep in mind that, so long as the individuals studied belong and conform to groups possessing a social-distance scale, the personal variations will be within the bounds of this scale. Variations among individuals along personal dimensions will all fall within a reference scale set by the social-distance norms. They cannot be used to explain the overall existence of prejudice (37, 72).

Research concerning individuals who do not conform to the social-distance scale, who reject stereotyped notions of out-groups, is sparse indeed. It is to be hoped that investigations in this area may avoid the pitfall of one-sided emphasis on personal factors or on sociocultural factors and instead approach the problem as one which must involve both kinds of factors. By studying these factors in a functionally interrelated way and noting their relative weights, an adequate account of the role of individual variations in acceptance or rejection of social-distance norms can be obtained.

Members of Minority Groups and the Social-Distance Scale

In previous sections we have been concerned with formation of prejudiced attitudes by individuals who are members of groups possessing social-distance norms. We noted the frequent tendency of members of subordinate groups to retain the established scale, while moving its own group from its low position up to the top of the scale. However, it should be noted that some individuals and some groups composed of minority members do reject the social-distance scale altogether as a result of bitter experiences as its victims.

Children who grow up as members of a group which is discriminated against may acquire clear-cut identification with their group even earlier than children of the dominant groups in society (41). In a study of Negro children, the Clarks (19, 20) found that Negro children become aware of their social designation very early. Along with this awareness comes the tragic fact of the low evaluation placed on their color group by others. Both in segregated and in mixed schools, the great majority of 3-year-old Negro children called brown children "bad" and said that the white child had a *nice* color. A more recent study in a biracial nursery school by Goodman (31) substantiated this finding. Four-year-old Negro children in this setting almost all preferred white dolls; often they called a colored doll "dirty" or "ugly." They seemed to reject the colored doll more than did the white children in the same school.

The psychological consequences of accepting the stereotypes and "place" assigned to the minority group member are not limited to his relationships with members of other groups (72). They pervade "private" areas of his life, including the goals he seeks and the sort of person he wants to become. The cruel limits which are placed on an individual's aspirations are illustrated by the following interview with a teen-age Negro girl in a northern state (22):

INTERVIEWER: What do you want to be, when you grow up?
GIRL: Oh . . . I guess I'm going to be a cleaning lady.
GIRL'S MOTHER (also in room):   Oh, don't tell the lady that! Tell her something *nice*—like working in an office.
GIRL: Okay. I guess I'll clean offices, then.

Members of subordinate groups are also citizens of the larger society. The relative positions on the social-distance scale are functionally related to one another. In this scheme of things, the group at the upper end of the scale, being more powerful in all areas of living, exerts greater weight than others. There is a strong tendency for the group at the upper end of the scale to serve as the main anchor. Strivings for living standards, status, occupation, and prestige are toward the level of the main anchor. When members of groups low on the social-distance scale find their moves upward barred because of systematic discrimination and segregation in occupational, educational, and social spheres, the psychological consequences are continual thwarting of aspirations, frustrations, and conflicts.

In periods of rapid change, these psychological consequences are intensified. During such periods, members of a discriminated minority come to realize more and more their potentialities on a par with any other group. The conception of self limited to a "place" subordinate to the dominant group tends to be rejected. And, in time of emergency, such as war, the larger society may not hesitate to require the same service demanded of any other citizen. Such times serve as a compelling reminder of the democratic ideals announced today as applying to all individuals. The demarcation lines prescribed by the social-distance scale stand in marked contrast to such values.

In summarizing the status of Negroes in the United States since World War II, Rose (69) points out how conditions brought on by the war speeded up changes already in process and brought new ones. These changing conditions produced great discrepancies for the individual. On one hand, Negroes served in the armed forces and in industry; on the other, they found themselves shut off from many opportunities available to others, restricted in the spheres of education, politics, legal protection, and housing.

Situations and opportunities which arise in periods of change tend to encourage, even to demand, that the member of a minority conceive of himself as a full-fledged citizen of the larger society like all other members. In this way the common standards for all groups become more compelling. But at the same time, the established demarcation lines between groups require that the member of a minority group conceive of himself, not just as different, but as inferior. Thus, he is placed simultaneously in two psychologically incompatible positions.

For the subordinate group low on the social-distance scale the problems of obtaining vital necessities, means of livelihood, adequate housing, medical, educational, and recreational facilities are matters of primary and central importance, as they are to any group. But if these things actually became available on an "equal but separate" basis while the established demarcation lines were drawn requiring that minority group members regulate their status relations and their aspirations in many areas of life at a lower level than the standards common for society, serious experiences of frustration and conflict would still be generated for individual members. The "equal but separate" formula requires the impossible psychological feat of conceiving of oneself and regulating one's strivings and aspirations in terms of two conflicting sets of standards. One set is common to citizens in the society. It is compelling as long as subordinate groups are expected and desire themselves to fulfill the duties and partake in opportunities of the larger society. The second set of standards is that established by the social-distance norms for an "inferior" group; it is implied as long as a

FIG. 19.1. "Separate educational facilities are inherently unequal." Supreme Court of the United States, May 17, 1954.

FIG. 19.2.

"separate" formula is upheld. Regulating the ego in terms of two such contradictory sets of standards is psychologically impossible, in the sense that it will always result in varying degrees of personal conflict, frustration, insecurity with all of their unfortunate by-products and personal consequences.

Members of minority groups face this discrepancy in a society where segregation of groups prevails in some or all areas of living. On May 17, 1954, the Supreme Court of the United States eliminated legal justification for this doctrine in the area of education with these words: "We conclude that in the field of public education the doctrine of 'separate but equal' has no place. Separate educational facilities are inherently unequal."

ATTITUDES OF PREJUDICE AND BEHAVIOR TOWARD OUT-GROUPS

In settled places and times, behavior exhibited by group members to ward out-groups is largely a function of the prescriptions of the social-distance scale. In those localities of the world where social changes lag or are deliberately retarded, this is still the case. Under these conditions, attitudes of prejudice are the weightier factors in the patterning of experience and behavior. However, they are never the only factors.

Ours is a time of great change and of increasing interdependence among groups within countries and between countries. It is true that within the United States, for example, the prevailing social-distance scale has its correlates in differential treatment and opportunities, in discrimination, hostilities, and maltreatment, in denial of rights and protection. But it is also true that influences other than attitudes of prejudice frequently prove weightier in structuring the trend and practice of intergroup relations. In this section we will note such influences which recur in empirical observations of intergroup behavior. There are others which cannot be included in our brief statement (see 72, chap. 8).

Shifts in the nature of functional relations between groups are conducive to changes in behavior toward the out-group. At times the new trends run counter to the prejudiced attitudes of individuals. Killian's investigation of southern white migrants in Chicago provides an instructive illustration of the point (46). The migrants came from certain areas in the South to definite local communities in Chicago. Other white groups on Chicago's West Side looked down on them as culturally inferior "hillbillies." Coming from an area where their native, white, Protestant stock assured them a position in the dominant southern group, the migrants regarded

Dan Weiner—Brackman Associates.

FIG. 19.3. Social distance norms have correlates in differential treatments. This man needs police escort to shop for groceries.

themselves as "real Americans" who were being unjustly disliked and mistreated. In the South, their position, though lowly, was definitely superior to that of Negroes and was supported by law and tradition. Their new situation in the poor section of Chicago was characterized both in work and in the city by nonsegregation of Negroes. Did they cling to their former behavior patterns of "asserting white supremacy"?

Killian found that some members tried to do so at first; but most came to realize the compellingness of their changed situation.

. . . The predominant reactions of the southern whites to non-segregation of Negroes were *acceptance* of the situation or *avoidance* by self-withdrawal; overt aggression or attempts to force withdrawal of Negroes were exceptional rather than normal. Acceptance was accompanied by certain standard explanations, including: (1) "When in Rome, do as the Romans do," (2) "you can't go against the law," and (3) "the Negroes are more powerful than the whites and you can't fight them." . . . Their behavior in the new situation did not conform to the old group norms of "asserting white supremacy"; in spite of lip-service paid to the old norms, behavior now conformed to the new norms of accommodation evolved in a novel situation [46].

Advances in technology which make the use of old devices, methods, or employment obsolete are conducive to changes in the scheme of human relations sanctioned by tradition. An authority on the caste system in India reported that "caste distinctions . . . invariably break down under the leveling influences of city and factory life" (6).

Individuals in modern societies are usually members of more than one group. In Chapter 18 we saw a number of examples of "inconsistency" in behavior stemming from conflicting group norms and trends of different reference groups. Individuals may say one thing and do another in a contradictory way. Frequently these contradictions result from being in one situation which favors behavior in line with the norm of one reference group, and then later being in another situation which favors behavior required by a conflicting norm or trend stemming from another reference group.

In states in which new trends and old norms exist simultaneously, one finds striking cases of contradictory intergroup behavior, particularly in public places. The following observation in Elmira, New York, illustrates the point: "Five Negroes (two of them fieldworkers) stopped in at another tavern to have a drink. The bartender was extremely friendly. A few hours later, white fieldworkers asked him if Negroes ever came to his place. He denied that they did. Another fieldworker put the same question to his wife a few days later. She also denied it" (23).

Among the influences which can affect intergroup behavior in directions contrary to attitudes of prejudice are trends and decisions taken by superordinate groups of a society (e.g., communities, states, national government). It is a commonly expressed belief that "prejudice cannot be legislated out of existence." The statement implies dire results of attempts by superordinate units to establish rules or norms running counter to the prevailing norms and attitudes in their subunits. This problem has important theoretical and practical implications.

In his survey of evidence concerning desegregation, Clark (18) noted the following conditions conducive to effecting desegregation efficiently and without "social disturbance":

A. A clear and unequivocal statement of policy by leaders with prestige and other authorities;

B. Firm enforcement of the changed policy by authorities and persistence in the execution of this policy in the face of initial resistance;

C. A willingness to deal with violations, attempted violations, and incitement to violations by a resort to the law and strong enforcement action;

D. A refusal of the authorities to resort to, engage in or tolerate subterfuges, gerrymandering or other devices for evading the principles and the fact of desegregation;

E. An appeal to the individuals concerned in terms of their religious principles of brotherhood and their acceptance of the American traditions of fair play and equal justice [18, p. 54].

PROBLEMS OF CHANGING PREJUDICED ATTITUDES

In Chapter 16 we discussed the essential problems of attitude formation and change. Formation and change of attitudes pertaining to in-group and out-group relations were among problems organically related to our discussion of formation and functioning of groups (Chapters 6–9). Intergroup attitudes, like prejudice, are ego-attitudes. They are experienced as personal stands by group members toward the members of an out-group and are manifested in their characteristically discriminatory reactions. Thus, the conclusions drawn earlier regarding formation and change of ego-attitudes apply to attitudes of prejudice as well. Here we shall take up a few implications of current interest in this area.

Many interested groups and agencies are engaged in attempts to alter attitudes of prejudice toward out-groups. Ordinarily, as noted in various contexts, the factors leading individuals to form attitudes of prejudice are not piecemeal, isolated influences. Rather, attitudes of prejudice are formed in the process of becoming a group member, in adopting a group and its norms as a main anchorage in the ego system.

After early childhood, the ego system embodies the demarcation lines prevalent in one's reference groups. Other groups are evaluated in terms of their relation (social proximity or distance) to the reference group. Lasting and consistent changes in attitudes toward out-groups can be expected (1) when individuals become psychologically related to a new reference group with differing norms toward out-groups or (2) when the norms established in the individual's present reference group are changed.

Lewin and Grabbe implied these conditions in their statement: "Reeducation influences conduct only when the new system of values and beliefs dominates the individual's perception. The acceptance of the new system is linked with the acceptance of a specific group, a particular role, a definite source of authority as points of reference" (51, p. 68).

The girls of conservative background who adopted the Bennington College community with its more liberal norms as their reference group changed their attitudes in the liberal direction. Those whose main anchorage remained the home, old friends, or small conservative groups in the Bennington setting continued to maintain their more conservative attitudes (see pp. 541–544).

Because attitudes are not formed in a piecemeal way, attempts to change them through discrete information or specific exposure to this or that item have been highly unrewarding on the whole. Attempts to change attitudes through various sorts of communication were discussed earlier (pp. 555–562).

Persons of good will often expressed the belief that *contact* breeds friendly association between members of different groups. It is obvious that contact is necessary for exchange of views between groups. However, it is a problem of great theoretical and practical importance to define the conditions under which contact between groups may be effective in changing attitudes of prejudice.

The difficulty is that contact may very well breed increased hostility and sharpened demarcations between groups (see pp. 548–551). Ram and Murphy's analysis of intergroup relations in India illustrates the point that contact between members of bitterly hostile in-groups exerts surprisingly little influence on the attitudes of group members when relations between groups are tense and strained (67). Even personal suffering at the hands of the out-group may contribute little to the individual's view of the out-group. Hindu refugees who had suffered in Muslim hands and those who had escaped without personal tragedy seemed equally hostile toward Muslims.

In discussing the effects of contact on intergroup attitudes, we must specify: What kind of contact? Contact in what capacity? Considerable evidence has been collected on this topic and is summarized in recent surveys by Saenger (71), Allport (4), Harding, Kutner, Proshansky, and Chein (34). The overall picture seems to be somewhat as follows:

While friendly associations with an individual member of an out-group held at considerable distance may become important in changing attitudes toward the out-group, it is more likely that the out-group member in question will be considered as an exceptional member and therefore exempt from stereotyped traits attributed to most other members. In situations in which in-group members meet with members of an out-group held at considerable distance on a very limited scale, such as a tea party, there is little likelihood of change in attitudes of in-group members.

When members of socially distant out-groups work in the same place of employment (e.g., a department store) with approximately equal status, and this condition is set forth in unequivocal terms as necessary for employment, individuals are likely to develop more favorable attitudes toward out-group members as parts of the employment situation (33). This development does not necessarily imply transfer of the newly acquired favorable view to other situations. The change tends to be specific to the employment situation.

When individuals of socially distant in-groups live in adjacent or in the same dwelling units, changes in attitudes toward the out-group may occur in either a positive or a negative direction, depending in part upon the opportunities for neighborly association made possible through being physically close or distant from out-group members (24, 77). Positive changes tend to occur among individuals *"who have relatively intimate contacts with Negroes and perceive these contacts as socially approved, and as a result change in their attitudes"* (77, p. 69, italics in original). The implication here is that attitudes toward Negroes change when both groups take a community as their reference group whose values are favorable to their association. However, there is indication that individuals who change to a more favorable attitude toward Negroes under these circumstances do not change in the same degree toward members of other out-groups (24, pp. 104 f.).

At the opposite pole from discrete contacts between individuals as members of different in-groups are situations in which members of traditionally hostile groups become members of a common reference group. In Chapter 16 we saw a striking instance of this among seamen on shipboard (pp. 543–544). When contact between members of socially distant out-groups involves joint participation as members in a group whose norms favor such participations, the individual's attitudes toward members of the out-group are likely to be altered.

However, as long as individuals belong to different groups with conflicting norms relating to out-groups, such changes may be relatively specific to the area of interaction. Conflicting norms of functionally related reference groups result in inconsistencies, for members of minority groups and for majority group members as well. In the latter case, personal conflict is sometimes minimized by socially established demarcations at points where one shifts from one set of norms to another. Thus, miners who work daily with Negroes as fellow workers leave the darkness underground, go to segregated washrooms, and live the rest of the day in a world having norms of superiority with comparative ease (59). Changes in attitudes

FIG. 19.4. Participation in groups whose norms favor crossing social-distance boundaries is conducive to reduction of prejudice.

FIG. 19.5. These high school students mix at school, but not outside of school.

which are consistent for all areas of life can be expected when the norms of a reference group relate to broad areas of life, or when the norms of various reference groups are themselves integrated. Under such circumstances, as G. W. Allport (4) has emphasized, overlapping loyalties to different reference groups need not conflict.

The reader who is particularly interested in problems of reducing group prejudice is referred to the discussion of intergroup relations and the experiment on reduction of intergroup hostility in Chapter 9 and to the general treatment of attitude change in Chapter 16.

Examination of factors that produce and perpetuate group prejudice suggests realistic measures which can be effectively applied for the reduction of prejudice and intergroup conflict. Evidence presented in this chapter and in earlier chapters (6–9) suggests the introduction of *superordinate goals* as an effective measure. The introduction of superordinate goals which are real and compelling is conducive to increased interaction and communication between contending groups. In this process, contending groups tend to pull together, rather than apart; available bits of information concerning the groups involved tend to acquire new, positive meanings; contact between groups tends to be utilized positively, rather than as occasion for exchanging accusations and increasing mutual irritation and conflict.

REFERENCES

1. Adams, Romanzo. *Interracial Marriage in Hawaii*. New York: Macmillan, 1937.
2. Adorno, T. W., et al. *The Authoritarian Personality*. New York: Harper, 1950.
3. Allport, G. W. Prejudice: a problem in psychological and social causation, *J. soc. Issues*, Supplement Series, No. 4, November, 1950.
4. Allport, G. W. *The Nature of Prejudice*. Cambridge: Addison-Wesley, 1954.
5. Allport, G. W., and Kramer, B. M. Some roots of prejudice, *J. Psychol.* (1946), 22:9–39.
6. Ambedkar, B., quoted in *Newsweek*, May 12, 1947, p. 40.
7. Anastasi, A., and Foley, J. P., Jr. *Differential Psychology*. New York: Macmillan, 1949.
8. Avigdor, R. The development of stereotypes as a result of group interaction. Doctorate dissertation, New York University, 1952.

9. Bayton, J. A. The racial stereotypes of Negro college students, *J. abnorm. & soc. Psychol.* (1941), 36:97–102.

10. Benedict, R. *Race and Cultural Relations.* Problems in American Life, No. 5. Washington: National Education Association, 1942.

11. Berry, B. *Race Relations.* Boston: Houghton Mifflin, 1951.

12. Bettelheim, B., and Janowitz, M. *Dynamics of Prejudice.* New York: Harper, 1950.

13. Blake, R., and Dennis, W. The development of stereotypes concerning the Negro, *J. abnorm. & soc. Psychol.* (1943), 38:525–531.

14. Bogardus, E. S. Changes in racial distances, *Internat. J. Opin. & Attit. Res.* (1947), 1:55–62.

15. Brophy, I. N. The luxury of anti-Negro prejudice, *Publ. Opin. Quart.* (1946), 10:456–466.

16. Christie, R. Authoritarianism Re-examined, in R. Christie and M. Jahoda (eds.), *Studies in the Scope and Method of "The Authoritarian Personality."* Glencoe, Ill.: Free Press, 1954.

17. Christie, R., and Garcia, J. Subcultural variation in authoritarian personality, *J. abnorm. & soc. Psychol.* (1951), 46:457–469.

18. Clark, K. B. Desegregation: An appraisal of the evidence, *J. soc. Issues* (1953), 9, No. 4.

19. Clark, K. B., and Clark, M. K. Skin color as a factor in racial identification of Negro pre-school children, *J. soc. Psychol.* (1940), 11:159–169.

20. Clark, K. B., and Clark, M. K. Racial identification and preference in Negro children, in T. M. Newcomb and E. L. Hartley (eds.), *Readings in Social Psychology.* New York: Holt, 1947.

21. Criswell, J. H. A sociometric study of race cleavages in the classroom, *Arch. Psychol.* (1939), No. 235.

22. Dean, John. Personal communication. Observation obtained during the Elmira Intergroup Relations Study, Cornell University, 1952.

23. Dean, J., and Kohn, M. L. Situational diagnosis and intergroup relations. Unpublished manuscript personally communicated by Professor Dean, Cornell University, 1952.

24. Deutsch, M., and Collins, M. E. *Interracial Housing.* Minneapolis: University of Minnesota Press, 1951.

25. Dodd, S. C. A social distance test in the Near East, *Amer. J. Sociol.* (1935), 41:194–204.

26. Dunn, L. C., and Dobzhansky, Th. *Heredity, Race, and Society.* New York: Mentor Books, rev. ed., 1952.

27. Eysenck, H. J., and Crown, S. National stereotypes: An experimental and methodological study, *Internat. J. Opin. & Attit. Res.* (1948), 2:26–49.

28. Freyre, G. Reported in O. Klineberg, *Tensions Affecting International*

Understanding. New York: Social Science Research Council, Bull. 62, 1950, pp. 192–193.

29. Gilbert, G. M. Stereotype persistence and change among college students, *J. abnorm. & soc. Psychol.* (1951), 46:245–254.

30. Goldstein, N. F. *The Roots of Prejudice Against the Negro in the United States*. Boston: Boston University Press, 1948.

31. Goodman, M. E. *Race Awareness in Young Children*. Cambridge: Addison-Wesley, 1952.

32. Guilford, J. P. Racial preferences of a thousand American university students, *J. soc. Psychol.* (1931), 2:179–204.

33. Harding, J., and Hogrefe, R. Attitudes of white department store employees toward Negro co-workers, *J. soc. Issues* (1952), 8:18–28.

34. Harding, J., Kutner, B., Proshansky, H., and Chein, I. Prejudice and Ethnic Relations, in G. Lindzey (ed.), *Handbook of Social Psychology*. Cambridge: Addison-Wesley, 1954, Vol. II.

35. Hartley, E. L. *Problems in Prejudice*. New York: King's Crown Press, 1946.

36. Hartley, E. L., Rosenbaum, M., and Schwartz, S. Children's use of ethnic frames of reference: An exploratory study of children's conceptualizations of multiple ethnic group membership, *J. Psychol.* (1948), 26:367–386; Children's perceptions of ethnic group membership, *ibid.*, 387–398; Note on children's role perception, *ibid.*, 399–405.

37. Hood, W. R., and Sherif, M. Personality oriented approaches to prejudice, *Sociol. & soc. Res.* (1955), 40:79–85.

38. Horowitz, E. L. The development of attitudes toward Negroes, *Arch. Psychol.* (1936), No. 194.

39. Horowitz, E. L. "Race" Attitudes, Part IV in O. Klineberg (ed.), *Characteristics of the American Negro*. New York: Harper, 1944.

40. Horowitz, E. L., and Horowitz, R. E. Development of social attitudes in children, *Sociometry* (1937), 1:301–338.

41. Horowitz, R. E. Racial aspects of self-identification in nursery school children, *J. Psychol.* (1939), 7:91–99.

42. Huxley, J. S., and Haddon, A. C. *We Europeans: A Survey of "Racial" Problems*. New York: Harper, 1936.

43. Hyman, H. H., and Sheatsley, P. B. "The Authoritarian Personality"—A Methodological Critique, in R. Christie and M. Jahoda (eds.), *Studies in the Scope and Method of "The Authoritarian Personality."* Glencoe, Ill.: Free Press, 1954.

44. Information Control Division, American Military Government in Germany. Survey reported in New York *Herald Tribune*, May 4, 1947.

45. Katz, D., and Braly, K. Racial stereotypes of one-hundred college students, *J. abnorm. & soc. Psychol.* (1933), 28:280–290.

46. Killian, L. M. Southern white laborers in Chicago's West Side. Doctorate dissertation, University of Chicago, 1949. Quotations from summaries kindly made available by the author.

47. Klineberg, O. *Tensions Affecting International Understanding*. New York: Social Science Research Council, Bull. 62, 1950.

48. Kusunoki, K. Mental characteristics of the Japanese race as seen by Japanese and American students, *Jap. J. appl. Psychol.* (1936), 4:232–237; reported by O. Klineberg (47).

49. LaPiere, R. T. Race prejudice: France and England, *Soc. Forces* (1928), 7:102–111.

50. Lasker, B. *Race Attitudes in Children*. New York: Holt, 1929.

51. Lewin, K. *Resolving Social Conflicts*. New York: Harper, 1948.

52. Lindgren, E. J. An example of culture contact without conflict, *Amer. Anthropologist* (1938), 40:605–621.

53. Linton, R. (ed.). *Acculturation in Seven American Indian Tribes*. New York: Appleton-Century, 1940.

54. Luchins, A. S. Rigidity and ethnocentrism: a critique, *J. Personal.* (1948–49), 17:449–466.

55. MacCrone, I. D. *Race Attitudes in South Africa*. London: Oxford University Press, 1937.

56. Masuoka, J. Race preference in Hawaii, *Amer. J. Sociol.* (1936), 41:635–641.

57. Meenes, M. A. A comparison of racial stereotypes of 1935 and 1942, *J. soc. Psychol.* (1943), 17:327–336.

58. Meltzer, H. Group differences in nationality and race preferences of children, *Sociometry* (1939), 2:86–105.

59. Minard, R. D. Race relationships in the Pocahontas coal field, *J. soc. Issues* (1952), 8:29–44.

60. Montagu, Ashley. *Statement on Race*. New York: Schuman, 1951.

61. Morse, N. C. Study summarized in G. W. Allport (3).

62. Murphy, G., and Likert, R. *Public Opinion and the Individual*. New York: Harper, 1938.

63. O'Reilly, C. T., and O'Reilly, E. J. Religious beliefs of Catholic college students and their attitudes toward minorities, *J. abnorm. & soc. Psychol.* (1954), 49:378–380.

64. Pierson, D. *Negroes in Brazil*. Chicago: University of Chicago Press, 1942.

65. Prothro, E. T., and Melikian, L. Social distance and social change in the Near East, *Sociol. & soc. Res.* (1952), 37:3–11.

66. Radke, M., Trager, H. G., and Davis, H. Children's perceptions and attitudes of children, *Genet. Psychol. Monogr.* (1949), 40:327–447.

67. Ram, P., and Murphy, G. Recent investigations of Hindu-Muslim relations in India, *Human Organiz.* (1952), 11:13–16.

68. Rose, A. *The Negro in America* (*A Condensation of an American Dilemma*). New York: Harper, 1948.
69. Rose, A. *The Negro in Postwar America*. New York: Anti-Defamation League of B'nai B'rith, 1950.
70. Rosenblith, J. F. A replication of "some roots of prejudice," *J. abnorm. & soc. Psychol.* (1949), 44:470–489.
71. Saenger, G. *The Social Psychology of Prejudice*. New York: Harper, 1953.
72. Sherif, M., and Sherif, C. W. *Groups in Harmony and Tension*. New York: Harper, 1953.
73. Stagner, R. Studies of aggressive social attitudes: I. Measurement and interrelations of selected attitudes, *J. soc. Psychol.* (1944), 20:109–120; II. Changes from peace to war, *ibid.*, 121–128; III. The role of personal and family scores, *ibid.*, 129–140.
74. United Nations, *Report of the United Nations Commission on the Racial Situation in the Union of South Africa*. General Assembly, Official Records: Eighth Session, Supplement No. 16, New York, 1953.
75. Willems, Emilio. Racial attitudes in Brazil, *Amer. J. Sociol.* (1949), 54:402–408.
76. Williams, R. M. *The Reduction of Intergroup Tensions*. New York: Social Science Research Council, Bull. 57, 1947.
77. Wilner, D. M., Walkley, R. P., and Cook, S. W. Residential proximity and intergroup relations in public housing projects, *J. soc. Issues* (1952), 8:45–69.
78. Zeligs, R., and Hendrickson, G. Racial attitudes of 200 sixth-grade children, *Sociol. & soc. Res.* (1933–34), 18:26–36.
79. Zeligs, R., and Hendrickson, G. Checking the social distance technique through the personal interview, *Sociol. & soc. Res.* (1933–34), 18:420–430.

VI

INDIVIDUALS AND SOCIAL CHANGE

CHAPTER **20**

Effects of Technology

Sitting in our living room, we can witness a new play being performed in New York, a concert in California, or a bull fight in Mexico. In a few seconds, we can speak to a friend on the other side of the world. Within some hours, we could join him for dinner.

The last 50 years alone have brought undreamed-of methods of communication and transportation, new sources of power, new methods of production, new foods, new fabrics, and new forms of entertainment. The world at mid-twentieth century faces developments in man's mastery of his environment which promise one thing surely: change. We face the development and utilization of atomic energy, whose birth and infancy were marked with tragedy and fear. We have caught tantalizing glimpses of factories, farms, and mines run automatically which eliminate long hours of arduous human effort. Dreams of the end of famine and deadly epidemic, of deserts transformed to fertile fields have become promises of the future.

The concept of "One World" has become meaningful today because of the growing realization, reinforced daily by concrete events, that twentieth-century developments in transportation, communication, production, tools, and arms have brought far-flung parts of the world into immediate contact and interdependence. Events and decisions made at a distant point of the globe can be known within minutes and can affect other points within hours. Even those parts of the world which were once isolated and somewhat self-contained are becoming functional parts of a world-wide industrial civilization.

There was a time when we could speak of "patterns of culture" comparatively complete within themselves. But today, when representatives from Samoa, Indonesia, and Africa come before the United Nations with

685

similar social and political aspirations, it is hardly realistic to speak of *closed* culture patterns. A functioning system is closed or self-sustaining only if the dominant factors are contributed by the system itself. If factors from outside the system intrude in a dominant way, one can no longer speak of a closed configuration. The stability of the system is upset. For the time being, the system is in a state of disequilibrium, in which internal forces tending to keep it intact come into conflict with the outside forces tending to establish a new balance.

This general trend toward a functionally interrelated world is reflected in the increasing concern of ethnologists with problems of culture change or "acculturation." Their concern with these problems is epitomized by the anthropologist Malinowski in these words "way back" in 1945:

> The anthropologist is becoming increasingly aware that the study of culture change must become one of his main tasks in field work and theory. The figment of the "uncontaminated" Native has to be dropped from research in field and study. The cogent reason for this is that the "uncontaminated" Native does not exist anywhere. The man of science has to study what is, and not what might have been. When his main interest lies in the reconstruction of the tribal past, he still has to study the Native as he is now, affected by Western influences. . . .
>
> The anthropologist could also usefully reflect on the fact that evolution and diffusion are processes not so different as they appear at first sight. Culture change in Africa does not differ profoundly from that which is at present transforming the rural and backward countries of Europe from peasant communities, living by indigenous age-long economic systems, by folklore and kinship organization, into a new type closely akin to the proletariat found in the industrial districts of the United States, England, or France [9, pp. 2–3].

In this chapter on social psychology we cannot attempt to encompass all the main problems of cultural change. We cannot delineate the various phases of the complicated relationships between technology and the mentality of those who use its products. Nor can we give even a partial account of the psychological effects of the automobile, the airplane, radio, movies, television, or atomic energy. Each of these is a complicated problem of the first order. Each is part of the general problem of the effects of technology or, more generally, of *material culture* upon the psychology of individuals.

Before stating that aspect of the technology-mentality relationship which is examined in this chapter, we must remind ourselves of the other social stimulus situations whose effects we have studied in other chapters. *The effects of technology are always upon individuals interacting with other individuals in group settings with particular organizations, concepts, values, and social norms.* Therefore, material culture or technology does not affect an individual discretely. The individual is a member of groups and large social organizations with structures and norms. His reactions toward a technological product are influenced in significant ways by his own attitudes derived from his group memberships and by active pressures from groups of individuals who are motivated to maintain the existing order of things or to influence his reactions in a particular way. In particular, the existing nonmaterial culture (e.g., concepts, values, norms) constitutes an important source of factors which determine the speed with which technological developments are accepted or propagated and with which they affect human relationships. In the United States, for example, there was considerable resistance for a time to automobiles, not only from manufacturers of horse-drawn vehicles, but also from many members of the older generation, in whose case it was not a matter of "vested interest."

As we have seen, there are socially approved and disapproved ways of looking at things, doing things, and living in everyday life. These social norms are important sources of the individual's own attitudes, and thus regulate and limit his outlook. Deviation from established ways by an individual, even deviation in a direction which is destined to become "normal" in the years to come, is almost invariably looked upon with suspicion at first. If the deviation pertains to a norm considered very important by the group, and especially if its vital interests are at stake, the deviate calls down the scorn and wrath of "good people" upon himself. Even when innovations are in a direction which in the long run proves to be a blessing, deviation is risky.

At times, scientists who stress the decisive effect of technological changes in shaping the mentality of man have been criticized for reducing everything to crude material determination. Yet those who have studied the topic have also been most concerned with resistance to innovations and the inevitable weight of nonmaterial culture in determining the results of innovations. In this chapter we can do no more than recognize the comprehensive problems implied by this interaction. Social psychology has hardly begun to consider the significance of the material part of the "man-made" environment for attitude formation and for changes in the individual's concepts and outlook. Our point of departure will be through simple but basic psychological principles with which we have already become familiar.

SOME ELEMENTARY EFFECTS OF TECHNOLOGY

In Chapters 2 and 3 we reviewed some basic principles of psychological structuring derived from well-known experiments on judgment. We have found these principles useful in analyzing and studying behavior in relation to other people, groups, and their products. Two of these principles pertained to the relative contribution of external factors and internal influences when the individual faces stimulus situations of varying objective structure (pp. 81–82). It will be recalled that when the external situation is unstructured, the relative contribution of internal influences is maximal. But when external stimuli provide clear-cut patterns, proportions, series, or gradations, fewer alternatives are available for psychological structuring. Experience is organized predominantly in terms of the objective properties of the stimulus field.

By and large, technological products are characterized by clear-cut objective structure, both in extrinsic properties and in their use and consequences in human activity. Therefore, we can take our lead from what we have learned about psychological structuring in relation to well-structured stimulus situations. First, we can recall the familiar experiments on perception in which definite objective lines, forms, patterns are presented; the objective structures and reference points become the compelling anchorages for experience (pp. 54–58). Then we can turn to studies of judgment. When individuals face or use certain magnitudes, weights, proportions repeatedly, they cannot help forming appropriate reference scales in relation to them. Subsequently, when they face these stimuli or others related to them, they react to them in a *relational* way as parts of that particular scale. Relevant stimuli are experienced in relation to their established reference scales. Thus, stimuli are experienced as too big, too small, too fast, too slow, too hard, too easy, as normal or extraordinary in relation to the person's established reference scales in these various dimensions.

In one experiment a college professor who was confronted with the task of judging a series of graded weights which varied within a kilogram gave a good many judgments of *heavy*, until he had made several series of judgments. Another person who habitually dealt with rather heavy weights in his daily work gave a good many judgments of *light* when first confronted with the same series of weights (14).

When individuals are accustomed to the same reference scales, or repeatedly face the same structured anchorages in the stimulus field, their reactions to a particular relevant stimulus become highly predictable. Tresselt and Volkmann (15) demonstrated that "uniform opinion" could be produced by such means through nonsocial stimulation. It will be recalled that in one experiment on "majority influence" Asch found that individuals faced with the task of matching one of two lines of obviously different lengths with a standard immediately made the correct choice, and laughed uproariously at a "planted" subject who chose the other one (p. 138). Such findings have direct and clear implications for understanding consensus in social groups and similarities in reactions of individual members. When objective stimuli are highly structured, individuals in groups reach agreement concerning them and respond to them in similar fashion. In these cases, consensus is not so much a result of social processes as of the compellingness of similar objective stimulation to which they are exposed.

In this chapter we will utilize such findings and principles toward understanding some well-known variations in experience in different material settings and certain alterations in attitudes and behavior produced by changes in technology. Then we can understand why a peasant from a primitive village, whose travel speed is regulated by the fact that he has to walk or ride a donkey, considers a trip in a worn-out bus a rare luxury and its leisurely progress a terrific speed. Utilizing the same basic principles, we can clarify the differential reactions of a multimillionaire and an ordinary working person upon receiving the sum of $500. We can comprehend a peasant's satisfaction, or even joy, if he attains a yearly income of $300.

Before going to concrete material pertaining to effects of technology, a few words are in order concerning the nature of the stimuli involved. In an experiment on judging weights or lines, the stimuli themselves have little motivational significance for the subject. On the other hand, objects and influences from material culture which people grow up with, which they face and use daily in vital activities, acquire considerable personal and motivational significance. Technological devices have significance in terms of actual efforts involved in using them, in terms of labor or time saved, in terms of pain or pleasure they produce, in terms of goals they aid in achieving. They acquire, at times, intensely personal significance. The farmer can scarcely conceive of himself without his plow and tractor. Reduced to a hand plow, he would be in state of personal misery. The traveling salesman's car becomes almost as much a part of himself as his own face. The grounded pilot has an empty existence until he sits at the controls of his plane once again.

Studying Effects of Technology

In the literature on "primitive" societies, a typical finding is that many of the concepts and attitudes toward the physical world differ considerably from those in technologically developed groups. We have referred to concrete examples in illustrating the effects of different anchorages in psychological organization (pp. 66–74) and in discussing relationships between concepts and cultural realities (pp. 456–458). Ethnologists are not usually content to record these exotic differences. They relate them to the conditions of life, vital activities, and sociocultural organizations in which they have developed and are used. One recurrent conclusion in this literature is that many basic concepts and attitudes are meaningful in terms of vital activities carried on in the society and the tools, devices, or vehicles utilized in them.

For example, Hallowell (2) reported on the ways distance, length, and area are conceived among the Saulteaux Indians of Canada. In contrast to the standard common units utilized in technologically developed societies, the Saulteaux's conceptions of distance, length, and area were extremely crude and variable. Distance was referred to through "units of activity." The length of a journey was measured in terms of "sleeps" or nights on the trip. Since horse and canoe were the means of transportation, experience of length might be determined much more by weather, high or low water, number of persons in the canoe, or size of the load than by distance as objectively measured. Unlike agricultural people, the Saulteaux, who are primarily hunters, do not make abstract delineations or comparisons of land areas. Hallowell suggests that this is the case because land has value only for hunting. The "yield" of a land area is not necessarily related to its size, for a small area may afford as many animals as a larger one.

One possible way of studying the effects of technology upon the formation of such elementary concepts and attitudes is to compare typical reactions in a group before, during, and after some new technological devices are introduced. Later in this chapter we shall examine a few examples obtained through such comparisons.

A second way of studying the effects of technology is to compare the reactions of groups in similar cultural areas whose life experiences differ

Standard Oil Co. (N.J.)

FIG. 20.1. Means of transportation available are important determinants of our experience of speed and distance.

Ewing Galloway.

chiefly in terms of how closely they are in contact with modern technology and industrial centers. Our first concrete example was obtained by such simultaneous comparison.

DIFFERENTIAL CONTACT WITH MODERN TECHNOLOGY IN FIVE TURKISH VILLAGES

In 1944, a study of technology-mentality relationships was made in five Turkish villages with varying degrees of isolation from more developed centers and with varying contact with modern technology. This study, by M. Sherif, was specifically designed to compare certain concepts and attitudes of groups within the same cultural setting but with differential contact with modern technology. Thus, the study represents a demonstration of relationships between technological developments and psychological data which recur in ethnological comparisons of different cultures.

All five villages studied had some contact with the world outside their boundaries. Along with the rest of the country, all were in a stage of transition. However, the most and least isolated villages present a striking contrast in terms of relative contact with technology. The three villages between these extremes represent roughly graded comparisons. All material was collected by graduate students who came from the villages and were intimate with village life. Thus, the difficulties that are connected with the use of informants and language barriers were not present in this study.

Two kinds of data were secured for comparisons: (1) data concerning material conditions and technological level of the villages; (2) data concerning related concepts and attitudes of the villagers.

The scope of the psychological data was deliberately limited to a few simple, but basic, phenomena. The units, their precision, and scope were ascertained in each village for the following:

Perceptions of space, distance, and time.

Standards for judging what is familiar and what is "strange."

Standards for judging wealth and "waste."

While simple, these data pertain to concepts and attitudes which are important in regulating the boundaries of an individual's activities, his expectations for himself and others, the degree and scope of his psychological mobility in undertaking vital activities, and his reactions within his group and toward out-groups.

In order to make the conditions of village life and the typical attitudes of villagers concrete and real, we will summarize the findings for the relatively most isolated and least isolated villages—Karlik in the western interior of Turkey and Beşikdüzü on the Black Sea coast. The villages of Kalinagil, Zanapa, and Isabey represent relatively intermediate isolation.

The Most Isolated Village: Karlik

Karlik is a village of 361 people (1944) situated in a rather mountainous region east of the Aegean coast. It is about 30 kilometers from a province capital, Afyon, and about 5 kilometers from a larger village, Şuhut. Although there is a dirt road between the two villages, the villagers usually travel to Şuhut on foot or donkey by a shorter path over the hills. During the winter, the stream at the village edge is flooded most of the time, thus cutting contact with Şuhut. Karlik has one telephone for official governmental use.

From Şuhut, there is occasional bus service to other towns. But the villagers of Karlik can take advantage of it only on exceptional occasions, for it is expensive to them. The railroad is 35 kilometers distant.

In Karlik, two or three families own about 200 *dönüm* (about 50 acres) of land each. Over 25 percent of the families own no land. They work on others' farms to earn their living. Between these two extremes, the remaining village families own 15–20 *dönüm* (4–5 acres) each. The villagers depend on farming grains for their livelihood. There are no animal herds of substantial value, except oxen, donkeys, horses, and cows kept for farm work, domestic use, and limited trade. No modern machinery is available; only primitive tools are used in farming. Some of the landless peasants go to Afyon for construction work between planting and harvest time. They also go occasionally to work, as transient help, in the provinces along the Aegean, returning to Karlik when they have saved a little money.

Since there are no stores in the village, villagers go to Şuhut on market days to sell their goods and buy a few necessities. Such trips are made by donkey; on ordinary days, the trip is made on foot.

A village school was founded six years prior to the study. The one teacher did not have the usual teacher's training. He teaches three classes and keeps attendance, which is no mean task because parents need their children for work.

Reactions of Villagers in Karlik

UNITS OF DISTANCE: The villagers express distances up to three or four kilometers with phrases such as: "Within a bullet's reach," "as far as my voice can go," "as far as (it takes) to smoke a cigarette." More precise or standard units of distance are not used.

Long distances, for example, 50 kilometers, are expressed as: "You start early in the morning and reach there by sunset," or "You reach there (by the time) you work on crops of one *dönüm* (of land)." The latter expression refers, of course, to work done without the use of modern agricultural tools and consequently varies considerably in terms of standard units. Guesses of distance based on time are always made in terms of the time a trip takes *on foot*. When villagers estimate long distances involving bus or train travel, they refer to the number of days, nights, and parts thereof (not hours) spent on the vehicle. Such distances are not comparable psychologically to so many shorter distances. The villagers do not translate them into walking time, which is their psychological unit for distance. As we shall see shortly, this results in great lack of precision and some interesting inaccuracies.

The greatest distances from the village in their experiences vary, in general, according to whether they are male or female and, among males, whether or not they have completed their military service. For women, the farthest distance is either the neighboring village of Şuhut or Afyon, the province capital 30 kilometers away. For males who have not yet left for military service, the greatest distance is Afyon or some other neighboring place where they have found temporary work to balance their annual budget. Young men who have completed military service have done so at some location within the country. Older men who fought in World War I and the Turkish War for Independence have traveled within the country as soldiers and some of them have gone outside of the country. Of other distant places or continents they have only vague notions.

Because distance on foot and distance by modern transportation cannot be translated into comparable units, the perceptions of both older and younger men for distances beyond their province are greatly distorted. The manner of the distortion depends on whether their visit was made on foot or by modern means. For example, the town of Haymana in the neighboring province, to which one has to walk, is considered farther away than Istanbul, which by railroad is actually almost twice as far.

The following illustration is even more striking: Older men who served in the army during World War I both in the province of Van, Turkey, (near the eastern border) and in Galicia (now mainly in Poland at a distance several times that of Van) claim that Van is farther away than Galicia. They had to walk most of the way to Van; they went to Galicia on the train. In other words, before precise units of distance are grasped, the *human effort spent* in reaching a place is a major factor in determining the experience of distance.

Units of Time: Instead of hours, the following expressions are generally used in Karlik for divisions of the day:"first rooster," dawn; "leaving of oxen" (for grazing), sunrise, midmorning (*Kuşluk*), noon; "return of oxen," sunset, evening, and midnight.

The day that stands out and regulates the *periodicity of the week* is the *market day* of Şuhut, the nearby larger village. Since they refer to this village as simply "the Town" (*Gasaba*), this day is called "Town Market" (*Gasaba Bazari*). It happens to fall on Saturday. Three other days of the week are known as market days for towns in the area and are so named. Thus, the week in Karlik starts on Saturday (Town Market), with Sunday, Monday, and Thursday given the names of market days. A few villagers know the conventional names of the days of the week and calendar months.

The months are classified according to the appearance of the moon. Divisions of the year are expressed as summer, winter, spring, fall, and, in addition, seasons denoting vital activities like "haying," "end of harvest," "sowing," and the like. There are others named after farming and animal-raising activities and a couple after religious holidays.

What Is Strange: All people who by their mode of life, clothing, or speech are different from the villagers, including government officials (*memur*), are considered strangers, even though they may be known to the villagers. Someone who comes from outside and settles in the village is still considered a stranger, to the extent that he deviates from village norms in his living, appearance, and expressions. Young men who return from military service make a point of coming home with a new suit. At first, the usual reaction to them is: "Hey, *Memet*, you kind of look like a stranger. I didn't recognize you at first glance." This joking but tolerant attitude is maintained until the new suit becomes indistinguishable from others, and other things purchased outside the village disappear. Deviations in speech are particularly singled out for teasing.

The villagers consider themselves in a rather strange place when they move two or three kilometers beyond their village. However, those men who have stayed in more prosperous surroundings express a desire to return or even to settle down in some form like: "It is better to live in a place like that, even for one day, than living forty days in a place like this [i.e., Karlik] on which the flies don't even like to make specks."

Standards of Riches: Within limits, the standards of riches vary according to the economic standing of the villagers. This standing is evaluated according to the amount of land, number of farm animals, and size of crops. The two or three families who own relatively large pieces of land are considered by the other villagers to possess wealth beyond anything in their own power to attain.

Except for those two or three men who own (to the villagers) these huge farms, the greatest sum of money the villagers can conceive of is about $80 for women and around $800 for men. However, neither men nor women have succeeded in amassing such enormous sums of money in spite of all their toil.

Villagers in Karlik consider the following as "waste" or luxury: buying a new suit when one has one already, even though it may be full of patches; buying shoes worn in towns instead of simple leather sandals; wearing clothes made of thin materials used in towns. They do not distinguish between "everyday" and "Sunday best." Everything other than bare necessities of living is considered a luxury.

The Least Isolated Village: Beşikdüzü

Beşikdüzü was the least isolated village studied. Unlike Karlik, it is a coastal village located on the Black Sea. It is about 4 kilometers from a somewhat larger village and about 51 kilometers from Trabzon, the province capital, which is also on the sea. At the time of the study, Beşikdüzü had a population of 842 people (1944).

Two conditions have been chiefly responsible for bringing the villagers into closer contact with modern technology than are the residents of Karlik. One is their location on the sea and the trading by boat of their main produce, which is hazelnuts. However, the businessmen of the village, not the producers, are most involved in this outside trading. The second condition is that in this area, like many places along the coast, tillable farms are squeezed between the hills. The scarcity of tillable land makes it difficult to raise enough of their staple food (corn) for their own use. During the years before the study, 80 percent of the villagers were unable to raise sufficient corn, and many were unable to sell enough hazelnuts to buy imported corn. As a result, many men leave the village temporarily or for long periods to find other jobs. Some work in coal mines at Zonguldak, the Karabük steel works, and the Divrik ore mines. Others work on boats, fishing or hauling small cargoes. A few had even been out of the country to work.

Means of transportation inland are scarce. Though there are occasional buses to the nearby village and to the city, the usual mode of travel inland is on foot. Some trading is done at the neighboring village, where villagers themselves sell hazelnuts, butter, and a few other products and buy soap, salt, sugar, clothing, and some manufactured goods.

Beşikdüzü has about 10 stores, a few coffee houses, 5 shoemakers and repairmen, and 8 hazelnut traders. All of the coffee houses have radios. People are much interested in listening and like to read newspapers that come into the village. There is an official telephone in the village.

There has been an elementary school since 1909, and most of the young men are literate. A few are high-school graduates. The young men, particularly those who have traveled, are aware of the outside world and its problems.

Reaction of Villagers in Beşikdüzü

UNITS OF DISTANCE: The villagers perceive distance differently depending on whether a trip involves sea travel or inland travel. Distance by sea between ports is usually expressed both in kilometers and in the travel time. Travel time is reckoned in days, hours, and minutes. Some of the young people who want to impress visitors use only kilometers. On the other hand, since inland trips are made on foot, inland distances are usually expressed in terms of time required to walk to the destination. Places which can be reached and returned from in one day are considered in the neighborhood. Points beyond this are considered distant.

Almost all parts of Turkey are known to the men, for many have gone to work in various provinces. A few men have worked out of the country, and these spontaneously compare conditions at home with those abroad. But to most women, who have stayed at home while their menfolks were away, these outside places are nothing more than names. Illiterate men who stick to the soil and have not left the village to work are only slightly different from the women. The conceptions of faraway places vary for literate men who have not been away themselves.

UNITS OF TIME: Old people usually locate events in the past in terms of past wars, the general emigration during World War I, or other memorable events. Within the year, the activities most closely connected with their vital activities serve as reference periods for time, e.g., "the hazelnut-gathering period," "the cutting of corn," and the like. The most important period is the hazelnut-collecting period. If the nuts are abundant, there is extraordinary rejoicing, singing and dancing. If the crop is poor, a general gloom prevails.

Days of the week are named for market days in the village and those in the vicinity. Time is generally designated in relation to their own market day—for example, as a day or two days after market day.

About 80 people in the village regularly use a calendar and a watch or clock. Villagers engaged exclusively in farming still rely on units based on natural phenomena (sunrise, sunset, etc.).

WHAT IS STRANGE: Since many villagers market in neighboring villages and have worked in various places, they do not usually consider city people or officials strange. They engage in lively conversation with them.

The people of Beşikdüzü do not seem to experience a feeling of strangeness on any seashore or place where there are hazelnut orchards. They have developed a capacity for making rapid adaptations even to places with different characteristics. The scarcity of land and the travel by boat have produced an actual mobility which has significantly affected their psychological mobility as well. The old folks react to this mobility quite unfavorably. In fact, they resist it. It is painful for them to break long-established ties with land and neighbors.

STANDARDS OF RICHES: In general, the amount of hazelnuts one raises and hoards for trading is used in gauging wealth. For the professional traders, money accumulated is becoming a more important standard of wealth.

A person who owns 50 *dönüm* of orchards and 25 *dönüm* of corn, and raises 4000–5000 kilograms of nuts and 2000 kilograms of corn, is considered wealthy. The farmers consider the accumulation of about $2000 a fortune; but for the village traders, a sum of a little over $5000 is a fortune.

Money spent on women, drink, and luxury items in clothing or furniture is considered wasted. However, some villagers indulge in such luxuries. But a man who leaves the village in threadbare clothes and sandals and returns in "city" clothes faces the ridicule of other villagers.

Summary of Effects of Differential Contacts with Modern Technology

On the basis of the findings in five Turkish villages with differing contact with modern technology, we may draw the following conclusions concerning the effects of differential contact in producing psychological variations:

1. When individuals in a social organization have little contact with modern technology and the internationally standardized units of distance, space, and time which accompany it, anchorages for the perception of

distance, space, and time are standardized. The nature of these anchorages depends largely on: (a) the periodicity of work activities and social-economic activities (like market days); (b) the periodicity of natural events (like sunrise-sunset, or cycles of the moon) and the appearances of compelling features in the surroundings (like a mountain peak); (c) the human effort involved in accomplishing tasks (e.g., walking, riding) with the means available. The anchorages standardized largely on these bases lack precision in varying degrees. Perception and other experiences are significantly affected by the particular nature of the anchorages developed and thus may not be comparable along a given dimension (e.g., distances traveled by train cannot be translated into distances walked).

2. As one passes from more isolated to less isolated, from technologically less-developed to more-developed villages, international units of distance, space, and time are used roughly in proportion to the degree of the impact of modern technology, and their use becomes correspondingly more precise.

3. A scale of wealth exists for every village. The limits of the scale are set by the financial levels of the rich and the poor in the village. The standards which an individual uses in judging wealth vary according to his own relative position on that scale.

4. The radius of the world in which the individual lives his daily life and to which he can adapt easily widens with the degree of contact with the products and facilities of modern technology. This applies particularly to modern means of transportation.

The individual's mobility increases in proportion to contact with modern technology and is further enhanced by the pressures of local conditions (e.g., economic scarcity) away from the community. In the two villages summarized (Karlik and Beşikdüzü), local conditions forced villagers to leave both places to seek work; however, those who left Karlik usually returned shortly while many who left Beşikdüzü were away for long periods or did not return. Ten families had left Beşikdüzü during the decade prior to the study and had not returned. In other words, the greater the degree of contact with modern means of transportation and other technological products, the greater is the *actual mobility* of individuals and the greater their *psychological mobility*. People with less contact with modern technology and long-established relatedness to familiar surroundings have less psychological mobility.

Although this study concentrated on the effects of material conditions, it was noted that existing values or norms frequently played an important

FIG. 20.2. Human effort required by available technology affects our conception of the world and our mobility from place to place.

part in regulating the experiences studied. The rather different reactions of young people and older people in Beşikdüzü constitute one example.

Differential Contact with Technology in America: The Hollow Folk

Conclusions concerning technology-mentality relationships derived from the study of five Turkish villages are substantiated by ethnological and sociological data from various parts of the world. For the most part, such data were collected in studying other problems. Rather than presenting further material from different culture areas, we will illustrate available evidence with an example from the United States, a country where technology has reached perhaps its highest and most widespread development.

In fairly recent years, it was possible to find groups of people in the United States who were isolated from the impact of modern technology. One such area in the Blue Ridge Mountains of Virginia, about 100 miles from the nation's capital, was studied for two years by a staff of social scientists and psychologists. The results were reported by Sherman and Henry in their book *Hollow Folk* (13). Four communities were studied. Starting with the most isolated, these were Colvin Hollow, Needles Hollow, Oakton Hollow, and Rigby Hollow, the least isolated. Briarsville, a small farm and sawmill town in the valley, was similar to other rural towns in different parts of the country.

The authors noted that the differences they found between the four Hollow communities did not seem due to differences in quality of land or natural resources. In this respect "all four communities are on an approximately equal plane. Yet because of the use of tools and equipment the output of Rigby yields incomes sufficiently large to maintain a standard of living far in excess of the three neighboring hollows" (p. 187). Thus, in the authors' opinion, it is the impact of modern technology which is at the root of the great differences found.

THE MOST ISOLATED COMMUNITY: Colvin Hollow was a scattered collection of cabins each with about two acres of garden. There was no road or system of communication with the outside world. The little trading done was carried on by one man who made about four trips a week across the almost trailless mountains to the valley. Over a high ridge, about three miles away by a narrow path, was a summer resort where some of the residents worked occasionally at unskilled jobs in the summer. The main means of livelihood was gardening, which was carried on with no modern tools. There were "rudiments of a home industry"—basket weaving. No one in the Hollow could read or write.

In many ways this community was more isolated, and the technological level was probably lower, than the most isolated Turkish village (Karlik). Perception of distance was even less precise. Residents did not ordinarily differentiate a quarter-mile from a mile. The usual designation for distances within this range was "over thar a piece." One child differentiated a short and long distance with the phrases "not a far piece over the hill" and "a good piece through the woods."

Expressions of time were also vague. Only three children in the community knew the days of the week. Even children in their teens did not ordinarily know one day from the other. "It is not vital for them to have this information because their way of living does not take into account time or days. All days are practically alike in Colvin Hollow" (p. 135). Three children had heard of Christmas and Thanksgiving but did not know what was done on those days.

People from outside the Hollow were viewed as strangers with great suspicion. The people knew almost nothing of the outside world, except the town at the foot of the mountains, which they visited occasionally. Because of the nature and limited radius of their world, the investigators found that people had few wants other than satisfying the most fundamental motives. The work tempo was observed to be very slow and irregular. As a result, people at the resort who sometimes employed the residents or ordered baskets tended to regard them as "unreliable."

THE LESS ISOLATED COMMUNITIES: Next to Colvin Hollow, the more isolated community was Needles Hollow, which was connected by a trail with a country road leading to the valley. Here farms averaged about five acres apiece and almost every family had a pig and a chicken. A few men were literate. In this Hollow, a scale of riches made its appearance, whereas in Colvin Hollow equal poverty was the rule. This scale was based mainly on land; and the investigators thought it significant that many of the farmers said that they had 20 or 30 acres of land when they actually had less. But in this Hollow the tempo of life is still so different from the outside world that few residents leave the community permanently. Even the former schoolteacher, who sold his belongings and moved to a small West Virginia town, found it difficult to adjust to the routine of life imposed by work in a sawmill. When asked why he came back:

" 'Wal,' he drawled, 'it's much better here. I gits up in the mornin' when I wants and I do what I wants. No gettin' up with a whistle and eating with a whistle here' " (p. 196).

The third community, Oakton Hollow, had more organized agriculture.

A surplus of apples and corn was traded in the valley. There was a store and post office, and nearly every home had a mail-order catalogue. Even the women made occasional trips to Briarsville in the valley. Here the scale of riches was clear-cut. Wealth was based on having a surplus of goods and the kind of clothes, house, and other articles which are outward signs of a surplus. The men of Oakton Hollow kept regular work routines when they worked outside the community. The community had lost population to the outside world, and the migrants tended to stay away if they left.

Rigby Hollow, the least isolated of all, was on a country road and was even more similar to other rural towns in different parts of the country. In Briarsville, the valley town with a sawmill and shopping center, regular working hours were maintained by the residents.

Thus, this study of the Hollow Folk illustrates the rather profound contrasts in concepts and attitudes found among people with differing degrees of contact with modern technology and the routines of life which accompany them. The investigators of the Hollow Folk observed that these differences were found even in the motives and aspirations of individuals. *In Colvin Hollow, the children hardly seemed to understand what was meant when asked "What do you want to be when you grow up?"* When it was explained, the usual answer was "I wants to be what I am" (p. 104). They had never come into contact with a diversity of occupations. Likewise, at each level, the desires and tastes of the residents were found to increase in number and variety. The authors concluded: "Wants develop only with experience, once elemental desires are attained" (p. 102).

TECHNOLOGICAL CHANGES CONDUCIVE TO CHANGING ORGANIZATIONS AND BEHAVIOR

On the basis of comparisons of groups with varying contact with modern technology, we can conclude that material and technological products provide highly structured stimulus situations which are significant factors in determining reference scales and standards for experiencing distance, space, time, wealth, and the radius of the world in which one feels at home. The study of the Hollow Folk indicated that the tempo of life and the objects which become goals are also affected in decisive ways by the material surroundings of individuals.

As noted earlier, however, material culture seldom affects individuals discretely. Its effects are almost always produced in interaction with existing social organization and social norms. The individuals who face technological products have interiorized social norms as ego-attitudes; and they are habitually interacting as members of groups with established interests, goals, and ways of living. In many cases, reaction to technological changes is influenced profoundly by the individual's established relatedness to his social environment and to active social pressures from that environment. At times, however, if an individual faces a concrete material situation in which behavior regulated by prevailing social norms is inappropriate, the compelling structure of the situation is a weightier determinant of his reactions.

Frequently, technological innovations alter the organization of man's vital activities and thus indirectly produce changed attitudes and behavior through the medium of social interaction. Such changes are studied by sociologists and ethnologists through longitudinal methods, starting prior to the technological changes and following through the resulting alterations in social organization and behavior. Most of the material referred to in the rest of the chapter was obtained in longitudinal and historical studies.

Some of the most significant personal ties which individuals form are within family organizations. Ego-attitudes formed in relation to family members are ordinarily earliest and among the most intimate. In his recent survey of "technology and the changing family," Ogburn (10) noted that, next to divorce, the change in the family most frequently mentioned by experts is the "decline in authority of the husband and father." Ogburn observed that this decline is a relative one which has been accompanied by a great increase in status for women and children. He proceeds to trace these changes in family organization and the changed attitudes and behavior which have accompanied them to the impetus of technological innovations.

In earlier times, women were usually parts of a joint family enterprise, whether farming or handicrafts, in which the husbands were actual and traditional managers. By and large, women were economically crucial but subordinate parts in the family organization. With the Industrial Revolution and especially with increasing mechanization, jobs outside of the home became available which, requiring little heavy muscular work, were suitable for women. At the same time that the factory system was creating jobs in factory, office, and shop which women could perform away from home, it "broke up the system of economic production in the home where the man of the house was the manager and the boss of the joint economic enterprise" (p. 191).

Ogburn concludes that the two new factors in women's economic role which have contributed to their increased status in the family are independent employment outside of the home and a money income. These are the chief sources of the woman's increased authority in the family. He notes, however, that the "residue of power" in American families still lies in the hands of the husband, who typically is the main, if not the sole, breadwinner. "But if one is interested in the changing aspect of the family situation, one will emphasize the increasing economic contribution of wives, and the accompanying increase in their authority" (p. 184).

The social norms concerning family organization and the woman's position put "limits" on the extent to which technological change affects her status. However, Ogburn cites survey evidence that in the United States there is increasing tendency for these norms to change in the direction of preferring that women work (p. 184). And he notes that social norms are not always the decisive influences in determining limits. Thus, in wartime, women assumed a much more active economic and social role than traditional norms would have indicated. Ogburn points out that the discrepancy between the norms and practice was greatest in Germany, where the shortage of males created a great demand for women workers and, on the other hand, the "official ideology" was the three K's (*Kinder, Kirche,* and *Kuchen*). Proportionally, more married women worked outside the home in Germany than in the United States.

It is well known that the number of children in a family has fallen off considerably with the coming of modern industrialization and the rise of great cities. An interesting ramification of this general fact in the United States concerns family size in rural areas, which were more recently exposed to modern technology and mechanized production methods. By the 1930's, the rate of decline in family size was actually greater in areas farthest from cities. Kolb and Brunner (4), who reported these findings, also noted that surveys in the early thirties revealed surprising changes from the older rural attitudes toward having children. The large majority of rural people advocated birth control. They saw these changes in attitude and behavior as an outgrowth of the increasing mechanization of agriculture, which made the labor of children less valuable.

Changing Kinship Ties and Attitudes in Periods of Rapid Transition

In these days of rapid industrialization in areas which have been less developed technologically, it is sometimes possible to glimpse within one or two generations changes in family organization and attitudes toward relatives, parents, husband, wife, or children. In such areas, this often involves comparison of peoples from rural, less developed communities as they move to newer, industrial centers. The changes observed are sometimes treated under "disorganization" in terms of traditional kinship organization. As Lewis (7) noted, the organizational and attitudinal changes do not necessarily imply breakdown of family life; they may indicate trends toward a new organizational stability.

Hunter (3) reported shifts in family organization and in attitudes toward relatives among the Pondo of South Africa as they move from reserves to work in the cities as laborers. The traditional coöperative unit, the *umzi*, breaks down completely in industrialized communities. Instead, the usual household group is the man, wife, and their minor children, like the typical modern family. *Accompanying this change, kinship terms and attitudes change.* In the traditional family organization, similar attitudes and behavior were observed for one's own father and brothers and for the father's brothers (uncles) and their children (cousins). On the other hand, relatives of the father and mother were clearly differentiated. In the industrial conditions, these similarities and differentiations become blurred. Even the differentiating terms are no longer used.

Perhaps the most dramatic illustration of changing family organization and attitudes in areas of rapid transition is Lang's report of field work carried out in China in 1935–1937 (5). A number of cases of rapid alterations were found as Chinese peasants came in larger numbers to participate in the accelerated industrial life of the country. Lang noted that the changes in the family came in two ways: "as a result of the new social and economic environment and the ideological influence of the West, the latter coming either through direct contact with the West or through the medium of modern Chinese schools, literature, etc., college education being the most potent medium of westernization" (p. 337). However, she added: "The environment is mainly—if not exclusively—responsible for the changes among the peasants and workers. They have heard very little, if anything, of modern ideas; but those who live in industrial cities or in rural districts where innovations have taken place and especially those who work in modern factories have seen their family life and relations changed by industrialization" (p. 337). The greatest changes in attitudes and behavior and the *greatest consistency of behavior was observed among those individuals who both lived in the new industrial environment and had been exposed to modern ideas.*

The survey showed a reversal in authority from the formerly powerful father to the children who became economically independent through participation in industrial life. The once-honored old fathers, far from being heads of their families, were treated with less respect and at times neglected by their children who worked in modern industry and supported them. Girls who worked in factories found that their status and treatment in the family changed. Their own attitudes toward parents were altered; their accustomed submission to parental authority gave way to independence, even to the point of their keeping the money they earned to spend on themselves. Wives who worked in factories found themselves with more authority and newly accorded respect from husbands and other family members. In some cases the wife who worked became the head of the family. One woman explained: "I have worked in the factory since I was very young and I know more of the world than my husband, who has never left his native village" (p. 206). In this family the roles of husband and wife were reversed. The wife dealt with the outside world and the husband with the home.

The family group is only one of various social organizations altered by new material conditions which change the functions of individual members and their relationships. The results have been altered expectations and behavior of its members and, ultimately, enduring attitudinal changes. One reason for the sensitivity of the family unit to such changed conditions is that it has both social-educational functions, intimate personal functions, and an important socioeconomic role. Studies of other human groups have also revealed changes in organization, behavior, and attitudes in varying degrees brought on by the impact of technological changes.

Technological Change and Changing Group Relations

As might be expected, the effect of technological changes can be detected most easily and directly in organizations whose chief functions are associated with the technological products in question. Work groups in a society or factory are obviously such organizations. In recent years there have been a number of detailed studies of the effects of technological innovation upon such groups.

Sayles (12) reported an intensive "case study" of a single department in a large manufacturing company whose function in the plant declined in importance owing to greatly improved machinery. The 35 men in this department were machine polishers; they were regarded by the other 1200 workers in the plant with "envy and awe." After the war, improved machinery eliminated the necessity for their work except for "special orders." The results included changes in the status of this group in the plant com-

Picking cotton by hand.

FIG. 20.3.   Technological innovations change man's occupations and his organizations.

Mechanical cotton pickers.

munity, changed relationships with other work groups, decreased participation in their union, "resurgent fears" of the plant management, and disintegration of their own informal work group. These changes imply altered intergroup relations, profound effects on in-group structure, and psychological effects as well.

This group had played a highly influential role in establishing the union in the first place. As "new production methods reduced the importance of their job, there was a decline in their participation in union affairs and, concomitantly, in their social status and group unity" (p. 14). Within the plant and the union, the group members became increasingly prone to feel that they were a "minority" group. "In a sense, social relations within the department mirrored these developments in 'foreign affairs.'" In-group solidarity was shattered; leadership changed. All of which had considerable effect on the experience and attitudes of individual members. "Ten years ago, individuals felt proud to be machine polishers. . . . The men felt anything but gloomy—they 'had the world by the tail.' Today self-satisfaction has been transformed into self-incrimination and internecine warfare" (p. 14).

BARBED-WIRE FENCING IN THE AMERICAN GREAT PLAINS: We sometimes tend to equate technology with industrial development and the cities. Technological innovations have played equally dramatic roles in group relationships and in the development of organizations in rural areas. One fascinating historical example is included in Walter Prescott Webb's account of the part played by transportation and fencing in the settlement of the Great Plains (16). It was, of course, the railroads which brought settlers to the Great Plains and made possible their trade with the East. But Webb observed: "It would be a mistake to assume that the railroads deserve all the credit for the settlement of the Great Plains. It would have been possible to build railroads in the Plains as early as 1850. But had railroads been built, it would have still been impossible for the farmer to occupy the country. His coming, trying enough at best, had to await certain other factors. . . . Not until then [1875] could the land of the Plains be fenced, and without fences agriculture is impossible in a country occupied by cattle" (p. 280).

The problem which necessitated some new solution began to come to a head as the farmers moved westward to the eastern edges of the "cattle country." Here the need for fences was most pressing and the rocks or timber which might have been used to build them were not available. It was then that groups of cattlemen and farmers came into direct and open conflict. Smooth wire fences and hedges of various kinds were tried out; but all were less than adequate. Wire fences were expensive; stock pushed through them without injury. Hedges required a period of growth. In the 1870's, several people developed barbed wire. As it began to spread, "there ensued a conflict, violent and sanguinary, between fence men and no-fence men. Fence-cutter wars broke out in Texas, Wyoming, New Mexico—wherever men began to fence and make private what hitherto had been free land and grass" (p. 313).

Newspapers and legislatures were immediately involved in this inter-group conflict. Laws were passed to regulate the actions of both sides. In the end, the wire-cutting cattlemen lost, less through legislation and force than by the irresistible production of barbed wire. This defeat is reflected in the colorful words of a Western cowboy who saw barbed-wire being produced:

"When I saw a barbed-wire machine at work manufacturing it and was told that there were thousands of them at the same work, I went home and told the boys they might just as well put up their cutters and quit splitting rails and use barbed wire instead. I was as confident then as I am today that wire would win . . . and that between barbed wire and railroads the cowboys' days were numbered." (16, p. 316).

Webb concluded that "Without barbed wire the Plains homestead could never have been protected from the grazing herds and, therefore, could not have been possible as an agricultural unit" (p. 317).

Organizational Changes Stemming from New Technology Alter Group Characteristics

There is evidence that some of the attitudes and behavior patterns characteristic of groups are changed with new material conditions in a society. Lewis' historical study of the effects of white contact on Blackfoot culture, for example, traces the effects of the introduction of the horse, gun, and fur trade upon the warfare of these Plains Indians (6). Pre-horse warfare among the Blackfoot involved concerted action of the tribe moti-vated chiefly by the desire to defend and expand tribal hunting grounds or by vengeance. Lewis finds no historical evidence of a static, unchanging "war complex." Rather, with the coming of horse, gun, and especially the fur trade, warfare became a more deadly business characterized by smaller raiding parties which utilized stealth and secrecy to secure the horses and guns which became so vital to their pursuit of the fur trade and for social status and prestige.

Among the Southern Ute of Colorado, the coming of the horse facili-
tated the development of "band" organization, in contrast to the pre-
horse family hunting groups. Opler (*11*), who reported on this change,
refers to Julian Seward's conclusion that for this area "the western limit of
the horse also was the western limit of true bands" (p. 154).

Among the Ute, warfare in pre-horse times was "mere localized defense
of one's kin." But with the development of the band organization, war
became a means of enriching the entire band. "The mobility afforded the
Ute band by the introduction of the horse led to a type of warfare motivated socially by a desire to loot." With this change, the qualifications for
leadership changed as well. A man had to prove his worth as a daring
scout and a wise organizer. The most popular camp leaders became those
"who called out most often that tonight they danced and tomorrow they
raided" (p. 164).

When the Utes and whites came into mortal conflict, the Utes had to
be subjugated by force of arms. Linton (*8*) observed that their level of
organization and reaction to white domination was in marked contrast to
those of a closely related group, the White Knife Shoshoni. The latter
accepted the new conditions brought on by white domination with "sly
sullenness." He accounted for the greater organization and warlike behavior of the Utes and the more fragmented family organization and do-
cility of the White Knife Shoshoni as follows:

> This difference must be seen as primarily a result of accidents of time and
> geographic location. The Utes, because of their more southern position, re-
> ceived horses first and were able to revolutionize certain aspects of their life be-
> fore White pressure became serious. The Shoshoni, on the other hand, received
> the horse late. Cultural modifications of the sort it produced among the Utes
> seem to have been under way but were still so poorly integrated with the rest
> of the culture that they were soon swept away. . . . The results of the ac-
> ceptance of the horse by the Utes are of particular interest in showing the speed
> with which important changes can be consummated in aboriginal cultures
> (p. 204).

INTERACTING EFFECTS OF TECHNOLOGICAL AND ORGANIZATIONAL CHANGES

In this chapter we have deliberately emphasized the role of technological products in the formation and change of simple standards and reference scales, in producing organizational changes and altered behavior and
attitudes. Such emphasis is needed in social psychology to keep its subject

matter in contact with a large and vital area of social stimulation—material culture. Our subject matter would not be balanced if we concentrated exclusively on language, social organization, social norms and values without regard to material conditions in which they function. On the other hand, we have emphasized at various points that these material conditions do not influence individuals independently of the above factors. Their effects are products of interaction with existing and emerging forms of social organization, social values, and ideologies.

As Quincy Wright (17) observed, technology cannot be said to *determine* the character of social orders single-handedly. "The effect of a particular technological invention or importation upon a particular social order depends upon the way in which it is utilized, and that utilization is in large measure influenced by the values and the culture of the social order" (p. 177). But, as he continues, neither are social orders *determined* by human wants, attitudes, ideals, or ideologies single-handedly. "Their effect in a particular social order depends in considerable degree upon the means for their realization which are made available in the existing culture." Social and political scientists recognize "that the emergence of social demands and opinions other than desire for the barest needs of physical life are in considerable measure conditioned by the state of technology. Unless the means of realization are on the horizon, ideas will not spread" (p. 178). As an example, Wright notes that the age-old desire of man to fly did not even attract wide interest until the internal-combustion engine had been invented.

The sweeping organizational and psychological changes which develop throughout historical periods from the interaction of material-technological changes and social forms and values are illustrated in Fromm's *Escape from Freedom* (1). The relevance of such changes for social psychology is apparent in the analysis he presents in this book. It implies alteration in the total conception of personal identity through changes in modes of production, ownership, and appropriate social organization. It is summarized here to suggest the importance of such analysis in understanding the social aspects of man's "nature" and its changing character.

During the Middle Ages, dominated by a feudal system and an all-embracing Church, the great majority of people in Europe were serfs—wretchedly poor and barely able to subsist. As parts of the feudal organization and children of the Church, on the whole, they experienced solidarity and security in a psychological sense. But they had no clear experience of themselves as distinct individuals. "Medieval society did not deprive the individual of his freedom, because the 'individual' did not yet exist; man was still related to the world by primary ties. He did not yet conceive of himself as an individual except through the medium of his social (which then was also his natural) role. He did not conceive of any other persons as 'individuals' either" (p. 43).

The gradual breakdown of the medieval feudal system, according to Wright (17) was hastened by the invention and utilization of the *gun* and *printing press* and accomplished by the Industrial Revolution. During the process, national states were formed and various religious formations independent of the Church arose (Protestantism). As Fromm points out, fundamental changes were brought about both in social organization and in psychological conceptions of self. The Industrial Revolution was carried out under private ownership and created a newly strengthened and propertied bourgeois class. As a rising capitalist or as a *petit bourgeois* or as a worker whose labor became a commodity to be hired, the individual came to experience individuality. But, owing to the highly competitive nature of the social organization, both among capitalists and among laborers, and the profound changes in human relationships it necessitated, the new individuality brought also the experiences of *insecurity, insignificance,* and *aloneness.* In Fromm's words: "While competition was certainly not completely lacking in medieval society, the feudal economic system was based on the principle of co-operation and was regulated—or regimented—by rules which curbed competition. With the rise of capitalism these medieval principles gave way more and more to a principle of individualistic enterprise. Each individual must go ahead and try his luck. He had to swim or to sink. Others were not allied with him in a common enterprise, they became competitors, and often he was confronted with the choice of destroying them or being destroyed" (p. 61).

REFERENCES

1. Fromm, E. *Escape from Freedom.* New York: Rinehart, 1941.
2. Hallowell, A. I. Some psychological aspects of measurement among the Saulteaux, *Amer. Anthropol.* (1942), 44:62–77.
3. Hunter, M. *Reaction to Conquest, Effects of Contact with Europeans on the Pondo of South-Africa.* London: Oxford University Press, 1936.
4. Kolb, J. H., and Brunner, E. deS. *A Study of Rural Society, Its Organization and Changes.* Boston: Houghton Mifflin, 1935.
5. Lang, O. *Chinese Family and Society.* New Haven: Yale University Press, 1946.

6. Lewis, O. The effects of White contact upon Blackfoot culture, *Monogr. Amer. Ethnolog. Soc.* (1942), 6.
7. Lewis, O. Tepoztlan restudied: A critique of the folk-urban conceptualization of social change, *Rural Sociol.* (1953), 18:121–134.
8. Linton, R. *Acculturation in Seven American Indian Tribes.* New York: Appleton-Century, 1940.
9. Malinwoski, B. *The Dynamics of Social Change, An Inquiry into Race Relations in Africa.* New Haven: Yale University Press, 1945.
10. Ogburn, W. F. *Technology and the Changing Family.* Boston: Houghton Mifflin, 1955.
11. Opler, M. K. The Southern Ute of Colorado, in R. Linton (ed.), *Acculturation in Seven American Indian Tribes.* New York: Appleton-Century, 1940.
12. Sayles, L. R. A case study of union participation and technological change, *Human Organiz.* (1952), 11:5–15.
13. Sherman, M., and Henry, T. R. *Hollow Folk.* New York: Crowell, 1933.
14. Tresselt, M. E. The influence of amount of practice upon formation of a scale of judgment, *J. exper. Psychol.* (1947), 37:251–260.
15. Tresselt, M. E., and Volkmann, J. The production of uniform opinion by nonsocial stimulation, *J. abnorm. & soc. Psychol.* (1942), 37:234–243.
16. Webb, W. P. *The Great Plains.* Boston: Houghton Mifflin, 1936, pp. 270–318.
17. Wright, Q. Modern Technology and the World Order, in W. F. Ogburn (ed.), *Technology and International Relations.* Chicago: University of Chicago Press, 1949.

CHAPTER **21**

Men in Critical Situations

The orderliness and stability of human relations and norms regulating them are not static in an absolute sense. They do not "stay put" permanently. Frustrations, deprivations, and aspirations of individuals; new technological devices introduced within the group or from out-groups; increased intergroup give-and-take through military, economic, political, and cultural interaction—all tend to bring about changes in the norms, structural arrangements, and practices of groups.

Even in relatively stable times, interaction within groups produces gradual changes which may not be readily perceptible. But in times of widespread and intensive interaction within and between groups, changes become easily visible to the naked eye. Interaction that is out-of-the-ordinary from the point of view of daily routine is referred to as *collective behavior*. In Chapter 10 we discussed collective behavior of rather short duration aroused by extraordinary events like a disaster, explosion, intergroup riot, or revival meeting. In events like these, we noted reactions which are different from daily, routine behavior.

Sudden and lasting changes in norms and behavior in groups are products of interaction in critical situations brought about by prolonged mass deprivation, prolonged mass insecurity, mass frustrations of various kinds. In time, critical situations are conducive to collective interactions which continue beyond one episode. The significance of such collective interaction is missed if we concentrate on behavior exhibited only at one point in the sequence. The behaviors exhibited during a given flare-up of interaction acquire their significance when their antecedents and the subsequent reactions stemming from them are examined.

When studied against the background of the motives of participating individuals and of prevailing sociocultural, political, and technological conditions, apparently discrete and irrational behavior exhibited during intense interaction acquires coherence. If we do not stop at merely noting extreme, emotional types of behavior but follow through the sequence of interaction, we usually find new and orderly forms of behavior stabilizing which express changes in social structure and the appearance of a new set of values or norms.

Like all collective interaction, interaction in a crisis situation has some focal aspect(s) (see pp. 345–352). When the focal aspect is brought into the picture, behavior in one episode ceases to appear rational, irrational, noble, or base in its own right. Items of behavior acquire significance in the light of the focal aspect, which gives a goal-directed character to collective interaction. Interaction in social movements and their extreme forms, namely, revolutions, has this goal-directed character. We can discover the directions by following the sequence of events rather than concentrating wholly on moments of extreme uncertainty, confusion, and violent flare-ups.

In determining the focal aspect of collective interaction, motivational influences (mass deprivation, frustration, insecurity) are certainly crucial. But motivational influences do not function independently of intellectual (cognitive) influences and external conditions. Prevailing ideas and beliefs, the degree of their hold on people at the time ("cultural lag"), the degree of certainty or uncertainty of the situation and hence the number of available alternatives for its resolution all come into the picture. The wider the scope of crisis and social unrest and the longer the duration of interaction episodes, the greater the dependence of intellectual, motivational, sociocultural, and political influences on one another. In the pages to follow we shall present a brief discussion of these functional relationships in collective interaction phenomena which produce marked changes in social norms and practices.

Behavior in Critical Situations

Our times have witnessed great mass deprivation and insecurity owing to prolonged unemployment, the most catastrophic of all wars in human history, economic and political unrest, and all of their products. The bitter products are hunger, lack of shelter and fuel, and a prevailing sense of insecurity and anxiety in all nations throughout the world today. Of course, an adequate analysis of these conditions goes far beyond the bounds of social psychology. As social psychologists, we can deal only with their effects on individuals and groups. These circumstances are changing men; and men, in turn, are changing the course of society. Even in less tempestuous times and societies, human deprivation is an important factor in bringing about culture change. This is apparent in the recently accumulating accounts of ethnologists. For example, Linton concluded from detailed study of various tribes in the process of transition: "Imperfections of cultural adaptations result in individual discomforts and dissatisfaction and these, in turn, provide the motives for cultural change" (15, p. 467).

Let us look briefly at some examples of collective interaction focused on alleviating deprivations. The specter of hunger knows no boundaries. We saw it in Austria in the period following World War II, where strikers carry a huge self-explanatory poster (Fig. 21.1). The unrest and the inevitable collective protest cut across age levels. In Figure 21.2 we see aged Parisian women demonstrating for more bread. In times of severe frustration and deprivation, the behavior of ordinarily civilized individuals may regress. Several news correspondents accompanying the advancing American armies in early 1945 reported mass looting of fuel and food by the usually well-disciplined German civilians (20). When the German city of Essen fell to the Allies in April, 1945, the troops "found the streets full of drunken civilians" (17). In the same city, Essen, as in many other places in postwar Europe, the typical human level of regulation of human relations in terms of a code of morals sank to a low ebb under the grinding impact of mass deprivation and frustration. In 1947 the mayor of Essen, Dr. Gustav Heinemann, stated: "There is no crime wave. People are just trying to live" (27). But human individuals do not live in such a state of "normlessness" for long. As soon as they get on their feet by securing the essentials of living, they stabilize themselves again with a code of ethics and other norms in various aspects of their lives.

Prolonged insecurity or continued threats of danger produce extreme forms of collective behavior. Right after the explosion of the atomic bomb in Hiroshima, some of the survivors tried to find refuge in a park. When it started to rain, a panic spread like wildfire: "The Americans are dropping gasoline. They're going to set fire to us!" (13, p. 52). In the tense and unsettled atmosphere of postwar Japan, a false radio announcement of the approach of a sea monster upset the people of Tokyo. "Tokyo was thrown into an uproar early tonight when a series of radio bulletins announced that a 20-foot-high sea monster was advancing into the center of the city. . . . Japanese police put out an alarm through all police boxes between here [Tokyo] and Yokohama. The number of Japanese telephoning for

FIG. 21.1. Mass deprivations impel people to collective unrest.

FIG. 21.2. Mass movements cut across age levels.

confirmation or denial was estimated in the thousands" (6). Such panic behavior is not the peculiarity of the Japanese psychology alone. During the tense days preceding World War II, thousands of people in the New York area were thrown into mass hysteria by Orson Welles' realistic radio presentation of H. G. Wells' play depicting an imaginary invasion by Martians (4). Similarly, reports of "flying disks" in the sky throughout the United States in recent years coincided with the intensification of war talk.

In such situations of real or apparent danger, uncertainty, or deprivation, thousands and even millions of people face the same fate *simultaneously*. Facing such situations in common, people cannot help sharing their experience, and this sometimes leads them to collective action of varying proportions. Of course, there are situations in which individually we face real or fancied dangers, insecurity, or deprivations. If these individual cases are numerous, they eventually have an impact on the life of the community. In this discussion we are interested in the impact of danger, insecurity, and deprivations which descend upon masses of people *simultaneously*.

Crises, Extreme Behavior, and Stabilization in Time

Critical situations, as represented by conditions of prolonged deprivation or insecurity, tend to break down, in varying degrees, established attitudes and modes of social behavior regulated by them. Under the impact of crisis, men become unusually susceptible to the acceptance of new formulations, whether or not these new formulations afford objective and lasting solutions. This fact is usually referred to as the increased *suggestibility* of the individual in critical situations. From Le Bon on, authors dealing with collective behavior have given detailed descriptions of the heightened "suggestibility and credulity of crowds" (e.g., *14*, pp. 34 ff. and 44 ff.).

Out-of-proportion predictions of what lay ahead, exaggeration and dramatization of what actually happened are vividly reported in Sinha's recent study of the reactions of people who had just lived through a catastrophic disaster (26).

In June 1950, Darjeeling, a beautiful 7000 ft. high hill-station in the Himalayas, with a population of 33,634 (1951 census provisional figure), suffered one of the worst disasters in its history. There had been landslides before, but nothing like this had ever happened. Loss of life and damage to property were heavy and extensive. . . . In the town itself houses collapsed and victims lay buried under the debris. For over two days, rain poured incessantly down the hill slopes which continued to loosen and slide. Collapsed houses and landslides lay across the roads, and mud flowed everywhere. . . .

Over a hundred and fifty persons lost their lives in the district, about thirty of them in the town itself. Over a hundred were injured. More than two hundred houses were damaged, and over 2000 people were rendered homeless. Refugees poured into the town from the outlying districts with tales of woe and misery [26, p. 200].

"Credulity had increased considerably. Statements were mainly believed without any desire to verify them" (26, p. 205). Observations of people were in the form of "a house had come *rolling down*" (26, p. 208). Distorted perceptions were rampant. "People reported, when they first saw Mt. Everest, that 'it had changed its shape,' that 'it appeared higher,' and that 'it was not as tapering and pointed as it used to be.' These cases of distorted perception strengthened and corroborated the rumours" (26, p. 209).

Under critical conditions men behave in ways which deviate markedly from the customarily expected modes of reactions prescribed by the prevailing norms of the social setting in question. Out-of-the-ordinary behavior thus produced, such as licentiousness, sadism, or, conversely, self-sacrifice or heroism, has been described in dramatic terms by various authors.

There is danger in stressing *only* the dramatic aspect of behavior in crisis situations. The analysis has to be extended longitudinally to include the consequences of the prolonged critical situations as well as the underlying conditions. If critical conditions, which may involve deprivations like hunger, insecurity concerning one's status or one's very identity, etc., are prolonged and affect masses of people, the end result is not chaos or perpetual continuation of extreme modes of behavior but the rise and standardization of new norms for human relationships and conduct. To toss around in the unstable fluidity of crisis is painful, especially after the initial stage of excitement has subsided. Man has to relate himself to his fellow men and to nature around him in some sort of established order. He tends to carry out the urgent business of living within the framework afforded by some relatively stable constellation of relationships. What we know about ego development and ego functioning leads us to posit the hypothesis that man strives to anchor himself securely within a frame of human and natural relationships; that an established constellation of such relationships is the basis of his personal identity; that his feeling of security, his freedom from anxiety depend primarily on being stably placed and on his experience in such a constellation of relationships (Chapter 17).

The end product of interaction in a crisis situation usually is the standardization of a new set of values, which, in time, become established as regulators of the new order of things. A glance at any revolution, successful or not, will convince one that it is the end product of more or less widespread critical tension experienced and shared by at least a part of the population. As Heberle aptly stated, "The rise of social movements in a society is a symptom of discontent with the existing social order. . . . Genuine social movements, as we have defined the concept, aim at changes in the social order" (12, p. 454).

In revolutionary situations, besides wholesale indictments of things opposed by the aroused crowd, there invariably arise crystallizations which express the cherished values of the proposed order embodied in appropriate *slogans*. Of course, this does not mean that the values and norms embodied in the slogans of a social upheaval will always bring about lasting stability. As Heberle stated, "The chances of an idea's becoming part of the creed of a mass movement depend not so much upon its intrinsic value as upon its appeal to the interests, sentiments, and resentments of certain strata and other groups" (12, p. 14). They may be solutions or values offered by powerful demagogues like a Mussolini or a Hitler. In such cases, of course, the crisis situations take new forms and even become intensified when viewed in a long-range perspective.

In terms of single individuals, such precarious solutions may reduce the individual to an automaton or to a regressed level. For example, individuals under the stress of chaotic conditions and precarious day-to-day existence may seek the protection and security promised by an all-powerful leader like Hitler. In such cases, as Fromm indicated, existence and security are obtained at the cost of individual autonomy (9). Henceforth, the values of the individual are handed down by the authoritarian leader. Security achieved through this kind of submission is not conducive to the formation of an autonomous ego, which is achieved through the person's own experiences in interpersonal and group relationships (see pp. 596–598).

As we have stressed in various contexts, the breakdown of established material and social moorings is painful for individuals whose psychological functioning on a higher cerebral level is not impaired (see pp. 600–602). The tendency is to reëstablish oneself with some degree of stability in a real or fancied way. Especially if individuals facing an unfortunate common lot are situated so that they can interact as a group toward alleviating their plight, some sort of group structure arises, determined by the peculiarities of the circumstances. Such group formations give the members a basis for an established personal identity and for a course of action directed toward relieving their plight within the framework of the newly emerging group. Group formations embodying some form of status hierarchy, mutual loyalties, and responsibilities among the downtrodden, wretched, and outcast demonstrate this fact, even though they may be precarious structures and may appear amorphous from outside (Chapters 5-6).

The more usual and consequential outcome in chaotic times is that many people are compellingly attracted by the formulations or slogans of the *leaders* of organized groups. These are the times when wretched people turn to the crystallizations of the pressure groups, even though their appeals may be merely demagoguery.

SOCIAL MOVEMENTS

Collective interaction and other activities contributing to a social movement are not usually affairs that occur within a few episodes. Their scope extends far beyond face-to-face encounters of a given number of individuals. The sequence of events may stretch over a long period and in some cases is taken over by a new generation of individuals. The national liberation movements in various countries under colonial rule in Asia and Africa, the rise of new religious sects in the United States, the labor union movements in industrialized countries are examples.

Social movements represent formative processes arising from some unrest, from some threat, deprivation, or aspiration keenly experienced by rather large numbers of individuals. The involvement in varying degrees of a large number of individuals in the same unrest, threat, deprivation, or aspiration is characteristic of social movements. If a small number of individuals band together because of a common motive but do not make appeals for a wider circle of adherents and followers, we have a group or organization of some kind. But such groups and organizations are not referred to as social movements.

A social movement is always possessed by a sense of mission. Underlying the sense of mission there is a message, a formula, a platform to be propagated with zeal to a class of people, to people in a certain age bracket or income bracket. There are also social movements whose platforms cut across such social demarcations and are proposed on a wider, all-embracing

Fig. 21.3. Collective action in a national liberation movement. Moroccan nationalists demonstrate their protests.

scope. Social movements centered around the virile ideologies of our times are examples of social movements whose platforms are of this all-embracing type.

General Characterization of Social Movements

A SOCIAL MOVEMENT IS A FORMATIVE STAGE: A social movement, then, is a formative stage of interaction in human relations. It expresses an ongoing process. It consists of attempts of a number of individuals or groups to propagate and give organizational form to a specific religious, social, political, or economic platform, or an all-embracing ideology.

If the attempt is successful, the social movement becomes established as a religious sect, a labor union, a political party, or a government. The American government, the French government, the Russian government that came into existence after successful revolutions began as social movements. The British Labour party was a crystallization of the Fabian movement into an organized agency seeking power. Protestantism and its various denominations were the outcome of a number of attempts to assert the new individualism which came into being as a consequence of budding "free enterprise" commercialism.

A social movement, then, is the term applied to the formative stage of attempts to realize a formula or a platform of action. If the attempts are successful, the movement is appropriately named in terms of the organization achieved. For example, it is then a government, political party, religious sect, or labor union. It is apparent that a social movement can best be understood as an ongoing trend.

MOTIVATIONAL BASIS IN SOCIAL MOVEMENTS: There is a small group of torchbearers in every social movement. The torchbearers are a necessary part of a social movement. They keep issues alive and in the foreground; they serve as catalyzers of emotion and action. Nevertheless, torchbearers are not sufficient to make a social movement, no matter how ingenious and fervent they may be. Social movements that have proportions of some significance are not the synthetic fabrications of a select elite, as Nietzsche or Carlyle would have had us believe.

At the basis of every great social movement and social upheaval there is unrest and discontent suffered simultaneously by a large number of individuals in one segment of the population (e.g., aged persons, people in a given profession, or a socioeconomic class) or by the majority of people in a country. Underlying the commonly experienced unrest or discontent, there may be lack of the essentials of living (food, shelter, clothing).

Underlying the unrest or discontent, there may be mass unemployment or inflation. There may be exploitation, oppression, or subjugation suffered at the hands of a ruthless ruling class or aristocracy. There may be the humiliation and indignity inflicted by foreign occupation or colonial rule. There may be widespread insecurity in people's social bearings or in relation to an uncertain future. Or, the motivational basis of the unrest and discontent may involve a combination of some or all of the deprivations, frustrations, and insecurities mentioned above.

In order to handle certain social movements, special mention should be made of real or induced *threat* experienced by a segment of people with common interests as a motivational basis. This inclusion is suggested by Heberle's discussion of "conservative" movements (*12*, pp. 50–62). During recent centuries people in established political and financial positions felt threatened by the rising tide of liberal and socialist movements and organizations. They launched their own movements and establishments to turn the tide from the threatening directions. In Heberle's words, "The old ruling classes rallied their forces in various kinds of groups and proceeded to the counter-attack in every field of social action. To speak of conservatism as a social movement is therefore not at all so paradoxical and contradictory as it would seem. In the course of time, the conservative movement received reinforcement from these elements of the bourgeoisie which found themselves content with the socio-political positions which they had reached" (*12*, p. 37). One good illustration is the strengthened royalist movement in France which utilized the disillusionment and misery of people during the decades following Napoleon's downfall.

SOCIOPOLITICAL MATURITY AND LEADERSHIP: Commonly experienced unrest and discontent prompted by frustration, deprivation, threat, insecurity, or blocking of widening aspirations are essential, but not sufficient in themselves, for the spread of a social movement. It can hardly be said that the Americans were more oppressed than peoples in other colonies at the time of their uprising for independence.

A social movement involves geographical distances and requires communication among the discontented and the aspiring. It involves the conception of prevailing conditions in a coördinated way. This becomes possible after a good many of the people in the same predicament develop a certain degree of intellectual and political maturity. When this stage is attained, people become more responsive to the communications, speeches, and exhortations of the torchbearers who constitute the leadership of the movement. We shall presently return to this point (pp. 732–735).

The leaders furnish an analysis of the situation. They formulate or specify an ideology containing their particular brand of explanation for problems and solutions which, explicitly or implicitly, states the values adhered to and the goals sought. They give short-cut expression to grievances and to the insufferable state of things. On the positive side, they write the articles of the platform to be achieved and short-cut formulas, viz., *slogans*, of the aspired-to goals. These formulations and slogans serve the purpose of giving definite structure and direction to the confusing yet goal-directed character of critical times. The declaration of human rights of the French Revolution, "The Unanimous Declaration of the thirteen United States of America," and the Soviet slogans at the time of the Russian Revolution are among the outstanding examples of such formulations.

COMPOSITION OF A SOCIAL MOVEMENT: In spite of the common motivational basis, all individuals psychologically involved in a social movement do not constitute a group. A social movement spreads from a nucleus. The nucleus consists of a group of individuals, who are committed in varying degrees to the same mission and who stand in definite status and role relations to one another. Around this nucleus, which increases its membership in time, there may be a large number of followers and sympathizers who may fluctuate in their interests. It becomes useful, therefore, to distinguish a social movement from an organized body like a church, a labor union, or a political party (*12*, p. 10).

If the unrest is sufficiently widespread, different and even rival nuclei may spring up, each contesting for supremacy in leading the movement. This seems to have happened in the American Revolution, in the French Revolution, and in the development of labor movements in various countries.

DEFINITION OF A SOCIAL MOVEMENT: Extracting the main points mentioned above, a definition of a social movement may be advanced: A social movement consists of a pattern of attempts through pronouncements, literature, meetings, and direct actions to establish or maintain a definite scheme of human relations and values prompted by a state of common unrest, common discontent, or common aspirations of a large number of individuals.

Social Movements Vary in Scope and Motivational Basis

The general characterization of social movements presented in the preceding paragraphs is extracted from the study of social movements of various scope and kind. It can be applied to social movements prompted by a circumscribed motivational basis and consequently limited in scope. Attempts to secure old-age pensions or to establish a new sect are examples of social movements of limited scope. Attempts to establish a new order during revolutionary periods or to form a new independent nation are illustrations of social movements with all-embracing scope.

The motivational basis and objective of a social movement may be limited to one or a few specific demands such as securing a certain wage level, or an old-age pension, or the franchise for women. In such cases the character of the movement and the *strategy* adopted are evolutionary. When the unrest and discontent are prompted by a wide range of motives (political, social, economic), the scope of the social movement permeates the population—as exemplified by great periods of transition. Then the social movement and the strategy adopted sometimes acquire revolutionary character (cf. 12). The American, French, and Russian revolutions and the great national liberation movements like the Turkish, Indian, and Indonesian independence struggles are good representatives of this type of great upheavals.

Some Illustrations of Social Movements

To make the points under discussion more concrete, we shall glance briefly at few social movements of limited scope. We shall not expand these illustrations. They embody the main features of collective interaction elaborated in Chapter 10. Relatively more space will be devoted in this chapter to brief presentations of great social upheavals and change in attitudes brought about by them. We shall not pass value judgments on these movements but simply report them against the setting from which they arose.

Even social movements of limited scope and objectives arise typically in rather unsettled, fluid settings or under extraordinary conditions such as depression, unemployment, and "war hysteria."

There was a series of such movements following the formation of the United States as a nation. One that developed into open conflict was the Whiskey Insurrection of 1794 in western Pennsylvania (24, pp. 2–20). Especially in the four western counties of the state people were hard hit by an excise tax on the distilling of whiskey, which constituted the main source of their livelihood. In that area the common gripe was why should people "meekly accept the imposition of a tax from a government that, after all, had done very little for them" (24, p. 3). One person hit by the law expressed the grievance in a petition as follows: "Why we should be made subject to a duty for drinking our grain more than eating it, seems a matter of astonishment to every reflecting mind."

This grievance found open and threatening expression in protest meetings at Brownsville, Washington (Pa.), Pittsburgh, and other places. The tax collectors in that area were tarred and feathered. Within a year various "Democratic Societies" were formed as action agencies to do away with the detested tax. The federal government restored order by force. The tax collection resumed its ordinary course. The insurgents were pardoned. Similar uprisings prompted by tax issues took place in that still formative, fluid period of the country (e.g., Frie's Rebellion in eastern Pennsylvania).

The business depression of 1893 gave rise to a number of spontaneous collective-action episodes throughout the country. The unrest culminated in the Commonweal movement, the high point of which was Coxey's march on Washington (24, pp. 86–91). "To focus the attention of Congress, and of the country at large, on the plight of those suffering from the depression, Coxey planned a march of the unemployed to Washington. The original army starting from Massillon, Ohio, gave the Cleveland administration little cause for worry. Conditions were such, however, that Coxey's idea quickly spread, and other armies were organized. Many hundreds of men started from remote points in the west" (pp. 87–88).

After the "boom and bust" following the First World War, the 1930's were pregnant years for the appearance of all kinds of social movements. The future was uncertain for an overwhelming majority of people in all walks of life. Mass unemployment reached unheard-of proportions. Many banks were ruined. Poverty reigned over a substantial proportion of the populace. Many able persons with doctor's degrees were willing to get employment as elevator operators and at other odd jobs. It was a heyday for demagogues as well as earnest leaders to launch new movements.

In this period, people were increasingly responsive to the appeals of their leaders and also to the appeals of demagogues fishing in the troubled waters. It was the fertile period for the rise or strengthening of various social movements. Abroad Hitler and Mussolini were riding roughshod over peoples. These were the years when both technocracy, which meant delegating the run of human affairs to a select group of technicians, and "Share the Wealth" slogans recruited some following. The period was marked by the appearance of all kinds of sects promising soothing havens to the insecure, the unemployed, the dejected. At the same time democratic movements with long-range plans and wide scope flourished.

In this period of socioeconomic insecurity, poverty, and confusion, the plight of old people was doubly insufferable. Even at relatively more normal periods in Western countries, the coming of old age is marked with an increased sense of insecurity and insignificance creating all sorts of ego problems. The spread of poverty and uncertainty to younger age levels rendered the plight and the psychological state of old people even more unbearable.

Therefore, when Dr. F. E. Townsend officially launched his old-age pension plan on New Year's Day, 1934, it aroused wide resonance. It spread like wildfire. By 1935 the Townsend movement was strong enough to hold a massive political rally in Chicago—a city quite a distance from the home headquarters of Dr. Townsend in southern California.

Townsend knew the plight of the old people from first-hand experience. He was in that age bracket himself, and he too was unemployed. He had seen old women pick scraps out of garbage cans to secure some nutrition (4). After expressing his indignation over the state of things, he could boil down the goals to a few essential items: "(1) All citizens of the United States, sixty years old or over, shall receive a monthly pension of $200. (2) Every person accepting this monthly pension shall agree under oath to spend it within the boundaries of the United States within thirty days. (3) The pensions will be financed by a two per cent tax on all business transactions" (p. 171). The measure proposed under item (2) was supposed to provide sufficient business activity to keep the wheels of industry running. This proposal had some appeal value to younger people unemployed at the time.

Becker (3) traced the development of a German youth movement called the Roamers around the turn of the century, its influence on adult-sponsored "tutelage" organizations, and ultimately the adoption and transformation of the movement by the Nazis into an official youth organization. The early movement sprang up among middle-class adolescents caught in conflict between "a dizzy whirl of social change" created by the rapid industrialization and political expansion of Germany during the latter nineteenth century, the middle-class values it nourished, and the surviving norms of feudal and peasant life (see 3, chap. 3). Although the movement had only a hazy program and even gloried in its "aimlessness," it attracted youth who longed "for new experience and emotionalized reciprocity with those sharing the same romantically rebellious mood" (p. 97). In their hikes into the country, informal clothing, glorification of folk culture, these youth found refreshing release from the contradictions, restraints, and conventional values of the adult world in close comradeship with others of their own kind and age.

Shortly before World War I, this youth movement consisted of numerous cults and clusters offering formulas representing almost every political, religious, and social doctrine of the time. They united in a loose kind of confederation. With World War I and the deepening crises of the twenties, disillusioned, deprived, and searching youth flocked in large numbers to youth groups, both those in the movement and conventional adult-sponsored organizations. By this time almost all youth groups had been affected in some degree by the youth movement. Most adopted the garb, folk activities, and romantic trips it featured. The leadership of the movement itself grew older. Along with a number of other political and religious groups, the Nazi party made active efforts to incorporate youth groups into its party organization. Success was found through utilizing forms of the youth movement with the appeal for German solidarity and rejuvenation which held such potent attraction to the disillusioned and frustrated youth of the time. In the process, the movement was effectively transformed into an integral part of the Nazi organization. In spite of its slogans of "Youth shall be led by youth" and its emphasis on "leadership training," the Hitler Youth was an integrated and subordinated part of the parent organization. After the Nazi seizure of power, all youth groups were brought under the control of the State Youth Organization.

MUSHROOMING OF SECTS: One of the interesting spectacles of our age is the mushrooming of diverse sects, especially in large cities like Los Angeles, Chicago, Philadelphia, New York, Paris, or Berlin. These large cities are full of sects promising security and a place in the sun to millions of men and women suffering inferior status or segregation, tossing in uncertain social bearings, anxiety-ridden because of confusion and bewilderment as to what tomorrow holds in store. The meeting announcements in newspapers of large cities make interesting reading. One discovers there all kinds of esoteric sects and other formations. Millions of people without stable social moorings desperately try to find some anchorage to achieve a sense of security. They may throw themselves at almost anything that appears promising. Every great city has its special Bohemias, each fostering its brand of formation consisting of artists and intellectuals trying to find an *escape* from a harsh and crass world.

Because it is a successful representative of other such collective formations, we shall briefly sketch the Kingdom of Father Divine. The Kingdom existed before the great crash of the 1930's. Until then the followers were chiefly lower-class Negroes. The early recruits found in the Heaven a place where they were not considered inferior. Father was preaching equality of status for all and was promising its fulfillment through his Heaven. It was more than the free banquets that lured the followers prior to the thirties. As Harris states, followers "say they came to Father because they were poor, they were Negroes and thought they were inferior, and because they knew that through all their whole lives long they would have no hope of being anything but inferior. . . . They knew they could not attend the same schools as white people attended and did not expect to be allowed to attend those schools. They knew they could not hold the same jobs as white people held and did not expect to hold those jobs. Therein, they tell today, lay the tragedy of their frustrations—*not in what they did not have but rather in what they could not expect*. It was not the reality of their lives that was so unbearable. It was the hopelessness behind the reality" (*11*, p. 27, italics ours).

Father Divine himself knew well the bitter experience of being treated as an inferior. As a young man he had held odd jobs for 50 cents a day. After long years of unsuccessful attempts at proving himself as a man of mission who could alleviate human ills, Father Divine came to establish a Heaven which provided in word and deed, *within its rather narrow confines*, an atmosphere of equality, an atmosphere of intimacy for the spontaneous expression of the burdens of heavy hearts, and, too, a place where the destitute could enjoy abundance of food and the luxury of a clean bed. Father Divine developed the ritual, hymns, frantic testimonials all carried out in collective interaction, all conducive to the convergence of experience and emotion on the focal figure of all their blessings, i.e., himself.

With the great depression the Heaven enlarged its activities. White followers entered the Kingdom. In the midst of deprivation, frustration, insecurity, Father Divine's Kingdom became an island of brotherhood, abundance, and comfort. In those days, about 5000–6000 people were fed through the abundance that Father provided within the bounds of Father's Heavens. Hundreds of destitute people were staying in the Divine dormitories.

In short, Father Divine's appeal was inclusive of body as well as soul. The Heaven operated an employment agency. The unemployed followers were taken care of. In return, those who already had jobs or obtained jobs were to turn over to Father at least part of their earnings.

For the angels, Father is all, and all is in Father. What they can hear, what they read, the associations they enjoy are all circumscribed by Father. They even acquire more heavenly names upon entering the Heaven. Earthly human relations, such as husband-wife, parent-child roles of the angels (followers) are to be subordinated to "brother" or "sister" in Heaven roles. All authority, love, and blessings emanate from Father. Father is a retributive force against any offenses to the Heaven.

As mentioned before, Father Divine's Heavens are only a few of the hundreds of sects that mushroomed under the conditions of frustration, insecurity, and perplexity of modern times.

CRYSTALLIZATION OF NEW VALUES IN GREAT SOCIAL MOVEMENTS

Intellectual Aspect in Social Change

In this section we shall consider briefly some social movements with broad scope and motivational basis. In their train, such movements bring profound changes in human relations and in social, political, economic, and, at times, religious attitudes of man.

As we mentioned earlier, the wider the scope of crisis and social unrest and the longer the duration of interaction episodes, the greater the weight of intellectual aspects in the propagation, organization, and execution of a social movement. The great religions of the world and the epoch-making revolutions in great transition periods are products of social movements of this kind. Therefore, we shall briefly discuss the role of intellectual influences before continuing the account of great social movements.

A great social movement does not drop suddenly out of nowhere. It forces its way against heavy odds. Tradition is pitted against it. And tradition does not just fade to a pale shadow while new trends overwhelm it. Tradition (established values or norms) is a part of the people. Tradition defines what people are and what they should be. People feel at a loss when their beliefs are questioned or rejected unless they gain new beliefs to hold to which define their new bearings. Hence, every significant social movement is born with a rationale for its existence. This rationale is its ideology. Short-cut expressions of its goals and strategy are formulated, usually expressed in clear-cut platforms and slogans (25). So in every great social movement some intellectuals are part of the leadership. They may be at the pinnacle of leadership, or they may directly inspire the organizational torchbearers with their analysis and formulations. Jefferson, Lenin, and Gandhi are examples of intellectuals who have played significant roles in social movements.

A great social movement does not take place in one locality in a day or a week, or in a few disjointed skirmishes and protest meetings. It simmers; it seeks expression and fulfillment over wide areas of human congregation and through years of ebbing and flowing tides. To be effective, a social movement requires a vision that integrates and coördinates various part processes of the broad unrest over a time span. Individuals with commensurate intellectual breadth and training who stake their personal fates on the fate of a social movement perform these functions.

Breaking loose from what prevails as customary, established, and respectable is no mean feat. Unless events have become highly fluid and unstable, making them malleable for shaping the new trend, taking a public stand on the side of what is new and unfamiliar brings a deluge of correctives upon a person's head.

Not many people can stand to be or to remain on the unpopular side of the fence, to carry the painful labels of "unsound," "crackpot," or even worse. Taking such a position requires men and women who can see with clarity and unwavering inner conviction a vision of a shape of the future and who can make this vision central in an integrated system of personal values.

An intellectual aspect is a necessary part of every significant social movement in formulating a platform and an ideology and in coördinating organization. Some of the intellectual leaders may emerge from the ranks of people who are most deprived, most frustrated in the social unrest. But there is no necessary correlation between the amount of frustration and the composition of leadership. Some leaders of great social movements have not come from the most deprived and frustrated segments of the population. These were men who tied their lives with those of people whose aspirations represented the new developing trend.

For example, Thomas Jefferson, Benjamin Franklin, Patrick Henry, and Tom Paine, who gave clear formulations to the American unrest for independence, were such men. It cannot be said that all these men were among the most frustrated of people on the Atlantic coast at that time. They were men who were especially influenced by the writings of the French *philos-*

ophes (7, 8, 22). The "social contract" ideas of Rousseau and the formulation of Locke were paramount in their visions.

The political philosophy of the chief author of the American Declaration of Independence, Thomas Jefferson, was (in the words of Parrington) "an amalgam of English and French liberalisms, supplemented by the conscious influence of the American frontier" (22, p. 343). The experience with the frontier had developed attitudes in Jefferson and his followers that made them particularly susceptible to the works of the French and English writers mentioned above (7, 22). Parrington describes Jefferson as springing from a society deep-rooted in an agrarian economy, a society he wished to preserve. "Born on the Virginia frontier, he had never seen a hamlet as large as twenty houses before his eighteenth year, his neighbors and associates were capable and vigorous frontier democrats, who managed the affairs of local government with the same homespun skill that went to their farming" (22, p. 345). It is not a coincidence, therefore, that the notions stressed by Jefferson were particularly acceptable to people along the frontier, through whose support he was elected President in 1801. Likewise, the torchbearers of the French Revolution were men well versed in the writings of the French *philosophes*, Voltaire, Montesquieu, Diderot, Rousseau, and others.

The leaders who gave a lucid formulation to the American aspirations for independence were men who knew British liberalism and the parliamentary system best and who, at the same time, had a close feel for the free and adventurous scene of the frontier. A somewhat similar parallel is found in the case of national liberation movements of more recent history. Some of the leading men in the long and heartbreaking independence movements, like Gandhi and Nehru in India, and Sokarno in Idonesia, were people who got their education in the very civilization against whose colonial policies they took their stand. Having been educated in England and Europe, they developed to claim for their own people the very human rights for freedom and development that the best thought in England and Holland proclaimed at home. Having seen the imperfections as well as the virtues in the home bases of their colonial masters, these leaders developed convictions in the equal potentialities of their people of India, Indonesia, and other countries.

In America, many of the individuals who are most actively participating in the movements to improve the status of Negroes and other underprivileged groups are physicians, lawyers, teachers, and other professional people who have been in closest contact with the intellectual life in the larger society (cf. *12*). As Wilson Record (*23*) stated in his analysis of intellectuals in social and racial movements: "One of the most notable characteristics of interracial cooperation movements is that they are composed primarily of intellectuals from both racial groups. . . . It is they who define the problems with which such movements will be concerned, and determine the techniques and strategies which will be followed" (p. 237). "They are substantially above average in educational attainments" (p. 238).

The periods of great social movements, like the rise of a propertied bourgeois class, the rise of modern industrialism, the Renaissance, the Reformation, and various revolutionary eras, are the times of most rapid social change. In these times, new values appeared, spread, and became established to regulate the new orders of human relationships.

Events during such periods of momentous social change seem to justify the formulations outlined in this chapter pertaining to great social movements. The American Revolution, the French Revolution, the Paris Commune, and the Russian Revolution are the best testing grounds for conceptualization of the psychology of social change. Since a book on social psychology is not the place for a detailed analysis of these momentous events, we shall restrict the discussion to the American and French revolutions.

The American Revolution

The intensification of the spirit of self-government and liberty among the colonists in the decade or so preceding the outbreak of the American Revolution was the product of the characteristic imperial attitude and conduct toward colonies. This characteristic attitude of the British oligarchy of the time has been summarized by the Beards as "the almost universal belief in England that the colonies were subordinate socially and intellectually as they were politically and economically" (*2*, p. 87). Hence, "the permanent subordination of the colonies to the interests of the British governing classes" was the generally accepted policy.

Whereas this attitude of the British ruling class did not meet active opposition *in the politically, intellectually, and economically less-developed colonies at that time*, it was opposed by the American colonists. Eighteenth-century Englishmen found these colonists "of a disposition haughty and insolent, impatient of rule, disdaining subjection" (quoted in *18*, p. 3). They had achieved political maturity. They had managed their local affairs through their legislative assemblies to a large extent. They saw themselves politically on a par with their English brethren. This attitude was expressed by George Mason of Virginia: "We claim nothing but the liberty and privileges of Englishmen, in the same degree, as if we had still continued among our brethren in Great Britain" (*18*, p. 168). Likewise, the American colonists were making rapid strides, on a domestic and international scale, in agriculture and commerce. "American business and agricultural enterprise was growing, swelling, and beating against the frontiers of English imperial control" (*1*, p. 201).

On the other hand, the British mercantilists saw no reason for altering their established course in relation to the colonies—in fact, no "impropriety in consigning the Western Hemisphere to a position of perpetual economic inferiority" (*18*, p. 5).

The bills curtailing colonial trade and the enactments of the British Parliament levying taxes caused serious discontent and resentment among different sections of the colonial population. The Royal Order of 1763 "reserving to the King the disposal of Western lands beyond a certain line" and the Sugar and Currency acts of 1764 were among the curtailments imposed upon the colonists. These and other grievances were destined to find glowing expression in the Declaration of Independence:

> Prudence, indeed, will dictate that Governments long established should not be changed for light and transient causes; and accordingly all experience hath shewn, that mankind are more disposed to suffer, while evils are sufferable, than to right themselves by abolishing the forms to which they are accustomed. But when a long train of abuses and usurpations, pursuing invariably the same Object, evinces a design to reduce them under absolute Despotism, it is their right, it is their duty, to throw off such Government, and to provide new Guards for their future security.—Such has been the patient sufferance of these Colonies; and such is now the necessity which constrains them to alter their former Systems of Government.

Nor did the business depression following the war with the French which ended in 1763 and which was so costly to the American colonies help matters. "In the swift reaction that followed, inflated prices collapsed, business languished, workmen in the towns were thrown out of employment, farmers and planters, burdened by falling prices, found the difficulties of securing specie steadily growing" (*1*, p. 211). The discontented urban laborers as well as the small farmers provided fertile soil for revolutionary ideas (*18*, p. 54).

The Stamp Act of 1765 "taxing numerous articles and transactions in America" solidified the in-group feelings of the colonists in their grievances against the mother country. For, unlike previous acts, this one hit everyone alike, "from the meanest peasant" to the "wealthy propertied class" (*18*, p. 129). It started a chain of violent mass actions and inspired the convening of the Stamp Act Congress which signaled American solidarity.

Patrick Henry's fiery speech in the Virginia House of Burgesses denouncing the measure found almost universal response in the colonists' hearts. The slogan "No taxation without representation" became the expression of colonial unrest and defined the stand at the time. The British-appointed stamp masters were violently denounced and actually driven out or prevented from carrying out the duties of their office, especially by the Sons of Liberty who began to spring up in all parts of the colonies (see *18*, chap. 6). "Henry had in fact expressed what thousands of colonists were thinking but dared not speak. His resolves dispelled the indecision and doubt which had prevented effective resistance to the Stamp Act; where the Old Dominion trod, the other colonies did *not fear to follow*. The resolves gave 'the Signal for a general outcry over the Continent' and made certain that resistance would be based upon a denial of Parliament's right to tax the colonies. In this sense, they mark the beginning of the revolutionary movement in the American colonies" (*18*, p. 126).

From that time on there was no end to the simmering of the colonial pot. The repeal of the Stamp Act, which soon followed, was hailed as a sign of the achievement of in-group solidarity and created confidence in the efficacy of collective action.

On the other side of the ocean, the British ministry and the Parliament were determined to keep their grip on the colonies. This determination was expressed in such acts as the Declaratory Act of 1766 "asserting the supremacy of the British Parliament in making laws for the colonies" and the Tea Act of 1767 "regulating importation of tea in British dominions in America in favor of the British East India Company." Such acts were not to be accepted any longer by the colonists, who were committed collectively to the principle of "no taxation without representation" and to defiance of laws not enacted by their own assemblies. The overwhelming attitude of defiance gave rise to a wave of collective outbursts, such as the Boston Tea Party, which spread like wildfire to other colonies. These actions were considered by them as being "of absolute moral and political necessity, and therefore exempt from even good laws" (*Virginia Gazette*, March 3, 1774, quoted in *18*, p. 349). Here we see clear instances of the breakdown of the existing rules and norms when they are no longer the cherished property of an in-group in the process of formation. Conversely, here are revealed the spontaneous acceptance and observance of new norms when they are products of the interaction of the newly emerging reference group.

The coercive acts to which the British resorted to keep peace and order, as they conceived these qualities, precipitated new and more violent conflicts between the opposing parties, such as the Boston Massacre of March 5, 1770. As the intensity of the crisis grew, the contending groups became immersed in the self-righteousness of their own cause and deeds and were prone to accept wholesale even the most exaggerated imputations concerning the other's conduct. Here we see another instance of the formation of negative attitudes when the functional relations between groups produce conflict (pp. 285–286).

In this tense atmosphere, colonial solidarity and a possible course of action were focalized in the first Continental Congress, which brought together representatives of the aroused colonies. In the prevailing uncertainty and vacillation, the radical elements were veering in the direction of a clear-cut course for independence, at first without success. But the population, with the exception of some of the gentry, was so aroused that pursuit of the course advocated by the more radical elements in the Congress was inevitable. The fateful series of events which culminated in the Declaration of Independence was motivated by this "surge of revolutionary temper from below." As the Beards concisely summarized the situation: "Strictly speaking, the movement for the break with Great Britain was spreading upward from the colonies to the Continental Congress, rather than downward to the colonies from the Congress" (2, p. 106). This spirit was expressed in Joseph Hawley's letter to Samuel Adams on April 1, 1776: "The People are now ahead of you, and the only way to prevent discord and dissension is to strike while the iron is hot. The People's blood is too hot to admit of delays. . . . All will be in confusion if independence is not declared immediately" (18, p. 485). This observation is an indication of the important functional relationship of *leadership-membership* roles in social movements. As we have already said (pp. 215–219), *leadership* stands in a definite functional relationship within the given hierarchy of a movement. A movement may be initiated at the outset by a handful of determined leaders who know the discontent and restlessness of the people to whom they appeal. But once the movement starts to acquire a definite leader-and-membership structure and gets under way, the leader is no longer free to stop or alter the course of action as his whims dictate. If he does, he is cut off from the movement, loses his position, and, at times, attracts the wrath of the erstwhile admiring members. In short, the leader leads as long as he understands the basic objective of the movement, keeps pace with it, and has foresight in charting its direction.

The crisis in America had gone too far to be settled by ordinary methods of discussion within the limits of cold logic. The popular movement was too active to be retracted; it would subside only after positive gains. "During the winter of 1774–1775, the 'menaces of blood and slaughter' which reverberated through the New England countryside became increasingly ominous. New Englanders were clearly preparing to take full advantage of the approval placed upon a defensive war by the Continental Congress; and, if the British troops ventured far from Boston they might well expect a warm reception from the Yankees" (*18*, p. 398).

The outbreak of open revolution thus awaited a relatively minor incident. And on April 18 and 19, 1775, at Lexington and Concord, "the shot heard round the world" provided that incident, and the clash became open. It is psychologically noteworthy that the identity of the group which fired the first shot is still a source of controversy. In the tense atmosphere of crisis in the 1770's, the incident might well have occurred at another spot and on another day on the American coast wherever the aroused antagonists faced each other. People—stirred, moved, restless—cannot remain in the agony of suspense forever. One way or another, the tension has to be resolved.

In the clash of the two groups, the Americans emerged as a distinct sovereign group with its own structure and definite in-group and out-group delineation. Before this distinct group or national entity found formal expression in the statutes, it shaped itself psychologically in the hearts of the people. In the course of events, "the mother country began to appear in American eyes as a foreign, despotic and 'Papist' power" (in the words of General Thomas Gage; see *18*, p. 374).

All of this found clear-cut crystallization in the resounding words of Tom Paine's *Common Sense* in January, 1776, and in the Declaration of Independence, which sums up the situation. In these documents, which were eagerly seized upon by the people as their own, the Americans found a glowing formulation of the thoughts and aspirations they were striving to express. These documents took the bull by the horns and removed the last vestige of doubt and vacillation. "Before *Common Sense*, Americans had professed to reverence the British Constitution and had declared that they were defending their own liberties and the rights of the King against the usurpation of Parliament. But Paine's attack upon the principle of monarchism struck at the very foundations of the British Constitution and largely destroyed its sanctity in the eyes of Americans. Its abuses and short-comings were now laid bare in order to persuade the colonists of the necessity of independence; the beauties which Americans had once beheld in it withered under the blasts of Tom Paine and his fellow propagandists" (18, p. 469).

The slogans that arose and became crystallized in the tense atmosphere of crisis, such as "Life, Liberty, and the Pursuit of Happiness," were destined to be the source of new established values which henceforth became the regulators of experience and conduct and, in time, solidified the cultural terrain of the new *status quo* and respectability.

On the one hand, the fact that the colonists were predominantly English in culture and language made it hard for them to take the fatal stand against the mother country and especially the Crown, which was perceived as a symbol of unity with their past. On the other hand, the very fact that they shared in the English culture and were politically conscious of representative government (unlike other colonies at the time) contributed to the rise of a leadership willing and committed to fight for their "inalienable rights." When the final break came in word and deed, there were still groups who could not make the move in line with the revolutionary upsurge. There were groups who vacillated. It was too big a jump to make in terms of their existing mode of life and their system of norms. These conservative and vacillating groups, as Miller tells us in his *Triumph of Freedom* (19), changed sides back and forth as the fortunes of the long-drawn-out war changed. *For many of the vacillating and opposing groups, the compelling hand of events unfolding became the decisive factors which determined the nature of their lasting attitudes on the issue.*

The French Revolution

The French Revolution which came into the open in 1789 constituted an epoch-making social transition and upheaval. The values that emerged as brilliant torches in the midst of crisis, violent collective action, bloodshed, and counterrevolution came to be the regulators of social relationships not only in France but also eventually in many other countries. Here we can mention only the bare essentials.

On one side, there was the growing influence of the propertied middle class, which was acquiring a dominant position in industry, commerce, etc. On the other, there were the decadent privileged aristocracy and the remnants of feudalism, with their survival trimmings. The existing setup cf rules and values did not express this social reality. There was no longer any correspondence between economic and social realities and the superstructure of norms and etiquette. The inevitable clash was long in the making. In the words of Mathiez, perhaps the greatest authority on the subject, the French Revolution "arose from the ever increasing divorce between reality and law, between institutions and men's way of living, between the letter and the spirit" (*16*, p. 1).

Consequently, the prevailing values of the day, which were products of feudal times and the heyday of the rule of aristocracy, rapidly lost their hold on great masses of people. Even long-entrenched religious values "no longer had any attractions" (p. 13). On the *intellectual side*, the writings of Voltaire, Diderot, Rousseau, and others had been doing the spadework for a new revolt against the worn-out institutions and modes of human relationships. The innovators were destined to win the day (p. 3).

The living conditions which rendered life intolerable in the years just preceding 1789 brought the conflict to a head. A few concrete instances of these conditions, which become more meaningful against the general background of social relationships characterized briefly above, will make the picture of crisis more clear. For example:

At Abbéville there were 12,000 workmen unemployed, at Lyons, 20,000 and the numbers at other places were in proportion. At the beginning of the winter, which was a very hard one, it was necessary in the large cities to organize workshops supported by charity, especially as the price of bread was constantly rising. The harvest of 1788 had been much below normal. The shortage of forage had been so great that the farmers had been forced to sacrifice part of their cattle and to leave some of their lands uncultivated, or else sow it without previous manuring. The markets were short of supplies. Not only was bread very dear, but there was a risk that it would run short. . . . The wretched people cast covetous glances upon the well-filled barns in which their lay and ecclesiastical lords stored up the proceeds of their tithes and their rents in kind [p. 34].

The counterpart of this critical situation in terms of single individuals is expressed by Taine in describing the plight of a peasant of the time:

I am miserable because they take too much from me. They take too much from me because they do not take enough from the privileged classes. Not only do the privileged classes make me pay in their stead but they levy upon me ecclesiastical and feudal dues. When from an income of a hundred francs, I have given fifty-three and more to the tax collector, I still have to give fourteen to my seignor and fourteen more for my tithe and out of the eighteen or nineteen francs I have left, I have yet to satisfy the excise-officer and the salt-tax-farmer. Poor wretch that I am, alone I pay for two governments—the one obsolete, local, which is today remote, useless, inconvenient, humiliating, and makes itself felt through its restraints, its injustices, its taxes; the other new, centralized, ubiquitous, which alone takes charge of every service, has enormous needs and pounces upon my weak shoulders with all its enormous weight [10, p. 39].

The collective action as an inevitable consequence of the clash of interests and the widespread deprivation faced by masses of individuals *simultaneously* in this critical situation is exemplified in the outbreak in Nantes. It typifies similar outbreaks throughout France and indicates the direction of the Revolution: "The rising was directed not only against those who were speculating in foodstuffs, against the old system of taxation, against internal tolls, and against feudalism, but against all those who exploit the populace and live upon its substance. It was closely connected with the political agitation. At Nantes the crowd besieged the Hotel de Ville with cries of 'Vive la Liberté' " (10, p. 35).

The great slogans such as "Liberty, Equality, and Fraternity," which moved millions of people to feeling and action during the eventful days of the Revolution, and the declaration of the rights of man, which crystallized the values of human relationships in the new era, remained as the established values for decades to come in spite of counterrevolutions and other events.

A fascinating study of the psychology of social change could be made, based on the great social movements and the critical conditions and events unrolling in our day. This would enable us to bring together all of the positive findings of social psychology concerning motivation, attitude change, group emergence, and action as they actually operate in human interaction under the out-of-the-ordinary circumstances of crises.

REFERENCES

1. Beard, C. A., and Beard, M. R. *The Rise of American Civilization*. New York: Macmillan, 1930, Vol. I.
2. Beard, C. A., and Beard, M. R. A *Basic History of the United States*. New York: New Home Library, 1944.
3. Becker, Howard. *German Youth: Bond or Free*. London: Kegan Paul, Trench, Trubner, 1946.
4. Cantril, H. *The Invasion from Mars*. Princeton: Princeton University Press, 1940.
5. Cantril, H. *The Psychology of Social Movements*. New York: Wiley, 1941.

6. Chapman, R., in the New York *Herald Tribune*, May 30, 1947.
7. Commager, H. S. *The American Mind.* New Haven: Yale University Press, 1950.
8. Curti, M. *The Growth of American Thought.* New York: Harper, 2nd ed., 1951.
9. Fromm, E. *Escape from Freedom.* New York: Rinehart, 1941.
10. Gottschalk, L. R. *The Era of the French Revolution, 1715–1815.* Boston: Houghton Mifflin, 1929.
11. Harris, S. *Father Divine: Holy Husband.* New York: Garden City (Perma-book ed.), 1954.
12. Heberle, R. *Social Movements: An Introduction to Political Sociology.* New York: Appleton-Century-Crofts, 1951.
13. Hersey, J. *Hiroshima.* New York: Knopf, 1946.
14. Le Bon, G. *The Crowd.* London: T. Fisher Unwin, 1914 ed.
15. Linton, R. *Acculturation in Seven American Tribes.* New York: Appleton-Century, 1940.
16. Mathiez, A. *The French Revolution.* New York: Knopf, 1929.
17. Mecklin, J. (reports to the newspaper) *PM*, 1945, March and April.
18. Miller, J. C. *Origins of the American Revolution.* Boston: Little, Brown, 1943.
19. Miller, J. C. *The Triumph of Freedom.* Boston: Little, Brown, 1948.
20. New York *Herald Tribune*, April 2 and 3, 1947.
21. New York *Times*, April 12, 1945.
22. Parrington, V. L. *Main Currents in American Thought.* New York: Harcourt, Brace, 1927, Vol. I.
23. Record, Wilson. Intellectuals in social and racial movements, *Phylon, The Atlanta University Review* (1954), 15:231–242.
24. Rich, B. M. *The Presidents and Civil Disorder.* Washington: The Brookings Institution, 1941.
25. Sherif, M. The psychology of slogans, *J. abnorm. & soc. Psychol.* (1937), 32:450–461.
26. Sinha, D. Behavior in a catastrophic situation: A psychological study of reports and rumours, *Brit. J. Psychol.* (1952), 43:200–209.
27. Unsigned article, Morals, *This Week Magazine*, New York *Herald Tribune*, August 10, 1947.

VII

PRESENT-DAY SOCIAL PSYCHOLOGY

A Glance at Social Psychology, Its Backgrounds and Present Trends

This chapter gives a brief glimpse of the historical background of social psychology, with the aim of appreciating better some of the important trends in its development. The rest of the chapter concerns (1) current social issues and social psychology and (2) major trends in present-day social psychology. These major trends are the use of scientific methods and techniques, achieving the necessary perspective for overcoming ethnocentrism, and the study of social behavior within a framework of interacting influences.

THE BACKGROUND IN A GLANCE[1]

Development of social psychology as a scientific study belongs to the modern historical period. But theories of social behavior and solutions for problems of social relationships are found in the grand literature of philosophy, history, jurisprudence, politics, and economics of past centuries. This literature from great writers reflects the glories and also the limitations of the times and conditions in which it was written. Plato in his *Republic* and Aristotle in *De Oratore* and *Ethics* and *Politics* dealt with topics of interest to social psychologists. St. Augustine pondered on man's sinful nature and on authority. Machiavelli sketched both theory and practical means for rulers to attain power, to manipulate groups and rivals. At the dawn of a changing world, Sir Thomas More envisioned his *Utopia* of harmonious human arrangements.

As the modern period approaches, we find theories and solutions which

[1] The reader who is particularly interested in historical precedents and developments in social psychology can consult the works of Murphy (46), Karpf (29, 30), Cottrell and Gallagher (14), and F. H. Allport (3).

crystallized as established viewpoints of various groups. Some have the status of "fact" in the realm of twentieth-century "common sense." With the rise of a flourishing capitalism in mid-seventeenth-century England, Hobbes wrote of man governed by self-interest, with fear his strongest motive—a man forced to form commonwealth if only to avoid destruction by other self-interested men. A similar view is heard even today as a popular picture of human nature and society, as is the eighteenth-century view of Bentham and other British empiricists of social behavior dominated by man's conscious search for pleasure and avoidance of pain.

In a period of groups seeking guides to freedom from the historic rights and tyrannies of feudal kings, John Locke pictured a creature of reason and forbearance who could live and govern in free association. In continental Europe, Jean Jacques Rousseau, sickened by a social world permeated with a decaying aristocracy, turned his back with an impassioned plea for a return to an "innocent" man in a beneficent nature. He saw man's efforts to govern himself fulfilled in the form of a "social contract" in which consensus of the governed was the key. The image of man sketched by Locke and Rousseau and their like shone in the minds of the men who wrote the Declaration of Independence in the American colonies.

The possibility of bringing social behavior within the realm of science was envisioned in various countries during the years following the French Revolution and the Napoleonic Wars. In France, Auguste Comte (1790–1851) set about to sketch outlines of a science of society. Disturbed at what he saw as the disorganized state of social arrangements, Comte turned to a study of society, which in his later years appeared to him and his sect-like followers as almost a revered personification.

In England the grandiose efforts of Herbert Spencer to achieve a "synthetic philosophy" dawned in the closing years of Comte's life in the second half of the nineteenth century. Immersed in the atmosphere of a triumphing colonial power, Spencer saw the evolutionary process as a "struggle for existence" in which individuals with superior force, intellect, and achievement triumphed in accordance with a law of "survival of the fittest." Starting with such biological analogies, he drew parallels first to human individuals and then to the evolution of societies, the result being that colonialism appeared as a natural outgrowth of evolutionary forces. Spencer's speculative work gained importance from Darwin's writings on biological evolution and was highly influential at the time in the United States as well as in England and continental Europe.

In Germany, Lazarus and Steinthal became interested in the "folk mind," in the differences in mental processes in various communities and nations. Their journal, founded in 1860, sought to further such study through individual psychology, in contrast to the approach of Comte and those who followed him in revering an almost omnipotent culture. Wundt, who has been termed the father of experimental psychology, became interested in such studies, believing that analysis of language provided a key to the psychic constitution of social groups.

More influential in shaping the immediate background from which modern social psychology has emerged were the writings of Tarde and Le Bon in France. Tarde sought to give a psychological explanation to social phenomena through the concept of imitation. In his *Laws of Imitation* (1890), he stated flatly that "Socially everything is either invention or imitation" (56, p. 3). In short, social behavior and relationships were to be derived from individual functioning. Le Bon likewise approached group processes through individual phenomena, especially inspired by studies on hysteria and suggestibility by the French psychiatrists Charcot and Liébeault. In his famous book *The Crowd* (1895), he showed how the individual became changed through the influence of a crowd or mob, which he viewed as a super-organism or beast to be feared (33).

At this point, the work of Freud as it relates to social psychology should be noted. Although his writings on social psychological topics came much later, largely after World War I, Freud's work and development of psychoanalysis began in the 1880's. From start to finish, psychoanalytic theory was individual-biased. Even the study of man in group life "can be nothing other than applied psychology" (24, p. 245). Interested in Le Bon's work on crowds, Freud took the further step toward individual explanations by rejecting Le Bon's observation that the crowd is responsible for the fact that the individual behaves one way in its presence and differently when alone. The "apparently new characteristics" shown by the individual in crowd situations were to Freud merely the manifestation of his "unconscious, in which all that is evil in the human mind is contained as a predisposition" (23, p. 10).

Before the end of the nineteenth century, the French sociologist Emile Durkheim was using empirical findings within a framework of theory (17, 18, 19). He contributed the notion of "collective representations," or social ideas, values, or social norms, which he correctly insisted could be studied in their own right (16). He enunciated the notion of "exteriority," namely, that social values or norms are at first external to the individual member of society. The influence of Durkheim's work is still appreciable in the United States, as evidenced by the recent editions of his works. It should be noted, therefore, that Durkheim further maintained that society exercised its influence in the form of "constraint." The morals and ideals of everything good in man thus became a direct product of society. The consequence was that Durkheim's view of individual-group relationships was one-sided, the emphasis being on the group, even as others mentioned above emphasized the individual side.

Developments in the United States

Influences from evolutionary sources, from German individual psychology, from both German and French sociology are evident in the works of early sociologists and psychologists on social psychological topics in the United States. Views reflecting one-sided emphasis on the individual and views emphasizing the group and society were developed and expanded by different authors. These simultaneously current views have persisted in systematic and text books on social psychology until recent decades. But even during the early development of psychology and sociology in the United States, views which were incompatible with one-sided emphasis on the individual or on the group were being shaped. While these early developments are not solely responsible for the shape of present-day social psychology, the overall view of individual-group relationship and many important insights and concepts are derived from these earlier works in psychology and sociology.

In his *Principles of Psychology* (Volume I, 1890), William James sketched a picture of the "social self" which influenced concepts of socialization for generations (28). At Princeton University, James Mark Baldwin was studying and observing children. Especially in his *Mental Development in the Child and the Race* (1895), Baldwin showed how the individual's notion of self emerges in the dialectic interaction between the individual and other persons (8). This work of Baldwin's, like much of James', is neglected today probably because of other views it contained which have since been discredited. For example, the "recapitulation theory" espoused by Baldwin, that child development parallels in general fashion the development of the species, is now regarded as a crude analogy. However, his name deserves a clear place in the history of social psychology. The works of James and Baldwin were among the influences on contemporary and later writers, including Cooley and Mead in the United States and Piaget abroad.

Charles H. Cooley developed the concept of self upon a firmer basis of sociological realities in his *Human Nature and the Social Order* (13, 1902). Both he and George H. Mead had a considerable influence on the development of social psychological thought. Mead began teaching a course on social psychology at the University of Chicago as early as 1900. He called his approach "social behaviorism." However, it had little in common with the behaviorism of John Watson, whose work epitomizes the term in psychology. Mead's approach was a social-psychological one, emphasizing in particular the distinctive role of language in the emergence of self identity, which he saw as dependent on social interaction (43, 44). Because Mead did not bring his ideas into one volume during his lifetime, his influence was largely through lectures and the work of students. The influence of Cooley's and Mead's writings did not become dominant in social psychology, especially among academic psychologists. Perhaps one reason is that their keen insights were not stated in terms of a concrete program of research and experiment. Attempts in this direction have been made in recent years.

Among the early sociologists, the name of William Graham. Sumner should be mentioned. His *Folkways* (55, 1906) was widely read and influential. Sumner emphasized the consequences of customs, traditions, mores in group life, and wrote of the tendency of groups to see and evaluate others from their own viewpoint (ethnocentrism). A group cherished by members was characterized as an "in-group," while other groups were regarded as "out-groups." Sumner suggested an inevitable tendency for in-group members to react against out-groups, tracing this negative reaction to a "fear of the strange," which he considered well-nigh universal. Sumner gave great weight to the power and enduring character of folkways. Thus his work contributed to the popular notion that "you can't legislate folkways," which has been a justification in retarding social legislation.

The first books with "social psychology" in their titles both appeared in 1908 (41, 52). One was written by E. A. Ross, a sociologist influenced particularly by Tarde and Le Bon, and one by William McDougall, the British psychologist. Both were widely read, probably McDougall's being more popular because of its colorful style and more systematic character. Against a background of evolutionary thought, McDougall started with the problem of instinct and emotion. Thus, he dramatized the problem of motivation, of irrational or organic aspects of behavior for a psychology which was, at the time, highly intellectualized.

Instincts were seen as innate tendencies of the individual predisposing him to perceive and strive in certain ways and accompanied by appropriate emotions. Social instincts—for example, gregariousness—were included. The fusion of instincts resulted in "sentiments." The view was exceedingly popular for a time in both psychology and other fields. Its weakest point, the doctrine of social instincts, was attacked both by psychologists, like Dunlap (15, 1919), and by sociologists, like Ellsworth Faris (21, 1921).

At the close of World War I, W. I. Thomas presented (with Znaniecki) his monumental study of *The Polish Peasant in Europe and America* (57). One significance of this work was its contribution of an empirical study within a framework of sociological and social-psychological theory. Thomas pointed out the relationship between social values, on the stimulus side, and attitudes, which individuals form in relation to social values. General psychology at this time was in fact not much concerned with social influences. Therefore, Thomas improvised psychological concepts, including his four "general patterns of wishes," which he used in support of his ideas on motivation. These four wishes have stood the test of time and research findings no better than classifications based on instinct theory. He called attention to the importance of the ways individuals perceive and evaluate social situations through his concept "definition of the situation." This concept highlighted a crucial problem for social psychology, namely, the shaping of social behavior in terms of the individual's evaluation of a situation.

In 1920 a German psychologist, Moede, published a series of laboratory studies showing the influence of the presence of other people on performance of various tasks (*Experimentelle Massenpsychologie*). In addition the effect of competition between teams and between individuals was studied. At Harvard, Münsterberg had carried on similar investigations. In 1924 F. H. Allport published his *Social Psychology* (1), in which he incorporated his own experiments along these lines within a framework of behavioristic psychology, then in its heyday. Social phenomena were explicitly reduced to matters of individual behavior. The differential effects of groups on performance were dealt with in terms of such concepts as "social facilitation," "increments," and "decrements" to individual performance. This same theoretical orientation was evident in his *Institutional Behavior* (2, 1933). (It should be noted that in recent years Professor Allport has modified his approach and views [4, 5].)

In the late twenties and early thirties a large number of empirical studies were carried out by sociologists and psychologists. The trend was toward empirical measurement, and for some years all sorts of attitudes, the influence of other people on performance in various tasks, and the like were tested in quantitative form, most frequently on a discrete basis with little attempt at theoretical integration. A convenient summary of these studies is found in Murphy and Murphy's *Experimental Social Psychology* (47, 1931), which marked the development of this new area of experimentation.

In sociology, one of the significant empirical developments during this period was a series of studies initiated by sociologists at Chicago, notably inspired by Robert Park, dealing with group functioning and relationships in specific ecological settings. From this research came Nels Anderson's *Hobo* (1923), Frederic Thrasher's *The Gang* (1927), Hiller's *The Strike* (1928), Landesco's *Organized Crime in Chicago* (1929), Zorbaugh's *The Gold Coast and the Slum* (1929), Clifford Shaw's *The Jack-Roller* (1930), *Natural History of a Delinquent Career* (1931), and a number of others.

More Recent Developments

In the years between the first edition of Murphy and Murphy's *Experimental Social Psychology* (1931) and the second edition (with T. M. Newcomb, 1937), a number of influences and trends became prominent which form the immediate background to the converging lines of social psychology today (48).

By that time, psychologists had become more aware of something which sociologists and ethnologists had long known, namely, that cultural factors have a profound influence in shaping individual behavior. The work and theories of Malinowski and Franz Boas and his students were among those which jolted many social psychologists from complacency in drawing conclusions based only on their own social setting. At the same time, the notion of "cultural relativism" gained greater popularity, to the point that it was sometimes considered that cultural forces were nearly all-sufficient in determining individual personalities and behavior.

In 1932, F. C. Bartlett's series of experiments on *Remembering* (9), which had started before World War I, was published. In this work the artificial classifications from traditional psychology separating perceiving, remembering, and imagining were broken down. Throughout, the integral role of the individual's interests, social attitudes, and past experiences in the patterning of experience and behavior was demonstrated. Bartlett was able to show how social-psychological principles valid in one culture could be carried to the study of social-psychological events in other cultures.

Piaget's studies on the development of children along social lines, in particular those presented in *Moral Judgment of the Child*, were translated from French and became known (49, 50, 51). The interplay between social factors, including language, and other influences in individual development was sketched theoretically on the basis of concrete empirical studies of children.

In 1934, the sociometric studies of J. L. Moreno (45) appeared in America, providing techniques for empirical study of role relationships in groups of various kinds. The individual was viewed within a web of personal relationships, and the study of the group and individuals in their interrelationship was emphasized. Since the publication of Moreno's book, studies of role relationships through sociometric techniques have accumulated rapidly.

Another work of this period was *The Psychology of Social Norms* (54, 1936), which brought together findings concerning behavior in groups and societies at a cultural level of study (e.g., Durkheim, Malinowski) and the rapidly developing experimental work on the psychology of perception and judgment to study the ways individuals come to perceive aspects of the world like other members of their social groups. The demonstration of some social factors in the process of perceiving in a strictly laboratory situation utilizing the autokinetic phenomenon resulted in many experiments on social influences in perceiving and judging. In the original presentation of the work with autokinesis (1935), it was stressed that social influence in the experimental situation did *not* represent all types of social influences. In fact, social influences in highly unstructured stimulus conditions typified by the autokinetic situation were presented only after a discussion of varying effects of social stimulus situations. It was noted that at the other extreme there are well-structured sociocultural stimulus conditions (e.g. technological products) in which the effects of social factors like social pressure and suggestion are minimal.

During this period, Kurt Lewin and his associates actively embarked on social-psychological experiments, notably on the effects of different "group atmospheres" on behavior and achievement within a group (36, 39, 40) and later on "group decision" in bringing about attitude change (37). Prior to this time, Lewin had contributed a series of theoretical and research writings. Particularly important were his contributions to child psychology and individual functioning (34, 35). Experiments on setting goals for performance ("level of aspiration") were carried out by his students in Germany and extended by students in the United States influenced by Lewin's work (22, 26). Particularly after this line of research was linked with current experiments pertaining to social factors in judging and perceiving by Chapman and Volkmann, Sears, and others, a body of research developed showing the effects of various social influences in setting goals (*12, 38, 53*).

Thus by World War II, trends were converging in social psychology toward studying social behavior within a frame of reference of interacting influences, in contrast to either an individual-centered or a group-centered emphasis. Social psychologists were at least aware of the fact that findings concerning forms of social behavior could not be generalized blithely from one culture to all others. Further, scientific methods and techniques appropriate for different problems and situations were developed and used by both sociologists and psychologists.

World War II brought large numbers of social psychologists, as well as psychologists and sociologists formerly interested in other topics, face to face with practical problems in social psychology. As Cartwright wrote: "Practical problems of social engineering sprang up over night which required solution before lunch" (*11*, p. 67). In many cases, social psychologists were requested or deeply desired to deliver goods which were not really ready to be delivered, in terms of the development of theory and research at the time. Nevertheless, numerous research programs on problems of civilian morale (including industrial morale), on problems of "psychological warfare," on leadership selection and like topics were carried out under the auspices of government, military, and private organizations.

Since the war, both government and private industry have shown interest in sponsoring research which might prove helpful in terms of their practical problems. These developments have had multiple consequences, among them bringing social psychologists close to the real-life situations which must be the ultimate testing grounds of their theories and hypotheses and involving them to a much greater extent than previously in organizational structures outside of academic life. This state of affairs has brought to the field both the progress and the problems which accompany the granting of considerable means for research agencies outside of academic life, as these affect relations within academic life and the directions taken in research and other activities.

CURRENT SOCIAL ISSUES AND SOCIAL PSYCHOLOGY

In social psychology, the tradition of sharply delineating between "pure" and "applied," between academic aloofness and tangible contact with practical issues of life, seems to have lost its high-handed grip.

This is as it should be. The psychologist does not move in a world of "bare existence" as Titchener would have had him. The supercilious attitude of divorcing pure and applied science is nothing more than an exhibition of aloofness. As aptly pointed out by Julian Huxley, one of the outstanding biologists of our time, sometimes it is not easy to separate what is pure and what is applied even in the physical sciences (27). Was research on atomic energy, for example, pure or applied science?

To begin with, topics of research do not drop down from the heavens on a few exceptional souls. They lie in the trend of the times. For example, the wonderful development of the physical sciences during the past centuries was prompted to a great extent by the demands of a rising business and industry. The really great men of science, like Galileo and Darwin, were men who responded effectively to the call of their respective times.

On the other hand, the temptation to swing altogether in the direction of delivering day-to-day devices and measures in response to demands and pressures of agencies engaged in practical work has become tremendous. Considerable work that is going on in social psychology at present is made to order for agencies and action groups who urgently hope for immediate solutions and prescriptions for more effective handling of their daily affairs.

A concrete idea of the scope of practical demands on the social psychologist can be conveyed by simply citing the kind of work carried out under such conditions. The sponsoring agencies and establishments naturally want short-cut devices to sell merchandise, ready-made techniques of communication to change people's attitudes in this or that direction. They require quick procedures for selecting effective leaders or foremen. They want to raise the morale and efficiency (e.g., productivity) of teams of men through "psychological" means. Some action groups feel impatient with the research man in human relations when they find him cautious concerning immediate cures for reducing prejudice. The feeling of urgency for solutions of practical problems is understandable.

On the other hand, men working in social psychology are interested also in developing a more rounded picture of their discipline, in attaining generalizations which will be valid for the many special cases which are studied at present in their own right and for their own sake.

The area of attitude measurement will illustrate the point. Literally hundreds of items are surveyed for their own sake. Attitudes pertaining to some aspect of the family, other groups, school subjects, religion, a particular social issue, a certain product are studied. The stand (attitude) of given samples of the population in regard to this or that matter is measured, and often such information is used for practical purposes. Sometimes these attitude surveys deliver the goods. An election may be successfully predicted within a few percentage points.

A survey may indicate the best way to advertise and distribute a motion picture. For example, if a representative sample turns thumbs down on the picture, it may be advertised widely and then distributed to the public in many theaters at once. Tickets are sold on the basis of the build-up before the audience has time to go about dropping the word that the picture is not worth seeing. But in many cases, it is not even possible for research men, practical men, or the public to check on the validity of the survey results through the outcome of concrete events.

In spite of all this research activity, it cannot be said that valid principles of attitude functioning are all established so that they can be applied in specific cases. Much basic work is needed on the persistent problems of this area. And these persistent problems pertain to more general topics of psychology—motivation, perception, judgment, the trend of socialization, and the like as these relate to behavior in groups.

When the aim is the advancement of the frontiers of social psychology, the immediate topic at hand becomes secondary. A topic of study and a problem are chosen so that the findings are applicable to much more than the specific issue under investigation. In the long run, the practical value of generalizations thus attained will be greater than piecemeal studies of this or that topic, because their applicability will be more comprehensive.

Basic work guided primarily by long-range theoretical and practical considerations advances, on the whole, at a painfully slow pace. There is place for this kind of work as well as for work prompted by more immediate objectives. These two kinds of investigation act and react on each other with mutual benefit.

When the aim of research is to build up social psychology as an established discipline, two considerations, among others, become important: (1) the formulation of studies in such a way that the results further the understanding of a scientific concept or principle, aside from their possible practical value at the moment; (2) the autonomous selection of a problem by the investigator. The topics which have relevance to persistent problems of a discipline may or may not coincide with those which sponsoring agencies consider important.

THREE OVERALL TRENDS IN PRESENT-DAY SOCIAL PSYCHOLOGY

In sketching the background of social psychology, some notable contributions were cited in broad historical sequence. It can be said that recent accelerated advances in the present formative stage of social psychology are due particularly to three trends of development in the mode of thinking and working of social psychologists:

1. The use of scientific methods and techniques.
2. The achievement of necessary perspective on problems and findings through checks against the ethnocentrism of the investigator himself.
3. The adoption of an approach that studies social behavior within a framework of interacting influences, rather than making either the individual or the group (or culture) the supreme determinant of man's social behavior.

The approach and work of a good many representative social psychologists are converging toward these three trends.

1. The Use of Scientific Methods and Techniques

Until supported by established facts, ideas advanced by theorists are no more than hunches to be tested. The necessity of testing and substantiating ideas and concepts led to the use of various methods and techniques in social psychology. Efforts to devise more refined methods and techniques for obtaining data (including the use of apparatus), and for measuring and manipulating data in quantitative form have been a characteristic activity in the field during recent years. The facts and generalizations in social psychology which are established have been verified through appropriate methods and techniques.

What is the best approach, the best method, the best mode of analyzing data? In terms of the existing state of social psychology, this question can be answered best in relation to how appropriate the particular approach, method, and analysis are to the problem at hand. The best methods and techniques in obtaining data and in their analysis are the ones that are the most effective tools in collecting data and treating results directly relevant to the problem raised and the hypotheses formulated. Since the problems raised and hypotheses tested vary considerably in nature, degree of specificity, and the like, the methods and techniques most appropriate are also bound to differ from one problem to another.

As noted above, no matter how brilliant a theory may appear, it is no more than a hunch until it is supported by evidence established through the use of scientific methods. It is equally true that methods and techniques are not ends in themselves. They are means and tools in answering or solving pertinent and significant problems. When techniques become masters of work in scientific study, especially in an area like social psychology which is still in a formative stage, they are not fulfilling the objectives for which they were devised. This may touch on one reason why established knowledge has not developed at an equal pace with the increasing number of experiments.

Probably far too many experiments in professional journals result from fascination with techniques, rather than fascination with significant problems. Of course, concepts and methods of science are on an "abstract" level. But if the level of abstraction has no bearing on actual events, the results can have no relation to significant and real problems. Concepts and methods in scientific work must refer to genuine problems if the efforts are to count in establishing knowledge in a field.

Many scientists have said that it is only through man's achievement of an outlook and techniques which yield to the run of things in nature that nature has yielded to man the secrets of its working. The first step in yielding to nature is to be able to put appropriate questions to it, that is, to formulate problems to which it will respond. Nature is deaf and dumb to questions which do not bear on its realities. Sometimes questions are asked which are unanswerable and not relevant to nature and human life. As a consequence, what is obtained is frequently an artifact.

In this connection, a statement of two outstanding physicists, Einstein and Infeld, is instructive for social psychology during its present formative stage: "The formulation of a problem is often more essential than its solution, which may be merely a matter of mathematical or experimental skill. To raise new questions, new possibilities, to regard old problems from a new angle, requires creative imagination and marks a real advance in science" (20, p. 95).

But crucial problems that have vital relevance to human relations cannot be drawn out of a hat. Crucial problems can be raised only after a sense of intimacy with the events in a problem area has been achieved. Murphy, Murphy, and Newcomb observed that solid lines of development in social psychology have come from those who first immersed themselves in the subject matter of their study (48).

Achieving the necessary familiarity with the run of events in an area requires an open mind, willing to describe them without preconceived notions, concepts, and modes of explanation. Otherwise, one's own misconceptions and ingrained formulations are imposed from the very start on every twist and turn of events. In short, he becomes not an observer but a partisan both in the choice of events to be noticed and in their explanation. Such preconceptions obstruct the faithful description of events as they occur, which should be the initial step in approaching problems of study.

This first step of getting a faithful, naturalistic picture of events at the start is referred to as a phenomenological approach (42). It consists largely of sheer description for the purpose of understanding events to be studied as they occur. The details of such description are not necessarily reported in the final account of an actual experiment or study.

This step of sheer description on a naturalistic level is only a first step. It helps in raising crucial problems. After raising the problems on this basis or with the support of already established generalizations, one can proceed to use appropriate methods and techniques, which can then serve as effective tools and not as masters of research.

Whenever feasible, the most effective methods and techniques are those used in experimentation. Experimental methods are preferable when and if they can be used without destroying or mutilating the essential characteristics of the problem chosen for study. Experimentation is a controlled kind of observation which allows systematic variation of just the aspect or aspects (variables) crucial to the problem, excluding other aspects or holding them constant.

The sound precaution in social psychology today is to use a *combination of methods* within the same study design whenever possible. For example, suppose we have the hypothesis that if a number of individuals interact with each other (talk, plan, work, etc.) toward goals desirable to all a social group will form in which each individual occupies a position (status) relative to the others. This hypothesis can be tested by placing individuals who are not acquainted with one another in "problem" situations requiring that they all act together to obtain a common goal (for example, preparing a meal when they are hungry). If it can be ascertained that relationships have developed and stabilized, involving each individual in a certain function or position relative to the others, the hypothesis is supported. This might be done by observing their behavior toward each other on several occasions, or by ratings of their relative standing by several observers. We could ask appropriate questions of the individuals (as is done in sociometric assessment). We could present tasks as part and parcel of the situations in which their expectations and attitudes toward others would be revealed through their judgments in the situation. However, if all of these techniques were used in combination, and the results of each technique confirmed the others, we would certainly be on sounder grounds to decide whether or not our hypothesis was correct. (Studies similar to this illustration were reported in Chapters 6 and 9.)

In the last decades, the effectiveness of methods and techniques for a scientific study of social psychology has been greatly enhanced by two other developing trends in the field, which are discussed in the following pages.

2. Achieving the Necessary Perspective

One established finding in social psychology is that what individuals notice or attend to is influenced by their attitudes and other motives. They evaluate objects, persons, and events in terms of standards, values, or social norms which they have assimilated or internalized as their own. This tendency is not peculiar to the members of any particular culture. It amounts to seeing things from given viewpoints and evaluating them from given premises. The major features of these viewpoints and premises are derived from one's own group. This tendency is referred to as *ethnocentrism*.

In many cases, ethnocentrism results in putting one's group at the center of things, as the model or ideal. When this is done, the values, norms, and practices of other groups tend to be evaluated unfavorably because they differ from those of one's own group.

Scientists have not always been immune to distortions and errors due to their ethnocentrisms. At times it has taken many years before biased, or one-sided, or incomplete accounts of a topic were put into proper focus through the efforts of other men who achieved the perspective necessary to see possibilities other than those prevalently conceived in their own cultural or academic group. Since the consequences of ethnocentrism and necessity of avoiding its pitfalls have implications both for theory and for practice, a few illustrations from the history of psychology are to the point.

Topics like "sensations" or "images" would not seem likely subjects for violent controversy. Certainly they do not when compared to "human nature," "prejudice," or other topics around which opinions commonly clash. Yet, in the history of psychology, hot controversy and contradictory research findings were poured on "sensations" and "images." Today these divergent views and findings can be traced to personal commitments of the participants to different scientific in-groups, and consequently to different theories. At Würzburg, Külpe and his students rarely found images; they were believers in imageless thought. Titchener and his students at

Cornell usually found them; they believed that thoughts are composed of images. Commitment to their own group, its theory and laboratory atmosphere decided what they would find and what they would not find (10).

A second illustration of the effects of ethnocentrism relates to a research area which is flourishing today, and strikes closer to home. During the decades 1910–1930 various scholars reported experimental results which seemed to prove that working in groups was inferior to working as individuals. It was sometimes concluded that there was a uniform tendency toward mediocrity in group interaction. During the last 20 years or so, it has been shown repeatedly that interaction in groups may be effective in bringing about changes in the attitudes and practices of individual members in positive and socially desirable directions as well. It is now established that group interaction can result in improving individual performance under certain circumstances. Mediocrity or leveling of performance is not an inevitable consequence of interaction in groups. The results of performance in any particular group depend both on the nature of the task and on the characteristics of the group in question.

The third and last example from many which might be given to illustrate the effect of ethnocentrism pertains to the characteristics of human groupings. In the decades preceding the 1930's, numerous attempts were made to arrange human groups in a hierarchy of supposedly inherent superiority or inferiority. Research results were cited to support the conclusion that certain human groups were inherently inferior in "intelligence," independent of educational and other blessings of their upbringing. The comparative and longitudinal research of Klineberg (31, 32) and others demonstrated that these presumably inherent rankings of various groups were altered under more favorable conditions.

Further, psychologists working in this area became aware that the tests on which various social and cultural groups were ranked as "superior" or "inferior" were standardized on the basis of performance by individuals from a rather narrow segment of the population (usually in the United States) on tasks important to achievement in certain areas of life (often academic). Anastasi has suggested the interesting possibility of standardizing tests using different segments of the population or different cultural groups on the basis of tasks important for achievement in the life circumstances of that group (6). The difference in results which would be obtained emphasizes the futility of ranking groups as innately different on a basis so clearly variable in terms of stimulus conditions. For example, a Draw-a-Man test was standardized on white American children. This might seem a "fair" task for children in any culture but it has not proved to be so. Similarly a Draw-a-Horse test, standardized on the basis of performance by American Indian children, worked to the decided disadvantage of white children. The performance of 11-year-old white children fell considerably below that achieved by the average Indian child.

Such illustrations of the narrowing and distorting effects of ethnocentrism are found in several areas of study. One cannot help finding a substantial grain of truth, therefore, in a concluding statement made by Anastasi and Foley after their extensive survey of "individual and group differences in behavior." "Since all types of behavior are influenced by the subject's stimulational background, it follows that psychological data obtained within any one cultural group cannot be generalized to cover all human behavior. Many statements offered under the heading of general psychology are not general at all, but are based upon human behavior as it develops within a single culture" (7, p. 838).

The social psychologist, as well as the student, has his own group identifications. Every group represents a point of view as it stands in relation to other groups. Every group has its explicit or implicit premises concerning the nature of human relations. From the outset, research and generalizations are doomed to be deflections or mere justifications of the point of view and premises of the group or groups with which one identifies himself, if one does not start his work with clear, deliberate recognition and neutralizing of his personal involvements in these issues. If this painful yet necessary process of deliberate recognition and neutralizing of one's personal involvements and commitments is not achieved, his autisms will greatly influence the design of his study and his collection and treatment of the data. The study design will be such that it is more suited to hit upon data in line with his own involvements. The likelihood of collecting data in a selective way not called for in the explicitly stated propositions will be considerable. If the social psychologist attempts solution of his complex problems without first recognizing his personal involvements as a consciously or unconsciously identified member of a socioeconomic class, as a member of a majority group, or a minority group, or a religious group, or a "school" of thought or "laboratory atmosphere," he may simply contribute his bit to the already existing muddle, and not to the scientific study of social psychology.

The demonstrated effects of ethnocentrism have to be eliminated from scientific work in social psychology if the objective is attaining principles and laws which are valid beyond the bounds of given cultures. There are procedures which can help in this process. These involve checking and cross-checking observations on which hypotheses are based and results of investigations against (1) findings from other cultures and from groups within societies in which life conditions differ, and (2) events occurring in different historical periods.

In actual practice such procedures mean *cross-cultural comparisons* covering as many different cultures as possible, *comparisons among groups within differentiated cultures* in which conditions of life differ significantly, and *historical comparisons* of events within the same culture. For example, if a genteel lady of seventeenth- or eighteenth-century America were to see her great-great-granddaughter of the mid-twentieth century at a beach or actively engaged in what was considered "man's work," she would be astounded as though encountering an entirely different world.

This emphasis on cross-cultural, intergroup, and historical comparisons is not in the least a plea for an unbridled cultural or historical relativism. Cultural relativism notes the fact of observed cultural variations in behavior and social relationships and adds the further unwarranted assumption that principles governing behavior and social relationships have to be derived separately for each culture in its own right. This amounts to a complete denial of processes and capacities common to all members of the human species, to asserting the total determination of behavior by cultural influences, and to reifying social organization (25).

Variations in the behavior of individuals in different cultures and in different historical periods are due to variations in stimulating conditions. They are not due to differences in the principles governing their basic psychological functioning. The members of different cultures do not function according to different psychological laws or principles. The underlying psychological functioning is the same. In fact, these general laws and principles can be attained only on the basis of cross-cultural and historical comparisons.

To take a documented example, adolescence in one culture may be a *relatively* smooth period of transition from childhood to adulthood. In another culture, adolescence may be a period of extreme conflict, stress, and tribulation with serious consequences for the later years of individuals involved. But whether smooth or turbulent, all these variations are due to the operation of the same psychological principles under different specified conditions. Thus the problems faced during adolescence within any cul-

tergroup relations, reference groups, attitude formation and change, ego-involvements, effects of language, technology, crisis situations and social movements (Chapters 4–21).

CONCLUDING REMARKS

In this chapter we have glanced briefly at the historical background from which present-day social psychology has developed. Social-psychological research at present faces the mixed blessing of being "in demand." This trend tends to bring social psychologists closer to the real-life events which must be the ultimate testing ground of their theories. At the same time, it suggests the danger that social-psychological research may become merely technical improvisation of premature answers to urgent practical questions, at a time when persistent and fundamental problems in the field are still to be solved.

Converging trends in the field have been noted which have led to an accelerated development, particularly (1) the use of scientific methods and techniques, (2) attempts to achieve the necessary perspective in theory and research through checks against the ethnocentrism of the investigator, and (3) the trend toward studying social behavior within a framework of interacting influences.

REFERENCES

1. Allport, F. H. *Social Psychology*. Boston: Houghton Mifflin, 1924.
2. Allport, F. H. *Institutional Behavior*. Chapel Hill: University of North Carolina Press, 1933.
3. Allport, F. H. Methods in the study of collective action phenomena, *J. soc. Psychol., SPSSI Bull.* (1942), 15:165–185.
4. Allport, F. H. The structuring of events: Outline of a general theory with applications to psychology, *Psychol. Rev.* (1954), 61:281–303.
5. Allport, F. H. *Theories of Perception and the Concept of Structure*. New York: Wiley, 1955.
6. Anastasi, A. Psychological Traits and Group Relations, in M. Sherif and M. O. Wilson (eds.), *Group Relations at the Crossroads*. New York: Harper, 1953.
7. Anastasi, A., and Foley, J. P. *Differential Psychology*. New York: Macmillan, rev. ed., 1949.
8. Baldwin, J. M. *Mental Development in the Child and the Race*. New York: Macmillan, 1900.
9. Bartlett, F. C. *Remembering: A Study in Experimental and Social Psychology*. Cambridge: University Press, 1932.

10. Boring, E. G. *Sensation and Perception in the History of Experimental Psychology.* New York: Appleton-Century, 1942.
11. Cartwright, D. American social psychology and the war, *J. consult. Psychol.* (1945), 9:67–72.
12. Chapman, D. W., and Volkmann, J. A social determinant of the level of aspiration, *J. abnorm. & soc. Psychol.* (1939), 34:225–238.
13. Cooley, C. H. *Human Nature and the Social Order.* New York: Scribner, 1902, 1922.
14. Cottrell, L. S., and Gallagher, R. Developments in social psychology, 1930–1940, *Sociometry Monogr.,* No. 1. New York: Beacon House, 1941.
15. Dunlap, Knight. Are there instincts? *J. abnorm. & soc. Psychol.* (1919), 14:307–311.
16. Durkheim, E. *Les Formes Elementaires de la Vie Religieuse.* Paris, 1912. Trans. *The Elementary Forms of Religious Life.* London: G. Allen and Unwin, 1915.
17. Durkheim, E. *Les Règles de la Méthode Sociologique.* Paris: F. Alcan, 1895. Trans. *The Rules of Sociological Method.* Chicago: University of Chicago Press, 1938.
18. Durkheim, E. *De la Division du Travail Social.* Paris: F. Alcan, 1893. Trans. *The Division of Labor in Society.* Glencoe, Ill.: Free Press, 1949.
19. Durkheim, E. *Le Suicide.* Paris: F. Alcan, 1897. Trans. *Suicide.* Glencoe, Ill.: Free Press, 1951.
20. Einstein, A., and Infeld, L. *The Evolution of Physics.* New York: Simon and Schuster, 1942.
21. Faris, E. Are instincts data or hypotheses? *Amer. J. Sociol.* (1921), 27:184–196.
22. Frank, J. D. Some psychological determinants of the level of aspiration, *Amer. J. Psychol.* (1935), 47:285–293.
23. Freud, S. *Group Psychology and the Analysis of the Ego.* London: Hogarth, 1922.
24. Freud, S. *New Introductory Lectures on Psychoanalysis.* New York: Norton, 1933.
25. Hartung, F. E. Cultural relativity and moral judgments, *Philos. of Science* (1954), 21:118–126.
26. Hoppe, F. Erfolg und Misserfolg, *Psychol. Forsch.* (1930), 14:1–62.
27. Huxley, J. Science and Its Relation to Social Needs, in *Scientific Progress* (Sir Halley Stewart Lecture). London: Allen and Unwin, 1935.
28. James, William. *The Principles of Psychology.* New York: Holt, 1890.
29. Karpf, F. B. *American Social Psychology.* New York: McGraw-Hill, 1932.
30. Karpf, F. B. American social psychology, 1951, *Amer. J. Sociol.* (1952–53), 58:187–193.
31. Klineberg, O. *Negro Intelligence and Selective Migration.* New York: Columbia University Press, 1935.

32. Klineberg, O. *Race Differences*. New York: Harper, 1935.

33. Le Bon, G. *Psychologie des Foules*. Paris, 1895. Trans. *The Crowd*. London: Fisher Unwin, 1917.

34. Lewin, K. Environmental Forces, in C. Murchison (ed.), *A Handbook of Child Psychology*. Worcester: Clark University Press, 2nd ed., 1933.

35. Lewin, K. *Dynamic Theory of Personality*. New York: McGraw-Hill, 1935.

36. Lewin, K. Field Theory and experiment in social psychology: Concepts and methods, *Amer. J. Sociol.* (1939), 44:868–896.

37. Lewin, K. *The Relative Effectiveness of a Lecture Method and a Method of Group Decision for Changing Food Habits*. Iowa City: State University of Iowa Child Welfare Research Station, 1942.

38. Lewin, K., Dembo, T., Festinger, L., and Sears, P. S. Levels of Aspiration, in J. McV. Hunt (ed.), *Personality and Behavior Disorders*. New York: Ronald, 1944, Vol. I.

39. Lewin, K., Lippitt, R., and White, R. K. Patterns of aggressive behavior in experimentally created "social climates," *J. soc. Psychol.* (1939), 10:271–300.

40. Lippitt, R. Field theory and experiment in social psychology: autocratic and democratic group atmospheres, *Amer. J. Sociol.* (1939), 45:26–49.

41. McDougall, William. *An Introduction to Social Psychology*. London: Methuen, 1908.

42. MacLeod, R. B. The Place of Phenomenological Analysis in Social Psychological Theory, in J. H. Rohrer and M. Sherif (eds.), *Social Psychology at the Crossroads*. New York: Harper, 1951.

43. Mead, G. H. The social self, *J. Philos., Psychol., sci. Meth.* (1913), 10:374–380.

44. Mead, G. H. The genesis of the self and social control, *Intern. Ethics* (1925), 35:251–277.

45. Moreno, J. L. *Who Shall Survive?* Washington: Nervous and Mental Disease Publishing Co., 1934.

46. Murphy, Gardner. *Historical Introduction to Modern Psychology*. New York: Harcourt, Brace, 1949.

47. Murphy, Gardner, and Murphy, L. B. *Experimental Social Psychology*. New York: Harper, 1931.

48. Murphy, Gardner, Murphy, L. B., and Newcomb, T. M. *Experimental Social Psychology*. New York: Harper, rev. ed., 1937, chap. 1.

49. Piaget, J. *Judgment and Reasoning in the Child*. New York: Harcourt, Brace, 1928.

50. Piaget, J. *The Child's Conception of Physical Causality*. New York: Harcourt, Brace, 1930.

51. Piaget, J. *The Moral Judgment of the Child*. London: Kegan Paul, 1932.

52. Ross, E. A. *Social Psychology*. New York: Macmillan, 1908.

53. Sears, P. S. Levels of aspiration in academically successful and unsuccessful children. *J. abnorm. & soc. Psychol.* (1940), 35:498–536.
54. Sherif, M. *The Psychology of Social Norms.* New York: Harper, 1936; also Study of Some Social Factors in Perception. *Arch. Psychol.* (1935), No. 187.
55. Sumner, W. G. *Folkways.* Boston: Ginn, 1906.
56. Tarde, G. *Les Lois de l'imitation.* Paris, 1890. Trans. by E. C. Parsons, *The Laws of Imitation.* New York: Holt, 1903.
57. Thomas, W. I., and Znaniecki, F. *The Polish Peasant in Europe and America.* Chicago: University of Chicago Press, 1918.

INDEXES

Abelson, R. P., 531, 535
Achilles, Paul S., 491
Adams, H. F., 250, 277
Adams, Romanzo, 652, 678
Adams, S., 473, 483
Adams, Samuel, 738
Adler, 372
Adorno, T. W., 666, 678
Aldrich, C. A., 392, 410
Alley, J., 271, 272, 273, 276, 277
Allison, Harry and Sarah, 597
Allport, F. H., 124, 127–128, 129, 131,
    132, 133, 134, 140, 182, 352, 491,
    493, 504, 534, 747 n., 752, 766
Allport, G. W., 95, 96, 114, 511, 534,
    586, 615, 656, 665, 666, 675, 678
Alper, T. G., 131, 132, 142
Ambedkar, B., 673, 678
Ambriere, Francis, 154, 174, 178
Ames, L. B., 396, 410
Anastasi, A., 588, 615, 658, 678, 762,
    763, 766
Anderson, Nels, 172, 178, 753
Ansbacher, H., 157, 158, 178, 417, 443
Arensberg, C. H., 282, 331
Aristotle, 656, 747
Asbury, H., 243, 277
Asch, S. E., 104, 136, 137, 138, 139, 140,
    264, 265, 279, 502, 534, 560, 608,
    615, 689
Atkinson, J. W., 419, 420, 445
Augustine, 747
Ausubel, D. P., 581, 594, 615
Avigdor, R., 300, 331, 654, 678

Back, K. W., 149, 178, 229, 233
Baldwin, James Mark, 750, 766
Bales, R. F., 222, 227, 228, 229, 231, 232,
    233
Barker, R. G., 386
Barnard, C. I., 148, 178
Baron, S. H., 263, 264, 278
Bartlett, F. C., 61, 63, 73, 74, 91–92, 114,
    416, 417, 433, 443, 459, 460, 461,
    483, 586, 753, 766

Barton, R. F., 457, 483
Bass, B. M., 157, 158, 178, 231, 233,
    234
Bavelas, Alex, 545
Bayton, J. A., 653, 679
Beach, F. A., 381, 386
Bean, C. H., 472, 483
Beard, C. A. and M. R., 735, 736, 738,
    742
Beaumont, H., 396, 410
Beaver, A. P., 597, 615
Becker, Howard, 123, 140, 729, 742
Beebe-Center, J., 51, 74
Beethoven, 583
Benary, W., 66, 74
Bendix, R., 633, 645
Benedict, Ruth, 657, 679
Benoit-Smullyan, E., 623, 624, 639, 645
Bentham, 748
Berelson, B., 511, 517, 534, 535, 566,
    569, 575, 576
Berenda, R. W., 139, 141
Bernard, Claude, 382
Berne, E. V. C., 597, 615
Berry, B., 657, 659, 679
Berry, M. F., 477, 483
Bettelheim, B., 666, 679
Bevan, W., Jr., 428, 444
Binet, A., 93, 114
Birch, H. G., 380, 386
Bird, C., 210, 234
Birney, R., 221, 234
Bitterman, M. E., 432, 433, 444
Blake, R. R., 135, 141, 266, 277, 504,
    537, 663, 679
Blankfort, M., 166, 178
Bleke, R. C., 586, 616
Bleuler, M. and R., 99, 115
Block, H., 502, 534
Blondel, C., 340, 360
Blos, P., 642, 645
Blumer, H., 346, 352, 353, 359, 360, 494,
    534
Boas, F., 70, 74, 753
Bodin, 656

Bogardus, E. S., 488, 510, 517, 518, 520, 521, 534, 648, 649, 650, 653, 679
Boring, E. G., 75, 115, 116, 483, 762, 767
Bovard, E. W., Jr., 226, 234, 264, 266, 267, 277
Bowman, P. H., 288, 331, 435, 436, 437, 444
Braly, K., 653, 664, 680
Breed, Warren, 635, 645
Brehm, J. W., 135, 141, 266, 277
Brian, C. R., 397, 410, 465, 484
Bridges, K. M. B., 390, 410, 597, 615
Bronson, W. C., 433, 445
Brophy, I. N., 544, 575, 679
Brown, R. W., 346, 360
Brozek, J., 433, 434, 435, 444
Brummitt, Jessie A., 173, 178
Bruner, J. S., 96, 115, 425, 426, 427, 432, 444, 445, 503, 536
Brunner, E. deS., 705, 713
Brunswik, Egon, 417
Buchanan, J. S., 271, 277
Buchanan, W., 513, 514, 534
Buck, P. H., 457, 483
Buehler, C., 505, 534
Burgess, E. W., 361
Butler, J., 546, 547, 576
Buxton, C. E., 41, 74

Campbell, A. A., 464, 484
Campbell, Donald T., 490, 497, 499, 534, 562, 577
Campbell, D. W., 558, 575
Cannon, W. B., 370, 377, 382, 386
Cantril, H., 149, 180, 204, 208, 342, 360, 402, 411, 494, 501, 513, 514, 516, 534, 536, 586, 594, 618, 634, 647, 719, 729, 742
Carlyle, 724
Carmichael, L., 410, 411, 461, 472, 483, 485
Carroll, J. B., 472, 483
Carter, J. H., 222, 234
Carter, L. F., 157, 158, 178, 212, 221, 231, 234, 426, 428, 444
Cartwright, D., 179, 229, 234, 235, 517, 534, 545, 569, 575, 576, 755, 767
Centers, R., 632, 633, 645
Chaffey, J., 643, 647
Chamberlain, A. J., 470, 483
Chamberlain, Houston, 658
Chamberlain, I. C., 470, 483
Chapman, D. W., 47, 51, 74, 93, 115, 624, 625, 645, 755, 767
Chapman, J., 350, 351, 360

Chapman, R., 719, 743
Charcot, 749
Charters, 638
Chave, E. J., 524, 525, 526, 527, 528, 536
Chein, I., 417, 420, 421, 422, 445, 675, 680
Cherrington, 557
Child, I. L., 644, 645
Chowdry, K., 219, 234
Christie, R., 665, 667, 679, 680
Clark, Lt. B. H., 108, 115
Clark, H., 132, 141
Clark, K. B., 418, 444, 586, 615, 662, 668, 673, 674, 679
Clark, M. K., 662, 668, 679
Clemmer, D., 243, 244, 277, 481, 483
Cohen, Edwin, 572, 575
Collins, M. E., 676, 679
Combs, A. W., 581, 618
Commager, H. S., 734, 743
Comte, Auguste, 748, 749
Considine, R., 446
Cook, S. W., 464, 483, 634, 645, 676, 682
Cooley, Charles H., 148, 751, 767
Cooper, E., 570, 575
Cope, L., 68, 74
Corbin, H. H., 88, 115
Corey, S. M., 498, 534
Cotten, Emmi, 42
Cottrell, L. S., 747 n., 767
Cowles, J. T., 466, 467, 484
Crisswell, J. H., 663, 679
Crown, S., 655, 679
Crutchfield, R. S., 250, 277, 423, 424, 445
Cunningham, R., 211, 234
Curti, M., 734, 743

Dale, E. C., 271, 272, 277
Dalton, M., 238, 277, 627
Darwin, 372, 748, 756
Dashiell, J. F., 124, 129, 131, 141
Davis, H., 662, 681
Davis, J., 592, 615
Davis, Kingsley, 474, 484, 593, 615, 642, 645
Dean, Dorothy J., 224, 225, 234
Dean, John, 668, 673, 679
Dembo, T., 386, 580, 617, 625, 646, 755, 768
Dennis, W., 663, 679
Deutsch, M., 230, 234, 634, 645, 676, 679
Dewey, E., 471, 472, 484

Dickson, W. J., 172, 173, 179, 238, 278, 627
Diderot, 734, 741
Dobzhansky, T., 657, 658, 679
Dodd, S. C., 549, 575, 652, 679
Dollard, J., 459, 485
Doob, L. W., 514, 516, 517, 534
Droba, D. D., 558, 575
Dukes, W. F., 428, 444
Dunlap, Knight, 752, 767
Dunn, L. C., 657, 658, 679
Durkheim, E., 126, 141, 247, 277, 339, 340, 360, 607, 615, 749, 750, 754, 767
Durr, C. J., 566, 575

Eckstein, M., 350, 351, 360
Edwards, A. L., 523, 527, 534, 586, 615
Edwards, W., 250, 277
Egan, J. P., 48–49, 75
Einstein, A., 759, 767
Eisenberg, P., 599, 615
Eisenson, J., 477, 483
Eldersveld, S., 575, 576
Elkin, F., 481, 484
Ellis, W. D., 74, 76
Esterhazy, Prince Paul, 633
Ewert, 109
Eysenck, H. J., 415, 416, 444, 655, 679

Faris, Ellsworth, 71, 74, 752, 767
Faris, R. E. L., 148, 178, 268, 277, 299, 331, 594, 615
Farnsworth, P. R., 136, 141
Fazil, 417
Fearing, Franklin, 564, 565, 575
Feldman, A. S., 351, 352, 361
Feldstein, M. J., 163, 179
Fenchel, G. H., 640, 645
Ferguson, L. W., 527, 535
Festinger, L., 149, 178, 231, 234, 523, 535, 549, 575, 580, 617, 625, 646, 755, 768
Fischer, J. W., 432, 446
Fleck, F. S., 430, 445
Flowerman, S., 563, 569, 575, 577
Foley, J. P., Jr., 658, 678, 763, 766
Ford, C. S., 381, 386
Forlano, G., 527, 536
Fortune, R. F., 69, 74
Frank, J. D., 51, 754, 767
Franklin, Benjamin, 733
Fraser, J. A., 44, 45, 74
Freedman, R., 29, 33, 164, 170, 172, 178
Freidson, E., 563, 575
French, J. R. P., Jr., 226, 234

Freud, S., 157, 178, 339, 340, 341, 360, 372, 386, 594, 615, 749, 767
Freyre, G., 652, 679
Fritz, C. E., 342, 343, 360
Fromm, E., 176 n., 178, 712, 713, 721, 743
Furniss, E. S., Jr., 242, 278

Gage, General Thomas, 739
Galileo, 756
Gallagher, R., 747 n., 767
Gandhi, 733, 734
Garcia, J., 665, 679
Gard, Wayne, 269, 270, 278
Gardner, B. B., 173, 178, 637, 647
Garmezy, N., 586, 616
Gaudet, H., 517, 535, 569, 576
Gellerman, L. W., 397, 410
Gesell, A., 390, 392, 395, 396, 410, 594, 595, 596, 597, 615, 616
Gibb, C. A., 157, 178, 210, 211, 212, 214, 221, 222, 231, 234
Gibson, J. J., 63, 74, 104, 461, 484
Gilbert, G. M., 653, 655, 680
Gilchrist, J. C., 96, 115, 422, 432, 433, 444, 446
Gillen, F. J., 458, 486
Gillin, J. S., 171, 178
Gist, N. P., 244, 278
Gladstone, A. I., 561, 576
Gobineau, Count de, 658
Goldman, I., 593, 616
Goldstein, K., 599, 600, 616
Goldstein, N. F., 653, 659, 660, 680
Goodenough, F. L., 397, 410, 465, 484, 596, 597, 616
Goodman, C. C., 425, 426, 444
Goodman, M. E., 668, 680
Gottschaldt, K., 58, 74
Gottschalk, L. R., 742, 743
Gouldner, A. W., 236
Grabbe, 674
Graham, Billy, 334, 336
Graybiel, Comdr. A., 108, 115
Green, E. H., 597, 616
Greenberg, P. J., 597, 616
Gropper, G. L., 433, 445
Guetzkow, H. S., 232, 234, 288, 331, 435, 436, 437, 444
Guilford, J. P., 651, 680
Guillaume, P., 470, 484
Gulliksen, H., 48, 74
Guttman, L., 521, 522, 535

Haddon, A. C., 658, 680
Haggard, E. A., 425, 444

Hallowell, A. I., 70, 72, 74, 450, 484, 690, 713
Hamilton, Sir William, 88
Hammond, K. R., 506–507, 509, 535, 585
Harding, J., 675, 676, 680
Hare, A. P., 123, 141, 229, 236
Harlow, H. F., 381, 386
Harris, R. E., 464, 483
Harris, S., 731, 743
Harrison, Benjamin, 270
Hartley, E. L., 115, 235, 236, 360, 361, 576, 634, 636, 640, 645, 651, 662, 664, 665, 679, 680
Hartley, R. E., 236, 634, 645
Hartmann, G. W., 418, 446
Hartung, F. E., 764, 767
Harvey, O. J., 107, 116, 192, 203, 205, 208, 263, 265, 279, 288, 293, 301, 331, 332, 602, 604, 605, 614, 616, 618
Haug, L. H., 57
Hawley, A. H., 29, 33, 164, 170, 172, 178
Hawley, Joseph, 738
Hayakawa, S. I., 454
Haythorn, W., 158, 178, 221, 231, 234, 235
Hebb, D. O., 411
Heberle, R., 721, 725, 726, 727, 735, 743
Heidbreder, E., 476, 484
Heinemann, Dr. Gustav, 717
Heintz, R., 65, 75
Hendrickson, G., 651, 663, 682
Henri, V., 48, 75
Henry, Patrick, 733, 737
Henry, T. R., 701, 714
Henschel, A., 433, 434, 435, 444
Hersey, J., 717, 743
Herskovits, M. J., 18, 28, 33, 607, 616
Hertzman, M., 104, 105, 116, 502, 534
Herz, M. F., 570, 575
Hetzer, H., 396, 410
Hicks, J. D., 410
Higham, T. M., 586, 587, 616
Hilgard, E. R., 48, 75, 464, 484
Hill, Virgil T., 606, 616
Hiller, E. T., 243, 278, 287, 331, 753
Himmelweit, H., 383, 386
Hinckley, E. D., 527, 528, 529, 531, 535, 558
Hirota, K., 597, 616
Hobbes, T., 368, 386, 748
Hocart, A. M., 456, 457, 484
Hochberg, J., 83, 115
Hoffman, E. L., 263, 264, 278

Hogan, H. P., 461, 483
Hogrefe, R., 676, 680
Holbrook, S. H., 218, 235
Hollander, E. P., 221, 235
Hollingshead, A. B., 149, 178
Hollingworth, L., 641, 645
Holmberg, A. R., 438, 439, 444, 458, 484
Holt, R. R., 588, 616
Holyoke, G. J., 148, 179
Homans, G. C., 124, 141, 229, 236
Hood, W. R., 192, 208, 288, 301 n., 331, 667, 680
Hoppe, F., 51, 754, 767
Horney, K., 176 n., 179
Horowitz, E. L., 287, 331, 662, 663, 664, 665, 680
Horowitz, R. E., 662, 663, 668, 680
Horrocks, J. E., 641, 645
Hough, W., 68, 75
Hovland, C. I., 65, 75, 288, 331, 464, 484, 486, 528, 531, 535, 536, 559, 560, 561, 562, 575, 576
Howes, D. H., 432, 444
Huddleston, S., 268, 278
Hughes, E. C., 176, 179, 359, 360, 582, 616, 638, 645
Hull, C. L., 476, 484
Humphrey, N. D., 354, 355
Hunt, J. L., 481, 484
Hunt, J. McV., 617, 646, 768
Hunter, M., 706, 713
Hurwitz, J. R., 158, 179, 231, 233, 235
Hutte, H. A., 231, 234
Huxley, J. S., 658, 680, 756, 767
Hyman, H. H., 175, 179, 516, 535, 569, 576, 626, 634, 645, 667, 680
Hymovitch, B., 158, 179, 231, 233, 235

Ibn-Khaldun, 656
Ilg, F. L., 390, 410, 594, 597, 615
Infeld, L., 759, 767
Ivy, E. R., 441, 444

Jackson, D. N., 430, 444
Jahoda, M., 570, 575, 634, 637, 645, 679, 680
James, B. B., 171, 179
James, William, 51, 76, 87, 90, 115, 372, 580, 616, 750, 767
Janis, I. L., 559, 560, 561, 562, 576
Janowitz, M., 666, 679
Jarrett, R. F., 560, 576
Jefferson, Thomas, 733, 734
Jenkins, W. O., 210, 235
Jenness, A., 133, 134, 141
Jennings, Helen H., 212, 235

Jersild, A. T., 390, 410
Jespersen, O., 477, 484
Jevons, 88
Johnson, C. S., 500, 535
Johnson, Wendell, 468
Jones, Harold E., 642, 645
Jones, M. C., 643, 647
Jones, S. V., 243, 278
Jung, 373

Kalish, H. I., 586, 616
Karowski, T. F., 53, 90, 116
Karpf, F. B., 747 n., 767
Katz, Daniel, 493, 517, 535, 575, 576,
    653, 664, 680
Katz, David, 30, 33, 54, 55, 75
Kaufman, E. L., 88, 115
Keller, Helen, 475
Keller, S., 634, 647
Kelley, H. H., 124, 141, 219, 229, 230,
    231, 235, 531, 535, 549, 559, 560,
    561, 562, 575, 576, 634, 645
Kellog, L. A. and W. N., 468, 484
Kelly, G., 505, 534
Kelly, W. H., 13, 33
Kelman, H., 265, 266, 278
Kent, G. H., 505, 535
Keys, A., 433, 434, 435, 444
Keys, John W., 477, 484
Killian, L. M., 339, 342, 346, 361, 634,
    638, 646, 671, 672, 681
Kilpatrick, P., 523, 534
Kitt, A. S., 634, 646
Klebanoff, S. G., 468, 484
Klein, G. S., 427, 444, 587, 616
Kleitman, N., 376, 386
Klineberg, O., 384, 386, 652, 679, 680,
    681, 762, 767, 768
Klisurich, Dana, 546
Kluckhohn, C., 13, 33, 451, 452, 453, 485
Kniffen, C. W., 432, 433, 444
Knop, C., 392, 410
Knower, F. H., 560, 576
Koffka, K., 60, 75, 582, 594, 616
Köhler, W., 52, 58, 75, 79–80, 115, 582,
    616
Kohn, M. L., 673, 679
Kolb, J. H., 150, 179, 705, 713
Korzybski, A., 468
Kramer, B. M., 96, 114, 665, 678
Kropotkin, P., 368, 386
Kubany, A. J., 508, 509, 535
Kuhlen, R. G., 641, 646
Kuhn, M. H., 621, 646
Külpe, O., 92–93, 115, 761

Kusunoki, K., 653, 681
Kutner, B., 675, 680

Lambert, P. E. C., 428, 445
Lambert, W. W., 427, 428, 445
Landecker, W. S., 29, 33, 164, 170, 172,
    178
Landesco, J., 173, 179, 753
Lang, O., 706, 713
Langfeld, H. S., 75, 115, 483
Lanzetta, J., 221, 234
LaPiere, R. T., 651, 681
Lashley, K. S., 373, 386
Lasker, B., 662, 681
Lazarsfeld, P. F., 515, 517, 535, 569,
    576, 599, 615, 646
Lazarus, 748
Learned, J., 396, 410
Leavitt, H. J., 232, 235
Le Bon, G., 126, 141, 339, 340, 352,
    361, 719, 743, 749, 751, 768
Lee, A. M., 354, 355, 360, 361, 565,
    575, 576
Leighton, Dorothea, 451, 452, 453, 485
Lenin, 733
Leuba, C. J., 130, 141, 597, 616
Levi, J. H., 427, 446
Levine, J. M., 417, 445, 546, 576, 586,
    616
Levine, R., 417, 420, 421, 422, 445
Levy, B., 586, 618
Lewin, Kurt, 147, 220, 235, 386, 393,
    410, 544, 545, 546, 576, 580, 582,
    617, 625, 636, 641, 646, 674, 681,
    754, 755, 768
Lewis, H. B., 104, 105, 116
Lewis, M. M., 9, 33, 398, 410, 470, 471,
    473, 484, 485
Lewis, Oscar, 284, 331, 706, 710, 714
Leytham, G., 433, 445
Liébeault, 749
Likert, R., 488, 510, 519, 520, 521, 522,
    535, 665, 681
Lindesmith, A. R., 475, 485, 634, 646
Lindgren, E. J., 659, 681
Lindsey, Almont, 148, 152, 179
Lindzey, G., 141, 234, 235, 236, 360,
    680
Line, W., 396, 410
Linnaeus, 657
Linton, R., 33, 622, 646, 681, 711, 714,
    717, 743
Lippitt, R., 220, 223, 235, 236, 754, 768
Lipset, S. M., 633, 645
Locke, John, 734, 748
Long, L., 410, 465, 473, 485, 486

Lord, M. W., 88, 115
Lowie, R. H., 593, 617
Luchins, A. S., 100, 102, 115, 666, 681
Ludeman, J. F., 96, 115, 433, 444
Lumsdaine, A. A., 561, 576
Lunt, P. S., 632, 647
Lynd, H. M., 369, 387, 582, 617
Lynd, R. S., 176, 179, 369, 386, 387, 582, 617
Lysak, W., 96, 115, 433, 444

McCarthy, D., 399, 411, 471, 472, 473, 485
McCarthy, P. J., 523, 535
McCarty, O., 441, 445
McClelland, D. C., 419, 420, 445
McCord, F., 264, 278
MacCrone, I. D., 657, 660, 681
McDougall, William, 352, 372, 382, 387, 592, 751, 768
McGarvey, H., 48, 50, 64, 65, 66, 75, 572
McGehee, W., 612, 617
McGinnies, E., 96, 115, 432, 445, 503, 536
McGranahan, D. V., 459, 485
McGregor, D., 501, 535
Machiavelli, 747
Machover, K., 104, 105, 116
McKay, H. D., 147, 180, 190, 208
McKeachie, W., 221, 234
MacLeod, R. B., 760, 768
McNemar, Q., 512, 523, 535
McPartland, T. S., 621, 646
Mahoney, Stanley, 597
Malinowski, B., 12–13, 33, 72, 75, 456, 457, 485, 592, 617, 686, 714, 753, 754
Malone, T. P., 231, 235
Mandell, W., 560, 576
Mandry, M., 392, 411
Manske, A. J., 558, 576
March, J. G., 217, 235
Marcuse, F. L., 386, 387
Marks, E. S., 71, 75, 342, 343, 360, 499, 500, 536, 573, 585
Marquis, D. P., 391, 392, 411
Marshall, D. G., 150, 179
Marshall, S. L. A., 345, 361
Martin, E. D., 339, 361
Martin, W. T., 535
Maslow, A. H., 378, 387
Mason, George, 736
Masuoka, J., 652, 681
Mathiez, A., 741, 743

Mauldin, Bill, 150, 159–160, 161, 165, 179
Mausner, B., 264, 265, 266, 278
Mayer, August, 126
Mayer, Kurt B., 633, 646
Mayo, Elton, 147
Mead, George Herbert, 594, 617, 750, 751, 768
Mead, Margaret, 592, 616, 617, 642, 646
Mecklin, J., 717, 743
Meenes, M. A., 653, 681
Meirowitz, B., 221, 234
Meissner, P. B., 104, 105, 116
Meister, D. E., 427, 444
Melikian, L., 652, 681
Meltzer, H., 651, 662, 681
Merei, F., 148, 179, 218, 219, 235
Merker, F., 11, 33, 457, 485
Merton, R. K., 568, 577, 634, 646
Metraux, R. W., 396, 410
Meumann, 126
Mickelsen, O., 433, 434, 435, 444
Miller, F. B., 132, 141
Miller, J. C., 287, 331, 735, 736, 737, 738, 739, 740, 743
Miller, L., 279
Miller, N. E., 288, 331, 459, 485
Mills, T. M., 232, 233
Millson, W. A. D., 560, 577
Minard, R. D., 676, 681
Miner, H. M., 29, 33, 164, 170, 172, 178
Mintz, A., 343, 361
Moede, 124, 752
Monderer, J. H., 640, 645
Montagu, Ashley, 658, 681
Montesquieu, 734
Moore, H. T., 136, 141
More, Sir Thomas, 747
Moreno, F. B., 148, 179
Moreno, J. L., 147, 149, 179, 230, 235, 754, 768
Morgan, C. T., 375 n., 383, 387, 466, 485
Morgan, J. H. B., 470, 485
Morgenau, H., 486
Morris, Charles, 450, 485
Morse, N. C., 665, 681
Moss, F. A., 387
Mosteller, F., 515, 536
Mowrer, 104
Munch, P. A., 163, 179
Munn, N. L., 397, 411
Münsterberg, H., 93, 94, 95, 115, 136, 752
Murchison, C., 141, 410, 768

Murfett, B. J., 537
Murger, H., 268, 278
Murphy, Gardner, 6, 33, 40, 75, 77, 83, 115, 124, 141, 371, 383, 384, 387, 395, 401, 411, 417, 420, 421, 422, 424, 427, 428, 429, 430, 431, 433, 445, 446, 505, 519, 527, 536, 548, 556, 557, 559, 577, 578, 579, 580, 586, 588, 589, 591, 594, 595, 598, 600, 616, 617, 665, 675, 681, 747 n., 753, 759, 768
Murphy, L. B., 124, 141, 371, 383, 384, 387, 556, 557, 559, 577, 578, 597, 598, 600, 617, 753, 759, 768
Mussen, P., 549, 577
Myers, R. C., 516, 536

Nehru, 734
Nekula, M., 392, 411
Nesberg, L. S., 422, 444
Newcomb, T. M., 115, 124, 141, 163, 179, 219, 234, 235, 360, 361, 371, 383, 384, 387, 521, 541, 542, 543, 544, 556, 557, 559, 576, 577, 578, 600, 617, 634, 638, 645, 646, 679, 753, 759, 768
Newman, E. B., 53, 54, 75, 90, 115
Newstetter, W. I., 163, 179
Nietzsche, 724
Nissen, H. W., 466, 487
Norfleet, B., 222, 235
Northrop, F. S. C., 486
Norval, M., 392, 410

O'Brien, R. W., 535
Ogburn, W. F., 704, 705, 714
Ogden, C. K., 485
Opler, M. K., 711, 714
O'Reilly, C. T. and E. J., 665, 681
Osborn, Max, 26
Osgood, C. E., 559, 578

Paine, Tom, 733, 739, 740
Park, R. E., 146, 352, 361, 517, 536, 635, 753
Parrington, V. L., 734, 743
Parrish, J. A., 562, 577
Parrish, R. E., 537
Parsons, T., 233
Parten, M. B., 148, 179, 512, 514, 536, 597, 617
Pear, T. H., 386, 444
Pearlin, L. I., 567, 568, 577
Pelz, D. C., 225, 235
Peterson, R. C., 523, 536, 557, 558, 577

Piaget, J., 7, 33, 149, 179, 246, 278, 401, 402, 403, 411, 594, 595, 596, 597, 617, 622, 750, 753, 754, 768
Pierson, D., 652, 681
Pintner, R., 527, 536
Plato, 747
Polansky, N., 223, 235, 236
Postman, L., 48–49, 75, 95, 96, 114, 115, 417, 423, 424, 430, 432, 433, 444, 445, 503, 536, 586
Prado, W., 537
Pratt, K. C., 390, 411
Preyer, W., 401, 411, 595, 617
Pringle, A. G., 481, 484
Pronko, N. H., 109, 110–112, 116
Prothro, E. T., 55, 59, 652, 681
Proshansky, H., 417, 424, 427, 428, 445, 506, 527, 536, 675, 680
Pyle, Ernie, 150, 179, 440, 445
Pyles, M. K., 465, 485

Radcliffe-Brown, A., 67–68, 75, 592, 593, 617
Rader, J. L., 271, 272, 277
Radin, P., 642, 646
Radke, M., 546, 662, 681
Ram, P., 577, 675, 681
Record, Wilson, 735, 743
Redl, F., 223, 236
Reese, E. P. and T. W., 88, 115
Ribot, T., 60–61, 75
Rice, C. D., 481, 482, 485
Rich, B. M., 727, 728, 743
Richards, I. A., 485
Riecken, H. W., 124, 141, 229, 236
Riess, B. F., 380, 387
Riley, J. W., Jr., 563, 577
Riley, M. W., 563, 577
Rivers, W. H. R., 403, 411, 592, 617
Rock, I., 430, 445
Rodhafer, I. A., 225, 236
Rodnick, E. H., 586, 616
Rodrigues, J. S., 427, 444
Roethlisberger, F. J., 172, 173, 179, 238, 278, 627, 636, 646
Rogers, S., 50, 64, 65, 75, 572
Rohrer, J. H., 34, 74, 76, 208, 263, 264, 278, 331, 332, 484, 485, 486
Rorschach, H., 505, 536
Rosanoff, A. J., 505, 535
Rose, Arnold, 659, 660, 669, 682
Rose, G. J., 425, 444
Roseborough, M. E., 124, 141, 157, 158, 179, 229, 232, 233, 236
Rosen, B. C., 643, 646
Rosen, W., 223, 235

Rosenbaum, M., 135, 141, 636, 645, 662, 680
Rosenberg, M., 567, 568, 577
Rosenblith, J. F. A., 665, 682
Rosenfeld, I. J., 537
Rosenthal, B. G., 427, 445, 446
Rosenzweig, S., 505, 506, 536
Ross, E. A., 126, 141, 751, 768
Rousseau, Jean Jacques, 368, 387, 734, 741, 748
Roy, Donald, 238, 278
Rubin, Edgar, 52, 53, 75, 82
Rugg, 514

Saadi, M., 136, 141
Saenger, G., 675, 682
Salter, P. J., 566, 575
Salusky, A. S., 597, 618
Sanford, F. H., 221, 236
Sanford, R. N., 418, 419, 433, 446
Sapir, E., 467, 485
Sarason, S., 393, 411
Sargent, S. S., 562, 564, 577
Sayles, L. R., 707, 714
Schachter, S., 149, 178, 229, 230, 236
Schafer, R., 417, 429, 430, 431, 446, 505, 536
Scheerer, M., 599, 600, 616
Schlesinger, H. J., 427, 444
Schlorff, P. W., 557, 577
Schlosberg, H., 38, 76, 88, 116
Schneirla, T. C., 10, 30, 34, 466, 467, 469, 485
Schoenfeld, N., 587, 616
Schooler, K., 426, 428, 444
Schrag, C. C., 535
Schwartz, M., 531, 535
Schwartz, S., 636, 645, 662, 680
Scott, E. L., 226, 236
Scott, J. P., 177, 179, 630, 646
Sears, P. S., 580, 617, 625, 646, 755, 768, 769
Sears, R. R., 288, 331
Sears, W. N., 464, 484
Seashore, R. H., 74
Seeleman, V., 418, 446, 586, 618
Semin, Refia Ugurel, 246, 278
Senden, M. V., 395, 411
Seward, Julian, 711
Shapiro, M. M., 219, 235
Shaw, Clifford R., 147, 149, 156, 180, 185, 190, 208, 644, 646, 753
Sheatsley, P. B., 569, 576, 667, 680
Sheffield, F. J., 561, 576

Sherif, C. W., 192, 195, 198, 199, 208, 223, 236, 285, 287, 288, 293, 295, 297, 298, 301 n., 331, 477, 486, 612, 618, 667, 668, 671, 682
Sherif, M., 30, 34, 65, 74, 75, 76, 79, 99, 100, 107, 115, 116, 134, 135, 142, 147, 149, 172, 178, 180, 192, 195, 198, 199, 202, 204, 205, 208, 223, 234, 236, 249, 263, 264, 265, 266, 278, 279, 285, 287, 288, 293, 295, 297, 298, 301, 331, 332, 402, 411, 417, 446, 477, 484, 485, 486, 494, 505, 528, 535, 536, 537, 552, 562, 564, 574, 577, 586, 594, 602, 604, 605, 609, 610, 614, 616, 618, 630, 634, 637, 646, 647, 667, 668, 671, 680, 682, 692, 733, 743, 754, 766, 769
Sherman, M., 390, 411, 701, 714
Sherriffs, A. C., 560, 576
Shibutani, T., 634, 647
Shils, E. A., 233
Shinn, M. W., 595, 618
Shirley, M. M., 396, 411
Shuey, A. M., 566, 578
Simmel, G., 123, 142, 244, 279
Simpson, W., 203
Singer, J. S., 468, 484
Sinha, Durganand, 264, 265, 279, 719, 720, 743
Slavson, S. R., 230, 236
Smith, E. W., 92, 116
Smith, F. T., 549, 578
Smith, Kate, 568
Smith, M. E., 399, 411, 471, 486
Smythe, D. W., 567, 578
Snyder, F. W., 109, 110–112, 116
Snygg, D., 581, 618
Sodhi, Kripal Singh, 264, 265, 279
Sokarno, 734
Solomon, R. L., 427, 432, 444, 445
Spencer, B., 458, 486
Spencer, Herbert, 368, 387, 748
Sperling, H. G., 264, 265, 279
Stagner, R., 53, 90, 116, 559, 578, 665, 682
Stanley, H. M., 71, 75
Steining, B. R., 397, 411
Steinthal, 748
Stellar, E., 383, 387
Stern, B. J., 594, 618
Stern, E., 634, 647
Stern, W., 93, 94, 116
Stevens, S. S., 76, 484
Stewart, F. D., 410
Stogdill, R. M., 210, 215, 236

Stolz, H. R., 643, 647
Stone, C. P., 387
Stonequist, E. V., 176, 180, 635, 647
Stouffer, S. A., 108, 116, 150, 180, 245, 279, 521, 522, 536, 637, 647
Stover, G. F., 558, 575
Stratton, 109
Strauss, A. L., 475, 485, 634, 646
Strodtbeck, F. L., 229, 231, 232, 233, 236
Sullivan, H. S., 176 n., 180, 602, 618
Sumner, William Graham, 751, 769
Swander, D., 263, 264, 278
Swanson, G. E., 115, 235, 360, 361, 576, 645

Taine, 741
Talland, G. A., 219, 236
Tarde, G., 352, 749, 751, 769
Taub, D., 65, 75
Taylor, H. L., 433, 434, 435, 444
Teska, 55, 59
Thibaut, J. W., 124, 141, 229, 231, 235
Thomas, W. I., 497, 536, 752, 769
Thompson, H., 390, 392, 396, 410, 594, 616
Thompson, L. M., 465, 486
Thompson, Laura, 23
Thorndike, R. L., 136, 142
Thrasher, F. M., 149, 152, 156, 172, 180, 185, 186, 208, 212, 216, 236, 247, 279, 287, 332, 753
Thrasher, James D., 103, 116, 263, 279
Thurstone, L. L., 488, 510, 523, 524, 525, 526, 527, 528, 533, 536, 557, 558, 577
Titchener, 756, 761
Toki, K., 216, 236
Tolman, E. C., 369, 387
Tomkins, S. S., 505, 537
Toscanini, 583–584
Townsend, Dr. F. E., 729
Trager, H. G., 662, 681
Travers, R. M. W., 498, 537
Tresselt, M. E., 49–50, 75, 248, 279, 586, 618, 688, 689, 714
Triplett, 130
Tsai, C., 378, 387
Tumin, M., 351, 352, 361

Van Gennep, A., 642, 647
Van Riper, C., 477, 486
Vanderplas, J. M., 504, 537
Veblen, T., 177, 633, 647
Venegas, F., 392, 410
Vernon, M. D., 395, 397, 411, 504

Vigotsky, L. S., 473, 486
Vinacke, W. E., 475, 486
Vitruvius, 656
Volkart, E. H., 561, 576
Volkmann, J., 47, 50, 51, 64, 65, 66, 74, 75, 88, 115, 248, 279, 464, 486, 572, 624, 625, 645, 689, 714, 755, 756, 767
Voltaire, 734, 741
Von Wiese, Leopold, 123, 140
Vosk, Marc, 548, 551, 578
Voth, A. C., 263, 279

Wainwright, General J. M., 441, 446, 599
Walker, R. N., 396, 410
Walkley, R. P., 676, 682
Wallen, R. W., 586, 618
Wallis, W. D., 70, 76
Wallon, H., 594, 618
Walter, A. A., 461, 483
Walter, Norman, 112, 116, 262, 279, 554, 578
Wapner, S., 104, 105, 116, 131, 132, 142
Warden, C. J., 378, 387, 464, 486
Ware, Caroline F., 268, 279
Waring, E. B., 465, 486
Warner, W. L., 593, 615, 631, 632, 647
Watson, John, 383, 751
Watson, P. D., 427, 445
Watson, W. S., 418, 446
Watts, A. F., 473, 476, 486
Webb, Walter Prescott, 269, 270, 279, 709, 710, 714
Webster, H., 67, 76, 642, 647
Weisbach, Werner, 25
Weiss, W., 559, 562, 576
Welch, L., 465, 473, 485, 486
Weld, H. P., 75, 115, 483
Wells, F. L., 62, 76
Wertheimer, M., 54, 55, 76, 104
Wever, E. G., 49, 76
Whiffen, T., 458, 486
Whipple, G. M., 93, 95, 116
White, B. J., 192, 205, 208, 288, 293, 301 n., 331, 332
White, L. A., 469, 486
White, R. K., 220, 235, 754, 768
White, R. W., 599, 618
White, W. H., Jr., 239, 279
White, William Allen, 566
Whittaker, E. M., 432, 446
Whorf, B., 453, 454, 486
Whyte, W. F., 147, 162, 163, 166, 178, 180, 184, 185, 186, 187–188, 190, 191, 202, 208, 215, 216, 217, 225,

Whyte—(*Continued*)
226, 233, 236, 239, 240, 244, 277, 279, 282, 332, 627, 637, 644, 647
Wilensky, H., 468, 484
Wilke, W. H., 558, 578
Willems, Emilio, 652, 682
Williams, R. M., Jr., 243, 279, 556, 578, 661, 682
Wilner, D. M., 676, 682
Wilson, M. O., 178, 180, 234, 646, 647, 766
Wispe, L. G., 423, 446
Witkin, H. A., 104, 105, 116
Wolfe, J. B., 466, 486
Woodrow, H., 47, 76
Woodworth, R. S., 38, 76, 88, 116
Wurster, C. R., 158, 178, 231, 233, 234
Wright, Frank Lloyd, 25, 26
Wright, Quincy, 712, 713, 714
Wundt, 749

Yeager, Charles E., 47, 76
Yerkes, R. M., 466, 467, 487
Yokoyama, 93, 116
Yoshida, Tetsuro, 24, 26
Young, D., 558, 578
Young, P. T., 378, 387, 441, 446

Zachry, C., 642, 647
Zander, A., 158, 179, 229, 231, 233, 234, 235, 545, 575, 576
Zangwill, O. L., 462, 463, 487
Zeaman, D., 610, 611, 612, 618
Zeligs, R., 651, 663, 682
Zener, K. E., 49, 76
Znaniecki, F., 497, 536, 752, 769
Zorbaugh, H. W., 149, 153, 180, 279, 753
Zuk-Kardos, 417

INDEX OF SUBJECTS

Acculturation, 686
    See also Social change
Adolescence, group formation in, 149,
    641 ff.
  in different cultures, 764 ff.
Adolescent attitudes, and reference
    groups, 641–644
Aloneness, 713
American Revolution, 356, 735–740
Anchorages, 46, 50, 62, 152
  and reference groups, 175 ff., 620 ff.
  conflicting, 109–113
  cultural variations in, 66–73
  definition of, 44, 83
  in judgments of number, 88 f.
  in social situations, 125 f.
  in structuring experience, 62–66
  loss of, 106–109, 601 f.
  norms as, 245, 260 ff.
Andamanese, 67 f., 383
Anxiety, and loss of anchorages, 601 f.
    See also Insecurity
Apartheid, 660 f.
Arunta, 458
Ashanti, 70
Assimilation effect, 64, 89
  and attitude change, 572 f.
Attention span, 86–90
Attitude change, 50, 538–574
  and assimilation effect, 572 f.
  and attitude formation, 538 ff.
  and "boomerang effect," 555 ff., 573
  and communication, 555–562
  and contact, 548–551
  and contrast effect, 572 f.
  and latitude of acceptance, 573
  and shifts of reference groups, 541 ff.
  and superordinate goals, 550 f.
  and technological change, 574
  external and internal factors in,
    570–574
  techniques for, 540 ff.

Attitude formation, 64–66, 404 f., 538 ff.
  and institutional preferences, 554
  and socialization, 398 ff., 594–598
  in autokinetic situation, 552 ff.
Attitude measurement, and "error choice
    technique," 507
  and imposed categories, 528 ff.
  and laboratory research, 498 ff.
  and method of paired comparisons,
    531 ff.
  and projective techniques, 505 ff.
  and thresholds of acceptance and re-
    jection, 529
  and unstructured stimuli, 529 ff.
  comparison of methods for, 532
  direct techniques for, 510–528
  indirect techniques for, 505–510
  own categories in, 528 f., 530
Attitudes, 77 f., 130, 366, 398, 490,
    494 ff., 752
  and behavior toward out-groups,
    671–674
  and emotions, 385
  and group norms, 173 ff.
  and material culture, 22, 685–714
  and reference groups, 634 f.
  and socialization, 490–494
  as sociogenic motives, 371, 413 f.
  based on status relations, 202–208
  criteria of, 494 ff.
  formed in group interaction, 155 f.
  in formation and change, 551–554
  in judging stimuli with varying struc-
    ture, 103 f.
  in remembering, 61, 63 f., 95, 430 ff.
  toward out-groups, 284, 285 ff., 294 ff.,
    298 f., 306–316
    See also Norms; Reference groups;
        Socialization; Stimulus struc-
        ture
Authoritarian leadership techniques,
    220 ff.

Authority, changes in, 706 f.
  delegation of, 214 f.
  legal and informal, 273 ff.
    See also Leadership; Power
Autokinetic movement, 99, 107, 112, 250 ff.

Band organization, 711
Barbed wire, introduction of, 709 f.
Behavior, and attitudes toward out-groups, 671–674
  and experience, 5 f.
  as data of psychology, 80
  individual, consistency of, 579 ff.
    See also Experience
Belongingness, experience of, 167 f.
Bennington attitude change study, 541 ff.
Biogenic motives, and infant behavior, 389–394
  characteristics of, 373, 375
  criteria of, 373–375
  definition of, 370
  deprivations of, 377 f., 379 ff.
  list of, 375
  periodicity of, 376 f., 436
    See also Deprivations; Motives
Biological endowment, 370
Biological value, and social significance, 377–378
Blackfoot warfare, 710
Bohemians, 149, 268
Brain injury, 468, 599 f.

Calendars, 66 f.
Catharsis, 299
Cerebral cortex, 10, 381, 383, 467 f.
Chinese family, 706 f.
Circular reaction, 352, 357
Class, 631 ff.
    See also Status
Clinical studies of motivation, 414 f.
Cognition, and motivation, 54, 79 f., 85, 716
  in collective behavior, 358 f., 716, 725 f., 732–735
    See also Judgment; Perception
Collective behavior, 333–361, 715 ff.
Collective interaction, 716 ff.
  accounting for, 355–358
  antecedents and consequences of, 720 ff.
  characterized, 336 ff.
  conditions conducive to, 353–355, 358, 360
  consequences of, 352, 358 ff.
  differential effects of, 339 ff.

Collective interaction—(*Continued*)
  focus of, 345 ff.
  processes in, 352 f.
  products of, 359 f., 732–742
  types of, 346–350
Collective representations, 247, 340, 749 f.
Collective unconscious, 372
Color classifications, 70 f.
"Common enemy," 300, 317
Communication, 9–11, 449–485
  and attitude change, 555–562
  and learning, 469–475
  and status relations, 225–233
  expression of emotions as, 384
  from mass media, 286, 562–570
  in disaster, 345
  in groups, 151, 216, 226 f., 232 f.
  in large organizations, 147
  in social movements, 725, 732 ff.
  in togetherness situations, 226 f.
  lines of, 182, 232
    See also Mass communication
Comparative psychology, 9–10, 177, 465–469
Competition, 130, 597
  among groups, 293 ff., 306–316
Concept formation, and attitudes, 495 f.
  and motivation, 398 ff.
  experiments on, 475 f.
  in social life, 481 f.
  neglected characteristics of, 476
Concepts, 9–11
  and individual behavior, 458–465
  and social influences, 128–132
  changes in, 454 f.
  in discrimination and learning, 463 ff.
  language, 449 ff.
  norms as, 170 ff., 240 f.
Conceptual level, 9–11, 177 f.
  and children's play, 148 f.
  and human motivation, 380 ff.
  and interaction, 151, 154
Conflict, and reference groups, 176 f., 191, 409 f.
  between groups, 295 ff., 301 ff., 306–316; reduction of, 316–328
  of anchorages, 109–113
Conformity, 7 f., 241–245
  and intergroup behavior, 283–285
  and prejudice, 665 f.
  and social attitudes, 173 ff.
  in autokinetic situation, 553
    See also Norms
Consensus, and stimulus structure, 689

Contact between groups, 317 f., 548–551, 675 ff.
Content analysis, 511
Continuity of personal identity, 579 ff.
Contrast effect, 51, 66, 71
and attitude change, 572 ff.
Convergence of judgments, 257 ff.
Criminal gangs, 173
See also Gangs
Crises, 719–722
See also Critical situations
Critical situations, 715–743
and changes in norms, 219, 732–742
and collective interaction, 353–355, 716 ff.
motives in, 370, 720 ff.
Crowds, 333 f., 339 ff., 346 ff., 350–352, 749
psychoanalytic accounts of, 340 f.
Cultural relativism, 753
Cultural variations, in anchorages, 66–73
Culture, and individual influences, 6–8
as stimulus conditions, 12, 18, 21–28
levels of analysis of, 28–31
man as creator of, 8
material, 21–27, 98, 686 ff.
nonmaterial, 27–28
See also Language; Norms; Organizations; Technology

Decision, group, speed of, 123 f.
See also Group decision
Definition of the situation, 752
Delayed reaction experiments, 466
Demagogues, 721 f.
Dependency of human children, 391–394
Deprivations, 377 f., 417, 433–443
and group formation, 152 ff.
and social change, 717 ff.
laboratory studies of, 418–424
See also Biogenic motives
Deviation, 172 f., 200, 229 f., 241–245, 329, 665 f., 687
and problem of intergroup behavior, 283–285
Differential effects of collective interaction, 151, 156–162, 339 ff.
of social situations, 119 ff., 128, 131
of togetherness and group situations, 184 ff.
Differentiation of response, 389–403
Disasters, 342–345
Discrimination, 87, 392, 394–398
effects of concepts in, 463 ff.
group, 668 ff., 672
See also Judgment

Discussion, 133 f., 290
groups, 227 ff., 232
method, 544 ff.; and cultural setting, 547 f.
Distance, concepts of, 690, 693, 697

Ego, 149, 155 f., 350, 407–410
and language, 596
and loss of anchorages, 601 f.
and other motives, 584–585
and prejudice, 662 ff., 674 ff.
and reference groups, 628 ff.
and social crises, 720 ff.
definition of, 581 f.
formation of, 401–403, 582, 594–598
integration of, 409
Ego-attitudes, 402, 580 ff.
and periodicity of motives, 585
and technology, 704 ff.
integrating personal identity, 589–591
motivational character of, 600 f.
See also Attitudes; Ego
Ego breakdowns, 598 ff.
Ego-involvements, 579–615
and competitive behavior, 592 f.
and coöperative behavior, 592 f.
and group relations, 619 ff.
and individual differences, 588 f.
and kinship, 593
and perception, 583 f.
and response to power, 224
and status, 622 ff.
cultural variations in, 591–594
definition of, 402
in interpersonal relations, 607 f.
in judging performance, 612 ff.
in social relations, 607
Emergent properties of behavior, 247 f.
See also Frame of reference
Emotional expression, 383 ff., 390
Emotions, 382 ff.
Equal-appearing intervals, 510, 526–528, 528 ff.
Ethnic groups, *see* Intergroup relations; Minority groups; Social distance
Ethnocentrism, 32, 75, 286
effects of, in psychology, 761 ff.
procedures for checking, 764
studies of, 666 f.
Expectations, 158
based on status relations, 202–208
in terms of status structure, 186 ff.
of leader's behavior, 217 f.
stabilization of, 163 ff.
violations of, 166 f., 189 f.
See also Deviation

Experience, and behavior a unity, 5 f., 38, 77 f.
    factors in structure of, 106
    tendency toward structure of, 80 f.
Experimental design, 193 ff.
Experimentation, 32, 760
    effects of observation in, 131 f.
    in the laboratory, 84, 85, 182
    on groups, 191 ff.
    on intergroup relations, 287–328
    on norm formation, 249 ff.
    stimulus conditions in, 12
    uncontrolled factors in, 129
        See also Scientific methods
Experiments, on deprivation, 435
    on effects of propaganda, 559–562
    on motivation, 416–433
    on norm formation, 251 ff., 262 ff.
    on togetherness situations, 126 ff.
Expression, of emotions, 383 ff.
External factors, 90 f.
        See also Stimulus situations

Factions, 284
Fads, 240
Failure, 39, 51
        See also Level of aspiration
Family, changes in, 704–707
Father Divine, 731 f.
Feudal system, 713
Field studies, 181, 185 ff., 191 f., 201 f., 208
Figure-ground relationship, 52 ff., 87, 406, 505
    and psychological selectivity, 84 ff.
    motives in determining, 429 ff.
    shifts in, 59 f.
    significance of ground in, 60
Folkways, 240, 751
        See also Norms
Frame of reference, 125, 157, 202, 247
    and reference group concept, 175 ff.
    and varying stimulus structure, 82 f.
    applied to collective behavior, 341 ff.
    definition of, 40 ff., 80
    for intergroup behavior, 282 ff.
    motives in, 365 ff.
    representation of, 79
French Revolution, 740 ff.
Friendship choices, 193, 196, 312, 325 f.
    reversals of, 200
Frontier, norm formation in, 268 ff.
Frustration, 288, 307, 383

Gangs, 147, 149, 152 f., 173, 184–191, 224 f.. 643–644

German youth, 729 f.
Goals, and group formation, 152–156
    in group experiments, 182, 194, 230, 289 f.
    in human learning, 405 f.
    reference scales of, 238 ff.
    superordinate, 291, 317–328, 330
    with biological significance, 404
        See also Biogenic motives; Motives
Ground, see Figure-ground relationship
Group, definition of, 144 f.
Group characteristics, and technological change, 710 f.
Group cohesion, see Solidarity
Group decision, 754
    studies of, 544–547
Group goals, 302 f.
        See also Goals
Group membership, 155 f.
        See also Group structure; Groups; Norms
Group norms, 240 ff.
        See also Norms
Group prejudice, 648–682
Group psychotherapy, 230 f.
Group relations, and ego-involvements, 619 ff.
    effects of technological change on, 707 ff.
Group sanctions, see Sanctions
Group situations, contrasted with togetherness situations, 124–126, 181–184
Group solidarity, 165–170
        See also Solidarity
Group structure, 15
    as property of groups, 151, 161–170
    definition of, 162
    formation of, 182 ff., 191 ff., 204 f., 303–306
    in collective interaction, 722
    in experimentally formed groups, 197 ff., 312 f.
    removing leader from, 216
    stability of, 165 ff., 205 ff.
        See also Leadership; Roles; Status
Group superiority doctrines, 656–661
Groups, and language, 451–458
    and togetherness situations, 124–126, 181–184
    as parts of large organizations, 18, 146, 147 f.
    as stimulus situations, 14–16
    children's, 148 f.
    concept of, and leadership, 215
    disintegration of, 154, 189

Groups—(*Continued*)
effects of intergroup relations on, 190 f., 294, 306, 309 ff.
experimental formation of, 191 ff., 204 f.
formally and informally organized, 147 f.
formation of, 303–306
informal, as prototypes, 146 ff.; generality of, 148–151
motives conducive to formation of, 152–156
norm formation in, 266 ff.
positive and negative effects of, 262
properties of, 143 ff., 151 ff.
relations between, *see* Intergroup relations
role of, in socialization, 408 ff.
study of, 28–31, 753
See also Norm formation

Hierarchy, in groups, 163 ff., 186 ff.
See also Group structure
Hollow Folk, 701 ff.
Homeostasis, 370, 377, 381 f.
Hopi, 453 f.
Human nature, 367–370, 372, 748 ff.

Ideology, 726, 732–735
Ifugao, 457
Illusions, 44 ff.
Imagining, and deprivation, 418 ff.
Imitation, 352, 357, 749
In-group, 751
definition of, 281
formation of, 151, 165 ff., 286 ff., 303–306, 438
See also Groups; Reference groups
Inconsistency of behavior, 637 f., 673
Indirect methods, in studying motivation, 414 ff.
of measuring attitudes, 505–510
Individual differences, 6, 104, 130
and deviation, 171
and effects of adult leadership, 221
and ego-involvements, 588 ff.
and interaction patterns, 231 f.
and norms, 74, 245 f.
and prejudice, 666 f.
and status, 162, 224 f.
during group formation, 182
in perception, 254, 257
in reaction to social influences, 265 f.
in semistarvation, 435 f.
in standards, 262 f.

Individual differences—(*Continued*)
of leaders, 210 ff.
See also Range of tolerable behavior
Individual-group relationship, 6–8, 146, 167 f.
See also Ego; Groups; Reference groups
Individual performance, and reference groups, 627 f.
Individuals, and language concepts, 458–465
and social-distance scales, 664–671
in critical situations, 715–743
Industrial organizations, 147, 172 f., 707, 709
Inferiority complex, 372
Informal groups, 146 ff.
See also Groups
Information, in attitude change, 317, 675, 678
Insecurity, and collective behavior, 717 ff.
and variability of reactions, 606 f.
effects of, 263
experimental demonstration of, 603 ff.
Institutions, formation and change of, 359 f.
Intellectual influences, in collective interaction, 716, 725 f., 732–735
Intellectual level, 356 f.
effects of collective interaction on, 358, 359
Interaction, analysis of, 227
and concept formation, 476 ff.
and language, 458, 481 ff.
basic to human relationships, 151
collective, *see* Collective interaction
differential effects of, 151, 156–162
effects on perception of, 247 f., 255 ff.
emergent properties of, 262 ff.
groups as products of, 145 f.
in togetherness and group situations, 184
motives in, 371 f., 406–410
norms formed in, 263 ff.
of influences on behavior, 6–8, 31 f., 765 f.
relative structure of, 125 f., 181 ff.
transitory, 124 ff.
typical level of, 9–11
See also Differential effects; Norm formation
Interdisciplinary approach, 29–31
Intergroup behavior, 281–286
Intergroup conflict, 276, 295 ff., 354 f., 675 ff.

Intergroup conflict—(*Continued*)
  production of, 306–316
  reduction of, 291, 299 f., 301 ff., 316–328
Intergroup coöperation, *see* Superordinate goals
Intergroup relations, 14, 15, 19, 194, 200 ff., 280 ff.
  and changed technology, 707 ff.
  and power relations, 224 f.
  experiments on, 287 ff.
  in American revolutionary period, 735–740
  of small groups, 281 f.
Internal factors, 80 ff., 85 f., 90 ff.
    See also Attitudes; Concepts; Ego-involvements; Motives, etc.
Internalization, of norms, 174 f., 246 f., 329 f.; and ego formation, 402 f.
  of social influences, 388 ff.
Interpersonal relations, 14–17
  and ego-involvements, 607 f.
  and social influences, 21
  indirect assessment of, 609 ff.

J-curve, 491
  and reference groups, 492 ff.
Judgment, 39 f., 51, 62, 69 ff., 87 ff.
  anchorages and reference scales of, 64–66, 104 f., 573 f.
  effect of majority on, 136 ff.
  effects of discussion on, 133 f.
  effects of conflicting anchorages on, 112 f., 554
  in social situations, 127 f.
  influenced by deprivation, 422
  of motive-relevant objects, 424–429
  of performance by group members, 312 ff.
  of stimuli with varying structure, 103–106, 688 ff.
  of time by group members, 307–309
  relativity of, 44, 45, 46–51
  revealing intergroup attitudes, 301, 312 f.
  revealing status relations, 202–208
Juvenile gangs, *see* Gangs

Kinship, 72, 593, 705 ff.

Labor organizations, 148, 152
Language, 9 f., 27 f., 66, 72, 148 f., 382, 449–485
  and communication, 151
  and ego, 596 f.
  and individual behavior, 458–465
  and realities of group life, 456 f.

Language—(*Continued*)
  and stereotyping, 655 f.
  differences in, 450–458
  "first words" of, 396
  learning of, 398 ff., 469–475
    See also Communication
Learning, 86 ff., 391
  and biogenic motives, 373 f., 381
  and socialization, 145 f.
  and sociogenic motives, 405 f.
  effects of concepts in, 463 ff.
  to communicate, 469–475
Leader-follower relations, 166 f., 189 f., 215–219
"Leaderless groups," 157 f., 211 ff.
Leaders, 166 f., 186
  differing conceptions of, 209 f., 214 f.
  in experimentally formed groups, 197 f., 309, 311
  in reducing intergroup conflict, 317
  in social crises, 722
  influence of, 139 f.
  range of tolerable behavior for, 217 ff.
  responsibilities of, 188
  selection of, 211 ff.
  traits of, 210 ff.
Leadership, 164
  as part of group structure, 210 f.
  changes of, 214 f., 217, 309, 311
  in collective interaction, 356 f.
  in formal and informal organizations, 219 f.
  in norm formation, 257
  in social movements, 725 f., 738 f.
  specific or general, 211–215
  techniques of democratic, 220–222
Level of aspiration, 51, 202, 754 f.
Levels, of analysis, 28–31
  of organization, 9–11
Libido, 372
Likert technique of attitude measurement, 519 f.

Majority opinion, 132, 136 ff.
Marginality, 635 ff.
Marquesans, 68
Masai, 457
Mass audience, 563 ff.
Mass communication, 286, 562 ff.
  and ego-involvements, 568 ff.
  content of, 566–568
  sources of, 564 ff.
Membership character, 48, 53, 81
Membership groups, 175 ff., 630 ff.
  definition of, 177
    See also Reference groups

Methods, 288 ff., 414 ff., 510
  combination of, 292, 312 ff., 324 ff.,
    760
Military organizations, 159 f., 226 f., 344
Minority groups, and social-distance
    scales, 651, 667–671
"Miracle at Sabana Grande," 350 ff.
Mobility, 631 f., 699 f.
Mobs, 346 f.
Morale, 150, 165 f.
Mores, 240
    See also Norms
Moroccans, 99
Motivation, and cognition, 54, 79 f., 85,
    716
  and perceptual selectivity, 95–97, 422 f.
  and technology, 689 f., 703
  effects on communication patterns,
    229 ff.
  emotional, 382–385
  in collective interaction, 345 f., 349 f.,
    356 ff., 716 ff.
  in concept formation, 476 f.
Motives, 38 f.
  and conceptual development, 398 ff.
  and social organization, 404
  and stimulus structure, 412, 415, 423 f.,
    429
  attitudes as, 489 ff.
  concept of, 367
  conducive to group formation, 151,
    152–156, 182, 185 f.
  emerging in interaction, 154 ff., 406–
    410
  in children's perceptions, 394–398
  in controversies over "human nature,"
    367–370
  in learning language, 471 ff.
  in social movements, 722, 724 f., 726 f.
  in social psychology, 365 ff.
  origin of, 370 ff.
  relationships among, 380 ff.
  relative weights of, 378–380
  study of, 413 ff.
    See also Biogenic motives; Ego;
      Sociogenic motives
Müller-Lyer illusion, 44–45
Multiple group membership, 175 ff., 245,
    629 ff.
    See also Reference groups

Name-calling, 296 ff., 307 f.
  decrease in, 326
Names, 459–465, 477–481
"Naming stage," 399 f., 471 f., 476

National liberation movements, 722 ff.,
    734
Navaho, 451 ff.
Nonconformity, 171, 173, 242–245, 329,
    665 f.
Norm formation, in collective interaction,
    358–360
  in groups, 266 ff.
  in the laboratory, 249 ff.
  in the Western frontier, 269 ff.
  problem of, 247 ff.
Norms, 15, 27 f., 62, 134, 185, 188
  and individual behavior, 245 f.
  and out-groups, 286 ff., 298, 306–316
  and range of tolerable behavior, 164,
    171 ff., 174
  and social attitudes, 173 ff.
  as group property, 144 ff., 152, 170–
    175
  changes by leaders, 219
  definition of, 170, 240 ff.
  evidence of, 172 ff.
  of social distance, 284, 285 ff., 649–
    656
  perception of, 245 f.
  products of interaction, 240 ff.
  regulating leadership, 217 ff.
  rising in social movements, 732–742
    See also Attitudes

Observation, 131 f., 312 ff., 324 ff.
Ojibwa, 450 f.
Oklahoma settlement, 270 ff.
One-way screen, 131 f.
Opinions, 515 ff.
    See also Attitudes
Organization, 185, 186–188
  and reaction in disasters, 343 f.
  as property of groups, 151, 161–170
  changed, and technology, 703–713
  community, 271 ff.
  formal and informal, 147–148
  in American frontier, 269 ff.
  in children's groups, 148 f.
  in collective interaction, 357 ff., 724 ff.
  large, 147 f., 226 f., 282
  leadership in, 215, 219 f.
  of a revival meeting, 334–336
    See also Group structure; Leader-
      ship; Role; Status
Orientation, 69, 106–109, 110 ff.
Out-groups, 165, 171, 751
  attitudes and behavior towards, 165,
    192, 201, 283 ff., 295–300, 671–674

Out-groups—(*Continued*)
    definition of, 281
    effects of, on in-groups, 190 f.
    stereotypes of, 286 ff., 298, 306–316
Own categories in attitude measurement,
    530

Panic, 342–345
Parent-youth conflict, 643
Participant observers, 196, 292 ff.
Perception, 38, 51–60, 79 ff., 253 ff.
    and language, 459, 472 ff.
    and stimulus structure, 81, 84 f., 100–
        106, 248, 255, 257, 263
    children's, 392, 394–398
    effects of technology in, 692 ff.
    of color, 70 f.
    of danger, 342 f.
    of patterns, 72
    of social relationships, 380 f.
    of speed, 47
    of time, 67 f.
    relativity of, 44 ff.
    studies of, 754
    See also Stimulus structure
"Perceptual defense," 95–97, 415 f.,
    432 f.
Perceptual selectivity, 87
    See also Psychological selectivity
Perceptual structure, 51–60, 79 ff.
Perceptual variations, and motives,
    420 ff.
Personal consistency, 580 ff., 585 ff.
Personal documents, 511
Personality, *see* Individual differences
Physiological states, 390 ff.
    See also Biogenic motives
Pondo, 706
Popularity, 197 ff.
Power, direct and indirect, 223 f.
    leaders' sources of, 220
Power relations, 197 f., 222–225, 242 f.
    and intergroup relations, 224 f.
    as aspect of status, 164
Prägnanz, 63
Prejudice, 96, 648–682
    formation of, 287, 661–664
    problems of changing, 674–678
    See also Attitude change
Prestige, 216 f.
    See also Status
Problem situations, 181 ff., 194, 289 ff.,
    306
    and superordinate goals, 318 ff.
Production norms, 172 f., 238, 627

Projection, 415 f.
Propaganda, 64–66, 557–562
Psychological mobility, 699
    See also Vertical mobility
Psychological organization, 41 ff., 78 ff.
Psychological selectivity, 54, 84–97, 406
    See also Selectivity
Psychophysics, 49 f.
    See also Judgment
Psychotherapy, group, 230 f.
Public opinion surveys, 497, 511–517
    and reference groups, 513

Questions, in surveys, 514

Race concept, 658
Race riots, 354 f.
Race superiority doctrines, 656–661
Range of tolerable behavior, 164, 171 ff.,
    174
    for leaders, 217 ff., 244 ff.
Rate busters, 173, 238
Rate setting in industrial plants, 172 f.,
    238, 627
Ratings, in interaction situations, 227 ff.
    of status, 205, 303
    of stereotypes, 300 f., 312, 326 f.
    See also Judgment
Reciprocal effects, of reference scales and
    anchorages, 573 f.
Reciprocities, in interaction process, 145,
    158 f.
    See also Roles; Status
Recognition thresholds, 95–97, 432 f.
Reference groups, 50, 83, 175 f., 188, 284,
    293, 503, 560
    and adolescent attitudes, 641 ff.
    and anchorages, 620 ff.
    and attitude change, 541 ff., 675 ff.
    and conformity (J-curve), 491–494
    and ego-involvements, 619 ff., 628 ff.
    and inconsistency of behavior, 637 ff.
    and marginality, 635–637
    and membership groups, 630 ff.
    and parent-youth conflict, 643
    and status equilibration, 639 f., 664 f.
    of rate busters, 238
    regulating performance, 627 f.
Reference points, 41, 47, 48, 50, 60
    See also Anchorages
Reference scales, 48–51, 501
    and anchorages, reciprocal effects of,
        64–66, 573–574
    established by group norms, 238 ff.
    of prejudice, 283 f.

Regression of ego, 598 ff.
Remembering, 60 f., 62–64, 91 f., 416 f.
and language forms, 459–463
cultural variations in, 73
selectivity of, 91 f., 93 ff.
Revivals, 334–336, 348 f.
Rhythm, 99 f.
Riots, 354 f.
Rivalry, 129
See also Competition
Roles, 200, 409 f.
See also Ego; Group structure;
Status
Rorschach ink blots, 99, 396, 505
Rosenzweig Picture-Frustration test, 505
Rumor, 108 f., 355, 357 f., 720
Rural areas, groups in, 149 f.

Sampling, stratified, 512
Sanctions, 172 f., 200, 244 ff.
Saulteaux, 70, 690
Scalability of items (Guttman tech-
nique), 520–523
Scale values, in Thurstone scales, 525
Schedules, adaptation to, 391 f.
Scientific methods, 32, 37 f., 114, 755 ff.
Sects, 70 f., 148 f., 171
Segregation, 355, 668 f., 673 ff.
Semistarvation, 288, 433–438
Selectivity of psychological activity, 54,
84–97, 377
and deprivations, 422 ff.
and mass communication, 568–570
changes in, 389–403
experiments on, 422 ff., 429–433
Self, 401, 581 ff.
See also Ego
Set, 62, 93
See also Attitude; Motives
Shoshoni, 711
Single stimuli, method of, 49
Siriono, 438 ff., 458
Situational factors, in togetherness and
groups, 161 f., 184, 232
Situational tests, 211 ff., 293
Slogans, 261 f., 360, 503, 721, 726, 740,
742
Small groups, see Groups
Social attitudes, 488–537
See also Attitudes
Social change, 219, 359 f., 685–743
intellectual aspects of, 732–735
Social class, 631 ff.
Social contact, and attitude change,
317 f., 548–551, 675 ff.

Social distance, 649–656, 665 ff.
between experimentally formed groups,
306 f.
Bogardus test of, 517 f., 649
Social-distance scales, 284, 329 f., 517 f.
and individuals, 664–671
formation of, 659 ff.
Social influences, and conceptual factors,
128–132
Social issues, and social psychology, 755 ff.
Social judgment, 71, 127, 136 ff., 202–
208, 301, 307–309 f.
See also Judgment
Social movements, 721–742
definition of, 726
general characterization of, 724 ff.
Social norms, 237–279
and technology, 687, 699 f., 704 f.,
712 f.
as generic term, 170 ff.
definition of, 240 ff.
See also Norms
Social perception, see Perception
Social psychology, and social issues, 755 ff.
backgrounds of, 747–755
definition of, 4 f.
level of analysis in, 28–31
perspective in, 32, 761–765
today, 31–32, 757–766
"Social self," 750
See also Ego; Self
Social situations, factors in, 121–124
laboratory studies of, 119 ff.
positive and negative effects of, 121,
128
Social stimulus situations, 4 f., 11–28,
66 f.
and attitudes, 490 ff., 496
classification of, 13 ff.
motivational relevance of, 106
well-structured, 98
See also Stimulus structure
Socialization, 7 f., 145 f., 167 f., 174
and attitudes, 488–494
and language, 473 ff.
and motives, 388 ff.
retardation in, 393
role of adults in, 407 f.
Sociogenic motives, 375, 388–409
attitudes as, 489 ff.
definition of, 370
orientation to, 403–410
See also Attitudes; Ego; Motives
Sociometric technique, 149, 196 ff., 203,
292, 325
Sociometric studies, 754

Sociopolitical maturity, 725 f., 732–735
Solidarity, 165–170, 188
  an index of, 241 f.
  and deprivations, 443
  importance of, in psychotherapy, 230 f.
  increase in intergroup conflict, 298, 311
Southern Ute, 711
Standards, in judgment, 47–51, 62
  of wealth, 695 f., 698 f., 702 f.
  See also Norms
Status, and ego-involvements, 622 ff.
  and power, 222, 224 f.
  as group property, 144 ff.
  definition of, 162, 164
  experiments on, 202–208
  strivings for, 374
  See also Leadership
Status equilibration, 624
  and reference groups, 639–641
Status relations, 125 f.
  stabilization of, 181, 184
  See also Group structure
Stereotypes, 71, 201, 653 ff.
  assessed by judgments, 300 f., 312, 326 f.
  change in, 271 f.
  children's, 662 f.
  of out-groups, 286 ff., 298, 306–316
Stimulus situations, 80
  See also Social stimulus situations; Stimulus structure
Stimulus structure, 81–83, 97 ff.
  and motivation, 202 f., 412, 415, 423 f., 429
  and naming, 462
  and perception, 54–60, 255, 257, 263
  and selectivity, 84 ff., 90 ff.
  and social influences, 137
  gradations of, 59 f., 100–106, 248 f.
Street Corner Boys, 184–191, 239 f.
Success, 39, 51
  See also Level of aspiration
Suggestibility, 719, 749
Suggestion, 89, 93, 101–103, 266, 352
Superordinate goals, 317–328, 330, 656–661, 678
  definition of, 291
  in changing attitudes, 550 f.
Swazi, 73, 91 f.
Symbols, 9–11
  and language concepts, 449 f.
  See also Language

Task, 158 f., 184, 229 ff., 231
Tasmanians, 458
Technological changes, and attitude change, 574, 703–713
  and group characteristics, 710 f.
  and group relations, 707 ff.
  and organizational change, 703–713
Technology, differential contact with, 692–703
  effects of, 685–714
  studies of, 690 ff.
Testimony, 93–95
Tests, for attitude measurement, 497 ff., 510–528
Thematic Apperception Test, 420, 505
Threshold of acceptance, 529
Threshold of rejection, 529
Thresholds, recognition, 95–97, 432 f.
Thurstone attitude scales, 523–528
Time, concepts of, 68, 455, 695, 697 f.
Togetherness situations, 144, 158
  and collective interaction, 337 f.
  and group situations, 124–126, 181–184
  and leadership, 212 ff.
Townsend movement, 729
Traits, attributed to out-groups, 653 ff.
  of leaders, 210 ff.
  See also Stereotypes
Trobriands, 72
Twins, language of, 477

Values, 7 f., 15
  in social movements, 732–742
  infants' first, 393
  See also Norms
Variability of response, 107 f., 113, 262 f.
Vertical mobility, 631 f.
Visual field, inversion of, 109–112
Vocabulary development, 399 f.
Voting, new methods of, 273 ff.

Wagiriama, 67
Warfare, changes in, 710 f.
Wish fulfillment, 421 f.
Witoto, 458
Women, changing conceptions and role of, 593 f., 704 f., 707
Words, 449–485
  See also Concepts; Language; Names

Youth movements. 729 f.